RANDOM HOUSE
ESSENTIAL
GERMAN
DICTIONARY

RANDOM HOUSE ESSENTIAL GERMAN DICTIONARY

Originally published as *The Random House German Dictionary, Second Vest Pocket Edition.*

Edited by
Jenni Karding Moulton
Under the general editorship of
Professor William G. Moulton
Princeton University

Revised by
Jennifer L. Hornor

BALLANTINE BOOKS • NEW YORK

Copyright © 1996 by Random House, Inc.

All rights reserved under International and Pan-American Copyright Conventions. No part of this book may be reproduced in any form or by any means, electronic or mechanical, including photocopying, without permission in writing from the publisher. All inquiries should be addressed to Reference & Information Publishing, Random House, Inc., 201 East 50th Street, New York, NY 10022-7703. Published in the United States by Ballantine Books, a division of Random House, Inc., New York, and simultaneously in Canada by Random House of Canada Limited, Toronto. This work was originally published as *The Random House German Dictionary, Second Vest Pocket Edition,* by Reference & Information Publishing, Random House, Inc., in 1996. It is a revised, updated, and completely retypeset edition of the *Random House German Dictionary, First Edition,* published in 1983.

Library of Congress Cataloging-in-Publication Data

Random House essential German dictionary / edited by Jenni Karding Moulton.
        p.   cm.
    ISBN 0-345-41080-7
    1. German language—Dictionaries—English. 2. English language—Dictionaries—German. I. Moulton, Jenni Karding.
PF3640.R33 1997
433'.21—dc20   96-35119
                                                                                         CIP

This edition published by arrangement with Random House, Inc.

Manufactured in the United States of America

First Ballantine Books Edition: February 1997

10 9 8 7 6 5 4 3 2 1

Concise Pronunciation Guide

Consonants

b Usually like English *b:* **Bett, graben.** But when final or before *s* or *t,* like English *p:* **das Grab, des Grabs, er gräbt.**

c In foreign words only. Before *a, o, u,* like English *k:* **Café´.** Before *ä, e, i* in words borrowed from Latin, like English *ts:* **Cicero;** otherwise usually with the foreign pronunciation.

ch After *a, o, u, au,* a scraping sound like Scottish *ch* in *loch,* made between the back of the tongue and the roof of the mouth: **Dach, Loch, Buch, auch.** In other positions, much like English *h* in *hue:* **Dächer, Löcher, Bücher, ich, manch, welch, durch.** In words borrowed from Greek or Latin, initial *ch* before *a, o, u, l, r* is like English *k:* **Charak´ter, Chor, Christ.** In words borrowed from French it is like German *sch:* **Chance.**

chs As a fixed combination, like English *ks:* **der Dachs,** *the badger.* But when the *s* is an ending, like German *ch* plus *s:* **des Dachs,** genitive of **das Dach,** *the roof.*

ck As in English: **backen, Stock.**

d Usually like English *d:* **Ding, Rede.** But when final or before *s,* like English *t:* **das Band, des Bands.**

dt Like English *tt:* **Stadt** just like **statt.**

f As in English: **Feuer, Ofen, Schaf.**

g Usually like English *g* in *get:* **Geld, schlagen, Könige, reinigen.** But when final or before *s* or *t,* like English *k:* **der Schlag, des Schlags, er schlägt.** However, *ig* when final or before *s* or *t* is like German *ich:* **der König, des Königs, er reinigt.** In words borrowed from French, *g* before *e* is like English *z* in *azure:* **Loge.**

h As in English: **hier.** But after vowels it is only a sign of vowel length, and is not pronounced: **gehen, Bahn, Kuh.**

j Like English *y:* **Jahr.** In a few words borrowed from French, like English *z* in *azure:* **Journal´.**

k As in English: **kennen, Haken, buk.**

l Not the "dark *l*" of English *mill, bill,* but the "bright *l*" of English *million, billion:* **lang, fallen, hell.**

m As in English: **mehr, kommen, dumm.**

n As in English: **neu, kennen, kann.**

ng Always like English *ng* in *singer,* never like English *ng* + g in *finger.* German **Finger, Hunger.**

p As in English: **Post, Rippe, Tip.**

pf Like English *pf* in *cupful:* **Kopf, Apfel, Pfund.**

ph As in English: **Philosophie´.**

qu Like English *kv:* **Quelle, Aqua´rium.**

r When followed by a vowel, either a gargled sound made between the back of the tongue and the roof of the mouth, or (less commonly) a quick flip of the tongue tip against the gum ridge: **Ring, Haare, bessere.** When not followed by a vowel, a sound much like the *ah* of English *yeah,* or the *a* of *sofa:* **Haar, besser.**

s Usually like English *z* in *zebra,* or *s* in *rose:* **sie, Rose.** But when final or before a consonant, like English *s* in *this:* **das, Wespe, Liste, Maske.**

sch Like English *sh* in *ship,* but with the lips rounded: **Schiff, waschen, Tisch.**

Consonants

sp } st }	At the beginning of a word, like *sch* + p, *sch* + t: **Spiel, Stahl.**
ss } ß }	Like English *ss* in *miss. ss* is written only after a short vowel when another vowel follows: **müssen.** Otherwise ß is written: finally **muß,** before a consonant **mußte,** or after a long vowel **Muße.**
t	As in English: **tun, bitter, Blatt.**
th	Always like *t*: **Thea´ter;** never like English *th.*
tion	Pronounced *tsyohn*: **Nation´, Aktion´.**
tsch	Like *t* + sch: **deutsch.**
tz	Like English *ts*: **sitzen, Platz.**
v	In German words, like English *f*: **Vater, Frevel.** In foreign words, like English *v*: **Novem´ber, Moti´ve;** but finally and before *s*, like *f* again: **das Motiv´, des Motivs´.**
w	Like English *v*: **Wagen, Löwe.**
x	As in English: **Hexe.**
z	Always like English *ts*: **zehn, Kreuz, Salz.**

Short vowels

a	Satz	Between English *o* in *hot* and *u* in *hut.*
ä e	Sätze } setze }	Like English *e* in *set.*
i	sitze	Like English *i* in *sit.*
o	Stock	Like English *o* in *gonna,* or the "New England short *o*" in *coat, road;* shorter than English *o* in *cost.*
ö	Stöcke	Tongue position as for short *e*, lips rounded as for short *o.*
u	Busch	Like English *u* in *bush.*
ü y	Büsche } mystisch }	Tongue position as for short *i*, lips rounded as for short *u.*

Unaccented short e

e	beginne	Like English *e* in *begin, pocket.*

Long vowels

a ah aa	Tal } Zahl } Saal }	Like English *a* in *father.*
ä äh	Täler } zählen }	In elevated speech, like English *ai* in *fair;* other wise just like German long *e.*
e eh ee	wer } mehr } Meer }	Like English *ey* in *they*, but with no glide toward a *y* sound.
ih ih ie	mir } ihr } Bier }	Like English *i* in *machine*, but with no glide toward a *y* sound.
o oh oo	Ton } Sohn } Boot }	Like English *ow* in *slow*, but with no glide toward a *w* sound.
ö öh	Töne } Söhne }	Tongue position as for long *e*, lips rounded as for long *o.*
u uh	Hut } Kuh }	Like English *u* in *rule*, but with no glide toward a *w* sound.
ü üh y	Hüte } Kühe } Typ }	Tongue position as for long *i*, lips rounded as for long *u.*

Diphthongs

ei	Seite }	
ai	Saite }	Like English *i* in *side*. Also spelled *ey*, *ay* in names: *Meyer, Bayern*.
au	Haut	Like English *ou* in *out*.
eu	heute }	
äu	Häute }	Like English *oi* in *oil*.

The spelling of vowel length	**Short**	**Long**
An accented vowel is always short when	schlaff	Schlaf
followed by a doubled consonant letter,	wenn	wen
but nearly always long when followed by a	still	Stil
single consonant letter.	offen	Ofen
	öffnen	Öfen
	Butter	Puter
Note that	dünne	Düne
ck counts as the doubled form of **k**:	hacken	Haken
tz counts as the doubled form of **z**:	putzen	duzen
ss counts as the doubled form of **ß**:	Masse	Maße
Vowels are always long when followed by	wann	Wahn
(unpronounced) **h**:	stelle	stehle
	irre	ihre
	Wonne	wohne
	gönne	Söhne
	Rum	Ruhm
	dünn	kühn
Vowels are always long when they are written	Stadt	Staat
double:	Bett	Beet
	Gott	Boot
In this respect, **ie** counts as the doubled form	bitte	biete
of **i**:		

German Accentuation

Most German words are accented on the first syllable: **Mo´nate, ar´bei**tete, Düsenkampfflugzeuge. However, the prefixes be-, emp-, ent-, er-, ge-, ver-, zer-, are never accented: **befeh´len, der Befehl´, empfan´gen, der Empfang´**, etc. Other prefixes are usually accented in nouns: **der Un´terricht**, but unaccented in verbs: **unterrich´ten**. Foreign words are often accented on a syllable other than the first: **Hotel´, Muse´um, Photographie´**.

Note particularly the accentuation of such forms as **übertre´ten, ich übertre´te** *I overstep*, where **über** is a prefix; but **ü´bertreten, ich trete . . . über** *I step over* where **über** is a separate word, despite the fact that **ü´bertreten** is spelled without a space. These two types will be distinguished in this dictionary by writing **übertre´ten** but **über•treten**.

German spelling does not indicate the place of the accent. In this dictionary, accent will be marked when it falls on a syllable other than the first: **Befehl´, unterrich´ten, Photographie´**. Where it is not marked, the accent is on the first syllable: **Monate, arbeit**ete, Düsenkampfflugzeuge, Unterricht, über•treten.

Nouns

This listing ↓	means this ↓
Wagen,-	plural is **Wagen.**
Vater,⸚	plural is **Väter.**
Tisch,-e	plural is **Tische.**
Sohn,⸚e	plural is **Söhne.**
Bild,-er	plural is **Bilder.**
Haus,⸚er	plural is **Häuser.**
Auge,-n	plural is **Augen.**
Ohr,-en	plural is **Ohren.**
Hotel´,-s	plural is **Hotels´.**
Muse´um,-e´en	plural is **Muse´en.**
Doktor,-o´ren	plural is **Dokto´ren.**
Kopie´,-i´en	plural is **Kopi´en,** with three syllables.
Kuß,⸚sse	final **ß** changes to medial **ss** because the **ü** is short.
Fuß,⸚e	final **ß** kept in all forms because the **ü** is long.
Junge,-n,-n	nominative singular is **Junge,** all other forms are **Jungen.**
Name(n),-	declined like **Wagen** (above), except that nominative singular is **Name.**
Beamt´-	takes adjective endings: **ein Beamter, der Beamte, zwei Beamte, die zwei Beamten.**
Milch	has no plural.
Leute, *n.pl.*	has no singular.

From almost any German noun meaning some kind of man or boy, a noun meaning the corresponding woman or girl can be formed by adding **-in: der Arbeiter** *worker (man or boy),* **die Arbeiterin** *worker (woman or girl);* **der Russe** *Russian (man or boy),* **die Russin** *Russian (woman or girl).*

Adjectives

Most German adjectives can also be used, without ending, as adverbs: **schlecht** *bad, badly.* The few which never occur without ending as adverbs are listed with a following hyphen: **link-** *left,* **ober-** *upper,* **zweit-** *second.* (The corresponding adverbs are **links** *to the left,* **oben** *above,* **zweitens** *secondly.*)

Adjectives which take umlaut in the comparative and superlative are listed as follows: **lang** (⸚), i.e., the comparative and superlative are **länger, längst-.**

Limiting or determining adjectives are listed in the nominative singular masculine, with an indication of the nominative singular neuter and feminine: **der, das, die, dieser, -es, -e; ein, -, -e.**

Descriptive adjectives take the following endings:

	Strong endings				Weak endings			
	masc.	neut.	fem.	pl.	masc.	neut.	fem.	pl.
nom.	-er	-es	-e	-e	-e	-e	-e	-en
acc.	-en	-es	-e	-e	-en	-e	-e	-en
dat.	-em	-em	-er	-er	-en	-en	-en	-en
gen.	-en	-en	-er	-er	-en	-en	-en	-en

Weak endings are used if the adjective is preceded by an inflected form of a limiting (determining) adjective; strong endings are used otherwise.

Verbs

Regular weak verbs are listed simply in the infinitive: **machen**. If a verb is used with a separable prefix (accented adverb), this is indicated by a raised dot: **auf•machen** (i.e., the infinitive is **aufmachen**, the present **ich mache . . . auf**, the past **ich machte . . . auf**, the past participle **aufgemacht**). An asterisk after a verb refers to the following lists of irregular weak and strong verbs. The sign † means that a verb takes the auxiliary verb **sein**; the sign ‡ means that a verb can take either **sein** or **haben**.

Irregular weak verbs

Infinitive	3rd sg. present	Past	Subjunctive	Past participle
haben	hat	hatte	hätte	gehabt
bringen	bringt	brachte	brächte	gebracht
denken	denkt	dachte	dächte	gedacht
brennen	brennt	brannte	brennte	gebrannt
kennen	kennt	kannte	kennte	gekannt
nennen	nennt	nannte	nennte	genannt
†rennen	rennt	rannte	rennte	gerannt
senden	sendet	sandte	sendete	gesandt
wenden	wendet	wandte	wendete	gewandt
dürfen	darf	durfte	dürfte	gedurft
können	kann	konnte	könnte	gekonnt
mögen	mag	mochte	möchte	gemocht
müssen	muß	mußte	müßte	gemußt
sollen	soll	sollte	sollte	gesollt
wollen	will	wollte	wollte	gewollt
wissen	weiß	wußte	wüßte	gewußt

Strong verbs

If a derived or compound verb is not listed, its forms may be found by consulting the simple verb. The sign + means that a regular weak form is also used.

Infinitive	3rd sg. present	Past	Subjunctive	Past participle
backen	bäckt	+buk	+büke	gebacken
befehlen	befiehlt	befahl	beföhle	befohlen
beginnen	beginnt	begann	begönne, begänne	begonnen
beißen	beißt	biß	bisse	gebissen
bergen	birgt	barg	bärge	geborgen
†bersten	birst	barst	bärste	geborsten
bewegen	bewegt	bewog	bewöge	bewogen
‡biegen	biegt	bog	böge	gebogen
bieten	bietet	bot	böte	geboten
binden	bindet	band	bände	gebunden
bitten	bittet	bat	bäte	gebeten
blasen	bläst	blies	bliese	geblasen
†bleiben	bleibt	blieb	bliebe	geblieben
braten	brät	briet	briete	gebraten
brechen	bricht	brach	bräche	gebrochen
dingen	dingt	+dang	+dänge	+gedungen
dreschen	drischt	drosch	drösche	gedroschen
†dringen	dringt	drang	dränge	gedrungen
†erbleichen	erbleicht	+erblich	+erbliche	+erblichen
erlöschen	erlischt	erlosch	erlösche	erloschen
essen	ißt	aß	äße	gegessen
‡fahren	fährt	fuhr	führe	gefahren
†fallen	fällt	fiel	fiele	gefallen
fangen	fängt	fing	finge	gefangen
fechten	ficht	focht	föchte	gefochten
finden	findet	fand	fände	gefunden
flechten	flicht	flocht	flöchte	geflochten
‡fliegen	fliegt	flog	flöge	geflogen
†fliehen	flieht	floh	flöhe	geflohen
†fließen	fließt	floß	flösse	geflossen
fressen	frißt	fraß	fräße	gefressen
frieren	friert	fror	fröre	gefroren
gären	gärt	+gor	+göre	+gegoren
gebären	gebiert	gebar	gebäre	geboren
geben	gibt	gab	gäbe	gegeben
†gedeihen	gedeiht	gedieh	gediehe	gediehen
†gehen	geht	ging	ginge	gegangen
†gelingen	gelingt	gelang	gelänge	gelungen
gelten	gilt	galt	gölte, gälte	gegolten
†genesen	genest	genas	genäse	genesen
genießen	genießt	genoß	genösse	genossen
†geschehen	geschieht	geschah	geschähe	geschehen
gewinnen	gewinnt	gewann	gewönne, gewänne	gewonnen
gießen	gießt	goß	gösse	gegossen
gleichen	gleicht	glich	gliche	geglichen
†gleiten	gleitet	glitt	glitte	geglitten
glimmen	glimmt	+glomm	+glömme	+geglommen
graben	gräbt	grub	grübe	gegraben
greifen	greift	griff	griffe	gegriffen
halten	hält	hielt	hielte	gehalten
hängen	hängt	hing	hinge	gehangen

Infinitive	3rd sg. present	Past	Subjunctive	Past participle
hauen	haut	+hieb	+hiebe	gehauen
heben	hebt	hob	höbe	gehoben
heißen	heißt	hieß	hieße	geheißen
helfen	hilft	half	hülfe, hälfe	geholfen
klimmen	klimmt	+klomm	+klömme	+geklommen
klingen	klingt	klang	klänge	geklungen
kneifen	kneift	kniff	kniffe	gekniffen
†kommen	kommt	kam	käme	gekommen
†kriechen	kriecht	kroch	kröche	gekrochen
laden	lädst	lud	lüde	geladen
lassen	läßt	ließ	ließe	gelassen
†laufen	läuft	lief	liefe	gelaufen
leiden	leidet	litt	litte	gelitten
leihen	leiht	lieh	liehe	geliehen
lesen	liest	las	läse	gelesen
liegen	liegt	lag	läge	gelegen
lügen	lügt	log	löge	gelogen
meiden	meidet	mied	miede	gemieden
messen	mißt	maß	mäße	gemessen
mißlingen	mißlingt	mißlang	mißlänge	mißlungen
nehmen	nimmt	nahm	nähme	genommen
pfeifen	pfeift	pfiff	pfiffe	gepfiffen
preisen	preist	pries	priese	gepriesen
quellen	quillt	quoll	quölle	gequollen
r aten	rät	riet	riete	geraten
reiben	reibt	rieb	riebe	gerieben
‡reißen	reißt	riß	risse	gerissen
‡reiten	reitet	ritt	ritte	geritten
riechen	riecht	roch	röche	gerochen
ringen	ringt	rang	ränge	gerungen
r innen	rinnt	rann	rönne	geronnen
rufen	ruft	rief	riefe	gerufen
saufen	säuft	soff	söffe	gesoffen
saugen	saugt	+sog	+söge	+gesogen
schaffen	schafft	schuf	schüfe	geschaffen
schallen	schallt	+scholl	+schölle	geschallt
‡scheiden	scheidet	schied	schiede	geschieden
scheinen	scheint	schien	schiene	geschienen
schelten	schilt	schalt	schölte	gescholten
scheren	schert	+schor	+schöre	+geschoren
schieben	schiebt	schob	schöbe	geschoben
schießen	schießt	schoß	schösse	geschossen
schinden	schindet	schund	schünde	geschunden
schlafen	schläft	schlief	schliefe	geschlafen
schlagen	schlägt	schlug	schlüge	geschlagen
†schleichen	schleicht	schlich	schliche	geschlichen
schleifen	schleift	schliff	schliffe	geschliffen
schließen	schließt	schloß	schlösse	geschlossen
schlingen	schlingt	schlang	schlänge	geschlungen
schmeißen	schmeißt	schmiß	schmisse	geschmissen
schmelzen	schmilzt	schmolz	schmölze	geschmolzen
schneiden	schneidet	schnitt	schnitte	geschnitten
schrecken	schrickt	schrak	schräke	geschrocken

Infinitive	3rd sg. present	Past	Subjunctive	Past participle
schreiben	schreibt	schrieb	schriebe	geschrieben
schreien	schreit	schrie	schriee	geschrie(e)n
†schreiten	schreitet	schritt	schritte	geschritten
schweigen	schweigt	schwieg	schwiege	geschwiegen
schwellen	schwillt	schwoll	schwölle	geschwollen
‡schwimmen	schwimmt	schwamm	schwömme	geschwommen
†schwinden	schwindet	schwand	schwände	geschwunden
schwingen	schwingt	schwang	schwänge	geschwungen
schwören	schwört	+schwur, schwor	+schwüre	+geschworen
sehen	sieht	sah	sähe	gesehen
†sein	ist	war	wäre	gewesen
sieden	siedet	+sott	+sötte	+gesotten
singen	singt	sang	sänge	gesungen
†sinken	sinkt	sank	sänke	gesunken
sinnen	sinnt	sann	sänne, sönne	gesonnen
sitzen	sitzt	saß	säße	gesessen
speien	speit	spie	spiee	gespie(e)n
spinnen	spinnt	spann	spönne, spänne	gesponnen
spleißen	spleißt	spliß	splisse	gesplissen
sprechen	spricht	sprach	spräche	gesprochen
sprießen	sprießt	sproß	sprösse	gesprossen
†springen	springt	sprang	spränge	gesprungen
stechen	sticht	stach	stäche	gestochen
stecken	steckt	+stak	+stäke	gesteckt
stehen	steht	stand	stände, stünde	gestanden
stehlen	stiehlt	stahl	stähle, stöhle	gestohlen
†steigen	steigt	stieg	stiege	gestiegen
†sterben	stirbt	starb	stürbe	gestorben
‡stieben	stiebt	+stob	+stöbe	+gestoben
stinken	stinkt	stank	stänke	gestunken
‡stoßen	stößt	stieß	stieße	gestoßen
streichen	streicht	strich	striche	gestrichen
streiten	streitet	stritt	stritte	gestritten
tragen	trägt	trug	trüge	getragen
treffen	trifft	traf	träfe	getroffen
‡treiben	treibt	trieb	triebe	getrieben
‡treten	tritt	trat	träte	getreten
trinken	trinkt	trank	tränke	getrunken
trügen	trügt	trog	tröge	getrogen
tun	tut	tat	täte	getan
verbleichen	verbleicht	verblich	verbliche	verblichen
verderben	verdirbt	verdarb	verdürbe	verdorben
verdrießen	verdrießt	verdroß	verdrösse	verdrossen
vergessen	vergißt	vergaß	vergäße	vergessen
verlieren	verliert	verlor	verlöre	verloren
†wachsen	wächst	wuchs	wüchse	gewachsen
wägen	wägt	wog	wöge	gewogen
waschen	wäscht	wusch	wüsche	gewaschen
weben	webt	+wob	+wöbe	+gewoben

Infinitive	3rd sg. present	Past	Subjunctive	Past participle
weichen	weicht	wich	wiche	gewichen
weisen	weist	wies	wiese	gewiesen
werben	wirbt	warb	würbe	geworben
†werden	wird	wurde, (ward)	würde	geworden
werfen	wirft	warf	würfe	geworfen
wiegen	wiegt	wog	wöge	gewogen
winden	windet	wand	wände	gewunden
wringen	wringt	wrang	wränge	gewrungen
‡ziehen	zieht	zog	zöge	gezogen
zwingen	zwingt	zwang	zwänge	gezwungen

Abbreviations

abbr.	abbreviation	*intr.*	intransitive
adj.	adjective	*jur.*	juridical
adv.	adverb	*m.*	masculine
arch.	architecture	*math.*	mathematics
art.	article	*med.*	medicine
bot.	botany	*mil.*	military
chem.	chemistry	*n.*	noun
comm.	commercial	*naut.*	nautical
conj.	conjunction	*nt.*	neuter
cpds.	compounds	*num.*	number
eccles.	ecclesiastical	*pl.*	plural
econ.	economics	*pol.*	politics
elec.	electricity	*pred.*	predicate
f.	feminine	*prep.*	preposition
fam.	familiar	*pron.*	pronoun
fig.	figuratively	*sg.*	singular
geogr.	geography	*tech.*	technical
geom.	geometry	*tr.*	transitive
gov't.	government	*typogr.*	typography
gram.	grammar	*vb.*	verb
interj.	interjection	*zool.*	zoology

GERMAN-ENGLISH

A

Aachen, *n.nt.* Aachen, Aix-la-Chapelle.

Aal, -e, *n.m.* eel.

ab, *adv.* down; off; **(ab Berlin)** leaving Berlin; **(ab heute)** from today on; **(ab und zu)** now and then; **(von jetzt ab)** from now on.

ab•ändern, *vb.* revise.

Abänderung, -en, *n.f.* variation, revision.

Abart, -en, *n.f.* variety, species.

Abbau, *n.m.* working; reduction, razing.

ab•bauen, *vb.* raze; mine.

Abbild, -er, *n.nt.* image, effigy.

ab•blenden, *vb.* dim (headlights).

ab•brechen*, *vb.* break off; cease, stop.

Abbruch, ⸚e, *n.m.* breaking off; cessation; damage.

ab•danken, *vb.* abdicate.

Abdankung, -en, *n.f.* abdication.

Abdruck, -e, *n.m.* (printed) impression, copy.

Abdruck, ⸚e, *n.m.* impress, mark, cast.

Abend, -e, *n.m.* evening; **(zu A. essen*)** dine, have dinner.

Abendbrot, -e, *n.nt.* supper.

Abenddämmerung, -en, *n.f.* dusk.

Abendessen, -, *n.nt.* dinner, supper.

Abendland, *n.nt.* Occident.

abendländisch, *adj.* occidental.

abendlich, *adj.* evening.

Abendmahl, -e, *n.nt.* Holy Communion, Lord's Supper.

abends, *adv.* in the evening.

Abenteuer, -, *n.nt.* adventure.

abenteuerlich, *adj.* adventurous.

Abenteurer, -, *n.m.* adventurer.

aber, *conj.* but.

Aberglaube(n), -, *n.m.* superstition.

abergläubisch, *adj.* superstitious.

abermals, *adv.* once again.

Abessi´nien, *n.nt.* Abyssinia.

ab•fahren*, *vb.* leave, depart.

Abfahrt, -en, *n.f.* departure; descent (skiing).

Abfahrtszeit, *n.f.* departure time.

Abfall, ⸚e, *n.m.* trash, rubbish; slope; decrease; defection.

ab•fallen*, *vb.* fall off; decrease; revolt.

abf ällig, *adj.* precipitous; derogatory.

ab•fangen*, *vb.* intercept.

ab•fassen, *vb.* draw up, compose.

ab•fertigen, *vb.* take care of, expedite.

ab•feuern, *vb.* discharge (gun).

ab•finden*, *vb.* **(sich a. mit)** put up with.

Abflug, *n.m.* departure (plane).

Abfluß, ⸚sse, *n.m.* drain(age); outlet.

ab•führen, *vb.* lead off.

Abführmittel, -, *n.nt.* laxative.

Abgabe, -n, *n.f.* levy.

Abgasbestimmungen, *n.f.pl.* emission controls.

Abgase, *n.pl.* exhaust fumes.

ab•geben*, *vb.* hand over; check (baggage); cast (vote).

abgebrüht, *adj.* hard-boiled.

abgedroschen, *adj.* trite.

abgelegen, *adj.* remote.

abgemacht, *adj.* settled, agreed.

abgeneigt, *adj.* averse, disinclined.

abgenutzt, *adj.* worn-out.

Abgeordnet-, *n.m.& f.* representative, deputy.

abgeschieden, *adj.* separated, secluded; departed.

abgesehen von, *prep.* aside from.

ab•gewinnen*, *vb.* gain from.

ab•gewöhnen, *vb.* give up (habit, smoking).

Abgott, ⸚er, *n.m.* idol.

Abgötterei´, -en, *n.f.* idolatry.

Abgrenzung, -en, *n.f.* demarcation.

Abgrund, ⸚e, *n.m.* abyss, precipice.

ab•halten*, *vb.* hold off, restrain, deter.

abhan´den, *adv.* missing; **(a. kommen*)** get lost.

Abhandlung, -en, *n.f.* treatise.

Abhang, ⸚e, *n.m.* slope.

ab•hängen*, *vb.* depend.

abhängig, *adj.* dependent.

Abhängigkeit, *n.f.* dependence.

ab•härten, *vb.* harden.

ab•helfen*, *vb.* remedy.

Abhilfe, -n, *n.f.* remedy, relief.

abhold, *adj.* averse, disinclined.

ab•holen, *vb.* go and get, pick up, call for.

ab•hören, *vb.* listen to, monitor.

Abitur´, -e, *n.nt.* final examination at end of secondary school; high school diploma.

Abkehr, *n.f.* turning away.

Abkomme, -n, -n, *n.m.* descendant, offspring.

Abkommen, -, *n.nt.* convention; agreement.

Abkömmling, -e, *n.m.* offspring, descendant; derivative.

ab•kühlen, *vb.* cool off.

ab•kürzen, *vb.* abbreviate; abridge.

Abkürzung, -en, *n.f.* abbreviation; abridgment; short cut.

ab•laden*, *vb.* unload.

Ablage, -n, *n.f.* depot, place of deposit.

Ablaß, ⁼sse, *n.m.* letting off, drainage; *(eccles.)* indulgence.

ab•lassen*, *vb.* let off, drain; desist.

Ablativ, -e, *n.m.* ablative.

Ablauf, *n.m.* running off, expiration.

ab•laufen*, *vb.* run off, expire.

Ablaut, -e, *n.m.* ablaut (vowel alteration, as in *si ngen, sa ng, gesu ngen*).

ab•legen, *vb.* discard, take off.

ab•lehnen, *vb.* decline, reject.

Ablehnung, -en, *n.f.* rejection.

ab•leiten, *vb.* derive.

Ableitung, -en, *n.f.* derivation.

ab•lenken, *vb.* divert, distract.

Ablenkung, -en, *n.f.* diversion, distraction.

ab•leugnen, *vb.* deny, disavow.

Ableugnung, -en, *n.f.* denial, disavowal.

ab•lichten, *vb.* photocopy.

Ablichtung, -en, *n.f.* photocopy.

ab•liefern, *vb.* deliver.

Ablieferung, -en, *n.f.* delivery.

ab•lösen, *vb.* relieve.

Ablösung, -en, *n.f.* relief.

Abmarsch, ⁼e, *n.m.* marching off, departure.

ab•melden, *vb.* report the departure of.

ab•mühen, *vb.* (sich a.) toil.

Abnahme, -n, *n.f.* decrease; purchase (business).

abnehmbar, *adj.* removable.

ab•nehmen*, *vb.* (*tr.*) take off, remove; (*intr.*) decrease, lose weight.

Abnehmer, -, *n.m.* purchaser.

Abneigung, -en, *n.f.* antipathy, dislike, aversion.

abnorm´, *adj.* abnormal.

ab•nötigen, *vb.* force from.

ab•nutzen, *vb.* wear (something) out.

Abnutzung, *n.f.* wearing out.

Abonnement´, -s, *n.nt.* subscription.

abonnie´ren, *vb.* subscribe.

Abordnung, -en, *n.f.* delegation.

Abort, -e, *n.m.* toilet.

Abort´, -e, *n.m.* abortion.

ab•rackern, *vb.* (sich a.) drudge.

ab•raten*, *vb.* dissuade.

ab•räumen, *vb.* clear off.

ab•rechnen, *vb.* settle accounts.

Abrechnung, -en, *n.f.* settlement of accounts.

Abrede, -n, *n.f.* (in A. stellen) deny.

Abreise, -n, *n.f.* departure.

ab•reisen, *vb.* depart.

ab•reißen*, *vb.* tear off; demolish.

Abriß, ⁼sse, *n.m.* outline, summary.

abrupt, *adj.* abrupt.

ab•rüsten, *vb.* disarm.

Abrüstung, -en, *n.f.* disarmament.

Absage, -n, *n.f.* refusal (of an invitation), calling off.

ab•sagen, *vb.* decline, revoke, cancel.

Absatz, ⁼e, *n.m.* paragraph; heel; landing; sale, market.

ab•schaben, *vb.* scrape off, abrade.

ab•schaffen*, *vb.* abolish, get rid of.

Abschaffung, -en, *n.f.* abolition.

ab•schätzen, *vb.* appraise, estimate.

Abschätzung, -en, *n.f.* appraisal, estimate.

Abschaum, *n.m.* dregs.

Abscheu, -e, *n.m.* abhorrence, loathing.

abscheu´lich, *adj.* abominable, detestable.

Abschied, -e, *n.m.* departure, leave, farewell.

Abschlag, ⁼e, *n.m.* chips; repulse; refusal.

ab•schlagen*, *vb.* chip off; repel; refuse.

abschlägig, *adj.* negative, refusing.

ab•schleifen*, *vb.* grind off, abrade.

ab•schließen*, *vb.* lock up, close off; conclude.

Abschluß, ⁼sse, *n.m.* conclusion.

Abschlußprüfung, -en, *n.f.* final exam.

Abschlußzeugnis, *n.nt.* diploma.

ab•schneiden*, *vb.* cut off.

Abschnitt, -e, *n.m.* section.

ab•schrecken, *vb.* frighten off.

abschreckend, *adj.* forbidding.

Abschreckung, *n.f.* deterrence.

Abschreckungsmittel, -, *n.nt.* deterrent.

ab•schreiben*, *vb.* copy.

Abschrift, -en, *n.f.* copy.

abschüssig, *adj.* precipitous.

ab•schweifen, *vb.* digress.

ab•schwören*, *vb.* abjure.

Abschwörung, -en, *n.f.* abjuration.

absehbar, *adj.* foreseeable.

ab•sehen*, *vb.* look away; see from; (a. von) give up; (auf mich abgesehen) aimed at me; (ist abzusehen) can be seen.

abseits, *adv.* aside, apart.

ab•senden*, *vb.* send off, mail.

Absender, -, *n.m.* sender.

Absendung, -en, *n.f.* dispatch.

ab•setzen, *vb.* set off, set down, depose.

Absicht, -en, *n.f.* intent, purpose; (mit A.) on purpose.

absichtlich, *adj.* intentional.

absolut´, *adj.* absolute.

absolvie´ren, *vb.* absolve; complete; finish (school); pass (an examination).

abson´derlich, *adj.* peculiar.

ab•sondern, *vb.* separate, detach; secrete.

absorbie´ren, *vb.* absorb.

Absorbie´rungsmittel, -, *n.nt.* absorbent.

Absorption´, -en, *n.f.* absorption.

ab•spannen, *vb.* loosen (tension), relax.

ab•spielen, *vb.* (sich a.) occur, take place.

ab•splittern, *vb.* chip.

Absprache, -n, *n.f.* agreement.

ab•sprechen*, *vb.* deny.

ab•springen*, *vb.* jump down, bail out (of a plane).

Absprung, ⸚e, *n.m.* jump down, parachute jump; digression.

ab•stammen, *vb.* be descended.

Abstammung, -en, *n.f.* descent, ancestry; derivation.

Abstand, ⸚e, *n.m.* distance, interval; (von etwas A. nehmen*) renounce.

ab•statten, *vb.* grant; (einen Besuch a.) pay a visit.

ab•stauben, *vb.* dust.

Abstecher, -, *n.m.* digression, side trip.

ab•stehen*, *vb.* stand off, stick out.

ab•steigen*, *vb.* descend, dismount; put up at (an inn).

ab•stellen, *vb.* put away; turn off.

ab•stempeln, *vb.* stamp, cancel.

ab•sterben*, *vb.* die out.

Abstieg, -e, *n.m.* descent.

ab•stimmen, *vb.* vote.

Abstimmung, -en, *n.f.* vote, plebiscite.

abstinent´, *adj.* abstinent.

Abstinenz´, *n.f.* abstinence.

ab•stoßen*, *vb.* knock off, repel, repulse.

abstoßend, *adj.* repulsive.

abstrahie´ren, *vb.* abstract.

abstrakt´, *adj.* abstract.

Abstraktion´, -en, *n.f.* abstraction.

ab•streifen, *vb.* strip.

Abstufung, -en, *n.f.* gradation.

ab•stumpfen, *vb.* become dull, blunt; make dull, blunt.

Absturz, ⸚e, *n.m.* fall, crash.

ab•stürzen, *vb.* fall, crash.

absurd´, *adj.* absurd.

Abszeß´, -sse, *n.m* abscess.

Abtei´, -en, *n.f.* abbey.

Abteil, -e, *n.nt.* compartment.

Abtei´lung, -en, *n.f.* division, section.

ab•tragen*, *vb.* wear out.

ab•treiben*, *vb.* drive off; cause an abortion.

Abtreibung, -en, *n.f.* abortion.

ab•trennen, *vb.* detach.

ab•treten*, *vb.* cede.

Abtretung, -en, *n.f.* withdrawal, cession, surrender.

Abtritt, -e, *n.m.* departure, exit; latrine.

ab•trocknen, *vb.* dry.

ab•tun*, *vb.* put aside, settle.

ab•wägen*, *vb.* weigh out, consider.

ab•wandeln, *vb.* change, inflect.

ab•wandern, *vb.* depart, migrate.

ab•warten, *vb.* wait (to see what will happen), bide one's time.

abwärts, *adv.* downwards.

ab•waschen*, *vb.* wash off.

Abwaschung, -en, *n.f.* ablution.

ab•wechseln, *vb.* alternate, take turns.

abwechselnd, *adj.* alternate.

Abwechs(e)lung, -en, *n.f.* change, alternation.

Abweg, -e, *n.m.* wrong way, devious path; (auf A.e gera´ten*) go astray.

abwegig, *adj.* errant.

Abwehr, *n.f.* warding off, defense.

Abwehrdienst, -e, *n.m.* counterintelligence service.

ab•wehren, *vb.* ward off, prevent.

Abwehrsystem, *n.nt.* immune system.

ab•weichen*, *vb.* deviate, depart.

Abweichung, -en, *n.f.* deviation, departure.

ab•weisen*, *vb.* send away, repulse.

ab•wenden*, *vb.* turn away, deflect, avert.

ab•werfen*, *vb.* throw down, shed.

ab•werten, *vb.* devaluate.

Abwertung, -en, *n.f.* devaluation.

abwesend, *adj.* absent.

Abwesend-, *n.m.& f.* absent person, absentee.

Abwesenheit, -en, *n.f.* absence.

ab•wickeln, *vb.* unwind.

ab•winken, *vb.* gesture "no."

ab•wischen, *vb.* wipe off.

Abwurf, ⸚e, *n.m.* throwing down; thing thrown down; (bombs) dropping; (sports) throw-out.

ab•zahlen, *vb.* pay off.

ab•zählen, *vb.* count off.

ab•zapfen, *vb.* draw off, tap.

ab•zehren, *vb.* waste away, consume.

Abzeichen, -, *n.nt.* badge, medal, insignia.

ab•ziehen*, *vb.* (tr.) draw off, subtract, deduct; (intr.) march off.

Abzug, ⸚e, *n.m.* marching off, departure; drawing off, subtraction, drain; print; trigger.

ab•zwingen*, *vb.* force away from, extort.

Acetylen´, *n.nt.* acetylene.

ach, *interj.* oh.

Achat´, -e, *n.m.* agate.

Achse, -n, *n.f.* axis, axle.

Achsel, -n, *n.f.* shoulder.

acht, *num.* eight.

acht-, *adj.* eighth.

Acht, *n.f.* attention, care; (sich in A. nehmen*) watch out, be on one's guard; (außer A. lassen*) pay no attention to, neglect.

Achtel, -, *n.nt.* eighth part; (ein a.) one-eighth.

achten, *vb.* respect; (a. auf) pay attention to.

ächten, *vb.* outlaw, ostracise.

achtern, *adv.* aft.

acht•geben*, *vb.* watch out, pay attention.

acht•haben*, *vb.* watch out, pay attention.

achtlos, *adj.* heedless.

achtsam, *adj.* attentive.

Achtung, *n.f.* attention, regard, esteem; **(A.!)** watch out! attention!

achtzehn, *num.* eighteen.

achtzehnt-, *adj.* eighteenth.

achtzig, *num.* eighty.

achtzigst-, *adj.* eightieth.

Achtzigstel, -, *n.nt.* eightieth part; **(ein a.)** one-eightieth.

ächzen, *vb.* groan, moan.

Acker, ∺, *n.m.* field.

Ackerbau, *n.m.* farming.

Adap´ter, -, *n.m.* adapter.

addie´ren, *vb.* add.

ade´, *interj.* adieu.

Adel, *n.m.* nobility.

Ader, -n, *n.f.* vein.

adieu, *interj.* adieu.

Adjektiv, -e, *n.nt.* adjective.

adjekti´visch, *adj.* adjectival.

Adjutant´, -en, -en, *n.m.* adjutant, aide, aide-de-camp.

Adler, -, *n.m.* eagle.

Adler-, *cpds.* aquiline.

adlig, *adj.* noble.

Adlig-, *n.m. & f.* nobleman, -woman.

Admiral´, -e, *n.m.* admiral.

Admiralität´, -en, *n.f.* admiralty.

adoptie´ren, *vb.* adopt.

Adoption´, -en, *n.f.* adoption.

Adres´se, -n, *n.f.* address.

adressie´ren, *vb.* address.

adrett´, *adj.* trim, smart.

Advent´, -e, *n.m.* Advent.

Adverb´, -ien, *n.nt.* adverb.

adverbial´, *adj.* adverbial.

Advokat´, -en, -en, *n.m.* lawyer.

Aeronau´tik, *n.f.* aeronautics.

Aff´ä´re, -n, *n.f.* affair, love affair.

Affe, -n, -n, *n.m.* ape, monkey.

Affekt´, -e, *n.m.* affect.

affektiert´, *adj.* affected.

Affektiert´heit, -en, *n.f.* affectation.

äffen, *vb.* ape, mock.

affig, *adj.* affected, vain.

Affix, -e, *n.nt.* affix.

Affront´, -s, *n.m.* affront, snub.

Afrika, *n.nt.* Africa.

Afrika´ner, -, *n.m.* African.

afrika´nisch, *adj.* African.

AG, *abbr.* (= Aktiengesellschaft) company.

Agent´, -en, -en, *n.m.* agent.

Agentur´, -en, *n.f.* agency.

Aggression´, -en, *n.f.* aggression.

aggressiv´, *adj.* aggressive.

agie´ren, *vb.* act.

Agno´stiker, -, *n.m.* agnostic.

Agno´stikerin, -nen, *n.f.* agnostic.

agno´stisch, *adj.* agnostic.

Ägyp´ten, *n.nt.* Egypt.

Ägyp´ter, -, *n.m.* Egyptian.

ägyp´tisch, *adj.* Egyptian.

Ahn, -en, *n.m.* ancestor.

Ahne, -n, *n.f.* ancestress.

ähneln, *vb.* resemble.

ahnen, *vb.* have any idea (that something will happen); forebode.

ähnlich, *adj.* similar.

Ähnlichkeit, -en, *n.f.* similarity.

Ahnung, -en, *n.f.* foreboding; hunch; **(ich habe keine A.)** I have no idea.

ahnungslos, *adj.* unsuspecting.

ahnungsvoll, *adj.* ominous.

Ahorn, -e, *n.m.* maple tree.

Ähre, -n, *n.f.* ear (of grain).

Aids, *n.* (no article), AIDS.

Ajatol´lah, -s, *n.m.* ayatollah.

Akademie´, -i´en, *n.f.* academy.

akade´misch, *adj.* academic.

Aka´zie, -n, *n.f.* acacia.

Akkord´, -e, *n.m.* chord.

akkreditie´ren, *vb.* accredit.

Akkumula´tor, -to´ren, *n.m.* battery.

Akkusativ, -e, *n.m.* accusative.

Akne, -n, *n.f.* acne.

Akrobat´, -en, -en, *n.m.* acrobat.

Akt, -e, *n.m.* act; nude (drawing).

Akte, -n, *n.f.* document, dossier, file.

Aktenmappe, -n, *n.f.* brief case.

Aktentasche, -n, *n.f.* attache case.

Aktie, -n, *n.f.* share (of stock).

Aktiengesellschaft, -en, *n.f.* corporation, stock company.

Aktion´, -en, *n.f.* action, undertaking.

Aktionär, -e, *n.m.* stockholder.

aktiv´, *adj.* active.

aktivie´ren, *vb.* activate.

Aktivie´rung, -en, *n.f.* activation.

aktuell´, *adj.* topical, current.

Akupunktur´, -en, *n.f.* acupuncture.

Aku´stik, *n.f.* acoustics.

aku´stisch, *adj.* acoustic.

akut´, *adj.* acute.

Akzent´, -e, *n.m.* accent.

akzentuie´ren, *vb.* accentuate.

Alarm´, -e, *n.m.* alarm, alert.

alarmie´ren, *vb.* alarm, alert.

Alaun´, -e, *n.m.* alum.

albern, *adj.* silly.

Albi´no, -s, *n.m.* albino.

Album, -en, *n.nt.* album.

Alchimie´, *n.f.* alchemy.

Alchimist´, -en, -en, *n.m.* alchemist.

Alge, -n, *n.f.* alga.

Algebra, *n.f.* algebra.

algebra´isch, *adj.* algebraic.

alias, *adv.* alias.

Alibi, -s, *n.nt.* alibi.

Aliment´, -e, *n.nt.* alimony.

Alka´li, -en, *n.nt.* alkali.

alka´lisch, *adj.* alkaline.

Alkohol, -e, *n.m.* alcohol.

Alkoho´liker, -, *n.m.* alcoholic.

alkoho´lisch, *adj.* alcoholic.

Alko´ven, -, *n.m.* alcove.

All, *n.nt.* universe.

all; aller, -es, -e, *pron. & adj.* all.

Allee´, -e´en, *n.f.* avenue.

Allegorie´, -i´en, *n.f.* allegory.

allein´, 1. *adv.* alone. **2.** *conj.* but.

allei´nig, *adj.* sole, only.

allemal, *adv.* always; **(ein für a.)** once and for all.

allenfalls, *adv.* in any case.

allenthal'ben, *adv.* everywhere.

aller-, *cpds.* of all; **allerbest'**, best of all; etc.

allerart, *adv.* all sorts of.

allerdings', *adv.* certainly, to be sure, indeed, admittedly.

Allergie', **-i'en,** *n.f.* allergy.

allerhand, *adv.* all sorts of; **(das ist ja a.)** that's tremendous, that's the limit.

allerlei, *adv.* all sorts of.

alles, *pron.* everything.

allesamt, *adv.* altogether.

allgemein, *adj.* general, common; **(im a. en)** generally, in general.

Allgemein'heit, -en, *n.f.* generality, general public.

Allianz', -en, *n.f.* alliance.

Alliga'tor, -o'ren, *n.m.* alligator.

alliie'ren, *vb.* ally.

Alliiert'-, *n.m.& f.* ally.

alljähr'lich, *adj.* annual.

allmäch'tig, *adj.* almighty, omnipotent.

allmäh'lich, *adj.* gradual.

allmo'natlich, *adj.* monthly.

allnächt'lich, *adj.* nightly.

Alltag, -e, *n.m.* weekday, tedium; everday life.

alltäg'lich, *adj.* daily, routine.

allzu, *adv.* all too.

Almanach, -e, *n.m.* almanac.

Almosen, -, *n.nt.* alms.

Alpdruck, ⸚e, *n.m.* nightmare.

Alpen, *n.pl.* Alps.

Alphabet', -e, *n.nt.* alphabet.

alphabe'tisch, *adj.* alphabetical.

alphabetisie'ren, *vb.* alphabetize.

Alptraum, ⸚e, *n.m.* nightmare.

als, *conj.* as, when; than.

alsbald', *adv.* immediately.

alsdann', *adv.* thereupon.

also, *adv.* so, thus, and so, hence, therefore.

alt, *adj.* old.

Alt, -e, *n.m.* alto.

Altar', ⸚e, *n.m.* altar.

Altar'diener, -, *n.m.* acolyte.

Alter, -, *n.nt.* age.

altern, *vb.* age.

alternativ', *adj.* alternative.

Alternati've, -n, *n.f.* alternative.

Altersgrenze, *n.f.* age limit.

Altersheim, -e, *n.nt.* nursing home.

Altertum, -ümer, *n.nt.* antiquity.

altertümlich, *adj.* archaic.

Altertumskunde, *n.f.* archaeology.

Ältest-, *n.m.* elder.

alther'gebracht, *adj.* traditional.

Altjahrsa'bend, -e, *n.m.* New Year's Eve.

altklug, ⸚, *adj.* precocious.

ältlich, *adj.* elderly.

altmodisch, *adj.* old-fashioned.

Altpapier, *n.nt.* waste paper (to be recycled).

Altruis'mus, *n.m.* altruism.

Altstimme, -n, *n.f.* alto.

Alumi'nium, *n.nt.* aluminum.

Amalgam', -e, *n.nt.* amalgam.

amalgamie'ren, *vb.* amalgamate.

Amateur', -e, *n.m.* amateur.

Amboß, -sse, *n.m.* anvil.

ambulant', *adj.* ambulatory.

Ameise, -n, *n.f.* ant.

Ame'rika, *n.nt.* America.

Amerika'ner, -, *n.m.* American.

Amerika'nerin, -nen, *n.f.* American.

amerika'nisch, *adj.* American.

Amethyst', -e, *n.m.* amethyst.

Ammoniak, *n.nt.* ammonia.

Amnestie', -i'en, *n.f.* amnesty.

Amö'be, -n, *n.f.* amoeba.

amoralisch, *adj.* amoral.

amortisie'ren, *vb.* amortize.

Ampere, -, *(pron.* **Ampär')** *n.nt.* ampere.

amphi'bisch, *adj.* amphibious.

amputie'ren, *vb.* amputate.

Amputiert'-, *n.m.& f.* amputee.

Amt, ⸚er, *n.nt.* office.

amtie'ren, *vb.* officiate.

amtlich, *adj.* official.

Amtseinführung, -en, *n.f.* inauguration.

Amtsschimmel, *n.m.* red tape.

amüsie'ren, *vb.* amuse; **(sich a.)** have a good time.

an, *prep.* at, on, to.

Anachronis'mus, -men, *n.m.* anachronism.

analog', *adj.* analogous.

Analogie', -i'en, *n.f.* analogy.

analo'gisch, *adj.* analogical.

Analphabet', -en, -en, *n.m.* illiterate.

Analphabe'tentum, *n.nt.* illiteracy.

Analy'se, -n, *n.f.* analysis.

analysie'ren, *vb.* analyze.

Analy'tiker, -, *n.m.* analyst.

analy'tisch, *adj.* analytic(al).

Anarchie', -i'en, *n.f.* anarchy.

Anästhesie', *n.f.* anesthesia.

Anatomie', -i'en, *n.f.* anatomy.

Anbau, -ten, *n.m.* cultivation; addition (to a house).

Anbeginn, *n.m.* origin.

anbei', *adv.* enclosed, herewith.

an•beten, *vb.* worship, adore.

Anbetracht, *n.m.* **(in A.)** in view of.

Anbetung, -en, *n.f.* adoration.

an•bieten*, *vb.* offer.

Anblick, -e, *n.m.* sight, view, appearance.

an•brechen*, *vb.* begin; break; **(der Tag bricht an)** day breaks, dawns.

Anbruch, ⸚e, *n.m.* beginning, (day)break, (night)fall.

Andacht, -en, *n.f.* devotion.

andächtig, *adj.* devout.

andauernd, *adj.* continual.

Andenken, -, *n.nt.* memory, memorial, souvenir.

ander-, *adj.* other, different.

and(e)rerseits, *adv.* on the other hand.

ändern, *vb.* change, alter, **(sich ä.)** change, vary.

anders, *adv.* otherwise, else, different.

anderswie, *adv.* otherwise.

anderswo, *adv.* elsewhere.

anderthalb, *num.* one and a half.

Änderung, -en, *n.f.* change, alteration.

an•deuten, *vb.* indicate, imply.

Andeutung, -en, *n.f.* indication, implication.

Andrang, *n.m.* rush, crowd.

an•drehen, *vb.* turn on.

an•eignen, (sich a.) seize, appropriate.

Aneignung, -en, *n.f.* seizure, appropriation.

aneinan´der, *adv.* to one another, together.

Anekdo´te, -n, *n.f.* anecdote.

an•ekeln, *vb.* disgust.

an•erkennen* (*or* **anerkennen***), *vb.* acknowledge, recognize.

anerkennenswert, *adj.* creditable.

Anerkennung, -en, *n.f.* acknowledgment, recognition.

an•fahren*, *vb.* drive up against, collide with, hit; speak sharply to.

Anfall, ⁼e, *n.m.* attack.

an•fallen*, *vb.* fall upon, attack.

Anfang, ⁼e, *n.m.* beginning.

an•fangen*, *vb.* begin.

Anf änger, -, *n.m.* beginner.

Anfängerin, -nen, *n.f.* beginner.

anf änglich, *adj.* initial.

anfangs, *adv.* in the beginning.

an•fassen, *vb.* take hold of, grasp, touch.

an•fechten*, *vb.* assail.

an•fertigen, *vb.* prepare, manufacture.

an•feuchten, *vb.* moisten.

an•feuern, *vb.* fire, incite, inspire.

an•flehen, *vb.* beseech.

an•fliegen*, *vb.* fly at, approach.

Anflug, ⁼e, *n.m.* approach flight, slight attack, touch.

an•fordern, *vb.* claim, demand.

Anfrage, -n, *n.f.* inquiry, application.

an•freunden, *vb.* **(sich a. mit)** befriend.

an•führen, *vb.* lead on; allege; cite; dupe.

Anführung, -en, *n.f.* leadership; quotation, allegation.

Anführungsstrich, -e, *n.m.* quotation mark.

Anführungszeichen, -, *n.nt.* quotation mark.

Angabe, -n, *n.f.* fact cited, statement, assertion; *(pl.)* data.

an•geben*, *vb.* cite as a fact, state, assert; brag, boast.

Angeber, -, *n.m.* boaster.

Angeberei´, -en, *n.f.* boast, boastfulness.

angeberisch, *adj.* boastful.

angeblich, *adj.* as stated, alleged.

angeboren, *adj.* innate, congenital.

Angebot, -e, *n.nt.* bid, offer.

angebracht, *adj.* proper.

angeheiratet, *adj.* related by marriage.

angeheitert, *adj.* tipsy.

an•gehen*, *vb.* concern.

angehend, *adj.* beginning, incipient.

an•gehören, *vb.* belong to.

angehörig, *adj.* belonging to.

Angehörig-, *n.m. & f.* dependent.

Angeklagt-, *n.m. & f.* accused, defendant.

Angel, -n, *n.f.* hinge, axis; fishing tackle.

angelegen, *adj.* important, of concern.

Angelegenheit, -en, *n.f.* matter, concern, affair.

angelehnt, *adj.* leaned against, ajar.

angeln, *vb.* fish, angle.

angemessen, *adj.* adequate, appropriate, suitable.

angenehm, *adj.* pleasant, agreeable.

angesehen, *adj.* respected, respectable.

Angesicht, -er, *n.nt.* face.

angesichts, *prep.* in view of.

angespannt, *adj.* tense.

Angestellt-, *n.m. & f.* employee.

angetrunken, *adj.* tipsy.

angewandt, *adj.* applied.

angewiesen, *adj.* dependent.

an•gewöhnen, *vb.* accustom to, get used to.

Angewohnheit, -en, *n.f.* habit, custom.

an•gleichen*, *vb.* assimilate, adjust.

Angleichung, -en, *n.f.* assimilation.

Angler, -, *n.m.* fisherman.

an•gliedern, *vb.* affiliate.

Angliederung, -en, *n.f.* affiliation.

angreifbar, *adj.* assailable.

an•greifen*, *vb.* attack, assault.

Angreifer, -, *n.m.* attacker, aggressor.

an•grenzen, *vb.* abut, border on.

angrenzend, *adj.* contiguous.

Angriff, -e, *n.m.* attack, aggression.

Angriffslust, *n.f.* aggressiveness.

Angst, ⁼e, *n.f.* fear; **(A. haben*)** be afraid.

ängstigen, *vb.* frighten.

ängstlich, *adj.* timid, anxious.

an•haben*, *vb.* have on, wear.

Anhalt, -e, *n.m.* hold; basis.

an•halten*, *vb.* *(tr.)* stop, arrest; *(intr.)* last, continue.

anhaltend, *adj.* lasting.

Anhaltspunkt, -e, *n.m.* point of reference, basis, clue.

Anhang, ⁼e, *n.m.* appendix; adherents.

Anhänger, -, *n.m.* follower; pendant; trailer.

an•häufen, *vb.* amass, accumulate.

Anhäufung, -en, *n.f.* accumulation.

an•heften, *vb.* affix, attach.

anheim´stellen, *vb.* submit.

Anhieb, -e, *n.m.* first stroke; **(auf A.)** right away, right off the bat.

an•hören, *vb.* listen to.

Anilin´, *n.nt.* aniline.

Ankauf, ⁼e, *n.m.* purchase.

an•kaufen, *vb.* buy.

Anker, -, *n.m.* anchor.

Ankerplatz, ⁼e, *n.m.* anchorage.

an•ketten, *vb.* chain.

Anklage, -n, *n.f.* accusation, indictment, impeachment.

an•klagen, *vb.* accuse, indict, impeach.

Ankläger, -, *n.m.* accuser, plaintiff.

an•klammern, *vb.* fasten (with a clamp); **(sich a.)** cling.

an•klopfen, *vb.* knock.

an•kommen*, *vb.* arrive; **(a. auf)** depend upon.

an•kündigen, *vb.* announce.

Ankunft, ⸗e, *n.f.* arrival.

an•kurbeln, *vb.* crank up, get started.

an•lächeln, *vb.* smile at.

Anlage, -n, *n.f.* arrangement, disposition, investment; enclosure; *(pl.)* grounds.

an•langen, *vb. (tr.)* concern; *(intr.)* arrive.

Anlaß, ⸗sse, *n.m.* cause, motivating factor.

an•lassen*, *vb.* leave on; start.

Anlasser, -, *n.m.* starter.

anläßlich, *prep.* on the occasion of.

Anlauf, ⸗e, *n.m.* start, warmup; attack.

an•laufen*, *vb.* run at, make for; swell, rise.

an•legen, *vb.* put on; invest; land.

an•lehnen, *vb.* lean against, leave ajar.

Anleihe, -n, *n.f.* loan.

an•leiten, *vb.* lead to, instruct.

Anleitung, -en, *n.f.* instruction.

an•lernen, *vb.* train.

an•lügen, *vb.* lie to.

an•machen, *vb.* fix, attach, turn on.

Anmarsch, *n.m.* (military) approach, advance.

an•maßen, *vb.* assume, presume.

anmaßend, *adj.* arrogant, presumptuous.

Anmaßung, -en, *n.f.* arrogance, presumption.

an•melden, *vb.* announce; register.

Anmeldung, -en, *n.f.* announcement, report, registration.

an•merken, *vb.* note.

Anmerkung, -en, *n.f.* (foot)note.

an•messen*, *vb.* measure for, fit.

Anmut, *n.f.* grace, charm.

anmutig, *adj.* graceful.

an•nähern, *vb.* **(sich a.)** approach.

annähernd, *adj.* approximate.

Annäherung, -en, *n.f.* approach, approximation.

Annahme, -n, *n.f.* acceptance, adoption; assumption, supposition.

annehmbar, *adj.* acceptable.

an•nehmen*, *vb.* accept, assume, suppose, infer; adopt.

Annehmlichkeit, -en, *n.f.* pleasure, agreeableness.

Annon´ce, -n, *n.f.* advertisement.

annoncie´ren, *vb.* advertise.

annullie´ren, *vb.* annul.

Anomalie´, -i´en, *n.f.* anomaly.

anonym´, *adj.* anonymous.

an•ordnen, *vb.* order, arrange.

Anordnung, -en, *n.f.* order, arrangement.

an•packen, *vb.* grab hold of, get started with.

an•passen, *vb.* adapt, fit, try on; **(sich a.)** conform.

Anpassung, -en, *n.f.* adaptation.

anpassungsfähig, *adj.* adaptable, adaptive.

an•pflanzen, *vb.* plant.

Anprall, *n.m.* collision, impact.

an•preisen*, *vb.* praise, recommend.

Anprobe, -n, *n.f.* fitting.

Anrecht, -e, *n.nt.* right, claim.

Anrede, -n, *n.f.* address, speech.

an•reden, *vb.* speak to, accost.

an•regen, *vb.* stimulate, incite.

Anregung, -en, *n.f.* stimulation; suggestion.

Anreiz, -e, *n.m.* stimulus, incentive.

an•reizen, *vb.* incite.

Anruf, -e, *n.m.* appeal, (telephone) call.

an•rufen*, *vb.* appeal to, invoke; call up.

Anrufbeantworter, *n.m.* answering machine.

Anrufung, *n.f.* invocation.

an•rühren, *vb.* touch; (cooking) mix.

an•sagen, *vb.* announce.

Ansager, -, *n.m.* announcer.

an•sammeln, *vb.* amass; **(sich a.)** congregate, gather.

Ansammlung, -en, *n.f.* collection, backlog.

ansässig, *adj.* resident.

Ansatz, ⸗e, *n.m.* start; estimate.

an•schaffen, *vb.* get, obtain; buy.

Anschaffung, -en, *n.f.* acquisition.

an•schauen, *vb.* look at.

anschaulich, *adj.* graphic, clear.

Anschauung, -en, *n.f.* view, opinion.

Anschein, -e, *n.m.* appearance.

anscheinend, *adj.* apparent.

Anschlag, -e, *n.m.* stroke; poster; estimate; plot.

an•schlagen*, *vb. (tr.)* strike, affix, fasten, post; estimate; *(intr.)* work, start to function.

an•schließen*, *vb.* fasten with a lock, adjoin; **(sich a.)** join; fit tight.

anschließend, *adv.* afterwards.

Anschluß, -sse, *n.m.* connection, annexation.

an•schnallen, *vb.* buckle on; **(sich a.)** fasten seatbelt.

an•schneiden*, *vb.* start cutting.

an•schreiben*, *vb.* write down, score, charge.

Anschrift, -en, *n.f.* address.

an•sehen*, *vb.* look at.

Ansehen, *n.nt.* reputation, repute.

ansehnlich, *adj.* handsome; considerable, notable.

an•setzen, *vb.* fix, affix; set; schedule; estimate.

Ansicht, -en, *n.f.* view, opinion.

an•siedeln, *vb.* settle, colonize.

an•spannen, *vb.* stretch, strain; harness.

Anspannung, -en, *n.f.* strain, tension.

an•spielen, *vb.* start to play; allude.

Anspielung, -en, *n.f.* allusion.

an•spornen, *vb.* spur on.

Ansprache, -n, *n.f.* pronunciation; talk.

an•sprechen*, *vb.* address, accost.

ansprechend, *adj.* attractive.

Anspruch, ⁼e, *n.m.* claim; **(A. machen auf)** lay claim to; **(in A. nehmen*)** require, take up.

anspruchslos, *adj.* unassuming.

anspruchsvoll, *adj.* pretentious.

an•stacheln, *vb.* goad, incite.

Anstalt, -en, *n.f.* arrangement, institution.

Anstand, *n.m.* propriety; objection.

anständig, *adj.* decent.

Anständigkeit, -en, *n.f.* decency.

an•starren, *vb.* stare at.

anstatt´, *adv.* instead of.

an•stecken, *vb.* pin on, put on; light, set fire to; **(a. mit)** infect; **(sich a.)** catch.

ansteckend, *adj.* contagious.

Ansteckung, -en, *n.f.* contagion.

an•stehen*, *vb.* line up, stand in line.

an•steigen*, *vb.* rise.

anstel´le, *prep.* instead of.

an•stellen, *vb.* place; hire, employ.

Anstellung, -en, *n.f.* employment.

Anstieg, -e, *n.m.* rise.

an•stiften, *vb.* incite, instigate.

an•stimmen, *vb.* intone, tune up.

Anstoß, ⁼e, *n.m.* shock; impetus; offense.

an•stoßen*, *vb.* knock, bump against, nudge; offend; clink glasses.

anstoßend, *adj.* adjoining.

anstößig, *adj.* offensive.

an•streben, *vb.* strive for.

an•streichen*, *vb.* paint; underline; mark.

an•strengen, *vb.* strain; **(sich a.)** exert oneself, try hard.

anstrengend, *adj.* strenuous.

Anstrengung, -en, *n.f.* effort, exertion.

Anstrich, -e, *n.m.* coat of paint; appearance; touch.

Ansturm, ⁼e, *n.m.* assault, run (on a bank).

Antark´tis, *n.f.* Antarctica.

antark´tisch, *adj.* antarctic.

Anteil, -e, *n.m.* share.

Anten´ne, -n, *n.f.* antenna.

antik´, *adj.* antique.

Anti´ke, *n.f.* antiquity, classical times.

Antilo´pe, -n, *n.f.* antelope.

Antimon´, *n.nt.* antimony.

antinuklear´, *adj.* antinuclear.

Antipathie´, -i´en, *n.f.* antipathy.

Antiquar´, -e, *n.m.* second-hand bookdealer, antique dealer.

Antiquariat´, -e, *n.nt.* second-hand bookstore.

antiqua´risch, *adj.* second-hand.

Antiquitä´ten, *n.pl.* antiques.

Antisemitis´mus, *n.m.* anti-Semitism.

antisep´tisch, *adj.* antiseptic.

antisozial´, *adj.* antisocial.

Antlitz, -e, *n.nt.* countenance.

Antrag, ⁼e, *n.m.* offer, proposal, motion.

an•treffen*, *vb.* meet up with.

an•treiben*, *vb.* drive on, propel, incite.

an•treten*, *vb.* enter into (office), start out on, step forward.

Antrieb, -e, *n.m.* impulse, impetus, force.

Antritt, -e, *n.m.* entrance into, start.

an•tun*, *vb.* put on, inflict, cause.

Antwort, -en, *n.f.* answer.

antworten, *vb.* answer.

an•vertrauen, *vb.* entrust; **(sich a.)** confide.

an•wachsen*, *vb.* grow, increase.

Anwalt, ⁼e, *n.m.* attorney, advocate.

Anwältin, -nen, *n.f.* attorney, advocate.

Anwärter, -, *n.m.* applicant, aspirant.

an•weisen*, *vb.* instruct, direct; assign.

Anweisung, -en, *n.f.* instruction, assignment; money order.

anwendbar, *adj.* applicable.

an•wenden*, *vb.* apply, use.

Anwendung, -en, *n.f.* application, use.

anwesend, *adj.* present.

Anwesenheit, -en, *n.f.* presence.

Anwurf, ⁼e, *n.m.* slur.

Anzahl, *n.f.* quantity, number.

an•zahlen, *vb.* make a down payment.

Anzahlung, -en, *n.f.* down payment.

an•zapfen, *vb.* tap (wire).

Anzeichen, -, *n.nt.* sign, symptom.

an•zeichnen, *vb.* mark, note.

Anzeige, -n, *n.f.* notice, advertisement; denunciation.

an•zeigen, *vb.* announce, advertise; denounce, report to police.

Anzeiger, -, *n.m.* advertiser; informer.

an•ziehen*, *vb.* draw along, attract; put on, dress; rise.

anziehend, *adj.* attractive.

Anziehungskraft, ⁼e, *n.f.* attraction; **(A. der Erde)** gravity.

Anzug, ⁼e, *n.m.* suit; approach.

an•zünden, *vb.* ignite, light.

an•zweifeln, *vb.* doubt, question.

apart, *adj.* out of the ordinary.

Apart'heid, *n.f.* apartheid.

Apathie', -i'en, *n.f.* apathy.

apa'thisch, *adj.* apathetic.

Apfel, ⁼, *n.m.* apple.

Apfelmus, *n.nt.* applesauce.

Apfelsi'ne, -n, *n.f.* orange.

apoplek'tisch, *adj.* apoplectic.

Apos'tel, -, *n.m.* apostle.

aposto'lisch, *adj.* apostolic.

Apostroph', -e, *n.m.* apostrophe.

Apothe'ke, -n, *n.f.* pharmacy.

Apothe'ker, -, *n.m.* pharmacist.

Apothe'kerin, -nen, *n.f.* pharmacist.

Apparat', -e, *n.m.* apparatus.

appellie'ren, *vb.* appeal.

Appetit', *n.m.* appetite.

appetit'lich, *adj.* appetizing, inviting.

applaudie'ren, *vb.* applaud.

Applaus', *n.m.* applause.

Apriko'se, -n, *n.f.* apricot.

April', *n.m.* April.

Aquarell', -e, *n.nt.* watercolor.

Aqua'rium, -ien, *n.nt.* aquarium.

Äqua'tor, *n.m.* equator.

äquatorial', *adj.* equatorial.

Araber, -, *n.m.* Arab.

Ara'berin, -nen, *n.f.* Arab.

ara'bisch, *adj.* Arabic, Arabian.

Arbeit, -en, *n.f.* work.

arbeiten, *vb.* work.

Arbeiter, -, *n.m.* worker, workman, laborer.

Arbeiterin, -nen, *n.f.* female worker.

Arbeiterschaft, *n.f.* labor.

Arbeitge'ber, -, *n.m.* employer.

Arbeiterklasse, *n.f.* working class.

Arbeitsamt, *n.nt.* employment office.

Arbeitserlaubnis, -se, *n.f.* work permit.

Arbeitsgenehmigung, -en, *n.f.* work permit.

arbeitslos, *adj.* unemployed.

Arbeitslosenunterstützung, *n.f.* unemployment support.

Arbeitslosigkeit, *n.f.* unemployment.

Arbeitsplatz, ⁼e, *n.m.* job, place of work.

Arbeitszimmer, -, *n.nt.* study.

Archäologie', *n.f.* archaeology.

Archipel', -e, *n.m.* archipelago.

Architekt', -en, -en, *n.m.* architect.

Architek'tin, -nen, *n.f.* architect.

architekto'nisch, *adj.* architectural.

Architektur', -en, *n.f.* architecture.

Archiv', -e, *n.nt.* archives.

Are'na, -nen, *n.f.* arena.

arg, *adj.* bad.

Argenti'nien, *n.nt.* Argentina.

Ärger, *n.m.* anger, annoyance, bother.

ärgerlich, *adj.* angry, annoying.

ärgern, *vb.* annoy, make angry, bother; (sich ä.) be angry.

Ärgernis, -se, *n.nt.* nuisance.

Arglist, *n.f.* guile.

arglos, *adj.* harmless, unsuspecting.

Argument', -e, *n.nt.* argument.

argumentie'ren, *vb.* argue.

Argwohn, *n.m.* suspicion.

argwöhnisch, *adj.* suspicious.

Arie, -n, *n.f.* aria.

Aristokrat', -en, -en, *n.m.* aristocrat.

Aristokratie', -i'en, *n.f.* aristocracy.

Aristokra'tin, -nen, *n.f.* aristocrat.

aristokra'tisch, *adj.* aristocratic.

Arithmetik', *n.f.* arithmetic.

Arka'de, -n, *n.f.* arcade.

arktisch, *adj.* arctic.

arm (⁼), *adj.* poor.

Arm, -e, *n.m.* arm.

Arm-, *n.m. & f.* pauper.

Armband, ⁼er, *n.nt.* bracelet.

Armbanduhr, -en, *n.f.* wristwatch.

Armee', -me'en, *n.f.* army.

Ärmel, -, *n.m.* sleeve.

Armleuchter, -, *n.m.* candelabrum.

armselig, *adj.* beggarly, miserable.

Armut, *n.f.* poverty, destitution.

Aro'ma, -s, *n.nt.* aroma.

arrangie'ren, *vb.* arrange.

arrogant', *adj.* arrogant.

Arroganz', -en, *n.f.* arrogance.

Arsen', *n.nt.* arsenic.

Art, -en, *n.f.* kind, sort, species; way, manner; (A. und Weise) way.

Arterie, -i'en, *n.f.* artery.

Arthri'tis, *n.f.* arthritis.

artig, *adj.* good, well-behaved.

Arti'kel, -, *n.m.* item, article.

artikulie'ren, *vb.* articulate.

Artillerie', -i'en, *n.f.* artillery.

Artischo'cke, -n, *n.f.* artichoke.

Arzt, ⁼e, *n.m.* physician, doctor; (praktischer A.) general practitioner.

Ärztin, -nen, *n.f.* physician, doctor.

ärztlich, *adj.* medical.

As, -se, *n.nt.* ace.

Asbest', -e, *n.m.* asbestos.

Asche, -n, *n.f.* ash; (glühende A.) embers.

Asch(en)becher, -, *n.m.* ashtray.

aschgrau, *adj.* ashen.

Asiat', -en, -en, *n.m.* Asian.

asia'tisch, *adj.* Asian.

Asien, *n.nt.* Asia.

Asket', -en, -en, *n.m.* ascetic.

aske'tisch, *adj.* ascetic.

Asphalt', -e, *n.m.* asphalt.

Aspirin', *n.nt.* aspirin.

assimilie'ren, *vb.* assimilate.

Assistent', -en, -en, *n.m.* assistant.

Assisten'tin, -nen, *n.f.* assistant.

assoziie'ren, *vb.* associate.

Ast, ⁼e, *n.m.* branch.

ästhe'tisch, *adj.* aesthetic.

Asthma, *n.nt.* asthma.

Astigmatis´mus, -men, *n.m.* astigmatism.

Astrologie´, -i´en, *n.f.* astrology.

Astronaut´, -en, -en, *n.m.* astronaut.

Astronau´tin, -nen, *n.f.* astronaut.

Astronomie´, -i´en, *n.f.* astronomy.

Asyl´, -e, *n.nt.* asylum.

Atelier´, -s, *n.nt.* studio.

Atem, -, *n.m.* breath.

atemlos, *adj.* breathless.

Atempause, -n, *n.f.* respite.

Atheist´, -en, -en, *n.m.* atheist.

Atheis´tin, -nen, *n.f.* atheist.

Äther, *n.m.* ether.

äthe´risch, *adj.* ethereal.

Athlet´, -en, -en, *n.m.* athlete.

athle´tisch, *adj.* athletic.

Atlan´tik, *n.m.* Atlantic Ocean.

atlan´tisch, *adj.* Atlantic.

Atlas, -lan´ten, *n.m.* atlas.

atmen, *vb.* breathe.

Atmen, *n.nt.* breathing.

Atmosphä´re, -n, *n.f.* atmosphere.

atmosphä´risch, *adj.* atmospheric.

Atmung, *n.f.* respiration.

Atom´, -e, *n.nt.* atom.

atomar´, *adj.* atomic.

atomisie´ren, *vb.* atomize.

Atom´müll, *n.m.* nuclear waste.

Atomsperr´vertrag, ⸗e, *n.m.* non-proliferation treaty.

Attaché´, -s, *n.m.* attaché.

Attentat´, -e, *n.nt.* attempt on someone's life, assassination attempt.

Attentä´ter, -, *n.m.* assassin.

Attest´, -e, *n.nt.* certificate.

ätzen, *vb.* etch; *(med.)* cauterize.

au, *interj.* ouch.

auch, *adv.* also, too; **(a. nicht)** not . . . either; **(a. jetzt)** even now.

Audienz´, -en, *n.f.* audience.

audiovisuell´, *adj.* audiovisual.

Audito´rium, -rien, *n.nt.* auditorium.

auf, *prep.* on, onto.

auf•atmen, *vb.* breathe a sigh of relief.

Aufbau, *n.m.* erection, construction; structure.

auf•bauen, *vb.* erect.

auf•blasen*, *vb.* inflate.

auf•bleiben*, *vb.* stay up.

auf•brechen*, *vb.* break open; start out.

auf•brauchen, *vb.* use up.

auf•decken, *vb.* uncover, unearth.

auf•drängen, *vb.* obtrude; **(sich a.)** obtrude.

aufdringlich, *adj.* obtrusive, importunate.

aufeinan´derfolgend, *adj.* successive, consecutive.

Aufenthalt, *n.m.* stay.

auf•erlegen, *vb.* impose.

Auferstehung, *n.f.* resurrection.

auf•fallen*, *vb.* be conspicuous.

auffällig, *adj.* noticeable, conspicuous, flashy.

Auffälligkeit, -en, *n.f.* conspicuousness, flashiness.

auf•fangen*, *vb.* catch; intercept.

auf•fassen, *vb.* conceive, interpret.

Auffassung, -en, *n.f.* conception, interpretation.

auf•flammen, *vb.* flash, flare up.

auf•fordern, *vb.* ask, invite, summon.

Aufforderung, -en, *n.f.* invitation, summons.

auf•frischen, *vb.* refresh.

auf•führen, *vb.* list; (theater) perform.

Aufführung, -en, *n.f.* performance.

Aufgabe, -n, *n.f.* task, assignment; (school) lesson.

Aufgang, ⸗e, *n.m.* rise.

auf•geben*, *vb.* give up, abandon; (luggage) check through; (food) serve; *(jur.)* waive.

Aufgebot, -e, *n.nt.* public notice; notice of intended marriage.

aufgebracht, *adj.* angry, provoked.

aufgedunsen, *adj.* bloated.

auf•gehen*, *vb.* (sun etc.) rise; *(math.)* leave no remainder; *(fig.)* be absorbed in.

auf•halten*, *vb.* hold open; stop, detain; **(sich a.)** stay.

auf•hängen*, *vb.* suspend; hang.

auf•heben*, *vb.* revoke, nullify; **(zeitweilig a.)** suspend; save.

Aufheben, *n.nt.* ado, fuss.

Aufhebung, -en, *n.f.* revocation, abolition.

auf•heitern, *vb.* cheer up.

auf•hören, *vb.* stop, quit.

Aufhören, *n.nt.* cessation.

auf•klären, *vb.* enlighten; tell the facts of life; **(sich a.)** clear.

Aufklärung, *n.f.* enlightenment.

Aufkleber, -, *n.m.* sticker.

auf•kommen*, *vb.* come into use; **(a. für)** be responsible for.

Auflage, -n, *n.f.* printing, circulation.

Auflauf, ⸗e, *n.m.* crowd, mob; soufflé.

auf•lösen, *vb.* dissolve; **(sich a.)** disperse, disappear.

Auflösung, -en, *n.f.* dissolution.

auf•machen, *vb.* open; **(sich a.)** set out for.

Aufmachung, -en, *n.f.* make-up.

aufmerksam, *adj.* attentive, polite; alert.

Aufmerksamkeit, -en, *n.f.* attention, attentiveness.

auf•muntern, *vb.* cheer up.

Aufnahme, -n, *n.f.* reception; (photo) shot; (phonograph, tape) recording.

auf•nehmen*, *vb.* take in; (phonograph, tape) record; film, photograph.

auf•opfern, *vb.* **(sich a.)** sacrifice oneself.

auf•passen, *vb.* pay attention, look out for.

auf•raffen, *vb.* **(sich a.)** bestir oneself; pull oneself together.

auf•räumen, *vb.* put in order, pick up; **(mit etwas a.)** debunk.

aufrecht, *adj.* upright.

aufrecht•erhalten*, *vb.* maintain, uphold.

Aufrechterhaltung, *n.f.* maintenance.

auf•regen, *vb.* excite, agitate; **(sich a.)** get excited.

Aufregung, -en, *n.f.* excitement.

aufreibend, *adj.* exhausting.

auf•reihen, *vb.* string.

auf•reißen*, *vb.* tear open.

auf•richten, *vb.* erect.

aufrichtig, *adj.* sincere, heartfelt.

Aufruf, -e, *n.m.* proclamation.

Aufruhr, *n.m.* riot; **(in A. geraten*)** riot.

aufrührerisch, *adj.* insurgent; inflammatory.

auf•sagen, *vb.* recite.

aufsässig, *adj.* rebellious.

Aufsatz, ⸗e, *n.m.* essay.

auf•saugen, *vb.* suck up, absorb.

auf•schieben*, *vb.* postpone, delay, procrastinate.

Aufschlag, ⸗e, *n.m.* surtax; (trousers, sleeve) cuff.

auf•schlagen*, *vb.* open; hit the ground.

auf•schließen*, *vb.* unlock.

Aufschluß, ⸗sse, *n.m.* information.

aufschlußreich, *adj.* informative.

Aufschnitt, *n.m.* cut; **(kalter A.)** cold cuts.

Aufschrift, -en, *n.f.* inscription; address; label.

Aufschub, *n.m.* postponement, stay.

Aufschwung, *n.m.* upward swing, boost.

auf•sehen*, *vb.* look up.

Aufsehen, *n.nt.* sensation.

aufsehenerregend, *adj.* spectacular.

Aufseher, -, *n.m.* supervisor.

Aufseherin, -nen, *n.f.* supervisor.

auf•setzen, *vb.* put on.

Aufsicht, *n.f.* supervision.

auf•speichern, *vb.* store up.

auf•springen*, *vb.* leap up; fly open; (skin) chap.

Aufstand, ⸗e, *n.m.* uprising, insurrection.

aufständisch, *adj.* insurgent.

Aufständisch-, *n.m.* insurgent.

auf•stapeln, *vb.* stack.

auf•stehen*, *vb.* get up, rise, arise.

auf•steigen*, *vb.* mount, ascend, rise.

auf•stellen, *vb.* put up; nominate.

Aufstieg, -e, *n.m.* ascent, advancement.

auf•suchen, *vb.* look up; seek.

auf•tauchen, *vb.* emerge.

auf•tauen, *vb.* thaw.

Auftrag, ⸗e, *n.m.* instruction, order.

auf•tragen*, *vb.* instruct, assign; lay on; wear out; (food) serve up.

auf•treiben*, *vb.* raise.

auf•trennen, *vb.* rip.

auf•treten*, *vb.* appear; act.

Auftreten, *n.nt.* appearance; **(sicheres A.)** poise.

auf•wachen, *vb.* awake.

Aufwand, *n.m.* expenditure, display.

auf•wärmen, *vb.* heat up, warm up; **(sich a.)** warm oneself up.

auf•warten, *vb.* wait upon; wait up.

aufwärts, *adv.* upward(s).

auf•wecken, *vb.* wake up (somebody else).

auf•wenden*, *vb.* expend.

auf•wiegen*, *vb.* balance.

auf•zählen, *vb.* enumerate; itemize.

auf•zeichnen, *vb.* record.

auf•ziehen*, *vb.* draw open; (watch) wind; (knitting) unravel; (child) rear.

Aufzug, ⸗e, *n.m.* lift, hoist, elevator; procession; (theater) act.

auf•zwingen*, *vb.* force upon.

Auge, -n, *n.nt.* eye; **(blaues A.)** black eye.

Augenarzt, ⸗e, *n.m.* oculist.

Augenärztin, -nen, *n.f.* oculist.

Augenblick, -e, *n.m.* moment, instant.

augenblicklich, *adj.* momentary, instant.

Augenbraue, -n, *n.f.* eyebrow.

Augenglas, ⸗er, *n.nt.* eyeglass.

Augenhöhle, -n, *n.f.* eye socket.

Augenlid, -er, *n.nt.* eyelid.

Augenschein, *n.m.* evidence.

augenscheinlich, *adj.* ostensible.

Augensicht, *n.f.* eyesight.

Augenwimper, -n, *n.f.* eyelash.

August´, *n.m.* August.

aus, *prep.* out of, from.

aus•arbeiten, *vb.* elaborate; **(sich a.)** work out.

aus•arten, *vb.* degenerate.

aus•atmen, *vb.* exhale.

aus•bessern, *vb.* repair, mend.

aus•beuten, *vb.* exploit.

aus•bilden, *vb.* educate, train.

aus•bleiben*, *vb.* stay out; fail to materialize.

Ausblick, -e, *n.m.* outlook; view.

aus•brechen*, *vb.* erupt.

aus•breiten, *vb.* spread, expand.

aus•brennen*, *vb.* burn out; *(med.)* cauterize.

Ausbruch, ⸗e, *n.m.* outbreak, outburst, eruption.

aus•brüten, *vb.* hatch.

aus•buchten, *vb.* (sich a.) bulge.

Ausdauer, *n.f.* endurance, stamina.

ausdauernd, *adj.* enduring.

aus•dehnen, *vb.* expand, extend; prolong; **(sich a.)** distend, dilate.

Ausdehnung, -en, *n.f.* expanse, expansion.

aus•denken*, *vb.* think up, invent.

aus•drehen, *vb.* turn off.

Ausdruck, ⸗e, *n.m.* expression, term.

aus•drücken, *vb.* express, phrase.

ausdrücklich, *adj.* explicit.

ausdrucksvoll, *adj.* expressive.

auseinan'der, *adv.* apart, asunder.

auseinan'der•gehen*, *vb.* part; diverge.

auseinan'der•nehmen*, *vb.* take apart.

auseinan'der•reißen*, *vb.* tear apart, disrupt.

auserlesen, *adj.* choice.

aus•fallen*, *vb.* fall out, not take place.

Ausflug, ⸚, *n.m.* excursion, outing.

aus•fragen, *vb.* interrogate, quiz.

Ausfuhr, *n.f.* export.

aus•führen, *vb.* carry out, execute; export.

ausführend, *adj.* executive.

ausführlich, *adj.* detailed, explicit.

Ausführung, -en, *n.f.* execution; statement.

aus•füllen, *vb.* fill out.

Ausgabe, -n, *n.f.* expense, expenditure; issuance; edition; (computer) output.

Ausgang, ⸚e, *n.m.* exit; end.

aus•geben*, *vb.* give out; spend, expend; issue; (sich a. für) pose as.

ausgefallen, *adj.* rare; odd.

aus•gehen*, *vb.* go out; date.

ausgelassen, *adj.* hilarious.

ausgenommen, *adj.* except for.

ausgestorben, *adj.* extinct.

ausgesucht, *adj.* select.

ausgezeichnet, *adj.* excellent.

aus•gleichen*, *vb.* balance, adjust.

aus•gleiten*, *vb.* slip.

aus•graben*, *vb.* excavate, dig up.

Ausguß, ⸚sse, *n.m.* sink.

aus•halten*, *vb.* hold out; bear.

aus•händigen, *vb.* hand out, over.

Aushilfe, -n, *n.f.* assistance; stopgap.

aus•hungern, *vb.* starve out.

aus•kennen, *vb.* (sich a.) know about something, know one's way around.

aus•kleiden, *vb.* (sich a.) undress.

aus•kommen*, *vb.* get along (with).

Auskommen, *n.nt.* livelihood.

Auskunft, ⸚e, *n.f.* information.

aus•lachen, *vb.* laugh at.

aus•laden*, *vb.* unload.

Auslage, -n, *n.f.* outlay; display.

Ausland, *n.nt.* foreign country; (im A.) abroad.

Ausländer, -, *n.m.* foreigner, alien.

ausländisch, *adj.* foreign, alien.

aus•lassen*, *vb.* leave out; let out.

aus•legen, *vb.* lay out; interpret; (money) advance.

Auslegung, -en, *n.f.* interpretation.

Auslese, -n, *n.f.* selection.

aus•liefern, *vb.* extradite.

aus•löschen, *vb.* extinguish, efface.

aus•lösen, *vb.* release, unleash.

Ausmaß, -e, *n.nt.* dimension.

Ausnahme, -n, *n.f.* exception.

aus•nutzen, *vb.* utilize; exploit.

aus•packen *vb.* unpack.

aus•pressen, *vb.* squeeze.

Auspuff, -e, *n.m.* exhaust.

aus•radieren, *vb.* erase, obliterate.

aus•rangieren, *vb.* scrap.

aus•rechnen, *vb.* figure out.

Ausrede, -n, *n.f.* excuse.

aus•reichen, *vb.* suffice.

aus•reißen*, *vb.* run away, bolt.

aus•renken, *vb.* dislocate.

aus•richten, *vb.* align; execute; deliver (a message).

aus•rotten, *vb.* exterminate, eradicate.

Ausruf, -e, *n.m.* exclamation.

aus•rufen*, *vb.* proclaim, exclaim.

Ausrufezeichen, -, *n.nt.* exclamation point.

aus•ruhen, *vb.* rest.

ausruhsam, *adj.* restful.

aus•rüsten, *vb.* equip.

Aussage, -n, *n.f.* statement; testimony.

aus•sagen, *vb.* testify.

Aussatz, *n.m.* leprosy.

aus•schalten, *vb.* eliminate; (elec.) disconnect; turn off.

Ausschalter, -, *n.m.* (elec.) cutout.

aus•scheiden*, *vb.* eliminate; (med.) secrete; (sich a.) retire, withdraw.

Ausscheidung, -en, *n.f.* elimination.

aus•schelten*, *vb.* berate.

aus•schimpfen, *vb.* scold, bawl out.

aus•schlafen*, *vb.* (sich a.) sleep as long as one wants to, sleep in.

Ausschlag, ⸚e, *n.m.* (med.) rash; (den A. geben*) clinch the matter.

aus•schließen*, *vb.* shut out, exclude.

ausschließlich, *adj.* exclusive.

Ausschluß, ⸚sse, *n.m.* exclusion.

aus•schmücken, *vb.* embellish.

Ausschnitt, -e, *n.m.* section; clipping; neck (of dress).

aus•schöpfen, *vb.* bail out (water), exhaust.

Ausschuß, ⸚sse, *n.m.* committee, board; waste.

aus•schweifen, *vb.* go far afield; dissipate.

aus•sehen*, *vb.* look, appear.

außen, *adv.* outside; (nach a.) outward.

Außenbezirk, -e, *n.m.* outskirts.

Außenseite, -n, *n.f.* outside.

Außenwelt, *n.f.* outside.

außer, *prep.* beside(s), except; out of; (a. sich) beside oneself.

äußer-, *adj.* exterior, external.

außerdem, *adv.* besides.

außergewöhnlich, *adj.* extraordinary.

äußerlich, *adj.* outward.

äußern, *vb.* utter.

außerordentlich, *adv.* exceedingly.

äußerst-, *adj.* extreme.

äußerst, *adv.* extremely.

Äußerst-, *n.nt.* extremity.

außerstan'de, *adv.* unable.

Äußerung, -en, *n.f.* utterance.

aus•setzen, *vb.* set out; expose, subject.

Aussetzung, -en, *n.f.* exposure.

Aussicht, -en, *n.f.* view; prospect.

aus•speien*, *vb.* disgorge.

Aussprache, -n, *n.f.* pronunciation.

aus•sprechen*, *vb.* enunciate, pronounce; **(falsch a.)** mispronounce.

aus•spucken, *vb.* spit (out).

aus•spülen, *vb.* rinse.

Ausstand, ⸚e, *n.m.* strike.

aus•statten, *vb.* equip, endow.

Ausstattung, -en, *n.f.* equipment, décor.

aus•stehen*, *vb.* bear, stand.

aus•steigen*, *vb.* get out.

aus•stellen, *vb.* show, exhibit; issue.

Ausstellung, -en, *n.f.* exhibit, exhibition.

aus•sterben*, *vb.* die out.

Aussterben, *n.nt.* extinction.

aus•stoßen*, *vb.* expel.

aus•strahlen, *vb.* radiate.

Ausstrahlung, -en, *n.f.* radiation.

aus•streichen*, *vb.* delete.

aus•strömen, *vb.* emanate.

aus•suchen, *vb.* choose, select.

Austausch, *n.m.* exchange.

austauschbar, *adj.* exchangeable.

aus•tauschen, *vb.* exchange.

aus•teilen, *vb.* distribute.

Auster, -n, *n.f.* oyster.

aus•tilgen, *vb.* expunge.

aus•tragen*, *vb.* deliver.

Austra'lien, *n, nt* Australia.

Austra'liler, -, *n.m.* Australian

Austra'lierin, -nen, *n.f.* Australian.

aus•treiben*, *vb.* drive out, exorcise.

aus•treten*, *vb.* step out; resign; secede.

aus•üben, *vb.* exercise, practice.

Ausübung, -en, *n.f.* exercise, practice.

Ausverkauf, *n.m.* sale.

Auswahl, -en, *n.f.* choice, selection, assortment.

aus•wählen, *vb.* select, pick.

aus•walzen, *vb.* roll out, laminate.

Auswanderer, -, *n.m.* emigrant.

aus•wandern, *vb.* emigrate.

auswärtig, *adj.* external.

Ausweg, -e, *n.m.* way out, escape.

aus•weichen*, *vb.* evade, dodge.

ausweichend, *adj.* evasive.

Ausweis, -e, *n.m.* pass, identification.

aus•weisen*, *vb.* evict; **(sich a.)** identify oneself.

Ausweisung, -en, *n.f.* eviction.

auswendig, *adj.* by heart; **(a. lernen)** memorize.

aus•werten, *vb.* evaluate; reclaim.

Auswertung, -en, *n.f.* evaluation; reclamation.

aus•wickeln, *vb.* unwrap.

aus•wirken, *vb.* work out; **(sich a.)** have an effect.

Auswirkung, -en, *n.f.* effect, impact.

aus•wischen, *vb.* wipe out.

Auswuchs, ⸚e, *n.m.* protuberance, excrescence.

aus•zahlen, *vb.* pay out.

aus•zeichnen, *vb.* distinguish; **(sich a.)** excel.

aus•ziehen*, *vb.* move out; (clothes) take off; **(sich a.)** undress.

Auszug, ⸚e, *n.m.* exodus; excerpt, extract.

authen'tisch, *adj.* authentic.

Auto, -s, *n.nt.* auto.

Autobahn, -en, *n.f.* superhighway.

Autobus, -se, *n.m.* bus.

Autogramm', -e, *n.nt.* autograph.

Automat', -en, -en, *n.m.* automaton; automaton.

Automation', *n.f.* automation.

automa'tisch, *adj.* automatic.

autonom', *adj.* autonomous.

Autonummer, *n.f.* license (plate) number.

Autor', -en, *n.m.* author.

Auto'rin, -nen, *n.f.* author.

autoritär', *adj.* authoritarian.

Autorität', -en, *n.f.* authority.

Autovermietung, *n.f.* car rental.

Autowaschanlage, *n.f.* car wash.

Axt, ⸚e, *n.f.* axe.

azur'blau, *adj.* azure.

B

Baby, -s, *n.nt.* baby.

Bach, ⸚e, *n.m.* brook.

Backe, -n, *n.f.* cheek, jowl.

backen*, *vb.* bake.

Bäcker, -, *n.m.* baker.

Bäckerin, -nen, *n.f.* baker.

Bäckerei', -en, *n.f.* bakery, pastry shop.

Backpflaume, -n, *n.f.* prune.

Backstein, -e, *n.m.* brick.

Bad, ⸚er, *n.nt.* bath.

Badeanstalt, -en, *n.f.* public bath.

Badeanzug, ⸚e, *n.m.* bathing suit.

Bademantel, -⸚, *n.m.* bathrobe.

baden, *vb.* bathe.

Badeort, -e, *n.m.* bathing resort.

Badewanne, -n, *n.f.* bathtub.

Badezimmer, -, *n.nt.* bathroom.

Bahn, -en, *n.f.* path, course.

Bahnhof, ⸚e, *n.m.* station.

Bahnsteig, -e, *n.m.* platform.

Bahre, -n, *n.f.* bier.

Bajonett´, -e, *n.nt.* bayonet.

Bakte´rie, -n, *n.f.* germ.

Bakte´rium, -rien, *n.nt.* bacterium.

balancie´ren, *vb.* balance.

bald, *adv.* soon, shortly.

Balken, -, *n.m.* beam.

Balkon´, -s *or* **-e,** *n.m.* balcony.

Ball, ≃e, *n.m.* ball.

ballen, *vb.* (fist) clench.

Ballett´, *n.nt.* ballet.

Ballon´, -s, *n.m.* balloon.

Balsam, -e, *n.m.* balsam, balm.

balsamie´ren, *vb.* embalm.

Bambus, -se, *n.m.* bamboo.

banal´, *adj.* banal.

Bana´ne, -n, *n.f.* banana.

Band, -e, *n.nt.* bond, tie.

Band, ≃e, *n.m.* (book) volume.

Band, ≃er, *n.nt.* band, ribbon, tape.

Bande, -n, *n.f.* band, gang.

bändigen, *vb.* tame.

Bandit´, -en, -en, *n.m.* bandit, desperado.

bang(e), *adj.* afraid.

Bank, -e, *n.f.* bench.

Bank, -en, *n.f.* bank.

Bankgeschäft, -e, *n.nt.* banking; banking firm.

Bankier´, -s, *n.m.* banker.

Bankkonto, -s, *n.nt.* bank account.

bankrott´, *adj.* bankrupt.

Bankrott´, *n.m.* bankruptcy.

Bann, -e, *n.m.* ban; (*eccles.*) excommunication.

bannen, *vb.* banish, outlaw.

Banner, -, *n.nt.* banner.

bar, *adj.* cash.

Bar, -s, *n.f.* bar.

Bär, -en, -en, *n.m.* bear; (**Große B.**) Big Dipper.

Barbar´, -en, -en, *n.m.* barbarian.

Barbarei´, -en, *n.f.* barbarism.

barba´risch, *adj.* barbarian, barbarous.

barfuß, *adj.* barefoot.

Bargeld, -er, *n.nt.* cash.

Bariton, -e, *n.m.* baritone.

Barium, *n.nt.* barium.

Barke, -n, *n.f.* bark.

barmher´zig, *adj.* merciful.

Barmixer, -, *n.m.* bartender.

barock´, *adj.* baroque.

Barome´ter, -, *n.nt.* barometer.

barome´trisch, *adj.* barometric.

Baron´, -e, *n.m.* baron.

Barones´se, -n, *n.f.* baroness.

Barrika´de, -n, *n.f.* barricade.

Bart, ≃e, *n.m.* beard.

Barthaar, -e, *n.nt.* whisker.

bärtig, *adj.* bearded.

bartlos, *adj.* beardless.

Barzahlung, -en, *n.f.* cash payment.

basie´ren, *vb.* base.

Basis, -sen, *n.f.* basis.

Baß, ≃sse, *n.m.* bass.

Bastard, -e, *n.m.* bastard.

basteln, *vb.* make with one's hands.

Bataillon´, -e, *n.nt.* battalion.

Batist´, -e, *n.m.* cambric; batiste.

Batterie´, -i´en, *n.f.* battery.

Bau, -ten, *n.m.* construction; building; structure.

Bauch, ≃e, *n.m.* belly.

bauen, *vb.* build, construct.

Bauer, -n, *n.m.* farmer, peasant; (chess) pawn.

Bäuerin, -nen, *n.f.* farmer, farmer's wife.

Bauernhaus, ≃er, *n.nt.* farmhouse.

Bauernhof, ≃e, *n.m.* farmyard.

baufällig, *adj.* dilapidated.

Baukunst, *n.f.* architecture.

Baum, ≃e, *n.m.* tree.

Baumeister, -, *n.m.* builder.

baumeln, *vb.* dangle; (**b. lassen***) dangle.

bäumen, *vb.* (**sich b.**) rear.

Baumstamm, ≃e, *n.m.* log.

Baumwolle, *n.f.* cotton.

bauschig, *adj.* baggy.

Bauunternehmer, -, *n.m.* contractor.

Bazar´, -e, *n.m.* bazaar.

Bazil´lus, -len, *n.m.* bacillus.

beab´sichtigen, *vb.* intend.

beach´ten, *vb.* notice, pay attention to.

beach´tenswert, *adj.* noteworthy.

beacht´lich, *adj.* remarkable.

Beach´tung, -en, *n.f.* notice, consideration.

Beamte´-, *n.m.* official.

bean´spruchen, *vb.* lay claim to.

bean´standen, *vb.* object to.

bean´tragen, *vb.* propose, move.

beant´worten, *vb.* answer.

bear´beiten, *vb.* work; adapt; handle, process.

beauf´sichtigen, *vb.* supervise.

beauf´tragen, *vb.* commission.

Beauf´tragt-, *n.m.* commissioner.

bebau´en, *vb.* till; build on.

beben, *vb.* quake, tremble.

Becher, -, *n.m.* beaker, goblet, cup.

Becken, -, *n.nt.* basin; pelvis.

Bedacht´, *n.m.* deliberation, care.

bedäch´tig, *adj.* cautious, deliberate.

bedan´ken, *vb.* (**sich bei jemandem für etwas b.**) thank someone for something.

Bedarf´, *n.m.* need, demand.

bedau´erlich, *adj.* regrettable.

bedau´ern, *vb.* regret.

Bedau´ern, *n.nt.* regret.

bede´cken, *vb.* cover over.

beden´ken*, *vb.* bear in mind.

Beden´ken, -, *n.nt.* compunction, misgiving.

bedeu´ten, *vb.* mean, signify.

bedeu´tend, *adj.* significant, important.

Bedeu´tung, -en, *n.f.* significance, meaning.

bedeu´tungslos, *adj.* insignificant.

bedie´nen, *vb.* serve, wait on; operate (machine); follow suit (cards); (**sich b.**) help oneself.

Bedie´ner, -, *n.m.* operator (of a machine).

Bedie´nerin, -nen, *n.f.* operator (of a machine).

Bedient´-, *n.m. & f.* servant, attendant.

Bedie´nung, *n.f.* service.

bedingt´, *adj.* conditional, qualified.

Bedin´gung, -en, *n.f.* condition.

bedin´gungslos, *adj.* unconditional.

bedrän´gen, *vb.* beset.

bedro´hen, *vb.* menace, threaten.

bedrü´cken, *vb.* oppress.

bedrü´ckend, *adj.* oppressive.

bedür´fen*, *vb.* have need of.

Bedürf´nis, -se, *n.nt.* need, requirement.

Bedürf´nisanstalt, -en, *n.f.* comfort station.

bedürf´tig, *adj.* indigent, needy; in need of.

beeh´ren, *vb.* honor.

beei´len, *vb.* **(sich b.)** hurry.

beein´drucken, *vb.* impress.

beein´flussen, *vb.* influence.

beein´trächtigen, *vb.* impair.

been´den, *vb.* end, finish.

been´digen, *vb.* end, finish.

beer´digen, *vb.* inter, bury.

Beer´digung, -en, *n.f.* funeral.

Beere, -n, *n.f.* berry.

bef ä´higen, *vb.* enable, qualify.

befahr´bar, *adj.* passable.

befal´len*, *vb.* fall upon, attack.

befan´gen, *adj.* embarrassed.

befas´sen, *vb.* touch; **(sich b. mit)** take up, attend to, deal with.

Befehl´, -e, *n.m.* command, order.

befeh´len*, *vb.* command, order.

Befehls´haber, -, *n.m.* commander.

befes´tigen, *vb.* fasten, fortify, confirm.

befeuch´ten, *vb.* moisten.

befin´den*, *vb.* find, deem; **(sich b.)** be located, feel.

befle´cken, *vb.* stain.

beflei´ßigen, *vb.* **(sich b.)** endeavor, take pains.

befol´gen, *vb.* follow, observe, obey.

beför´dern, *vb.* advance, promote, transport.

Beför´derungsmittel, *n.nt.* conveyance.

befra´gen, *vb.* question, interrogate.

befrei´en, *vb.* liberate, exempt.

Befrei´ung, -en, *n.f.* liberation, release.

befrem´den, *vb.* appear strange to, alienate.

befreun´den, *vb.* befriend; **(sich b. mit)** make friends with.

befrie´digen, *vb.* satisfy.

befrie´digend, *adj.* satisfactory.

Befrie´digung, -en, *n.f.* satisfaction.

befruch´ten, *vb.* fertilize, fructify.

Befug´nis, -se, *n.f.* authority.

befugt´, *adj.* authorized.

befüh´len, *vb.* feel, finger.

Befund´, *n.m.* finding(s).

befürch´ten, *vb.* fear.

befür´worten, *vb.* advocate, recommend.

begabt´, *adj.* gifted.

Bega´bung, -en, *n.f.* talent.

bege´ben*, *vb.* **(sich b.)** betake oneself; occur.

begeg´nen, *vb.* meet, encounter.

Begeg´nung, -en, *n.f.* meeting, encounter.

bege´hen*, *vb.* commit.

begeh´ren, *vb.* desire, covet.

begeis´tern, *vb.* inspire.

begeis´tert, *adj.* enthusiastic.

Begeis´terung, *n.f.* enthusiasm.

Begier´de, -n, *n.f.* desire, lust.

begie´rig, *adj.* eager, desirous.

begie´ßen*, *vb.* water.

Beginn´, *n.m.* beginning.

begin´nen*, *vb.* begin.

Begin´nen, *n.nt.* inception.

beglau´bigen, *vb.* certify, accredit.

Beglau´bigungsschreiben, -, *n.nt.* credentials.

beglei´chen*, *vb.* settle.

beglei´ten, *vb.* accompany.

beglei´tend, *adj.* concomitant.

Beglei´ter, -, *n.m.* companion, escort; accompanist.

Beglei´terin, -nen, *n.f.* companion; accompanist.

Beglei´tung, -en, *n.f.* accompaniment.

beglück´wünschen, *vb.* congratulate.

begna´digen, *vb.* pardon.

begnü´gen, *vb.* **(sich b. mit)** content oneself with.

begra´ben*, *vb.* bury.

Begräb´nis, -se, *n.nt.* burial, funeral.

begrei´fen*, *vb.* comprehend.

begreif´lich, *adj.* understandable.

begren´zen, *vb.* limit.

Begren´zung, -en, *n.f.* limitation.

Begriff´, -e, *n.m.* concept; **(im B. sein*)** be about to.

begrün´den, *vb.* establish; justify.

begrü´ßen, *vb.* greet.

Begrü´ßung, -en, *n.f.* greeting, salutation.

begün´stigen, *vb.* favor, support.

Begün´stigung, -en, *n.f.* favoritism, encouragement.

behä´big, *adj.* portly.

beha´gen, *vb.* please.

Beha´gen, *n.nt.* comfort, pleasure.

behag´lich, *adj.* comfortable, pleasant.

behal´ten*, *vb.* keep.

Behäl´ter, -, *n.m.* container.

behan´deln, *vb.* treat.

Behand´lung, -en, *n.f.* treatment.

Behang´, ⸗e, *n.m.* drapery.

behar´ren, *vb.* persevere, insist.

beharr´lich, *adj.* constant, persistent.

Beharr´lichkeit, *n.f.* perseverance.

behaup´ten, *vb.* assert, maintain; allege.

Behaup´tung, -en, *n.f.* assertion.

behe´ben*, *vb.* remove.

Behelf´, -e, *n.m.* expedient, makeshift.

behel´fen*, *vb.* **(sich b. mit)** make do with.

behel´ligen, *vb.* bother.

behen´d(e), *adj.* nimble, agile.

beher´bergen, *vb.* shelter, lodge.

beherr´schen, *vb.* rule, govern; control; master; dominate.

Beherr´schung, *n.f.* rule, mastery.

beher´zigen, *vb.* take to heart.

beherzt, *adj.* courageous, game.

behilf´lich, *adj.* helpful.

behin´dern, *vb.* impede.

behin´dert, *adj.* disabled, handicapped.

Behin´dert, -, *n.m. & f.* disabled person, handicapped person.

Behin´derung, -en, *n.f.* impediment.

Behör´de, -n, *n.f.* governing office, authority.

Behuf´, -e, *n.m.* purpose; benefit.

behufs´, *prep.* for the purpose of.

behü´ten, *vb.* guard, protect, keep from; (**Gott behüte**) God forbid.

behut´sam, *adj.* cautious.

bei, *prep.* at, near, by; in connection with; (**b. mir**) at my house, on my person.

bei•behalten*, *vb.* retain.

Beibehaltung, -en, *n.f.* retention.

Beiblatt, ⁼er, *n.nt.* supplement.

bei•bringen*, *vb.* bring forward; (**jemandem etwas b.**) make something clear to someone, teach someone something.

Beichte, -n, *n.f.* confession.

beichten, *vb.* confess.

Beichtstuhl, ⁼e, *n.m.* confessional.

Beichtvater, ⁼, *n.m.* confessor.

beide, *adj. & pron.* both.

Beifall, ⁼e, *n.m.* applause.

Beifallsruf, -e, *n.m.* cheer.

bei•fügen, *vb.* add, enclose, attach, include.

Beifügung, -en, *n.f.* attachment.

Beihilfe, -n, *n.f.* assistance.

bei•kommen*, *vb.* get at.

Beil, -e, *n.nt.* hatchet.

Beilage, -n, *n.f.* enclosure; supplement; side dish.

beiläufig, *adj.* incidental.

bei•legen, *vb.* add, attach to, enclose.

Beileid, *n.nt.* condolences.

bei•messen*, *vb.* attribute.

Beimessung, -en, *n.f.* attribution.

Beimischung, -en, *n.f.* admixture.

Bein, -e, *n.nt.* leg.

beinahe, *adv.* almost.

bei•ordnen, *vb.* adjoin, coordinate.

bei•pflichten, *vb.* agree with.

beir´ren, *vb.* confuse.

beisam´men, *adv.* together.

Beisein, *n.nt.* presence.

beisei´te, *adv.* aside, apart.

Beispiel, -e, *n.nt.* example.

beispiellos, *adj.* unheard of.

beißen*, *vb.* bite.

beißend, *adj.* biting, acrid.

Beistand, ⁼e, *n.m.* assistance.

bei•stehen*, *vb.* assist.

bei•stimmen, *vb.* agree.

Beitrag, ⁼e, *n.m.* contribution.

bei•tragen*, *vb.* contribute.

Beiträger, -, *n.m.* contributor.

bei•treten*, *vb.* join.

Beitritt, -e, *n.m.* joining.

bei•wohnen, *vb.* attend, witness.

Beiwort, ⁼er, *n.nt.* epithet.

Beize, *n.f.* corrosion, stain.

beizei´ten, *adv.* in good time.

beizen, *vb.* corrode, stain.

bejah´en, *vb.* affirm, say yes to.

bejah´end, *adj.* affirmative.

bejahrt´, *adj.* aged.

bejam´mern, *vb.* deplore.

bejam´mernswert, *adj.* deplorable.

bekäm´pfen, *vb.* combat.

bekannt´, *adj.* well-known; acquainted.

Bekannt´-, *n.m. & f.* acquaintance.

bekannt´•geben*, *vb.* make known, announce.

bekannt´lich, *adv.* as is well known.

bekannt´•machen, *vb.* acquaint, make known.

Bekannt´machung, -en, *n.f.* proclamation.

Bekannt´schaft, -en, *n.f.* acquaintance.

bekeh´ren, *vb.* convert.

beken´nen*, *vb.* confess.

Bekennt´nis, -se, *n.nt.* confession.

bekla´gen, *vb.* deplore, lament; (**sich b. über**) complain about.

bekla´genswert, *adj.* deplorable, lamentable.

Beklagt´-, *n.m. & f.* accused, defendant.

beklei´den, *vb.* clothe, cover; fill (a position).

Beklei´dung, -en, *n.f.* clothing, covering.

beklem´men*, *vb.* oppress.

Beklom´menheit, *n.f.* anxiety.

bekom´men*, *vb.* get, obtain, receive; agree with, suit.

bekös´tigen, *vb.* feed, board.

bekräf´tigen, *vb.* confirm, corroborate.

beküm´mern, *vb.* grieve, distress.

Beküm´mernis, -se, *n.f.* grief, distress.

bekun´den, *vb.* manifest.

bela´den, *vb.* load, burden.

Belag´, ⁼e, *n.m.* covering, surface; (food) spread.

bela´gern, *vb.* besiege.

Bela´gerung, -en, *n.f.* siege.

Belang´, -e, *n.m.* importance.

belan´gen, *vb.* concern; sue.

belang´los, *adj.* unimportant, irrelevant.

belang´reich, *adj.* important, relevant.

belas´ten, *vb.* load, burden, strain; incriminate.

beläs´tigen, *vb.* annoy, bother, molest.

Belas´tung, -en, *n.f.* strain; inconvenience; incrimination.

belau´fen*, *vb.* (**sich b. auf**) amount to.

bele´ben, *vb.* animate, enliven.

Beleg´, -e, *n.m.* proof, evidence, documentation.

bele´gen, vb. attest; reserve (seat); sign up for (academic subject).

belegt´, adj. **(belegtes Brot)** sandwich.

beleh´ren, vb. teach.

belei´digen, vb. insult.

Belei´digung, -en, n.f. insult.

beleuch´ten, vb. illuminate.

Beleuch´tung, -en, n.f. illumination.

Belgien, n.nt. Belgium.

Belgier, -, n.m. Belgian.

Belgierin, -nen, n.f. Belgian.

belgisch, adj. Belgian.

belich´ten, vb. expose.

Belich´tung, -en, n.f. exposure.

belie´ben, vb. please.

Belie´ben, n.nt. pleasure, discretion; **(nach B.)** as you please.

belie´big, adj. any (you wish); **(eine beliebige Zahl)** any number you want.

beliebt´, adj. popular.

Beliebt´heit, n.f. popularity.

bellen, vb. bark.

beloh´nen, vb. reward.

Beloh´nung, -en, n.f. reward.

belü´gen*, vb. lie to.

belus´tigen, vb. amuse, entertain.

bema´len, vb. paint.

beman´nen, vb. man.

bemerk´bar, adj. noticeable, perceptible.

bemer´ken, vb. notice; remark.

bemer´kenswert, adj. notable.

Bemer´kung, -en, n.f. remark.

bemit´leiden, vb. pity, feel sorry for.

bemü´hen, vb. trouble; **(sich b.)** take pains, try hard.

benach´bart, adj. neighboring.

benach´richtigen, vb. notify.

Benach´richtigung, -en, n.f. notification.

benach´teiligen, vb. put at a disadvantage, handicap.

beneh´men*, vb. take away; **(sich b.)** behave.

Beneh´men, n.nt. behavior.

benei´den, vb. envy.

benei´denswert, adj. enviable.

Bengel, -, n.m. rascal.

benom´men, adj. groggy, confused.

benö´tigen, vb. need.

benut´zen, vb. use.

Benut´zung, -en, n.f. use.

Benzin´, n.nt. gas, gasoline.

beob´achten, vb. observe.

Beob´achtung, -en, n.f. observation.

bequem´, adj. comfortable, convenient.

Bequem´lichkeit, -en, n.f. comfort.

bera´ten*, vb. advise; **(sich b.)** deliberate.

Bera´ter, -, n.m. adviser, consultant.

berau´ben, vb. rob, deprive of.

Berau´bung, -en, n.f. deprivation.

berau´schen, vb. intoxicate.

bere´chenbar, adj. calculable.

berech´nen, vb. calculate, compute.

berech´nend, vb. calculating.

Berech´nung, -en, n.f. calculation, computation.

berech´tigen, vb. justify, entitle.

Berech´tigung, -en, n.f. justification.

bere´den, vb. persuade.

Bered´samkeit, n.f. eloquence.

beredt´, adj. eloquent.

Bereich´, -e, n.m. domain, scope.

berei´chern, vb. enrich.

berei´sen, vb. tour.

bereit´, adj. ready, prepared.

berei´ten, vb. make ready, prepare.

bereits´, adv. already.

bereit´willig, adj. willing (to oblige).

bereu´en, vb. repent, regret.

Berg, -e, n.m. mountain.

bergab´, adv. downhill.

bergan´, adv. uphill.

Bergarbeiter, -, n.m. miner.

bergauf´, adv. uphill.

Bergbau, n.m. mining.

bergen*, vb. save, rescue, recover.

Bergkette, -n, n.f. mountain range.

Bergrutsch, -e, n.m. land slide.

Bergsteiger, -, n.m. mountain climber.

Bergsteigerin, -nen, h.f. mountain climber.

Bergung, n.f. salvage.

Bergwerk, -e, n.nt. mine.

Bericht´, -e, n.m. report.

berich´ten, vb. report.

Bericht´erstatter, -, n.m. reporter.

Bericht´erstatterin, -nen, n.f. reporter.

berich´tigen, vb. report.

Berich´tigung, -en, n.f. correction.

bersten*, vb. burst.

berüch´tigt, adj. notorious.

berück´sichtigen, vb. consider, take into consideration; allow for.

Beruf´, -e, n.m. profession.

beru´fen*, vb. call, appoint; **(sich b. auf)** refer to, appeal to.

Berufs´beratung, n.f. career guidance.

berufs´mäßig, adj. professional.

Beru´fung, -en, n.f. summons, appointment; appeal.

beru´hen, vb. rest, be based.

beruh´igen, vb. quiet, calm.

Beru´higungsmittel, -, n.nt. sedative.

berühmt´, adj. famous.

Berühmt´heit, -en, n.f. celebrity, fame.

berüh´ren, vb. touch.

Berüh´rung, -en, n.f. touch.

besa´gen, vb. say, indicate, mean.

besagt´, adj. (afore)said.

besänf´tigen, vb. soften, soothe.

Besatz´, ≃e, n.m. border, trimming, facing.

Besat´zung, -en, n.f. occupying forces; crew.

beschä´digen, vb. damage.

Beschä´digung, -en, n.f. damage.

beschaf´fen, *vb.* get, obtain, procure; provide.

beschaf´fen, *adj.* constituted; **(so b.)** of such a nature.

Beschaf´fenheit, -en, *n.f.* nature, quality.

beschäf´tigen, *vb.* employ, occupy, keep busy.

beschäf´tigt, *adj.* busy, engaged.

Beschäf´tigung, -en, *n.f.* occupation, employment.

beschä´men, *vb.* shame.

beschämt´, *adj.* ashamed.

beschat´ten, *vb.* shade.

beschau´en, *vb.* look at, contemplate.

beschau´lich, *adj.* contemplative.

Bescheid´, -e, *n.m.* answer, decision; information; **(B. geben*)** let know; **(B. wissen* über)** know all about.

beschei´den*, *vb.* allot, apportion; inform.

beschei´den, *adj.* modest.

Beschei´denheit, *n.f.* modesty.

beschei´nigen, *vb.* certify.

Beschei´nigung, -en, *n.f.* certificate, certification.

beschen´ken, *vb.* **(b. mit)** make a present of.

beschie´ßen*, *vb.* shoot at, shell, bombard.

Beschie´ßung, -en, *n.f.* bombardment.

beschimp´fen, *vb.* abuse, insult.

Beschim´pfung, -en, *n.f.* abuse, insult.

beschir´men, *vb.* protect.

Beschlag´, ⸗e, *n.m.* metal fitting, coating, condensation; **(in B. nehmen*)** confiscate.

beschla´gen*, *vb.* cover with, coat, mount; **(sich b.)** become coated, tarnish.

beschla´gen, *adj.* experienced, proficient.

Beschlag´nahme, -n, *n.f.* seizure, confiscation.

beschlag´nahmen, *vb.* seize, confiscate.

beschleu´nigen, *vb.* quicken, accelerate.

beschlie´ßen*, *vb.* finish, conclude, decide, make up one's mind.

Beschluß´, ⸗sse, *n.m.* decision, conclusion.

beschmie´ren, *vb.* smear, spread on.

beschmut´zen, *vb.* make dirty, soil.

beschnei´den*, *vb.* cut off, clip, circumcise.

beschö´nigen, *vb.* make pretty; gloss over, excuse.

beschrän´ken, *vb.* limit.

beschränkt´, *adj.* limited, of limited abilities.

Beschränk´ung, -en, *n.f.* limitation.

beschrei´ben*, *vb.* describe.

Beschrei´bung, -en, *n.f.* description.

beschul´digen, *vb.* blame, accuse, incriminate.

Beschul´digung, -en, *n.f.* incrimination.

beschüt´zen, *vb.* protect.

Beschwer´de, -n, *n.f.* complaint, burden, trouble.

beschwe´ren, *vb.* burden; **(sich bei jemandem über etwas b.)** complain to someone about something.

beschwer´lich, *adj.* burdensome.

beschwich´tigen, *vb.* appease, soothe.

Beschwich´tigung, -en, *n.f.* appeasement.

beschwipst´, *adj.* tight, tipsy.

beschwö´ren*, *vb.* swear to; implore.

Beschwö´rung, -en, *n.f.* swearing by oath; entreaty; exorcism.

besei´tigen, *vb.* remove.

Besei´tigung, *n.f.* removal.

Besen, -, *n.m.* broom.

beses´sen, *adj.* mad, possessed.

beset´zen, *vb.* occupy, fill; trim.

besetzt´, *adj.* occupied, taken; (telephone) busy.

Beset´zung, *n.f.* occupation.

besich´tigen, *vb.* view, inspect, look around in.

Besich´tigung, -en, *n.f.* view, inspection, sight-seeing.

besie´deln, *vb.* settle, colonize.

Besie´d(e)lung, -en, *n.f.* settlement, colonization.

besie´geln, *vb.* seal.

besie´gen, *vb.* defeat.

besin´nen*, *vb.* **(sich b.)** remember, think over; **(sich anders b.)** change one's mind.

Besin´nung, -en, *n.f.* consideration, recollection; senses, consciousness.

besin´nungslos, *adj.* senseless, unconscious.

Besitz´, *n.m.* possession, property.

besit´zen*, *vb.* possess, own.

Besit´zer, -, *n.m.* proprietor.

besitz´gierig, *adj.* possessive.

Besit´zung, -en, *n.f.* possession.

besof´fen, *adj.* drunk.

besoh´len, *vb.* sole.

beson´der-, *adj.* special.

Beson´derheit, -en, *n.f.* peculiarity.

beson´ders, *adv.* especially.

beson´nen, *adj.* thoughtful, cautious.

besor´gen, *vb.* take care of, get, buy.

Besorg´nis, -se, *n.f.* apprehension, anxiety.

besorgt´, *adj.* anxious, worried.

Besor´gung, -en, *n.f.* management, care; errand.

bespöt´teln, *vb.* ridicule.

bespre´chen*, *vb.* discuss, talk over.

Bespre´chung, -en, *n.f.* discussion, review, conference.

besprit´zen, *vb.* spatter.

besser, *adj.* better.

bessern, *vb.* make better, improve.

Besserung, -en, *n.f.* amelioration, improvement; **(gute B.!)** I hope you get well soon.

best-, *adj.* best.

Bestand´, ⁼e, *n.m.* duration, stability; supply, stock.

bestän´dig, *adj.* steady, stable, constant.

Bestand´teil, -e, *n.m.* constituent, ingredient.

bestär´ken, *vb.* strengthen.

bestä´tigen, *vb.* confirm, acknowledge, verify.

Bestä´tigung, -en, *n.f.* confirmation, verification.

bestat´ten, *vb.* bury.

Bestat´tung, -en, *n.f.* burial.

beste´chen*, *vb.* bribe.

beste´chend, *adj.* attractive, tempting.

Beste´chung, -en, *n.f.* bribery, graft, corruption.

Besteck´, -e, *n.nt.* cutlery; knife, fork, and spoon.

beste´hen*, *vb.* exist; survive; (test) pass; **(b. auf)** insist on; **(b. aus)** consist of.

Beste´hen, *n.nt.* existence; insistence.

besteh´len*, *vb.* steal from, rob.

bestei´gen*, *vb.* climb up, ascend; mount; go on board.

bestel´len, *vb.* order; send for; give a message; appoint; till.

Bestel´lung, -en, *n.f.* order; message; appointment; cultivation.

Bestel´lungsnummer, *n.f.* order number.

Bestel´lungsschein, *n.m.* order form.

bestens, *adv.* very well.

besteu´ern, *vb.* tax.

Besteu´erung, -en, *n.f.* taxation.

Bestie, -n, *n.f.* beast.

bestimm´bar, *adj.* definable, ascertainable, assignable.

bestim´men, *vb.* determine, decide, specify, designate, destine, dispose.

bestimmt´, *adj.* definite.

Bestim´mungsort, -e, *n.m.* destination.

bestra´fen, *vb.* punish.

bestrah´len, *vb.* irradiate, treat with rays.

bestre´ben, *vb.* **(sich b.)** strive.

Bestre´bung, -en, *n.f.* effort.

bestreit´bar, *adj.* disputable.

bestrei´ten*, *vb.* contest, dispute, deny.

bestri´cken, *vb.* entangle, ensnare, captivate, charm.

bestür´men, *vb.* storm, attack, implore.

bestürzt´, *adj.* dismayed.

Bestür´zung, -en, *n.f.* dismay.

Besuch´, -e, *n.m.* visit, call; visitor, company; attendance.

besu´chen, *vb.* visit, attend.

Besu´cher, -, *n.m.* visitor.

betagt´, *adj.* aged.

betä´tigen, *vb.* operate; show; **(sich b.)** be active.

betäu´ben, *vb.* stun, deafen, stupefy.

betäu´bend, *adj.* stupefying; narcotic, anesthetic.

Bete, -n, *n.f.* beet.

betei´ligen, *vb.* cause to share in; **(sich b.)** take part.

Betei´ligung, -en, *n.f.* participation.

beten, *vb.* pray.

beteu´ern, *vb.* assert, swear.

Beteu´erung, -en, *n.f.* assertion.

beti´teln, *vb.* entitle.

Beton´, -s, *n.m.* concrete.

beto´nen, *vb.* stress.

Beto´nung, -en, *n.f.* stress.

betö´ren, *vb.* infatuate.

Betracht´, *n.m.* consideration.

betrach´ten, *vb.* look at, consider, observe, contemplate.

beträcht´lich, *adj.* considerable.

Betrach´tung, -en, *n.f.* consideration, contemplation.

Betrag´, ⁼e, *n.m.* amount, sum.

betra´gen*, *vb.* amount to; **(sich b.)** behave.

Betra´gen, *n.nt.* behavior.

betrau´ern, *vb.* mourn for, deplore.

Betreff´, *n.m.* reference.

betref´fen*, *vb.* affect, concern.

betreffs´, *prep.* in regard to.

betrei´ben*, *vb.* carry on.

betre´ten*, *vb.* step upon, enter.

betreu´en, *vb.* take care of.

Betrieb´, -e, *n.m.* works, management, activity; **(in B.)** running.

Betriebs´anleitung, -en, *n.f.* operating instructions.

Betriebs´leitung, *n.f.* management.

betrin´ken*, *vb.* **(sich b.)** get drunk.

betrof´fen, *adj.* taken aback; affected.

betrü´ben, *vb.* grieve.

Betrüb´nis, -se, *n.f.* grief.

Betrug´, *n.m.* deceit, deception, fraud.

betrü´gen*, *vb.* deceive, cheat.

betrü´gerisch, *adj.* deceitful, crooked.

betrun´ken, *adj.* drunk, drunken.

Bett, -en, *n.nt.* bed.

Bettdecke, -n, *n.f.* bedspread.

betteln, *vb.* beg.

Bettler, -, *n.m.* beggar.

Bettlerin, -nen, *n.f.* beggar.

Bettplatz, ⁼e, *n.m.* berth.

Bettzeug, *n.nt.* bedding, bedclothes.

beugen, *vb.* bend.

Beugung, -en, *n.f.* bend; inflection.

Beule, -n, *n.f.* swelling, bump, lump.

beun´ruhigen, *vb.* disturb, agitate.

Beun´ruhigung, -en, *n.f.* alarm, agitation.

beur´kunden, *vb.* authenticate.

beur´lauben, *vb.* give leave (of absence) to.

beur´teilen, *vb.* judge.

Beute, -n, *n.f.* booty, loot.

Beutel, -, *n.m.* bag, purse, pouch.

Bevöl´kerung, -en, *n.f.* population.

bevoll´mächtigen, *vb.* authorize, give full power to.

Bevoll´mächtigung, -en, *n.f.* authorization.

bevor´, *conj.* before.

bevor´•stehen*, *vb.* be about to happen, be in store for.

bevor´stehend, *adj.* imminent.

bevor´zugen, *vb.* favor.

bewa´chen, *vb.* guard, watch.

bewaff´nen, *vb.* arm.

Bewaff´nung, -en, *n.f.* armament.

bewah´ren, *vb.* keep, preserve.

bewäh´ren, *vb.* (**sich b.**) prove itself.

Bewah´rung, -en, *n.f.* conservation.

bewäl´tigen, *vb.* overcome, master.

bewan´dert, *adj.* (**b. in**) experienced in, conversant with.

bewe´gen*, *vb.* induce.

bewe´gen, *vb.* move.

Beweg´grund, ⸗e, *n.m.* motive.

beweg´lich, *adj.* movable, active.

Bewe´gung, -en, *n.f.* movement, motion, exercise.

bewe´gungslos, *adj.* motionless.

bewei´nen, *vb.* bewail, deplore.

Beweis´, -e, *n.m.* proof, evidence.

bewei´sen*, *vb.* prove, demonstrate.

bewer´ben*, *vb.* (**sich b. um**) apply for.

Bewer´ber, -, *n.m.* applicant, contestant, competitor, suitor.

Bewer´berin,, -nen, *n.f.* applicant, contestant, competitor.

Bewer´bung, -en, *n.f.* application.

bewer´ten, *vb.* evaluate, grade.

bewil´ligen, *vb.* approve, appropriate.

Bewil´ligung, -en, *n.f.* approval, appropriation.

bewir´ken, *vb.* cause, effect.

bewir´ten, *vb.* be host to, entertain.

bewohn´bar, *adj.* habitable.

bewoh´nen, *vb.* inhabit.

Bewoh´ner, -, *n.m.* inhabitant, occupant.

bewölkt´, *adj.* cloudy.

bewun´dern, *vb.* admire.

bewun´dernswert, *adj.* admirable.

Bewun´derung, *n.f.* admiration.

bewußt´, *adj.* conscious, aware.

bewußt´los, *adj.* unconscious.

Bewußt´sein, *n.nt.* consciousness; (**bei B.**) conscious.

bezah´len, *vb.* pay.

Bezah´lung, -en, *n.f.* pay, payment.

bezau´bern, *vb.* bewitch, enchant.

bezeich´nen, *vb.* mark, designate, signify.

bezeich´nend, *adj.* characteristic.

Bezeich´nung, -en, *n.f.* designation.

bezeu´gen, *vb.* testify, attest.

bezie´hen*, *vb.* cover with, upholster, put on clean sheets; move into; draw (pay); (**sich b.**) cloud over; (**sich b. auf**) refer to.

Bezie´hung, -en, *n.f.* reference, relation; pull, drag.

Bezirk´, -e, *n.m.* district.

Bezug´, ⸗e, *n.m.* cover(ing), case; supply; reference.

Bezug´nahme, *n.f.* reference.

bezwe´cken, *vb.* have as one's purpose, aim at.

bezwei´feln, *vb.* doubt.

BH, -s, *n.m.* bra.

Bibel, -n, *n.f.* Bible.

Biber, -, *n.m.* beaver.

Bibliothek´, -en, *n.f.* library.

Bibliothekar´, -e, *n.m.* librarian.

Bibliotheka´rin, -nen, *n.f.* librarian.

biblisch, *adj.* Biblical.

bieder, *adj.* upright, bourgeois.

biegen*, *vb.* bend; (**sich b.**) buckle.

biegsam, *adj.* flexible, pliable.

Biegung, -en, *n.f.* bend.

Biene, -n, *n.f.* bee.

Bier, -e, *n.nt.* beer.

Bierlokal, -e, *n.nt.* tavern, pub.

Biest, -er, *n.nt.* beast; brute.

bieten*, *vb.* bid, offer.

Bieter, -, *n.m.* bidder.

Bieterin, -nen, *n.f.* bidder.

bifokal´, *adj.* bifocal.

Bigamie´, *n.f.* bigamy.

bigott´, *adj.* bigoted.

Bild, -er, *n.nt.* picture, painting.

bilden, *vb.* form.

bildend, *adj.* educational, formative.

Bildhauer, -, *n.m.* sculptor.

Bildhauerin, -nen, *n.f.* sculptor.

bildhauern, *vb.* sculpture.

bildlich, *adj.* figurative.

Bildung, *n.f.* learning, education, refinement.

Billard, *n.nt.* billiards.

Billett´, -e, *n.nt.* ticket.

billig, *adj.* cheap; equitable.

billigen, *vb.* approve.

Billigkeit, -en, *n.f.* cheapness; justness.

Billion´, -en, *n.f.* billion.

Binde, -n, *n.f.* bandage; (**Damenbinde**) sanitary napkin.

binden*, *vb.* tie; bind.

bindend, *adj.* binding.

Bindestrich, -e, *n.m.* hyphen.

Bindfaden, ⸗, *n.m.* string.

Bindung, -en, *n.f.* tie, bond; (ski) binding; *(fig.)* obligation.

binnen, *prep.* within.

Binnenland, ⸗er, *n.nt.* inland.

Biographie´, -i´en, *n.f.* biography.

biogra´phisch, *adj.* biographical.

Biologie´, -i´en, *n.f.* biology.

biolo´gisch, *adj.* biological.

Biosignalrück´gabe, -n, *n.f.* biofeedback.

Birke, -n, *n.f.* birch.

Birne, -n, *n.f.* pear.

bis, *adv. & prep.* till, until.

Bischof, ⸗e, *n.m.* bishop.

bisher´, *adv.* hitherto.

Biskuit´, -e, *n.nt.* biscuit.

Bißchen, -, *n.nt.* bit; (**ein b.**) a bit, a little.

Bissen, -, *n.m.* bite, mouthful.

Bit, -s, *n.nt.* (computer) bit.

bitte, *interj.* please; you are welcome.

Bitte, -n, *n.f.* request, plea.

bitten*, *vb.* ask, request; beg.

bitter, *adj.* bitter.

bizarr´, *adj.* bizarre, freak.

Bizeps, -e, *n.m.* biceps.

blähen, *vb.* bloat, puff up.

Blama´ge, -n, *n.f.* disgrace.

blamie´ren, *vb.* disgrace.

blank, *adj.* bright, shining; (without money) broke.

Blase, -n, *n.f.* bubble; bladder; blister.

Blasebalg, ˝e, *n.m.* bellows.

blasen*, *vb.* blow.

blaß, *adj.* pale.

Blässe, *n.f.* paleness.

Blatt, ˝er, *n.nt.* leaf; piece of paper.

Blattern, *n.pl.* smallpox.

blau, *adj.* blue; drunk.

Blaubeere, -n, *n.f.* blueberry.

Blech, *n.nt.* tin.

Blei, *n.nt.* lead.

bleiben*, *vb.* stay, remain.

bleich, *adj.* pale; (b. werden) blanch.

bleichen, *vb.* bleach.

bleiern, *adj.* leaden.

bleifrei, *adj.* unleaded.

Bleistift, -e, *n.m.* pencil.

blenden, *vb.* blind, dazzle.

blended, *adj.* great splendid.

Blick, -e, *n.m.* look, glance.

blicken, *vb.* look, glance.

blind, *adj.* blind.

Blinddarm, ˝e, *n.m.* appendix.

Blinddarmentzündung, -en, *n.f.* appendicitis.

Blindheit, -en, *n.f.* blindness.

blinken, *vb.* blink.

Blinklicht, -er, *n.nt.* blinker.

blinzeln, *vb.* blink; wink.

Blitz, -e, *n.m.* lightning.

blitzen, *vb.* flash, emit lightning.

blitzsauber, *adj.* immaculate.

Block, -s, *n.m.* bloc; block; (paper) pad.

Blocka´de, -n, *n.f.* blockade.

blockfrei, *adj.* non-aligned.

blockie´ren, *vb.* block; (account) freeze.

blöd(e), *adj.* stupid, dumb.

Blödsinn, *n.m.* idiocy, nonsense.

blödsinnig, *adj.* idiotic.

blond, *adj.* blond.

bloß, 1. *adj.* bare. **2.** *adv.* only, merely.

Blöße, -n, *n.f.* nakedness; (*fig.*) weak spot.

Bloßstellung, -en, *n.f.* exposure.

Bluejeans, *n.pl.* blue jeans.

Bluff, -s, *n.m.* bluff.

bluffen, *vb.* bluff.

blühen, *vb.* bloom; flourish.

blühend, *adj.* prosperous.

Blume, -n, *n.f.* flower.

Blumengeschäft, -e, *n.nt.* flower shop.

Blumenhändler, -, *n.m.* florist.

Blumenhändlerin, -nen, *n.f.* florist.

Blumenkohl, -e, *n.m.* cauliflower.

Blumenstrauß, ˝e, *n.m.* bouquet.

blumig, *adj.* flowery.

Bluse, -n, *n.f.* blouse.

Blut, *n.nt.* blood.

blutarm, *adj.* anemic; (*fig.*) penniless.

Blutarmut, *n.f.* anemia.

Blutdruck, -e, *n.m.* blood pressure.

Blüte, -n, *n.f.* bloom, blossom; (*fig.*) prime.

bluten, *vb.* bleed.

blütenreich, *adj.* florid.

Bluterguß, ˝sse, *n.m.* hemorrhage.

Bluterkrankheit, *n.f.* hemophilia.

Bluthund, -e, *n.m.* bloodhound.

blutig, *adj.* bloody.

Blutspender, -, *n.m.* blood donor.

Blutspenderin, -nen, *n.f.* blood donor.

blutlos, *adj.* bloodless.

blutunterlaufen, *adj.* bloodshot.

Blutvergießen, *n.nt.* bloodshed.

Blutvergiftung, -en, *n.f.* blood poisoning.

Bö, -en, *n.f.* squall.

Bock, ˝e, *n.m.* buck.

bockig, *adj.* obstinate.

Bockwurst, ˝e, *n.f.* sausage.

Boden, ˝, *n.m.* ground, soil, bottom, floor; attic; **(Grund und B.)** real estate.

bodenlos, *adj.* bottomless; outrageous.

Bodensatz, *n.m.* dregs.

Bogen, ˝, *n.m.* arch; bow; (paper) sheet.

Bogenschießen, *n.nt.* archery.

Bogenschütze, -n, -n, *n.m.* archer.

Böhme, -n, -n, *n.m.* Bohemian.

Böhmen, *n.nt.* Bohemia.

böhmisch, *adj.* Bohemian.

Bohne, -n, *n.f.* bean; (grüne B.) string bean.

bohren, *vb.* bore, drill.

Bohrer, -, *n.m.* drill.

Boli´vien, *n.nt.* Bolivia.

Bollwerk, -e, *n.nt.* bulwark.

bombardie´ren, *vb.* bombard.

Bombe, -n, *n.f.* bomb, bombshell.

bomben, *vb.* bomb.

Bombenflugzeug, -e, *n.nt.* bomber.

bombensicher, *adj.* bombproof.

Boot, -e, *n.nt.* boat.

Bord, -e, *n.nt.* shelf; board; **(an B.)** aboard; **(an B. gehen)** board.

Bordell´, -e, *n.nt.* brothel.

Bordstein, -e, *n.m.* curb, curbstone.

borgen, *vb.* borrow.

borniert´, *adj.* stupid.

Börse, -n, *n.f.* purse; stock exchange.

Borste, -n, *n.f.* bristle.

Borte, -n, *n.f.* trimming, braid.

Bös-, *n.nt.* evil.

bösartig, *adj.* malicious; (*med.*) malignant.

Böschung, -en, *n.f.* bank, embankment.

böse, *adj.* bad, evil; angry, mad.

Bösewicht, -e, *n.m.* scoundrel.

boshaft, *adj.* malicious.

Bosheit, -en, *n.f.* malice.

böswillig, *adj.* malevolent.

Botanik, *n.f.* botany.

botanisch, *adj.* botanical.

Bote, -n, -n, *n.m.* messenger.

Botin, -nen, *n.f.* messenger.

Botschaft, -en, *n.f.* message; embassy.

Botschafter, -, *n.m.* ambassador.

Botschafterin, -nen, *n.f.* ambassador.

Bouillon´, -s, *n.f.* consommé.

boxen, *vb.* box, spar.

Boxkampf, ̈e, *n.m.* boxing match.

Boykott´, -e, *n.m.* boycott.

boykottie´ren, *vb.* boycott.

Brand, ̈e, *n.m.* conflagration; blight.

branden, *vb.* surge.

brandmarken, *vb.* brand.

Brandstifter, -, *n.m.* arsonist.

Brandstiftung, -en, *n.f.* arson.

Brandung, -en, *n.f.* surf, breakers.

Branntwein, -e, *n.m.* brandy.

Brasilien, *n.nt.* Brazil.

braten*, , *vb.* roast, fry.

Braten, -, *n.m.* roast.

Bratpfanne, -n, *n.f.* frying pan, griddle.

Bratrost, -e, *n.m.* oven rack; broiler.

Bratsche, -n, *n.f.* viola.

Bräu, *n.nt.* brew.

Brauch, ̈e, *n.m.* custom, usage.

brauchbar, *adj.* useful.

brauchen, *vb.* need, require; use.

brauen, *vb.* brew.

Brauer, -, *n.m.* brewer.

Brauerei´, -en, *n.f.* brewery.

braun, *adj.* brown.

bräunen, *vb.* brown; tan.

brausen, *vb.* roar.

Braut, ̈e, *n.f.* bride.

Brautführer, -, *n.m.* usher (at a wedding).

Bräutigam, -e, *n.m.* bridegroom.

Brautjungfer, -n, *n.f.* bridesmaid.

brav, *adj.* upright; (of children) good.

Bravour´, *n.f.* bravado.

brechen*, *vb.* break; (med.) fracture.

Brechmittel, -, *n.nt.* emetic.

Brei, -e, *n.m.* pap; porridge; (fig.) pulp.

breit, *adj.* broad, wide.

Breite, -n, *n.f.* breadth, width; latitude.

Bremse, -n, *n.f.* brake; horsefly.

bremsen, *vb.* brake, put on the brake.

brennbar, *adj.* combustible.

brennen*, *vb.* burn, scorch.

brennend, *adj.* burning; fervid.

Brenner, -, *n.m.* burner.

Brennholz, *n.nt.* firewood.

Brennpunkt, -e, *n.m.* focus.

Brennstoff, -e, *n.m.* fuel.

brenzlich, *adj.* risky, precarious.

Brett, -er, *n.nt.* board, plank.

Bretterbude, -n, *n.f.* shack.

Brezel, -n, *n.f.* pretzel.

Brief, -e, *n.m.* letter.

Briefkasten, ̈, *n.m.* mailbox.

Briefmarke, -n, *n.f.* stamp.

Briefpapier, *n.nt.* stationery.

Brieftasche, -n, *n.f.* wallet, billfold.

Briefträger, -, *n.m.* mail carrier.

Briefträgerin, -nen, *n.f.* mail carrier.

Briefumschlag, ̈e, *n.m.* envelope.

Briefwechsel, *n.m.* correspondence.

Briga´de, -n, *n.f.* brigade.

Brille, -n, *n.f.* spectacles, glasses.

bringen*, *vb.* bring; take.

Brise, -n, *n.f.* breeze.

Britannien, *n.nt.* Britain.

Brite, -n, -n, *n.m.* Briton.

Britin, -nen, *n.f.* Briton.

britisch, *adj.* British.

Brocken, -, *n.m.* crumb.

Brombeere, -n, *n.f.* blackberry.

bronchial´, *adj.* bronchial.

Bronchitis, *n.f.* bronchitis.

Bronze, -n, *n.f.* brooch.

Broschü´re, -n, *n.f.* pamphlet, booklet.

Brot, -e, *n.nt.* bread; (belegtes B.) sandwich.

Brötchen, -, *n.nt.* roll, bun.

Bruch, ̈e, *n.m.* break, breach, fracture; hernia; (fig.) violation.

brüchig, *adj.* brittle.

Bruchrechnung, *n.f.* fractions.

Bruchstück, -e, *n.nt.* fragment.

Bruchteil, -e, *n.m.* fraction.

Brücke, -n, *n.f.* bridge.

Bruder, ̈, *n.m.* brother.

brüderlich, *adj.* brotherly, fraternal.

Brüderschaft, -en, *n.f.* fraternity; intimate friendship.

Brühe, -n, *n.f.* broth.

brühen, *vb.* scald.

brüllen, *vb.* yell, bellow, howl.

brummen, *vb.* hum, buzz; grumble.

brünett´, *adj.* dark-haired.

Brunnen, -, *n.m.* well, fountain.

brünstig, *adj.* fervent.

brüsk, *adj.* brusque.

Brust, ̈e, *n.f.* breast, chest.

brüsten, *vb.* (sich b.) boast.

Brut, -en, *n.f.* brood.

brutal´, *adj.* brutal.

Brutalität´, -en, *n.f.* brutality.

brüten, *vb.* brood.

brutto, *adj.* gross.

Bube, -n, -n, *n.m.* boy; (cards) jack.

Buch, ̈er, *n.nt.* book.

Buchbinderei´, -ei´en, *n.f.* bookbindery.

Buche, -n, *n.f.* beech.

buchen, *vb.* book, reserve (plane seat, hotel).

Bücherei´, -en, *n.f.* library.

Bücherregal´, -e, *n.nt.* bookshelf.

Bücherschrank, ̈e, *n.m.* bookcase.

Buchführung, -en, *n.f.* accounting, bookkeeping.

Buchhalter, -, *n.m.* accountant, bookkeeper.

Buchhalterin, -nen, *n.f.* accountant, bookkeeper.

Buchhändler, -, *n.m.* book-seller.

Buchhändlerin, -nen, *n.f.* book-seller.

Buchhandlung, -en, *n.f.* bookstore.

Büchse, -n, *n.f.* can.

Büchsenöffner, -, *n.m.* can opener.

Buchstabe(n), -, (or **-n, -n),** *n.m.* letter (of the alphabet).

buchstabie´ren, *vb.* spell; **(falsch b.)** misspell.

buchstäblich, *adj.* literal.

Bucht, -en, *n.f.* bay.

Buchweizen, *n.m.* buck-wheat.

Buckel, -, *n.m.* hump, pro-tuberance; hunchback.

buckelig, *adj.* hunchbacked.

bücken, *vb.* **(sich b.)** bend down, stoop.

Bude, -n, *n.f.* booth, stall, stand.

Büfett, -s, *n.nt.* buffet.

Büffel, -, *n.m.* buffalo.

Bug, -e, *n.m.* bow.

Bügeleisen, -, *n.nt.* flatiron.

bügeln, *vb.* iron, press.

Bühne, -n, *n.f.* stage.

Bühnenausstattung, -en, *n.f.* scenery.

Bulldogge, -n, *n.f.* bulldog.

Bulle, -n, -n, *n.m.* bull.

Bummel, -n, *n.m.* spree, stroll.

bummeln, *vb.* stroll.

Bund, ¨e, *n.m.* league, fed-eration.

Bund, -e, *n.nt.* bunch, bun-dle.

Bündel, -, *n.nt.* bundle.

Bundes, *cpds.* federal.

Bundesbahn, *n.f.* German Federal Railway.

Bundeskanzler, *n.m.* chan-cellor of Germany.

Bundesrat, *n.m.* upper house of German parliament.

bundesstaatlich, *adj.* federal.

Bundestag, *n.m.* lower house of German parliament.

Bündnis, -se, *n.nt.* alliance.

bunt, *adj.* colorful; varicol-ored, motley.

Bürde, -n, *n.f.* burden.

Bürge, -n, -n, *n.m.* sponsor, guarantor.

Bürger, -, *n.m.* citizen.

Bürgerin, -nen, *n.f.* citizen.

bürgerlich, *adj.* civil; bour-geois.

Bürgermeister, -, *n.m.* mayor.

Bürgermeisterin, -nen, *n.f.* mayor.

Bürgerrechte, *n.pl.* civil rights.

Bürgerschaft, *n.f.* citizenry.

Bürgersteig, -e, *n.m.* side-walk.

Burgfriede(n), -n, *n.m.* truce.

Bürgschaft, -en, *n.f.* guar-anty, bond, bail.

Burgun´der, -, *n.m.* bur-gundy (wine).

Büro´, -s, *n.nt.* office, bu-reau.

Bursche, -n, -n, *n.m.* chap, fellow.

Bürste, -n, *n.f.* brush.

bürsten, *vb.* brush.

Bus, -se, *n.m.* bus.

Busch, ¨e, *n.m.* bush, shrub.

Büschel, -, *n.nt.* bunch.

buschig, *adj.* bushy.

Busen, -, *n.m.* bosom.

Buße, -n, *n.f.* atonement, penitence; fine, penalty.

büßen, *vb.* do penance, atone for.

Büste, -n, *n.f.* bust.

Büstenhalter, -, *n.m.* brassiere.

Butter, *n.f.* butter.

Butterblume, -n, *n.f.* butter-cup.

Butterbrot, -e, *n.nt.* slice of bread and butter.

Buttermilch, *n.f.* buttermilk.

buttern, *vb.* churn.

C

Café´, -s, *n.nt.* café.

CD-Spieler, *n.m.* compact disk player.

Cellist´, -en, -en, *n.m.* cel-list.

Cellis´tin, -nen, *n.f.* cellist.

Cello, -s, *n.nt.* cello.

Chance, -n, *n.f.* opportunity, odds.

chao´tisch, *adj.* chaotic.

Charak´ter, -e´re, *n.m.* character.

charakterisie´ren, *vb.* char-acterize.

charakteris´tisch, *adj.* char-acteristic.

Charis´ma, *n.nt.* charisma.

Charme, *n.m.* charm.

Charterflug, ¨e, *n.m.* char-ter flight.

Chauffeur´, -e, *n.m.* chauf-feur.

Chaussee´, -e´en, *n.f.* high-way.

Chef, -s, *n.m.* chef; boss.

Chefin, -nen, *n.f.* boss.

Chemie´, *n.f.* chemistry.

Chemika´lien, *n.pl.* chemi-cals.

Chemiker, -, *n.m.* chemist.

Chemikerin, -nen, *n.f.* chemist.

chemisch, *adj.* chemical.

Chemotherapie´, *n.f.* chemotherapy.

Chiffre, -n, *n.f.* cipher.

China, *n.nt.* China.

Chine´se, -n, -n, *n.m.* Chi-nese.

Chinesin, -nen, *n.f.* Chinese.

chine´sisch, *adj.* Chinese.

Chinin´, *n.nt.* quinine.

Chiroprak´tiker, -, *n.m.* chi-ropractor.

Chiroprak´tikerin, -nen, *n.f.* chiropractor.

Chirurg´, -en, -en, *n.f.* sur-geon.

Chirur´gin, -nen, *n.f.* sur-geon.

Chirurgie´, *n.f.* surgery.

Chlor, -s, *n.nt.* chlorine.

Chloroform´, *n.nt.* chloro-form.

Cholera, *n.f.* cholera.

chole´risch, *adj.* choleric.

Chor, -s, ¨e, *n.m.* choir; chorus.

Chorgang, ¨e, *n.m.* aisle.

Chorsänger, -, *n.m.* chorister.

Christ, -en, -en, *n.m.* Christian.

Christenheit, *n.f.* Christendom.

Christentum, *n.nt.* Christianity.

christlich, *adj.* Christian.

Christus, *n.m.* Christ.

Chrom, *n.nt.* chrome, chromium.

Chronik, -en, *n.f.* chronicle.

chronisch, *adj.* chronic.

Chronologie´, -i´en, *n.f.* chronology.

chronolo´gisch, *adj.* chronological.

Chrysanthe´me, -en, *n.f.* chrysanthemum.

Clown, -s, *n.m.* clown.

Cocktail, -s, *n.m.* cocktail.

College, -s, *n.nt.* college.

Compu´ter, -, *n.m.* computer.

Comu´terspiel, -e, *n.nt.* computer game.

Couch, -es, *n.f.* couch.

Coupon´, -s, *n.m.* coupon.

Cousin´, -s, *n.m.* (male) cousin.

Cousi´ne, -en, *n.f.* (female) cousin.

Cowboy, -s, *n.m.* cowboy.

Crème, -s, *n.f.* cream.

D

da, 1. *conj.* because, since, as. **2.** *adv.* there; here; then.

dabei´, *adv.* near it; present; in so doing, at the same time.

Dach, ⸚er, *n.nt.* roof.

Dachrinne, -n, *n.f.* eaves.

Dachstube, -n, *n.f.* garret.

Dachtraufe, -n, *n.f.* gutter.

dadurch´, *adv.* thereby.

dafür´, *adv.* for that; instead.

dage´gen, *adv.* against it; on the other hand.

daher´, *adv.* therefore, hence.

dahin´, *adv.* (to) there.

dahin´ter, *adv.* behind it.

damals, *adv.* then, at that time.

Dame, -n, *n.f.* lady; checkers.

Damebrett, -er, *n.nt.* checkerboard.

Damenhut, ⸚e, *n.m.* lady's hat.

Damenunterwäsche, *n.f.* lingerie.

Damespiel, *n.nt.* checkers.

damit´, 1. *conj.* in order that. **2.** *adv.* with it, with them, at that.

Damm, ⸚e, *n.m.* dam, causeway, levee.

dämmern, *vb.* dawn.

Dämmerung, -en, *n.f.* twilight.

Dämon, -o´nen, *n.m.* demon.

Dampf, ⸚e, *n.m.* steam, vapor fume.

Dampfboot, -e, *n.nt.* steamboat.

dampfen, *vb.* steam.

dämpfen, *vb.* muffle; (cooking) steam.

Dampfer, -, *n.m.* steamship.

Däne, -n, -n, *n.m.* Dane.

Dänemark, *n.nt.* Denmark.

dänisch, *adj.* Danish.

dank, *prep.* owing to.

Dank, *n.m.* thanks.

dankbar, *adj.* thankful, grateful.

Dankbarkeit, -en, *n.f.* gratitude.

danken, *vb.* thank.

dann, *adv.* then, after that.

darauf´, *adv.* on it, on them; after that, thereupon.

dar•bieten*, *vb.* present.

Darbietung, -en, *n.f.* presentation; entertainment.

dar•legen, *vb.* state.

Darlegung, -en, *n.f.* exposé, exposition.

Darlehen, -, *n.nt.* loan.

Darm, -e, *n.m.* intestine.

dar•stellen, *vb.* represent, constitute; present; portray.

Darstellung, -en, *n.f.* presentation; representation; depiction; **(graphische D.)** diagram.

Dasein, *n.nt.* existence.

daß, *conj.* that.

Datenverarbeitung, -en, *n.f.* data processing.

datie´ren, *vb.* date.

Dattel, -n, *n.f.* date.

Datum, -ten, *n.nt.* date.

Dauer, -, *n.f.* duration, length.

dauerhaft, *adj.* durable, lasting.

Dauerhaftigkeit, *n.f.* durability.

dauern, *vb.* last, continue; take (a while).

dauernd, *adj.* lasting, continual.

Dauerwelle, -n, *n.f.* permanent wave.

Daumen, -, *n.m.* thumb.

Daune, -n, *n.f.* down.

dazu´, *adv.* in addition.

dazwi´schen•kommen*, *vb.* intervene.

dazwi´schen•treten*, *vb.* intercede.

Dazwi´schentreten, *n.nt.* intervention.

DDR (Deutsche Demokratische Republik) East Germany (German Democratic Republic).

Deba´kel, -, *n.nt.* debacle.

Debat´te, -n, *n.f.* debate.

Debet, -s, *n.nt.* debit.

Debüt´, -s, *n.nt.* debut.

Debütan´tin, -nen, *n.f.* debutante.

Deck, -s, *n.nt.* deck.

Decke, -n, *n.f.* cover; blanket; ceiling.

Deckel, -n, *n.m.* lid.

decken, *vb.* cover; **(sich d.)** coincide, jibe.

Deckung, -en, *n.f.* cover(ing); collateral.

defekt´, *adj.* defective.

Defekt´, -e, *n.m.* defect.

Defensi´ve, -n, *n.f.* defensive.

Definition´, -en, *n.f.* definition.

definitiv´, *adj.* definite; definitive.

Defizit, -e, *n.nt.* deficit.

Deflation´, -en, *n.f.* deflation.

Degen, -, *n.m.* sword; epée.

Degeneration´, *n.f.* degeneration.

degeneriert´, *adj.* degenerate.

degradie´ren, *vb.* demote.

dehnen, *vb.* stretch, expand; drawl.

Dehnung, -en, *n.f.* stretch(ing), expansion.

Deich, -e, *n.m.* dike.

Dekan´, -e, *n.m.* dean.

Deklamation´, -en, *n.f.* declamation.

deklamie´ren, *vb.* declaim.

deklarie´ren, *vb.* declare.

Deklination´, -en, *n.f.* declension.

deklinie´ren, *vb.* decline.

Dekorateur´, -e, *n.m.* decorator; window dresser.

Dekorateu´rin, -nen, *n.f.* decorator, window dresser.

dekorativ´, *adj.* decorative, ornamental.

dekorie´ren, *vb.* decorate.

Dekret´, -e, *n.nt.* decree.

Delegation´, -en, *n.f.* delegation.

delegie´ren, *vb.* delegate.

Delegiert´, -, *n.m. & f.* delegate.

delikat´, *adj.* delicate, dainty.

Delikates´se, -n, *n.f.* delicacy.

Deli´rium, -rien, *n.nt.* delirium.

Demago´ge, -n, -n, *n.m.* demagogue.

demgemäß, *adv.* accordingly.

demnächst´, *adv.* shortly, soon.

demobilisie´ren, *vb.* demobilize.

Demobilisie´rung, -en, *n.f.* demobilization.

Demokrat´, -en, -en, *n.m.* democrat.

Demokratie´, -n, *n.f.* democracy.

demokra´tisch, *adj.* democratic.

demolie´ren, *vb.* wreck.

demonstrativ´, *adj.* demonstrative.

demonstrie´ren, *vb.* demonstrate.

demoralisie´ren, *vb.* demoralize.

Demut, *n.f.* humility.

demütig, *adj.* humble.

demütigen, *vb.* humiliate.

Demütigung, -en, *n.f.* humiliation.

demzufolge, *adv.* accordingly; consequently.

denkbar, *adj.* imaginable.

denken*, *vb.* think, reason.

Denker, -, *n.m.* thinker.

Denkmal, -̈er, *n.nt.* monument, memorial.

Denkungsart, *n.f.* mode of thinking, mentality.

denkwürdig, *adj.* memorable.

denn, 1. *conj.* for. 2. *adv.* do tell me; I wonder.

dennoch, *adv.* still, yet, nevertheless.

denunzie´ren, *vb.* denounce, inform.

Deportation´, -en, *n.f.* deportation.

deportie´ren, *vb.* deport.

Depot´, -s, *n.nt.* depot.

Depression´, -en, *n.f.* depression.

deprimie´ren, *vb.* depress.

der, das, die, 1. *art. & adj.* the, that. 2. *pron.* he, she, it, they; that one. 3. *rel. pron.* who, which, that.

derart, 1. *adj.* such, of such a kind. 2. *adv.* in such a way.

derb, *adj.* coarse; stout; earthy.

dermaßen, *adv.* to such a degree, in such a manner.

Deserteur´, -e, *n.m.* deserter.

Desertion´, -en, *n.f.* desertion.

deshalb, *adv.* therefore, hence.

Desi´gner, -, *n.m.* designer.

Desi´gnerin, -nen, *n.f.* designer.

desinfizie´ren, *vb.* disinfect.

desodorisie´ren, *vb.* deodorize.

Despot´, -en, -en, *n.m.* despot.

despo´tisch, *adj.* despotic.

Destillation´, -en, *n.f.* distillation.

destillie´ren, *vb.* distill.

desto, *adv.* **(d. besser)** so much the better; **(je mehr, d. besser)** the more the better.

deswegen, *adv.* therefore, that's why.

Detail´, -s, *n.nt.* detail.

Detektiv´, -e, *n.m.* detective.

deuten, *vb.* interpret; point.

deutlich, *adj.* clear, distinct.

deutsch, *adj.* German.

Deutsch-, *n.m. & f.* German.

Deutschland, *n.nt.* Germany.

Deutung, -en, *n.f.* interpretation.

Dezem´ber, -, *n.m.* December.

dezentralisie´ren, *vb.* decentralize.

Dezi´bel, -n, *n.f.* decibel.

Dezimal´-, *cpds.* decimal.

dezimie´ren, *vb.* decimate.

Diagno´se, -n, *n.f.* diagnosis.

diagnostizie´ren, *vb.* diagnose.

diagonal´, *adj.* diagonal.

Diagramm´, -e, *n.nt.* graph.

Dialekt´, -e, *n.m.* dialect.

Dialog´, -e, *n.m.* dialogue.

Diamant´, -en, *n.m.* diamond.

diametral´, *adj.* diametrical.

Diät´, -en, *n.f.* diet.

diät´gemäß, *adj.* dietary.

dicht, *adj.* dense, thick; tight.

Dichte, *n.f.* density.

Dichter, -, *n.m.* poet.

Dichterin, -nen, *n.f.* poet.

dichterisch, *adj.* poetic.

Dichtheit, *n.f.* thickness.

Dichtung, -en, *n.f.* poetry; *(tech.)* packing, gasket.

dick, *adj.* thick, fat, stout.

Dickdarm, *n.m.* colon.

Dicke, *n.f.* thickness.

dicken, *vb.* thicken.

Dickicht, -e, *n.nt.* thicket, brush.

dicklich, *adj.* chubby.

Dieb, -e, *n.m.* thief, robber.

Diebin, -nen, *n.f.* thief, robber.

Diebstahl, -̈e, *n.m.* theft, larceny.

Diele, -n, *n.f.* hall, hallway.

dienen, *vb.* serve.

Diener, -, *n.m.* valet, butler.

Dienerin, -nen, *n.f.* maid, servant.

Dienerschaft, -en, *n.f.* servant.

Dienst, -e, *n.m.* service.

Dienstag, -e, *n.m.* Tuesday.

dienstbeflissen, *adj.* assiduous; officious.

Dienstmädchen, -, *n.nt.* maid.

Dienstpflicht, *n.f.* compulsory military service, draft.

Dienstvorschrift, -en, *n.f.* regulation.

Dieselmotor, -en, *n.m.* diesel engine.

dieser, -es, -e, *pron. & adj.* this.

differential´, *adj.* differential.

differenzie´ren, *vb.* differentiate.

Diktat´, -e, *n.nt.* dictation.

Dikta´tor, -o´ren, *n.m.* dictator.

diktato´risch, *adj.* dictatorial.

Diktatur´, -en, *n.f.* dictatorship.

diktie´ren, *vb.* dictate.

Dilem´ma, -s, *n.nt.* dilemma, predicament.

Dilettant´, -en, -en, *n.m.* dilettante.

Dill, *n.m.* dill.

Ding, -e, *n.nt.* thing.

dingen*, *vb.* hire.

Diphtherie´, *n.f.* diphtheria.

Diplom´, -e, *n.nt.* diploma.

Diplomat´, -en, -en, *n.m.* diplomat.

Diploma´tin, -nen, *n.f.* diplomat.

Diplomatie´, *n.f.* diplomacy.

diploma´tisch, *adj.* diplomatic.

direkt´, *adj.* direct; downright.

Direkti´ve, -n, *n.f.* directive.

Direk´tor, -o´ren, *n.m.* director, manager.

Direkto´rin, -nen, *n.f.* director, manager.

Direkto´rium, -ien, *n.nt.* directorate, directory.

Dirigent´, -en, -en, *n.m.* conductor.

Dirigen´tin, -nen, *n.f.* conductor.

dirigie´ren, *vb.* conduct.

Diskont´, -e, *n.m.* discount.

Diskont´satz, ´-e, *n.m.* interest rate.

Diskothek´, -en, *n.f.* discotheque.

diskret´, *adj.* discreet.

Diskretion´, *n.f.* discretion.

diskrimi´nie ren, *vb.* discriminate.

Diskriminie´rung, -en, *n.f.* discrimination.

Diskussion´, -en, *n.f.* discussion.

diskutie´ren, *vb.* discuss.

disqualifizie´ren, *vb.* disqualify.

Dissertation´, -en, *n.f.* dissertation.

Diszip´lin´, *n.f.* discipline.

disziplinie´ren, *vb.* discipline.

Diva, -s, *n.f.* diva.

divers´, *adj.* miscellaneous.

Division´, -en, *n.f.* division.

D-Mark, -, *n.f.* (= deutsche Mark) mark, German unit of currency.

doch, 1. *conj.* yet. **2.** *adv.* yet; indeed; oh yes.

Docht, -e, *n.m.* wick.

Dock, -s, *n.nt.* dock.

docken, *vb.* dock.

Dogma, -men, *n.nt.* dogma.

dogma´tisch, *adj.* dogmatic.

Doktor, -o´ren, *n.m.* doctor.

Doktorat´, -e, *n.nt.* doctorate.

doktinär´, *adj.* doctrinaire.

Dokument´, -e, *n.nt.* document.

dokumenta´risch, *adj.* documentary.

dokumentie´ren, *vb.* document, authenticate.

Dolch, -e, *n.m.* dagger.

Dollar, -s, *n.m.* dollar.

dolmetschen, *vb.* interpret.

Dolmetscher, -, *n.m.* interpreter.

Dolmetscherin, -nen, *n.f.* interpreter.

Dom, -e, *n.m.* cathedral, dome.

Domi´nion, -s, *n.nt.* dominion.

Donau, *n.f.* Danube.

Donner, -, *n.m.* thunder.

donnern, *vb.* thunder.

Donnerstag, -e, *n.m.* Thursday.

Donnerwetter, *n.nt.* **(zum D.)** confound it!; (what) in thunder.

Doppel-, *cpds.* double, dual.

Doppelgänger, -, *n.m.* double.

doppelkohlensaur, *adj.* **(d. es Natron)** bicarbonate of soda.

Doppelpunkt, -e, *n.m.* colon.

doppelt, *adj.* double.

Dorf, ´-er, *n.nt.* village.

Dorn, -en, *n.m.* thorn.

dörren, *vb.* dry, parch.

dort, *adv.* there.

Dose, -n, *n.f.* (small) box, can.

dösen, *vb.* doze.

Dosie´rung, -en, *n.f.* dosage.

Dosis, -sen, *n.f.* dose.

Drache, -n, -n, *n.m.* dragon.

Draht, ´-e, *n.m.* wire.

Drahtaufnahmegerät, -e, *n.nt.* wire recorder.

drahtlos, *adj.* wireless.

drall, *adj.* buxom.

Drama, -men, *n.nt.* drama.

Drama´tiker, -, *n.m.* dramatist.

drama´tisch, *adj.* dramatic.

dramatisie´ren, *vb.* dramatize.

Drang, ´-e, *n.m.* urge.

drängeln, *vb.* crowd.

drängen, *vb.* urge, press.

Drangsal, -e, *n.f.* distress.

drapie´ren, *vb.* drape.

drastisch, *adj.* drastic.

draußen, *adv.* outside.

Dreck, *n.m.* dirt, mud.

dreckig, *adj.* filthy.

Drehbuch, ´-er, *n.nt.* scenario (film).

drehen, *vb.* turn; make (a movie).

Drehpunkt, -e, *n.m.* pivot, fulcrum.

Drehung, -en, *n.f.* turning.

drei, *num.* three.

Dreieck, -e, *n.nt.* triangle.

dreifach, *adj.* triple.

dreif ältig, *adj.* threefold.

dreimal, *adv.* thrice, three times.

Dreirad, ≈er, *n.nt.* tricycle.

dreißig, *num.* thirty.

dreißigst-, *adj.* thirtieth.

Dreißigstel, -, *n.nt.* thirtieth part; **(ein d.)** one-thirtieth.

dreist, *adj.* bold; fresh, nervy.

dreizehn, *num,* thirteen.

dreschen*, *vb.* thresh, thrash.

Drill, *n.m.* drill.

Drillbohrer, -, *n.m.* drill.

dringen*, *vb.* force one's way, penetrate; insist.

dringend, *adj.* urgent.

dringlich, *adj.* pressing.

Dringlichkeit, *n.f.* urgency.

drinnen, *adv.* inside.

dritt-, *adj.* third.

Drittel, -, *n.nt.* third part; **(ein d.)** one-third.

drittens, *adv.* in the third place, thirdly.

Dritte Welt, *n.f.* Third World.

drittletzt, *adj.* third from last.

Droge, -n, *n.f.* drug.

Drogerie´, -i´en, *n.f.* drug store.

Drogist, -en, *n.m.* druggist.

Drogis´tin, -nen, *n.f.* druggist.

drohen, *vb.* threaten.

dröhnen, *vb.* sound, boom, roar.

Drohung, -en, *n.f.* threat.

drollig, *adj.* droll, funny.

Droschke, -n, *n.f.* hack, cab.

Drossel, -n, *n.f.* thrush.

drosseln, *vb.* throttle, cut down.

drüben, *adv.* over there.

Druck, -e, *n.m.* print(ing), impression.

Druck, ≈e, *n.m.* pressure.

drucken, *vb.* print.

Drucken, *n.nt.* printing.

drücken, *vb.* press, squeeze; oppress; **(sich d.)** get out of work, shirk.

drückend, *adj.* pressing, oppressive.

Druckerpresse, -n, *n.f.* printing-press.

drunter, *adv.* underneath.

Drüse, -n, *n.f.* gland.

Dschungel, -, *n.m. or nt.* (-*n f.*), jungle.

du, *pron.* you (familiar); thou.

ducken, *vb.* **(sich d.)** duck.

Duell´, -e, *n.nt.* duel.

Duett´, -e, *n.nt.* duet.

Duft, ≈e, *n.m.* fragrance.

duftig, *adj.* fragrant.

dulden, *vb.* tolerate.

duldsam, *adj.* tolerant.

Duldsamkeit, *n.f.* tolerance.

dumm(≈), *adj.* stupid, dumb.

Dummheit, -en, *n.f.* stupidity.

Dummkopf, ≈e, *n.m.* dullard, idiot.

dumpf, *adj.* dull, musty.

Düne, -n, *n.f.* dune.

Dung, *n.m.* dung.

düngen, *vb.* fertilize.

Dünger, *n.m.* fertilizer, manure.

dunkel, *adj.* dark; obscure.

Dunkel, *n.nt.* dark(ness).

Dünkel, *n.m.* pretension.

dünken, *vb.* seem; **(mich dünkt)** methinks.

dünn, *adj.* thin.

Dunst, ≈e, *n.m.* haze, vapor.

dunsten, *vb.* steam, fume.

dünsten, *vb.* steam, stew.

dunstig, *adj.* hazy.

Duplikat´, -e, *n.nt.* duplicate.

Dur, *n.nt.* major; **(A-Dur)** A-major.

durch, *prep.* through; by means of.

durchaus´, *adv.* entirely, by all means.

durchblät´tern, *vb.* leaf through.

Durchblick, -e, *n.m.* view (through something); grasp.

durch·blicken, *vb.* look through; be visible.

durchbli´cken, *vb.* see through, discern.

durchboh´ren, *vb.* pierce.

Durchbruch, ≈e, *n.m.* break-through.

durchdacht´, *adj.* thought out.

durch·drehen, *vb.* panic.

durch·dringen*, *vb.* force one's way through, penetrate.

durchdrin´gen*, *vb.* permeate, impregnate.

durcheinan´der, *adv.* through one another; all mixed up.

Durcheinan´der, *n.nt.* confusion, turmoil, mess.

Durchfahrt, -en, *n.f.* passage, transit.

Durchfall, *n.m.* diarrhea.

durch·fallen*, *vb.* fail (a test).

durchführbar, *adj.* practicable.

durch·führen, *vb.* carry out.

Durchgang, ≈e, *n.m.* passage through; passageway; **(D. gesperrt!)** closed to traffic.

durch·gehen*, *vb.* go through; bolt, run away.

durchgehend, *adj.* nonstop.

durch·helfen*, *vb.* help through; **(sich d.)** get along somehow.

durch·kreuzen, *vb.* cross out.

durchkreu´zen, *vb.* cross, intersect; thwart.

durch·leuchten, *vb.* shine through.

durchleuch´ten, *vb.* illuminate, irradiate, X-ray.

durchlö´chern, *vb.* perforate, puncture.

Durchlö´cherung, -en, *n.f.* perforation.

Durchmesser, -, *n.m.* diameter.

durchnäs´sen, *vb.* drench, soak.

Durchreise, -n, *n.f.* journey through; **(auf der D.)** passing through.

durch·schauen, *vb.* look through.

durchschau´en, *vb.* see through, understand.

durch·schneiden*, *vb.* cut in two.

durchschnei´den*, *vb.* cut, bisect, intersect.

Durchschnitt, -e, *n.m.* average.

durchschnittlich, *adj.* average.

durch·sehen*, *vb.* see through.

durchse´hen*, *vb.* look over, scrutinize; revise.

durch·setzen, *vb.* put through, get accepted.

durchset´zen, *vb.* intersperse, permeate.

Durchsicht, *n.f.* view; perusal.

durchsichtig, *adj.* transparent.

durch•sickern, *vb.* leak through, seep through.

durch•stechen*, *vb.* stick through.

durchste´chen*, *vb.* puncture, pierce.

durchsu´chen, *vb.* search.

Durchsu´chung, **-en**, *n.f.* search.

durch•wählen, *vb.* dial direct.

durchwüh´len, *vb.* ransack.

dürfen*, *vb.* be permitted, may.

dürftig, *adj.* meager.

dürr, *adj.* dry, barren; skinny.

Dürre, **-n**, *n.f.* drought, barrenness.

Durst, *n.m.* thirst.

dürsten, *vb.* thirst.

durstig, *adj.* thirsty.

Dusche, **-n**, *n.f.* shower.

Düse, **-n**, *n.f.* nozzle, jet.

Dusel, *n.m.* good luck.

duselig, *adj.* fizzy; stupid.

Düsenflugzeug, **-e**, *n.nt.* jet plane.

Düsenkampfflugzeug, *n.nt.* jet fighter plane.

düster, *adj.* gloomy.

Düsterheit, *n.f.* gloom.

Dutzend, **-e**, *n.nt.* dozen.

duzen, *vb.* call a person *du.*

Dyna´mik, *n.f.* dynamics.

dyna´misch, *adj.* dynamic.

Dynamit´, *n.nt.* dynamite.

Dyna´mo, **-s**, *n.m.* dynamo.

Dynastie´, **-i´en**, *n.f.* dynasty.

Dyslexie´, *n.f.* dyslexia.

D-Zug, **⸚e**, *n.m.* (= Durchgangszug) train with corridors in the cars; express train.

E

Ebbe, *n.f.* low tide.

ebben, *vb.* ebb.

eben, *adj.* even, level.

eben, *adv.* just; exactly.

Ebene, **-n**, *n.f.* plain, level ground; plane.

ebenfalls, *adv.* likewise.

ebenso, *adv.* likewise; (**e. groß**) just as big.

ebnen, *vb.* level, make smooth.

Echo, **-s**, *n.nt.* echo.

echt, *adj.* genuine, real.

Echtheit, **-en**, *n.f.* authenticity, genuineness.

Ecke, **-n**, *n.f.* corner.

eckig, *adj.* angular.

edel, *adj.* noble.

Edelstein, **-e**, *n.m.* jewel.

Efeu, *n.m.* ivy.

EG (**Europäische Gemeinschaft**), *n.f.* European Community.

egal´, *adj.* equal; (**es ist mir e.**) I don't care, it makes no difference to me.

Egois´mus, *n.m.* egoism.

Egoist´, **-en**, **-en**, *n.m.* egotist.

Egotis´mus, *n.m.* egotism.

ehe, *conj.* before.

Ehe, **-n**, *n.f.* marriage, matrimony.

Ehebrecher, **-**, *n.m.* adulterer.

Ehebrecherin, **-nen**, *n.f.* adulteress.

Ehebruch, **⸚e**, *n.m.* adultery.

ehedem, *adv.* formerly.

Ehefrau, **-en**, *n.f.* wife.

Ehegatte, **-n**, **-n**, *n.m.* spouse; husband.

Ehegattin, **-nen**, *n.f.* wife.

Eheleute, *n.pl.* married people.

ehelich, *adj.* marital; legitimate.

ehelos, *adj.* celibate.

Ehelosigkeit, *n.f.* celibacy.

ehemalig, *adj.* former.

ehemals, *adv.* formerly.

Ehemann, **⸚er**, *n.m.* husband.

Ehepaar, **-e**, *n.nt.* married couple.

eher, *adv.* sooner, earlier; rather.

ehern, *adj.* brazen, brass.

Ehescheidung, **-en**, *n.f.* divorce.

Ehestand, *n.m.* matrimony.

ehrbar, *adj.* honorable.

Ehre, **-n**, *n.f.* honor.

ehren, *vb.* honor.

ehrenamtlich, *adj.* honorary, unpaid.

Ehrengast, **⸚e**, *n.m.* guest of honor.

Ehrenplatz, **⸚e**, *n.m.* place of honor.

ehrenvoll, *adj.* honorable.

ehrenwert, *adj.* worthy.

Ehrenwort, *n.nt.* word of honor.

ehrerbietig, *adj.* respectful.

Ehrerbietung, **-en**, *n.f.* reverence, obeisance.

Ehrfurcht, *n.f.* awe, respect, reverence.

Ehrgeiz, *n.m.* ambition.

ehrgeizig, *adj.* ambitious.

ehrlich, *adj.* honest, sincere.

Ehrlichkeit, **-en**, *n.f.* honesty.

ehrlos, *adj.* dishonorable.

Ehrlosigkeit, *n.f.* dishonor.

ehrsam, *adj.* honest, respectable.

Ehrsamkeit, *n.f.* respectability.

Ehrung, **-en**, *n.f.* tribute.

ehrwürdig, *adj.* reverend, venerable.

Ei, **-er**, *n.nt.* egg.

Eiche, **-n**, *n.f.* oak.

Eichhörnchen, **-**, *n.nt.* squirrel.

Eid, **-e**, *n.m.* oath.

eidesstattlich, *adj.* under oath; (**eidesstattliche Erklä´rung**) affidavit.

Eidgenosse, **-n**, **-n**, *n.m.* confederate.

Eidgenossenschaft, **-en**, *n.f.* confederation; (**Schweizerische E.**) Swiss Confederation.

eidgenössisch, *adj.* federal; Swiss.

Eifer, *n.m.* zeal, eagerness.

Eifersucht, *n.f.* jealousy.

eifersüchtig, *adj.* jealous.

eifrig, *adj.* zealous, eager, ardent.

Eigelb, **-e**, *n.nt.* yolk.

eigen, *adj.* own; typical of.

Eigenart, -en, *n.f.* peculiarity, inherent nature.

eigenartig, *adj.* peculiar.

Eigenheit, -en, *n.f.* peculiarity.

eigenmächtig, *adj.* arbitrary.

Eigenname(n), -, *n.m.* proper name.

Eigennutz, *n.m.* selfishness.

eigennützig, *adj.* selfish.

Eigenschaft, -en, *n.f.* quality.

Eigenschaftswort, ⸚er, *n.nt.* adjective.

Eigensinn, *n.m.* obstinacy, willfulness.

eigensinnig, *adj.* obstinate, willful.

eigentlich, 1. *adj.* actual. **2.** *adv.* as a matter of fact.

Eigentum, *n.nt.* property.

Eigentümer, -, *n.m.* owner.

Eigentümerin, -nen, *n.f.* owner.

Eigentumswohnung, -en, *n.f.* condominium.

eigenwillig, *adj.* willful; individual.

eignen, *vb.* **(sich e.)** be suited.

Eilbote, -n, -n, *n.m.* special delivery messenger; **(per E.n)** by special delivery.

Eilbrief, -e, *n.m.* special delivery letter.

Eile, *n.f.* haste, hurry.

eilen, *vb.* hurry.

eilig, *adj.* hasty, urgent.

Eilpost, *n.f.* special delivery.

Eimer, -, *n.m.* pail.

ein, -, -e, *art. & adj.* a, an; (stressed) one.

einan´der, *pron.* one another, each other.

ein•äschern, *vb.* cremate.

Einäscherung, -en, *n.f.* cremation.

ein•atmen, *vb.* inhale.

Einbahn-, *cpds.* one-way.

Einband, ⸚e, *n.m.* binding.

ein•bauen, *vb.* install.

ein•behalten*, *vb.* withhold.

ein•berufen*, *vb.* summon, convoke.

ein•bilden, *vb.* **(sich e.)** imagine.

Einbildung, -en, *n.f.* imagination; conceit.

ein•binden*, *vb.* bind.

Einblick, -e, *n.m.* insight.

Einbrecher, -, *n.m.* burglar.

ein•bringen*, *vb.* yield.

Einbruch, ⸚e, *n.m.* burglary.

Einbuchtung, -en, *n.f.* dent; bay.

ein•bürgern, *vb.* naturalize.

Einbuße, *n.f.* forfeiture.

ein•büßen, *vb.* forfeit.

ein•dämmen, *vb.* dam.

eindeutig, *adj.* clear, unequivocal.

ein•drängen, *vb.* **(sich e.)** encroach upon.

ein•dringen*, *vb.* penetrate, intrude, invade.

Eindringling, -e, *n.m.* intruder.

Eindruck, ⸚e, *n.m.* impression.

eindrucksvoll, *adj.* impressive.

ein•engen, *vb.* hem in.

einer, -es, -e, *pron.* one, a person; one thing.

einerlei´, *adj.* of one kind; **(es ist mir e.)** it's all the same to me.

einerseits, *adv.* on the one hand.

einfach, *adj.* simple, plain.

Einfachheit, *n.f.* simplicity.

Einfahrt, -en, *n.f.* gateway, entrance.

Einfall, -e, *n.m.* collapse; bright idea.

ein•fallen*, *vb.* fall in; invade; occur to.

einf ältig, *adj.* simple.

Einfamilienhaus, ⸚er, *n.nt.* one family home.

ein•fassen, *vb.* edge, trim.

ein•finden*, *vb.* **(sich e.)** present oneself, show up.

ein•flößen, *vb.* administer, instill.

Einfluß, ⸚sse, *n.m.* influence.

einflußreich, *adj.* influential.

ein•fordern, *vb.* demand, reclaim.

einförmig, *adj.* uniform.

ein•fügen, *vb.* insert; **(sich e.)** adapt oneself.

Einfuhr, *n.f.* import, importation.

ein•führen, *vb.* import, induct.

Einführung, -en, *n.f.* induction; introduction.

Eingabe, -n, *n.f.* petition; (computer) input.

Eingang, ⸚e, *n.m.* entrance.

ein•geben*, *vb.* give; inspire.

eingebildet, *adj.* conceited.

eingeboren, *adj.* native, indigenous.

Eingeboren-, *n.m. & f.* native.

Eingebung, -en, *n.f.* inspiration.

eingedenk, *adj.* mindful.

eingefleischt, *adj.* inveterate.

ein•gehen*, *vb.* enter; shrink; cease, perish.

eingehend, *adj.* detailed, thorough.

Eingemacht-, *n.nt.* preserves.

eingenommen, *adj.* partial, prejudiced.

Eingesessen-, *n.m. & f.* inhabitant.

Eingeständnis, -se, *n.nt.* confession, admission.

ein•gestehen*, *vb.* confess, admit.

Eingeweide, *n.pl.* intestines.

ein•gewöhnen, *vb.* acclimate.

ein•graben*, *vb.* bury.

ein•greifen*, *vb.* interfere.

Eingriff, -e, *n.m.* intervention.

ein•halten*, *vb.* check, stop; observe, keep.

ein•händigen, *vb.* hand in.

einheimisch, *adj.* native.

Einheimisch-, *n.m. & f.* native.

Einheit, -en, *n.f.* unit.

einheitlich, *adj.* uniform.

einher´, *adv.* along.

ein•holen, *vb.* gather; overtake.

ein•hüllen, *vb.* wrap up, enfold.

einig, *adj.* united, agreed.

einige, *pron. & adj.* some, several.

einigen, *vb.* unite; **(sich e.)** agree.

einigermaßen, *adv.* to some extent, somewhat.

Einigkeit, *n.f.* unity.

ein•impfen, *vb.* inoculate.

ein•kassieren, *vb.* collect.

Einkauf, ⁼e, *n.m.* purchase.

ein•kaufen, *vb.* purchase.

Einkaufsbummel, *n.m.* shopping spree.

ein•kehren, *vb.* put up (at an inn).

ein•kerkern, *vb.* incarcerate.

ein•klammern, *vb.* bracket; put in parentheses.

Einklang, ⁼e, *n.m.* harmony.

ein•kleiden, *vb.* clothe.

ein•klemmen, *vb.* wedge in.

Einkommen, -, *n.nt.* income.

Einkommensteuer, -n, *n.f.* income tax.

ein•kreisen, *vb.* encircle.

Einkünfte, *n.pl.* revenue.

ein•laden*, *vb.* invite.

Einladung, -en, *n.f.* invitation.

Einlage, -n, *n.f.* enclosure, filling; deposit.

Einlaß, ⁼sse, *n.m.* admission, entrance.

ein•laufen*, *vb.* enter; shrink.

ein•legen, *vb.* insert; deposit; pickle.

ein•leiten, *vb.* introduce.

einleitend, *adj.* introductory.

Einleitung, -en, *n.f.* introduction.

ein•leuchten, *vb.* make sense.

einleuchtend, *adj.* plausible.

ein•lösen, *vb.* redeem; cash.

Einlösung, -en, *n.f.* redemption.

ein•machen, *vb.* preserve, can.

einmal, *adv.* once; **(auf e.)** all of a sudden; **(noch e.)** once again; **(nicht e.)** not even.

einmalig, *adj.* occurring only once, single, unique.

Einmarsch, ⁼e, *n.m.* marching into, entry.

ein•mauern, *vb.* wall in.

ein•mengen, *vb.* mix in; **(sich e.)** interfere.

ein•mischen, *vb.* mix in; **(sich e.)** intervene, meddle.

Einmischung, -en, *n.f.* intervention.

Einnahme, -n, *n.f.* receipt; capture.

ein•nehmen*, *vb.* take; captivate.

Einöde, *n.f.* desolate place, solitude.

ein•ordnen, *vb.* arrange, file.

ein•packen, *vb.* pack up, wrap up.

ein•pflanzen, *vb.* plant.

ein•prägen, *vb.* impress.

ein•rahmen, *vb.* frame.

ein•räumen, *vb.* concede; put away.

ein•rechnen, *vb.* include, allow for.

Einrede, -n, *n.f.* objection.

ein•reden, *vb.* talk into, persuade.

ein•reihen, *vb.* arrange.

ein•reißen*, *vb.* tear down.

ein•richten, *vb.* furnish, arrange, establish.

Einrichtung, -en, *n.f.* arrangement, institution.

ein•rücken, *vb.* move in; indent.

eins, *num.* one.

einsam, *adj.* lone(ly), lonesome.

Einsamkeit, *n.f.* loneliness, solitude.

ein•sammeln, *vb.* gather in.

Einsatz, ⁼e, *n.m.* inset; stake (in betting); *(mil.)* sortie; mission.

ein•schalten, *vb.* switch on, shift into, tune in.

ein•schärfen, *vb.* inculcate.

ein•schätzen, *vb.* assess, estimate.

ein•schiffen, *vb.* **(sich e.)** embark.

ein•schlafen*, *vb.* go to sleep.

Einschlag, ⁼e, *n.m.* impact; envelope.

ein•schlagen*, *vb.* drive in; strike, break; take.

einschlägig, *adj.* pertinent, relevant.

ein•schließen*, *vb.* lock up, in; enclose, include, involve.

einschließlich, *adj.* inclusive.

ein•schmeicheln, *vb.* **(sich e.)** insinuate oneself.

ein•schnappen, *vb.* snap shut; get annoyed.

Einschnitt, -e, *n.m.* cut, notch, segment.

ein•schränken, *vb.* limit, restrict.

Einschränkung, -en, *n.f.* restriction.

Einschreibebrief, -e, *n.m.* registered letter.

ein•schreiben*, *vb.* inscribe; **(sich e.)** register.

ein•schüchtern, *vb.* intimidate.

Einschüchterung, -en, *n.f.* intimidation.

ein•segnen, *vb.* consecrate, confirm.

ein•sehen*, *vb.* look into, realize.

ein•seifen, *vb.* soap, lather.

einseitig, *adj.* one-sided.

ein•setzen, *vb.* set in; appoint; install.

Einsicht, -en, *n.f.* insight; inspection.

Einsiedler, -, *n.m.* hermit.

ein•spannen, *vb.* stretch; harness, enlist.

ein•sperren, *vb.* lock up, imprison.

ein•spritzen, *vb.* inject.

Einspritzung, -en, *n.f.* injection.

Einspruch, ⁼e, *n.m.* protest; **(E. erhe´ben*)** to protest.

einst, *adv.* once, one day.

ein•stecken, *vb.* put in one's pocket.

ein•stehen*, *vb.* **(e. für)** stand up for, take the place of.

ein•steigen*, *vb.* get in; **(e.!)** allaboard!

ein•stellen, *vb.* put in, tune in, engage; stop, suspend.

Einstellung, -en, *n.f.* attitude; adjustment; suspension.

ein•stimmen, *vb.* chime in, join in, agree.

einstimmig, *adj.* unanimous.

Einstimmigkeit, *n.f.* unanimity.

Einsturz, ⁼e, *n.m.* collapse.

einstweilen, *adv.* in the meantime.

ein•tauchen, *vb.* dip.

ein•tauschen, *vb.* exchange, swap.

ein•teilen, *vb.* divide, arrange, classify.

Einteilung, -en, *n.f.* classification.

eintönig, *adj.* monotonous.

Eintracht, *n.f.* harmony, concord.

ein•tragen*, *vb.* register, enter, record; bring in.

einträglich, *adj.* profitable.

Eintragung, -en, *n.f.* entry.

ein•treffen*, *vb.* arrive, happen.

ein•treten*, *vb.* enter.

Eintritt, -e, *n.m.* entry; beginning; admission.

Eintrittskarte, -n, *n.f.* ticket of admission.

ein•üben, *vb.* practice.

ein•verleiben, *vb.* incorporate, annex.

Einvernehmen, -, *n.nt.* accord.

Einverständnis, -se, *n.nt.* agreement.

Einwand, -̈e, *n.m.* objection.

Einwanderer, -, *n.m.* immigrant.

ein•wandern, *vb.* immigrate.

Einwanderung, -en, *n.f.* immigration.

einwandfrei, *adj.* sound, unobjectionable; perfect.

ein•wechseln, *vb.* change, cash.

ein•weichen, *vb.* soak.

ein•weihen, *vb.* consecrate, initiate.

Einweihung, -en, *n.f.* consecration, inauguration.

ein•wenden*, *vb.* wrap up.

ein•werfen*, *vb.* throw in; object, interject.

ein•wickeln, *vb.* wrap up.

ein•willigen, *vb.* consent.

Einwilligung, -en, *n.f.* consent, approval.

Einwirkung, -en, *n.f.* influence.

Einwohner, -, *n.m.* inhabitant, resident.

Einwohnerin, -nen, *n.f.* inhabitant, resident.

Einwurf, -̈e, *n.m.* slot; objection.

ein•zahlen, *vb.* pay in, deposit.

Einzahlung, -en, *n.f.* deposit.

Einzäunung, -en, *n.f.* enclosure.

ein•zeichnen, *vb.* inscribe.

Einzelheit, -en, *n.f.* detail.

einzeln, *adj.* single, individual.

ein•ziehen*, *vb.* *(tr.)* pull in, furl, seize, draft; *(intr.)* move in, march in.

einzig, *adj.* only, sole, single.

einzigartig, *adj.* unique.

Einzug, -̈e, *n.m.* entry.

ein•zwängen, *vb.* force in, squeeze in.

Eis, *n.nt.* ice; ice cream.

Eisberg, -e, *n.m.* iceberg.

Eisdiele, -n, *n.f.* ice-cream parlor.

Eisen, *n.nt.* iron.

Eisenbahn, -en, *n.f.* railroad.

Eisenbahnwagen, -, *n.m.* railroad coach.

Eisenwaren, *n.pl.* hardware.

eisern, *adj.* iron.

eisig, *adj.* icy.

eiskalt, *adj.* ice cold.

Eiskunstlauf, *n.m.* figure skating.

Eisregen, *n.m.* sleet.

Eisschrank, -̈e, *n.m.* refrigerator.

eitel, *adj.* vain.

Eitelkeit, -en, *n.f.* vanity.

Eiter, *n.m.* pus.

Eiterbeule, -n, *n.f.* abscess.

Eitergeschwulst, -̈e, *n.f.* abscess.

Eiweiß, -e, *n.nt.* white of egg.

Ekel, *n.m.* disgust.

ekelerregend, *adj.* nauseating.

ekelhaft, *adj.* disgusting.

ekeln, *vb.* arouse disgust; **(sich e. vor)** be disgusted by.

EKG (Elektrokardiogramm´, -e), *n.nt.* electrocardiogram.

Ekstase, -n, *n.f.* ecstasy.

ekstatisch, *adj.* ecstatic.

Ekzem´, -e, *n.nt.* eczema.

elastisch, *adj.* elastic.

Elefant´, -en, -en, *n.m.* elephant.

elegant´, *adj.* elegant, chic, smart.

Eleganz´, *n.f.* elegance.

elektrifizie´ren, *vb.* electrify.

Elek´triker, -, *n.m.* electrician.

elek´trisch, *adj.* electric.

Elektrizität´, *n.f.* electricity.

Elek´tron, -o´nen, *n.nt.* electron.

Elektro´nenrechner, -, *n.m.* computer.

Elektro´nenwissenschaft, *n.f.* electronics.

Element´, -e, *n.nt.* element.

elementar´, *adj.* elemental, elementary.

Elend, *n.nt.* misery.

elend, *adj.* miserable, wretched; sick.

elf, *num.* eleven.

Elfenbein, *n.nt.* ivory.

elft-, *adj.* eleventh.

Elftel, -, *n.nt.* eleventh part; **(ein e.)** one-eleventh.

Eli´te, *n.f.* elite.

Elixier´, -e, *n.nt.* elixir.

Ellbogen, -, *n.m.* elbow.

Elle, -, *n.f.* ell, yard.

Elsaß, *n.nt.* Alsace.

elterlich, *adj.* parental.

Eltern, *n.pl.* parents.

Emai´lle, *n.f.* enamel.

emanzipie´ren, *vb.* emancipate.

Embar´go, -s, *n.nt.* embargo.

Emblem´, -e, *n.nt.* emblem.

Embryo, -s, *n.m.* embryo.

Empfang´, -̈e, *n.m.* reception.

empfan´gen*, *vb.* receive; conceive (child).

Empf äng´er, -, *n.m.* receiver, recipient, addressee.

empf äng´lich, *adj.* susceptible.

Empfäng´nisverhütung, *n.f.* birth control, contraception.

Empfangs´bestätigung, *n.f.* receipt.

empfeh´len*, *vb.* recommend, commend.

empfeh´lenswert, *adj.* (re)commendable.

Empfeh´lung, -en, *n.f.* recommendation.

empfin´den*, *vb.* feel, sense.

empfind´lich, *adj.* sensitive.

empfind´sam, *adj.* sentimental; sensitive.

Empfin´dung, -en, *n.f.* feeling, sensation.

empfin'dungslos, *adj.* insensitive.

empor', *adv.* upward, aloft.

empö'ren, *vb.* make indignant; **(sich e.)** be furious; rebel.

empor'•ragen, *vb.* rise up, tower.

empor'schwingen*, *vb.* **(sich e.)** soar upward.

Empö'rung, -en, *n.f.* indignation; rebellion.

emsig, *adj.* busy, industrious.

Emulsion', -en, *n.f.* emulsion.

Ende, -n, *n.nt.* end.

enden, *vb.* end.

endgültig, *adj.* definitive, conclusive, final.

endigen, *vb.* end.

endlich, 1. *adj.* final; finite. **2.** *adv.* at last.

endlos, *adj.* endless.

Endstation, -en, *n.f.* terminus.

Energie', -n, *n.f.* energy.

energie'los, *adj.* languid.

ener'gisch, *adj.* energetic.

eng, *adj.* narrow, tight.

engagie'ren, *vb.* engage, hire.

Enge, -n, *n.f.* narrowness; narrow place; **(in die E. treiben*)** drive into a corner.

Engel, -, *n.m.* angel.

England, *n.nt.* England.

Engländer, -, *n.m.* Englishman.

Engländerin, -nen, *n.f.* Englishwoman.

englisch, *adj.* English.

engstirnig, *adj.* narrowminded.

Enkel, -, *n.m.* grandson.

Enkelin, -nen, *n.f.* granddaughter.

Enkelkind, -er, *n.nt.* grandchild.

enorm', *adj.* enormous.

Ensem'ble, -s, *n.nt.* ensemble.

entar'ten, *vb.* degenerate.

entbeh'ren, *vb.* go without.

entbehr'lich, *adj.* dispensable.

Entbeh'rung, -en, *n.f.* privation.

entbin'den*, *vb.* set free; deliver.

Entbin'dung, -en, *n.f.* delivery.

entblö'ßen, *vb.* denude, uncover, bare.

entde'cken, *vb.* discover.

Entde'ckung, -en, *n.f.* discovery.

Ente, -n, *n.f.* duck.

enteh'ren, *vb.* dishonor.

enteig'nen, *vb.* dispossess.

enter'ben, *vb.* disinherit.

entfa'chen, *vb.* kindle.

entfal'len*, *vb.* be cancelled; slip from (memory).

entfal'ten, *vb.* unfold.

entfer'nen, *vb.* remove.

Entfer'nung, -en, *n.f.* removal; distance.

entfes'seln, *vb.* unchain, release.

entflam'men, *vb.* inflame.

entflie'hen*, *vb.* flee, escape.

entfrem'den, *vb.* estrange, alienate.

entfüh'ren*, *vb.* carry off, abduct, kidnap.

Entfüh'rung, -en, *n.f.* abduction.

entge'gen, *adv.& prep.* opposite, contrary to; towards.

entge'gengesetzt, *adj.* opposite.

entge'gen•kommen*, *vb.* come towards; be obliging.

entge'gen•setzen, *vb.* oppose.

entgeg'nen, *vb.* reply, retort.

entge'hen*, *vb.* elude.

Entgelt', -, *n.nt.* remuneration.

entglei'sen*, *vb.* jump the track; make a slip.

Entglei'sung, -en, *n.f.* derailment; blunder.

enthal'ten*, *vb.* hold, contain; **(sich e.)** refrain.

enthalt'sam, *adj.* abstemious.

Enthalt'samkeit, -en, *n.f.* abstinence.

Enthal'tung, *n.f.* forbearance.

enthe'ben*, *vb.* oust.

Enthe'bung, -en, *n.f.* ouster.

enthül'len, *vb.* unveil, disclose.

Enthül'lung, -en, *n.f.* disclosure, exposé.

Enthusiast', -en, -en, *n.m.* enthusiast.

entklei'den, *vb.* undress, divest.

entkom'men*, *vb.* escape.

entkräf'ten, *vb.* debilitate.

entla'den*, *vb.* unload.

entlang', *adv.& prep.* along.

entlas'sen*, *vb.* dismiss, release.

Entlas'sung, -en, *n.f.* dismissal, release.

entlau'fen*, *vb.* run away.

entle'digen, *vb.* free from, exempt.

entle'gen, *adj.* remote.

entmilitarisie'ren, *vb.* demilitarize.

entmu'tigen, *vb.* discourage.

Entmu'tigung, -en, *n.f.* discouragement.

entneh'men*, *vb.* take from, infer from.

entner'ven, *vb.* enervate.

entrah'men, *vb.* skim.

enträt'seln, *vb.* decipher.

entrei'ßen*, *vb.* snatch from.

entrich'ten, *vb.* pay, settle.

entrin'nen*, *vb.* run away from.

entrüs'ten, *vb.* make indignant; **(sich e.)** become indignant.

entrüs'tet, *adj.* indignant.

Entrüs'tung, -en, *n.f.* indignation.

entsa'gen, *vb.* renounce, abjure.

entschä'digen, *vb.* compensate, indemnify.

Entschä'digung, -en, *n.f.* compensation, indemnification.

entschei'den*, *vb.* decide.

entschei'dend, *adj.* decisive.

Entschei'dung, -en, *n.f.* decision.

entschie'den, *adj.* decided, definite.

entschlie'ßen*, *vb.* **(sich e.)** decide.

entschlo'ssen, *adj.* determined.

Entschlos´senheit, *n.f.* determination.

entschlüp´fen, *vb.* slip away from.

Entschluß´, ⸗sse, *n.m.* decision.

entschul´digen, *vb.* excuse; **(sich e.)** apologize.

Entschul´digung, -en, *n.f.* excuse, apology.

entset´zen, *vb.* dismiss; horrify; **(sich e.)** be horrified.

Entset´zen, *n.nt.* horror.

entsetz´lich, *adj.* horrible.

entsin´nen*, *vb.* **(sich e.)** recollect.

Entsor´gung, *n.f.* safe disposal of waste.

entspan´nen, *vb.* relax.

Entspan´nung, *n.f.* détente; relaxation.

entspre´chen*, *vb.* correspond.

entspre´chend, *adj.* corresponding (to), respective.

entste´hen*, *vb.* arise, originate.

entstel´len, *vb.* disfigure, deform, distort, mutilate, garble.

enttäu´schen, *vb.* disappoint.

Enttäu´schung, -en, *n.f.* disappointment.

entthro´nen, *vb.* dethrone.

entwaff´nen, *vb.* disarm.

entwäs´sern, *vb.* drain.

entweder, *conj.* **(e. . . . oder)** either . . . or.

entwei´chen*, *vb.* escape.

entwen´den*, *vb.* steal.

entwer´fen*, *vb.* sketch, draft, plan.

entwer´ten, *vb.* depreciate; cancel.

entwi´ckeln, *vb.* develop.

Entwick´ler, -, *n.m.* developer.

Entwicklung, -en, *n.f.* development.

Entwick´lungshilfe, *n.f.* foreign aid.

Entwick´lungsland, ⸗er, *n.nt.* developing nation.

entwir´ren, *vb.* disentangle.

entwi´schen, *vb.* slip away from.

entwöh´nen, *vb.* wean; cure (from drugs).

entwür´digen, *vb.* dishonor.

Entwurf´, ⸗e, *n.m.* sketch, design, draft, plan.

entzie´hen*, *vb.* remove, extract.

entzü´cken, *vb.* delight.

Entzü´cken, -, *n.nt.* delight.

entzü´ckend, *adj.* delightful, charming.

Entzü´ckung, -en, *n.f.* rapture.

entzünd´bar, *adj.* inflammable.

entzün´den, *vb.* inflame.

entzün´det, *adj.* infected.

Entzün´dung, -en, *n.f.* inflammation, infection.

entzwei´, *adv.* in two, apart.

Enzy´klika, -ken, *n.f.* encyclical.

Enzyklopädie´, -i´en, *n.f.* encyclopaedia.

Epidemie´, -i´en, *n.f.* epidemic.

epide´misch, *adj.* epidemic.

Epilepsie´, *n.f.* epilepsy.

Epilog´, -e, *n.m.* epilogue.

Episo´de, -n, *n.f.* episode.

Epo´che, -n, *n.f.* epoch.

Epos (pl. Epopen), *n.nt.* epic poem.

er, *pron.* he, it.

erach´ten, *vb.* consider.

erbar´men, *vb.* have pity; **(sich e.)** pity.

Erbar´men, *n.nt.* pity.

erbärm´lich, *adj.* pitiful.

erbar´mungslos, *adj.* pitiless.

erbau´en, *vb.* construct; edify.

erbau´lich, *adj.* edifying.

Erbau´ung, *n.f.* edification.

Erbe, -, -n, *n.m.* heir.

Erbe, *n.nt.* inheritance, heritage.

erben, *vb.* inherit.

Erbfolge, *n.f.* succession.

erbie´ten*, *vb.* **(sich e.)** offer, volunteer.

Erbin, -nen, *n.f.* heiress.

erbit´ten, *vb.* ask for.

erbit´tern, *vb.* embitter.

erblas´sen, *vb.* turn pale.

erblei´chen*, *vb.* turn pale.

erblich, *adj.* hereditary.

Erblichkeit, *n.f.* heredity.

erblicken, *vb.* catch sight of.

erbo´sen, *vb.* make angry; **(sich e.)** get angry.

erbre´chen*, *vb.* break open; **(sich e.)** vomit.

Erbschaft, -en, *n.f.* inheritance.

Erbse, -n, *n.f.* pea.

Erbstück, -e, *n.nt.* heirloom.

Erdbeben, -, *n.nt.* earthquake.

Erdbeere, -n, *n.f.* strawberry.

Erdboden, *n.m.* ground, soil.

Erde, *n.f.* earth.

erden, *vb.* ground.

erden´ken*, *vb.* think up.

erdenk´lich, *adj.* imaginable.

Erdgeschoß, *n.nt.* ground floor.

Erdhügel, -, *n.m.* mound.

erdich´ten, *vb.* invent, imagine.

erdich´tet, *adj.* fictional.

Erdich´tung, *n.f.* fiction.

erdig, *adj.* earthy.

Erdkreis, -e, *n.m.* sphere.

Erdkugel, -n, *n.f.* globe.

Erdkunde, *n.f.* geography.

Erdnuß, ⸗sse, *n.f.* peanut.

Erdöl, -e, *n.nt.* petroleum.

erdrei´sten, *vb.* **(sich e.)** so bold.

erdros´seln, *vb.* strangle.

erdrü´cken, *vb.* crush (to death), stifle.

Erdteil, -e, *n.m.* continent.

erdul´den, *vb.* endure.

ereig´nen, *vb.* **(sich e.)** happen.

Ereig´nis, -se, *n.nt.* event.

ereig´nisreich, *adj.* eventful.

erfah´ren*, *vb.* come to know, learn, experience.

erfah´ren, *adj.* experienced, adept.

Erfah´rung, -en, *n.f.* experience.

erfas´sen, *vb.* grasp, realize; apprehend.

erfin´den*, *vb.* invent; contrive.

Erfin´der, -, *n.m.* inventor.

Erfin´derin, -nen, *n.f.* inventor.

erfin´derisch, *adj.* inventive; ingenious.

Erfin´dung, -en, *n.f.* invention.

Erfolg´, -e, *n.m.* success.

erfolg´los, *adj.* unsuccessful.

erfolg´reich, *adj.* successful; (**e. sein***) to succeed.

erfor´derlich, *adj.* required.

erfor´dern, *vb.* require.

Erfor´dernis, *-se*, *n.nt.* requirement, requisite.

erfor´schen, *vb.* explore.

Erfor´schung, *-en*, *n.f.* exploration.

erfreu´en, *vb.* delight, gratify; (**sich e.**) enjoy.

erfreu´lich, *adj.* enjoyable, pleasing; welcome.

erfrie´ren*, *vb.* freeze.

erfri´schen, *vb.* refresh, invigorate.

Erfri´schung, *-en*, *n.f.* refreshment.

erfül´len, *vb.* fill; fulfill.

Erfül´lung, *-en*, *n.f.* fulfillment.

ergän´zen, *vb.* supplement; amend.

Ergän´zung, *-en*, *n.f.* supplement, complement.

erge´ben*, *vb.* yield; result in; (**sich e.**) result, follow; surrender.

erge´ben, *adj.* devoted.

Ergeb´nis, *-se*, *n.nt.* result, outcome.

ergie´big, *adj.* productive.

ergöt´zen, *vb.* delight.

ergötz´lich, *adj.* delectable.

ergrei´fen*, *vb.* grasp, seize.

Ergrif´fenheit, *n.f.* emotion.

Erguß´, *=sse*, *n.m.* effusion.

erha´ben, *adj.* elevated; lofty, sublime.

Erha´benheit, *n.f.* grandeur.

erhal´ten*, *vb.* maintain, preserve; get, obtain.

Erhal´tung, *n.f.* maintenance, preservation; acquisition.

erhär´ten, *vb.* harden.

erha´schen, *vb.* snatch.

erhe´ben*, *vb.* raise.

erheb´lich, *adj.* considerable.

erhei´tern, *vb.* brighten, cheer.

erhel´len, *vb.* illuminate.

erhit´zen, *vb.* heat.

erhö´hen, *vb.* raise, heighten; ennoble.

Erhö´hung, *-en*, *n.f.* elevation, rise; enhancement; increase.

erho´len, *vb.* (**sich e.**) get better, recuperate.

Erho´lung, *n.f.* recuperation, recreation.

erhö´ren, *vb.* hear.

erin´nern, *vb.* remind; (**sich e.**) remember, recollect.

Erin´nerung, *-en*, *n.f.* remembrance, memory.

erkäl´ten, *vb.* (**sich e.**) catch cold.

Erkäl´tung, *-en*, *n.f.* cold.

erken´nen*, *vb.* recognize.

erkennt´lich, *adj.* recognizable; thankful.

Erkennt´nis, *-se*, *n.f.* realization, knowledge.

erklä´ren, *vb.* explain, declare.

erklä´rend, *adj.* explanatory.

Erklä´rung, *-en*, *n.f.* explanation; declaration.

erklet´tern, *vb.* climb up, scale.

erklin´gen*, *vb.* (re)sound.

erkran´ken, *vb.* be taken ill.

erkun´digen, *vb.* (**sich e.**) inquire.

Erkun´digung, *-en*, *n.f.* inquiry.

erlan´gen, *vb.* obtain, attain.

Erlaß´, *-sse*, *n.m.* decree.

erlas´sen*, *vb.* decree; forgive.

erlau´ben, *vb.* allow, permit.

Erlaub´nis, *-se*, *n.f.* permission, permit.

erläu´tern, *vb.* illustrate; elucidate.

Erläu´terung, *-en*, *n.f.* illustration; elucidation.

Erleb´nis, *-se*, *n.nt.* event, experience.

erle´digen, *vb.* take care of, settle.

erle´digt, *adj.* settled; exhausted.

erleich´tern, *vb.* lighten, facilitate; relieve.

Erleich´terung, *-en*, *n.f.* ease, relief.

erlei´den*, *vb.* suffer.

erle´sen, *adj.* chosen, choice, select.

erleuch´ten, *vb.* illuminate.

erlie´gen*, *vb.* succumb.

Erlös´, *n.m.* proceeds.

erlö´schen*, *vb.* go out, be extinguished; become extinct.

erlö´sen, *vb.* deliver, redeem.

Erlö´ser, *n.m.* redeemer.

Erlö´sung, *-en*, *n.f.* deliverance, redemption.

ermäch´tigen, *vb.* empower, enable.

Ermäch´tigung, *-en*, *n.f.* authorization.

ermah´nen, *vb.* admonish.

erman´geln, *vb.* lack.

ermä´ßigen, *vb.* reduce.

Ermä´ßigung, *-en*, *n.f.* reduction.

ermat´ten, *vb.* tire.

ermes´sen*, *vb.* calculate; comprehend.

ermit´teln, *vb.* ascertain.

Ermitt´lung, *-en*, *n.f.* detection; investigation.

ermög´lichen, *vb.* make possible, enable.

ermor´den, *vb.* murder.

Ermor´dung, *-en*, *n.f.* murder, assassination.

ermü´den, *vb.* tire; (**sich e.**) get tired.

ermun´tern, *vb.* rouse; cheer up.

ermu´tigen, *vb.* encourage.

Ermu´tigung, *-en*, *n.f.* encouragement.

ernäh´ren, *vb.* nourish, nurture.

Ernäh´rung, *n.f.* nourishment, nutrition.

ernen´nen*, *vb.* appoint, nominate.

Ernen´nung, *-en*, *n.f.* appointment, nomination.

erneu´ern, *vb.* renew.

Erneu´erung, *-en*, *n.f.* renewal.

ernie´drigen, *vb.* debase, degrade.

Ernie´drigung, *-en*, *n.f.* degradation.

ernst, *adj.* earnest; severe, serious.

Ernst, *n.m.* earnestness; gravity, seriousness.

Ernte, *-n*, *n.f.* harvest, crop.

ernten, *vb.* harvest, reap.

Ero´berer, *-*, *n.m.* conqueror.

ero'bern, *vb.* conquer.

Ero'berung, -en, *n.f.* conquest.

eröff'nen, *vb.* open.

Eröff'nung, -en, *n.f.* opening.

erör'tern, *vb.* discuss, debate.

Erör'terung, -en, *n.f.* discussion, debate.

Ero'tik, *n.f.* eroticism.

ero'tisch, *adj.* erotic.

erpicht', *adj.* intent.

erpres'sen, *vb.* blackmail.

Erpres'sung, -en, *n.f.* blackmail, extortion.

erqui'cken, *vb.* refresh.

erra'ten*, *vb.* guess.

erre'gen, *vb.* arouse, excite.

Erre'gung, -en, *n.f.* excitement; emotion.

errei'chen, *vb.* reach; achieve.

errich'ten, *vb.* erect, establish.

Errich'tung, -en, *n.f.* erection.

errin'gen*, *vb.* achieve; gain.

Errun'genschaft, -en, *n.f.* achievement, attainment.

Ersatz', *n.m.* compensation; substitute; *cpds.* spare.

erschaf'fen*, *vb.* create.

Erschaf'fung, -en, *n.f.* creation.

erschei'nen*, *vb.* appear.

Erschei'nung, -en, *n.f.* appearance; apparition; phenomenon.

erschie'ßen*, *vb.* shoot (dead).

erschla'gen*, *vb.* slay.

erschlie'ßen*, *vb.* open, unfold.

erschöp'fen, *vb.* exhaust.

erschöpft', *adj.* weary, exhausted.

Erschöp'fung, *n.f.* exhaustion.

erschre'cken, *vb.* scare, frighten, startle.

erschre'cken*, *vb.* become scared, become frightened, be startled.

erschü'ttern, *vb.* shake, shock.

Erschüt'terung, -en, *n.f.* shock; vibration.

erschwe'ren, *vb.* make more difficult, aggravate.

erschwing'lich, *adj.* within one's means.

erse'hen*, *vb.* see, learn.

erset'zen, *vb.* make good, replace; supersede.

ersicht'lich, *adj.* evident.

ersin'nen*, *vb.* devise.

erspa'ren, *vb.* save.

erst, **1.** *adj.* first. **2.** *adv.* not until, only.

erstar'ren, *vb.* get numb, stiffen; congeal.

erstat'ten, *vb.* refund, recompense.

erstau'nen, *vb.* astonish, amaze.

Erstau'nen, *n.nt.* amazement, astonishment.

erstaun'lich, *adj.* amazing.

erste'hen*, *vb.* arise; get, obtain.

erstei'gen*, *vb.* climb.

erstens, *adv.* in the first place, firstly.

erster-, *adj.* former.

ersti'cken, *vb.* stifle, suffocate, smother.

Ersti'ckung, -en, *n.f.* suffocation, asphyxiation, choking.

erstklassig, *adj.* first-class, first-rate.

erstre'ben, *vb.* aspire to.

erstreck'en, *vb.* (**sich e.**) extend, range.

ersu'chen, *vb.* request.

ertap'pen, *vb.* catch, surprise.

ertei'len, *vb.* give, administer.

Ertrag', ⸚e, *n.m.* yield, return.

ertrag'bar, *adj.* bearable.

ertra'gen*, *vb.* bear, endure.

erträg'lich, *adj.* passable, tolerable.

erträn'ken, *vb.* (*tr.*) drown.

ertrin'ken*, *vb.* (*intr.*) drown.

erü'brigen, *vb.* (**sich e.**) not be necessary.

erwa'chen, *vb.* wake.

erwach'sen*, *vb.* arise, grow, grow up.

erwach'sen, *adj.* grown, grown-up, adult.

Erwach'sen-, *n.m. & f.* adult.

erwä'gen, *vb.* deliberate, ponder.

Erwä'gung, -en, *n.f.* consideration.

erwäh'nen, *vb.* mention.

Erwäh'nung, -en, *n.f.* mention.

erwar'ten, *vb.* expect, await.

Erwar'tung, -en, *n.f.* expectation, anticipation.

erwe'cken, *vb.* awaken.

erwei'chen, *vb.* soften, mollify; (**sich e. lassen***) relent.

erwei'sen*, *vb.* prove; render.

erwei'tern, *vb.* widen, extend.

erwer'ben*, *vb.* acquire.

Erwer'bung, -en, *n.f.* acquisition.

erwi'dern, *vb.* reply; return, reciprocate.

Erwi'derung, -en, *n.f.* reply; return.

erwir'ken, *vb.* bring about.

erwi'schen, *vb.* catch, get hold of.

erwünscht', *adj.* desired.

erwür'gen, *vb.* strangle.

erzäh'len, *vb.* tell, narrate, relate.

Erzäh'lung, -en, *n.f.* story, narrative, tale.

Erzbischof, ⸚e, *n.m.* archbishop.

Erzdiözese, -n, *n.f.* archdiocese.

erzeu'gen, *vb.* create, produce; (*elec.*) generate.

Erzeug'nis, -se, *n.nt.* product.

Erzherzog, ⸚e, *n.m.* archduke.

erzie'hen*, *vb.* educate.

Erzie'her, -, *n.m.* educator.

Erzie'herin, -nen, *n.f.* governess, educator, teacher.

erzie'herisch, *adj.* education; breeding.

Erzie'hung, *n.f.* upbringing; education.

Erzie'hungsanstalt, *n.f.* reform school.

erzür'nen, *vb.* (**sich e.**) become angry.

erzwin'gen*, *vb.* force.

es, *pron.* it.

Esche, -n, *n.f.* ash (tree).

Esel, -, *n.m.* donkey, ass, jackass.

Eskalation´, *n.f.* escalation.

eskalie´ren, *vb.* escalate.

eßbar, *adj.* edible.

essen*, *vb.* eat.

Essen, *n.nt.* food.

Essenz´, -en, *n.f.* essence; flavoring.

Essig, *n.m.* vinegar.

Eßlöffel, -, *n.m.* tablespoon.

Eßstäbchen, -, *n.nt.* chopstick.

Eßzimmer, -, *n.nt.* dining room.

Estland, *n.nt.* Estonia.

Eta´ge, -n, *n.f.* floor, story.

Etat´, -s, *n.m.* budget.

ethnisch, *adj.* ethnic.

Etikett´, -e, *n.nt.* tag, label, sticker.

Etiket´te, *n.f.* etiquette.

etliche, *pron.* several.

etwa, *adv.* about, approximately, more or less, maybe.

etwaig, *adj.* eventual.

etwas, 1. *pron.* something. **2.** *adv.* somewhat.

Eule, -n, *n.f.* owl.

Euro´pa, *n.nt.* Europe.

Europä´er, -, *n.m.* European.

Europä´erin, -nen, *n.f.* European.

europä´isch, *adj.* European.

Europä´ische Gemeinschaft, *n.f.* European Community.

evakuie´ren, *vb.* evacuate.

evange´lisch, *adj.* evangelical, Protestant.

Evangelist´, -en, -en, *n.m.* evangelist.

Evange´lium, *n.nt.* gospel.

Eventualität´, -en, *n.f.* contingency.

eventuell´, *adj.* possible, potential.

ewig, 1. *adj.* eternal, everlasting. **2.** *adv.* forever.

Ewigkeit, -en, *n.f.* eternity.

Exa´men, -, *n.nt.* examination.

Exemplar´, -e, *n.nt.* specimen, copy.

exerzie´ren, *vb.* drill.

Existenz´, -en, *n.f.* existence.

existie´ren, *vb.* exist.

exo´tisch, *adj.* exotic.

Experiment´, -e, *n.nt.* experiment.

experimentie´ren, *vb.* experiment.

Exper´te, -n, *n.m.* expert.

explodie´ren, *vb.* explode, detonate.

Explosion´, -en, *n.f.* explosion.

explosiv´, *adj.* explosive.

Export´, -e, *n.m.* export.

exportie´ren, *vb.* export.

Expreß´, -sse, *n.m.* express train.

extra, *adj.* extra; on purpose.

Extravaganz, -en, *n.f.* extravagance.

extrem´, *adj.* extreme.

Exzellenz´, -en, *n.f.* Excellency.

exzen´trisch, *adj.* eccentric.

Exzentrizität´, -en, *n.f.* eccentricity.

F

Fabel, -n, *n.f.* fable.

fabelhaft, *adj.* fabulous, wonderful.

Fabrik´, -en, *n.f.* factory, plant.

Fabrikant´, -en, -en, *n.m.* manufacturer.

Fabrikat´, -e, *n.nt.* manufactured article; **(deutsches F.)** made in Germany.

Fach, ¨er, *n.nt.* compartment; profession; (academic) subject.

Fächer, -, *n.m.* fan.

f ächern, *vb.* fan.

Fachhochschule, -n, *n.f.* technical university.

fachmännisch, *adj.* professional.

Fachwort, -er, *n.nt.* technical term.

Fackel, -, *n.f.* torch.

fade, *adj.* flavorless, insipid.

Faden, ¨, *n.m.* thread, filament.

fadenscheinig, *adj.* threadbare.

f ähig, *adj.* able, capable, competent.

Fähigkeit, -en, *n.f.* ability, capability, competence.

fahnden, *vb.* search.

Fahne, -n, *n.f.* flag.

Fahnenflucht, *n.f.* desertion.

Fahnenflüchtig-, *n.m.* deserter.

Fähnrich, -e, *n.m.* ensign.

Fahrbahn, -en, *n.f.* lane.

Fähre, -n, *n.f.* ferry.

fahren*, *vb.* drive, ride, go.

Fahrer, -, *n.m.* driver.

Fahrerin, -nen, *n.f.* driver.

Fahrgeld, -er, *n.nt.* fare.

Fahrgemeinschaft, *n.f.* car pool.

Fahrkarte, -n, *n.f.* ticket.

Fahrkartenautomat, -en, *n.m.* ticket machine.

Fahrkartenschalter, -, *n.m.* ticket office.

fahrlässig, *adj.* negligent.

Fahrplan, ¨e, *n.m.* timetable, schedule.

fahrplanmäßig, *adj.* scheduled.

Fahrpreis, -e, *n.m.* fare.

Fahrrad, ¨er, *n.nt.* bicycle.

Fahrrinne, -n, *n.f.* lane.

Fahrschein, -e, *n.m.* ticket.

Fahrstuhl, ¨e, *n.m.* elevator.

Fahrt, -en, *n.f.* ride; trip.

Fährte, -n, *n.f.* track, trail.

Fahrzeug, -e, *n.nt.* vehicle, conveyance.

Faktor, -o´ren, *n.m.* factor.

Fakultät´, -en, *n.f.* faculty.

fakultativ´, *adj.* optional.

Fall, ¨e, *n.m.* fall; case.

Falle, -n, *n.f.* trap; pitfall.

fallen*, *vb.* fall, drop; **(f. lassen*)** drop.

f ällen, *vb.* fell.

f ällig, *adj.* due; **(f. werden*)** become due, mature.

Fälligkeit, *n.f.* maturity.

falls, *conj.* in case, if.

falsch, *adj.* false, wrong; fake; deceitful.

fälschen, *vb.* forge, counterfeit.

Fälscher, -, *n.m.* forger.

Falschheit, -en, *n.f.* falseness, deceit.

Fälschung, -en, *n.f.* forgery.

Falte, -n, *n.f.* fold, crease, pleat; wrinkle.

falten, *vb.* fold, pleat, crease.

familiär´, *adj.* familiar; intimate.

Fami´lie, -n, *n.f.* family.

Fami´liennamme(n), -, *n.m.* surname.

famos´, *adj.* splendid.

Fana´tiker, -, *n.m.* fanatic.

fana´tisch, *adj.* fanatic, rabid.

Fanatis´mus, *n.m.* fanaticism.

Fanfa´re, -n, *n.f.* fanfare.

Fang, ≃e, *n.m.* catch.

fangen*, *vb.* catch, capture.

Fänger, -, *n.m.* catcher.

Farbe, -n, *n.f.* color; paint; dye; (cards) suit.

färben, *vb.* color, dye.

farbenreich, *adj.* colorful.

Färber, -, *n.m.* dyer.

farbig, *adj.* colored.

farblos, *adj.* colorless, drab.

Farbstoff, -e, *n.m.* dye (stuff).

Farbton, ≃e, *n.m.* shade.

Farbtönung, -en, *n.f.* tint.

Färbung, -en, *n.f.* coloring, hue.

Farce, -n, *n.f.* farce.

Farmer, -, *n.m.* farmer.

Fasching, *n.m.* carnival, Mardi Gras.

Faschis´mus, *n.m.* fascism.

Faschist´, -en, -en, *n.m.* fascist.

faschis´tisch, *adj.* fascist.

faseln, *vb.* talk nonsense.

Faser, -n, *n.f.* fiber.

Faß, ≃sser, *n.nt.* barrel, keg, vat, cask.

Fassa´de, -n, *n.f.* façade.

fassen, *vb.* grasp; seize; (sich f.) compose oneself; **(fasse dich kurz!)** make it short.

Fasson´, -s, *n.f.* shape.

Fassung, -en, *n.f.* version; gem setting; *(fig.)* composure; **(aus der F. bringen*)** rattle.

fassungslos, *adj.* bewildered, staggered.

Fassungsvermögen, -, *n.nt.* capacity; comprehension.

fast, *adv.* almost, nearly.

fasten, *vb.* fast.

Fastenzeit, *n.f.* Lent.

faszinie´ren, *vb.* fascinate.

fauchen, *vb.* puff; (of cats) spit.

faul, *adj.* lazy; rotten.

faulenzen, *vb.* loaf.

Faulenzer, -n, *n.m.* loafer.

Faulenzerin, -nen, *n.f.* loafer.

Fäulnis, *n.f.* decay, putrefaction.

Faultier, -e, *n.nt.* sloth.

Faust, ≃e, *n.f.* fist.

faxen, *vb.* fax.

Februar, -e, *n.m.* February.

fechten*, *vb.* fence.

Feder, -n, *n.f.* feather, plume; pen.

federleicht, *adj.* feathery.

federn, *vb.* feather; have good springs.

Fee, Fe´en, *n.f.* fairy.

Fegefeuer, *n.nt.* purgatory.

Fehde, -n, *n.f.* feud.

fehlbar, *adj.* fallible.

fehlen, *vb.* lack; be absent or missing.

Fehler, -, *n.m.* mistake, error; flaw, imperfection, defect; blunder.

fehlerfrei, *adj.* flawless.

fehlerhaft, *adj.* faulty, imperfect, defective.

fehlerlos, *adj.* faultless.

fehl•gebären*, *vb.* abort, have a miscarriage.

Fehlgeburt, -en, *n.f.* miscarriage, abortion.

fehl•gehen*, *vb.* err, go astray.

Fehlschlag, ≃e, *n.m.* failure; setback.

Fehltritt, -e, *n.m.* slip.

Feier, -n, *n.f.* celebration.

Feierabend, *n.m.* end of work.

feierlich, *adj.* ceremonious; solemn.

Feierlichkeit, -en, *n.f.* ceremony, solemnity.

feiern, *vb.* celebrate.

Feiertag, -e, *n.m.* holiday.

feige, *adj.* cowardly.

Feige, -n, *n.f.* fig.

Feigheit, -en, *n.f.* cowardice.

Feigling, -e, *n.m.* coward.

Feile, -n, *n.f.* file.

feilen, *vb.* file.

feilschen, *vb.* bargain, haggle.

fein, *adj.* fine, delicate; elegant; subtle.

Feind, -e, *n.m.* foe, enemy.

Feindin, -nen, *n.f.* enemy.

feindlich, *adj.* hostile.

Feindschaft, -en, *n.f.* enmity; feud.

Feindseligkeit, -en, *n.f.* hostility.

Feingefühl, *n.nt.* sensitivity.

Feinheit, -en, *n.f.* purity; delicacy; elegance; subtlety.

Feinschmecker, -, *n.m.* gourmet.

feinsinnig, *adj.* ingenious.

feist, *adj.* fat, plump.

Feld, -er, *n.nt.* field.

Feldbett, -en, *n.nt.* cot.

Feldherr, -n, -en, *n.m.* commander.

Feldstecher, -, *n.m.* binoculars.

Feldzug, ≃e, *n.m.* campaign.

Fell, -e, *n.nt.* skin, pelt, hide.

Fels(en), -), *n.m.* rock, boulder.

Felsblock, ≃e, *n.m.* boulder.

felsig, *adj.* rocky, craggy.

Fenster, -, *n.nt.* window.

Fensterladen, ≃, *n.m.* shutter.

Fensterscheibe, -n, *n.f.* windowpane.

Ferien, *n.pl.* vacation.

Ferienort, -e, *n.m.* resort.

fern, *adj.* far, distant, remote.

Fernanruf, -e, *n.m.* long-distance call.

ferner, *adv.* moreover, furthermore.

Ferngespräch, -e, *n.nt.* long-distance call.

Fernglas, ≃er, *n.nt.* binocular(s).

Fernrohr, -e, *n.nt.* telescope.

Fernsehen, *n.nt.* television.

Fernsprecher, -, *n.m.* telephone.

Ferse, -n, *n.f.* heel.

fertig, *adj.* finished, complete, ready, done; **(f. sein*)** be through; **(f. bringen*)** complete, accomplish.

Fertigkeit, -en, *n.f.* dexterity, knack.

fesch, *adj.* chic.

Fessel, -n, *n.f.* fetter, irons, handcuffs; ankle.

Fesselgelenk, -e, *n.nt.* ankle.

fesseln, *vb.* chain; *(fig.)* captivate, fascinate.

fest, *adj.* firm, solid; fixed, steady; tight.

Fest, -e, *n.nt.* feast, celebration.

Feste, -n, *n.f.* fort, stronghold.

Festessen, -, *n.nt.* banquet, feast.

fest•fahren*, *vb.* run aground; *(fig.)* come to an impasse.

fest•halten*, *vb.* hold fast to, adhere to; detain.

festigen, *vb.* solidify, consolidate.

Festigkeit, *n.f.* firmness, solidity.

fest•klammern, *vb.* clamp; **(sich f.)** hold fast.

Festland, *n.nt.* mainland.

fest•legen, *vb.* fix, lay down.

festlich, *adj.* festive.

Festlichkeit, -en, *n.f.* festivity.

fest•machen, *vb.* fasten, make fast.

Festmahl, -e, *n.nt.* feast.

Festnahme, -n, *n.f.* arrest.

fest•nehmen*, *vb.* arrest.

fest•setzen, *vb.* fix, establish; determine.

Festspiel, -e, *n.nt.* festival.

fest•stehen*, *vb.* be stable; be certain.

feststehend, *adj.* stationary.

fest•stellen, *vb.* determine, ascertain; state.

Festtag, -e, *n.m.* holiday.

Festung, -en, *n.f.* fortress.

Fete, -n, *n.f.* party.

fett, *adj.* fat, greasy.

Fett, -e, *n.nt.* fat, grease.

fetten, *vb.* grease.

fettig, *adj.* fatty, greasy, oily.

fettleibig, *adj.* obese.

Fetzen, -, *n.m.* rag; scrap.

feucht, *adj.* moist, damp, humid.

Feuchtigkeit, *n.f.* moisture, dampness, humidity.

feuchtkalt, *adj.* clammy.

Feuer, -, *n.nt.* fire, *(fig.)* verve.

Feueralarm, -e, *n.m.* fire alarm.

feuergefährlich, *adj.* inflammable.

Feuerleiter, -n, *n.f.* fire escape.

Feuermelder, -, *n.m.* fire alarm (box).

feuern, *vb.* fire.

Feuersbrunst, *n.f.* conflagration.

Feuerspritze, -n, *n.f.* fire engine.

Feuerstein, -e, *n.m.* flint.

Feuerwaffe, -n, *n.f.* firearm.

Feuerwechsel, -, *n.m.* skirmish.

Feuerwehrmann, ∻er, *n.m.* fireman.

Feuerwerk, -e, *n.nt.* fireworks.

Feuerzeug, -e, *n.nt.* cigarette lighter.

feurig, *adj.* fiery.

Fichte, -n, *n.f.* pine, fir.

fidel´, *adj.* jolly.

Fieber, *n.nt.* fever.

fieberhaft, *adj.* feverish.

fiebern, *vb.* be feverish.

Fieberwahnsinn, -e, *n.m.* delirium.

Fiedel, -n, *n.f.* fiddle.

Figur´, -en, *n.f.* figure.

figür´lich, *adj.* figurative.

Fiktion´, -en, *n.f.* figment; fiction.

Filet´, -s, *n.nt.* fillet.

Filiale, -n, *n.f.* branch.

Film, -e, *n.m.* film, movie, motion-picture.

filmen, *vb.* film.

Filmschauspieler, -, *n.m.* movie actor.

Filmschauspielerin, -nen, *n.f.* movie actress.

Filter, -, *n.m.* filter.

filtrie´ren, *vb.* filter.

Filz, -e, *n.m.* felt.

Finale, -s, *n.nt.* finale.

Finan´zen, *n.pl.* finances.

finanziell´, *adj.* financial.

finanzie´ren, *vb.* finance.

Finanz´mann, ∻er, *n.m.* financier.

Finanz´wirtschaft, -en, *n.f.* finance.

finden*, *vb.* find, locate.

Finderlohn, *n.m.* reward (for returning lost articles).

findig, *adj.* ingenious, resourceful.

Findigkeit, *n.f.* ingenuity.

Findling, -e, *n.m.* foundling.

Finger, -, *n.m.* finger.

Fingerabdruck, ∻e, *n.m.* fingerprint.

Fingernagel, ∻, *n.m.* fingernail.

fingie´ren, *vb.* feign, simulate.

fingiert´, *adj.* fictitious.

finster, *adj.* dark; saturnine.

Finsternis, -se, *n.f.* darkness; eclipse.

Firma (*pl.* **Firmen**), *n.f.* firm, company.

Firnis, -se, *n.m.* varnish.

firnissen, *vb.* varnish.

Fisch, -e, *n.m.* fish.

fischen, *vb.* fish.

Fischer, -, *n.m.* fisherman.

Fischgeschäft, -e, *n.nt.* fishstore.

Fixie´rung, -en, *n.f.* fixation.

flach, *adj.* flat, shallow.

Fläche, -n, *n.f.* plane, area.

Flachheit, -en, *n.f.* flatness.

Flachs, *n.m.* flax.

flackern, *vb.* flare, flicker.

Flagge, -n, *n.f.* flag.

Flak, -(s), *n.f.* (= Fliegerabwehrkanone) antiaircraft (fire, troops).

Flak-, *cpds.* antiaircraft.

Flame, -n, -n, *n.m.* Fleming.

Flamme, -n, *n.f.* flame, blaze.

flammend, *adj.* flaming; *(fig.)* enthusiastic.

Flanell´, -e, *n.m.* flannel.

Flanke, -n, *n.f.* flank.

flankie´ren, *vb.* flank.

Flasche, -n, *n.f.* bottle, flask.

Flaschenöffner, -, *n.m.* bottle opener.

flattern, *vb.* flutter, flap.

flau, *adj.* slack, dull.

Flaum, *n.m.* down, fuzz.

flaumig, *adj.* downy, fuzzy, fluffy.

Flechte, -n, *n.f.* braid.

flechten*, *vb.* weave, plait, bind.

Fleck, -e, *n.m.* spot, stain, blotch.

Fledermaus, ⸗e, *n.f.* bat.

Flegel, -, *n.m.* rowdy, boor.

flehen, *vb.* implore, beseech.

flehentlich, *adj.* beseeching.

Fleisch, *n.nt.* flesh, meat.

Fleischerei´, *n.f.* butcher's shop.

fleischig, *adj.* fleshy.

fleischlich, *adj.* carnal.

Fleiß, *n.m.* diligence, hard work.

fleißig, *adj.* industrious, hard working.

flicken, *vb.* patch.

Flicken, -, *n.m.* patch.

Flickwerk, *n.nt.* patchwork.

Flieder, *n.m.* lilac.

Fliege, -n, *n.f.* fly.

fliegen*, *vb.* fly.

Flieger, -, *n.m.* flier, aviator.

fliehen*, *vb.* flee.

Fliese, -n, *n.f.* tile, flagstone.

fließen*, *vb.* flow.

fließend, *adj.* fluent.

flimmern, *vb.* flicker.

flink, *adj.* nimble, spry.

Flirt, -s, *n.m.* flirt, flirtation.

flirten, *vb.* flirt.

Flitterwochen, *n.pl.* honeymoon.

Flocke, -n, *n.f.* flake.

Floh, ⸗e, *n.m.* flea.

Floß, ⸗e, *n.nt.* float, raft.

Flosse, -n, *n.f.* fin.

Flöte, -n, *n.f.* whistle; flute.

flott, *adj.* afloat; smart, dashing.

Flotte, -n, *n.f.* fleet, navy.

Fluch, ⸗e, *n.m.* curse.

fluchen, *vb.* swear, curse.

Flucht, *n.f.* escape, flight, getaway; **(in die F. schlagen*)** rout.

flüchten, *vb.* flee.

flüchtig, *adj.* fleeting, cursory; superficial.

Flüchtling, -en, *n.m.* refugee, fugitive.

Flug, ⸗e, *n.m.* flight.

Flugblatt, ⸗er, *n.nt.* leaflet.

Flügel, -, *n.m.* wing.

Flughafen, ⸗, *n.m.* airport.

Flugpersonal, *n.nt.* flight attendants.

Flugzeug, -e, *n.nt.* airplane.

Flunder, -n, *n.nf.* flounder.

flunkern, *vb.* fib.

fluoresze´rend, *adj.* fluorescent.

Fluß, ⸗sse, *n.m.* river; flux.

flüssig, *adj.* liquid, fluid; **(f. machen)** liquefy.

Flüssigkeit, -en, *n.f.* fluid, liquid.

flüstern, *vb.* whisper.

Flut, -en, *n.f.* flood, high tide.

fluten, *vb.* flood.

Föhn, *n.m.* foehn wind.

Folge, -n, *n.f.* consequence, outgrowth; succession; **(zur F. haben*)** result in.

folgen, *vb.* follow; succeed.

folgend, *adj.* subsequent.

folgenreich, *adj.* consequential.

folgenschwer, *adj.* momentous.

folgerichtig, *adj.* consistent.

folgern, *vb.* infer, deduce.

Folgerung, -en, *n.f.* inference, deduction.

folglich, *adv.* consequently.

Folter, -n, *n.f.* torture.

Fön, *n.m.* hair-dryer.

Fond, -s, *n.m.* fund.

Fondant´, -s, *n.m.* bonbon.

Förderer, -, *n.m.* sponsor.

förderlich, *adj.* helpful, conducive.

fordern, *vb.* demand.

fördern, *vb.* promote, further; *(mining)* mine, haul.

Forderung, -en, *n.f.* demand, claim.

Förderung, -en, *n.f.* furtherance, advancement.

Forel´le, -n, *n.f.* trout.

Form, -en, *n.f.* form, shape; mold; **(in F. sein*)** be fit, be in fine shape.

Formalität´, -en, *n.f.* formality.

Format´, -e, *n.nt.* format; *(fig.)* stature.

Formation´, -en, *n.f.* formation.

Formel, -n, *n.f.* formula.

formell´, *adj.* formal.

formen, *vb.* form, shape, mold.

Förmlichkeit, -en, *n.f.* formality.

formlos, *adj.* formless.

Formular´, -e, *n.nt.* form, blank.

formulie´ren, *vb.* formulate.

forschen, *vb.* explore, search.

Forscher, -, *n.m.* investigator, researcher.

Forscherin, -nen, *n.f.* investigator, researcher.

Forschung, -en, *n.f.* research.

fort, *adv.* away, gone; forward.

Fortbildung, *n.f.* further education, training.

Fortdauer, *n.f.* continuity.

fortdauernd, *adj.* continuous.

fort•fahren*, *vb.* drive away; proceed, continue.

fort•gehen*, *vb.* leave; continue.

fortgeschritten, *adj.* advanced.

fort•pflanzen, *vb.* propagate.

fort•schreiten*, *vb.* progress.

Fortschritt, -e, *n.m.* progress, advance.

fortschrittlich, *adj.* progressive.

fort•setzen, *vb.* continue.

Fortsetzung, -en, *n.f.* continuation.

fortwährend, *adj.* continuous.

Foto, -s, *n.nt.* photograph.

Fotograf´, -en, *n.m.* photographer.

Fotografin, -nen, *n.f.* photographer.

Fotokopie´, -n, *n.f.* photocopy.

Foyer´, -s, *n.nt.* foyer.

Fracht, -en, *n.f.* freight, cargo.

Frachtbrief, -e, *n.m.* bill of lading.

Frachter, -, *n.m.* freighter.

Frachtschiff, -e, *n.nt.* freighter.

Frachtspesen, *n.pl.* freight charges.

Frage, -n, *n.f.* question.

Fragebogen, ≈, *n.m.* questionnaire.

fragen, *vb.* ask, inquire.

fragend, *adj.* interrogative.

Fragezeichen, -, *n.nt.* question mark.

fraglich, *adj.* questionable.

fragmenta´risch, *adj.* fragmentary.

fragwürdig, *adj.* questionable.

Fraktur´, *n.f.* (*med.*) fracture; German type (*print*).

Frankreich, *n.nt.* France.

Franse, -n, *n.f.* fringe.

Franzo´se, -n, -n, *n.m.* Frenchman.

Franzö´sin, -nen, *n.f.* Frenchwoman.

franzö´sisch, *adj.* French.

frappant´, *adj.* striking.

fraternisie´ren, *vb.* fraternize.

Fratze, -n, *n.f.* grimace; face, mug.

Frau, -en, *n.f.* woman, wife; Mrs.

Frauenarzt, ≈e, *n.m.* gynecologist.

Frauenärztin, -nen, *n.f.* gynecologist.

Frauenrechtler, -, *n.m.* feminist.

Frauenrechtlerin, -nen, *n.f.* feminist.

Fräulein, -, *n.nt.* Miss.

fraulich, *adj.* womanly.

frech, *adj.* impudent; saucy.

Frechheit, -en, *n.f.* impertinence, effrontery.

frei, *adj.* free; frank; vacant.

Frei-, *n.nt.* outdoors.

Freibad, ≈er, *n.nt.* open-air swimming pool.

Freier, -, *n.m.* suitor.

freigebig, *adj.* generous.

Freigebigkeit, *n.f.* liberality, generosity.

freigestellt, *adj.* optional.

frei•halten*, *vb.* keep free; treat.

Freiheit, -en, *n.f.* liberty, freedom.

Freiherr, -n, -en, *n.m.* baron.

frei•lassen*, *vb.* free; leave blank.

freilich, *adv.* to be sure.

Freimarke, -n, *n.f.* stamp.

Freimaurer, -, *n.m.* Mason.

freimütig, *adj.* candid, heart-to-heart.

freisinnig, *adj.* liberal.

frei•sprechen*, *vb.* acquit, absolve.

Freispruch, ≈e, *n.m.* acquittal.

Freitag, -e, *n.m.* Friday.

freiwillig, *adj.* voluntary; (**sich f. melden**) volunteer; enlist.

Freiwillig-, *n.m. & f.* volunteer.

Freizeit, *n.f.* leisure time.

fremd, *adj.* strange; foreign, alien.

Fremd-, *n.m. & f.* stranger.

Fremdenführer, -, *n.m.* guide.

Fremdenführerin, -nen, *n.f.* guide.

Fremdenverkehr, *n.m.* tourism.

Fremdenverkehrsbüro, *n.nt.* tourist office.

Fremdenzimmer, -, *n.nt.* guest room, room to let.

frequentie´ren, *vb.* habituate.

Frequenz´, -en, *n.f.* frequency.

Fresko, -ken, *n.nt.* fresco.

fressen*, *vb.* (of animals) eat; stuff oneself.

Freude, -n, *n.f.* joy, pleasure.

Freudenfeuer, -, *n.nt.* bonfire.

freudig, *adj.* joyful, joyous.

freudlos, *adj.* cheerless.

freuen, *vb.* make glad; (**sich f.**) be glad, rejoice.

Freund, -e, *n.m.* friend.

Freundin, -nen, *n.f.* friend (female).

freundlich, *adj.* friendly, kind.

freundlicherweise, *adv.* kindly.

Freundlichkeit, *n.f.* kindness, friendliness.

freundlos, *adj.* friendless.

Freundschaft, -en, *n.f.* friendship.

freundschaftlich, *adj.* amicable.

Frevel, -, *n.m.* outrage.

frevelhaft, *adj.* sacrilegious; flagrant.

Friede(n), *n.m.* peace.

Friedensvertrag, ≈e, *n.m.* peace treaty.

friedfertig, *adj.* peaceable.

Friedhof, ≈e, *n.m.* cemetery, graveyard.

friedlich, *adj.* peaceable, peaceful.

frieren*, *vb.* freeze.

Frikassee´, -s, *n.nt.* fricassee.

frisch, *adj.* fresh, crisp.

Frische, *n.f.* freshness.

Friseur´, -e, *n.m.* barber, hairdresser.

Friseu´se, -n, *n.f.* hairdresser (female).

frisie´ren, *vb.* dress the hair; (*fig.*) tamper with.

Frist, -en, *n.f.* limited period; respite; deadline.

Frisur´, -en, *n.f.* coiffure, hairdo.

frivol´, *adj.* frivolous.

froh, *adj.* glad.

fröhlich, *adj.* gay, cheerful, happy, merry.

Fröhlichkeit, *n.f.* cheerfulness, merriment.

frohlo´cken, *vb.* rejoice.

fromm (≈, -), *adj.* pious, religious, devout.

Frömmelei´, -en, *n.f.* bigotry.

Frömmigkeit, *n.f.* piety.

Frömmler, -, *n.m.* bigot.

frönen, *vb.* indulge.

Front, -en, *n.f.* front.

Frosch, ≈e, *n.m.* frog.

Frost, ≈e, *n.m.* frost, chill.

frösteln, *vb.* feel chilly.

frostig, *adj.* frosty.

Frucht, ≈e, *n.f.* fruit.

fruchtbar, *adj.* fruitful, fertile; prolific.

Fruchtbarkeit, *n.f.* fertility.

fruchtlos, *adj.* fruitless.

früh, *adj.* early.

früher, *adj.* earlier; former.

Frühjahr, -e, *n.nt.* spring.

Frühling, -e, *n.m.* spring.

frühreif, *adj.* precocious.

Frühstück, -e, *n.nt.* breakfast.

frühzeitig, *adj.* early.

Fuchs, ≈e, *n.m.* fox.

fügen, *vb.* join; (**sich f.**) comply, submit.

fügsam, *adj.* docile.

fühlbar, *adj.* tangible.

fühlen, *vb.* feel, sense.

führen, *vb.* lead, guide, direct.

Führer, -, *n.m.* leader, guide.

Führerin, -nen, *n.f.* leader, guide.

Führerschein, -e, *n.m.* driver's license.

Fülle, *n.f.* fullness, wealth; **(in Hülle und F.)** galore.

füllen, *vb.* fill.

Füllfederhalter, -, *n.m.* fountain pen.

Füllung, -en, *n.f.* filling.

Fund, -e, *n.m.* find, discovery.

Fundament´, -e, *n.nt.* foundation.

fundie´ren, *vb.* base.

fünf, *num.* five.

fünft´-, *adj.* fifth.

Fünftel, -, *n.nt.* fifth part; **(ein f.)** one-fifth.

fünfzig, *num.* fifty.

fünfzigst-, *adj.* fiftieth.

Fünfzigstel, -, *n.nt.* fiftieth part; **(ein f.)** one-fiftieth.

Funke(n), -, *n.m.* spark.

funkeln, *vb.* sparkle.

funkelnagelneu, *adj.* brand-new.

funken, *vb.* radio.

Funktion´, -en, *n.f.* function.

Funktionär´, -e, *n.m.* functionary, official.

Funktionärin, -nen, *n.f.* functionary, official.

funktionie´ren, *vb.* function.

für, *prep.* for.

Furche, -n, *n.f.* furrow.

Furcht, *n.f.* fright, fear, dread.

furchtbar, *adj.* terrible.

fürchten, *vb.* fear; **(sich f. vor)** be afraid of.

furchtlos, *adj.* fearless.

Furchtlosigkeit, *n.f.* fearlessness.

furchtsam, *adj.* fearful.

Fürsorge, *n.f.* care; welfare.

Fürst, -en, -en, *n.m.* prince, ruler.

Fürstin, -nen, *n.f.* princess.

fürstlich, *adj.* princely.

Furt, -en, *n.f.* ford.

Furun´kel, -n, *n.f.* boil.

Fürwort, ⁼er, *n.nt.* pronoun.

Fusion´, -en, *n.f.* fusion, merger.

Fuß, ⁼e, *n.m.* foot.

Fußball, ⁼e, *n.m.* football.

Fußboden, ⁼, *n.m.* floor; flooring.

Fußgänger, -, *n.m.* pedestrian.

Fußgängerzone, -n, *n.f.* pedestrian zone.

Fußnote, -n, *n.f.* footnote.

Fußpfleger, -, *n.m.* chiropodist.

Futter, -, *n.nt.* feed, fodder; lining.

füttern, *vb.* feed; (clothing) line.

Futurologie´, *n.f.* futurology.

G

Gabardine, *n.m.* gabardine.

Gabe, -n, *n.f.* gift, donation; faculty.

Gabel, -n, *n.f.* fork.

gaffen, *vb.* gape.

gähnen, *vb.* yawn.

galant´, *adj.* gallant.

Galanterie´, -en, *n.f.* gallantry.

Gala-Uniform, *n.f.* full dress.

Galerie´, -i´en, *n.f.* gallery.

Galgen, -, *n.m.* gallows.

Galle, -n, *n.f.* gall, bile.

Gallenblase, -n, *n.f.* gall bladder.

gallertartig, *adj.* gelatinous.

gallig, *adj.* bilious.

Galopp´, -s, *n.m.* gallop; **(leichter G.)** canter.

galoppie´ren, *vb.* gallop.

galvanisie´ren, *vb.* galvanize.

Gang, ⁼e, *n.m.* walk; corridor, aisle; course; (auto) gear.

Gangrän´, -e, *n.nt.* gangrene.

Gangster, -, *n.m.* gangster.

Gans, ⁼e, *n.f.* goose.

Gänsemarsch, *n.m.* single file.

ganz, 1. *adj.* whole, entire. **2.** *adv.* quite, rather; **(g. gut)** pretty good; **(g. und gar)** completely.

Ganz-, *n.nt.* whole (thing).

Ganzheit, *n.f.* entirety.

gänzlich, *adj.* complete.

Ganztagsbeschäftigung, *n.f.* full-time job.

gar, 1. *adj.* cooked, done. **2.** *adv.* **(g. nicht)** not at all; **(g. nichts)** nothing at all.

Gara´ge, -n, *n.f.* garage.

Garantie´, -i´en, *n.f.* guarantee.

garantie´ren, *vb.* guarantee, warrant.

Garbe, -n, *n.f.* sheaf.

Gardero´be, -n, *n.f.* clothes; cloakroom.

gären*, *vb.* ferment.

Garn, -e, *n.nt.* yarn; thread.

Garne´le, -n, *n.f.* shrimp.

garnie´ren, *vb.* garnish.

Garnison´, -en, *n.f.* garrison.

Garnitur´, -en, *n.f.* set.

garstig, *adj.* nasty.

Garten, ⁼, *n.m.* garden, yard.

Gartenbau, *n.m.* horticulture.

Gärtner, -, *n.m.* gardener.

Gärtnerin, -nen, *n.f.* gardener.

Gas, -e, *n.nt.* gas.

Gashebel, -, *n.m.* accelerator.

gasig, *adj.* gassy.

Gasse, -n, *n.f.* narrow street, alley.

Gast, ⁼e, *n.m.* guest.

Gastarbeiter, -, *n.m.* foreign worker.

gastfrei, *adj.* hospitable.

Gastfreiheit, *n.f.* hospitality.

gastfreundlich, *adj.* hospitable.

Gastfreundschaft, *n.f.* hospitality.

Gastgeber, -, *n.m.* host.

Gastgeberin, -nen, *n.f.* hostess.

Gasthaus, ⁼er, *n.nt.* inn; restaurant.

gastrono´misch, *adj.* gastronomical.

Gaststube, -n, *n.f.* taproom; restaurant.

Gatte, -n, -n, *n.m.* husband.

Gattin, -nen, *n.f.* wife.

Gattung, -en, *n.f.* species, genus.

Gau, -e, *n.m.* district, province.

Gaul, ⸚e, *n.m.* nag.

Gaumen, -, *n.m.* palate.

Gaze, -n, *n.f.* gauze.

Geäch'tet-, *n.m.* outlaw.

Gebäck', *n.nt.* pastry.

Gebär'de, -n, *n.f.* gesticulation; gesture.

geba'ren, *vb.* **(sich g.)** behave.

gebä'ren*, *vb.* bear.

Gebäu'de, -, *n.nt.* building.

geben*, *vb.* give; deal (cards); **(es gibt)** there is, there are.

Geber, -, *n.m.* giver.

Gebet', -e, *n.nt.* prayer.

Gebiet', -e, *n.nt.* territory, region, field.

gebie'ten*, *vb.* command.

Gebie'ter, -, *n.m.* master.

Gebil'de, -, *n.nt.* form, structure.

gebil'det, *adj.* educated, civilized, cultured.

Gebir'ge, -, *n.nt.* mountainous area, mountains; mountain range.

gebir'gig, *adj.* mountainous.

Gebiß', -sse, *n.nt.* teeth; denture; (horse) bit.

Geblüt', *n.nt.* descent, family.

gebo'ren, *adj.* born.

Gebor'genheit, *n.f.* safety.

Gebot', -e, *n.nt.* command(ment).

Gebräu', -e, *n.nt.* brew, concoction.

Gebrauch', ⸚e, *n.m.* use; usage, custom.

gebrau'chen, *vb.* use.

gebräuch'lich, *adj.* customary.

Gebrauchs'anweisung, -en, *n.f.* directions (for use).

gebraucht', *adj.* secondhand, used.

Gebre'chen, -, *n.nt.* infirmity.

gebrech'lich, *adj.* decrepit.

Gebrü'der, *n.pl.* brothers.

Gebrüll', *n.nt.* roar, howl.

gebückt', *adj.* stooped.

Gebühr', -en, *n.f.* charge, fee; **(nach G.)** duly; **(über alle G.)** excessively.

gebüh'ren, *vb.* be due; **(sich g.)** be proper.

gebüh'rend, *adj.* duly.

gebühr'lich, *adj.* proper.

Geburt', -en, *n.f.* birth; childbirth; **(von G. an)** congenital.

Gebur'tenkontrolle, *n.f.* birth control.

gebür'tig, *adj.* native.

Geburts'datum, -ten, *n.nt.* date of birth.

Geburts'helfer, -, *n.m.* obstetrician.

Geburts'ort, -e, *n.m.* birthplace.

Geburts'schein, -e, *n.m.* birth certificate.

Geburts'tag, -e, *n.m.* birthday.

Gebüsch', -e, *n.nt.* bushes, shrubbery.

Geck, -en, -en, *n.m.* dandy.

Gedächt'nis, -se, *n.nt.* memory.

Gedächt'nisfeier, -n, *n.f.* commemoration.

Gedan'ke(n), -, *n.m.* thought, idea.

gedan'kenlos, *adj.* thoughtless, unthinking.

gedan'kenvoll, *adj.* thoughtful.

Gedeck', -e, *n.nt.* cover, table setting.

gedei'hen*, *vb.* thrive.

geden'ken*, *vb.* remember; commemorate.

Gedicht', -e, *n.nt.* poem.

gedie'gen, *adj.* solid.

Gedrän'ge, *n.nt.* crush, crowd.

gedrängt', *adj.* concise.

Geduld', *n.f.* patience.

gedul'den, *vb.* **(sich g.)** have patience, forbear.

gedul'dig, *adj.* patient.

geehrt', *adj.* honored.

geeig'net, *adj.* qualified; suitable.

Gefahr', -en, *n.f.* danger, jeopardy.

gef䨨r'den, *vb.* endanger, jeopardize.

gef䨨r'lich, *adj.* dangerous.

gefahr'los, *adj.* without danger.

Gef䨨r'te, -n, -n, *n.m.* companion.

gefal'len*, *vb.* please; **(es gefällt mir)** I like it.

Gefal'len, -, *n.m.* favor.

gef䨨l'lig, *adj.* obliging, pleasing.

Gefan'gen-, *n.m. & f.* prisoner, captive.

Gefan'gennahme, -n, *n.f.* capture.

Gefan'genschaft, -en, *n.f.* captivity.

Gef䨨ng'nis, -se, *n.nt.* prison, jail.

Gef䨨ng'niswärter, -, *n.m.* jailer.

Gef䨨ß', -e, *n.nt.* container.

gefaßt', *adj.* composed.

Gefecht', -e, *n.nt.* battle, engagement.

gefeit', *adj.* fortified against.

Gefie'der, *n.nt.* plumage.

gefleckt', *adj.* dappled.

geflis'sentlich, *adj.* intentional; studied.

Geflü'gel, *n.nt.* poultry.

Geflüs'ter, *n.nt.* whispering.

Gefol'ge, *n.nt.* retinue.

gefrä'ßig, *adj.* gluttonous.

Gefreit'-, *n.m.* corporal.

gefrie'ren*, *vb.* freeze.

Gefrier'fach, ⸚er, *n.nt.* freezer (in refrigerator).

Gefro'ren-, *n.nt.* ice (cream).

gefü'gig, *adj.* compliant.

Gefühl', -e, *n.nt.* feeling, sensation; emotion, sentiment.

gefühl'los, *adj.* insensible, callous.

gefühls'mäßig, *adj.* emotional.

gefühl'voll, *adj.* sentimental.

gegen, *prep.* against; toward; about.

Gegenangriff, -e, *n.m.* counterattack.

Gegend, -en, *n.f.* region.

Gegengewicht, -e, *n.nt.* counterbalance.

Gegengift, -e, *n.nt.* antidote, antitoxin.

Gegenmaßnahme, -n, *n.f.* countermeasure.

Gegensatz, ⸚e, *n.m.* contrast, opposite.

gegenseitig, *adj.* mutual.

Gegenstand, ⸚e, *n.m.* object.

Gegenteil, *n.nt.* reverse, opposite.

gegenü´ber, *prep. & adv.* opposite.

gegenü´ber•stellen, *vb.* confront.

Gegenwart, *n.f.* present, presence.

gegenwärtig, *adj.* present.

Gegenwirkung, -en, *n.f.* counteraction.

Gegner, -, *n.m.* adversary, opponent.

Gehalt´, -e, *n.m.* content, substance.

Gehalt´, ⸚er, *n.nt.* salary, pay.

gehar´nischt, *adj.* armed; *(fig.)* vehement.

gehäs´sig, *adj.* malicious.

Gehäu´se, -, *n.nt.* casing.

geheim´, *adj.* secret, cryptic.

Geheim´dienst, -e, *n.m.* secret service.

geheim•halten*, *vb.* keep secret.

Geheim´nis, -se, *n.nt.* secret, mystery.

geheim´nisvoll, *adj.* secretive, mysterious.

Geheiß´, *n.nt.* command, behest.

gehemmt´, *adj.* inhibited, self-conscious.

gehen*, *vb.* go, walk; **(wie geht es Ihnen?)** how are you?

gehen•lassen*, *vb.* **(sich g.)** let oneself go.

Gehil´fe, -n, -n, *n.m.* helper, assistant.

Gehil´fin, -nen, *n.f.* assistant.

Gehirn´, -e, *n.nt.* brain.

Gehirn´erschütterung, -en, *n.f.* concussion.

Gehöft´, -e, *n.nt.* farmstead.

Gehölz´, -e, *n.nt.* woods.

Gehör´, *n.nt.* hearing.

gehor´chen, *vb.* obey.

gehö´ren, *vb.* belong to.

gehö´rig, *adj.* belonging to; thorough, sound; appropriate.

gehor´sam, *adj.* obedient.

Gehor´sam, *n.m.* obedience, allegiance.

Geige, -n, *n.f.* violin.

geil, *adj.* horny, *(fam.)* awesome.

Geisel, -n, *n.m.* hostage.

Geiser, -, *n.m.* geyser.

Geißel, -n, *n.f.* whip, scourge.

geißeln, *vb.* flagellate, scourge.

Geist, -er, *n.m.* mind, spirit; ghost; **(Heiliger G.)** Holy Spirit, Ghost.

geistesabwesend, *adj.* absent-minded.

Geistesgegenwart, *n.f.* presence of mind.

geistesgestört, *adj.* deranged.

Geisteswissenschaften, *n.pl.* arts.

geistig, *adj.* mental, spiritual.

geistlich, *adj.* ecclesiastic(al).

Geistlich -, *n.m.& f.* minister, clergy.

Geistlichkeit, *n.f.* clergy.

geistlos, *adj.* inane, vacuous.

geistreich, *adj.* bright, witty.

geisttötend, *adj.* tedious.

Geiz, -e, *n.m.* avarice, meanness.

Geizhals, ⸚e, *n.m.* miser.

Geizkragen, -, *n.m.* miser.

geizig, *adj.* avaricious, miserly.

Geklap´per, *n.nt.* clatter.

Gekrit´zel, *n.nt.* scribbling.

gekün´stelt, *adj.* contrived.

Geläch´ter, *n.nt.* laughter.

Gela´ge, -, *n.nt.* banquet.

gelähmt´, *adj.* crippled.

Gelän´de, -, *n.nt.* terrain.

Gelän´der, -, *n.nt.* railing, banister.

gelan´gen, *vb.* reach, get to.

gelas´sen, *adj.* placid, composed.

Gelati´ne, -n, *n.f.* gelatine.

geläu´fig, *adj.* familiar, fluent.

Geläu´figkeit, *n.f.* fluency.

gelaunt´, *adj.* **(gut g.)** in good humor.

gelb, *adj.* yellow.

gelbbraun, *adj.* tan.

Geld, -er, *n.nt.* money.

Geldbeutel, -, *n.m.* purse.

geldlich, *adj.* monetary.

Geldschein, -, *n.m.* bill.

Geldschrank, ⸚e, *n.m.* safe.

Geldstrafe, -n, *n.f.* fine; **(zu einer G. verurteilen)** fine.

Geldwechsler, -, *n.m.* money-changer.

Gelee´, -s, *n.nt.* jelly.

gele´gen, *adj.* situated; opportune.

Gele´genheit, -en, *n.f.* occasion, chance.

Gele´genheitskauf, *n.m.* bargain.

gele´gentlich, *adj.* occasional.

Gelehr´samkeit, *n.f.* erudition, scholarship.

gelehrt´, *adj.* learned, erudite.

Gelehr´t-, *n.m.& f.* scholar.

Gelei´se, -, *n.nt.* track.

Geleit´, *n.nt.* accompaniment; **(freies G.)** safe conduct.

gelei´ten, *vb.* escort.

Geleit´zug, -e, *n.m.* convoy.

Gelenk´, -e, *n.nt.* joint.

gelen´kig, *adj.* supple.

geliebt´, *adj.* beloved.

Gelieb´t-, *n.m.& f.* beloved, lover.

gelind´, *adj.* mild, light.

gelin´gen*, *vb.* succeed.

gellen, *vb.* shriek.

gellend, *adj.* shrill.

gelo´ben, *vb.* vow, pledge.

gelten*, *vb.* be valid, apply, hold; be intended for; be considered; **(das gilt nicht)** that's not fair.

Geltung, *n.f.* standing, value.

Gelüb´de, -, *n.nt.* vow.

Gelüst´, -e, *n.nt.* lust.

gemach´, *adv.* slowly, gently.

Gemach´, ⸚er, *n.nt.* chamber.

gemäch´lich, *adj.* leisurely, slow and easy.

Gemahl´, -e, *n.m.* husband; consort.

Gemah´lin, -nen, *n.f.* wife.

gemäß´, *prep.* according to.

gemä´ßigt, *adj.* moderate.

gemein´, 1. *adj.* mean, vile, vicious. **2.** *adv.* in common.

Gemein´de, -n, *n.f.* community; municipality; congregation.

gemein´gültig, *adj.* generally accepted.

Gemein´platz, ⁼e, *n.m.* platitude.

gemein´sam, *adj.* common, joint.

Gemein´schaft, *n.f.* community, fellowship.

Gemur´mel, -, *n.nt.* murmur.

Gemü´se, -, *n.nt.* vegetable.

Gemüt´, -er, *n.nt.* mind, spirit, temper, heart.

gemüt´lich, *adj.* comfortable, homey, genial.

Gemüts´art, -en, *n.f.* temperament.

Gemüts´ruhe, *n.f.* placidity.

genau´, *adj.* accurate, exact; fussy.

Genau´igkeit, -en, *n.f.* accuracy.

geneh´migen, *vb.* grant, approve.

Geneh´migung, -en, *n.f.* permission, license.

geneigt´, *adj.* inclined.

General´, ⁼e, *n.m.* general.

Genera´tor, -o´ren, *n.m.* generator.

gene´sen*, *vb.* recover.

Gene´sung, *n.f.* convalescence, recovery.

genial´, *adj.* ingenious, having genius.

Genialität´, *n.f.* ingenuity, genius.

Genie´, -s, *n.nt.* genius.

genie´ren, *vb.* embarrass.

genie´ßen*, *vb.* enjoy, relish.

Genitiv, -e, *n.m.* genitive.

Genos´se, -n, *n.m.* companion; *(derogatory)* character.

Genos´senschaft, -en, *n.f.* association, co-operative society.

genug´, *adj.* enough.

genü´gen, *vb.* be enough, suffice.

genü´gend, *adj.* satisfactory, sufficient.

genüg´sam, *adj.* modest.

Genüg´samkeit, *n.f.* frugality.

Genug´tuung, -en, *n.f.* satisfaction.

Genuß´, ⁼sse, *n.m.* enjoyment; relish.

Geograph´, -en, -en, *n.m.* geographer.

Geographie´, *n.f.* geography.

geogra´phisch, *adj.* geographical.

Geometrie´, *n.f.* geometry.

geome´trisch, *adj.* geometric.

geord´net, *adj.* orderly.

Gepäck´, *n.nt.* luggage, baggage.

Gepäck´träger, -, *n.m.* porter.

Gepäck´schein, -e, *n.m.* baggage check.

Geplau´der, *n.nt.* chat, small talk.

Geprä´ge, *n.nt.* stamp; character.

gera´de, 1. *adj.* straight, even. **2.** *adv.* just; **(g. aus)** straight ahead.

gera´de·stehen*, *vb.* stand straight; answer for.

geradezu´, *adv.* downright.

Gerad´heit, *n.f.* erectness; directness.

Gerät´, -e, *n.nt.* tool, appliance, utensil.

Geratewohl´, *n.nt.* **(aufs G.)** at random, haphazardly.

geraum´, *adj.* considerable.

geräu´mig, *adj.* spacious.

Geräusch´, -e, *n.nt.* noise.

geräusch´los, *adj.* noiseless.

gerben, *vb.* tan (leather).

gerecht´, *adj.* just, fair.

Gerech´tigkeit, *n.f.* justice.

Gere´de, *n.nt.* chatter; **(ins G. bringen)** make someone the talk of the town.

gereift´, *adj.* mellow.

gereizt´, *adj.* irritated, edgy.

Gereizt´heit, *n.f.* irritability.

gereu´en, *vb.* repent, regret.

Gericht´, -e, *n.nt.* court, bar, tribunal; (food) course; **(Jüngstes G.)** doomsday, judgment day.

gericht´lich, *adj.* legal, judicial, forensic.

Gerichts´barkeit, *n.f.* jurisdiction.

Gerichts´gebäude, -, *n.nt.* courthouse.

Gerichts´saal, -säle, *n.m.* courtroom.

Gerichts´verhandlung, -en, *n.f.* court proceedings, trial.

gerie´ben, *adj.* cunning, sly.

gering´, *adj.* slight, slim.

gering´achten, *vb.* look down upon.

gering´fügig, *adj.* negligible, petty.

gering´schätzen, *vb.* hold in low esteem.

gering´schätzig, *adj.* disparaging, derogatory.

gerin´nen*, *vb.* curdle, clot, coagulate.

Gerip´pe, -, *n.nt.* skeleton.

geris´sen, *adj.* shrewd.

Germa´ne, -n, -n, *n.m.* Teuton.

germa´nisch, *adj.* Germanic.

gern, *adv.* gladly, readily; **(g. haben*)** like, be fond of; **(g. tun*)** like to do.

Gerste, -n, *n.f.* barley.

Gerstenkorn, ⁼er, *n.nt.* barleycorn; sty.

Geruch´, ⁼e, *n.m.* smell, odor, scent.

Gerücht´, -e, *n.nt.* rumor.

geru´hen, *vb.* **(g. zu)** deign.

Gerüst´, -e, *n.nt.* scaffold, scaffolding.

gesamt´, *adj.* total.

Gesamt´heit, *n.f.* entirety.

Gesandt´, -n.m.&f. ambassador, envoy.

Gesandt´schaft, -en, *n.f.* legation.

Gesang´, ⁼e, *n.m.* song, chant.

Gesang´buch, ⁼er, *n.nt.* hymnal.

Geschäft´, -e, *n.nt.* business, deal; shop, store.

geschäf´tig, *adj.* busy.

Geschäf´tigkeit, -en, *n.f.* bustle.

Geschäfts´mann, ⁼er, *or* **-leute,** *n.m.* businessman.

geschäfts´mäßig, *adj.* businesslike.

Geschäfts´viertel, -, *n.nt.* downtown, business section.

Geschäfts´zeiten, *n.pl.* hours of business.

gesche′hen*, *vb.* occur, happen.

Gescheh′nis, -se, *n.nt.* happening, occurrence.

gescheit′, *adj.* bright, clever.

Geschenk′, -e, *n.nt.* present.

Geschich′te, -n, *n.f.* story; history.

Geschick′, *n.nt.* skill.

Geschick′lichkeit, -en, *n.f.* dexterity, facility.

geschickt′, *adj.* skillful, clever, deft.

Geschirr′, -e, *n.nt.* dishes; harness.

Geschlecht′, -er, *n.nt.* genus, sex; gender; lineage, family.

geschlecht′lich, *adj.* sexual.

Geschmack′, ⸚e, *n.m.* taste, flavor.

geschmack′los, *adj.* tasteless; in bad taste.

geschmei′dig, *adj.* lithe.

Geschöpf′, -e, *n.nt.* creature.

Geschoß′, -sse, *n.nt.* missile, projectile.

Geschrei′, *n.nt.* clamor.

Geschütz′, -e, *n.nt.* gun.

Geschwa′der, -, *n.nt.* squadron.

Geschwätz′, *n.nt.* idle talk, babble.

geschwät′zig, *adj.* talkative, gossipy.

geschwind′, *adj.* swift.

Geschwin′digkeit, -en, *n.f.* speed, velocity.

Geschwin′digkeitsgrenze, -n, *n.f.* speed limit.

Geschwo′ren-, *n.m.& f.* juror; *(pl.)* jury.

Geschwulst′, -e, *n.nt.* swelling, growth.

Geschwür′, -e, *n.nt.* abscess, ulcer.

geseg′net, *adj.* blessed.

Gesel′le, -n, -n, *n.m.* journeyman; fellow.

gesel′len, *vb.* **(sich g.)** join.

gesel′lig, *adj.* sociable, gregarious.

Gesell′schaft, -en, *n.f.* society; company; party.

Gesell′schafter, -, *n.m.* companion.

Gesell′schafterin, -nen, *n.f.* companion.

gesell′schaftlich, *adj.* social.

Gesell′schaftskleidung, -en, *n.f.* evening dress, dress clothes.

Gesell′schaftsreise, -n, *n.f.* group tour.

Gesetz′, -e, *n.nt.* law, act.

Gesetz′antrag, ⸚e, *n.m.* bill.

gesetz′gebend, *adj.* legislative.

Gesetz′geber, -, *n.m.* legislator.

Gesetz′geberin, -nen, *n.f.* legislator.

Gesetz′gebung, *n.f.* legislation.

gesetz′lich, *adj.* lawful, legal.

gesetz′los, *adj.* lawless.

gesetz′mäßig, *adj.* legal.

Gesetz′mäßigkeit, *n.f.* legality.

gesetz′widrig, *adj.* illegal, unlawful.

Gesicht′, -er, *n.nt.* face.

Gesichts′ausdruck, ⸚e, *n.m.* facial expression, mien.

Gesichts′farbe, *n.f.* complexion.

Gesichts′kreis, -e, *n.m.* horizon.

Gesichts′massage, -n, *n.f.* facial.

Gesichts′punkt, -e, *n.m.* point of view, aspect.

Gesichts′zug, ⸚e, *n.m.* feature.

Gesin′del, *n.nt.* rabble.

gesinnt′, *adj.* **(g. sein*)** be of a mind, be disposed.

Gesin′nung, -en, *n.f.* attitude, way of thinking, views.

gesit′tet, *adj.* well-mannered, civilized.

gespannt′, *adj.* tense; eager to know, curious.

Gespenst′, -er, *n.nt.* ghost.

Gespie′le, -n, -n, *n.m.* playmate.

Gespräch′, -e, *n.nt.* talk, conversation.

gesprä′chig, *adj.* talkative.

Gestalt′, -en, *n.f.* figure, form, shape.

gestal′ten, *vb.* form, shape, fashion.

Gestal′tung, -en, *n.f.* formation, fashioning.

Gestam′mel, *n.nt.* stammering.

gestän′dig, *adj.* **(g. sein*)** make a confession.

Geständ′nis, -se, *n.nt.* confession, avowal.

Gestank′, *n.m.* stench.

gestat′ten, *vb.* permit.

Geste, -n, *n.f.* gesture.

geste′hen*, *vb.* confess, avow.

Gestein′, *n.nt.* rock.

Gestell′, -e, *n.nt.* stand, rack, frame.

gestern, *adv.* yesterday.

gestikulie′ren, *vb.* gesticulate.

Gestirn′, -e, *n.nt.* star; constellation.

Gestirns′bahn, -en, *n.f.* orbit.

Gesträpp′, *n.nt.* scrub, brush.

Gesuch′, -e, *n.nt.* application, petition, request.

gesucht′, *adj.* far-fetched, contrived.

gesund′, *adj.* healthy, sound, wholesome.

gesun′den, *vb.* recover.

Gesund′heit, *n.f.* health, fitness; **(geistige G.)** sanity.

Gesund′heitsamt, *n.nt.* Department of Public Health.

Gesund′heitsattest, -e, *n.nt.* certificate of health.

gesund′heitsschädlich, *adj.* unhealthy.

Gesund′heitswesen, *n.nt.* sanitation.

Gesun′dung, *n.f.* recovery.

Getö′se, *n.nt.* uproar.

Getränk′, -e, *n.nt.* drink, beverage; **(alkoholfreies G.)** soft drink.

getrau′en, *vb.* **(sich g.)** dare.

Getrei′de, *n.nt.* grain, cereal.

getrennt′, *adj.* separate.

getreu′, *adj.* faithful.

Getrie′be, -n, *n.nt.* gear.

getrost′, *adv.* confidently.

Getu′e, *n.nt.* fuss.

geübt′, *adj.* experienced.

Gewächs′, -e, *n.nt.* growth.

gewagt′, *adj.* daring, hazardous.

Gewähr′, *n.f.* guarantee.

gewäh′ren, *vb.* grant.

gewähr′leisten, *vb.* warrant, guarantee.

Gewahr´sam, *n.m.* custody.

Gewalt´, -en, *n.f.* force, power.

Gewalt´herrschaft, *n.f.* despotism.

gewal´tig, *adj.* powerful, tremendous.

gewalt´sam, *adj.* forcible, violent.

gewalt´tätig, *adj.* violent.

Gewalt´tätigkeit, -en, *n.f.* violence.

Gewand´, ⸚er, *n.nt.* garb, garment.

gewandt´, *adj.* facile, versatile.

Gewandt´heit, -en, *n.f.* deftness.

gewär´tig, *adv.* **(g. sein*)** be prepared.

Gewäs´ser, *n.nt.* waters.

Gewe´be, -, *n.nt.* tissue, texture.

Gewehr´, -e, *n.nt.* rifle, gun.

Gewer´be, -, *n.nt.* trade, business.

Gewerk´schaft, -en, *n.f.* labor union.

Gewicht´ -e, *n.nt.* weight.

gewiegt´, *adj.* crafty.

gewillt´, *adj.* willing.

Gewinn´, -e, *n.m.* gain, profit.

gewinn´bringend, *adj.* lucrative.

gewin´nen*, *vb.* win, gain.

Gewin´ner, -, *n.m.* winner.

Gewin´nerin, -nen, *n.f.* winner.

gewinn´süchtig, *adj.* mercenary, greedy.

Gewirr´, *n.nt.* tangle, confusion.

gewiß´, *adj.* certain.

Gewis´sen, -, *n.nt.* conscience.

gewis´senhaft, *adj.* conscientious.

gewis´senlos, *adj.* unprincipled.

Gewis´sensbiß, -sse, *n.m.* remorse, qualms.

gewisserma´ßen, *adv.* so to speak, as it were.

Gewiß´heit, -en, *n.f.* certainty.

Gewit´ter, -, *n.nt.* thunderstorm.

gewit´zigt, *adj.* clever.

gewo´gen, *adj.* **(g. sein*)** be disposed towards.

gewöh´nen, *vb.* accustom; **(sich g. an)** become accustomed to.

Gewohn´heit, -en, *n.f.* habit, custom, practice.

gewohn´heitsmäßig, *adj.* customary, habitual.

gewöhn´lich, *adj.* ordinary, usual, regular; common, vulgar.

gewohnt´, *adj.* accustomed.

Gewöl´be, -, *n.nt.* vaulting, vault.

Gewühl´, *n.nt.* shuffle, melee.

gewun´den, *adj.* coiled; sinuous.

Gewürz´, -e, *n.nt.* spice, condiment, seasoning.

Gewürz´kraut ⸚er, *n.nt.* herb.

Gezei´ten, *n.pl.* tide.

gezie´men, *vb.* be proper, befit.

Gicht, -en, *n.f.* gout, arthritis.

Giebel, -, *n.m.* gable.

Gier, *n.f.* greed(iness).

gierig, *adj.* greedy.

gießen*, *vb.* pour; cast (metal).

Gift, -e, *n.nt.* poison.

giftig, *adj.* poisonous.

Giftmüll, *n.m.* toxic waste.

Gilde, -n, *n.f.* guild.

Gin, -s, *n.m.* gin.

Gipfel, -, *n.m.* peak.

Gipfelkonferenz, *n.f.* summit.

gipfeln, *vb.* culminate.

Gips, -e, *n.m.* gypsum, plaster.

Giraf´fe, -n, *n.f.* giraffe.

Girant´, -en, -en, *n.m.* endorser.

Girat´, -en, -en, *n.m.* endorsee.

girie´ren, *vb.* endorse (a check, note, etc.), put into circulation.

Giro, -s, *n.nt.* endorsement, circulation (of endorsed notes, etc.).

Girokonto, -s, *n.nt.* checking account.

Gischt, -e, *n.m.* spray, foam.

Gitar´re, -n, *n.f.* guitar.

Gitter, -, *n.nt.* grating; gate.

Gitterwerk, -e, *n.nt.* grating.

glaciert´, *adj.* glacé.

Glanz, *n.m.* shine, sheen, gloss; brilliance, splendor.

glänzen, *vb.* shine.

glänzend, *adj.* shiny, brilliant.

Glas, ⸚er, *n.nt.* glass.

Glaser, -, *n.m.* glazier.

gläsern, *adj.* made of glass.

glasie´ren, *vb.* glaze.

glasig, *adj.* glassy.

Glasscheibe, -n, *n.f.* pane.

Glasur, -en, *n.f.* glaze.

Glasware, -n, *n.f.* glassware.

glatt, *adj.* smooth, slippery; outright.

glätten, *vb.* smooth.

Glatzkopf, ⸚e, *n.m.* bald head.

Glaube(n), -, *n.m.* belief, faith.

glauben, *vb.* believe.

Glaubensbekenntnis, -se, *n.nt.* confession of faith; creed.

glaubhaft, *adj.* believable.

gläubig, *adj.* believing, devout.

Gläubig-, *n.m.& f.* believer; creditor.

glaublich, *adj.* credible.

glaubwürdig, *adj.* credible.

Glaubwürdigkeit, *n.f.* credibility.

gleich, 1. *adj.* equal, same, even. **2.** *adv.* right away.

gleichaltig, *adj.* of the same age.

gleichartig, *adj.* similar, homogeneous.

gleichberechtigt, *adj.* having equal rights.

Gleichberechtigung, -en, *n.f.* equality of rights.

gleichen*, *vb.* be like, equal, resemble.

gleichfalls, *adv.* likewise.

gleichförmig, *adj.* uniform.

gleichgesinnt, *adj.* likeminded.

gleichgestellt, *adj.* coordinate.

Gleichgewicht, *n.nt.* equilibrium.

gleichgültig, *adj.* indifferent.

Gleichgültigkeit, *n.f.* indifference.

Gleichheit, *n.f.* equality.

gleich•machen, *vb.* equalize.

Gleichmaß, *n.nt.* proportion, symmetry.

gleichmäßig, *adj.* even, regular.

Gleichmut, *n.m.* equanimity.

gleichmütig, *adj.* even-tempered.

Gleichnis, -se, *n.nt.* simile, parable.

gleichsam, *adv.* as it were.

gleichseitig, *adj.* equilateral.

gleich•setzen, *vb.* equate.

Gleichstrom, ≈e, *n.m.* direct current.

gleich•tun*, *vb.* do like, match up to.

Gleichung, -en, *n.f.* equation.

gleichwertig, *adj.* equivalent.

gleich´wie, *adv. & conj.* just as.

gleich´wohl, *adv.* nevertheless.

gleichzeitig, *adj.* simultaneous.

Gleis, -e, *n.nt.* track.

gleiten*, *vb.* glide, slide, slip.

Gletscher, -, *n.m.* glacier.

Gletscherspalte, -n, *n.f.* crevasse.

Glied, -er, *n.nt.* limb; link.

gliedern, *vb.* segment, classify.

Gliederung, -en, *n.f.* arrangement, structure.

Gliedmaßen, *n.pl.* limbs, extremities.

glimmen*, *vb.* glow, glimmer.

glitschig, *adj.* slippery.

glitzern, *vb.* glitter.

Globus, -ben (-busse), *n.m.* globe.

Glocke, -n, *n.f.* bell.

Glockenschlag, ≈e, *n.m.* stroke of the clock.

Glockenspiel, -e, *n.nt.* chimes, carillon.

Glockenturm, ≈, *n.m.* belfry, bell-tower.

Glorie, -n, *n.f.* glory.

Glorienschein, -e, *n.m.* halo.

glorreich, *adj.* glorious.

glotzen, *vb.* stare.

Glück, *n.nt.* happiness, luck.

gluckern, *vb.* gurgle.

glücklich, *adj.* happy.

glücklicherweise, *adj.* fortunately.

glückse´lig, *adj.* blissful.

Glückse´ligkeit, -en, *n.f.* bliss.

glucksen, *vb.* gurgle.

Glücksfall, ≈e, *n.m.* stroke of luck.

Glücksspiel, -e, *n.nt.* gamble; gambling.

Glücksspieler, -, *n.m.* gambler.

Glücksspielerin, -nen, *n.f.* gambler.

Glückwunsch, ≈e, *n.m.* congratulation.

Glühbirne, -n, *n.f.* electric light bulb.

glühen, *vb.* glow.

glühend, *adj.* glowing, incandescent; ardent.

Glut, -en, *n.f.* heat, live coals; ardor, passion.

Glyzerin´, -e, *n.nt.* glycerine.

G.m.b.H., *abbr.* (= Gesell´schaft mit beschränk´ter Haftung) incorporated, inc.

Gnade, *n.f.* grace, mercy.

gnadenreich, *adj.* merciful.

gnädig, *adj.* gracious, merciful; **(g.e Frau)** madam.

Gold, *n.nt.* gold.

Goldbarren, -, *n.m.* bullion.

golden, *adj.* golden.

Goldfisch, -e, *n.m.* goldfish.

goldig, *adj.* darling, cute.

Goldschmied, -e, *n.m.* goldsmith.

Golf, -e, *n.m.* gulf, bay.

Golf, *n.nt.* golf.

Golfplatz, ≈e, *n.m.* golf course.

Gondel, -n, *n.f.* gondola.

gönnen, *vb.* grant, not begrudge; **(sich g.)** allow oneself; **(das gönne ich ihm!)** that serves him right!

Gör, -en, *n.nt.* brat, kid.

Goril´la, -s, *n.m.* gorilla.

Gosse, -n, *n.f.* gutter, drain.

Gotik, *n.f.* Gothic architecture.

gotisch, *adj.* Gothic.

Gott, ≈er, *n.m.* god, deity.

gottähnlich, *adj.* godlike.

Götterdämmerung, *n.f.* twilight of the gods.

Gottesacker, ≈, *n.m.* cemetery.

Gottesdienst, -e, *n.m.* (church) service.

Gottesgabe, -, *n.f.* godsend.

Gotteshaus, ≈er, *n.nt.* church.

Gotteslästerung, -en, *n.f.* blasphemy.

Gottheit, -en, *n.f.* deity, divinity.

Göttin, -nen, *n.f.* goddess.

göttlich, *adj.* godly, divine.

gottlob´, *interj.* praise God.

gottlos, *adj.* godless.

Götze, -n, -n, *n.m.* idol, false god.

Götzenbild, -er, *n.nt.* idol.

Götzendienst, -e, *n.m.* idolatry.

Gouvernan´te, -n, *n.f.* governess.

Gouverneur´, -e, *n.m.* governor.

Gouverneu´rin, -nen, *n.f.* governor.

Gouverneurs´amt, ≈er, *n.nt.* governorship.

Grab, ≈er, *n.nt.* grave.

graben*, *vb.* dig.

Graben, ≈, *n.m.* trench, ditch.

Grablegung, -en, *n.f.* burial.

Grabmal, ≈er, *n.nt.* tomb(stone).

Grabschrift, -en, *n.f.* epitaph.

Grabstein, -e, *n.m.* gravestone.

Grad, -e, *n.m.* degree.

Graf, -en, -en, *n.m.* count.

Gräfin, -nen, *n.f.* countess.

Grafschaft, -en, *n.f.* county.

Gram, *n.m.* grief, care.

grämen, *vb.* **(sich g.)** grieve, fret.

Gramm, -, *n.nt.* gram.

Gramma´tik, -en, *n.f.* grammar.

Gramma´tiker, -, *n.m.* grammarian.

Gramma´tikerin, -nen, *n.f.* grammarian.

gramma´tisch, *adj.* grammatical.

Grammophon´, -e, *n.nt.* phonograph.

Granat´, -e, *n.m.* garnet.

Grana´te, -n, *n.f.* grenade.

Granit´, -e, *n.m.* granite.

granulie´ren, *vb.* granulate.

Graphiker, -, *n.m.* illustrator, commercial artist.

Graphikerin, -nen, *n.f.* illustrator, commercial artist.

graphisch, *adj.* graphic.

Gras, ¨er, *n.nt.* grass.

grasartig, *adj.* grasslike, grassy.

grasen, *vb.* graze.

grasig, *adj.* grassy.

gräßlich, *adj.* hideous.

Grat, -e, *n.m.* ridge.

Gräte, -n, *n.f.* bone (of a fish).

gratis, *adj.* gratis.

Gratisprobe, -n, *n.f.* free sample.

gratulie´ren, *vb.* congratulate.

grau, *adj.* gray.

Grauen, *n.nt.* horror.

grauenhaft, *adj.* ghastly.

grausam, *adj.* cruel.

grausig, *adj.* lurid.

Graveur´, -e, *n.m.* engraver.

Graveu´rin, -nen, *n.f.* engraver.

gravie´ren, *vb.* engrave.

gravitie´ren, *vb.* gravitate.

Grazie, -n, *n.f.* grace, charm.

graziös´, *adj.* graceful.

greifbar, *adj.* tangible.

greifen*, *vb.* seize, grasp.

Greis, -e, *n.m.* old man.

Greisenalter, -, *n.nt.* old age.

Greisin, -nen, *n.f.* old woman.

grell, *adj.* garish, gaudy, shrill.

Grenze, -n, *n.f.* limit, border, boundary.

grenzen, *vb.* **(g. an)** border on.

grenzenlos, *adj.* boundless.

Greuel, -, *n.m.* horror, outrage.

greulich, *adj.* horrible.

Grieche, -, -n, *n.m.* Greek.

Griechenland, *n.nt.* Greece.

Griechin, -nen, *n.f.* Greek.

griechisch, *adj.* Greek.

Griesgram, -e, *n.m.* grouch.

griesgrämig, *adj.* sullen.

Grieß, -e, *n.m.* semolina, coarse meal; gravel.

Griff, -e, *n.m.* grasp, grip, handle.

Grill, -s, *n.m.* grill; grillroom.

Grille, -n, *n.f.* cricket; whim.

grillen, *vb.* broil.

grillenhaft, *adj.* whimsical.

Grimas´se, -n, *n.f.* grimace.

Grimm, *n.m.* anger.

grimmig, *adj.* angry.

grinsen, *vb.* grin.

Grinsen, *n.nt.* grin.

Grippe, -n, *n.f.* grippe, influenza.

grob(-), *adj.* coarse, rough, crude.

Grobian, -e, *n.m.* boor, ruffian.

Grog, -s, *n.m.* grog.

Groll, *n.m.* anger, grudge.

grollen, *vb.* be angry, bear a grudge.

Gros, -se, *n.nt.* gross.

Groschen, -, *n.m.* ten pfennig piece; 1/100 of an Austrian schilling.

groß(-), *adj.* big, tall, great.

großartig, *adj.* grand, magnificent.

Großbritan´ien, *n.nt.* Great Britain.

Größe, -n, *n.f.* size, height, greatness.

Großeltern, *n.pl.* grandparents.

großenteils, *adv.* in large part, largely.

Größenwahnsinn, *n.m.* megalomania.

Großhandel, *n.m.* wholesale trade.

großherzig, *adj.* magnanimous.

großjährig, *adj.* of age.

Großmacht, ¨e, *n.f.* major power.

Großmut, *n.m.* magnanimity, generosity.

großmütig, *adj.* magnanimous, generous.

Großmutter, ¨, *n.f.* grandmother.

Großrechenanlage, -n, *n.f.* (computer) mainframe.

großsprecherisch, *adj.* boastful.

Großstaat, -en, *n.m.* major power.

Großstadt, ¨e, *n.f.* large city, metropolis.

Großstädter, -e, *n.m.* big city person.

Großstädterin, -nen, *n.f.* big city person.

größtenteils, *adv.* for the most part, mostly.

groß•tun*, *vb.* act big, boast.

Großvater, ¨, *n.m.* grandfather.

groß•ziehen*, *vb.* bring up, raise.

großzügig, *adj.* on a grand scale, generous, broadminded.

grotesk´, *adj.* grotesque.

Grotte, -n, *n.f.* grotto.

Grube, -n, *n.f.* pit; mine.

grübeln, *vb.* brood.

Grubenarbeiter, -, *n.m.* miner.

Gruft, ¨e, *n.f.* crypt, vault.

grün, *adj.* green.

Grund, ¨e, *n.m.* ground, bottom, basis, reason; **(G. und Boden)** land, real estate.

Grundbegriff, -e, *n.m.* basic concept.

Grundbesitz, -e, *n.m.* landed property.

Grundbesitzer, -, *n.m.* landholder.

Grundbesitzerin, -nen, *n.f.* landholder.

gründen, *vb.* found.

Grundgesetz, -e, *n.nt.* basic law; constitution.

Grundlage, -n, *n.f.* basis.

grundlegend, *adj.* fundamental.

gründlich, *adj.* thorough.

Grundlinie, -n, *n.f.* base.

grundlos, *adj.* bottomless; unfounded.

Grundriß, -sse, *n.m.* outline, sketch.

Grundsatz, ¨e, *n.m.* principle.

grundsätzlich, *adj.* fundamental, on principle.

Grundschule, -n, *n.f.* elementary school.

Grundstoff, -e, *n.m.* basic material.

Grundstück, -e, *n.nt.* lot.

Gründung, -en, *n.f.* founding, establishment.

grunzen, *vb.* grunt.
Gruppe, -n, *n.f.* group.
gruppie´ren, *vb.* group.
gruselig, *adj.* uncanny, creepy.
Gruß, ⸗e, *n.m.* greeting; salute.
grüßen, *vb.* greet; salute.
gucken, *vb.* look.
gültig, *adj.* valid.
Gültigkeit, *n.f.* validity.
Gummi, -s, *n.m.* rubber; eraser.
Gummi, -s, *n.nt.* gum.
gummiartig, *adj.* gummy.
Gummiband, ⸗er, *n.nt.* rubber band.
Gummischuhe, *n.pl.* overshoes, galoshes, rubbers.
Gunst, ⸗e, *n.f.* favor.
günstig, *adj.* favorable.
Günstling, -e, *n.m.* favorite.
Gurgel, -n, *n.f.* throat, gullet.
gurgeln, *vb.* gargle.

Gurke, -n, *n.f.* cucumber; **(saure G.)** pickle.
Gurt, -e, *n.m.* girth, harness.
Gürtel, -, *n.m.* belt, girdle.
gürten, *vb.* gird.
Guru, -s, *n.m.* guru.
Guß, ⸗sse, *n.m.* downpour; frosting; casting.
Gußstein, -e, *n.m.* sink, drain.
gut, 1. *adj.* good. **2.** *adv.* well.
Gut, ⸗er, *n.nt.* property; landed estate; *(pl.)* goods.
Gutachten, -, *n.nt.* (expert) opinion, (legal) advice.
gutaussehend, *adj.* good-looking.
Gutdünken, *n.nt.* opinion, discretion.
Güte, *n.f.* kindness; quality, purity.
gutgläubig, *adj.* credulous.

Guthaben, -, *n.nt.* credit; assets.
gut•heißen*, *vb.* approve.
gutherzig, *adj.* good-hearted.
gütig, *adj.* kind, friendly, gracious.
gütlich, *adj.* kind, friendly.
gut•machen, *vb.* make good; **(wieder g.)** make amends for.
gutmütig, *adj.* good-natured.
gut•schreiben*, *vb.* credit.
Gutschrift, -en, *n.f.* credit.
Gymna´sium, -ien, *n.nt.* secondary school preparing for university.
Gymnas´tik, *n.f.* gymnastics.
gymnas´tisch, *adj.* gymnastic.
Gynäkologe, -n, *n.m.* gynaecologist.
Gynäkologin, -nen, *n.f.* gynaecologist.

H

ha, *abbr.* (= Hektar´) hectare.
Haar, -e, *n.nt.* hair.
haarig, *adj.* hairy.
Haarklammer, -n, *n.f.* bobby pin.
Haarnadel, -n, *n.f.* hairpin.
haarscharf, *adj.* very sharp.
Haarschneiden, *n.nt.* haircut.
Haarschnitt, -e, *n.m.* (style of) haircut.
Haarspray, *n.m.* hairspray.
haarsträubend, *adj.* hair-raising.
Habe, -n, *n.f.* property; **(Hab und Gut)** goods and chattels, all one's property.
haben*, *vb.* have.
Haben, *n.nt.* credit; **(Soll und H.)** debit and credit.
Habgier, *n.f.* greed.
habgierig, *adj.* greedy.
Habseligkeiten, *n.pl.* belongings.
Habsucht, *n.f.* greed.
habsüchtig, *adj.* greedy.
Hacke, -n, *n.f.* hoe, pick; heel.
hacken, *vb.* chip.
Hader, *n.m.* quarrel, strife.

hadern, *vb.* quarrel.
Hafen, ⸗, *n.m.* harbor, port.
Hafenstadt, ⸗e, *n.f.* seaport.
Hafer, *n.m.* oats.
Hafergrütze, *n.f.* oatmeal.
Haft, *n.f.* arrest, detention.
haftbar, *adj.* liable.
Haftbefehl, -e, *n.m.* warrant.
haften, *vb.* stick, adhere; be responsible.
Haftpflicht, -en, *n.f.* liability.
Hagel, *n.m.* hail.
Hagelwetter, -, *n.nt.* hailstorm.
hager, *adj.* gaunt.
Hahn, ⸗e, *n.m.* rooster; faucet.
Hähnchen, -, *n.nt.* chicken.
Haifisch, -e, *n.m.* shark.
Hain, -e, *n.m.* grove.
Haken, -, *n.m.* hook.
halb, *adj.* half.
halber, *prep.* because of, for the sake of.
halbie´ren, *vb.* halve.
Halbinsel, -n, *n.f.* peninsula.
halbjährlich, *adj.* semiannual.
Halbkreis, -e, *n.m.* semicircle.

Halbkugel, -n, *n.f.* hemisphere.
Halbmesser, -, *n.m.* radius.
Halbschuhe, *n.pl.* shoes.
halbtags, *adv.* part-time, half-day.
halbwegs, *adv.* halfway.
Hälfte, -n, *n.f.* half.
Halfter, -, *n.nt.* halter.
Halle, -n, *n.f.* hall.
hallen, *vb.* sound, echo.
Hallenbad, ⸗er, *n.nt.* indoor swimming pool.
Halm, -e, *n.m.* blade, stalk.
hallo, *interj.* hello.
Hals, ⸗e, *n.m.* neck.
Halsband, ⸗er, *n.nt.* necklace.
halsbrecherisch, *adj.* breakneck.
Halskette, -n, *n.f.* necklace.
Halsschmerzen, *n.pl.* sore throat.
halsstarrig, *adj.* obstinate.
Halstuch, ⸗er, *n.nt.* kerchief.
Halsweh, *n.nt.* sore throat.
halt, *interj.* halt.
halt, *adv.* after all; I think.
Halt, -e, *n.m.* halt; hold, support.

haltbar, *adj.* tenable; durable; not perishable.

halten*, *vb.* hold, keep, stop; **(h. für)** consider as.

Halter, -, *n.m.* holder.

Haltestelle, -n, *n.f.* stop.

halt•machen, *vb.* halt, stop.

Haltung, -en, *n.f.* attitude, posture.

Hammelbraten, -, *n.m.* roast mutton.

Hammelfleisch, *n.nt.* mutton.

Hammelkeule, -n, *n.f.* leg of mutton.

Hammer, ⸗, *n.m.* hammer.

hämmern, *vb.* hammer.

Hämorrhoi´de, -n, *n.f.* hemorrhoid.

hamstern, *vb.* hoard.

Hand, ⸗e, *n.f.* hand.

Handarbeit, -en, *n.f.* manual labor; needlework.

Handbremse, -n, *n.f.* hand brake.

Handbuch, ⸗er, *n.nt.* handbook, manual.

Händedruck, *n.m.* handshake.

Handel, *n.m.* trade, commerce.

handeln, *vb.* act, trade, deal; **(es handelt sich um . . .)** it is a question of . . .

Handelsabkommen, *n.nt.* trade agreement.

Handelsgeist, *n.m.* commercialism.

Handelsmarine, *n.f.* merchant marine.

Handelsreisend-, *n.m. & f.* traveling salesperson.

handfest, *adj.* sturdy.

Handfläche, -n, *n.f.* palm.

Handgelenk, -e, *n.nt.* wrist.

handhaben, *vb.* handle, manage.

Handikap, -s, *n.nt.* handicap.

Handlanger, -, *n.m.* handy man.

Händler, -, *n.m.* dealer, trader.

Händlerin, -nen, *n.f.* dealer, trader.

handlich, *adj.* handy.

Handlung, -en, *n.f.* action; plot.

Handschelle, -n, *n.f.* handcuff.

Handschrift, -en, *n.f.* handwriting.

Handschuh, -e, *n.m.* glove.

Handtasche, -n, *n.f.* pocketbook.

Handtuch, ⸗er, *n.nt.* towel.

Handvoll, *n.f.* handful.

Handwerk, *n.nt.* handicraft, handiwork.

Handwerker, -, *n.m.* craftsman, artisan.

Handwerkerin, -nen, *n.f.* craftswoman, artisan.

Hang, ⸗e, *n.m.* slope; inclination.

Hängebrücke, -n, *n.f.* suspension bridge.

Hängematte, -n, *n.f.* hammock.

hängen*, *vb.* (*intr.*) hang, be suspended; **(an jemandem h.)** be attached to someone; (*tr.*) hang, suspend.

Hans, *n.m.* Hans; **(H. Dampf in allen Gassen)** jack-of-all-trades.

hänseln, *vb.* tease.

hantie´ren, *vb.* handle, manipulate.

hapern, *vb.* get stuck, be wrong.

Happen, -, *n.m.* morsel.

Harfe, -n, *n.f.* harp.

Harke, -n, *n.f.* rake.

harken, *vb.* rake.

Harm, *n.m.* grief.

harmlos, *adj.* harmless.

Harmonie´, -i´en, *n.f.* harmony.

Harmo´nika, -s, *n.f.* harmonica.

harmo´nisch, *adj.* harmonious.

harmonisie´ren, *vb.* harmonize.

Harn, *n.m.* urine.

Harnblase, -n, *n.f.* (urinary) bladder.

harnen, *vb.* urinate.

Harnisch, -e, *n.m.* harness; armor.

Harpu´ne, -n, *n.f.* harpoon.

hart (⸗), *adj.* hard, severe.

Härte, -n, *n.f.* hardness, severity.

härten, *vb.* harden, temper.

hartgekocht, *adj.* hard-boiled.

hartherzig, *adj.* hard-hearted.

hartnäckig, *adj.* stubborn.

Harz, -e, *n.nt.* resin, rosin.

Hasch, *n.nt.* marijuana.

haschen, *vb.* catch, snatch.

Hase, -n, -n, *n.m.* hare.

Haselnuß, ⸗sse, *n.f.* hazelnut.

Hasenbraten, -, *n.m.* roast hare.

Haspe, -n, *n.f.* hasp, hinge.

Haß, *n.m.* hatred.

hassen, *vb.* hate.

häßlich, *adj.* ugly.

Häßlichkeit, *n.f.* ugliness.

Hast, *n.f.* haste, hurry.

hasten, *vb.* hasten, hurry.

hastig, *adj.* hasty.

Haube, -n, *n.f.* hood.

Hauch, -e, *n.m.* breath.

hauchdünn, *adj.* extremely thin.

hauen*, *vb.* hew, chop, strike, spank; **(sich h.)** fight.

Haufen, -, *n.m.* pile, heap; crowd.

häufen, *vb.* heap.

häufig, *adj.* frequent.

Häufigkeit, -en, *n.f.* frequency.

Häufung, -en, *n.f.* accumulation.

Haupt, ⸗er, *n.nt.* head.

Hauptamt, ⸗er, *n.nt.* main office.

Hauptbahnhof, ⸗e, *n.m.* main railroad station.

Häuptling, -e, *n.m.* chieftain.

Hauptmann, -leute, *n.m.* captain.

Hauptquartier, -e, *n.nt.* headquarters.

Hauptsache, -n, *n.f.* main, essential thing; principal matter.

hauptsächlich, *adj.* main, principal.

Hauptstadt, ⸗e, *n.f.* capital.

Hauptwort, ⸗er, *n.nt.* noun, substantive.

Haus, ⸗er, *n.nt.* house.

Hausangestellt-, *n.m. & f.* servant.

Hausarbeit, -en, *n.f.* housework.

Hausaufgabe, -n, *n.f.* homework.

hausbacken, *adj.* homemade; plain.

hausen, *vb.* dwell, reside.

Häuserblock, -s, *n.m.* block.

Hausfrau, -en, *n.f.* housewife.

Haushalt, -e, *n.m.* household.

haus•halten*, *vb.* economize.

Haushälterin, -nen, *n.f.* housekeeper.

Haushaltung, *n.f.* housekeeping.

hausie´ren, *vb.* peddle.

Hausie´rer, -, *n.m.* peddler.

häuslich, *adj.* domestic.

Hausmeister, -, *n.m.* janitor.

Hausrat, *n.m.* household goods.

Hausschuh, -e, *n.m.* slipper.

Haut, =e, *n.f.* skin, hide.

hautstraffend, *adj.* astringent.

Hebamme, -n, *n.f.* midwife.

Hebel, -, *n.m.* lever.

heben*, *vb.* raise, lift.

Hebrä´er, -, *n.m.* Hebrew.

Hebrä´erin, -nen, *n.f.* Hebrew.

hebrä´isch, *adj.* Hebrew.

hecheln, *vb.* heckle.

Hecht, -e, *n.m.* pike (fish).

Heck, -e, *n.nt.* stern, rear, tail.

Hecke, -n, *n.f.* hedge.

Heer, -e, *n.nt.* army.

Heft, -e, *n.nt.* notebook; handle, hilt.

heften, *vb.* fasten, pin, stitch, tack.

Hefter, -, *n.m.* folder.

heftig, *adj.* vehement.

Heftigkeit, *n.f.* vehemence.

Heftklammer, -n, *n.f.* staple.

Heftzweche, -n, *n.f.* thumbtack.

hegen, *vb.* nurture.

Heide, -n, -n, *n.m.* heathen.

Heide, -n, *n.f.* heath.

Heidelbeere, -n, *n.f.* huckleberry.

heidnisch, *adj.* heathen.

heikel, *adj.* ticklish, tricky, delicate.

Heil, *n.nt.* welfare, safety, salvation.

heil, *adj.* whole; well, healed, unhurt.

Heiland, *n.m.* Savior.

Heilbad, =er, *n.nt.* spa.

heilbar, *adj.* curable.

Heilbutt, -e, *n.m.* halibut.

heilen, *vb.* heal, cure.

heilig, *adj.* holy, sacred.

Heilig, -, *n.m.& f.* saint.

Heiligabend, *n.m.* Christmas Eve.

heiligen, *vb.* hallow, sanctify.

Heiligenschein, -e, *n.m.* halo.

Heiligkeit, *n.f.* holiness, sanctity.

Heiligtum, =er, *n.nt.* sanctuary.

Heiligung, -en, *n.f.* sanctification, consecration.

Heilmittel, -, *n.nt.* remedy, cure.

Heilung, -en, *n.f.* healing, cure.

Heim, -e, *n.nt.* home.

heim, *adv.* home.

Heimat, *n.f.* home (town, country).

Heimatland, =er, *n.nt.* homeland.

heimatlich, *adj.* native.

heimatlos, *adj.* homeless.

Heimchen, -, *n.nt.* cricket.

heimisch, *adj.* domestic, home-like.

heimlich, *adj.* secret.

heim•suchen, *vb.* scourge.

Heimsuchung, -en, *n.f.* scourge.

heimtückisch, *adj.* malicious, treacherous.

heimwärts, *adv.* homeward.

Heimweh, *n.nt.* homesickness.

Heirat, -en, *n.f.* marriage.

heiraten, *vb.* marry.

Heiratsantrag, =e, *n.m.* proposal.

heiser, *adj.* hoarse.

heiß, *adj.* hot.

heissen*, *vb.* be called, be named; mean; call, order.

heiter, *adj.* cheerful; clear.

heizen, *vb.* heat, have the heat on.

Heizkörper, -, *n.m.* radiator.

Heizvorrichtung, -en, *n.f.* heater.

Hektar´, -e, *n.m.* hectare.

hektisch, *adj.* hectic.

Hektogramm´, -e, *n.nt.* hectogram.

Held, -en, -en, *n.m.* hero.

heldenhaft, *adj.* heroic.

Heldenmut, *n.m.* heroism.

Heldin, -nen, *n.f.* heroine.

helfen*, *vb.* help, aid, assist.

Helfer, -, *n.m.* helper.

Helferin, -nen, *n.f.* helper.

Helfershelfer, -, *n.m.* confederate, accomplice.

hell, *adj.* bright, light.

Helligkeit, *n.f.* brightness.

Helm, -e, *n.m.* helmet.

Hemd, -en, *n.nt.* shirt.

hemmen, *vb.* stop, hinder.

Hemmnis, -se, *n.nt.* hindrance, obstacle.

Hemmschuh, -e, *n.m.* brake.

Hemmung, -en, *n.f.* restraint, inhibition.

hemmungslos, *adj.* uninhibited, unrestrained.

Henkel, -, *n.m.* handle.

Henker, -, *n.m.* executioner.

Henna, *n.f.* henna.

Henne, -n, *n.f.* hen.

her, *adv.* towards here; ago.

herab´, *adv.* downwards.

herab´•hängen, *vb.* droop.

herab´•lassen*, *vb.* let down; (sich h.) condescend.

herab´lassend, *adj.* condescending.

Herab´lassung, -en, *n.f.* condescension.

herab´•setzen, *vb.* set down, lower, reduce, disparage.

Herab´setzung, -en, *n.f.* reduction, disparagement.

heran´, *adv.* up to, toward.

heran´•gehen*, *vb.* walk up to, approach.

heran´•nahen, *vb.* approach, draw near.

heran´•wachsen*, *vb.* grow up.

herauf´, *adv.* upwards.

heraus´, *adv.* out.

heraus´•bringen*, *vb.* bring out, publish.

Heraus´forderer, -, *n.m.* challenger.

heraus´·fordern, vb. challenge.

heraus´fordernd, adj. defiant.

Heraus´forderung, -en, n.f. challenge, defiance.

heraus´·geben*, vb. edit, publish.

Heraus´geber, -, n.m. editor, publisher.

Heraus´geberin, -nen, n.f. editor, publisher.

heraus´·kommen*, vb. come out, be published.

heraus´·lassen*, vb. let out.

heraus´·putzen, vb. dress up.

heraus´·stellen, vb. put out; (sich h.) turn out to be.

heraus´·ziehen*, vb. extract.

herb, adj. tart, bitter.

herbei´, adv. toward here.

herbei´·schaffen, vb. procure.

Herberge, -n, n.f. hostel.

herbergen, -n, vb. shelter, lodge.

Herbheit, -en, n.f. tartness.

Herbst, -e, n.m. fall, autumn.

herbstlich, adj. autumnal.

Herd, -e, n.m. kitchen stove; hearth.

Herde, -n, n.f. herd.

herein´, adv. in; (h.!) come in!

Hergang, -̈e, n.m. course of events.

hergebracht, adj. customary.

hergelaufen, adj. of uncertain origin.

Hering, -e, n.m. herring.

Herkommen, -, n.nt. tradition; origin.

herkömmlich, adj. traditional.

Herkunft, -̈e, n.f. origin, extraction.

her·leiten, vb. derive.

herme´tisch, adj. hermetic.

hernach´, adv. afterwards.

hernie´der, adv. downwards, from above.

Herr, -n, -en, n.m. Mr., gentleman, lord, master.

Herrenbekleidung, n.f. menswear.

Herrenfriseur, -e, n.m. men's barber.

Herrenvolk, -̈er, nt. master race.

her·richten, vb. set up, arrange.

Herrin, -nen, n.f. mistress.

herrisch, adj. imperious.

herrlich, adj. wonderful, splendid.

Herrlichkeit, n.f. glory, magnificence.

Herrschaft, n.f. rule, reign; estate.

Herrschaften, n.pl. master and mistress of the house; people of high rank; (meine H.) ladies and gentlemen.

herrschen, vb. rule, reign.

herrschend, adj. ruling, prevailing.

Herrscher, -, n.m. ruler.

Herrscherin, -nen, n.f. ruler.

herrschsüchtig, adj. imperious, tyrannical.

her·sagen, vb. recite.

her·stellen, vb. make, manufacture.

Herstellung, -n, n.f. manufacture.

Hertz, n.nt. hertz.

herü´ber, adv. over (towards here).

herum´, adv. around, about.

herum´·kriegen, vb. talk over, win over.

herum´·lungern, vb. loaf around.

herum´·nörgeln, vb. nag.

herum´·pfuschen, vb. tamper.

herum´·schnüffeln, vb. pry, snoop.

herum´·stehen*, vb. stand around, loiter.

herun´ter, adv. down.

herun´tergekommen, adj. run-down, down at the heels.

herun´ter·lassen*, vb. lower.

herun´ter·machen, vb. dress down, tear apart, pan.

hervor´, adv. forth, forward.

hervor´·brechen*, vb. erupt.

hervor´·bringen*, vb. bring forth, produce.

hervor´·heben*, vb. emphasize.

hervor´·quellen*, vb. gush; ooze.

hervor´ragend, adj. prominent, outstanding, superb.

hervor´·rufen*, vb. evoke; provoke.

hervor´·schießen*, vb. spurt.

hervor´·stehen*, vb. protrude.

Herz(en), -, n.nt. heart.

her·zeigen, vb. show.

herzen, vb. hug, cuddle.

herzhaft, adj. hearty.

herzig, adj. lovable, darling.

Herzinfarkt, -e, n.m. heart attack.

herzlich, adj. cordial, affectionate.

Herzlichkeit, n.f. cordiality.

herzlos, adj. heartless.

Herzog, -̈e, n.m. duke.

Herzogin, -nen, n.f. duchess.

Herzogtum, -̈er, n.nt. dukedom, duchy.

heterosexuell´, adj. heterosexual.

Hetze, -n, n.f. rush; agitation, inflammatory talk; hassle.

hetzen, vb. rush; hound, agitate, rabble-rouse.

Hetzerei´, -en, n.f. rush; demagoguery.

hetzerisch, adj. inflammatory, demagogic.

Hetzredner, -, n.m. rabble rouser, demagogue.

Heu, n.nt. hay.

Heuchelei´, -en, n.f. hypocrisy.

heucheln, vb. fake, feign; play the hypocrite.

Heuchler, -, n.m. hypocrite.

Heuchlerin, -nen, n.f. hypocrite.

heuchlerisch, adj. hypocritical.

heuer, adv. this year.

Heugabel, -n, n.f. pitchfork.

Heuhaufen, -, n.m. haystack.

heulen, vb. howl; cry.

heurig, adj. of this year.

Heuschnupfen, -, n.m. hay fever.

heute, adv. today; (h. abend) tonight.

heutig, adj. today's.

heutzutage, adv. nowadays.

Heuwiese, -n, n.f. hayfield.

Hexe, -n, n.f. witch.

hexen, *vb.* perform witchcraft; be a magician.

Hexenschuß, *n.m.* lumbago.

Hieb, -e, *n.m.* blow, stroke.

hienie´den, *adv.* here below.

hier, *adv.* here.

hierar´chisch, *adj.* hierarchical.

hierbei, *adv.* hereby.

hierher, *adv.* hither.

hiermit, *adv.* hereby, herewith.

Hifi, *n.nt.* high fidelity.

Hilfe, -n, *n.f.* help, aid.

hilfeflehend, *adj.* imploring.

Hilfeleistung, -en, *n.f.* assistance, aid.

hilflos, *adj.* helpless, defenseless.

Hilflosigkeit, *n.f.* helplessness.

hilfreich, *adj.* helpful.

hilfsbedürftig, *adj.* needy.

hilfsbereit, *adj.* cooperative.

Hilfsmittel, -, *n.nt.* aid.

Hilfsquelle, -n, *n.f.* resource.

Himbeere, -n, *n.f.* raspberry.

Himmel, -, *n.m.* heaven, sky.

Himmelfahrt, -en, *n.f.* ascension to heaven; **(H. Christi)** Ascension (Day) (40 days after Easter); **(Mari´ä H.)** Assumption (of the Blessed Virgin) (August 15).

himmelhochjauchzend, *adj.* jubilant.

himmelschreiend, *adj.* scandalous.

Himmelsrichtung, -en, *n.f.* point of the compass, direction.

himmlisch, *adj.* heavenly.

hin, *adv.* to there; gone; **(h. und her)** back and forth; **(h. und wieder)** now and then.

hinab´, *prep.* down.

hinaus´, *adv.* out.

hinaus´•zögern, *vb.* procrastinate.

Hinblick, *n.m.* aspect. **(in H. auf . . .)** with regard to . . .

hinderlich, *adj.* hindering, inconvenient.

hindern, *vb.* hinder, deter.

Hindernis, -se, *n.nt.* hindrance, obstacle.

hin•deuten, *vb.* point to.

hinein´, *adv.* in.

hin•fallen*, *vb.* fall down.

Hingabe, *n.f.* fervency.

hin•geben*, *vb.* give away, up; **(sich h.)** devote oneself; surrender.

Hingebung, *n.f.* devotion.

hingestreckt, *adj.* prostrate.

hin•halten*, *vb.* (*fig.*) delay.

hinken, *vb.* limp.

hin•legen, *vb.* lay down; **(sich h.)** lie down.

hin•purzeln, *vb.* tumble.

hin•reißen*, *vb.* **(sich h. lassen)** let oneself be carried away.

hinreißend, *adj.* captivating, ravishing.

hin•richten, *vb.* execute.

Hinrichtung, -en, *n.f.* execution.

Hinsicht, -en, *n.f.* respect, regard.

hinsichtlich, *prep.* in regard to, regarding, concerning.

hinten, *adv.* behind.

hintenherum´, *adv.* from behind; (*fig.*) roundabout, through the back door.

hinter, *prep.* behind, beyond.

hinter-, *adj.* hind, back.

Hintergedanke(n), -, *n.m.* ulterior motive.

Hintergrund, ⁼e, *n.m.* background.

Hinterhalt, -e, *n.m.* ambush.

hinterher´, *adv.* afterward(s).

Hinterland, *n.nt.* hinterland.

hinterle´gen, *vb.* deposit.

Hinterlist, *n.f.* insidiousness, underhanded act.

hinterlistig, *adj.* insidious, designing, underhanded.

Hintern, *n.m.* (*fam.*) bottom, behind.

Hintertreffen, *n.nt.* **(ins H. geraten)** fall behind.

Hintertür, -en, *n.f.* back door; (*fig.*) loophole.

hinterzie´hen*, *vb.* (*fig.*) defraud.

hinü´ber, *adv.* over, across.

hinun´ter, *adv.* down.

Hinweis, -e, *n.m.* reference; indication.

hin•weisen*, *vb.* point, refer, allude.

hinzu´•fügen, *vb.* add.

Hirn, -e, *n.nt.* brain.

Hirsch, -e, *n.m.* stag.

Hirschleder, -, *n.nt.* deerskin.

Hirt, -en, -en (*Biblical* **Hirte, -n, -n**), *n.m.* shepherd.

hissen, *vb.* hoist.

Histo´riker, -, *n.m.* historian.

Historikerin, -nen, *n.f.* historian.

histo´risch, *adj.* historic(al).

Hitze, *n.m.* heat.

hitzig, *adj.* heated, fiery, heady.

hitzköpfig, *adj.* hot-headed.

Hitzschlag, ⁼e, *n.m.* heatstroke.

Hobel, -, *n.m.* plane.

hobeln, *vb.* plane.

hoch (hoh-, höher, höchst), 1. *adj.* high, tall. **2.** *adv.* up.

Hochebene, -n, *n.f.* plateau.

hochachtungsvoll, *adv.* yours sincerely.

Hochdeutsch, *n.nt.* standard High German.

hocherfreut, *adj.* elated.

hochgradig, *adj.* intense, extreme.

Hochmut, *n.m.* haughtiness, pride.

hochmütig, *adj.* haughty, arrogant.

Hochsaison, *n.f.* peak season.

hoch•schätzen, *vb.* treasure.

Hochschule, -n, *n.f.* university.

Hochsommer, -, *n.m.* midsummer.

höchst, *adv.* highly, extremely.

Hochstapler, -, *n.m.* swindler, impersonator.

höchstenfalls, *adv.* at best, at the outside.

höchstens, *adv.* at best, at the outside.

Höchstgrenze, -n, *n.f.* top limit.

hochtrabend, *adj.* pompous, grandiloquent.

Hochverrat, *n.m.* high treason.

Hochzeit, -en, *n.f.* wedding.

Hochzeitsreise, -n, *n.f.* honeymoon.

hoch•ziehen*, *vb.* hoist.

hocken, *vb.* squat.

Hocker, -, *n.m.* stool.

Höcker, -, *n.m.* bump, hump.

Hockey, *n.nt.* hockey.

Hof, ̈e, *n.m.* court, courtyard; **(den H. machen)** court.

hoffen, *vb.* hope.

hoffentlich, *adv.* I hope.

Hoffnung, -en, *n.f.* hope.

hoffnungslos, *adj.* hopeless.

hoffnungsvoll, *adj.* hopeful.

höfisch, *adj.* courtly.

höflich, *adj.* polite, courteous, respectful, civil.

Höflichkeit, -en, *n.f.* courtesy.

Höhe, -n, *n.f.* height, altitude, elevation.

Hoheit, -en, *n.f.* Highness.

Höhepunkt, -e, *n.m.* high point, highlight, climax, culmination.

höher, *adj.* higher.

hohl, *adj.* hollow.

Höhle, -n, *n.f.* cave, den.

Hohlraum, ̈e, *n.m.* hollow space, vacuum.

Hohn, *n.m.* mockery, derision.

höhnisch, *adj.* derisive, mocking.

hohnlächeln, *vb.* sneer, deride.

hold, *adj.* gracious, lovely.

holdselig, *adj.* gracious.

holen, *vb.* (go and) get, fetch.

Holland, *n.nt.* Holland.

Holländer, -, *n.m.* Dutchman.

Holländerin, -nen, *n.f.* Dutchwoman.

holländisch, *adj.* Dutch.

Hölle, *n.f.* inferno, hell.

höllisch, *adj.* infernal, hellish.

Hologramm´, -e, *n.nt.* hologram.

Holographie´, *n.f.* holography.

holprig, *adj.* bumpy.

Holz, ̈er, *n.nt.* wood, lumber, timber.

hölzern, *adj.* wooden.

Holzklotz, ̈e, *n.m.* block (of wood); log.

Holzkohle, -n, *n.f.* charcoal.

Holzschnitt, -e, *n.m.* woodcut.

homosexuell´, *adj.* homosexual.

Honig, *n.m.* honey.

Honorar´, -e, *n.nt.* honorarium.

honorie´ren, *vb.* honor; remunerate.

Hopfen, -, *n.m.* hop(s).

hopsen, *vb.* hop, skip.

hops•gehen*, *vb.* go down the drain, go west.

hörbar, *adj.* audible.

horchen, *vb.* listen to; eavesdrop.

Horde, -n, *n.f.* horde.

hören, *vb.* hear.

Hörensagen, *n.nt.* hearsay.

Hörer, -, *n.m.* (telephone) receiver; (student) auditor.

hörig, *adj.* submissive; subservient.

Horizont´, -e, *n.m.* horizon.

horizontal´, *adj.* horizontal.

Hormon´, -e, *n.nt.* hormone.

Horn, ̈er, *n.nt.* horn.

hörnern, *adj.* horny.

Hornhaut, ̈e, *n.f.* callous skin; cornea.

hornig, *adj.* horny.

Hornis´se, -en, *n.f.* horoscope.

Horoskop´, -e, *n.nt.* horoscope.

Hörsaal, -säle, *n.m.* lecture hall.

Hort, -e, *n.m.* hoard; refuge, retreat.

Hörweite, -n, *n.f.* earshot.

Hose, -n, *n.f.* trousers, pants.

Hosenband, ̈er, *n.nt.* garter.

Hostie, *n.f.* host.

Hotel´, -s, *n.nt.* hotel.

Hotel´boy, -s, *n.m.* bellboy.

Hovercraft, *n.nt.* hovercraft.

hübsch, *adj.* pretty, handsome.

Hubschrauber, -, *n.m.* helicopter.

Huf, -e, *n.nt.* hoof.

Hüfte, -n, *n.f.* hip.

Hügel, -, *n.m.* hill.

Huhn, ̈er, *n.nt.* chicken, fowl.

Hühnerauge, -n, *n.nt.* corn (on the foot).

huldigen, *vb.* do homage to.

Hülle, -n, *n.f.* covering, casing; **(in H. und Fülle)** abundantly, in profusion.

hüllen, *vb.* clothe, wrap, envelop.

Hülse, -n, *n.f.* hull, husk; case.

human´, *adj.* humane.

Humanis´mus, *n.m.* humanism.

Humanist´, -en, -en, *n.m.* humanist.

humanitär´, *adj.* humanitarian.

Humanität´, *n.f.* humanity.

Hummel, -n, *n.f.* bumble bee.

Hummer, -, *n.m.* lobster.

Humor´, *n.m.* humor, wit.

Humorist´, -en, -en, *n.m.* humorist.

humor´voll, *adj.* humorous.

humpeln, *vb.* hobble.

Hund, -e, *n.m.* dog, hound.

hundert, *num.* a hundred.

Hundert, -e, *n.nt.* hundred.

Hundertjahr´feier, -n, *n.f.* centenary, centennial.

hundertjährig, *adj.* centennial.

hundertst -, *adj.* hundredth.

Hundertstel, -, *n.nt.* hundredth part; **(ein h.)** one one-hundredth.

Hundezwinger, -, *n.m.* kennel.

Hündin, -nen, *n.f.* bitch.

hünenhaft, *adj.* gigantic.

Hunger, *n.m.* hunger.

hungern, *vb.* starve.

Hungersnot, ̈e, *n.f.* famine.

Hungertod, *n.m.* starvation.

hungrig, *adj.* hungry.

Hupe, -n, *n.f.* auto horn.

hupen, *vb.* blow the horn.

hüpfen, *vb.* hop.

Hürde, -n, *n.f.* hurdle.

Hure, -n, *n.f.* whore.

husten, *vb.* cough.

Husten, *n.m.* cough.

Hut, ̈e, *n.m.* hat.

Hut, *n.f.* care, protection; **(auf der H. sein*)** be on the alert.

hüten, *vb.* tend; **(sich h.)** beware, be careful not to do.
Hütte, -n, *n.f.* hut; shed, hovel; *(tech.)* foundry.
Hyazin´the, -n, *n.f.* hyacinth.
Hydrant´, -en, -en, *n.m.* hydrant.
Hygie´ne, *n.f.* hygiene.

hygie´nisch, *adj.* hygienic, sanitary.
Hymne, -n, *n.f.* hymn, anthem.
Hypno´se, -n, *n.f.* hypnosis.
hypno´tisch, *adj.* hypnotic.
hypnotisie´ren, *vb.* hypnotize.

Hypothek´, -en, *n.f.* mortgage.
Hypothe´se, -n, *n.f.* hypothesis.
hypothe´tisch, *adj.* hypothetical.
Hysterie´, *n.f.* hysteria, hysterics.
hyste´risch, *adj.* hysterical.

I

ich, *pron.* I.
Ich, *n.nt.* ego.
ideal´, *adj.* ideal.
Ideal´, -e, *n.nt.* ideal.
idealisie´ren, *vb.* idealize.
Idealis´mus, *n.m.* idealism.
Ideé, -e´en, *n.f.* idea, notion; **(fixe I.)** obsession.
identifizier´bar, *adj.* identifiable.
identifizie´ren, *vb.* identify.
iden´tisch, *adj.* identical.
Identität´, -en, *n.f.* identity.
Idiot´, -en, -en, *n.m.* idiot.
idio´tisch, *adj.* idiotic.
Idyll´, -e, *n.nt.* idyl.
idyl´lisch, *adj.* idyllic.
ignorie´ren, *vb.* ignore.
illuminie´ren, *vb.* illuminate.
illuso´risch, *adj.* illusive, illusory.
Illustration´, -en, *n.f.* illustration.
illustrie´ren, *vb.* illustrate.
imaginär´, *adj.* imaginary.
Imam, -e, *n.m.* imam.
Imbiß, -sse, *n.m.* snack.
Imbißstube, -n, *n.f.* snack bar.
Imita´tor, -o´ren, *n.m.* impersonator.
imitie´ren, *vb.* imitate.
immatrikulie´ren, *vb.* **(sich i.)** register in a university.
immer, *adv.* always.
immergrün, *adj.* evergreen.
immerhin´, *adv.* after all, anyway.
Immobi´lien, *n.pl.* real estate.
immun´, *adj.* immune.
Immun´schwäche, *n.f.* immunodeficiency.
Immunität´, -en, *n.f.* immunity.

Imperfekt, -e, *n.nt.* imperfect tense.
Imperialis´mus, *n.m.* imperialism.
imperialis´tisch, *adj.* imperialist.
impfen, *vb.* vaccinate.
Impfstoff, -e, *n.m.* vaccine.
Impfung, -en, *n.f.* vaccination.
implizi´te, *adv.* by implication.
implizie´ren, *vb.* imply, implicate.
imponie´ren, *vb.* impress.
Import´, -e, *n.m.* import.
importie´ren, *vb.* import.
imposant´, *adj.* imposing.
impotent´, *adj.* impotent.
Impotenz´, *n.f.* impotence.
imprägnie´ren, *vb.* waterproof.
Impresa´rio, -s, *n.m.* impresario.
improvisie´ren, *vb.* improvise.
Impuls´, -e, *n.m.* impulse.
impulsiv´, *adj.* impulsive.
Impulsivität´, *n.f.* spontaneity.
imstan´de, *adj.* able, capable.
in, *prep.* in, into.
Inbegriff, -e, *n.m.* essence, embodiment.
inbegriffen, *adj.* included; implicit.
Inbrunst, *n.f.* ardor, fervor.
inbrünstig, *adj.* zealous, ardent.
Inder, -, *n.m.* Indian.
Inderin, -nen, *n.f.* Indian.
Index, -e *or* **-dizes,** *n.m.* index.
India´ner, -, *n.m.* (American) Indian, Native American.

India´nerin, -nen, *n.f.* *American) Indian, Native American.
india´nisch, *adj.* (American) Indian, Native American.
Indien, *n.nt.* India.
Indikativ, -e, *n.m.* indicative.
Indika´tor, -o´ren, *n.m.* indicator.
indirekt, *adj.* indirect.
indisch, *adj.* Indian.
indiskret, *adj.* indiscreet.
Individualität´, -en, *n.f.* individuality.
individuell´, *adj.* individual.
Indivi´duum, -duen, *n.nt.* individual.
Indone´sien, *n.nt.* Indonesia.
Induktion´, -en, *n.f.* induction.
induktiv´, *adj.* inductive.
Industrie´, -i´en, *n.f.* industry.
industriell´, *adj.* industrial.
Industriell´e, -n, -n, *n.m.&f.* industrialist.
induzie´ren, *vb.* induce.
infam´, *adj.* infamous; beastly.
Infanterie, -n, *n.f.* infantry.
Infanterist, -en, -en, *n.m.* infantryman.
infiltrie´ren, *vb.* infiltrate.
Infinitiv, -e, *n.m.* infinitive.
infizie´ren, *vb.* infect.
Inflation´, -en, *n.f.* inflation.
infolgedes´sen, *adv.* consequently.
informie´ren, *vb.* inform.
Ingenieur´, -e, *n.m.* engineer.
Ingenieu´rin, -nen, *n.f.* engineer.
Ingwer, *n.m.* ginger.
Inhaber, -, *n.m.* proprietor; (of an apartment) occupant.

Inhaberin, -nen, *n.f.* proprietor; (of an apartment) occupant.

Inhalt, *n.m.* content, volume, capacity.

Inhaltsangabe, -n, *n.f.* table of contents.

inhaltschwer, *adj.* momentous, weighty.

Inhaltsverzeichnis, -se, *n.nt.* table of contents, index.

Initiati´ve, -n, *n.f.* initiative.

inkog´nito, *adv.* incognito.

Inland, -e, *n.nt.* homeland; **(im In- und Ausland)** at home and abroad.

inländisch, *adj.* domestic.

inmit´ten, *prep.* amid, in the midst of.

innen, *adv.* inside.

Innen-, *cpds.* interior, inner; domestic.

Innenpolitik, *n.f.* domestic policy.

Innenseite, -n, *n.f.* inside.

inner-, *adj.* inner, interior, internal.

Inner-, *n.nt.* interior, inside; soul.

innerhalb, *prep.* within.

innerlich, *adj.* inward, intrinsic.

innerst-, *adj.* innermost.

innig, *adj.* intimate; fervent.

Innigkeit, *n.f.* fervor.

Innung, -en, *n.f.* guild.

Input, -s, *n.m.* input.

Insasse, -n, -n, *n.m.* occupant; inmate.

Insassin, -nen, *n.f.* occupant; inmate.

insbeson´dere, *adv.* especially.

Inschrift, -en, *n.f.* inscription.

Insekt´, -en, *n.nt.* insect.

Insek´tenpulver, -, *n.nt.* insecticide.

Insel, -n, *n.f.* island.

Inserat´, -e, *n.nt.* advertisement.

Inserent´, -en, -en, *n.m.* advertiser.

insgeheim´, *adv.* secretly.

insgesamt´, *adv.* altogether.

Insig´nien, *n.pl.* insignia.

inso´fern, inso´weit, *adv.* to that extent, to this extent.

insofern´, insoweit´, *conj.* insofar as, to the extent that.

Inspek´tor, -o´ren, *n.m.* inspector.

Inspekto´rin, -nen, *n.f.* inspector.

inspizie´ren, *vb.* inspect.

Installation´, -en, *n.f.* installation.

instand•´halten*, *vb.* keep up, keep in good repair.

Instand´haltung, *n.f.* maintenance.

inständig, *adj.* earnest.

instand•´setzen, *vb.* repair, recondition; enable.

Instanz´, -en, *n.f.* instance.

Instan´zenweg, -e, *n.m.* stages of appeal, channels.

Instinkt´, -e, *n.m.* instinct.

instinktiv´, *adj.* instinctive.

Institut´, -e, *n.nt.* institute, institution.

Instrument´, -e, *n.nt.* instrument.

Insulin´, *n.nt.* insulin.

inszenie´ren, *vb.* stage.

Inszenie´rung, -en, *n.f.* scenario.

intakt´, *adj.* intact.

integrie´ren, *vb.* integrate.

Intellekt´, *n.m.* intellect.

intellektuell´, *adj.* intellectual.

Intellektuell-´, *n.m. & f.* intellectual, highbrow, egghead.

intelligent´, *adj.* intelligent.

Intelligenz´, *n.f.* intelligence.

intensiv´, *adj.* intense, intensive.

interessant´, *adj.* interesting.

Interes´se, -n, *n.nt.* interest, concern.

interessie´ren, *vb.* interest.

interjektion´, -en, *n.f.* interjection.

Internat´, -e, *n.nt.* boarding school.

international´, *adj.* international.

internie´ren, *vb.* intern.

Internist´, -en, -en, *n.m.* specialist for internal medicine.

interpretie´ren, *vb.* interpret.

interpunktie´ren, *vb.* punctuate.

Interpunktion´, *n.f.* punctuation.

Interview´, -s, *n.nt.* interview.

interview´en, *vb.* interview.

intim´, *adj.* intimate.

Intoleranz´, *n.f.* intolerance.

intransitiv, *adj.* intransitive.

intravenös´, *adj.* intravenous.

Intri´ge, -n, *n.f.* intrigue.

intrigie´ren, *vb.* plot, scheme.

Intuition´, -en, *n.f.* intuition.

intuitiv´, *adj.* intuitive.

Invali´de, -n, -n, *n.m.* invalid.

Invasion´, -en, *n.f.* invasion.

Inventar´, -e, *n.nt.* inventory.

investie´ren, *vb.* invest.

inwendig, *adj.* inward, inner.

inzwi´schen, *adv.* in the meantime.

Irak´, *n.nt.* Iraq.

Iran´, *n.nt.* Iran.

irdisch, *adj.* earthly.

Ire, -n, -n, *n.m.* Irishman.

irgendein, -, *adj.* any (at all), any old.

irgendeiner, -e, *pron.* anyone, anybody.

irgendetwas, *pron.* something or other, anything at all.

irgendjemand, *pron.* somebody or other.

irgendwann´, *adv.* sometime.

irgendwelcher, -es, -e, *adj.* any.

irgendwie´, *adv.* somehow.

irgendwo´, *adv.* somewhere, anywhere.

irgendwohin´, *adv.* (to) somewhere, anywhere.

Irin, -nen, *n.f.* Irishwoman.

irisch, *adj.* Irish.

Irland, *n.nt.* Ireland.

Irländer, -, -, *n.m.* Irishman.

Irländerin, -nen, *n.f.* Irishwoman.

Ironie´, *n.f.* irony.

iro´nisch, *adj.* ironical.

irre, *adj.* astray, wrong; wandering, lost; insane.

irre•führen, *vb.* mislead.

irreführend, *adj.* misleading.

irren, *vb.* err, go astray; **(sich i.)** err, be mistaken.

irrig, *adj.* mistaken.

irritie´ren, *vb.* irritate, annoy.

Irrsinn, *n.m.* nonsense, lunacy.

irrsinnig, *adj.* lunatic.

Irrtum, ⸗**er,** *n.m.* error.

irrtümlich, *adj.* erroneous.

Isolationist´, **-en, -en,** *n.m.* isolationist.

Isola´tor, -o´ren, *n.m.* insulator.

isolie´ren, *vb.* isolate; insulate.

Isolie´rung, -en, *n.f.* isolation; insulation.

Israel, *n.nt.* Israel.

Israe´li, -s, *n.m.* Israeli.

israe´lisch, *adj.* Israeli.

Israelit´, -en, -en, *n.m.* Israelite.

Ita´lien, *n.nt.* Italy.

Italie´ner, -, *n.m.* Italian.

Italie´nerin, -nen, *n.f.* Italian.

italie´nisch, *adj.* Italian.

J

ja, 1. *interj.* yes. **2.** *adv.* as is well known, to be sure.

Jacht, -en, *n.f.* yacht.

Jacke, -n, *n.f.* jacket.

Jade, *n.m.* jade.

Jagd, -en, *n.f.* hunt; chase, pursuit.

jagen, *vb.* hunt; chase.

Jäger, -, *n.m.* hunter.

jäh, *adj.* sudden.

Jahr, -e, *n.nt.* year.

jahraus´, jahrein´, *adv.* year in, year out.

Jahrbuch, ⸗**er,** *n.nt.* yearbook, almanac, annual; *(pl.)* annals.

Jahrestag, -e, *n.m.* anniversary.

Jahreszeit, -en, *n.f.* season.

Jahrgang, ⸗**e,** *n.m.* (school) class; (wine) vintage.

Jahrhun´dert, -e, *n.nt.* century.

jährlich, *adj.* yearly, annual.

Jahrmarkt, ⸗**e,** *n.m.* fair.

Jahrzehnt´, -e, *n.nt.* decade.

Jähzorn, *n.m.* quick temper.

jähzornig, *adj.* quick-tempered.

Jammer, *n.m.* misery.

jämmerlich, *adj.* miserable; dismal.

Januar, -e, *n.m.* January.

Japan, *n.nt.* Japan.

Japa´ner, -, *n.m.* Japanese.

Japanerin, -nen, *n.f.* Japanese.

japa´nisch, *adj.* Japanese.

Jargon´, -s, *n.m.* jargon, slang.

jäten, *vb.* weed.

jauchzen, *vb.* jubilate, cheer.

jawohl´, *interj.* yes, sir.

Jazz, *n.m.* jazz.

je, *adv.* ever; apiece; each; **(j. nach)** in each case according to; **(j. nachdem´)** according to whether, as the case may be; **(je mehr, je desto, umso besser)** the more the better.

Jeans, *n.pl.* jeans.

Jeansstoff, -e, *n.m.* denim.

jeder, -es, -e, *pron. & adj.* each, every.

jedoch´, *conj.* yet; nevertheless.

jemals, *adv.* ever.

jemand, *pron.* someone, somebody; anyone, anybody.

jener, -es, -e, *pron & adj.* that, yonder; the former.

jenseits, *adv. & prep.* beyond, on the other side.

Jenseits, *n.nt.* beyond, life after death.

Jeru´salem, *n.nt.* Jerusalem.

Jesuit´, -en, -en, *n.m.* Jesuit.

jetzig, *adj.* present.

jetzt, *adv.* now.

jeweilig, *adj.* in question, under consideration.

Joch, -e, *n.nt.* yoke.

Jockei, -s, *n.m.* jockey.

Jod, *n.nt.* iodine.

jodeln, *vb.* yodel.

Joghurt´, *n.m. or nt.* yogurt.

johlen, *vb.* howl.

Joker, -, *n.m.* joker.

jonglie´ren, *vb.* juggle.

Jota, -s, *n.nt.* iota.

Journalist´, -en, -en, *n.m.* journalist.

Journalis´tin, -nen, *n.f.* journalist.

Jubel, *n.m.* jubilation, rejoicing.

jubeln, *vb.* shout with joy, rejoice.

Jubilä´um, -en, *n.nt.* jubilee.

jucken, *vb.* itch.

Jude, -n, -n, *n.m.* Jew.

Judentum, *n.nt.* Judaism, Jewry.

Judenverfolgung, -en, *n.f.* pogrom.

Jüdin, -nen, *n.f.* Jew.

jüdisch, *adj.* Jewish.

Jugend, *n.f.* youth.

Jugendherberge, -n, *n.f.* youth hostel.

jugendlich, *adj.* youthful; adolescent, juvenile.

Jugendverbrecher, -, *n.m.* juvenile delinquent.

Jugendzeit, -en, *n.f.* youth, adolescence.

Jugosla´we, -n, -n, *n.m.* Yugoslav.

Jugosläwin, -nen, *n.f.* Yugoslav.

Jugosla´wien, *n.nt.* Yugoslavia.

jugosla´wisch, *adj.* Yugoslavian.

Juli, *n.m.* July.

jung (⸗), *adj.* young.

Jung-, *n.nt.* young (of an animal).

Junge, -n, -n, *n.m.* boy.

jungenhaft, *adj.* boyish.

Jünger, -, *n.m.* disciple.

Jungfer, -n, *n.f.* **(alte J.)** old maid, spinster.

Jungfrau, -en, *n.f.* virgin.

Junggeselle, -n, -n, *n.m.* bachelor.

Jüngling, -e, *n.m.* young man.

Juni, *n.m.* June.

Junker, -, *n.m.* aristocratic landowner (especially in Prussia).

Jurist´, -en, -en, *n.m.* jurist, lawyer; law student.

Juris´tin, -nen, *n.f.* jurist, lawyer; law student.

juris´tisch, *adj.* juridical, legal.

Justiz´, *n.f.* justice.

Juwel´, -en, *n.nt.* jewel.

Juwelier´, -e, *n.m.* jeweler.

Juwelie´rin, -nen, *n.f.* jeweler.

Jux, *n.m.* fun.

K

Kabarett´, -e, *n.nt.* cabaret.

Kabel, -, *n.nt.* cable; cablegram.

Kabeljau, -e, *n.m.* cod.

kabeln, *vb.* cable.

Kabi´ne, -n, *n.f.* cabin, stateroom.

Kabinett´, -e, *n.nt.* cabinet.

Kabriolett´, -s, *n.nt.* convertible.

Kachel, -n, *n.f.* tile.

Kada´ver, -, *n.m.* carcass.

Kadett´, -en, -en, *n.m.* cadet.

Käfer, -, *n.m.* beetle, bug.

Kaffee, *n.m.* coffee.

Kaffein´, *n.nt.* caffeine.

Käfig, -e, *n.m.* cage.

kahl, *adj.* bald; bare.

Kahn, ¨e, *n.m.* boat, barge.

Kaiser, -, *n.m.* emperor.

Kajü´te, -n, *n.f.* cabin (on a boat).

Kaka´o, -s, *n.m.* cocoa.

Kalb, ¨er, *n.nt.* calf.

Kalbfleisch, *n.nt.* veal.

Kalbleder, -, *n.nt.* calfskin.

Kalen´der, -, *n.m.* calendar.

Kali, *n.nt.* potash, potassium.

Kali´ber, -, *n.nt.* caliber.

Kalium, *n.nt.* potassium.

Kalk, -n.m. lime, chalk, calcium.

Kalkstein, *n.m.* limestone.

Kalorie´, -i´en, *n.f.* calorie.

kalt(¨), *adj.* cold.

kaltblütig, *adj.* cold-blooded.

Kälte, -n, *n.f.* cold(ness).

Kalva´rienberg, *n.m.* Calvary.

Kalzium, *n.nt.* calcium.

Kame´e, -n, *n.f.* cameo.

Kamel´, -e, *n.nt.* camel.

Kamera, -s, *n.f.* camera.

Kamerad´, -en, -en, *n.m.* companion, friend; comrade.

Kamera´din, -nen, *n.f.* companion, friend.

Kamerad´schaft, -en, *n.f.* comradeship, camaraderie; friendship.

Kamil´le, -n, *n.f.* camomile.

Kamin´, -e, *n.m.* fireplace, hearth; fireside.

Kamm, ¨e, *n.m.* comb; (mountain) crest.

kämmen, *vb.* comb.

Kammer, -n, *n.f.* room; chamber.

Kammermusik, *n.f.* chamber music.

Kampag´ne, -n, *n.f.* campaign.

Kampf, ¨e, *n.m.* fight, fighting, combat.

kämpfen, *vb.* fight.

Kampfer, *n.m.* camphor.

Kämpfer, -, *n.m.* fighter, combatant; champion.

kampfunfähig, *adj.* disabled.

Kanada, *n.nt.* Canada.

Kana´dier, -, *n.m.* Canadian.

Kana´dierin, -nen, *n.f.* Canadian.

kana´disch, *adj.* Canadian.

Kanal´, ¨e, *n.m.* canal, channel; duct.

Kanalisation´, *n.f.* canalization; sewer.

kanalisie´ren, *vb.* canalize; drain by sewer.

Kana´rienvogel, ¨, *n.m.* canary.

Kanda´re, -n, *n.f.* curb (of a horse); **(an die K. nehmen)** take a person in hand.

Kandidat´, -en, -en, *n.m.* candidate, nominee.

Kandida´tin, -nen, *n.f.* candidate, nominee.

Kandidatur´, -en, *n.f.* candidacy, nomination.

kandiert´, *adj.* candied.

Känguruh´, -s, *n.nt.* kangaroo.

Kanin´chen, -, *n.nt.* rabbit, bunny.

Kanne, -n, *n.f.* can, jug, pitcher.

Kanniba´le, -n, -n, *n.m.* cannibal.

Kanon, -s, *n.m.* canon.

Kanona´de, -n, *n.f.* cannonade.

Kano´ne, -n, *n.f.* cannon.

Kano´nenboot, -e, *n.nt.* gunboat.

Kanonier´, -e, *n.m.* cannoneer.

kano´nisch, *adj.* canonical.

kanonisie´ren, *vb.* canonize.

Kanta´te, -n, *n.f.* cantata.

Kante, -n, *n.f.* edge, border.

Kanti´ne, -n, *n.f.* canteen.

Kanu´, -s, *n.nt.* canoe.

Kanzel, -n, *n.f.* pulpit.

Kanzlei´, -en, *n.f.* chancellery.

Kanzler, -, *n.m.* chancellor.

Kap, -s, *n.nt.* cape.

Kapaun´, -e, *n.m.* capon.

Kapel´le, -n, *n.f.* chapel; orchestra, band.

Kapell´meister, -, *n.m.* conductor, bandmaster.

kapern, *vb.* capture.

kapie´ren, *vb.* understand.

kapital´, *adj.* capital.

Kapital´, -ien, *n.nt.* capital (funds).

kapitalisie´ren, *vb.* capitalize.

Kapitalis´mus, *n.m.* capitalism.

kapitalis´tisch, *adj.* capitalistic.

Kapitän´, -e, *n.m.* captain.

Kapi´tel, -, *n.nt.* chapter.

kapitulie´ren, *vb.* capitulate.

Kappe, -n, *n.f.* cap, hood.

Kapsel, -n, *n.f.* capsule.

kaputt´, *adj.* broken, busted; **(k. machen)** bust, wreck.

Kapu´ze, -n, *n.f.* hood.

Karabi´ner, -, *n.m.* carbine.

Karaf´fe, -n, *n.f.* decanter, carafe.

Karamel´, *n.nt.* caramel.

Kara´te, *n.nt.* karate.

Karawa´ne, -n, *n.f.* caravan.

Karbid´, *n.nt.* carbide.

Karbun´kel, -, *n.m.* carbuncle.

Kardinal´, ⸗e, *n.m.* cardinal.

Karfrei´tag, *n.m.* Good Friday.

Karies, *n.f.* caries.

Karikatur´, -en, *n.f.* caricature; cartoon.

karikie´ren, *vb.* caricature.

karmin´rot(⸗), *adj.* crimson.

Karneval, -s, *n.m.* carnival.

Karo, *n.nt.* (cards) diamond(s).

Karpfen, -, *n.m.* carp.

Karre, -n, *n.f.* cart.

Karree´, -s, *n.nt.* square.

Karren, -, *n.m.* cart.

Karrie´re, -n, *n.f.* career; **(K. machen)** be successful, get far in one's profession.

Karte, -n, *n.f.* card; chart, map.

Kartei´, -en, *n.f.* card index, file.

Kartell´, -e, *n.nt.* cartel.

Kartenspiel, -e, *n.nt.* card game; deck of cards.

Kartof´fel, -n, *n.f.* potato.

Karton´, -s, *n.m.* carton.

Karussell´, -s, *n.nt.* merrygo-round.

Karwoche, *n.f.* Holy Week.

Kaschmir, -e, *n.m.* cashmere.

Käse, *n.m.* cheese.

Kaser´ne, -n, *n.f.* barracks.

Kasi´no, -s, *n.nt.* casino.

Kasse, -n, *n.f.* cash box; cash register; box-office; **(bei K. sein*)** be flush; **(an der K. bezahlen)** pay the cashier.

Kassenzettel, -, *n.m.* sales slip.

Kasset´te, -n, *n.f.* cassette.

kassie´ren, *vb.* collect (money due); dismiss.

Kassie´rer, -, *n.m.* teller, cashier.

Kassie´rerin, -nen, *n.f.* teller, cashier.

Kaste, -n, *n.f.* caste.

kastei´en, *vb.* chastise, mortify.

Kasten, ⸗, *n.m.* box, case.

Katalog´, -e, *n.m.* catalogue.

Katapult´, -e, *n.m.* catapult.

Katarrh´, -e, *n.m.* catarrh.

Katas´ter, -, *n.nt.* register.

katastrophal´, *adj.* disastrous, ruinous.

Katastro´phe, -n, *n.f.* disaster.

Katechis´mus, -men, *n.m.* catechism.

Kategorie´, -i´en, *n.f.* category.

katego´risch, *adj.* categorical.

Kater, -, *n.m.* tomcat; hangover.

Kathedra´le, -n, *n.f.* cathedral.

Katho´de, -n, *n.f.* cathode.

Katholik´, -en, -en, *n.m.* Catholic.

katho´lisch, *adj.* Catholic.

Katholizis´mus, -men, *n.m.* Catholicism.

Kattun´, -e, *n.m.* gingham, calico.

Kätzchen, -, *n.nt.* kitten.

Katze, -n, *n.f.* cat.

katzenartig, *adj.* feline.

Katzenjammer, *n.m.* hangover.

kauen, *vb.* chew.

kauern, *vb.* crouch, cower.

Kauf, ⸗e, *n.m.* purchase.

kaufen, *vb.* purchase, buy.

Käufer, -, *n.m.* buyer.

Käuferin, -nen, *n.f.* buyer.

Kauffrau, -en, *n.f.* businesswoman.

Kaufkontrakt, -e, *n.m.* bill of sale.

Kaufmann, -leute, *n.m.* businessman, merchant.

kaufmännisch, *adj.* commercial.

Kaugummi, -s, *n.nt.* chewing gum.

kaum, *adv.* scarcely, hardly, barely.

Kausalität´, -en, *n.f.* causation.

Kaution´, -en, *n.f.* surety; security; bail.

Kavalier´, -e, *n.m.* cavalier.

Kavallerie´, -n, *n.f.* cavalry.

Kaviar, *n.m.* caviar.

keck, *adj.* saucy.

Kegel, -, *n.m.* cone.

kegelförmig, *adj.* conic.

kegeln, *vb.* bowl.

Kehle, -n, *n.f.* throat.

Kehlkopfentzündung, -en, *n.f.* laryngitis.

kehren, *vb.* turn; brush, sweep.

Kehricht, *n.m.* sweepings; garbage.

Kehrseite, -n, *n.f.* reverse side; other side of the picture.

kehrt•machen, *vb.* turn around, about-face.

Kehrtwendung, *n.f.* about face.

keifen, *vb.* nag, scold.

Keil, -e, *n.m.* wedge.

Keilerie´, -en, *n.f.* fracas, brawl.

Keim, -e, *n.m.* germ, bud.

keimen, *vb.* germinate.

keimfrei, *adj.* germ free, sterile.

keimtötend, *adj.* germicidal.

kein, -, -e, *adj.* not a, not any, no.

keiner, -es, -e, *pron.* no one, not any, none.

keinerlei, *adj.* not of any sort.

keineswegs, *adv.* by no means.

Keks, -e, *n.m.* biscuit, cookie.

Kelch, -e, *n.m.* cup, goblet, chalice; calyx.

Kelchglas, ⸗er, *n.nt.* goblet.

Kelle, -n, *n.f.* ladle, scoop.

Keller, -, *n.m.* cellar.

Kellner, -, *n.m.* waiter.

Kellnerin, -nen, *n.f.* waitress.

kennen*, *vb.* know, be acquainted with.

kennen•lernen, *vb.* meet, become acquainted with.

Kenner, -, *n.m.* connoisseur.

Kennerin, -nen, *n.f.* connoisseur, expert.

Kennkarte, -n, *n.f.* identity card.

kenntlich, *adj.* recognizable.

Kenntnis, -se, *n.f.* knowledge, notice.

Kennzeichen, -, *n.nt.* sign, distinguishing mark, feature.

kennzeichnen, *vb.* mark, stamp, distinguish, characterize.

kentern, *vb.* capsize.

Kera´mik, -en, *n.f.* ceramics.

kera´misch, *adj.* ceramic.

Kerbe, -n, *n.f.* notch.

kerben, *vb.* notch.

Kerker, -, *n.m.* jail, prison.

Kerl, -e, *n.m.* fellow, guy.

Kern, -e, *n.m.* kernel, pit, core; nucleus; gist.

Kernenergie, *n.f.* nuclear energy.

Kerngehäuse, -, *n.nt.* core.

Kernhaus, -er, *n.nt.* core.

Kernkraftwerk, -e, *n.nt.* nuclear power plant.

Kernphysik, *n.f.* nuclear physics.

Kernspaltung, -en, *n.f.* nuclear fission.

Kerosin´, *n.nt.* kerosene.

Kerze, -n, *n.f.* candle.

Kessel, -, *n.m.* kettle, boiler.

Kette, -n, *n.f.* chain.

ketten, *vb.* chain, link.

Kettenreaktion, -en, *n.f.* chain reaction.

Ketzer, -, *n.m.* heretic.

Ketzerei´, *n.f.* heresy.

keuchen, *vb.* gasp.

Keuchhusten, *n.m.* whooping-cough.

Keule, -n, *n.f.* club, cudgel; (meat) leg, joint.

keusch, *adj.* chaste.

Keuschheit, *n.f.* chastity.

kichern, *vb.* giggle.

Kiefer, -, *n.m.* jaw.

Kiefer, -n, *n.f.* pine.

Kiel, -e, *n.m.* keel.

Kielwasser, *n.nt.* wake.

Kieme, -n, *n.f.* gill.

Kiepe, -n, *n.f.* basket (carried on the back).

Kies, -e, *n.m.* gravel.

Kilo, -, *n.nt.* kilogram.

Kilohertz, *n.nt.* kilohertz.

Kilome´ter, *n.m. or nt.* kilometer.

Kilowatt´, -, *n.nt.* kilowatt.

Kind, -er, *n.nt.* child.

Kinderarzt, -e, *n.m.* pediatrician.

Kinderärztin, -nen, *n.f.* pediatrician.

Kinderbett, -en, *n.nt.* crib.

Kindergarten, -, *n.m.* kindergarten.

Kinderlähmung, -en, *n.f.* infantile paralysis, polio.

kinderlos, *adj.* childless.

Kinderraub, *n.m.* kidnapping.

Kinderräuber, -, *n.m.* kidnapper.

Kindersportwagen, -, *n.m.* stroller.

Kinderwagen, -, *n.m.* baby carriage.

Kinderzimmer, -, *n.nt.* nursery.

Kindheit, -en, *n.f.* childhood.

kindisch, *adj.* childish.

kindlich, *adj.* childlike.

Kinn, -e, *n.nt.* chin.

Kino, -s, *n.nt.* movie theater.

Kiosk´, -e, *n.m.* kiosk, newsstand.

kippen, *vb.* tip, tilt.

Kirche, -n, *n.f.* church.

Kirchenlied, -er, *n.nt.* hymn.

Kirchenschiff, -e, *n.nt.* nave.

Kirchenstuhl, -e, *n.m.* pew.

Kirchhof, -e, *n.m.* churchyard.

kirchlich, *adj.* ecclesiastical.

Kirchspiel, -e, *n.nt.* parish.

Kirchturm, -e, *n.m.* steeple.

Kirsche, -n, *n.f.* cherry.

Kissen, -e, *n.nt.* cushion, pillow.

Kissenbezug, -e, *n.m.* pillowcase.

Kiste, -n, *n.f.* crate, chest.

Kitsch, *n.m.* trash.

Kittel, -, *n.nt.* smock.

kitzeln, *vb.* tickle.

kitzlig, *adj.* ticklish.

klaffen, *vb.* gape, yawn.

Klage, -n, *n.f.* complaint; suit.

Kläger, -, *n.m.* plaintiff.

Klägerin, -nen, *n.f.* plaintiff.

kläglich, *adj.* miserable.

Klammer, -n, *n.f.* clamp, clasp; parenthesis.

Klamot´ten, *n.pl.* duds, rags, stuff.

Klampe, -n, *n.f.* cleat.

Klang, -e, *n.m.* sound, ring(ing).

Klappbett, -en, *n.nt.* folding bed.

Klappe, -n, *n.f.* flap, lid, valve.

klappen, *vb. (tr.)* flap, fold; *(intr.)* come out right.

klappern, *vb.* clatter, chatter, rattle.

Klaps, -e, *n.m.* slap.

klar, *adj.* clear.

klären, *vb.* clear.

Klarheit, -en, *n.f.* clarity.

Klarinet´te, -n, *n.f.* clarinet.

klar•legen, *vb.* clarify.

klar•stellen, *vb.* clarify.

Klasse, -n, *n.f.* class.

Klassenkamerad, -en, -en, *n.m.* classmate.

Klassenkameradin, -nen, *n.f.* classmate.

Klassenzimmer, -, *n.nt.* classroom.

klassifizie´ren, *vb.* classify.

Klassifizie´rung, -en, *n.f.* classification.

klassisch, *adj.* classic(al).

Klatsch, *n.m.* gossip.

klatschen, *vb.* clap; gossip.

Klaue, -n, *n.f.* claw.

klauen, *vb.* snitch.

Klausel, -n, *n.f.* clause, proviso.

Klavier´, -e, *n.nt.* piano.

Klebemittel, -, *n.nt.* glue, adhesive.

kleben, *vb.* paste; stick.

Klebgummi, *n.m.* mucilage.

klebrig, *adj.* sticky.

Klebstoff, -e, *n.m.* paste.

kleckern, *vb.* spill, make a spot.

Klecks, -e, *n.m.* spot, stain.

Klee, *n.m.* clover.

Kleid, -er, *n.nt.* dress; *(pl.)* clothes.

kleiden, *vb.* clothe, dress.

Kleiderbügel, -, *n.m.* hanger.

Kleiderhändler, -, *n.m.* clothier.

Kleiderschrank, -e, *n.m.* clothes closet, wardrobe.

kleidsam, *adj.* becoming.

Kleidung, -en, *n.f.* clothing.

Kleidungsstück, -e, *n.nt.* garment.

klein, *adj.* little, small.

Kleingeld, -er, *n.nt.* change.

Kleinheit, -en, *n.f.* smallness.

Kleinigkeit, -en, *n.f.* trifle.

kleinlaut, *adj.* meek, subdued.

kleinlich, *adj.* petty.

Kleinod, -ien, *n.nt.* jewel, gem.

Kleister, -, *n.m.* paste.

Klemme, -n, *n.f.* clamp; dilemma, jam, tight spot.

klemmen, *vb.* pinch, jam.

Klempner, -, *n.m.* plumber.

Klepper, -, *n.m.* hack.

klerikal', *adj.* clerical.

Kleriker, -, *n.m.* clergyman.

Klerus, *n.m.* clergy.

klettern, *vb.* climb.

klicken, *vb.* click (computer).

Klient', -en, -en, *n.m.* client.

Klien'tin, -nen, *n.f.* client.

Klima, -a'te, *n.nt.* climate.

Klimaanlage, -n, *n.f.* air conditioning (system).

klima'tisch, *adj.* climatic.

klimatisie'ren, *vb.* air-condition.

klimmen*, *vb.* climb.

Klinge, -n, *n.f.* blade.

Klingel, -n, *n.f.* (small) bell; buzzer.

klingeln, *vb.* ring.

klingen*, *vb.* ring, sound.

Klinik, -en, *n.f.* clinic, hospital.

klinisch, *adj.* clinical.

Klippe, -n, *n.f.* cliff, crag.

Klistier', -e, *n.nt.* enema.

Klo, -s, *n.nt.* (short for **Klosett'**) bathroom, toilet.

Kloa'ke, -n, *n.f.* sewer, drain.

klobig, *adj.* clumsy.

klopfen, *vb.* knock, beat.

Klops, -e, *n.m.* meatball.

Klosett', -e, *n.nt.* water closet.

Kloß, ⸚e, *n.m.* clump; dumpling.

Kloster, ⸚, *n.nt.* monastery, nunnery.

Klosterbruder, ⸚, *n.m.* friar.

Klostergang, ⸚e, *n.m.* cloister(s).

Klotz, ⸚e, *n.m.* block.

Klub, -s, *n.m.* club (social).

Kluft, ⸚e, *n.f.* gap, cleft, fissure.

klug(⸚), *adj.* clever, smart.

Klugheit, -en, *n.f.* cleverness.

Klumpen, -, *n.m.* lump.

klumpig, *adj.* lumpy.

knabbern, *vb.* nibble.

Knabe, -n, -n, *n.m.* lad, youth.

knacken, *vb.* click.

Knall, -e, *n.m.* bang, crack, pop.

knallen, *vb.* bang, pop.

knapp, *adj.* scarce, scant, tight, terse.

Knappheit, -en, *n.f.* scarcity, shortage, terseness.

knarren, *vb.* creak, rattle.

Knäuel, -, *n.m. or nt.* clew, ball; throng, crowd.

knauserig, *adj.* stingy.

Knebel, -, *n.m.* cudgel; gag.

knebeln, *vb.* bind, gag.

Knecht, -e, *n.m.* servant, farm hand.

Knechtschaft, -en, *n.f.* bondage, servitude.

kneifen*, *vb.* pinch.

Kneifzange, -n, *n.f.* pliers.

Kneipe, -n, *n.f.* tavern, pub, joint.

kneten, *vb.* knead.

Knick, -e, *n.m.* bend, crack.

knicken, *vb.* bend, fold, crack.

Knicks, -e, *n.m.* curtsy.

Knie, -i'e, *n.nt.* knee.

kni'en, *vb.* kneel.

Kniff, -e, *n.m.* pinch; trick.

knifflig, *adj.* tricky.

knipsen, *vb.* snap, punch (ticket), take a snapshot, snap one's fingers.

knirschen, *vb.* grate, crunch; gnash (teeth).

knistern, *vb.* crackle.

knittern, *vb.* wrinkle.

Knöchel, -, *n.m.* knuckle.

Knochen, -, *n.m.* bone.

knochenlos, *adj.* boneless.

knochig, *adj.* bony.

Knödel, -, *n.m.* dumpling.

Knopf, ⸚e, *n.m.* button.

Knopfloch, ⸚er, *n.nt.* buttonhole.

Knorpel, -, *n.m.* cartilage.

Knorren, -, *n.m.* knot, gnarl.

knorrig, *adj.* knotty, gnarled.

Knospe, -n, *n.f.* bud.

knospen, *vb.* bud.

Knoten, -, *n.m.* knot.

knoten, *vb.* knot.

Knotenpunkt, -e, *n.m.* junction.

knüpfen, *vb.* tie, knot.

Knüppel, -, *n.m.* cudgel, club.

knurren, *vb.* growl.

knusp(e)rig, *adj.* crisp, crusty.

Kobalt, *n.m.* cobalt.

Koch, ⸚e, *n.m.* cook.

Kochbuch, ⸚er, *n.nt.* cookbook.

kochen, *vb.* cook, boil.

Köchin, -nen, *n.f.* cook.

Kode, -s, *n.m.* code.

Kodein', *n.nt.* codein.

ködern, *vb.* decoy.

Kodex, -dizes, *n.m.* code.

kodifizie'ren, *vb.* codify.

Koffein', -e, *n.nt.* caffeine.

koffein'frei, *adj.* decaffeinated.

Koffer, -, *n.m.* suitcase, trunk.

Kofferkuli, -s, *n.m.* baggage cart (airport).

Kofferraum, *n.m.* trunk (auto).

Kognak, -s, *n.m.* brandy, cognac.

Kohl, -e, *n.m.* cabbage.

Kohle, -n, *n.f.* coal.

kohlen, *vb.* char.

Kohlenoxyd', *n.nt.* carbon monoxide.

Kohlenstoff, -e, *n.m.* carbon.

Koje, -n, *n.f.* bunk.

Kokain', *n.nt.* cocaine.

kokett', *adj.* coquettish.

Koket'te, -n, *n.f.* coquette.

kokettie'ren, *vb.* flirt.

Kokon', -s, *n.m.* cocoon.

Koks, -e, *n.m.* coke.

Kolben, -, *n.m.* butt; piston.

Kolle'ge, -n, -n, *n.m.* colleague.

Kolle'gin, -nen, *n.f.* colleague.

kollektiv', *adj.* collective.

Koller, -, *n.m.* rage, frenzy.

kölnisch Wasser, *n.nt.* eau-de-cologne.

kolonial', *adj.* colonial.

Kolonial´waren, *n.pl.* groceries.

Kolonial´warenhändler, -, *n.m.* grocer.

Kolonie´, -i´en, *n.f.* colony.

Kolonisation´, *n.f.* colonization.

kolonisie´ren, *vb.* colonize.

Kolon´ne, -n, *n.f.* column.

Kolorit´, -e, *n.nt.* color(ing).

kolossal´, *adj.* colossal.

Koma, *n.nt.* coma.

Kombi, -s, *n.m.* station wagon.

Kombination´, -en, *n.f.* combination.

kombinie´ren, *vb.* combine.

Komet´, -en, -en, *n.m.* comet.

Komiker, -, *n.m.* comedian.

Komikerin, -nen, *n.f.* comedienne.

komisch, *adj.* funny.

Komitee´, -s, *n.nt.* committee.

Komma, -s, *(or* -ta), *n.nt.* comma.

Kommandant´, -en, -en, *n.m.* commander, commanding officer.

Kommandantur´, -en, *n.f.* commander's office.

kommen*, *vb.* come.

Kommentar´, -e, *n.m.* commentary.

Kommenta´tor, -o´ren, *n.m.* commentator.

kommentie´ren, *vb.* comment on.

Kommissar´, -e, *n.m.* commissary, commissioner.

Kommissa´rin, -nen, *n.f.* commissary, commissioner.

Kommission´, -en, *n.f.* commission.

Kommo´de, -n, *n.f.* bureau.

kommunal´, *adj.* communal, municipal.

Kommunikant´, -en, -en, *n.m.* communicant.

Kommunion´, -en, *n.f.* communion.

Kommuniqué, -s, *n.nt.* communiqué.

Kommunis´mus, *n.m.* communism.

Kommunist´, -en, -en, *n.m.* communist.

Kommunis´tin, -nen, *n.f.* communist.

kommunis´tisch, *adj.* communistic.

kommunizie´ren, *vb.* commune; communicate.

Komödiant´, -en, -en, *n.m.* comedian.

Komödian´tin, -nen, *n.f.* comedienne.

Komö´die, -n, *n.f.* comedy.

Kompagnon, -s, *n.m.* (business) partner.

kompakt´, *adj.* compact.

Komparative, -e, *n.m.* comparative (degree).

Kompaß, -sse, *n.m.* compass.

kompensie´rend, *adj.* compensatory.

kompetent´, *adj.* competent, authoritative.

Kompetenz´, -en, *n.f.* competence, authority, jurisdiction.

komplex´, *adj.* complex.

Komplex´, -e, *n.m.* complex.

Komplikation´, -en, *n.f.* complication.

Kompliment´, -e, *n.nt.* compliment.

Kompli´ze, -n, -n, *n.m.* accomplice.

Kompli´zin, -nen, *n.f.* accomplice.

komplizie´ren, *vb.* complicate.

kompliziert´, *adj.* complicated.

Komplott´, -e, *n.nt.* plot.

komponie´ren, *vb.* compose.

Komponist´, -en, -en, *n.m.* composer.

Komponis´tin, -nen, *n.f.* composer.

Komposition´, -en, *n.f.* composition.

Kompott´, -e, *n.nt.* compote.

Kompres´se, -n, *n.f.* compress.

Kompression´, -en, *n.f.* compression.

Kompres´sor, -o´ren, *n.m.* compressor.

Kompromiß´, -sse, *n.m.* compromise.

kompromittie´ren, *vb.* compromise.

Kompu´ter, -, *n.m.* computer.

Kondensation´, -en, *n.f.* condensation.

Kondensa´tor, -o´ren, *n.m.* condenser.

kondensie´ren, *vb.* condense.

Kondi´tor, -o´ren, *n.m.* confectioner, pastry baker.

Konditorei´, -ei´en, *n.f.* café and pastry shop.

Kondom´, -e, *n.m.* condom.

Konfekt´, -e, *n.nt.* candy.

Konfektion´, *n.f.* readymade clothing.

Konferenz´, -en, *n.f.* conference.

Konfirmation´, -en, *n.f.* confirmation.

konfiszie´ren, *vb.* confiscate.

Konfitü´re, -n, *n.f.* jam.

Konflikt´, -e, *n.m.* conflict.

konform´, *adj.* in conformity.

konfrontie´ren, *vb.* confront.

konfus´, *adj.* confused.

Kongreß´, -sse, *n.m.* congress.

König, -e, *n.m.* king.

Königin, -nen, *n.f.* queen.

königlich, *adj.* royal.

Königreich, -e, *n.nt.* kingdom.

Königtum, *n.nt.* kingship, royalty.

Konjugation´, -en, *n.f.* conjugation.

konjugie´ren, *vb.* conjugate.

Konjunktion´, -en, *n.f.* conjunction.

Konjunktiv, -e, *n.m.* subjunctive.

konkav´, *adj.* concave.

konkret´, *adj.* concrete.

Konkurrent´, -en, -en, *n.m.* competitor.

Konkurren´tin, -nen, *n.f.* competitor.

Konkurrenz´, -en, *n.f.* competition.

konkurrie´ren, *vb.* compete.

Konkurs´, -e, *n.m.* bankruptcy.

können*, *vb.* can, be able.

konsequent´, *adj.* consistent.

Konservatis´mus, *n.m.* conservatism.

konservativ´, *adj.* conservative.

Konservato´rium, -en, *n.nt.* conservatory.

Konser´venfabrik, -en, *n.f.* cannery.

konservie′ren, vb. preserve.

Konservie′rung, -en, n.f. conservation.

Konsistenz′, n.f. consistency.

konsolidie′ren, vb. consolidate.

Konsonant′, -en, -en, n.m. consonant.

konstant′, adj. constant.

Konstellation′, -en, n.f. constellation.

konstituie′ren, vb. constitute.

Konstitution′, -en, f. constitution.

konstitutionell′, adj. constitutional.

konstruie′ren, vb. construct.

Konstrukteur′, -e, n.m. constructor, designer.

Konstruktion′, -en, n.f. construction.

Konsul, -n, n.m. consul.

konsula′risch, adj. consular.

Konsulat′, -e, n.nt. consulate.

Konsum′, -s, n.m. consumption; (short for Konsum′laden, ⸚, n.m.) cooperative store, co-op.

Konsument′, -en, -en, n.m. consumer.

Konsum′verein, -e, n.m. cooperative (society).

Kontakt′, -e, n.m. contact.

Kontinent, -e, n.m. continent.

kontinental′, adj. continental.

Konto, -s or -ten or -ti, n.nt. account.

Kontobuch, ⸚er, n.nt. bankbook, account book.

Kontor′, -e, n.nt. office.

Kontorist′, -en, -en, n.m. clerk.

Kontoris′tin, -nen, n.f. clerk.

Kontrast′, -e, n.m. contrast.

Kontroll′abschnitt, -e, n.m. stub.

Kontrol′le, -n, n.f. control, check.

kontrollier′bar, adj. controllable.

kontrollie′ren, vb. control, check.

Kontroll′marke, -n, n.f. check.

Kontur′, -en, n.f. contour, outline.

Konvaleszenz′, n.f. convalescence.

Konvention′, -en, n.f. convention.

konventionell′, adj. conventional.

konvergie′ren, vb. converge.

konvertie′ren, vb. convert.

konvex′, adj. convex.

Konvulsion′, -en, n.f. convulsion.

konvulsiv′, adj. convulsive.

Konzentration′, -en, n.f. concentration.

Konzentrations′lager, -, n.nt. concentration camp.

konzentrie′ren, vb. concentrate.

konzen′trisch, adj. concentric.

Konzept′, -e, n.nt. plan, draft; (aus dem K. bringen*) confuse.

Konzern′, -e, n.m. (business) trust, pool.

Konzert′, -e, n.nt. concert.

Konzert′saal, -säle, n.m. concert hall.

Konzession′, -en, n.f. concession.

koordinie′ren, vb. coordinate.

Kopf, ⸚e, n.m. head.

Kopfhaut, ⸚e, n.f. scalp.

Kopfhörer, -, n.m. earphone.

Kopfkissen, -, n.nt. pillow.

Kopfsalat, -e, n.m. lettuce.

Kopfschmerzen, n.pl. headache.

Kopfsprung, ⸚e, n.m. dive.

Kopftuch, ⸚er, n.nt. kerchief.

Kopie, -i′en, n.f. copy.

kopie′ren, vb. copy, duplicate.

Kopier′maschine, -n, n.f. photocopier; copying machine.

koppeln, vb. couple.

Koral′le, -n, n.f. coral.

Korb, ⸚e, n.m. basket.

Korbball, ⸚e, n.m. basketball.

Korbwiege, -n, n.f. bassinet.

Korduanleder, -, n.nt. cordovan.

Kore′a, n.nt. Korea.

Korin′the, -n, n.f. currant.

Kork, -e, n.m. cork (material).

Korken, -, n.m. cork (stopper).

Korkenzieher, -, n.m. corkscrew.

Korn, -, n.m. grain whiskey.

Korn, -e, n.nt. (type of) grain.

Korn, ⸚er, n.nt. (individual) grain.

Körnchen, -, n.nt. granule.

Kornett′, -e, n.nt. cornet.

körnig, adj. granular.

Kornkammer, -n, n.f. granary.

Kornspeicher, -, n.m. granary.

Körper, -, n.m. body.

Körperbau, n.m. physique.

Körperbehinderung, -en, n.f. physical disability.

Körperchen, -, n.nt. corpuscle.

Körperkraft, n.f. physical strength.

körperlich, adj. physical, corporeal.

Körperpflege, n.f. hygiene.

Körperschaft, -en, n.f. corporation.

Korps, -, n.nt. corps.

korpulent′, adj. corpulent.

korrekt′, adj. correct.

Korrekt′heit, -en, n.f. correctness.

korrektiv′, adj. corrective.

Korrespondent′, -en, -en, n.m. correspondent.

Korresponden′tin, -nen, n.f. correspondent.

Korrespondenz′, -en, n.f. correspondence.

korrespondie′ren, vb. correspond.

Korridor, -e, n.m. corridor.

korrigie′ren, vb. correct.

korrumpie′ren, vb. corrupt.

korrupt′, adj. corrupt.

Korruption′, -en, n.f. corruption.

Korsett′, -s, n.nt. corset.

kosen, vb. fondle, caress.

Kosename(n), -, n.m. pet name.

Kosme′tik, n.f. cosmetics.

kosme′tisch, adj. cosmetic.

kosmisch, adj. cosmic.

kosmopoli′tisch, adj. cosmopolitan.

Kosmos, *n.m.* cosmos.

Kost, *n.f.* food, fare, board.

kostbar, *adj.* costly, precious.

kosten, *vb.* cost; taste.

Kosten, *n.pl.* cost, charges, expenses.

Kostenanschlag, ⸚e, *n.m.* estimate.

kostenfrei, *adj.* free of charge.

kostenlos, *adj.* free, without cost.

Kostgänger, -, *n.m.* boarder.

köstlich, *adj.* delicious.

kostspielig, *adj.* expensive.

Kostspieligkeit, -en, *n.f.* costliness.

Kostüm´, -e, *n.nt.* costume; matching coat and skirt.

Kot, *n.m.* dirt, mud, filth.

Kotelett´, -s, *n.nt.* cutlet, chop.

Köter, -, *n.m.* cur.

kotzen, *vb.* vomit.

Krabbe, -n, *n.f.* shrimp, crab.

Krach, -e, *or* -s, *n.m.* bang, crash, racket; row, fight.

krachen, *vb.* crash.

Kraft, ⸚e, *n.f.* strength, force, power.

kraft, *prep.* by virtue of.

Kraftbrühe, -, *n.f.* bouillon.

Kraftfahrer, -, *n.m.* motorist.

Kraftfahrerin, -nen, *n.f.* motorist.

Kraftfahrzeug, -e, *n.nt.* motor vehicle.

kräftig, *adj.* strong.

kraftlos, *adj.* powerless.

kraftstrotzend, *adj.* vigorous.

kraftvoll, *adj.* powerful.

Kraftwagen, -, *n.m.* automobile.

Kragen, -, *n.m.* collar.

Krähe, -n, *n.f.* crow.

Kralle, -n, *n.f.* claw.

Kram, ⸚e, *n.m.* stuff, junk; business, affairs; retail trade, goods.

kramen, *vb.* rummage.

Krämer, -, *n.m.* small tradesman.

Krampf, ⸚e, *n.m.* cramp, spasm.

krampfhaft, *adj.* spasmodic.

Kran, ⸚e, *n.m.* crane, derrick.

Kranich, -e, *n.m.* crane.

krank(⸚), *adj.* sick.

kranken, *vb.* suffer from, ail.

kränken, *vb.* offend.

Krankenauto, -s, *n.nt.* ambulance.

Krankenhaus, ⸚er, *n.nt.* hospital.

Krankenkasse, *n.f.* health insurance.

Krankenpfleger, -, *n.m.* male nurse.

Krankenschwester, -n, *n.f.* nurse.

Krankenwagen -, *n.m.* ambulance.

krankhaft, *adj.* morbid.

Krankheit, -en, *n.f.* sickness, disease.

kränklich, *adj.* sickly.

Kränkung, -en, *n.f.* offense.

Kranz, ⸚e, *n.m.* wreath.

kraß, *adj.* crass, gross.

Kraßheit, -en, *n.f.* grossness.

kratzen, *vb.* scrape, scratch.

kraus, *adj.* curly, crisp.

Krause, -n, *n.f.* frill.

kräuseln, *vb.* curl, ruffle.

Kraut, ⸚er, *n.nt.* herb, plant.

Krawat´te, -n, *n.f.* necktie.

Krebs, -e, *n.m.* crayfish; *(med.)* cancer.

krebserregend, *adj.* carcinogenic.

kreden´zen, *vb.* serve, offer.

Kredit´, -e, *n.m.* credit.

Kredit´karte, -n, *n.f.* credit card.

Kreide, -n, *n.f.* chalk.

kreidig, *adj.* chalky.

Kreis, -e, *n.m.* circle; district.

Kreisbahn, -en, *n.f.* orbit.

kreischen, *vb.* shriek.

Kreisel, -, *n.m.* top.

kreiseln, *vb.* spin like a top, gyrate.

kreisen, *vb.* circle, revolve.

kreisförmig, *adj.* circular.

Kreislauf, ⸚e, *n.m.* circulation, circuit.

Kremato´rium, -ien, *n.nt.* crematorium.

Krempe, -n, *n.f.* brim.

Krepp, *n.m.* crepe.

Kretonn´e, -s, *n.m.* cretonne.

Kreuz, -e, *n.nt.* cross; back; *(music)* sharp.

kreuzen, *vb.* cross; cruise, tack.

Kreuzer, -, *n.m.* cruiser.

Kreuzgang, ⸚e, *n.m.* cloister.

kreuzigen, *vb.* crucify.

Kreuzigung, -en, *n.f.* crucifixion.

kreuz und quer, *adv.* crisscross.

Kreuzung, -en, *n.f.* cross-(breed); crossing, intersection.

Kreuzverhör, -e, *n.nt.* cross-examination.

Kreuzzug, ⸚e, *n.m.* crusade.

Kreuzzügler, -, *n.m.* crusader.

kribbelig, *adj.* jittery.

kriechen*, *vb.* crawl, creep; grovel.

Krieg, -e, *n.m.* war.

kriegen, *vb.* get.

Krieger, -, *n.m.* warrior.

kriegerisch, *adj.* warlike.

Kriegsdienst, -e, *n.m.* military service.

Kriegsdienstverweigerer, -, *n.m.* conscientious objector.

Kriegsgefangen-, *n.m.* prisoner of war.

Kriegsgericht, -e, *n.nt.* court-martial.

Kriegslist, -en, *n.f.* stratagem.

Kriegslust, ⸚e, *n.f.* belligerence.

kriegslustig, *adj.* bellicose.

Kriegsmacht, ⸚e, *n.f.* military forces.

Kriegsschiff, -e, *n.nt.* warship.

Kriegsverbrechen, -, *n.nt.* war crime.

kriegsversehrt, *adj.* disabled (by war).

Kriegszug, ⸚e, *n.m.* military expedition.

Kriegszustand, ⸚e, *n.m.* state of war.

kriminal´, *adj.* criminal.

Kriminal´film, -e, *n.m.* thriller.

Krippe, -n, *n.f.* crib.

Krise, -n, *n.f.* crisis.

Kristall´, -e, *n.nt.* crystal.

kristal´len, *adj.* crystal, crystalline.

kristallisie´ren, *vb.* crystallize.

Kritik´, -en, *n.f.* criticism, critique, review.

Kritiker, -, *n.m.* critic.
Kritikerin, -nen, *n.f.* critic.
kritisie, *adj.* critical.
kritisie´ren, *vb.* criticize.
kritzeln, *vb.* scribble.
Krocket´spiel, -e, *n.nt.* croquet.
Krokodil´, -e, *n.nt.* crocodile.
Krone, -n, *n.f.* crown.
krönen, *vb.* crown.
Kronleuchter, -, *n.m.* chandelier.
Kronprinz, -en, -en, *n.m.* crown prince.
Krönung, -en, *n.f.* coronation.
Kropf, ⸚e, *n.m.* crop; goiter.
Krücke, -n, *n.f.* crutch.
Krug, ⸚e, *n.m.* pitcher.
Krümel, -, *n.m.* crumb.
krümeln, *vb.* crumble.
krumm (⸚, -), *adj.* crooked.
krümmen, *vb.* bend; **(sich k.)** warp, buckle, double up (with pain or laughter).
Krümmung, -en, *n.f.* bend, curve; curvature.
Krüppel, -, *n.m.* cripple.
Kruste, -n, *n.f.* crust.
Kruzifix, -e, *n.nt.* crucifix.
Kübel, -, *n.m.* bucket.
Kubik´, *cpds.* cubic.
kubisch, *adj.* cubic.
Küche, -n, *n.f.* kitchen.
Kuchen, -, *n.m.* cake.
Küchenchef, -s, *n.m.* chef.
Küchenzettel, -, *n.m.* menu, bill of fare.
Kugel, -n, *n.f.* sphere, ball, bullet.
kugelförmig, *adj.* spherical; globular.
Kuh, ⸚e, *n.f.* cow.
kühl, *adj.* cool.
Kühle, *n.f.* coolness.
kühlen, *vb.* cool.
Kühler, -, *n.m.* auto radiator.
Kühlschrank, ⸚e, *n.m.* refrigerator.
kühn, *adj.* bold.

Kühnheit, -en, *n.f.* boldness.
Küken, -, *n.nt.* chick.
kulina´risch, *adj.* culinary.
Kult, -e, *n.m.* cult.
kultivie´ren, *vb.* cultivate.
kultiviert´, *adj.* cultured.
Kultivie´rung, *n.f.* cultivation.
Kultur´, -en, *n.f.* culture.
kulturell´, *adj.* cultural.
Kümmel, *n.m.* caraway.
Kummer, -, *n.m.* sorrow, grief.
kümmerlich, *adj.* miserable.
kümmern, *vb.* grieve, trouble, concern; **(sich k. um)** care about, look out for.
kummervoll, *adj.* sorrowful.
kund, *adj.* known.
Kunde, -n, -n, *n.m.* customer, client.
Kundin, -nen, *n.f.* customer, client.
Kunde, -n, *n.f.* knowledge, information.
kund•geben*, *vb.* make known.
Kundgebung, -en, *n.f.* demonstration.
kundig, *adj.* well informed, knowing.
kündigen, *vb.* give notice; cancel.
Kündigung, -en, *n.f.* cancellation.
Kundschaft, -en, *n.f.* clientele.
künftig, *adj.* future.
Kunst, ⸚e, *n.f.* art.
künsteln, *vb.* contrive.
kunstfertig, *adj.* skillful.
Künstler, -, *n.m.* artist.
Künstlerin, -nen, *n.f.* artist.
künstlerisch, *adj.* artistic.
Künstlertum, *n.nt.* artistry.
künstlich, *adj.* artificial.
kunstlos, *adj.* artless.
Kunstseide, -n, *n.f.* rayon.
Kunststoff, -e, *n.m.* plastic.
Kunststück, -e, *n.nt.* feat, stunt.

kunstvoll, *adj.* artistic.
Kunstwerk, -e, *n.nt.* work of art.
Kunstwissenschaft, *n.f.* fine arts.
Kupfer, *n.nt.* copper.
kuppeln, *vb.* couple; join; pander.
Kuppelung, -en, *n.f.* clutch.
Kur, -en, *n.f.* cure.
Kurbel, -n, *n.f.* crank.
Kürbis, -se, *n.m.* pumpkin, gourd.
Kurier´, -e, *n.m.* courier.
kurie´ren, *vb.* cure.
kurios´, *adj.* odd, strange.
Kuriosität´, -en, *n.f.* curio.
Kurio´sum, -sa, *n.nt.* freak.
Kurort, -e, *n.m.* resort.
Kurs, -e, *n.m.* course; rate of exchange.
Kursbuch, ⸚er, *n.nt.* timetable.
kursie´ren, *vb.* circulate.
kursiv´, *adj.* italic.
Kursus, Kurse, *n.m.* course.
Kurve, -n, *n.f.* curve.
kurz(⸚), *adj.* short; **(k. und bündig)** short and to the point.
Kürze, -n, *n.f.* shortness, brevity.
kürzen, *vb.* shorten.
kürzlich, *adj.* recently.
Kurzschluß, *n.m.* short circuit.
kurzsichtig, *adj.* nearsighted.
kurzum´, *adv.* in short.
Kürzung, -en, *n.f.* shortening, cut.
Kurzwaren, *n.pl.* notions.
Kusi´ne, -n, *n.f.* cousin.
Kuß, ⸚sse, *n.m.* kiss.
küssen, *vb.* kiss.
Küste, -n, *n.f.* coast, shore.
Küster, -, *n.m.* sexton.
Kutsche, -n, *n.f.* coach.
Kuvert´, -s, *n.nt.* envelope.

L

Labe, -n, *n.f.* refreshment, comfort.
laben, *vb.* refresh, comfort.
Laborato´rium, -rien, *n.nt.* laboratory.

Labsal, -e, *n.nt.* refreshment, comfort.
Labyrinth´, -e, *n.nt.* labyrinth.
Lache, -n, *n.f.* puddle.
lächeln, *vb.* smile.

Lächeln, *n.nt.* smile.
lachen, *vb.* laugh.
Lachen, *n.nt.* laugh(ing).
lächerlich, *adj.* ridiculous.
Lachs, *n.m.* salmon.

Lack, -e, *n.m.* lacquer.

Lackleder, *n.nt.* patent leather.

Lade, -n, *n.f.* box, chest, drawer.

laden*, *vb.* load, charge; summon.

Laden, ⸗, *n.m.* shop; shutter.

Ladendieb, -e, *n.m.* shop-lifter.

Ladendiebin, -nen, *n.f.* shop-lifter.

Ladenkasse, -n, *n.f.* till.

Ladentisch, -e, *n.m.* counter.

Ladung, -en, *n.f.* load, cargo, shipment; charge.

Lage, -n, *n.f.* location, situation, condition.

Lager, -, *n.nt.* camp, lair, bed; deposit, depot, supply; bearing.

Lagerhaus, ⸗er, *n.nt.* storehouse.

lagern, *vb.* lay down, store, deposit; **(sich l.)** camp; be deposited.

Lagerung, -en, *n.f.* storage, bearing; stratification, grain.

Lagu´ne, -n, *n.f.* lagoon.

lahm, *adj.* lame.

lähmen, *vb.* lame, cripple, paralyze.

Lähmung, -en, *n.f.* paralysis.

Laib, -e, *n.m.* loaf.

Laie, -n, -n, *n.m.* layman.

Laienstand, *n.m.* laity.

Laken, -, *n.nt.* sheet.

Lamm, ⸗er, *n.nt.* lamb.

Lampe, -n, *n.f.* lamp.

lancie´ren, *vb.* launch.

Land, ⸗er, *n.nt.* land, country.

Landbau, *n.m.* agriculture.

Landebahn, -en, *n.f.* flight strip, runway.

landen, *vb.* land.

Landesverrat, *n.m.* high treason.

Landkarte, -n, *n.f.* map.

landläufig, *adj.* usual, ordinary.

ländlich, *adj.* rural.

Landschaft, -en, *n.f.* landscape, countryside.

Landser, -, *n.m.* common soldier, GI.

Landsmann, -leute, *n.m.* compatriot.

Landsmännin, -en, *n.f.* compatriot.

Landstraße, -n, *n.f.* highway.

Landstrich, -e, *n.m.* region.

Landung, -en, *n.f.* landing.

Landwirt, -e, *n.m.* farmer.

Landwirtin, -nen, *n.f.* farmer.

Landwirtschaft, *n.f.* agriculture.

landwirtschaftlich, *adj.* agricultural.

lang (⸗), *adj.* long, tall.

lange, *adv.* for a long time.

Länge, -n, *n.f.* length; longitude.

langen, *vb.* hand; suffice.

Langeweile, *n.f.* boredom.

langlebig, *adj.* long-lived.

länglich, *adj.* oblong.

Langmut, *n.m.* patience.

langmütig, *adj.* long-suffering.

längs, *adv. & prep.* along.

langsam, *adj.* slow.

Langsamkeit, *n.f.* slowness.

längst, *adv.* long since.

langweilen, *vb.* bore.

langweilig, *adj.* boring.

langwierig, *adj.* lengthy.

Lanze, -n, *n.f.* lance.

Lappa´lie, -n, *n.f.* trifle.

Lappen, -, *n.m.* rag; lobe.

Lärm, *n.m.* noise.

Larve, -n, *n.f.* mask; larva.

Laserstrahl, -en, *n.m.* laser beam.

lassen*, *vb.* let, permit; cause to, have (someone do something, something done); leave; leave off, stop.

lässig, *adj.* indolent, careless.

Last, -en, *n.f.* burden, encumbrance; load, weight, cargo.

Lastauto, -s, *n.nt.* truck.

lasten, *vb.* weigh heavily, be a burden.

Laster, -, *n.nt.* vice.

lasterhaft, *adj.* vicious, wicked.

lästern, *vb.* slander, blaspheme.

lästig, *adj.* troublesome, disagreeable.

Lastkraftwagen, -, *n.m.* (motor) truck.

Lastwagen, -n, *n.m.* (motor) truck.

Latein´, *n.nt.* Latin.

latei´nisch, *adj.* Latin.

Later´ne, -n, *n.f.* lantern.

Latri´ne, -n, *n.f.* latrine.

latschen, *vb.* shuffle, slouch.

Latz, ⸗e, *n.m.* bib, flap.

lau, *adj.* tepid, lukewarm.

Laub, *n.nt.* foliage.

Lauer, *n.f.* ambush.

lauern, *vb.* lurk, lie in wait for.

Lauf, -, *n.m.* course, race, run; (gun) barrel.

Laufbahn, -en, *n.f.* career; runway, race track.

laufen*, *vb.* run, walk.

laufend, *adj.* running, current.

Läufer, -, *n.m.* runner; stair carpet; (chess) bishop.

Läuferin, -nen, *n.f.* runner.

Lauge, -n, *n.f.* lye.

Laune, -n, *n.f.* whim, caprice, fancy; mood, humor.

launenhaft, *adj.* capricious.

launig, *adj.* humorous.

launisch, *adj.* moody.

Laus, ⸗e, *n.f.* louse.

lauschen, *vb.* listen.

lausig, *adj.* lousy.

laut, *adj.* loud, aloud.

laut, *prep.* according to.

Laut, -e, *n.m.* sound.

Laute, -n, *n.f.* lute.

lauten, *vb.* read, say.

läuten, *vb.* ring, peal, sound.

lauter, *adj.* pure, sheer, nothing but.

Lauterkeit, -en, *n.f.* purity.

läutern, *vb.* purify.

lautlos, *adj.* soundless, silent.

Lautsprecher, -, *n.m.* loudspeaker.

lauwarm, *adj.* lukewarm; half-hearted.

Lava, *n.f.* lava.

Laven´del, *n.m.* lavender.

lax, *adj.* lax.

Laxheit, *n.f.* laxity.

leben, *vb.* live, be alive.

Leben, -, *n.nt.* life.
lebend, *adj.* living.
leben´dig, *adj.* living, alive; lively.
Leben´digkeit, *n.f.* liveliness, vivacity.
lebenserfahren, *adj.* experienced, sophisticated.
Lebensgefahr, -en, *n.f.* danger (to life).
lebensgefährlich, *adj.* highly dangerous.
Lebenskraft, *n.f.* vitality.
lebenslänglich, *adj.* lifelong, for life.
Lebensmittel, *n.pl.* provisions, groceries.
Lebensmittelgeschäft, -e, *n.nt.* grocery store.
Lebensstandard, *n.m.* standard of living.
Lebensstil, *n.m.* life style.
Lebensunterhalt, *n.m.* livelihood.
Leber, -n, *n.f.* liver.
Lebewesen, -, *n.nt.* living being, organism.
lebewohl´, *interj.* farewell, adieu.
lebhaft, *adj.* lively.
leblos, *adj.* lifeless.
Lebzeiten, *n.pl.* lifetime.
lechzen, *vb.* thirst, languish.
leck, *adj.* leaky, having a leak.
Leck, -e, *n.nt.* leak.
lecken, *vb.* leak; lick.
lecker, *adj.* tasty, appetizing.
Leder, -, *n.nt.* leather.
ledern, *adj.* leather(y).
ledig, *adj.* unmarried, single; vacant; exempt.
lediglich, *adv.* merely.
leer, *adj.* empty, vacant, blank.
Leere, -, *n.f.* emptiness.
leeren, *vb.* empty.
Leerlauf, *n.m.* neutral (gear).
legal, *adj.* legal.
legalisie´ren, *vb.* legalize.
Legat´, -e, *n.nt.* bequest.
legen, *vb.* lay, place, put; **(sich l.)** lie down, subside.
legendär´, *adj.* legendary.
Legen´de, -n, *n.f.* legend.
Legie´rung, -en, *n.f.* alloy.
Legion´, -en, *n.f.* legion.
legitim´, *adj.* legitimate.

legitimie´ren, *vb.* legitimize; **(sich l.)** prove one's identity.
Lehm, *n.m.* loam, clay.
Lehne, -n, *n.f.* back, arm (of a chair), support.
lehnen, *vb.* lean.
Lehnstuhl, ¨e, *n.m.* armchair.
Lehrbuch, ¨er, *n.nt.* textbook.
Lehre, -n, *n.f.* doctrine, teaching, lesson; apprenticeship.
lehren, *vb.* teach.
Lehrer, -, *n.m.* teacher.
Lehrerin, -nen, *n.f.* teacher.
Lehrgang, ¨e, *n.m.* course of instruction.
Lehrplan, ¨e, *n.m.* curriculum.
lehrreich, *adj.* instructive.
Lehrsatz, ¨e, *n.m.* proposition.
Lehrstunde, -n, *n.f.* lesson.
Leib, -er, *n.m.* body; abdomen; womb.
leibhaft(ig), *adj.* incarnate, personified.
leiblich, *adj.* bodily.
Leiche, -n, *n.f.* corpse.
leicht, *adj.* light; easy.
Leichtathletik, *n.f.* track and field.
Leichter, -, *n.m.* barge.
leichtfertig, *adj.* frivolous.
Leichtfertigkeit, *n.f.* frivolity.
leichtgläubig, *adj.* gullible, credulous.
Leichtigkeit, -en, *n.f.* ease.
Leichtsinn, *n.m.* frivolity.
leichtsinnig, *adj.* frivolous, reckless.
leid, *adj.* **(es tut* mir l.)** I'm sorry.
Leid, *n.nt.* suffering, sorrow, harm.
leiden*, *vb.* suffer; stand, endure; **(gern l. mögen*)** like.
Leiden, -, *n.nt.* suffering; illness.
Leidenschaft, -en, *n.f.* passion.
leidenschaftlich, *adj.* passionate.
leidenschaftslos, *adj.* dispassionate.

leider, *adv.* unfortunately.
leidig, *adj.* unpleasant.
leidlich, *adj.* tolerable.
Leier, -n, *n.f.* lyre.
leihen*, *vb.* lend; borrow.
leihweise, *adv.* on loan.
Leim, *n.m.* glue.
leimen, *vb.* glue.
Leine, -n, *n.f.* line, leash.
leinen, *adj.* linen.
Leinen, -, *n.nt.* linen.
Leinsamen, *n.m.* linseed.
Leinwand, *n.f.* canvas; (movie) screen.
leise, *adj.* soft, quiet, gentle.
leisten, *vb.* perform, accomplish; **(sich l.)** afford.
Leisten, -, *n.m.* last.
Leistung, -en, *n.f.* performance, accomplishment, achievement, output.
leistungsf ähig, *adj.* efficient.
Leitartikel, -, *n.nt.* editorial.
leiten, *vb.* lead, direct, conduct, manage.
Leiter, -, *n.m.* leader, director, manager.
Leiter, -n, *n.f.* ladder.
Leiterin, -nen, *n.f.* leader, director, manager.
Leitfaden, ¨, *n.m.* key, guide.
Leitsatz, ¨e, *n.m.* guiding principle.
Leitung, -en, *n.f.* guidance, direction, management; wire, line, duct, tube; conduction.
Leitungswasser, *n.nt.* tap water.
Leitungsrohr, -e, *n.nt.* conduit.
Lektion´, -en, *n.f.* lesson.
Lektor, -o´ren, *n.m.* university instructor.
Lekto´rin, -nen, *n.f.* university instructor.
Lektü´re, -n, *n.f.* reading.
Lende, -n, *n.f.* loin.
Lendenstück, -e, *n.nt.* sirloin.
lenkbar, *adj.* steerable, dirigible, manageable.
lenken, *vb.* direct, steer, guide.
Lenkung, -en, *n.f.* guidance, steering, control.
Lenz, -e, *n.m.* spring.

Leopard´, -en, -en, *n.m.* leopard.

Lerche, -n, *n.f.* lark.

lernen, *vb.* learn.

Lesart, -en, *n.f.* reading, version.

lesbar, *adj.* legible; worth reading.

lesbisch, *adj.* lesbian.

Lese, -n, *n.f.* vintage.

Lesebuch, ˝er, *n.nt.* reader.

lesen*, *vb.* read; lecture; gather.

Leser, -, *n.m.* reader.

leserlich, *adj.* legible.

Lethargie´, *n.f.* lethargy.

lethar´gisch, *adj.* lethargic.

Lettland, *n.nt.* Latvia.

letzt-, *adj.* last.

letzter-, *adj.* latter.

leuchten, *vb.* give forth light, shine.

Leuchter, -, *n.m.* candlestick.

Leuchtschirm, -e, *n.m.* fluorescent screen, television screen.

Leuchtsignal, -e, *n.nt.* flare.

Leuchtturm, ˝e, *n.m.* lighthouse.

leugnen, *vb.* deny.

Leukoplast´, *n.nt.* adhesive tape, band-aid.

Leumund, -e, *n.m.* reputation.

Leute, *n.pl.* people.

Leutnant, -s *or* -e, *n.m.* lieutenant.

leutselig, *adj.* affable.

Lexikon, -ka, *n.nt.* dictionary.

Liaison´, -s, *n.f.* liaison.

liberal´, *adj.* liberal.

Liberalis´mus, *n.m.* liberalism.

Libret´to, -s, *n.nt.* libretto.

Licht, -er, *n.nt.* light.

Lichtbild, -er, *n.nt.* photograph.

Lichtschimmer, -, *n.m.* glint.

Lichtspiel, -e, *n.nt.* moving picture.

Lid, -er, *n.nt.* eyelid.

lieb, *adj.* dear.

liebäugeln, *vb.* make eyes at.

Liebchen, -, *n.nt.* dearest, darling.

Liebe, -n, *n.f.* love.

Liebelei´, -en, *n.f.* flirtation.

liebeln, *vb.* flirt, make love.

lieben, *vb.* love.

liebenswert, *adj.* lovable.

liebenswürdig, *adj.* amiable, kind.

lieber, *adv.* rather.

Liebesaff äre, -n, *n.f.* love affair.

liebevoll, *adj.* loving, affectionate.

lieb•haben*, *vb.* love.

Liebhaber, -, *n.m.* lover.

Liebhaberei´, -en, *n.f.* hobby.

liebkosen, *vb.* fondle, caress.

Liebkosung, -en, *n.f.* caress.

lieblich, *adj.* lovely.

Liebling, -e, *n.m.* darling.

Lieblings-, *cpds.* favorite.

lieblos, *adj.* loveless.

Liebreiz, -e, *n.m.* charm.

Liebschaft, -en, *n.f.* love affair.

Liebst-, *n.m. & f.* dearest, sweetheart.

Lied, -er, *n.nt.* song.

liederlich, *adj.* slovenly; dissolute.

Lieferant´, -en, -en, *n.m.* supplier.

liefern, *vb.* supply, deliver.

Lieferung, -en, *n.f.* delivery.

Lieferwagen, -, *n.m.* delivery van.

liegen*, *vb.* lie, be located.

Lift, -e, *n.m.* elevator.

Likör´, -e, *n.m.* liqueur.

lila, *adj.* lilac, purple.

Lilie, -n, *n.f.* lily.

Limona´de, -n, *n.f.* lemonade.

Limo´ne, -n, *n.f.* lime.

Limousi´ne, -n, *n.f.* limousine, sedan.

lind, *adj.* mild, gentle.

lindern, *vb.* alleviate, ease, soothe.

Lineal´, -e, *n.nt.* ruler.

linear´, *adj.* linear.

Linguist´, -en, -en, *n.m.* linguist.

Linguis´tin, -nen, *n.f.* linguist.

linguis´tisch, *adj.* linguistic.

Linie, -n, *n.f.* line.

link-, *adj.* left.

Link-, *n.f.* left.

linkisch, *adj.* awkward, clumsy.

links, *adv.* to the left.

Linse, -n, *n.f.* lens; lentil.

Lippe, -n, *n.f.* lip.

Lippenstift, -e, *n.m.* lipstick.

liquidie´ren, *vb.* liquidate.

lispeln, *vb.* lisp, whisper.

List, -en, *n.f.* cunning, trick, ruse.

Liste, -n, *n.f.* list.

listig, *adj.* cunning, crafty.

Litanei´, *n.f.* litany.

Litauen, *n.nt.* Lithuania.

Liter, -, *n.m. or nt.* liter.

litera´risch, *adj.* literary.

Literatur´, -en, *n.f.* literature.

Lithographie´, -i´en, *n.f.* lithograph(y).

Liturgie´, -i´en, *n.f.* liturgy.

litur´gisch, *adj.* liturgical.

Livree´, -e´en, *n.f.* livery.

Lizenz´, -en, *n.f.* license.

Lob, -e, *n.nt.* praise.

loben, *vb.* praise.

lobenswert, *adj.* praiseworthy.

löblich, *adj.* praiseworthy.

lobpreisen, *vb.* praise, extol.

Lobrede, -n, *n.f.* eulogy.

Loch, ˝er, *n.nt.* hole.

lochen, *vb.* put a hole in, punch.

Locke, -n, *n.f.* lock, curl.

locken, *vb.* curl; lure.

locker, *adj.* loose.

lockern, *vb.* loosen.

lockig, *adj.* curly.

lodern, *vb.* blaze.

Löffel, -, *n.m.* spoon.

Logbuch, ˝er, *n.nt.* log.

Loge, -n, *n.f.* loge, box; (fraternal) lodge.

Logik, *n.f.* logic.

logisch, *adj.* logical.

Lohn, ˝e, *n.m.* reward; wages.

lohnen, *vb.* reward, pay, be of value; (sich l.) be worth the trouble.

Lohnerhöhung, (-en) *n.f.* raise.

lokal´, *adj.* local.

Lokal´, -e, *n.nt.* night club, bar, place of amusement; premises.

Lokomoti´ve, -n, *n.f.* locomotive.

Lokus, -se, *n.m.* toilet.

los, *adj.* loose; wrong; **(was ist l.?)** what's the matter?

Los, -e, *n.nt.* lot.

lösbar, *adj.* soluble.

los•binden*, *vb.* untie.

Loschblatt, *-er, n.nt.* blotter.

löschen, *vb.* extinguish, quench; unload.

lose, *adj.* loose, slack, lax, dissolute.

Lösegeld, -er, *n.nt.* ransom.

lösen, *vb.* undo, solve, dissolve; buy (a ticket).

los•fahren*, *vb.* start out.

los•gehen*, *vb.* start out, go off, begin.

los•kommen*, *vb.* get loose.

los•lassen*, *vb.* get loose, let go.

los•lösen, *vb.* disconnect.

los•machen, *vb.* unfasten, free.

Lösung, -en, *n.f.* solution.

Lösungsmittel, -, *n.nt.* solvent.

los•werden*, *vb.* get rid of.

Lot, -e, *n.nt.* lead, plumbline.

löten, *vb.* solder.

lotrecht, *adj.* perpendicular.

Lotse, -n, -n, *n.m.* pilot.

lotsen, *vb.* pilot.

Lotterie´, -i´en, *n.f.* lottery.

Löwe, -n, -n, *n.m.* lion.

Lücke, -n, *n.f.* gap.

lückenhaft, *adj.* with gaps, incomplete.

lückenlos, *adj.* without gaps, complete.

Luder, -, *n.nt.* scoundrel, slut; carrion.

Luft, ¨e, *n.f.* air.

Luftabwehr, *n.f.* anti-aircraft, air defense.

Luftangriff, -e, *n.m.* air raid.

Luftballon, -s, *n.m.* balloon.

Luftblase, -n, *n.f.* bubble.

Luftbrücke, -n, *n.f.* air lift.

luftdicht, *adj.* airtight.

Luftdruck, -e, *n.m.* air pressure.

lüften, *vb.* air, ventilate.

Luftfahrt, *n.nt.* aviation.

Luftflotte, -n, *n.f.* air fleet.

luftig, *adj.* airy.

luftkrank, ¨, *adj.* air-sick.

Luftlinie, -n, *n.f.* air line.

Luftpirat, -en, -en, *n.m.* hijacker.

Luftpost, *n.f.* airmail.

Luftsack, ¨e, *n.m.* airbag (automobile).

Luftschiff, -e, *n.nt.* airship, dirigible.

Luftsprung, ¨e, *n.m.* caper.

Luftstützpunkt, -e, *n.m.* air base.

Lüftung, *n.f.* ventilation.

Luftverpestung, *n.f.* air pollution.

Luftverschmutzung, *n.f.* air pollution.

Luftwaffe, -n, *n.f.* air force.

Luftzug, ¨e, *n.m.* draft.

Lüge, -n, *n.f.* lie.

lugen, *vb.* peep.

lügen*, *vb.* lie.

Lügner, -, *n.m.* liar.

Lügnerin, -nen, *n.f.* liar.

Lümmel, -, *n.m.* lout.

Lump, -en, -en, *n.m.* bum.

Lumpen, -, *n.m.* rag.

Lunge, -n, *n.f.* lung.

Lungenentzündung, -en, *n.f.* pneumonia.

Lust, ¨e, *n.f.* pleasure, desire; **(L. haben*)** feel like (doing something).

lüstern, *adj.* lecherous.

lustig, *adj.* merry, gay.

Lüstling, -e, *n.m.* libertine.

lustlos, *adj.* listless.

Lustspiel, -e, *n.nt.* comedy.

Luthera´ner, -, *n.m.* Lutheran.

lutherisch, *adj.* Lutheran.

lutschen, *vb.* suck.

luxuriös, *adj.* luxurious.

Luxus, *n.m.* luxury.

Luxus-, *cpds.* de luxe.

Lymphe, -n, *n.f.* lymph.

lynchen, *vb.* lynch.

Lyrik, *n.f.* lyric poetry.

lyrisch, *adj.* lyric.

Lyze´um, -e´en, *n.nt.* girls' high school.

M

Maat, -e, *n.m.* mate.

machbar, *adj.* feasible.

machen, *vb.* make, do.

Macht, ¨e, *n.f.* power.

Machterweiterung, -en, *n.f.* aggrandizement.

mächtig, *adj.* powerful.

machtlos, *adj.* powerless.

Mädchen, -, *n.nt.* girl.

mädchenhaft, *adj.* girlish.

Mädel, -, *n.nt.* girl.

Mafia, *n.f.* mafia.

Magazin´, -e, *n.nt.* magazine, storeroom, store.

Magd, -e, *n.f.* hired girl.

Magen, - or ¨, *n.m.* stomach.

Magenbeschwerden, *n.pl.* indigestion.

Magengeschwür, -e, *n.nt.* stomach ulcer.

Magenschmerzen, *n.pl.* stomach ache.

Magenverstimmung, -en, *n.f.* stomach upset.

mager, *adj.* lean.

Magermilch, *n.f.* skim milk.

Magie´, *n.f.* magic.

magisch, *adj.* magic.

Magnat´, -en, -en, *n.m.* magnate, tycoon.

Magne´sium, *n.nt.* magnesium.

Magnet´, -e, *or* **-en, -en,** *n.m.* magnet.

magne´tisch, *adj.* magnetic.

Magnetophon´, -e, *n.nt.* tape recorder.

Mahago´ni, *n.nt.* mahogany.

mähen, *vb.* mow.

Mahl, -e, *or* **¨er,** *n.nt.* meal, repast.

mahlen, *vb.* grind.

Mahlzeit, -en, *n.f.* meal.

mahnen, *vb.* remind, urge, warn, dun.

Mahnung, -en, *n.f.* admonition, warning.

Mähre, -n, *n.f.* mare.

Mai, *n.m.* May.

Mais, -, *n.m.* corn, maize.

Maiskolben, -, *n.m.* corncob.

Majestät´, -en, *n.f.* majesty.

majestä´tisch, *adj.* majestic.

Major´, -e, *n.m.* major.

Majorität´, -en, *n.f.* majority.

Majus´kel, -n, *n.f.* capital letter.

Makel, -, *n.m.* stain, blemish, flaw.

makellos, *adj.* spotless, flawless, immaculate.

Makkaro´ni, *n.pl.* macaroni.

Makler, -, *n.m.* broker.

Maklerin, -nen, *n.f.* broker.

Makre´le, -n, *n.f.* mackerel.

Makro´ne, -n, *n.f.* macaroon.

¹Mal, -e, *n.nt.* mark, sign, spot, mole.

²Mal, -e, *n.nt.* time; **(das erste M.)** the first time; **(2 mal 2)** 2 times 2.

mal, *adv.* (= einmal) once, just; **(nicht m.)** not even.

Mala´ria, *n.f.* malaria.

malen, *vb.* paint.

Maler, -, *n.m.* painter.

Malerei´, -en, *n.f.* painting.

Malerin, -nen, *n.f.* painter.

malerisch, *adj.* picturesque.

Malz, *n.m.* malt.

man, *pron.* one, a person.

Manager, -, *n.m.* manager.

Managerin, -nen, *n.f.* manager.

mancher, -es, -e, *pron. & adj.* many, many a.

mancherlei, *adj.* various.

manchmal, *adv.* sometimes.

Mandat´, -e, *n.nt.* mandate.

Mandel, -n, *n.f.* almond; tonsil.

Mandoli´ne, -n, *n.f.* mandolin.

Mangel, ⸗, *n.m.* lack, dearth, defect.

Mangel, -n, *n.f.* mangle.

mangelhaft, *adj.* faulty.

mangeln, *vb.* be lacking, deficient; **(es mangelt mir an . . . .)** I lack . . . .

mangels, *prep.* for lack of.

Manie´, -i´en, *n.f.* mania.

Manier´, -en, *n.f.* manner.

manier´lich, *adj.* mannerly, polite.

manikü´ren, *vb.* manicure.

manipulie´ren, *vb.* manipulate.

Manko, -s, *n.nt.* defect, deficiency.

Mann, ⸗er, *n.m.* man, husband.

Männchen, -, *n.nt.* male (animal).

Mannesalter, *n.nt.* manhood.

mannhaft, *adj.* manly.

mannigfach, *adj.* manifold.

mannigfaltig, *adj.* manifold.

Mannigfaltigkeit, -en, *n.f.* diversity.

männlich, *adj.* male, masculine.

Männlichkeit, *n.f.* manliness.

Mannschaft, -en, *n.f.* crew, team, squad; *(pl.)* enlisted men.

Manö´ver, -, *n.nt.* maneuver.

manövrie´ren, *vb.* maneuver.

Manschet´te, -n, *n.f.* cuff.

Mantel, ⸗, *n.m.* overcoat.

Manufaktur´, -en, *n.f.* manufacture, factory.

Manuskript´, -e, *n.nt.* manuscript.

Mappe, -n, *n.f.* portfolio, briefcase, folder.

Märchen, -, *n.nt.* fairy tale.

märchenhaft, *adj.* fabulous.

Märchenland, ⸗er, *n.nt.* fairyland.

Margari´ne, *n.f.* margarine.

Marihua´na, *n.nt.* marijuana.

Mari´ne, -n, *n.f.* navy.

marinie´ren, *vb.* marinate.

Marionet´te, -n, *n.f.* marionette, puppet.

Mark, -, *n.f.* mark (unit of money); **(Deutsche M.)** German mark.

Mark, -en, *n.f.* border(land).

Marke, -n, *n.f.* mark; brand, sort; postage stamp, check, ticket.

markie´ren, *vb.* mark.

Marki´se, -n, *n.f.* awning.

Markstein, -e, *n.m.* boundary stone, landmark.

Markt, ⸗e, *n.m.* market.

Marktplatz, ⸗e, *n.m.* market place.

Marmela´de, -n, *n.f.* jam.

Marmor, -e, *n.m.* marble.

Maro´ne, -n, *n.f.* chestnut.

Marot´te, -n, *n.f.* whim, fad.

Marsch, ⸗e, *n.m.* march.

Marsch, -en, *n.f.* marsh.

Marschall, ⸗e, *n.m.* marshal.

marschie´ren, *vb.* march.

Marter, -n, *n.f.* torture.

martern, *vb.* torture.

Märtyrer, -, *n.m.* martyr.

Märtyrerin, -nen, *n.f.* martyr.

Märtyrertum, *n.nt.* martyrdom.

März, *n.m.* March.

Marzipan´, -e, *n.m. or nt.* marzipan, almond paste.

Masche, -n, *n.f.* stitch, mesh.

Maschi´ne, -n, *n.f.* machine.

Maschi´nenbau, *n.m.* mechanical engineering.

Maschi´nengewehr, -e, *n.nt.* machine gun.

Maschinist´, -en, -en, *n.m.* machinist.

Masern, *n.pl.* measles.

Maske, -n, *n.f.* mask.

Maskera´de, -n, *n.f.* masquerade.

maskie´ren, *vb.* mask.

Maskot´te, -n, *n.f.* mascot.

maskulin´, *adj.* masculine.

Maß, -e, *n.nt.* measure(ment), dimension, extent, rate, proportion.

Massa´ge, -n, *n.f.* massage.

Masse, -n, *n.f.* mass.

massenhaft, *adj.* in large quantity.

Massenmedien, *n.pl.* mass media.

Massenversammlung, -en, *n.f.* mass meeting.

massenweise, *adv.* in large numbers.

Masseur´, -e, *n.m.* masseur.

Masseu´se, -n, *n.f.* masseuse.

maßgebend, *adj.* authoritative, standard.

maßgeblich, *adj.* authoritative, standard.

massie´ren, *vb.* massage.

massig, *adj.* bulky, solid.

mäßig, *adj.* moderate.

mäßigen, *vb.* moderate.

Mäßigkeit, *n.f.* temperance.

Mäßigung, *n.f.* moderation.

massiv´, *adj.* massive.

maßlos, *adj.* immoderate, excessive.

Maßnahme, -n, *n.f.* measure, step.

Maßregel, -n, *n.f.* measure, step.

maßregelnd, *adj.* disciplinary.

Maßstab, ⁼e, *n.m.* scale, rate, gauge, standard.

maßvoll, *adj.* moderate.

Mast, -e *or* -en, *n.m.* mast.

mästen, *vb.* fatten.

Material´, -ien, *n.nt.* material.

Materialis´mus, *n.m.* materialism.

Mate´rie, -n, *n.f.* matter, stuff.

materiell´, *adj.* material.

Mathematik´, *n.f.* mathematics.

Mathema´tiker, -, *n.m.* mathematician.

Mathema´tikerin, -nen, *n.f.* mathematician.

mathema´tisch, *adj.* mathematical.

Matrat´ze, -n, *n.f.* mattress.

Mätres´se, -n, *n.f.* mistress.

Matro´se, -n, -n, *n.m.* sailor.

matschig, *adj.* muddy, slushy; pulpy.

matt, *adj.* dull, tired.

Matte, -n, *n.f.* mat.

Mattigkeit, *n.f.* lassitude.

Mätzchen, -, *n.nt.* antic, foolish trick.

Mauer, -n, *n.f.* (outside) wall.

Maul, ⁼er, *n.nt.* mouth, snout.

Maulkorb, ⁼e, *n.m.* muzzle.

Maultier, -e, *n.nt.* mule.

Maulwurf, ⁼e, *n.m.* mole.

Maure, -n, -n, *n.m.* Moor.

Maurer, -, *n.m.* mason, bricklayer.

Maus, ⁼e, *n.f.* mouse.

Mausole´um, -le´en, *n.nt.* mausoleum.

maximal´, *adj.* maximum.

Maximum, -ma, *n.nt.* maximum.

Mayonnai´se, -n, *n.f.* mayonnaise.

m. E., *abbr.* (= meines Erach´tens) in my opinion.

Mecha´nik, *n.f.* mechanics, mechanism.

Mecha´niker, -, *n.m.* mechanic.

Mecha´nikerin, -nen, *n.f.* mechanic.

mecha´nisch, *adj.* mechanical.

mechanisie´ren, *vb.* mechanize.

Mechanis´mus, -men, *n.m.* mechanism.

Medai´lle, -n, *n.f.* medal.

Medikament´, -e, *n.nt.* drug, medicine.

Medium, -ien, *n.nt.* medium.

Medizin´, -en, *n.f.* medicine.

Medizi´ner, -, *n.m.* medical man, medical student.

Medizi´nerin, -nen, *n.f.* medical student.

medizi´nisch, *adj.* medical.

Meer, -e, *n.nt.* sea.

Meerbusen, -, *n.m.* bay.

Meerenge, -n, *n.f.* strait.

Meeresboden, *n.m.* seabed.

Meeresbucht, -en, *n.f.* bay.

Meerrettich, -e, *n.m.* horseradish.

Meerschweinchen, -, *n.nt.* guinea pig.

Megahertz, *n.nt.* megahertz.

Mehl, *n.nt.* flour, meal.

mehr, *adj.* more.

mehren, *vb.* increase.

mehrere, *adj.* several.

mehrfach, *adj.* multiple.

Mehrheit, -en, *n.f.* majority.

mehrmalig, *adj.* repeated.

mehrmals, *adv.* repeatedly.

Mehrwertsteuer, -n, *n.f.* value-added tax.

Mehrzahl, -en, *n.f.* majority; plural.

meiden*, *vb.* avoid.

Meile, -n, *n.f.* mile.

Meilenstein, -e, *n.m.* milestone.z

mein, -, -e, *adj.* my.

Meineid, *n.m.* perjury.

meinen, *vb.* mean, think.

meiner, -es, -e, *pron.* mine.

meinetwegen, *adv.* for my sake; for all I care.

Meinung, -en, *n.f.* opinion.

Meinungsumfrage, -n, *n.f.* poll.

Meißel, -, *n.m.* chisel.

meist, **1.** *adj.* most (of). **2.** *adv.* mostly, usually.

meistens, *adv.* mostly, usually.

Meister, -, *n.m.* master; champion.

meisterhaft, *adj.* masterly.

Meisterin -nen, *n.f.* master; champion.

Meisterschaft, -en, *n.f.* championship.

Meisterstück, -e, *n.nt.* masterpiece.

Melancholie´, *n.f.* melancholy.z

melancho´lisch, *adj.* melancholy.

Melas´se, *n.f.* molasses.

melden, *vb.* announce, notify, report.

Meldung, -en, *n.f.* announcement, notification, report.

melken, *vb.* milk.

Melodie´, -i´en, *n.f.* melody, tune.

melo´disch, *adj.* melodious.

Melo´ne, -n, *n.f.* melon; derby.

Membra´ne, -n, *n.f.* membrane.

Memoi´ren, *n.pl.* memoirs.

Memoran´dum, -den, *n.nt.* memorandum.

Menagerie´, -i´en, *n.f.* menagerie.

Menge, -n, *n.f.* quantity; crowd, multitude; (**eine M.**) a lot.

Mensa, -sen, *n.f.* cafeteria.

Mensch, -en, -en, *n.m.* human being, person; man.

Menschenfeind, -e, *n.m.* misanthrope.

Menschenfreund, -e, *n.m.* humanitarian.

Menschenliebe, *n.f.* philanthropy.

Meschenmenge, -n, *n.f.* mob.

Menschenrechte, *n.pl.* human rights.

Menschenverstand, *n.m.* (**gesunder M.**) common sense.

Menschheit, *n.f.* mankind, humanity.

menschlich, *adj.* human; humane.

Menschlichkeit, *n.f.* humanity.

Menstruation´, *n.f.* menstruation.

Mentalität´, *n.f.* mentality.

Menthol´, *n.nt.* menthol.

Menü, -s, *n.nt.* menu.

merken, *vb.* realize; notice; **(sich m.)** keep in mind; **(sich nichts m. lassen*)** not give oneself away.

Merkmal, -e, *n.nt.* mark, characteristic.

merkwürdig, *adj.* peculiar, odd, queer.

Messe, -n, *n.f.* fair; *(eccles.)* mass.

messen*, *vb.* measure; gauge; **(sich m.)** match.

Messer, -, *n.nt.* knife.

Messi´as, *n.m.* Messiah.

Messing, *n.nt.* brass.

Metall´, -e, *n.nt.* metal.

metal´len, *adj.* metallic.

Metall´waren, *n.pl.* hardware.

Meteor´, -e, *n.m. or nt.* meteor.

Meteorologie´, *n.f.* meteorology.

Meter, -, *n.m. or nt.* meter.

Metho´de, -n, *n.f.* method.

metrisch, *adj.* metric.

Metzger, -, *n.m.* butcher.

Metzgerei´, -en, *n.f.* butcher shop.

Meuterei´, -en, *n.f.* mutiny.

meutern, *vb.* mutiny.

Mexika´ner, -, *n.m.* Mexican.

Mexika´nerin, -nen, *n.f.* Mexican.

mexika´nisch, *adj.* Mexican.

Mexiko, *n.nt.* Mexico.

Mieder, -, *n.nt.* bodice.

Miene, -n, *n.f.* mien.

Mienenspiel, -e, *n.nt.* pantomine.

Miete, -n, *n.f.* rent, rental.

mieten, *vb.* rent, lease, hire.

Mieter, -, *n.m.* tenant.

Mieterin, -nen, *n.f.* tenant.

Mietvertrag, ⸚e, *n.m.* lease.

Mietwagen, -, *n.m.* rented car.

Mietwohnung, -en, *n.f.* flat, apartment.

Migrä´ne, *n.f.* migraine.

Mikro´be, -n, *n.f.* microbe.

Mikrofilm, -e, *n.m.* microfilm.

Mikrophon´, -e, *n.nt.* microphone.

Mikroskop´, -e, *n.nt.* microscope.

Milbe, -n, *n.f.* mite.

Milch, *n.f.* milk.

Milchhändler, -, *n.m.* dairyman.

milchig, *adj.* milky.

Milchmann, ⸚er, *n.m.* milkman.

Milchwirtschaft, -en, *n.f.* dairy.

mild, *adj.* mild, gentle, lenient.

Milde, *n.f.* mildness, leniency, clemency.

mildern, *vb.* mitigate, alleviate, soften; **(mildernde Umstände)** extenuating circumstances.

Milderung, -en, *n.f.* alleviation.

Militär´, -s, *n.nt.* military.

Militär´dienstpflicht, -en, *n.f.* conscription.

militä´risch, *adj.* military.

Militaris´mus, *n.m.* militarism.

militaris´tisch, *adj.* militaristic.

Miliz´, -en, *n.f.* militia.

Millime´ter, -, *n.nt.* millimeter.

Million´, -en, *n.f.* million.

Millionär´, -e, *n.m.* millionaire.

Millionä´rin, -nen, *n.f.* millionairess.

Milz, -en, *n.f.* spleen.

Minderheit, -en, *n.f.* minority.

minderjährig, *adj.* minor, not of age.

Minderjährigkeit, *n.f.* minority.

mindern, *vb.* reduce.

minderwertig, *adj.* inferior.

Minderwertigkeitskomplex, *n.m.* inferiority complex.

mindestens, *adv.* at least.

Mine, -n, *n.f.* mine.

Mineral´, -e *or* -ien, *n.nt.* mineral.

minera´lisch, *adj.* mineral.

Miniatur´, -en, *n.f.* miniature.

minimal´, *adj.* minimum, minute.

Minimum, -ma, *n.nt.* minimum.

Mini´ster, -, *n.m.* (cabinet) minister.

Mini´sterin, -nen, *n.f.* (cabinet) minister.

Ministe´rium, -rien, *n.nt.* ministry, department.

Mini´sterpräsident, -en, -en, *n.m.* prime minister.

Mini´sterpräsidentin, -nen, *n.f.* prime minister.

minus, *adv.* minus.

Minu´te, -n, *n.f.* minute.

Minz´e, -n, *n.f.* mint.

mischen, *vb.* mix, mingle, blend.

Mischmasch, -e, *n.m.* hodgepodge.

Mischung, -en, *n.f.* mixture, blend.

mißachten, *vb.* disregard; slight.

Mißachtung, -en, *n.f.* disdain.

Mißbildung, -en, *n.f.* abnormality, deformity.

mißbilligen, *vb.* disapprove.

Mißbrauch, ⸚e, *n.m.* abuse, misuse.

mißbrau´chen, *vb.* abuse.

mißdeu´ten, *vb.* misconstrue.

missen, *vb.* do without.

Mißerfolg, -e, *n.m.* failure.

Missetat, -en, *n.f.* misdeed, crime.

Missetäter, -, *n.m.* offender.

mißfal´len*, *vb.* displease.

Mißfallen, *n.nt.* displeasure.

Mißgeburt, -en, *n.f.* freak.

Mißgeschick, -e, *n.nt.* adversity, misfortune.

mißglü´cken, *vb.* fail.

mißglückt´, *adj.* unsuccessful, abortive.

mißgön´nen, *vb.* begrudge.

mißhan´deln, *vb.* mistreat, maltreat.

Mission´, -en, *n.f.* mission.

Missionar´, -e, *n.m.* missionary.

Missiona´rin, -nen, *n.f.* missionary.

Mißklang, ⸚e, *n.m.* discord.

mißlin´gen*, *vb.* miscarry, fail.

mißra´ten, *adj.* ill-bred, low.

mißtrau´en, *vb.* distrust.
Mißtrauen, *n.nt.* distrust.
mißtrauisch, *adj.* suspicious, distrustful.
mißvergnügt, *adj.* cranky.
Mißverhältnis, -se, *n.nt.* disproportion.
Mißverständnis, -se, *n.nt.* misunderstanding.
mißverstehen*, *vb.* misunderstand.
Mist, *n.m.* manure, muck.
mistig, *adj.* misty.
mit, *prep.* with.
Mitarbeit, *n.f.* cooperation, collaboration.
mit•arbeiten, *vb.* collaborate.
Mitarbeiter, -, *n.m.* collaborator; colleague; (**anonymer M.**) ghost writer.
Mitarbeiterin, -nen, *n.f.* collaborator; colleague.
Mitbewerber, -, *n.m.* competitor.
mit•bringen*, *vb.* bring along; bring a present.
Mitbürger, -, *n.m.* fellow citizen.
Mitbürgerin, -nen, *n.f.* fellow citizen.
miteinan´der, *adv.* together, jointly.
mitein´begriffen, *adj.* included; implied.
mitempfunden, *adj.* sympathizing; vicarious.
mit•fühlen, *vb.* sympathize.
mitfühlend, *adj.* sympathetic.
Mitgefühl, *n.nt.* sympathy.
mitgenommen, *adj.* the worse for wear.
Mitgift, -en, *n.f.* dowry.
Mitglied, -er, *n.nt.* member, fellow.
Mitgliedschaft, *n.f.* membership.
Mithelfer, -, *n.m.* accessory.
Mithelferin, -nen, *n.f.* accessory.
Mitleid, *n.nt.* pity, compassion; mercy.
mitleidig, *adj.* compassionate.
mit•machen, *vb.* string along, join, conform.

Mitmacher, -, *n.m.* conformer.
Mitmensch, -en, -en, *n.m.* fellow-man.
Mitschuld, *n.f.* complicity.
mitschuldig, *adj.* being an accessory.
Mitschüler, -, *n.m.* classmate.
Mitschülerin, -nen, *n.f.* classmate.
Mitspieler, -, *n.m.* player.
Mitspielerin, -nen, *n.f.* player.
Mittag, *n.m.* midday, noon.
Mittagessen, -, *n.nt.* noon meal, lunch, dinner.
Mittäter, -, *n.m.* accomplice.
Mitte, -n, *n.f.* middle, midst, center.
mitteilbar, *adj.* communicable.
mit•teilen, *vb.* inform, communicate.
Mitteilung, -en, *n.f.* information, communication.
Mittel, -, *n.nt.* means, measure, expedient; medium.
mittel, *adj.* mean.
Mittelalter, *n.nt.* Middle Ages.
mittelalterlich, *adj.* medieval.
mittellos, *adj.* penniless, destitute.
mittelmäßig, *adj.* mediocre.
Mittelmeer, *n.nt.* Mediterranean Sea.
Mittelpunkt, -e, *n.m.* center, focus.
mittels, *prep.* by means of.
Mittelstand, *n.m.* middle class.
Mitternacht, *n.f.* midnight.
mittler-, *adj.* medium, middle.
Mittler-Osten, *n.m.* Middle East.
mittschiffs, *adv.* amidships.
Mittwoch, -e, *n.m.* Wednesday.
mit•wirken, *vb.* cooperate, assist, contribute.
mitwirkend, *adj.* contributory.
Möbel, -, *n.nt.* piece of furniture; (*pl.*) furniture.
Möbelwagen, -, *n.m.* moving van.

mobil´, *adj.* mobile; (*fig.*) hale and hearty.
mobilisie´ren, *vb.* mobilize.
mobilisiert´, *adj.* mobile.
möblie´ren, *vb.* furnish.
Mode, -n, *n.f.* mode, fashion.
Modell´, -e, *n.nt.* model.
modellie´ren, *vb.* model.
Modenschau, *n.f.* fashion show.
modern, *vb.* rot.
modern´, *adj.* modern, fashionable.
modernisie´ren, *vb.* modernize.
Modeschöpfer, -, *n.m.* designer.
modifizie´ren, *vb.* modify.
modisch, *adj.* modish, fashionable.
Mofa, -s, *n.nt.* moped.
mögen*, *vb.* like; may.
möglich, *adj.* possible; potential.
möglicherweise, *adv.* possibly.
Möglichkeit, -en, *n.f.* possibility; potential; facility.
Mohammeda´ner, -, *n.m.* Moslem.
Mohammeda´nerin, -nen, *n.f.* Moslem.
Mohr, -en, -en, *n.m.* Moor.
Mohrrübe, -n, *n.f.* carrot.
Mole, -n, *n.f.* mole, jetty, breakwater.
Molkerei´, -en, *n.f.* dairy.
Moll, *n.nt.* minor.
mollig, *adj.* plump; snug.
Moment´, -e, *n.m.* moment, instant.
Moment´, -e, *n.nt.* factor, impulse, motive.
momentan´, *adj.* momentary.
Monarch´, -en, -en, *n.m.* monarch.
Monarchie´, -i´en, *n.f.* monarchy.
Monat, -e, *n.m.* month.
monatlich, *adj.* monthly.
Monatschrift, -en, *n.f.* monthly.
Mönch, -e, *n.m.* monk.
Mond, -e, *n.m.* moon.
Mondschein, *n.m.* moonlight.

Mondsichel, -n, *n.f.* crescent moon.

Monolog´, -e, *n.m.* monologue.

Monopol´, -e, *n.m.* monopoly.

monopolisie´ren, *vb.* monopolize.

monoton´, *adj.* monotonous.

Monotonie´, *n.f.* monotony.

monströs´, *adj.* monstrous, freak.

Montag, -e, *n.m.* Monday.

Montan´union, *n.f.* European Coal and Steel Community.

montie´ren, *vb.* assemble, mount.

monumental´, *adj.* monumental.

Moor, -e, *n.nt.* moor.

Moos, -e, *n.nt.* moss.

Mop, -s, *n.m.* mop.

Moral´, *n.f.* morals; morality; morale.

mora´lisch, *adj.* moral, ethical.

Moralist´, -en, -en, *n.m.* moralist.

Morast´, -e, *n.m.* morass, bog.

Mord, -e, *n.m.* murder, assassination.

morden, *vb.* murder.

Mörder, -, *n.m.* murderer.

Mörderin, -nen, *n.f.* murderess.

Mords-, *cpds.* mortal; heck of a . . . .

morgen, *adv.* tomorrow.

Morgen, -, *n.m.* morning; acre.

Morgendämmerung, -en, *n.f.* dawn.

Morgenrock, ⸚e, *n.m.* dressing gown.

morgens, *adv.* in the morning.

Morphium, *n.nt.* morphine.

morsch, *adj.* rotten.

Mörser, -, *n.m.* mortar.

Mörtel, -, *n.m.* mortar.

Mosaik´, -e, *n.nt.* mosaic.

Moschee´, -n, *n.f.* mosque.

Moskau, *n.nt.* Moscow.

Most, -e, *n.m.* grape juice, new wine; **(Apfelmost)** cider.

Mostrich, *n.m.* mustard.

Motiv´, -e, *n.nt.* motif.

motivie´ren, *vb.* motivate.

Motivie´rung, -en, *n.f.* motivation.

Motor(´), -o´ren, *n.m.* motor, engine.

motorisie´ren, *vb.* motorize, mechanize.

Motor(´)rad, ⸚er, *n.nt.* motorcycle.

Motte, -n, *n.f.* moth.

Motto, -s, *n.nt.* motto.

Mücke, -n, *n.f.* mosquito.

mucksen, *vb.* stir.

müde, *adj.* tired, sleepy; weary.

Müdigkeit, *n.f.* fatigue.

Muff, -e, *n.m.* muff.

muffig, *adj.* musty.

Mühe, -n, *n.f.* trouble, inconvenience; effort; **(machen Sie sich keine M.)** don't bother.

mühelos, *adj.* effortless.

mühen, *vb.* **(sich m.)** try, take the trouble.

Mühle, -n, *n.f.* mill.

Muhme, -n, *n.f.* aunt.

Mühsal, -e, *n.f.* trouble, hardship.

mühsam, *adj.* difficult, tedious, inconvenient.

mühselig, *adj.* laborious.

Mull, *n.m.* gauze.

Müll, *n.m.* garbage.

Mullah, -s, *n.m.* mullah.

Müller, -, *n.m.* miller.

Müllerin, -nen, *n.f.* miller.

multinational´, *adj.* multinational.

Multiplikation´, -en, *n.f.* multiplication.

multiplizie´ren, *vb.* multiply.

Mumie, -n, *n.f.* mummy.

München, *n.nt.* Munich.

Mund, ⸚er, *n.m.* mouth.

Mundart, -en, *n.f.* dialect.

Mündel, -, *n.nt.* ward.

münden, *vb.* run, flow into, end.

mündlich, *adj.* oral, verbal.

Mündung, -en, *n.f.* (river) mouth; (gun) muzzle.

Munition´, -en, *n.f.* ammunition, munition.

munkeln, *vb.* rumor.

Münster, *n.nt.* cathedral.

munter, *adj.* awake; sprightly, lusty.

Münze, -n, *n.f.* coin; mint.

mürbe, *adj.* mellow; (meat) tender; (cake) crisp; *(fig.)* weary.

murmeln, *vb.* murmur, mutter.

murren, *vb.* grumble.

mürrisch, *adj.* disgruntled, petulant, glum.

Mürrischkeit, *n.f.* glumness.

Muschel, -n, *n.f.* shell; mussel, clam.

Muse, -n, *n.f.* muse.

Muse´um, -e´en, *n.nt.* museum.

Musik´, *n.f.* music.

musika´lisch, *adj.* musical.

Musikant´, -en, -en, *n.m.* musician.

Musiker, -, *n.m.* musician.

Musikerin, -nen, *n.f.* musician.

Musik´kapelle, -n, *n.f.* band, orchestra.

Musik´pavillon, -s, *n.m.* bandstand.

Muskat´, -n, *n.m.* nutmeg.

Muskel, -n, *n.m.* muscle.

Muskelkraft, ⸚e, *n.f.* muscular strength, brawn.

muskulös´, *adj.* muscular.

Muße, -n, *n.f.* leisure.

Musselin´, -e, *n.m.* muslin.

müssen*, *vb.* must, have to.

müßig, *adj.* idle.

Müßigkeit, *n.f.* idleness.

Muster, -, *n.nt.* model; sample; pattern, design.

Musterbeispiel, -e, *n.nt.* paragon, perfect example.

mustergültig, *adj.* exemplary, model.

musterhaft, *adj.* exemplary.

mustern, *vb.* examine; *(mil.)* muster.

Musterung, -en, *n.f.* examination; *(mil.)* muster; (pattern) figuring.

Mut, *n.m.* courage, fortitude.

Mutation´, -en, *n.f.* mutation.

mutig, *adj.* courageous.

Mutigkeit, *n.f.* pluck.

mutmaßen, *vb.* conjecture.

mutmaßlich, *adj.* presumable.

Mutmaßung, -en, *n.f.* conjecture.

Mutter, ≈, *n.f.* mother.

Mutterleib, *n.m.* womb.

mütterlich, *adj.* maternal.

Mutterschaft, *n.f.* maternity.

mutterseelenallein´, *adj.* all alone.

Muttersprache, -n, *n.f.* native language.

mutwillig, *adj.* deliberate, wilful.

Mütze, -n, *n.f.* cap, bonnet.

Myrte, -n, *n.f.* myrtle.

mysteriös´, *adj.* mysterious.

Mystik, *n.f.* mysticism.

mystisch, *adj.* mystic.

Mythe, -n, *n.f.* myth.

Mythologie´, *n.f.* mythology.

N

na, *interj.* well; **(n. also)** there you are; **(n. und ob)** I should say so.

Nabe, -n, *n.f.* hub.

nach, *prep.* towards, to; after; according to; **(n. und n.)** by and by, gradually.

nach•affen, *vb.* ape, imitate.

nach•ahmen, *vb.* imitate, simulate.

Nachahmung, -en, *n.f.* imitation.

Nachbar, (-n,) -n, *n.m.* neighbor.

Nachbarin, -nen, *n.f.* neighbor.

Nachbarschaft, -en, *n.f.* neighborhood.

nachdem´, *conj.* after.

nach•denken*, *vb.* think, meditate, reflect.

nachdenklich, *adj.* contemplative, pensive.

Nachdruck, *n.m.* emphasis.

nachdrücklich, *adj.* emphatic.

nach•eifern, *vb.* emulate.

Nachfolger, -, *n.m.* successor.

Nachfolgerin, -nen, *n.f.* successor.

Nachforschung, -en, *n.f.* investigation; research.

Nachfrage, -en, *n.f.* inquiry; **(Angebot und N.)** supply and demand.

nach•fühlen, *vb.* understand, appreciate.

nach•füllen, *vb.* refill.

nach•geben*, *vb.* give in, yield.

nach•gehen*, *vb.* follow; seek; (clock) be slow.

nachgiebig, *adj.* compliant.

nachhaltig, *adj.* lasting.

nach•helfen*, *vb.* assist, boost.

nachher, *adv.* afterward(s).

Nachhilfe, *n.f.* assistance.

Nachhilfelehrer, -, *n.m.* tutor.

Nachhilfelehrerin, -nen, *n.f.* tutor.

nach•holen, *vb.* make up for.

Nachkomme, -n, -n, *n.m.* descendant.

Nachlaß, ≈sse, *n.m.* estate.

nach•lassen*, *vb.* abate, subside.

nachlässig, *adj.* negligent, careless, derelict.

Nachlässigkeit, -en, *n.f.* negligence, carelessness.

nach•machen, *vb.* imitate.

Nachmittag, -e, *n.m.* afternoon.

Nachmittagsvorstellung, -en, *n.f.* matinée.

Nachnahme, -n, *n.f.* **(per N.)** C.O.D.

nach•prüfen, *vb.* check up, verify.

Nachricht, -en, *n.f.* information, message, notice; *(pl.)* news.

Nachrichtensendung, -en, *n.f.* newscast.

nach•schlagen*, *vb.* look up, refer to.

Nachschrift, -en, *n.f.* postscript.

nach•sehen*, *vb.* look after; look up; examine, check; *(fig.)* excuse, indulge.

Nachsehen, *n.nt.* **(das N. haben*)** be the loser.

nach•senden*, *vb.* forward, send on.

Nachsicht, -en, *n.f.* indulgence, forbearance.

nachsichtig, *adj.* lenient, indulgent.

Nachspiel, -e, *n.nt.* postlude.

nach•spüren, *vb.* track down.

nächst-, *adj.* next nearest.

nach•stehen*, *vb.* be inferior.

nach•stellen, *vb.* pursue; (clock) put back.

Nächstenliebe, *n.f.* charity.

nächstens, *adv.* soon.

Nacht, ≈e, *n.f.* night.

Nachteil, -e, *n.m.* disadvantage, drawback.

nachteilig, *adj.* disadvantageous, adverse.

Nachthemd, -en, *n.nt.* nightgown.

Nachtigall, -en, *n.f.* nightingale.

Nachtisch, -e, *n.m.* dessert.

nächtlich, *adj.* nocturnal.

Nachtlokal, -e, *n.nt.* night club.

Nachtrag, ≈e, *n.m.* supplement.

nach•tragen*, *vb.* carry behind; *(fig.)* resent, bear a grudge.

nachträglich, *adj.* belated.

Nachtwache, -n, *n.f.* vigil.

Nachweis, -e, *n.m.* proof, certificate.

nachweisbar, *adj.* demonstrable.

nach•weisen*, *vb.* demonstrate, prove.

Nachwelt, *n.f.* posterity.

Nachwirkung, -en, *n.f.* aftereffect.

nach•zählen, *vb.* count over again, count up.

nach•zeichnen, *vb.* trace.

nackt, *adj.* naked, nude; bare.

Nacktheit, *n.f.* nakedness, bareness.

Nadel, -n, *n.f.* needle, pin.

Nagel, ≈, *n.m.* nail.

nagen, *vb.* gnaw.

Nagetier, -e, *n.nt.* rodent.

nah(e) (näher, nächst-), *adj.* near.

Nähe, *n.f.* vicinity, proximity.

nähen, *vb.* sew.

Näherin, -nen, *n.f.* seamstress.

nähern, *vb.* (sich n.) approach.

nähren, *vb.* nourish; nurture.

nahrhaft, *adj.* nutritious, nourishing.

Nahrung, -en, *n.f.* nourishment, food.

Nahrungsmittel, *n.pl.* foodstuffs.

Naht, ²e, *n.f.* seam.

naiv´, *adj.* naïve.

Name(n), -, -n, *n.m.* name.

namentlich, *adv.* by name, namely; considerable.

namhaft, *adj.* renowned.

nämlich, *adv.* that is to say, namely.

nanu´, *interj.* well, what do you know?

Naphtha, *n.nt.* naphtha.

Narbe, -n, *n.f.* scar.

Narko´se, -n, *n.f.* anesthetic.

narko´tisch, *adj.* narcotic, anesthetic.

Narr, -en, -en, *n.m.* fool; (zum N. halten*) fool, make a fool of.

narrensicher, *adj.* foolproof.

närrisch, *adj.* foolish, daffy.

Narzis´se, -n, *n.f.* narcissus; (gelbe N.) daffodil.

nasal´, *adj.* nasal.

naschen, *vb.* nibble (secretly) on sweets.

Nase, -n, *n.f.* nose.

näselnd, *adj.* nasal.

Nasenbluten, *n.nt.* nosebleed.

Nasenloch, ²er, *n.nt.* nostril.

Nasenschleim, *n.m.* mucus.

naseweis, *adj.* fresh, know-it-all.

naß(²), *adj.* wet.

Nässe, *n.f.* wetness, moisture.

nässen, *vb.* wet.

Nation´, -en, *n.f.* nation.

national´, *adj.* national.

Nationalis´mus, *n.m.* nationalism.

Nationalität´, -en, *n.f.* nationality.

National´ökonomie, *n.f.* political economics.

Natrium, *n.nt.* sodium.

Natron, *n.nt.* sodium.

Natur´, -en, *n.f.* nature.

Natura´lien, *n.pl.* food produce.

naturalisie´ren, *vb.* naturalize.

Naturalist´, -en, -en, *n.m.* naturalist.

Natur´forscher, -, *n.m.* naturalist.

Natur´forscherin, -nen, *n.f.* naturalist.

Natur´kunde, *n.f.* nature study.

natür´lich, 1. *adj.* natural. **2.** *adv.* of course.

Natür´lichkeit, *n.f.* naturalness.

Natur´wissenschaftler, *n.m.* scientist.

Natur´wissenschaftlerin, -nen, *n.f.* scientist.

nautisch, *adj.* nautical.

Navigation´, *n.f.* navigation.

Nebel, -, *n.m.* fog, mist.

Nebelfleck, -e, *n.m.* nebula.

nebelhaft, *adj.* nebulous.

neb(e)lig, *adj.* foggy.

neben, *prep.* beside.

Nebenanschluß, ²sse, *n.m.* (telephone) extension.

nebenbei´, *adv.* besides; by the way, incidentally.

Nebenbuhler, -, *n.m.* rival.

nebeneinan´der, *adv.* beside one another, abreast.

Nebengebäude, -, *n.nt.* annex.

Nebenprodukt, -e, *n.nt.* byproduct.

Nebensache, -n, *n.f.* incidental matter.

nebensächlich, *adj.* incidental, irrelevant.

Nebenweg, -e, *n.m.* byway.

nebst, *prep.* with, including.

necken, *vb.* tease, kid.

neckisch, *adj.* playful, cute.

Neffe, -n, -n, *n.m.* nephew.

negativ´, *adj.* negative.

Negativ, -e, *n.nt.* negative.

Neger, -, *n.m.* Negro.

Negligé, -s, *n.nt.* negligée.

nehmen*, *vb.* take.

Neid, *n.m.* envy.

neidisch, *adj.* envious.

neigen, *vb.* (tr.) incline, bow, bend; (intr.) lean, slant; (fig.) tend.

Neigung, -en, *n.f.* inclination; slant; tendency, trend; affection.

nein, *interj.* no.

Nelke, -n, *n.f.* carnation.

nennen*, *vb.* name, call.

nennenswert, *adj.* considerable, worth mentioning.

Nenner, -, *n.m.* denominator.

Nennwert, -e, *n.m.* denomination; face value.

Neon, *n.nt.* neon.

Nerv, -en, *n.m.* nerve.

Nervenarzt, ²e, *n.m.* neurologist.

Nervenärztin, -nen, *n.f.* neurologist.

Nervenkitzel, -, *n.m.* thrill.

nervös´, *adj.* nervous, jittery; high-strung.

Nervosität´, *n.f.* nervousness.

Nerz, -e, *n.m.* mink.

Nessel, -n, *n.f.* nettle.

Nest, -er, *n.nt.* nest.

nett, *adj.* nice, enjoyable.

netto, *adj.* net.

Netz, -e, *n.nt.* net, web; network.

Netzhaut, ²e, *n.f.* retina.

neu, *adj.* new; (aufs neue, von neuem) anew.

Neubelebung, -en, *n.f.* revival.

Neuerung, -en, *n.f.* innovation.

Neugierde, *n.f.* curiosity.

neugierig, *adj.* curious, inquisitive.

Neuheit, -en, *n.f.* novelty.

Neuigkeit, -en, *n.f.* news; novelty.

Neujahr, *n.nt.* New Year; (Fröhliches N.) Happy New Year.

neulich, *adv.* the other day, recently.

Neuling, -e, *n.m.* novice.

neun, *num.* nine.

neunt-, *adj.* ninth.

Neuntel, -, *n.nt.* ninth part; (ein n.) one-ninth.

neunzig, *num.* ninety.

neunzigst-, *adj.* ninetieth.

Neunzigstel, -, *n.nt.* ninetieth part; (ein n.) one-ninetieth.

Neuralgie´, *n.f.* neuralgia.

neuro´tisch, *adj.* neurotic.

neutral´, *adj.* neutral.

Neutralität´, *n.f.* neutrality.

Neutron, -o´nen, *n.nt.* neutron.

Neutro´nenbombe, -n, *n.f.* neutron bomb.

nicht, *adv.* not; (**n. wahr**) isn't that so, don't you, aren't we, won't they, etc.

Nichtachtung, *n.f.* disregard, disrespect.

Nichtanerkennung, -en, *n.f.* nonrecognition; repudiation.

Nichtbeachtung, *n.f.* disregard.

Nichte, -n, *n.f.* niece.

nichtig, *adj.* null, void.

nichts, *pron.* nothing.

Nichts, *n.nt.* nothingness, nonentity.

nichtsdestoweniger, *adv.* notwithstanding, nevertheless.

Nichtswisser, -, *n.m.* ignoramus.

nichtswürdig, *adj.* worthless, condemnable.

Nickel, *n.nt.* nickel.

nicken, *vb.* nod.

nie, *adv.* never.

nieder, *adv.* down.

Niedergang, *n.m.* decline.

niedergedrückt, *adj.* depressed.

niedergeschlagen, *adj.* dejected.

Niederkunft, *n.f.* childbirth.

Niederlage, -n, *n.f.* defeat; branch office.

Niederlande, *n.pl.* Netherlands.

Niederländer, -, *n.m.* Netherlander, Dutchman.

Niederländerin, -nen, *nf.* Dutchwoman.

niederländisch, *adj.* Netherlandic, Dutch.

nieder•lassen*, *vb.* (**sich n.**) settle.

Niederlassung, -en, *n.f.* settlement.

nieder•metzeln, *vb.* massacre.

Niederschlag, ⸚e, *n.m.* precipitation; sediment.

Niedertracht, *n.f.* meanness, infamy.

niederträchtig, *adj.* mean, vile, infamous.

niedlich, *adj.* pretty, cute.

niedrig, *adj.* low; base, menial.

niemals, *adv.* never.

niemand, *pron.* no one, nobody.

Niere, -n, *n.f.* kidney.

nieseln, *vb.* drizzle.

niesen, *vb.* sneeze.

Niete, -n, *n.f.* rivet; (lottery) blank; failure, washout.

Nihilis´mus, *n.m.* nihilism.

Nikotin´, *n.nt.* nicotine.

nimmer, *adv.* never.

nimmermehr, *adv.* never again.

nirgends, nirgendwo, *adv.* nowhere.

Nische, -n, *n.f.* recess, niche.

nisten, *vb.* nestle.

Niveau´, -s, *n.nt.* level.

nobel, *adj.* noble; liberal.

noch, *adv.* still, yet; (**n. einmal**) once more; (**n. ein**) another, an additional; (**weder . . . n.**) neither . . . nor.

nochmalig, *adj.* additional, repeated.

nochmal(s), *adv.* once more.

Noma´de, -n, -n, *n.m.* nomad.

nominal´, *adj.* nominal.

Nonne, -n, *n.f.* nun.

Nonnenkloster, ⸚e, *n.nt.* convent.

Nord, Norden, *n.m.* north.

nördlich, *adj.* northern; to the north.

Nordos´ten, *n.m.* northeast.

nordöst´lich, *adj.* northeastern; to the northeast.

Nordpol, *n.m.* North Pole.

Nordwes´ten, *n.m.* northwest.

nordwest´lich, *adj.* northwestern; to the northwest.

nörgeln, *vb.* gripe.

Norm, -en, *n.f.* norm, standard.

normal´, *adj.* normal.

Norwegen, *n.nt.* Norway.

Norweger, -, *n.m.* Norwegian.

Norwegerin, -nen, *n.f.* Norwegian.

norwegisch, *adj.* Norwegian.

Not, ⸚e, *n.f.* need, necessity; hardship; distress.

Notar´, -e, *n.m.* notary.

Notausgang, ⸚e, *n.m.* emergency exit.

Notbehelf, *n.m.* makeshift, stop-gap.

Notdurft, *n.f.* want; need.

notdürftig, *adj.* scanty, bare.

Note, -n, *n.f.* note; grade.

Notfall, ⸚e, *n.m.* emergency.

notgedrungen, *adv.* perforce.

notie´ren, *vb.* note, make a note.

Notie´rung, -en, *n.f.* quotation.

nötig, *adj.* necessary.

nötigen, *vb.* urge.

Notiz´, -en, *n.f.* note.

Notiz´block, ⸚e, *n.m.* notepaper pad.

Notiz´buch, ⸚er, *n.nt.* notebook.

notleidend, *adj.* needy.

notwendig, *adj.* necessary.

Notwendigkeit, -en, *n.f.* necessity.

Novel´le, -n, *n.f.* short story; novella.

Novem´ber, *n.m.* November.

Nu, *n.m.* jiffy.

nüchtern, *adj.* sober; (**auf nüchternen Magen**) on an empty stomach.

Nüchternheit, *n.f.* sobriety; unimaginativeness.

Nudeln, *n.pl.* noodles.

nuklear´, *adj.* nuclear.

Null, -en, *n.f.* cipher; zero.

numerie´ren, *vb.* number.

Num´mer, -, -n, *n.f.* number.

nun, *adv.* now; (**von n. an**) henceforth.

nur, *adv.* only.

Nuß, ⸚sse, *n.f.* nut.

Nußschale, -n, *n.f.* nutshell.

Nüster, -n, *n.f.* nostril.

Nutzbarkeit, *n.f.* utility.

Nutzen, -, *n.m.* benefit.

nützen, *vb.* (*tr.*) use, utilize; (*intr.*) be of use, help, benefit.

nützlich, *adj.* useful, beneficial.

nutzlos, *adj.* useless, futile.

Nutzlosigkeit, *n.f.* futility.

Nylon, *n.nt.* nylon.

Nymphe, -n, *n.f.* nymph.

O

Oa´se, -n, *n.f.* oasis.
ob, *conj.* whether; **(als o.)** as if.
Obdach, *n.nt.* shelter.
obdachlos, *adj.* homeless.
oben, *adv.* above; upstairs.
ober-, *adj.* upper.
Ober, -, *n.m.* (= Oberkellner) headwaiter, waiter; **(Herr O.!)** waiter!
Oberbefehlshaber, -, *n.m.* commander-in-chief.
Oberfläche, -n, *n.f.* surface.
oberflächlich, *adj.* superficial.
Oberhaupt, ⸚er, *n.nt.* chief.
Oberherrschaft, *n.f.* sovereignty.
Oberschicht, *n.f.* upper stratum; upper classes.
oberst-, *adj.* supreme, paramount.
Oberst, -en, -en, *n.m.* colonel.
Oberstleut´nant, -s, *n.m.* lieutenant colonel.
obgleich´, *conj.* although.
Obhut, *n.f.* keeping, charge.
obig, *adj.* above, aforesaid.
Objekt´ -e, *n.nt.* object.
objektiv´, *adj.* objective.
Objektiv´, -e, *n.nt.* objective; lens.
Objektivität´, *n.f.* objectivity, detachment.
Obliegenheit, -en, *n.f.* duty, obligation.
Obligation´, -en, *n.f.* bond; obligation.
obligato´risch, *adj.* obligatory.
Obrigkeit, -en, *n.f.* authorities, government.
obschon´, *conj.* although.
ob•siegen, *vb.* be victorious over.
Obst, *n.nt.* fruit.
Obstgarten, ⸚, *n.m.* orchard.
obszön´, *adj.* obscene.
Obus, -se, *n.m.* (= Oberleitungsomnibus) trolley bus.
ob•walten, *vb.* prevail, exist.
obwohl´, *conj.* although.

Ochse, -n, -n or **Ochs, -en, -en,** *n.m.* ox.
öde, *adj.* bleak, desolate.
Öde, -n, *n.f.* bleakness, waste place.
oder, *conj.* or.
Ofen, ⸚, *n.m.* stove, oven, furnace.
offen, *adj.* open, frank.
offenbar, *adj.* evident.
offenba´ren, *vb.* reveal.
Offenba´rung, -en, *n.f.* revelation.
Offenba´rungsschrift, -en, *n.f.* scripture.
Offenheit, *n.f.* frankness.
offenkundig, *adj.* manifest.
offensichtlich, *adj.* obvious.
Offensi´ve, -n, *n.f.* offense, offensive.
öffentlich, *adj.* public.
Öffentlichkeit, *n.f.* public.
offiziell´, *adj.* official.
Offizier´, -e, *n.m.* officer.
öffnen, *vb.* open.
Öffnung, -en, *n.f.* opening, aperture.
Öffnungszeiten, *n. pl.* opening hours.
oft (⸚), *adv.* often.
öfters, *adv.* quite often.
oftmals, *adv.* often (times).
Oheim, -e, *n.m.* uncle.
ohne, *prep.* without.
ohneglei´chen, *adv.* unequalled.
ohnehin, *adv.* in any case.
Ohnmacht, *n.f.* faint, unconsciousness; **(in O. fallen*)** faint.
ohnmächtig, *adj.* in a faint, powerless.
Ohr, -en, *n.nt.* ear.
Öhr, -e, *n.nt.* eye (of a needle, etc.).
Ohrenschmerzen, *n.pl.* earache.
Ohrfeige, -n, *n.f.* slap.
Ohrring, -e, *n.m.* earring.
okay, *pred. adv.* okay.
okkult´, *adj.* occult.
Ökologie´, *n.f.* ecology.
ökologisch, *adj.* ecological.
Ökonom´, -en, -en, *n.m.* farmer, manager.

Ökonomie´, -i´en, *n.f.* economy; agriculture.
ökono´misch, *adj.* economical.
Okta´ve, -n, *n.f.* octave.
Okto´ber, *n.m.* October.
ökume´nisch, *adj.* ecumenical.
Okzident, *n.m.* occident.
Öl, -e, *n.nt.* oil.
ölen, *vb.* oil.
ölig, *adj.* oily.
Oli´ve, -n, *n.f.* olive.
Ölung, -en, *n.f.* oiling; anointment; **(letzt Ö.)** extreme unction.
Oma, -s, *n.f.* granny, grandma.
Ombudsmann, ⸚er, *n.m.* ombudsman.
Omelett´, -e, *n.nt.* omelet.
Omnibus, -se, *n.m.* (omni)bus.
ondulie´ren, *vb.* wave (hair).
Onkel, -, *n.m.* uncle.
Opa, -s, *n.m.* grandpa.
Opal´, -e, *n.m.* opal.
Oper, -n, *n.f.* opera.
Operation´, -en, *n.f.* operation.
operativ´, *adj.* operative.
Operet´te, -n, *n.f.* operetta.
operie´ren, *vb.* operate.
Opernglas, ⸚er, *n.nt.* opera glasses.
Opfer, -, *n.nt.* offering, sacrifice; victim, casualty.
opfern, *adv.* sacrifice.
Opium, *n.nt.* opium.
opponie´ren, *vb.* oppose.
Opposition´, -en, *n.f.* opposition.
Optik, *n.f.* optics.
Optiker, -, *n.m.* optician.
Optikerin, -nen, *n.f.* optician.
Optimis´mus, *n.m.* optimism.
optimis´tisch, *adj.* optimistic.
optisch, *adj.* optic.
Oran´ge, -n, *n.f.* orange.
Orches´ter, -, *n.nt.* orchestra.
Orchide´e, -n, *n.f.* orchid.

Orden, -, *n.m.* order, medal, decoration.
ordentlich, *adj.* orderly, decent, regular.
ordinär, *adj.* vulgar.
ordnen, *vb.* put in order, sort, arrange.
Ordnung, -en, *n.f.* order.
Organ´, -e, *n.nt.* organ.
Organisation´, -en, *n.f.* organization.
orga´nisch, *adj.* organic.
organisie´ren, *vb.* organize; scrounge.
Organis´mus, -men, *n.m.* organism.
Organist´, -en, -en, *n.m.* organist.
Organis´tin, -nen, *n.f.* organist.
Orgel, -n, *n.f.* organ.

Orgie, -n, *n.f.* orgy.
Orient, *n.m.* Orient.
orienta´lisch, *adj.* oriental.
orientie´ren, *vb.* orient(ate).
Orientie´rung, -en, *n.f.* orientation.
Original´, -e, *n.nt.* original.
Originalität´, -en, *n.f.* originality.
originell´, *adj.* original.
Ort, -e, *n.m.* place, locality, town.
Orter, -, *n.m.* navigator.
orthodox´, *adj.* orthodox.
örtlich, *adj.* local.
ortsansässig, *adj.* resident, indigenous.
Ortschaft, -en, *n.f.* town, village.
Ortsgespräch, -e, *n.nt.* local call.

Ost, Osten, *n.m.* east.
Ostblockstaaten, *n.m.pl.* Eastern European nations.
Ostern, *n.nt.* Easter.
Österreich, *n.nt.* Austria.
Österreicher, -, *n.m.* Austrian.
Österreicherin, -nen, *n.f.* Austrian.
österreichisch, *adj.* Austrian.
östlich, *adj.* eastern, easterly.
Ostsee, *n.f.* Baltic Sea.
ostwärts, *adv.* eastward.
Otter, -, *n.m.* otter.
Otter, -n, *n.f.* adder.
Ouvertü´re, -n, *n.f.* overture.
oval´, *adj.* oval.
Ozean, -e, *n.m.* ocean.
Ozeandampfer, -, *n.m.* ocean liner.
Ozon´, -e, *n.nt.* ozone.

P

Paar, -e, *n.nt.* pair, couple;
(ein paar) a few.
paaren, *vb.* mate.
Pacht, -en, *n.f.* lease, tenure.
Pachtbrief, -e, *n.m.* lease (document).
pachten, *vb.* lease (from).
Pächter, -, *n.m.* tenant.
Pächterin, -nen, *n.f.,* tenant.
Pachtzins, *n.m.* rent (money).
Pack, ⸚e, *n.m.* pack; rabble.
Päckchen, -, *n.nt.* parcel.
packen, *vb.* pack, seize, thrill.
Packen, -, *n.m.* pack.
Packung, -en, *n.f.* packing, wrapper, pack(age).
Pädago´ge, -n, -n, *n.m.* pedagogue.
Pädago´gik, *n.f.* pedagogy.
Pädago´gin, -nen, *n.f.* pedagogue.
Paddel, -, *n.nt.* paddle.
paff, *interj.* bang.
Page, -n, -n, *n.m.* page.
Paket´, -e, *n.nt.* package.
Pakt, -e, *n.m.* pact.
Palast´, ⸚e, *n.m.* palace.
Palet´te, -n, *n.f.* palette.
Palme, -n, *n.f.* palm.
Pampelmu´se, -n, *n.f.* grapefruit.
Panik, *n.f.* panic.

Panne, -n, *n.f.* breakdown; flat tire.
Panora´ma, -men, *n.nt.* panorama.
Panther, -, *n.m.* panther.
Pantof´fel, -n, *n.f.* slipper.
Pantomi´me, -n, *n.f.* pantomime.
Panzer, -, *n.m.* armor; tank.
Panzer-, *cpds.* armored.
Papagei´, -en, -en, *n.m.* parrot.
Papier´, -e, *n.nt.* paper.
Papier´bogen, ⸚, *n.m.* sheet of paper.
Papier´korb, ⸚e, *n.m.* wastebasket.
Papier´krieg, -e, *n.m.* red tape, paperwork.
Papier´waren, *n.pl.* stationery.
Papp, -e, *n.m.* pap, paste.
Pappe, -n, *n.f.* cardboard.
Papst, ⸚e, *n.m.* pope.
päpstlich, *adj.* papal.
Papsttum, *n.nt.* papacy.
Para´de, -n, *n.f.* parade.
Paradies´, *n.nt.* paradise.
paradox´, *adj.* paradoxical.
Paradox´, -e, *n.nt.* paradox.
Paraffin´, -e, *n.nt.* paraffin.
Paragraph´, -en, -en, *n.m.* paragraph.

parallel´, *adj.* parallel.
Paralle´le, -n, *n.f.* parallel.
Paraly´se, -n, *n.f.* paralysis.
Parenthe´se, -n, *n.f.* parenthesis.
Parfüm´, -e, *n.nt.* perfume.
pari, *adv.* at par.
Pari, *n.nt.* par.
Paris´, *n.nt.* Paris.
Pari´ser, -, *n.m.* Parisian.
Pari´serin, -nen, *n.f.* Parisian.
Park, -e *or* **-s,** *n.m.* park.
parken, *vb.* park.
Parkuhr, -en, *n.f.* parking meter.
Parkverbot, -e, *n.nt.* no parking.
Parlament´, -e, *n.nt.* parliament.
parlamenta´risch, *adj.* parliamentary.
Parodie´, -i´en, *n.f.* parody.
Paro´le, -n, *n.f.* password.
Partei´, -en, *n.f.* party.
Partei´genosse, -n, -n, *n.m.* party comrade.
partei´isch, *adj.* partisan, biased.
partei´lich, *adj.* partisan, biased.
partei´los, *adj.* impartial.

Parter´re, -s, *n.nt.* ground floor; orchestra (seats in theater).

Partie´, -i´en, *n.f.* match.

Partisan´, (-en,) -en, *n.m.* partisan; guerilla.

Partitur´, -en, *n.f.* score.

Partizip´, -ien, *n.nt.* participle.

Partner, -, *n.m.* partner, associate.

Partnerin, -nen, *n.f.* partner, associate.

Parzel´le, -n, *n.f.* lot, plot.

Paß, ⸗sse, *n.m.* pass; passport.

passa´bel, *adj.* passable.

Passagier´, -e, *n.m.* passenger.

Passant´, -en, -en, *n.m.* passer-by.

passen, *vb.* suit, fit; **(p. zu)** match.

passend, *adj.* fitting, suitable, proper.

passie´ren, *vb.* happen; pass.

Passion´, *n.f.* passion.

passiv, *adj.* passive.

Passiv, -e, *n.nt.* passive.

Pasta, -sten, *n.f.* paste.

Paste, -n, *n.f.* paste.

Paste´te, -n, *n.f.* meat pie.

pasteurisie´ren, *vb.* pasteurize.

Pastil´le, -n, *n.f.* lozenge.

Pastor, -o´ren, *n.m.* minister.

Pate, -n, -n, *n.m.* godfather.

Pate, -n, *n.f.* godmother.

Patenkind, -er, *n.nt.* godchild.

Patenonkel, -, *n.m.* godfather.

Patent´, -e, *n.nt.* patent.

Patentante, -n, *n.f.* godmother.

Pathos, *n.nt.* pathos.

Patient´, -en, -en, *n.m.* patient.

Patien´tin, -nen, *n.f.* patient.

Patin, -nen, *n.f.* godmother.

Patriot´, -en, -en, *n.m.* patriot.

patrio´tisch, *adj.* patriotic.

Patriotis´mus, *n.m.* patriotism.

Patro´ne, -n, *n.f.* cartridge; pattern.

Patrouil´le, -n, *n.f.* patrol.

Pauschal´preis, -e, *n.m.* total price.

Pause, -n, *n.f.* pause, intermission, recess.

Pavillon, -s, *n.m.* pavillion.

Pazifis´mus, *n.m.* pacifism.

Pazifist´, -en, -en, *n.m.* pacifist.

Pech, *n.nt.* pitch, bad luck.

Pedal´, -e, *n.nt.* pedal.

Pedant´, -en, -en, *n.m.* pedant.

Pein, *n.f.* pain, agony.

peinigen, *vb.* torment.

peinlich, *adj.* embarrassing; meticulous.

Peitsche, -n, *n.f.* whip.

peitschen, *vb.* whip.

Pelz, -e, *n.m.* fur.

Pelzhändler, -, *n.m.* furrier.

Pendel, -, *n.m. or nt.* pendulum.

pendeln, *vb.* swing, oscillate.

Pendler, -, *n.m.* commuter.

Penis, -se, *n.m.* penis.

Penizillin´, *n.nt.* penicillin.

Pension´, -en, *n.f.* pension; board, boarding house.

pensionie´ren, *vb.* pension; **(sich p. lassen*)** retire.

per, *prep.* per, by, with.

perfekt´, *adj.* perfect.

Perfekt´, -e, *n.nt.* perfect (tense).

Pergament´, -e, *n.nt.* parchment.

Perio´de, -n, *n.f.* period, term.

perio´disch, *adj.* periodic.

Peripherie´, -i´en, *n.f.* periphery.

Perle, -n, *n.f.* pearl.

Perlmutter, *n.f.* mother-of-pearl.

Persia´ner, *n.m.* Persian lamb.

Persien, *n.nt.* Persia.

Person´, -en, *n.f.* person.

Personal´, *n.nt.* personnel, staff.

Persona´lien, *n.pl.* personal data.

Perso´nenzug, ⸗e, *n.m.* passenger train.

persön´lich, *adj.* personal.

Persön´lichkeit, -en, *n.f.* personage; personality.

Perspekti´ve, -n, *n.f.* perspective.

pervers´, *adj.* perverse.

Pessimis´mus, *n.m.* pessimism.

pessimis´tisch, *adj.* pessimistic.

Pest, *n.f.* plague, pestilence.

Petersi´lie, *n.f.* parsley.

Petro´leum, *n.nt.* petroleum.

Petschaft, -en, *n.f.* seal.

Pfad, -e, *n.m.* path.

Pfadfinder, -, *n.m.* boy scout.

Pfahl, ⸗e, *n.m.* pole, pile, post, stake.

Pfand, ⸗er, *n.m.* pawn, pledge, security; deposit.

Pfandbrief, -e, *n.m.* bond, mortgage bond.

pfänden, *vb.* seize, attach, impound.

Pfandhaus, ⸗er, *n.nt.* pawnshop.

Pfanne, -n, *n.f.* pan.

Pfannkuchen, -, *n.m.* pancake.

Pfarrer, -, *n.m.* minister, priest.

Pfau, -e, *n.m.* peacock.

Pfeffer, -n, *n.m.* pepper.

Pfefferkuchen, -, *n.m.* gingerbread.

Pfeffermin´ze, *n.f.* peppermint.

Pfeife, -n, *n.f.* pipe, whistle.

pfeifen*, *vb.* whistle.

Pfeil, -e, *n.m.* arrow.

Pfeiler, -, *n.m.* pillar, pier.

Pfennig, -e, *n.m.* penny.

Pferd, -e, *n.nt.* horse.

Pferdestärke, -n, *n.f.* horsepower.

Pfiff, -e, *n.m.* whistle; trick.

pfiffig, *adj.* tricky, sly.

Pfingsten, *n.m.* Pentecost, Whitsuntide.

Pfirsich, -e, *n.m.* peach.

Pflanze, -n, *n.f.* plant.

pflanzen, *vb.* plant.

Pflaster, -, *n.nt.* plaster; pavement.

pflastern, *vb.* plaster, pave.

Pflaume, -n, *n.f.* plum.

Pflege, -n, *n.f.* care, nursing, cultivation.

Pflegeeltern, *n.pl.* foster parents.

pflegen, vb. take care of, nurse, cultivate; be accustomed.

Pflicht, -en, n.f. duty.

pflichtgemäß, adj. dutiful.

Pflock, ⸗e, n.m. peg.

pflücken, vb. pick, gather.

Pflug, ⸗e, n.m. plow.

pflügen, vb. plow.

Pforte, -n, n.f. gate, door, entrance.

Pförtner, -, n.m. janitor, doorman.

Pfosten, -, n.m. post, jamb.

Pfote, -n, n.f. paw.

Pfropf, -e, Pfropfen, -, n.m. stopper, plug.

pfropfen, vb. graft.

Pfund, -e, n.nt. pound.

pfuschen, vb. botch, bungle.

Pfütze, -n, n.f. puddle.

Phänomen´, -e, n.nt. phenomenon.

Phantasie´, -i´en, n.f. fantasy.

phantas´tisch, adj. fantastic.

Phase, -n, n.f. phase.

Philosoph´, -en, -en, n.m. philosopher.

Philosophie´, -i´en, n.f. philosophy.

Philoso´phin, -nen, n.f. philosopher.

philoso´phisch, adj. philosophical.

phlegma´tisch, adj. phlegmatic.

phone´tisch, adj. phonetic.

Phosphor, n.m. phosphorus.

Photoapparat, -e, n.m. camera.

photoelek´trisch, adj. photoelectric.

Photograph´, -en, -en, n.m. photographer.

Photographie´, -i´en, n.f. photograph(y).

Photogra´phin, -nen, n.f. photographer.

Photokopie´, -i´en, n.f. photocopy.

photokopie´ren, vb. photocopy.

Photokopier´maschine, -n, n.f. photocopier.

Physik´, n.f. physics.

Physiker, -, n.m. physicist.

Physikerin, -nen, n.f. physicist.

Physiologie´, n.f. physiology.

physisch, adj. physical.

Pianist´, -en, -en, n.m. pianist.

Pianis´tin, -nen, n.f. pianist.

Pickel, -, n.m. pimple; ice axe.

picken, vb. peck.

Picknick, -s, n.nt. picnic.

piepsen, vb. peep.

Pier, -s, n.m. pier.

Pietät´, n.f. piety.

Pigment´, -e, n.nt. pigment.

pikant´, adj. piquant.

Pilger, -, n.m. pilgrim.

Pilgerin, -nen, n.f. pilgrim.

Pille, -n, n.f. pill.

Pilot´, -en, -en, n.m. pilot.

Pilo´tin, -nen, n.f. pilot.

Pilz, -e, n.m. mushroom.

Pinsel, -, n.m. brush.

Pinzet´te, -n, n.f. tweezers.

Pionier´, -e, n.m. pioneer; (mil.) engineer.

Pisto´le, -n, n.f. pistol.

Pisto´lenhalter, -, n.m. holster.

Pizza, -s, n.f. pizza.

Plackerei´, -en, n.f. drudgery.

plädie´ren, vb. plead.

Plädoyer´, -s, n.nt. plea.

Plage, -n, n.f. trouble, affliction.

plagen, vb. plague, annoy, afflict.

Plagiat´, n.nt. plagiarism.

Plakat´, -e, n.nt. placard, poster.

Plan, ⸗e, n.m. plan.

planen, vb. plan.

Planet´, -en, -en, n.m. planet.

Planke, -n, n.f. plank.

planlos, adj. aimless.

planmäßig, adj. according to plan; scheduled.

planschen, vb. splash.

Planta´ge, -n, n.f. plantation.

Plappermaul, ⸗er, n.nt. chatterbox.

plappern, vb. babble.

Plasma, -men, n.nt. plasma.

Plastik, -en, n.f. sculpture.

plastisch, adj. plastic.

Plateau´, -s, n.nt. plateau.

Platin, n.nt. platinum.

platt, adj. flat.

Plättbrett, -er, n.nt. ironing board.

Platte, -n, n.f. plate, slab, sheet, tray; (photographic) slide; (phonograph) record.

Plätteisen, -, n.nt. (flat) iron.

plätten, vb. iron.

Plattenspieler, -, n.m. record player.

Plattform, -en, n.f. platform.

Plattfuß, ⸗e, n.m. flat foot.

plattie´ren, vb. plate.

Platz, ⸗e, n.m. place, seat, square.

platzen, vb. burst.

Plauderei´, -en, n.f. chat.

plaudern, vb. chat.

pleite, adj. broke.

Plombe, -n, n.f. (tooth) filling.

plötzlich, adj. sudden.

plump, adj. clumsy, tactless.

Plunder, n.m. old clothes, rubbish.

plündern, vb. plunder, pillage.

Plünderung, -en, n.f. pillage.

Plural, -e, n.m. plural.

plus, adv. plus.

Plüsch, -e, n.m. plush.

Plutokrat´, -en, -en, n.m. plutocrat.

pneuma´tisch, adj. pneumatic.

Pöbel, n.m. mob, rabble.

pöbelhaft, adj. vulgar.

pochen, vb. knock, throb.

Pocke, -n, n.f. pock; (pl.) smallpox.

Podium, -ien, n.nt. rostrum.

Poesie´, i´en, n.f. poetry.

Poet´, -en, -en, n.m. poet.

poe´tisch, adj. poetic.

Poin´te, -n, n.f. point (of a joke), punch line.

Pokal´, -e, n.m. goblet, cup.

Pol, -e, n.m. pole.

polar´, adj. polar.

Polar´stern, n.m. North Star.

Pole, -n, -n, n.m. Pole.

Polen, n.nt. Poland.

Poli´ce, -n, n.f. (insurance) policy.

polie´ren, vb. polish.

Politik´, n.f. politics, policy.

Poli´tiker, -, n.m. politician.

Poli´tikerin, -nen, n.f. politician.

poli´tisch, adj. politic(al).

Politur', -en, *n.f.* polish.

Polizei', -en, *n.f.* police.

polizei'lich, *adj.* by the police.

Polizei'präsident, -en, -en, *n.m.* chief of police.

Polizei'präsidium, -ien, *n.nt.* police headquarters.

Polizei'revier, -e, *n.nt.* police station.

Polizei'richter, -, *n.m.* police state.

Polizei'staat, -en, *n.m.* police state.

Polizei'stunde, -n, *n.f.* curfew.

Polizei'wache, -n, *n.f.* police station.

Polizist', -en, -en, *n.m.* policeman.

Polizis'tin, -nen, *n.f.* police officer.

polnisch, *adj.* Polish.

Polonä'se, -n, *n.f.* polonaise.

Polster, -, *n.nt.* pad, cushion.

polstern, *vb.* pad, upholster.

Polsterung, -en, *n.f.* padding, upholstery.

poltern, *vb.* rattle, bluster.

Polygamie', *n.f.* polygamy.

Poly'pen, *n.pl.* adenoids.

Polytech'nikum, -ken, *n.nt.* technical college.

Pomeran'ze, -n, *n.f.* orange.

Pommes frites, *n.pl.* French fries.

Pony, -s, *n.nt.* pony; *(pl.)* bangs.

populär', *adj.* popular.

popularisie'ren, *vb.* popularize.

Popularität', *n.f.* popularity.

Pore, -n, *n.f.* pore.

porös', *adj.* porous.

Portal', -e, *n.nt.* portal.

Portefeuille', -s, *n.nt.* portfolio.

Portemonnaie', -s, *n.nt.* purse.

Portier', -s, *n.m.* doorman, concierge.

Portion', -en, *n.f.* portion, helping.

Porto, *n.nt.* postage.

Porträt', -s, *n.nt.* portrait.

Portugal, *n.nt.* Portugal.

Portugie'se, -n, -n, *n.m.* Portuguese.

Portugie'sin, -nen, *n.f.* Portuguese.

portugie'sisch, *adj.* Portuguese.

Porzellan', -en, *n.nt.* porcelain, china.

Posau'ne, -n, *n.f.* trumpet.

Pose, -n, *n.f.* pose.

posie'ren, *vb.* strike a pose.

Position', -en, *n.f.* position.

positiv, *adj.* positive.

Posse, -n, *n.f.* prank, antic; farce.

Post, *n.f.* mail; post office.

Postamt, ⸗er, *n.nt.* post office.

Postanweisung, -en, *n.f.* money order.

Postbote, -n, -n, *n.m.* mail carrier.

Postbotin, -nen, *n.f.* mail carrier.

Posten, -, *n.m.* post, station; item.

Postfach, ⸗er, *n.nt.* post office box.

Postkarte, -n, *n.f.* postcard.

postlagernd, *adv.* general delivery.

Postleitzahl, -en, *n.f.* zip code.

Poststempel, -, *n.m.* postmark.

Pracht, *n.f.* splendor.

prächtig, *adj.* splendid.

prachtvoll, *adv.* gorgeous.

Prädikat', -e, *n.nt.* predicate.

Präfix, -e, *n.nt.* prefix.

prägen, *vb.* stamp, coin, impress.

Prägung, -en, *n.f.* coinage.

prähistorisch, *adj.* prehistoric.

prahlen, *vb.* boast.

praktisch, *adj.* practical.

Prali'ne, -n, *n.f.* chocolate candy.

prallen, *vb.* bounce, be reflected.

Prämie, -n, *n.f.* premium, prize.

präparie'ren, *vb.* prepare.

Präposition', -en, *n.f.* preposition.

Präsens, *n.nt.* present.

präsentie'ren, *vb.* present.

Präservativ', -e, *n.nt.* condom.

Präsident', -en, -en, *n.m.* president.

Präsiden'tin, -nen, *n.f.* president.

prasseln, *vb.* patter, crackle.

Praxis, *n.f.* practice; doctor's office.

Präzedenz'fall, ⸗e, *n.m.* precedent.

Präzision', *n.f.* precision.

predigen, *vb.* preach.

Prediger, -, *n.m.* preacher.

Predigt, -en, *n.f.* sermon.

Preis, -e, *n.m.* price, cost; prize, praise.

Preiselbeere, -n, *n.f.* cranberry.

preisen*, *vb.* praise.

Preisgabe, -n, *n.f.* surrender, abandonment.

preis•geben*, *vb.* surrender, abandon.

prellen, *vb.* toss; cheat.

Premie're, -n, *n.f.* première.

Premier'minister, -, *n.m.* prime minister.

Premier'ministerin, -nen, *n.f.* prime minister.

Presse, *n.f.* press.

pressen, *vb.* press.

Prestige', *n.nt.* prestige.

Preuße, -n, -n, *n.m.* Prussian.

Preußen, *n.nt.* Prussia.

preußisch, *adj.* Prussian.

Priester, -, *n.m.* priest.

prima, *adj.* first class, swell.

primär', *adj.* primary.

Primel, -n, *n.f.* primrose.

primitiv', *adj.* primitive.

Prinz, -en, -en, *n.m.* prince.

Prinzes'sin, -nen, *n.f.* princess.

Prinzip', -ien, *n.nt.* principle.

Priorität', -en, *n.f.* priority.

Prise, -n, *n.f.* pinch.

Prisma, -men, *n.nt.* prism.

privat', *adj.* private.

Privileg', -ien, *n.nt.* privilege.

pro, *prep.* per.

Probe, -n, *n.f.* experiment, test; rehearsal; sample.

proben, *vb.* rehearse.

probeweise, *adj.* tentative.

Probezeit, -en, *n.f.* probation.

probie'ren, *vb.* try (out).

Problem', -e, *n.nt.* problem.

Produkt', -e, *n.nt.* product.

Produktion´, *n.f.* production.

produktiv´, *adj.* productive.

Produzent´, **-en, -en,** *n.m.* producer.

produzie´ren, *vb.* produce.

profan´, *adj.* profane.

Profes´sor, **-o´ren,** *n.m.* professor.

Professo´rin, **-nen,** *n.f.* professor.

Profil´, **-e,** *n.nt.* profile.

Profit´, **-e,** *n.m.* profit.

profitie´ren, *vb.* profit.

Progno´se, **-n,** *n.f.* prognosis.

Programm´, **-e,** *n.nt.* program.

Projekt´, **-e,** *n.nt.* project.

Projektion´, **-en,** *n.f.* projection.

Projek´tor, **-o´ren,** *n.m.* projector.

projizie´ren, *vb.* project.

Proklamation´, **-en,** *n.f.* proclamation.

Prokurist´, **-en, -en,** *n.m.* manager.

Prokuris´tin, **-nen,** *n.f.* manager.

Proletariat´, *n.nt.* proletariat.

Proleta´rier, **-,** *n.m.* proletarian.

proleta´risch, *adj.* proletarian.

Prolog´, **-e,** *n.m.* prologue.

prominent´, *adj.* prominent.

Prono´men, **-mina,** *n.nt.* pronoun.

Propagan´da, *n.f.* propaganda, publicity.

Propel´ler, **-,** *n.m.* propeller.

Prophet´, **-en, -en,** *n.m.* prophet.

prophe´tisch, *adj.* prophetic.

prophezei´en, *vb.* prophesy.

Prophezei´ung, **-en,** *n.f.* prophecy.

Proportion´, **-en,** *n.f.* proportion.

proppenvoll´, *adj.* chock full.

Prosa´, *n.f.* prose.

prosa´isch, *adj.* prosaic.

Prospekt´, **-e,** *n.m.* prospectus.

Prostituiert´-, *n.f.* prostitute.

Protein´, *n.nt.* protein.

Protest´, **-e,** *n.m.* protest.

Protestant´, **-en, -en,** *n.m.* Protestant.

protestie´ren, *vb.* protest.

Protokoll´, **-e,** *n.nt.* minutes, record.

protzen, *vb.* show off.

protzig, *adj.* gaudy.

Proviant´, *n.m.* food, supplies.

Provinz´, **-en,** *n.f.* province.

provinziell´, *adj.* provincial.

Provision´, **-en,** *n.f.* commission.

proviso´risch, *adj.* temporary.

Provokation´, **-en,** *n.f.* provocation.

provozie´ren, *vb.* provoke.

Prozent´, **-e,** *n.nt.* per cent.

Prozent´satz, **⸚e,** *n.m.* percentage.

Prozeß´, **-sse,** *n.m.* process; trial, lawsuit.

Prozession´, **-en,** *n.f.* procession.

prüde, *adj.* prudish.

prüfen, *vb.* test, examine, verify.

Prüfung, **-en,** *n.f.* test, examination, scrutiny.

Prügel, **-,** *n.m.* cudgel; *(pl.)* beating.

Prügelei´, **-en,** *n.f.* brawl.

prügeln, *vb.* beat, thrash.

Prunk, *n.m.* pomp, show.

prunkvoll, *adj.* pompous, showy.

PS, *abbr.* (= Pferdestärke) horsepower.

Psalm, **-en,** *n.m.* psalm.

Pseudonym´, **-e,** *n.nt.* pseudonym.

psychede´lisch, *adj.* psychedelic.

Psychia´ter, **-,** *n.m.* psychiatrist.

Psychia´terin, **-nen,** *n.f.* psychiatrist.

Psychiatrie´, *n.f.* psychiatry.

Psychoanaly´se, **-n,** *n.f.* psychoanalysis.

Psycholo´ge, **-n, -n,** *n.m.* psychologist.

Psychologie´, *n.f.* psychology.

Psycholo´gin, **-nen,** *n.f.* psychologist.

psycholo´gisch, *adj.* psychological.

Psycho´se, **-n,** *n.f.* psychosis.

Pubertät´, *n.f.* puberty.

Publikation´, **-en,** *n.f.* publication.

Publikum, *n.nt.* public, audience.

publizie´ren, *vb.* publish.

Pudding, **-e,** *n.m.* pudding.

Pudel, **-,** *n.m.* poodle.

Puder, **-,** *n.nt.* powder.

Puderdose, **-n,** *n.f.* compact.

pudern, *vb.* powder.

Puderquaste, **-n,** *n.f.* powder puff.

Puffer, **-,** *n.m.* buffer.

Pulli, **-s,** *n.m.* sweater.

Pullo´ver, **-,** *n.m.* sweater.

Puls, **-e,** *n.m.* pulse.

Pulsader, **-n,** *n.f.* artery.

Pulsar, **-s,** *n.m.* pulsar.

pulsie´ren, *vb.* pulsate, throb.

Pult, **-e,** *n.nt.* desk, lectern.

Pulver, **-,** *n.nt.* powder.

Pumpe, **-n,** *n.f.* pump.

pumpen, *vb.* pump; borrow, lend.

Pumps, *n.pl.* pumps.

Punkt, **-e,** *n.m.* point, dot, period.

Punktgleichheit, *n.f.* tie.

Punktion´, **-en,** *n.f.* puncture.

pünktlich, *adj.* punctual.

Punktzahl, **-en,** *n.f.* score.

Punsch, *n.m.* punch.

Pupil´le, **-n,** *n.f.* pupil.

Puppe, **-n,** *n.f.* doll; chrysalis.

pur, *adj.* pure; (alcohol) straight.

Püree´, **-s,** *n.nt.* purée.

Purpur, *n.m.* purple.

purpurn, *adj.* purple.

Puter, **-,** *n.m.* turkey.

Putsch, **-e,** *n.m.* attempt to overthrow the government.

Putz, *n.m.* finery.

putzen, *vb.* clean, polish.

Putzfrau, **-en,** *n.f.* cleaning woman.

putzig, *adj.* funny, droll, quaint.

Putzwaren, *n.pl.* millinery.

Puzzle, **-n,** *n.nt.* puzzle.

Pyja´ma, **-s,** *n.m.* pajamas.

Pyrami´de, **-n,** *n.f.* pyramid.

Q

quadraphon´, *adj.* quadraphonic.

Quadrat´, **-e**, *n.nt.* square.

Quadrat´-, *cpds.* square.

quadra´tisch, *adj.* square.

quaken, *vb.* quack, croak.

Qual, **-en**, *n.f.* torment, agony, ordeal.

quälen, *vb.* torment, torture.

Qualifikation´, **-en**, *n.f.* qualification.

qualifizie´ren, *vb.* qualify.

Qualität´, **-en**, *n.f.* quality.

qualmen, *vb.* smoke.

qualvoll, *adj.* agonizing.

Quantität´, **-en**, *n.f.* quantity.

Quarantä´ne, **-n**, *n.f.* quarantine.

Quark, *n.m.* curds.

Quarkkäse, *n.m.* cottage cheese.

Quartal´, **-e**, *n.nt.* quarter of a year.

Quartett´, **-e**, *n.nt.* quartet.

Quartier´, **-e**, *n.nt.* lodging, billet.

Quarz, **-e**, *n.m.* quartz.

Quasar, *n.m.* quasar.

Quaste, **-n**, *n.f.* tuft.

Quatsch, *n.m.* nonsense, bunk, baloney.

Quecksilber, *n.nt.* mercury.

Quelle, **-n**, *n.f.* spring, source, well, fountain.

quellen*, *vb.* well, gush, flow.

quer, *adj.* cross(wise), diagonal.

Querschnitt, **-**, *n.m.* cross section.

Querstraße, **-n**, *n.f.* cross street.

Querverweis, **-e**, *n.m.* cross reference.

quetschen, *vb.* squeeze, bruise.

Quetschung, **-en**, *n.f.* contusion.

quietschen, *vb.* squeak.

Quintett´, **-e**, *n.nt.* quintet.

quitt, *adj.* quits, even, square.

quittie´ren, *vb.* receipt.

Quittung, **-en**, *n.f.* receipt.

Quote, **-n**, *n.f.* quota.

R

Rabatt´, **-e**, *n.m.* discount.

Rabau´ke, **-n**, **-n**, *n.m.* tough.

Rabbi´ner, **-**, *n.m.* rabbi.

Rabe, **-n**, **-n**, *n.m.* raven.

Rache, *n.f.* revenge.

rächen, *vb.* revenge, avenge.

Rachen, **-**, *n.m.* throat, jaws.

Rad, **ër**, *n.nt.* wheel.

Radar, *n.nt.* radar.

Radau´, *n.m.* noise, racket.

radeln, *vb.* (bi)cycle.

rad·fahren*, *vb.* (bi)cycle.

Radfahrer, **-**, *n.m.* (bi)cyclist.

Radfahrerin, **-nen**, *n.f.* bicyclist.

radie´ren, *vb.* erase; etch.

Radier´gummi, **-s**, *n.m.* (rubber) eraser.

Radie´rung, **-en**, *n.f.* etching.

Radies´chen, **-**, *n.nt.* radish.

radikal´, *adj.* radical.

Radio, **-s**, *n.nt.* radio.

radioaktiv´, *adj.* radioactive.

radioaktiv´-Niederschlag, *n.m.* fallout.

Radioapparat, **-e**, *n.m.* radio set.

Radioempf änger, **-**, *n.m.* radio receiver.

Radiosender, **-**, *n.m.* radio transmitter, broadcasting station.

Radiosendung, **-en**, *n.f.* radio broadcast.

Radium, *n.nt.* radium.

Radius, **-ien**, *n.m.* radius.

Radspur, **-en**, *n.f.* rut.

Radweg, **-e**, *n.m.* bike path.

raffinie´ren, *vb.* refine.

raffiniert´, *adj.* tricky, shrewd; sophisticated.

ragen, *vb.* extend, loom.

Rahm, *n.m.* cream.

rahmen, *vb.* frame.

Rahmen, **-**, *n.m.* frame.

Rake´te, **-n**, *n.f.* rocket.

Rake´tenwaffe, **-n**, *n.f.* missile.

rammen, *vb.* ram.

Rampe, **-n**, *n.f.* ramp.

Rand, **ër**, *n.m.* edge, brim, margin.

Rang, **ë**, *n.m.* rank.

rangie´ren, *vb.* switch, shunt.

Rangordnung, **-en**, *n.f.* hierarchy.

ranzig, *adj.* rancid.

Rapier´, **-e**, *n.nt.* foil.

rasch, *adj.* quick.

rascheln, *vb.* rustle.

rasen, *vb.* rage.

Rasen, *n.m.* lawn, turf.

rasend, *adj.* frenzied.

Raserei´, **-en**, *n.f.* frenzy.

Rasierapparat, **-e**, *n.m.* safety razor.

rasie´ren, *vb.* shave.

Rasier´klinge, **-n**, *n.f.* razor blade.

Rasier´messer, **-**, *n.nt.* (straight) razor.

Rasse, **-n**, *n.f.* race; breed.

rasseln, *vb.* rattle.

Rast, **-en**, *n.f.* rest.

rasten, *vb.* rest.

rastlos, *adj.* restless.

Rasur´, **-en**, *n.f.* erasure; shave.

Rat, **ë**, *n.m.* advice; councilor.

Rate, **-n**, *n.f.* payment, installment.

raten*, *vb.* guess, advise.

Ratenzahlung, *n.f.* payment by installments.

ratifizie´ren, *vb.* ratify.

Ration´, **-en**, *n.f.* ration.

rationell´, *adj.* rational, reasonable.

rationie´ren, *vb.* ration.

ratlos, *adj.* helpless, perplexed, at one's wit's end.

Ratlosigkeit, *n.f.* perplexity.

ratsam, *adj.* advisable.

Ratsamkeit, *n.f.* advisability.

Rätsel, **-**, *n.nt.* riddle, puzzle; enigma, mystery.

rätselhaft, *adj.* puzzling, mysterious.

Ratte, -n, *n.f.* rat.

rattern, *vb.* rattle.

Raub, *n.m.* robbery, plunder.

rauben, *vb.* rob.

Räuber, -, *n.m.* robber.

Rauch, *n.m.* smoke.

rauchen, *vb.* smoke.

Raucher, -, *n.m.* smoker.

räuchern, *vb.* smoke (fish, meat).

raufen, *vb.* pull, tear; **(sich r.)** fight, brawl.

Rauferei´, -en, *n.f.* brawl.

rauh, *adj.* rough; harsh; rugged.

Rauheit, -en, *n.f.* roughness.

Raum, ⸚e, *n.m.* room, space.

räumen, *vb.* vacate.

Raumfahrt, *n.f.* space travel.

Rauminhalt, *n.m.* volume, capacity, contents.

räumlich, *adj.* spatial.

Raumtransporter, *n.m.* space shuttle.

Räumung, *n.f. (comm.)* clearance; *(mil.)* evacuation.

raunen, *vb.* whisper.

Rausch, ⸚e, *n.m.* intoxication.

rauschen, *vb.* roar, rustle.

Rauschgift, -e, *n.nt.* narcotic, dope.

Razzia, -ien, *n.f.* raid.

reagie´ren, *vb.* react, respond.

Reaktion´, -en, *n.f.* reaction, response.

Reaktionär´, -e, *n.m.* reactionary.

reaktionär´, *adj.* reactionary.

reaktivie´ren, *vb.* recommission.

Reak´tor, -o´ren, *n.m.* reactor.

realisie´ren, *vb.* realize, put into effect.

Realisie´rung, -en, *n.f.* realization.

Realis´mus, *n.m.* realism.

Realist´, -en, -en, *n.f.* realist.

Realität´, -en, *n.f.* reality.

Rebe, -n, *n.f.* vine; grape.

Rebstock, ⸚e, *n.m.* vine.

Rechen, -, *n.m.* rake.

Rechenaufgabe, -n, *n.f.* arithmetic problem.

Rechenmaschine, -n, *n.f.* calculating machine.

Rechenschaft, *n.f.* account, responsibility; **(R. able- gen)** account for.

Rechenschieber, -, *n.m.* slide rule.

rechnen, *vb.* count, do sums, figure.

Rechnen, *n.nt.* arithmetic.

Rechnung, -en, *n.f.* figuring, computation; bill; **(R. tra- gen*)** take into account.

Rechnungsbuch, ⸚er, *n.nt.* account book.

recht, *adj.* right; **(r. haben*)** be right.

Recht, -e, *n.nt.* right; (system of) law.

Rechteck, -e, *n.nt.* rectangle.

rechteckig, *adj.* rectangular, oblong.

rechtfertigen, *vb.* justify; vindicate.

Rechtfertigung, -en, *n.f.* justification.

rechtlich, *adj.* legal, judicial.

rechtmäßig, *adj.* lawful.

rechts, *adv.* (to the) right.

Rechtsanwalt, ⸚e, *n.m.* lawyer.

Rectsanwältin, -nen, *n.f.* lawyer.

rechtschaffen, *adj.* honest, righteous.

Rechtschaffenheit, *n.f.* honesty, righteousness.

Rechtschreibung, *n.f.* orthography, spelling.

Rechtsgelehrt-, *n.m.* jurist.

Rechtsprechung, *n.f.* jurisdiction.

Rechtsspruch, ⸚e, *n.m.* judgment, sentence.

Rechtsstreit, -e, *n.m.* litigation.

Rechtswissenschaft, *n.f.* jurisprudence.

recken, *vb.* stretch.

Redakteur´, -e, *n.m.* editor.

Redaktion´, -en, *n.f.* editorial office; editor.

Rede, -n, *n.f.* speech, talk; **(eine R. halten*)** give a speech; **(keine R. sein* von)** be no question of;

(jemanden zur R. stellen) confront a person with, take to task.

redegewandt, *adj.* eloquent.

Redekunst, *n.f.* rhetoric, oratory.

reden, *vb.* talk, speak; **(vernünftig r. mit)** reason with.

Redensart, -en, *n.f.* way of speaking; saying, idiom.

Redeteil, -e, *n.m.* part of speech.

Redewendung, -en, *n.f.* phrase, figure of speech.

redlich, *adj.* honest, upright.

Redner, -, *n.m.* speaker, orator.

Rednerin, -nen, *n.f.* speaker, orator.

redselig, *adj.* loquacious.

Reduktion´, -en, *n.f.* reduction.

reduzie´ren, *vb.* reduce.

reell´, *adj.* honest, sound.

reflektie´ren, *vb.* reflect.

Reflex´, -e, *n.m.* reflex.

Reflexion´, -en, *n.f.* reflection.

Reform´, -en, *n.f.* reform.

reformie´ren, *vb.* reform.

Refrain´, -s, *n.m.* refrain.

Regal´, -e, *n.nt.* shelf.

rege, *adj.* alert; active.

Regel, -n, *n.f.* rule.

regelmäßig, *adj.* regular.

Regelmäßigkeit, *n.f.* regularity.

regeln, *vb.* regulate.

regelrecht, *adj.* regular, downright.

Regelung, -en, *n.f.* regulation.

regen, *vb.* **(sich r.)** stir, move.

Regen, *n.m.* rain.

Regenbogen, ⸚, *n.m.* rainbow.

Regenguß, ⸚sse, *n.m.* downpour.

Regenmantel, ⸚, *n.m.* raincoat.

Regenschirm, -e, *n.m.* umbrella.

Regie, *n.f.* direction.

regie´ren, *vb.* govern.

Regie´rung, -en, *n.f.* government.

Regi´me, -s, *n.nt.* regime.

Regiment´, -er, *n.nt.* regiment.

Region´, -en, *n.f.* region.

Regisseur´, -e, *n.m.* director.

Regis´ter, -, *n.nt.* register, index.

Registrie´rung, -en, *n.f.* registration.

regnen, *vb.* rain.

regnerisch, *adj.* rainy.

regsam, *adj.* alert, quick.

regulie´ren, *vb.* regulate.

Reh, -e, *n.nt.* deer, roe.

rehabilitie´ren, *vb.* rehabilitate.

Rehleder, -, *n.nt.* deerskin.

Reibe, -n, *n.f.* grater.

reiben*, *vb.* rub; grate; chafe.

Reibung, -en, *n.f.* friction.

reich, *adj.* rich.

Reich, -e, *n.nt.* kingdom, empire, realm.

reichen, *vb.* (*tr.*) pass, hand, reach; (*intr.*) extend.

reichlich, *adj.* plentiful, ample, abundant.

Reichtum, ⁼er, *n.m.* wealth, affluence.

Reichweite, *n.m.* reach, range.

reif, *adj.* ripe, mature.

Reife, *n.f.* maturity.

reifen, *vb.* ripen, mature.

Reifen, -, *n.m.* hoop; (auto, etc.) tire.

Reifenpanne, -n, *n.f.* puncture, blowout.

reiflich, *adj.* carefully considerate.

Reigen, -, *n.m.* (dance) round; (music) song.

Reihe, -n, *n.f.* row; series, succession.

reihen, *vb.* (sich r.) rank.

Reihenfolge, -n, *n.f.* sequence, succession.

Reim, -, *n.m.* rhyme.

rein, *adj.* clean, pure.

Reinfall, ⁼e, *n.m.* flop.

rein•fallen*, *vb.* be taken in.

Reinheit, *n.f.* purity.

reinigen, *vb.* clean, cleanse.

Reinigung, -en, *n.f.* cleaning, cleansing; (chemische R.) dry-cleaner, dry-cleaning.

rein•legen, *vb.* trick, take in.

Reis, *n.m.* rice.

Reise, -n, *n.f.* trip, journey.

Reiseandenken, -, *n.nt.* souvenir.

Reisebüro, -s, *n.nt.* travel agency.

Reiseführer, -, *n.m.* guidebook.

reisen, *vb.* travel.

Reisend-, *n.m.& f.* traveler.

Reiseroute, -n, *n.f.* itinerary.

Reisescheck, -s, *n.m.* traveler's check.

reißen*, *vb.* rip, tear; (sich r. um) scramble for.

reißend, *adj.* rapid, racing.

Reißer, -, *n.m.* thriller, bestseller.

reiten*, *vb.* ride, horseback.

Reiter, -, *n.m.* rider.

Reiterin, -nen, *n.f.* rider.

Reiz, -e, *n.m.* charm, appeal; irritation.

reizbar, *adj.* sensitive, irritable.

reizen, *vb.* excite, tempt; irritate.

reizend, *adj.* adorable, lovely.

Reizfaktor, -en, *n.m.* irritant.

Reizmittel, -, *n.nt.* stimulant.

Reizung, -en, *n.f.* irritation.

rekeln, *vb.* (sich r.) stretch, sprawl.

Rekla´me, *n.f.* advertisement, advertising, publicity.

reklamie´ren, *vb.* reclaim; complain.

Rekord´, -e, *n.m.* record.

Rekrut´, -en, -en, *n.m.* draftee, recruit.

Rektor, -o´ren, *n.m.* headmaster; (university) president, chancellor.

relativ´, *adj.* relative.

Religion´, -en, *n.f.* religion.

religiös´, *adj.* religious.

Rendezvous, -, *n.nt.* rendezvous, tryst.

Rennen, -, *n.nt.* race.

rennen*, *vb.* run, dash; race.

Renntier, -e, *n.nt.* reindeer.

renovie´ren, *vb.* renovate.

renta´bel, *adj.* profitable.

Rente, -n, *n.f.* pension, income.

rentie´ren, *vb.* (sich r.) be profitable.

Reparation´, -en, *n.f.* reparation.

Reparatur´, -en, *n.f.* repair.

reparie´ren, *vb.* repair.

repatriie´ren, *vb.* repatriate.

Repertoire´, -s, *n.nt.* repertoire.

Repor´ter, -, *n.m.* reporter.

Repor´terin, -nen, *n.f.* reporter.

Repräsentant´, -en, -en, *n.m.* representative.

Repräsentation´, -en, *n.f.* representation.

reproduzie´ren, *vb.* reproduce.

Reptil´, -e *or* **-ien,** *n.nt.* reptile.

Republik´, -en, *n.f.* republic.

republika´nisch, *adj.* republican.

requirie´ren, *vb.* requisition.

Requisition´, -en, *n.f.* requisition.

Reservation´, -en, *n.f.* reservation.

Reser´ve, -n, *n.f.* reserve.

reservie´ren, *vb.* reserve.

Reservoir´, -s, *n.nt.* reservoir.

Residenz´, -en, *n.f.* residence.

Resignation´, -en, *n.f.* resignation.

resignie´ren, *vb.* resign.

resolut´, *adj.* determined.

resonant´, *adj.* resonant.

Resonanz´, -en, *n.f.* resonance.

Respekt´, *n.m.* respect, regard.

Rest, -e, *n.m.* rest, remnant.

Restaurant´, -s, *n.nt.* restaurant.

restaurie´ren, *vb.* restore.

Restbestand, ⁼e, *n.m.* residue.

restlos, *adj.* without remainder, entire.

Resultat´, -e, *n.nt.* result.

Resümee´, -s, *n.nt.* résumé.

retten, *vb.* rescue, save, salvage.

Retter, -, *n.m.* savior.

Rettung, -en, *n.f.* rescue; salvation.

Rettungsboot, -e, *n.nt.* lifeboat.

rettungslos, *adj.* irretrievable, hopeless.

Rettungsring, -e, *n.m.* life preserver.

Rettungswagen, -, *n.m.* ambulance.

Reue, *n.f.* repentance.

reuevoll, *adj.* repentant.

reuig, *adj.* penitent.

Revan'che, -n, *n.f.* revenge; return match.

Revers', -e, *n.m.* lapel.

revidie'ren, *vb.* revise.

Revier', -e, *n.nt.* district.

Revision', -en, *n.f.* revision.

Revol'te, -n, *n.f.* revolt.

revoltie'ren, *vb.* revolt.

Revolution', -en, *n.f.* revolution.

revolutionär', *adj.* revolutionary.

Revol'ver, -, *n.m.* revolver, gun.

Rezept', -e, *n.nt.* receipt; recipe; prescription.

Rhabar'ber, *n.m.* rhubarb.

Rhapsodie', -i'en, *n.f.* rhapsody.

Rhein, *n.m.* Rhine.

rheto'risch, *adj.* rhetorical.

Rheuma, *n.nt.* rheumatism.

Rheumatis'mus, *n.m.* rheumatism.

rhythmisch, *adj.* rhythmical.

Rhythmus, -men, *n.m.* rhythm.

richten, *vb.* set right; **(r. auf)** turn to; **(sich r. an)** turn to; **(sich r. nach)** go by, be guided by, depend on; *(jur.)* judge.

Richter, -, *n.m.* judge.

Richterin, -nen, *n.f.* judge.

richterlich, *adj.* judicial, judiciary.

Richteramt, *n.nt.* judiciary.

richtig, *adj.* true, correct.

Richtigkeit, *n.f.* correctness.

Richtung, -en, *n.f.* direction; tendency.

riechen*, *vb.* smell.

Riecher, -, *n.m.* *(fig.)* hunch.

Riegel, -, *n.m.* bolt.

Riemen, -, *n.m.* strap; oar.

Riese, -n, -n, *n.m.* giant.

riesenhaft, *adj.* gigantic.

riesig, *adj.* tremendous, vast.

rigoros', *adj.* rigorous.

Rind, -er, *n.nt.* ox, cow, cattle.

Rinde, -n, *n.f.* bark.

Rindfleisch, *n.nt.* beef.

Rindsleder, -, *n.nt.* cowhide.

Ring, -e, *n.m.* ring.

ringeln, *vb.* curl.

ringen*, *vb.* struggle, wrestle.

Ringkampf, ⸚e, *n.m.* wrestling match.

Rinne, -n, *n.f.* rut, groove.

rinnen*, *vb.* run, flow.

Rinnstein, -e, *n.m.* curb, gutter.

Rippe, -n, *n.f.* rib.

Rippenfellentzündung, -en, *n.f.* pleurisy.

Risiko, -s or **-ken,** *n.nt.* risk, hazard, gamble.

riskie'ren, *vb.* risk, gamble.

Riß, -sse, *n.m.* tear, crack.

Ritt, -e, *n.m.* ride.

Ritter, -, *n.m.* knight.

ritterlich, *adj.* chivalrous.

rittlings, *adv.* astride.

Rituele', *n.nt.* ritual.

rituell', *adj.* ritual.

Ritus, -en, *n.m.* rite.

Ritze, -n, *n.f.* crack.

Riva'le, -n, -n, *n.m.* rival.

Riva'lin, -nen, *n.f.* rival.

rivalisie'ren, *vb.* rival.

Rivalität', -en, *n.f.* rivalry.

Rizinusöl, *n.nt.* castor oil.

Robbe, -n, *n.f.* seal.

Roboter, -, *n.m.* robot.

robust', *adj.* robust.

röcheln, *vb.* breathe heavily.

Rock, ⸚e, *n.m.* (men) jacket; (women) skirt; (music) rock.

Rockmusik, *n.f.* rock music.

rodeln, *vb.* go sledding.

Rodelschlitten, -, *n.m.* sled.

Rogen, -, *n.m.* roe.

Roggen, *n.m.* rye.

roh, *adj.* raw, crude; *(fig.)* brutal.

Roheit, -en, *n.f.* crudeness, brutality.

Rohling, -e, *n.m.* rowdy.

Rohr, -e, *n.nt.* pipe; (gun) barrel; (bamboo, sugar) cane.

Röhre, -n, *n.f.* pipe, tube.

Rohrflöte, -n, *n.f.* reed pipe.

Rolle, -n, *n.f.* roll, coil; spool; role, part.

rollen, *vb.* roll.

Roller, -, *n.m.* scooter.

Rolltreppe, -n, *n.f.* escalator.

Rom, *n.nt.* Rome.

Roman', -e, *n.m.* novel.

roma'nisch, *adj.* Romance.

Roman'schriftsteller, -, *n.m.* novelist.

Roman'schriftstellerin, -nen, *n.f.* novelist.

Roman'tik, *n.m.* romanticism, Romantic Movement.

roman'tisch, *adj.* romantic.

Roman'ze, -n, *n.f.* romance.

Römer, -, *n.m.* Roman.

Römerin, -nen, *n.f.* Roman.

römisch, *adj.* Roman.

röntgen, -s *vb.* x-ray.

Röntgenaufnahme, -n, *n.f.* x-ray.

Röntgenstrahlen, *n.pl.* x-rays.

rosa, *adj.* pink.

Rose, -n, *n.f.* rose.

Rosenkranz, ⸚e, *n.m.* rosary.

rosig, *adj.* rosy.

Rosi'ne, -n, *n.f.* raisin.

Roß, -sse, *n.nt.* horse, steed.

Rost, *n.m.* rust; (oven) grate.

rosten, *vb.* rust.

rösten, *vb.* roast; toast.

rostig, *adj.* rusty.

rot (⸚), *adj.* red.

rotbraun, *adj.* red-brown, maroon.

Röteln, *n.pl.* German measles.

rotie'ren, *vb.* rotate.

Rotwein, -e, *n.m.* red wine, claret.

Roué', -s, *n.m.* roué, rake.

Rouge, *n.nt.* rouge.

Roula'de, -n, *n.f.* meat roll.

Route, -n, *n.f.* route.

Routi'ne, -n, *n.f.* routine.

routiniert', *adj.* experienced.

Rowdy, -s, *n.m.* hoodlum.

Rübe, -n, *n.f.* **(gelbe R.)** carrot; **(rote R.)** beet; **(weisse R.)** turnip.

Rubin', -e, *n.m.* ruby.

Rubrik', -en, *n.f.* category, heading.

ruchbar, *adj.* notorious.

ruchlos, *adj.* infamous, profligate.

Ruck, -e, *n.m.* jerk, wrench.

Rückantwort, -en, *n.f.* reply.

ruckartig, *adj.* jerky.

rückbezüglich, *adj.* reflexive.

Rückblick, *n.m.* retrospect.

rücken, *vb.* move, move over.

Rücken, -, *n.m.* back.

rückerstatten, *vb.* refund.

Rückfahrkarte, -n, *n.f.* return ticket.

Rückfahrt, -en, *n.f.* return trip.

Rückfall, ⁼e, *n.m.* relapse.

Rückgabe, *n.f.* return, restitution.

Rückgang, ⁼e, *n.m.* retrogression, decline.

rückgängig, *adj.* declining; **(r. machen)** cancel, revoke.

Rückgrat, -e, *n.nt.* spine, backbone.

Rückhalt, *n.m.* support, reserve.

rückhaltlos, *adj.* unreserved, frank.

Rückhand, ⁼, *n.f.* backhand.

Rückkaufswert, -e, *n.m.* equity (mortgage, etc.).

Rückkehr, *n.f.* return; reversion.

Rückkopplung, -en, *n.f.* feedback.

Rückmarsch, ⁼e, *n.m.* retreat.

Rucksack, ⁼e, *n.m.* knapsack.

Rückschlag, ⁼e, *n.m.* reverse, upset.

Rückschluß, ⁼sse, *n.m.* conclusion.

Rückseite, -n, *n.f.* reverse, rear.

Rücksicht, -en, *n.f.* consideration.

Rücksichtnahme, *n.f.* consideration.

rücksichtslos, *adj.* inconsiderate; reckless, ruthless.

Rücksichtslosigkeit, -en, *n.f.* lack of consideration, ill-mannered behavior; ruthlessness.

rücksichtsvoll, *adj.* thoughtful, considerate.

Rückstand, ⁼e, *n.m.* arrears; **(in R. geraten*)** fall behind, lag.

rückständig, *adj.* in arrears; backward, antiquated.

Rücktritt, -e, *n.m.* resignation.

rückwärts, *adv.* backward(s).

Rückwärtsgang, ⁼e, *n.m.* reverse (gear).

ruckweise, *adv.* by fits and starts.

Rückzug, ⁼e, *n.m.* retreat.

Rudel, -, *n.nt.* pack.

Ruder, -, *n.nt.* oar.

Ruderboot, -e, *n.nt.* row-boat.

rudern, *vb.* row.

Ruf, -e, *n.m.* call; reputation, standing.

rufen*, *vb.* call, shout.

Rufnummer, -n, *n.f.* (telephone) number.

Rüge, -n, *n.f.* reprimand.

rügen, *vb.* reprimand.

Ruhe, *n.f.* rest; calmness, tranquility; silence.

ruhelos, *adj.* restless.

ruhen, *vb.* rest, repose.

Ruhestand, *n.m.* retirement.

Ruhestätte, -n, *n.f.* resting place.

ruhig, *adj.* calm, composed; quiet; **(das kannst du r. machen)** go ahead and do it.

Ruhm, *n.m.* fame, glory.

rühmen, *vb.* praise, extol.

rühmenswert, *adj.* praiseworthy.

rühmlich, *adj.* laudable.

ruhmlos, *adj.* inglorious.

ruhmreich, *adj.* glorious.

Ruhr, *n.f.* dysentery.

Rührei, -er, *n.nt.* scrambled eggs.

rühren, *vb.* move, stir; **(sich r.)** stir.

rührend, *adj.* touching, pathetic.

rührig, *adj.* lively, bustling.

Rührung, *n.f.* emotion, compassion.

Rui´ne, -n, *n.f.* ruin.

ruinie´ren, *vb.* ruin.

Rum, *n.m.* rum.

Rummel, *n.m.* hubbub, racket.

Rummelplatz, *n.m.* amusement park, fair.

rumpeln, *vb.* rumble.

Rumpf, -e, *n.m.* torso, fuselage, hull.

rund, *adj.* round, circular.

Runde, -n, *n.f.* round; (sports) lap.

Rundfunk, *n.m.* radio.

Rundfunksendung, -en, *n.f.* broadcast.

Rundfunksprecher, -, *n.m.* broadcaster.

Rundfunkübertragung, -en, *n.f.* broadcast.

rundlich, *adj.* plump.

Rundreise, -n, *n.f.* tour.

Rundschreiben, -, *n.nt.* circular.

Runzel, -n, *n.f.* wrinkle.

runzeln, *vb.* wrinkle; **(die Stirn r.)** frown.

rupfen, *vb.* pluck.

Rüsche, -n, *n.f.* ruffle.

Ruß, *n.m.* soot, grime.

Russe, -n, *n.m.* Russian.

Rüssel, -n, *n.m.* trunk.

Russin, -nen, *n.f.* Russian.

russisch, *adj.* Russian.

Rußland, *n.nt.* Russia.

rüsten, *vb.* prepare; *(mil.)* arm.

rüstig, *adj.* vigorous, spry.

Rüstung, -en, *n.f.* armament; armor.

rutschen, *vb.* slide, skid.

rütteln, *vb.* shake, jolt.

S

Saal, Säle, *n.m.* large room, hall.

Saat, -en, *n.f.* seed, sowing.

Sabbat, -en, *n.m.* Sabbath.

Säbel, -, *n.m.* saber.

Sabota´ge, *n.f.* sabotage.

Saboteur´, -e, *n.m.* saboteur.

sabotie´ren, *vb.* sabotage.

Sacharin´, *n.nt.* saccharine.

Sache, -n, *n.f.* thing, matter; cause.

Sachkundig-, *n.m.* expert.

sachlich, *adj.* objective, relevant, matter-of-fact; (art) functional.

Sachlichkeit, *n.f.* objectivity, detachment.

sacht, *adj.* soft.

sachte, *adv.* cautiously, gingerly.

Sachverständig-, *n.m. & f.* expert.

Sack, ≃e, *n.m.* sack, bag.

Sadis´mus, *n.m.* sadism.

Sadist´, -en, -en, *n.m.* sadist.

sadis´tisch, *adj.* sadistic.

säen, *vb.* sow.

Saft, ≃e, *n.m.* juice, sap.

saftig, *adj.* juicy, succulent.

Sage, -n, *n.f.* myth.

Säge, -n, *n.f.* saw.

sagen, *vb.* say, tell.

sägen, *vb.* saw.

sagenhaft, *adj.* mythical, fabulous.

Sago, *n.nt.* tapioca.

Sahne, *n.f.* cream.

Sahneeis, *n.nt.* ice cream.

Saison´, -s, *n.f.* season.

Saite, -n, *n.f.* string, chord.

Sakrament´, -e, *n.nt.* sacrament.

Sakrileg´, -e, *n.nt.* sacrilege.

Sakristei, -en, *n.f.* sacristy, vestry.

Salat´, -e, *n.m.* salad.

Salat´soße, -n, *n.f.* salad dressing.

Salbe, -n, *n.f.* salve, ointment.

salben, *vb.* anoint.

Saldo, -den, *n.m.* balance, remainder.

Salm, -e, *n.m.* salmon.

Salon´, -s, *n.m.* salon.

salopp´, *adj.* nonchalant.

salutie´ren, *vb.* salute.

Salve, -n, *n.f.* salvo.

Salz, -e, *n.m.* salt.

salzen, *vb.* salt.

salzig, *adj.* salty.

Salzwasser, -, *n.nt.* brine.

Samen, -, *n.m.* seed.

sammeln, *vb.* collect, gather; **(sich s.)** *(mil.)* rally.

Sammler, -, *n.m.* collector.

Sammlerin, -nen, *n.f.* collector.

Sammlung, -en, *n.f.* collection.

Samstag, -e, *n.m.* Saturday.

Samt, *n.m.* velvet.

samt, *adv. & prep.* together with.

sämtlich, *adj.* entire.

Sanato´rium, -rien, *n.nt.* sanatorium.

Sand, -e, *n.m.* sand.

Sanda´le, -n, *n.f.* sandal.

sandig, *adj.* sandy.

Sandtorte, -n, *n.f.* pound cake.

sanft, *adj.* gentle, meek.

Sanftmut, *n.m.* gentleness.

sanftmütig, *adj.* gentle, meek.

Sänger, -, *n.m.* singer.

Sängerin, -nen, *n.f.* singer.

sang- und klanglos, *adv.* quietly.

Sankt, *adj.* Saint.

Saphir´, -e, *n.m.* sapphire.

Sardel´le, -n, *n.f.* anchovy.

Sardi´ne, -n, *n.f.* sardine.

Sarg, ≃e, *n.m.* coffin.

Sarkas´mus, *n.m.* sarcasm.

sarkas´tisch, *adj.* sarcastic.

Satan, *n.m.* Satan.

sata´nisch, *adj.* diabolical.

Satellit´, -en, -en, *n.m.* satellite.

Satin´, -s, *n.m.* satin.

Sati´re, -n, *n.f.* satire.

sati´risch, *adj.* satirical.

satt, *adj.* satiated; **(ich bin s.)** I have had enough to eat; **(ich habe es s.)** I am sick of it; **(sich s. essen*, sehen*)** have one's fill.

Sattel, -, *n.m.* saddle.

satteln, *vb.* saddle.

sättigen, *vb.* satiate, saturate.

Sättigung, *n.f.* satiation, saturation.

sattsam, *adv.* sufficiently.

Satz, ≃e, *n.m.* *(gram.)* sentence, clause; *(music)* movement; *(dishes, tennis)* set.

Satzlehre, *n.f.* syntax.

Satzung, -en, *n.f.* statute, by-law.

Satzzeichen, -, *n.nt.* punctuation mark.

Sau, ≃e, *n.f.* sow.

sauber, *adj.* clean, neat.

Sauberkeit, *n.f.* cleanliness, neatness.

säuberlich, *adj.* clean, careful.

säubern, *vb.* cleanse, purge.

Säuberungsaktion, -en, *n.f.* purge.

sauer, *adj.* sour, acid.

Säuerlichkeit, -en, *n.f.* acidity.

Sauerstoff, *n.m.* oxygen.

saufen*, *vb.* drink heavily, guzzle.

Säufer, -, *n.m.* drunkard.

saugen*, *vb.* suck.

Saugen, *n.nt.* suction.

Sauger, -, *n.m.* nipple (baby's bottle).

Säugetier, -e, *n.nt.* mammal.

Säugling, -e, *n.m.* infant, baby.

Säule, -n, *n.f.* pillar, column.

Saum, ≃e, *n.m.* seam, hem.

säumen, *vb.* hem; delay.

säumig, *adj.* tardy, delinquent.

Säure, -n, *n.f.* acid.

säuseln, *vb.* rustle.

sausen, *vb.* (wind) whistle; run, dash.

S-Bahn, *n.f.* city and suburban train.

schaben, *vb.* scrape.

Schabernack, -e, *n.m.* hoax.

schäbig, *adj.* shabby.

Schach, *n.nt.* chess; **(in S. halten*)** keep at bay.

Schachbrett, -er, *n.nt.* chessboard.

Schachfigur, -en, *n.f.* chessman.

schachmatt´, *adj.* checkmate; *(fig.)* exhausted.

Schachspiel, -e, *n.nt.* chess.

Schacht, ≃e, *n.m.* shaft.

Schachtel, -n, *n.f.* box.

schade, *adv.* too bad.

Schädel, -, *n.m.* skull.

schaden, *vb.* harm; be harmful.

Schaden, ≃, *n.m.* harm, damage.

Schadenersatz, *n.m.* indemnity, compensation, damages.

schadenfroh, *adj.* gloating; **(s. sein*)** gloat.

schadhaft, *adj.* defective.

schädigen, *vb.* wrong, damage.

schädlich, *adj.* harmful, injurious.

Schädling, -e, *n.m.* pest, destructive insect.

Schädlingsbekämpfungsmittel, *n.nt.* pesticide.

Schaf, -e, *n.nt.* sheep.

Schäfer, -, *n.m.* shepherd.

schaffen*, *vb.* make, create.

schaffen, *vb.* get done, achieve; **(sich zu s. machen mit)** to busy oneself with, tangle.

Schaffner, -, *n.m.* conductor.

Schaffnerin, -nen, *n.f.* conductor.

Schafott´, -e, *n.nt.* scaffold.

Schafskopf, ²e, *n.m.* idiot.

Schaft, ²e, *n.m.* shaft.

Schakal´, -e, *n.m.* jackal.

Schal, -s, *n.m.* shawl, scarf.

schal, *adj.* stale.

Schale, -n, *n.f.* skin, rind; shell; dish, bowl.

schälen, *vb.* pare, peel.

Schalk, ²e, *n.m.* rogue.

schalkhaft, *adj.* roguish.

Schall, ²e, *n.m.* sound, ring.

Schalldämpfer, -, *n.m.* (auto) muffler; (gun) silencer.

schallen*, *vb.* ring, resound.

Schallgrenze, -n, *n.f.* sound barrier.

Schallplatte, -n, *n.f.* phonograph record.

Schalot´te, -n, *n.f.* scallion.

Schaltanlage, -n, *n.f.* switchboard.

Schaltbrett, -er, *n.nt.* switchboard; control panel.

schalten, *vb.* shift; command; **(s. und walten)** do as one pleases.

Schalter, -, *n.m. (elec.)* switch; (ticket, etc.) window.

Schaltjahr, -e, *n.nt.* leap year.

Schaltung, -en, *n.f. (elec.)* connection; (auto) shift.

Scham, *n.f.* shame; chastity.

schämen, *vb.* shame; **(sich s.)** be ashamed.

Schamgefühl, -e, *n.nt.* sense of modesty.

schamhaft, *adj.* modest, chaste.

schamlos, *adj.* shameless, infamous.

Schamlosigkeit, *n.f.* shamelessness.

Schampun´, -s, *n.nt.* shampoo.

schandbar, *adj.* shameful, disgraceful.

Schande, *n.f.* shame, dishonor.

schänden, *vb.* dishonor, ravish.

Schandfleck, -e, *n.m.* blemish, stigma.

schändlich, *adj.* infamous.

Schandtat, -en, *n.f.* crime.

Schändung, -en, *n.f.* desecration; rape.

Schankstube, -n, *n.f.* barroom.

Schanze, -n, *n.f.* entrenchment; **(sein Leben in die S. schlagen*)** risk one's life.

Schar, -en, *n.f.* flock, group, host.

scharf (²), *adj.* sharp, acute, keen.

Scharfblick, *n.m.* quick eye; acuteness.

Schärfe, -n, *n.f.* sharpness, acuteness.

schärfen, *vb.* sharpen.

Scharfrichter, -, *n.m.* executioner.

Scharfsinn, *n.m.* acumen, discernment.

scharfsinnig, *adj.* acute, shrewd.

Scharlach, *n.m.* scarlet fever.

scharlachrot, *adj.* scarlet.

Scharnier´, -e, *n.nt.* hinge.

Schärpe, -n, *n.f.* sash.

Scharte, -n, *n.f.* crack.

Schatten, -, *n.m.* shade; shadow.

Schattenbild, -er, *n.nt.* silhouette.

Schattengestalt, -en, *n.f.* phantom, phantasm.

Schattenseite, -n, *n.f.* shady side; *(fig.)* disadvantage, drawback.

schattie´ren, *vb.* shade.

schattig, *adj.* shady.

Schatz, ²e, *n.m.* treasure.

schätzen, *vb.* treasure, prize; estimate, gauge; esteem.

schätzenswert, *adj.* estimable.

Schatzmeister, -, *n.m.* treasurer.

Schätzung, -en, *n.f.* estimate.

schätzungsweise, *adv.* approximately.

Schau, *n.f.* show, exhibition; **(zur S. tragen*)** display.

Schauder, -, *n.m.* shudder, shiver.

schauderhaft, *adj.* horrible, ghastly.

schaudern, *vb.* shudder.

schauen, *vb.* see, look.

Schauer, -, *n.m.* shower; (fever) chill.

schauerlich, *adj.* gruesome.

Schaufel, -n, *n.f.* shovel; dustpan.

Schaufenster, -, *n.nt.* store window, display window.

Schaukel, -n, *n.f.* swing.

schaukeln, *vb.* swing, rock.

Schaukelstuhl, ²e, *n.m.* rocking chair.

Schaum, *n.m.* froth, foam; lather.

schäumen, *vb.* froth, foam; lather.

Schaumgummi, *n.m.* foam rubber.

Schaumwein, -e, *n.m.* champagne.

Schauplatz, ²e, *n.m.* scene, theater, locale.

schaurig, *adj.* horrible.

Schauspiel, -e, *n.nt.* drama; spectacle.

Schauspieler, -, *n.m.* actor.

Schauspielerin, -nen, *n.f.* actress.

Schaustellung, *n.f.* exhibition; ostentation.

Scheck, -s, *n.m.* check.

scheel, *adj.* **(s. an•sehen*)** look askance at.

Scheffel, -, *n.m.* bushel.

Scheibe, -n, *n.f.* disk; slice; pane.

Scheibenwischer, -, *n.m.* windshield wiper.

Scheich, -e, *n.m.* sheikh.

Scheide, -n, *n.f.* sheath; (water) divide; vagina.

scheiden*, *vb.* leave, part; **(sich s. lassen*)** get divorced.

Scheidewand, ²e, *n.f.* partition.

Scheideweg, -e, *n.m.* crossroads.

Scheidung, -en, *n.f.* divorce.

Schein, *n.m.* shine, light, shimmer; brilliance.

scheinbar, *adj.* apparent; imaginary.

scheinen*, vb. shine; seem.

scheinheilig, adj. hypocritical.

Scheinwerfer, -, n.m. spotlight; headlight.

Scheinwerferlicht, n.nt. floodlight.

Scheitel, -, n.m. part (in the hair).

scheitern, vb. fail.

Schelle, -n, n.f. bell.

schellen, vb. ring.

Schelm, -e, n.m. rogue.

schelmisch, adj. roguish, mischievous.

Schelte, n.f. scolding.

schelten*, vb. scold.

Schema, -s, n.nt. scheme.

Schenke, -n, n.f. tavern, bar.

Schenkel, -, n.m. thigh.

schenken, vb. give (as a present).

Schenkstube, -n, n.f. taproom, bar.

Schenkung, -en, nf. donation.

Schere, -n, n.f. scissors, shears.

scheren*, vb. shear.

Schererei´, -en, n.f. bother.

Scherz, -e, n.m. joke, jest.

scherzen, vb. joke, jest, kid.

scherzhaft, adj. jocular.

scheu, adj. shy.

Scheu, n.f. timidity.

scheuchen, vb. scare, shoo.

scheuen, vb. shy, shun.

Scheuer, -n, n.f. barn, shed.

scheuern, vb. scour.

Scheuklappe, -n, n.f. blinder.

Scheune, -n, n.f. barn, shed.

Scheusal, -e, n.nt. monster, fright.

scheußlich, adj. horrible.

Schi, -er, n.m. ski.

Schicht, -en, n.f. layer, stratum, class.

schick, adj. chic, stylish.

Schick, n.m. skill; stylishness.

schicken, vb. send; (sich s.) be proper.

Schickeri´a, n.f. (slang) jet-set.

schicklich, adj. proper.

Schicksal, -e, n.nt. fate.

schicksalsschwer, adj. fateful.

Schickung, n.f. providence.

Schiebedach, n.nt. sun-roof.

schieben*, vb. push, shove; engage in illegal transactions.

Schieber, -, n.m. profiteer.

Schiebung, -en, n.f. racketeering.

Schiedsrichter, -, n.m. umpire, referee.

schief, adj. crooked, askew.

Schiefer, n.m. slate.

schielen, vb. be cross-eyed, look cross-eyed.

Schienbein, -e, n.nt. shin.

Schiene, -n, n.f. rail; (med.) splint.

schier, 1. adj. sheer, pure. **2.** adv. almost.

Schierling, n.m. hemlock.

schießen*, vb. shoot.

Schießgewehr, -e, n.nt. gun.

Schiff, -e, n.nt. ship; nave (of a church).

Schiffahrt, n.f. navigation.

schiffbar, adj. navigable.

Schiffbau, n.m. ship building.

Schiffbruch, ⁼e, n.m. shipwreck.

Schiffer, -, n.m. mariner.

Schiffsrumpf, ⁼e, n.m. hull.

schi•laufen*, vb. ski.

Schild, -e, n.m. shield.

Schild, -er, n.nt. sign.

Schilddrüse, -n, n.f. thyroid gland.

schildern, vb. portray.

Schilderung, -en, n.f. portrayal.

Schildkröte, -n, n.f. turtle, tortoise.

Schilf, n.nt. reed.

Schilift, -s, n.m. ski lift.

schillern, vb. be iridescent.

Schilling, -e, n.m. shilling.

Schimmel, -, n.m. mold, mildew; white horse.

schimmelig, adj. moldy.

Schimmer, -, n.m. glimmer, gleam.

Schimpan´se, -n, -n, n.m. chimpanzee.

Schimpf, -e, n.m. insult, abuse, disgrace.

schimpfen, vb. insult, abuse; complain, gripe.

Schimpfwort, -e, n.nt. term of abuse.

schinden*, vb. flay; (fig.) torment; (sich s.) work hard, slave.

Schinken, -, n.m. ham.

Schirm, -e, n.m. screen; umbrella, parasol; shelter.

schirmen, vb. protect.

Schirmherr, -n, -en, n.m. patron.

Schlacht, -en, n.f. battle.

schlachten, vb. slaughter.

Schlächter, -, n.m. butcher.

Schlachtfeld, -er, n.nt. battlefield.

Schlachtschiff, -e, n.nt. battleship.

Schlacke, -n, n.f. slag, clinker, cinder.

Schlaf, n.m. sleep.

Schlafanzug, ⁼e, n.m. pajamas.

Schläfe, -n, n.f. temple.

schlafen*, vb. sleep, be asleep.

Schlafenszeit, -en, n.f. bedtime.

schlaff, adj. limp.

Schlaffheit, n.f. limpness, laxity.

Schlaflosigkeit, n.f. insomnia.

Schlafmittel, -, n.nt. sleeping pill.

schläfrig, adj. sleepy.

Schlafrock, ⁼e, n.m. dressing gown.

Schlafwagen, -, n.m. sleeping car.

Schlafzimmer, -, n.nt. bedroom.

Schlag, ⁼e, n.m. blow, stroke, shock.

Schlagader, -n, n.f. artery.

Schlaganfall, ⁼e, n.m. stroke; apoplexy.

Schlagbaum, ⁼e, n.m. wooden bar, (railroad customs) barrier.

schlagen*, vb. hit, strike, beat; fell (trees); coin (money).

Schlager, -, n.m. hit (song, play, book).

Schläger, -, n.m. hitter; bat, club.

Schlägerei´, -en, n.f. brawl.

Schlagholz, ⁼er, n.nt. bat, club.

Schlagobers, *n.nt.* whipped cream.

Schlagsahne, *n.f.* whipped cream.

Schlagseite, *n.f.* list.

Schlagwort, -e, *n.nt.* slogan.

Schlagzeile, -n, *n.f.* headline.

Schlamm, *n.m.* muck, mud.

schlampig, *adj.* frowsy.

Schlange, -n, *n.f.* snake, serpent.

schlängeln, *vb.* **(sich s.)** wind, wriggle.

schlank, *adj.* slender, slim.

schlapp, *adj.* slack, flabby.

Schlappe, -n, *n.f.* rebuff, setback, defeat.

schlau, *adj.* sly, clever, astute.

Schlauch, ⸚e, *n.m.* hose, tube.

Schlaufe, -n, *n.f.* loop.

schlecht, *adj.* bad.

schlechterdings, *adv.* absolutely.

schlechthin, *adv.* quite, simply.

Schlegel, -, *n.m.* mallet, sledge hammer, drumstick.

schleichen*, *vb.* sneak, slink, crawl.

Schleier, -, *n.m.* veil.

schleierhaft, *adj.* veil-like; inexplicable, mysterious.

Schleife, -n, *n.f.* bow.

schleifen, *vb.* drag.

schleifen*, *vb.* grind, polish, sharpen.

Schleifmittel, -, *n.nt.* abrasive.

Schleifstein, -e, *n.m.* grindstone.

Schleim, *n.m.* slime; mucus.

Schleimhaut, ⸚e, *n.f.* mucous membrane.

schleimig, *adj.* slimy; mucous.

schlendern, *vb.* saunter, stroll.

schlenkern, *vb.* shamble, dangle, swing.

Schleppe, -n, *n.f.* train.

schleppen, *vb.* drag, lug, haul, tow.

Schlepper, -, *n.m.* tugboat, tractor.

Schleuder, -n, *n.f.* slingshot, catapult, centrifuge.

schleudern, *vb.* hurl, fling; skid.

schleunig, *adj.* speedy.

Schleuse, -n, *n.f.* sluice, lock.

Schlich, -e, *n.m.* trick.

schlicht, *adj.* plain, simple.

schlichten, *vb.* smooth; arbitrate.

Schlichter, -, *n.m.* arbitrator.

Schlichtung, -en, *n.f.* arbitration.

schließen*, *vb.* shut; close; conclude.

Schließfach, ⸚er, *n.nt.* baggage locker.

schließlich, 1. *adj.* final. **2.** *adv.* at last.

Schliff, -e, *n.m.* cut, polish(ing), grind(ing); good manners, style; **(letzter S.)** final touch.

schlimm, *adj.* bad, serious.

Schlinge, -n, *n.f.* sling, noose.

schlingen*, *vb.* twist, wind; gulp.

schlingern, *vb.* roll; *(fig.)* stagger.

Schlips, -e, *n.m.* necktie.

Schlitten, -, *n.m.* sled, sleigh.

Schlittschuh, -e, *n.m.* skate.

schlittschuh•laufen*, *vb.* skate.

Schlitz, -e, *n.m.* slit, slot, slash.

Schloß, ⸚sser, *n.nt.* lock; castle.

Schlot, -e, *n.m.* chimney, flue.

schlottern, *vb.* hang loosely, flop, shake.

Schlucht, -en, *n.f.* gorge, gulch.

schluchzen, *vb.* sob.

Schluck, -e, *n.m.* swallow.

Schluckauf, *n.m.* hiccup(s).

Schlückchen, -, *n.nt.* nip.

schlucken, *vb.* swallow.

Schlummer, *n.m.* slumber.

schlummern, *vb.* slumber.

Schlund, ⸚e, *n.m.* throat, gullet; chasm.

schlüpfen, *vb.* slip.

Schlüpfer, -, *n.m.* panties.

schlüpfrig, *adj.* slippery.

schlürfen, *vb.* sip.

Schluß, ⸚sse, *n.m.* end, close, conclusion.

Schlüssel, -, *n.m.* key.

Schlußfolgerung, -e, *n.f.* deduction, conclusion.

Schmach, *n.f.* disgrace, insult.

schmachten, *vb.* languish.

schmächtig, *adj.* slim, slight.

schmachvoll, *adj.* ignominious.

schmackhaft, *adj.* tasty.

schmähen, *vb.* abuse, revile.

schmal (-, ⸚), *adj.* narrow.

schmälern, *vb.* curtail, detract from.

Schmalz, *n.nt.* lard.

schmarotzen, *vb.* sponge (on).

Schmarot´zer, -, *n.m.* hanger-on; parasite.

schmatzen, *vb.* smack one's lips.

Schmaus, ⸚e, *n.m.* feast.

schmausen, *vb.* feast.

schmecken, *vb.* taste.

Schmeichelei´, -en, *n.f.* flattery.

schmeichelhaft, *adj.* flattering.

schmeicheln, *vb.* flatter.

schmeißen*, *vb.* throw, hurl, chuck, hit.

schmelzen*, *vb.* melt.

Schmerz, -en, *n.m.* ache, pain.

schmerzen, *vb.* ache, pain, hurt.

Schmerzgeld, *n.nt.* punitive damages.

schmerzhaft, *adj.* painful.

schmerzlos, *adj.* painless.

Schmetterling, -e, *n.m.* butterfly.

schmettern, *vb.* dash, smash; bray, blare.

Schmied, -e, *n.m.* blacksmith.

Schmiede, -n, *n.f.* forge.

schmieden, *vb.* forge.

schmiegen, *vb.* bend, press close, nestle, cling.

schmiegsam, *adj.* pliant, flexible.

Schmiere, -n, *n.f.* grease.

schmieren, *vb.* grease, smear, scribble; **(wie geschmiert´)** like clockwork.

schmierig, *adj.* greasy, dirty, sordid.

Schmiermittel, -, *n.nt.* lubricant.

Schminke, -n, *n.f.* rouge, make-up, grease paint.

schminken, *vb.* put on make-up.

Schmiß, -sse, *n.m.* stroke, cut; dueling scar; verve.

schmökern, *vb.* browse.

schmollen, *vb.* pout, sulk.

schmoren, *vb.* stew.

schmuck, *adj.* smart, trim.

Schmuck, *n.m.* ornament, jewelry.

schmücken, *vb.* decorate.

Schmucknadel, -n, *n.f.* clip.

Schmuggel, -, *n.m.* smuggling.

schmuggeln, *vb.* smuggle.

Schmuggelware, -n, *n.f.* contraband.

Schmuggler, -, *n.m.* smuggler.

schmunzeln, *vb.* smirk, grin.

schmusen, *vb.* cuddle, neck.

Schmutz, *n.m.* dirt, filth.

schmutzig, *adj.* dirty.

Schnabel, ∻, *n.m.* beak.

Schnake, -n, *n.f.* gnat.

Schnalle, -n, *n.f.* buckle, clasp.

schnallen, *vb.* buckle.

schnalzen, *vb.* click (one's tongue), snap (one's fingers), crack (a whip).

schnappen, *vb.* snap, snatch, grab, catch, gasp (for breath).

Schnappschuß, -sse, *n.m.* snapshot.

Schnaps, ∻, *n.m.* hard liquor, whisky, brandy.

schnarchen, *vb.* snore.

schnarren, *vb.* buzz, whir, rattle, burr.

schnattern, *vb.* cackle.

schnauben, *vb.* pant, snort.

schnaufen, *vb.* breathe hard.

Schnauze, -, *n.f.* snout.

Schnecke, -n, *n.f.* snail.

Schnee, *n.m.* snow.

Schneepflug, ∻e, *n.m.* snowplow.

Schneesturm, ∻e, *n.m.* blizzard.

Schneid, *n.m.* bravado.

Schneide, -n, *n.f.* edge.

schneiden*, *vb.* cut.

schneidend, *adj.* cutting, scathing.

Schneider, -, *n.m.* tailor.

Schneiderin, -nen, *n.f.* dressmaker.

schneidig, *adj.* dashing.

schneien, *vb.* snow.

schnell, *adj.* quick.

schnellen, *vb.* flip, jerk.

Schnelligkeit, -en, *n.f.* swiftness.

Schnellzug, ∻e, *n.m.* express train.

schneuzen, *vb.* (**sich s.**) blow one's nose.

schnippisch, *adj.* saucy.

Schnitt, -e, *n.m.* cut, slice, incision.

Schnittbohne, -n, *n.f.* string bean.

Schnitte, -n, *n.f.* slice, sandwich.

Schnittlauch, *n.m.* chive(s).

Schnittmuster, -, *n.nt.* pattern.

Schnittpunkt, -e, *n.m.* intersection.

Schnittstelle, -n, *f.* (computer) interface.

Schnittwaren, *n.pl.* dry goods.

Schnittwunde, -n, *n.f.* cut.

Schnitzel, -, *n.nt.* chip; cutlet.

schnitzen, *vb.* carve, whittle.

Schnitzwerk, -e, *n.nt.* carving.

schnodd(e)rig, *adj.* insolent.

schnöde, *adj.* scornful, base.

Schnorchel, -, *n.m.* snorkel.

schnüffeln, *vb.* sniffle, snoop.

Schnuller, -, *n.m.* pacifier.

Schnupfen, -, *n.m.* cold (in the head).

Schnupftuch, ∻er, *n.nt.* handkerchief.

Schnuppe, -n, *n.f.* shooting star; (**das ist mir S.**) I don't care a hoot.

Schnur, ∻e, *n.f.* cord, string.

schnüren, *vb.* lace.

Schnurrbart, ∻e, *n.m.* mustache.

Schnürsenkel, -, *n.m.* shoelace.

Schock, -s, *n.m.* shock.

schockieren, *vb.* shock.

schofel(ig), *adj.* shabby, mean.

Schokolade, -n, *n.f.* chocolate.

Scholle, -n, *n.f.* clod, soil.

schon, *adv.* already; even.

schön, *adj.* beautiful, nice.

schonen, *vb.* treat carefully, spare.

Schönheit, -en, *n.f.* beauty.

Schönheitssalon, -s, *n.m.* beauty parlor.

Schonung, -en, *n.f.* careful treatment, consideration.

schonungslos, *adj.* merciless.

Schopf, ∻e, *n.m.* forelock, crown.

schöpfen, *vb.* draw (water, breath); take from.

Schöpfer, *n.m.* creator.

schöpferisch, *adj.* creative.

Schöpfkelle, -n, *n.f.* scoop.

Schöpflöffel, -, *n.m.* ladle, dipper.

Schöpfung, *n.f.* creation.

Schoppen, -, *n.m.* glass of beer or wine; pint.

Schorf, *n.m.* scab.

Schornstein, -e, *n.m.* chimney, smokestack.

Schoß, ∻e, *n.m.* lap.

Schößling, -e, *n.m.* shoot.

Schote, -n, *n.f.* pod.

Schotte, -n, -n, *n.m.* Scotsman.

Schottin, -nen, *n.f.* Scotswoman.

schottisch, *adj.* Scotch.

Schottland, *n.nt.* Scotland.

schräg, *adj.* oblique.

Schrägschrift, *n.f.* italics.

Schramme, -n, *n.f.* scratch.

Schrank, ∻e, *n.m.* wardrobe, locker, cupboard, cabinet.

Schranke, -n, *n.f.* barrier.

Schrapnell, -s, *n.nt.* shrapnel.

Schraube, -n, *n.f.* screw.

schrauben, *vb.* screw.

Schraubenschlüssel, -, *n.m.* wrench.

Schraubenzieher, -, *n.m.* screwdriver.

Schreck, -e, *n.m.* fright, scare.

schrecken*, *vb.* frighten.

Schrecken, -, *n.m.* terror, fear.

schreckhaft, *adj.* easily frightened.

schrecklich, *adj.* awful, terrible.

Schrei, -e, *n.m.* cry, scream, shout.

schreiben*, *vb.* write.

Schreiben, -, *n.nt.* letter.

Schreiber, -, *n.m.* clerk, scribe.

Schreibheft, -e, *n.nt.* notebook.

Schreibkraft, =e, *n.f.* typist; clerk.

Schreibmaschine, -n, *n.f.* typewriter.

Schreibtisch, -e, *n.m.* desk.

Schreibung, -en, *n.f.* spelling.

Schreibwaren, *n.pl.* stationery.

schreien*, *vb.* cry, scream, shout.

schreiend, *adj.* flagrant.

Schrein, -e, *n.m.* shrine, casket, cabinet.

schreiten*, *vb.* stride, step.

Schrift, -en, *n.f.* writing, script; (Heilige S.) scripture(s).

Schriftführer, -, *n.m.* secretary (of an organization).

schriftlich, *adj.* written, in writing.

Schriftsatz, =e, *n.m.* type.

Schriftsteller, -, *n.m.* writer, author.

Schriftstellerin, -nen, *n.f.* writer, author.

schrill, *adj.* shrill.

Schritt, -e, *n.m.* step, pace; crotch (of trousers).

schroff, *adj.* steep, abrupt, curt.

Schrotmehl, *n.m.* coarse meal, grits.

schrubbe(r)n, *vb.* scrub.

Schrulle, -n, *n.f.* whim.

schrumpfen, *vb.* shrink.

Schub, =e, *n.m.* shove, thrust; batch.

Schublade, -n, *n.f.* drawer.

Schubschiff, -e, *n.nt.* tugboat.

schüchtern, *adj.* shy, bashful.

Schüchternheit, -en, *nf.* bashfulness, shyness.

Schuft, -e, *n.m.* cad, scoundrel.

schuften, *vb.* work hard, drudge.

schuftig, *adj.* mean, shabby.

Schuh, -e, *n.m.* shoe.

Schuhmacher, -, *n.m.* shoemaker.

Schuhmacherin, -nen, *n.f.* shoemaker.

Schuhputzer, -, *n.m.* bootblack.

Schuhwerk, -e, *n.nt.* footwear.

Schularbeiten, *n.pl.* homework.

Schulbeispiel, -e, *n.nt.* typical example.

Schuld, -en, *n.f.* fault, guilt, blame, debt.

schulden, *vb.* owe.

schuldhaft, *adj.* culpable.

schuldig, *adj.* guilty; due, owing.

Schuldigkeit, *n.f.* duty.

Schuldigsprechung, -en, *n.f.* conviction.

Schuldirektor, -en, *n.m.* headmaster, principal.

Schuldirekto'rin, -nen, *n.f.* headmistress, principal.

schuldlos, *adj.* guiltless.

Schuldner, -, *n.m.* debtor.

Schuldnerin, -nen, *n.f.* debtor.

Schule, -n, *n.f.* school.

schulen, *vb.* train, indoctrinate.

Schüler, -, *n.m.* (boy) pupil.

Schülerin, -nen, *n.f.* (girl) pupil.

Schulgeld, -er, *n.nt.* tuition.

Schulter, -n, *n.f.* shoulder.

schultern, *vb.* shoulder.

schummeln, *vb.* cheat.

Schund, *n.m.* trash.

Schupo, -s, *n.m.* (= Schutzpolizist) cop.

Schuppe, -n, *n.f.* scale; (pl.) dandruff.

Schuppen, -, *n.m.* shed, hangar.

schüren, *vb.* poke, stir up, foment.

Schurke, -n, -n, *n.m.* villain, scoundrel.

Schürze, -n, *n.f.* apron.

Schuß, =sse, *n.m.* shot.

Schüssel, -n, *n.f.* dish, bowl.

schustern, *vb.* repair shoes.

Schuster, -, *n.m.* shoemaker.

Schutt, *n.m.* rubbish.

schütteln, *vb.* shake.

schütten, *vb.* shed, pour.

Schutz, *n.m.* protection.

Schütze, -n, -n, *n.m.* rifleman, marksman, shot.

schützen, *vb.* protect.

Schutzengel, -, *n.m.* guardian angel.

Schützengraben, =, *n.m.* trench, dugout.

Schutzhaft, *n.f.* protective custody.

Schutzheilig-, *n.m. & f.* patron saint.

Schutzherr, -n, -en, *n.m.* patron.

schutzlos, *adj.* unprotected, defenseless.

Schutzmann, =er, *n.m.* patrolman.

Schutzmarke, -n, *n.f.* trade mark.

schwach (=), *adj.* weak.

Schwäche, -n, *n.f.* weakness.

schwächen, *vb.* weaken.

Schwachheit, -en, *n.f.* frailty.

schwächlich, *adj.* feeble.

Schwächling, -e, *n.m.* weakling.

Schwachsinn, *n.m.* feeblemindedness.

schwachsinnig, *adj.* feebleminded.

Schwager, =r, *n.m.* brother-in-law.

Schwägerin, -nen, *n.f.* sister-in-law.

Schwalbe, -n, *n.f.* swallow.

Schwall, -e, *n.m.* flood.

Schwamm, =e, *n.m.* sponge.

Schwan, =e, *n.m.* swan.

schwanger, *adj.* pregnant.

Schwangerschaft, -en, *n.f.* pregnancy.

Schwangerschaftsverhütung, *n.f.* contraception.

schwankern, *vb.* totter, sway, vacillate, waver.

Schwankung, -en, *n.f.* fluctuation.

Schwanz, =e, *n.m.* tail.

schwänzen, *vb.* cut (a class).

Schwarm, =e, *n.m.* swarm.

schwärmen, vb. swarm; (s. für) be crazy about.

Schwärmer, -, n.m. enthusiast.

schwarz(⸚), adj. black; illegal.

Schwarz-, n. m. & f. Black (person).

Schwarzbrot, -e, n.nt. black bread.

schwärzen, vb. blacken.

Schwarzmarkt, ⸚e, n.m. black market.

Schwarzseher, -, n.m. alarmist, pessimist.

schwatzen, schwätzen, vb. chatter, gab.

Schwebe, n.f. suspense, suspension; (in der S.) undecided.

schweben, vb. hover, be suspended, be pending.

Schwebezustand, ⸚e, n.m. abeyance.

Schwede, -n, -n, n.m. Swede.

Schweden, n.nt. Sweden.

Schwedin, -nen, n.f. Swede.

schwedisch, adj. Swedish.

Schwefel, n.m. sulphur.

Schweif, -e, n.m. tail, train.

schweifen, vb. roam, range.

schweigen*, vb. keep quiet, be silent.

Schweigen, n.nt. silence.

schweigsam, adj. silent.

Schwein, -e, n.nt. swine, hog, pig; good luck.

Schweinebraten, -, n.m. roast of pork.

Schweinefleisch, n.nt. pork.

Schweinerei´, -en, n.f. awful mess, dirty business.

Schweinestall, ⸚e, n.m. pigsty.

Schweinsleder, n.nt. pigskin.

Schweiß, n.m. sweat.

Schweiz, n.f. Switzerland.

Schweizer, -, n.m. Swiss.

Schweizerin, -nen, n.f. Swiss.

schweizerisch, adj. Swiss.

schwelen, vb. smolder.

schwelgen, vb. revel.

Schwelgerei´, -en, n.f. revelry.

Schwelle, -n, n.f. sill, threshold; (railroad) tie.

schwellen*, vb. swell.

schwenken, vb. wave, flourish, brandish.

schwer, adj. heavy; difficult.

Schwere, n.f. heaviness.

schwerf ällig, adj. clumsy, ponderous, stolid.

Schwergewicht, n.nt. heavyweight.

schwerhörig, adj. hard of hearing.

Schwerkraft, n.f. gravity.

schwerlich, adj. with difficulty, hardly.

Schwermut, n.f. melancholy.

schwermütig, adj. moody, melancholy.

Schwerpunkt, n.m. center of gravity; emphasis.

Schwert, -er, n.nt. sword; centerboard.

schwerwiegend, adj. grave.

Schwester, -n, n.f. sister; nurse.

Schwiegereltern, n.pl. parents-in-law.

Schwiegermutter, ⸚, n.f. mother-in-law.

Schwiegersohn, ⸚e, n.m. son-in-law.

Schwiegertochter, ⸚, n.f. daughter-in-law.

Schwiegervater, ⸚, n.m. father-in-law.

Schwiele, -n, n.f. callous, weal.

schwielig, adj. callous.

schwierig, adj. difficult.

Schwierigkeit, -en, n.f. difficulty, trouble.

Schwimmbad, ⸚er, n.nt. swimming pool.

schwimmen*, vb. swim.

Schwimmweste, -n, n.f. life-jacket.

Schwindel, -, n.m. dizziness; swindle, hoax; bunk.

Schwindelgefühl, n.nt. vertigo.

schwindeln, vb. swindle, cheat, fraud.

schwinden*, vb. disappear.

Schwindler, -, n.m. swindler, cheat, fraud.

schwindlig, adj. dizzy.

Schwindsucht, n.f. consumption.

schwindsüchtig, adj. consumptive.

schwingen*, vb. swing, brandish, oscillate.

Schwingung, -en, n.f. oscillation.

Schwips, n.m. (einen S. haben*) be tipsy.

schwirren, vb. whir.

schwitzen, vb. sweat.

schwören*, vb. swear.

schwul, adj. homosexual.

schwül, adj. sultry, muggy.

Schwulst, ⸚e, n.m. bombast.

Schwund, n.m. disappearance, loss.

Schwung, ⸚e, n.m. swing, verve, animation, motion.

Schwungkraft, n.f. drive.

schwunglos, adj. lackadaisical.

schwungvoll, adj. spirited.

Schwur, ⸚e, n.m. oath.

sechs, num. six.

sechst-, adj. sixth.

Sechstel, -, n.nt. sixth part; (ein s.) one-sixth.

sechzig, num. sixty.

sechzigst-, adj. sixtieth.

Sechzigstel, -, n.nt. sixtieth part; (ein s.) one-sixtieth.

See, Se´en, n.m. lake.

See, Se´en, n.f. sea.

See-, cpds. naval, marine.

Seegang, n.m. (rough, calm) sea.

Seehund, -e, n.m. seal.

seekrank, adj. seasick.

Seekrankheit, n.f. seasickness.

Seele, -n, n.f. soul, spirit, mind.

Seeleute, n.pl. seamen.

seelisch, adj. spiritual.

Seelsorge, n.f. ministry.

Seemann, -leute, n.m. mariner.

Seemeile, -n, n.f. nautical mile.

Seeräuber, -, n.m. pirate.

Seereise, -n, n.f. cruise.

Seetang, n.m. seaweed.

seetüchtig, adj. seaworthy.

Seezunge, -n, n.f. sole.

Segel, -, n.nt. sail.

Segelboot, -e, n.nt. sailboat.

Segelflug, n.m. gliding.

Segelflugzeug, -e, n.nt. glider, sailplane.

segeln, vb. sail.

Segeltuch, *n.nt.* canvas, duck.

Segen, -, *n.m.* blessing.

Segment´, -e, *n.nt.* segment.

segnen, *vb.* bless.

Segnung, -en, *n.f.* blessing, benediction.

sehen*, *vb.* see.

sehenswert, *adj.* worth seeing.

Sehenswürdigkeit, -en, *n.f.* sight(s).

Seher, -, *n.m.* seer, prophet.

Sehkraft, ⸚e, *n.f.* (power of) sight, vision.

Sehne, -n, *n.f.* tendon, ligament, sinew.

sehnen, *vb.* (sich s.) long, yearn.

Sehnsucht, *n.f.* longing.

sehnsüchtig, *adj.* longing.

sehnsuchtsvoll, *adj.* longing.

sehr, *adv.* very, much, a lot.

Sehweite, -n, *n.f.* range of sight.

seicht, *adj.* shallow, insipid.

Seide, -n, *n.f.* silk.

Seidel, -, *n.nt.* beer mug.

seiden, *adj.* silk.

Seidenpapier, *n.nt.* tissue paper.

seidig, *adj.* silky.

Seife, -n, *n.f.* soap.

Seifenschaum, *n.m.* suds.

seihen, *vb.* strain.

Seil, -e, *n.nt.* rope, cable.

Seilbahn, -en, *n.f.* cableway.

sein*, *vb.* be.

sein, -, -e, *adj.* his, its.

Sein, *n.nt.* being.

seiner, -es, -e, *pron.* his, its.

seinerseits, *adv.* for his part.

seinerzeit, *adv.* at the time.

seinesgleichen, *pron.* equal to him, such as he.

seinetwegen, *adv.* for his sake; for all he cares.

seinetwillen, *adv.* (um s.) for his sake, because of him.

seit, 1. *prep.* since, for. 2. *conj.* since.

seitab´, *adv.* aside.

seitdem, 1. *conj.* since. 2. *adv.* since then.

Seite, -n, *n.f.* side; page.

seitenlang, *adj.* going on for pages.

seitens, *prep.* on behalf of.

Seitensprung, ⸚e, *n.m.* escapade.

Seitenstraße, -n, *n.f.* side street.

Seitenzahl, -en, *n.f.* number of pages.

seither, *adv.* since then.

seitlich, *adj.* lateral.

seitwärts, *adv.* sideways.

Sekretär´, -e, *n.m.* secretary.

Sekretä´rin, -nen, *n.f.* secretary.

Sekt, -e, *n.m.* champagne.

Sekte, -n, *n.f.* sect, denomination.

Sekundant´, -en, -en, *n.m.* second (at a duel).

sekundär´, *adj.* secondary.

Sekun´de, -n, *n.f.* second.

selb-, *adj.* same.

selber, *adv.* (my-, your-, him-, etc.) self; (our-, your-, them-)selves.

selbst, *adv.* even; (my-, your-, him-, etc.) self; (our-, your-, them-) selves.

Selbstachtung, *n.f.* self-respect.

selbständig, *adj.* independent.

Selbständigkeit, *n.f.* independence.

Selbstbeherrschung, *n.f.* self-control.

Selbstbestimmung, *n.f.* self-determination.

selbstbewußt, *adj.* self-conscious.

Selbstbiographie, -n, autobiography.

selbstgefällig, *adj.* self-satisfied, smug.

selbstgefertigt, *adj.* home-made.

selbstgerecht, *adj.* self-righteous.

Selbstgespräch, -e, *n.nt.* monologue.

selbstlos, *adj.* unselfish.

Selbstmord, -e, *n.m.* suicide.

selbstredend, *adj.* self-evident.

selbstsicher, *adj.* self-confident.

Selbstsucht, *n.f.* selfishness.

selbstsüchtig, *adj.* selfish.

selbsttätig, *adj.* automatic.

selbstverständlich, *adj.* obvious.

Selbstverwaltung, *n.f.* home rule.

selbstzufrieden, *adj.* complacent.

Selbstzufriedenheit, *n.f.* complacency.

selig, *adj.* blessed; blissfully happy; deceased, late.

Seligkeit, -en, *n.f.* salvation, bliss.

selig•sprechen*, *vb.* beatify.

Sellerie, *n.m.* celery.

selten, 1. *adj.* rare, scarce. 2. *adv.* seldom.

Seltenheit, -en, *n.f.* rarity.

Selters, Selter(s)wasser, *n.nt.* soda water.

seltsam, *adj.* strange, queer, curious.

Seman´tik, *n.f.* semantics.

seman´tisch, *adj.* semantic.

Semes´ter, -, *n.nt.* semester, term.

Semiko´lon, -s, *n.nt.* semicolon.

Seminar´, -e, *n.nt.* seminar(y).

Semit´, -en, -en, *n.m.* Semite.

semi´tisch, *adj.* Semitic.

Semmel, -n, *n.f.* roll.

Senat´, -e, *n.m.* senate.

Sena´tor, -o´ren, *n.m.* senator.

senden*, *vb.* send, ship.

senden, *vb.* broadcast.

Sender, -, *n.m.* sender, transmitter, broadcasting station.

Sendung, -en, *n.f.* shipment; broadcast, transmission.

Senf, *n.m.* mustard.

sengen, *vb.* scorch, singe.

Senior, -o´ren, *n.m.* senior citizen.

senken, *vb.* sink, lower, reduce.

senkrecht, *adj.* perpendicular.

Senkung, -en, *n.f.* depression, reduction.

Sensation´, -en, *n.f.* sensation, thrill.

sensationell´, *adj.* sensational.

Sense, -n, *n.f.* scythe.

sensi´bel, *adj.* sensitive.

sentimental´, *adj.* sentimental.

Septem´ber, -, *n.m.* September.

Serbe, -n, -n, *n.m.* Serbian.

Serbien, *n.nt.* Serbia.

Serbin, -nen, *n.f.* Serbian.

serbisch, *adj.* Serbian.

Serie, -n, *n.f.* series.

Serum, -ra, *n.nt.* serum.

Servi´ce, *n.nt.* service, set.

servie´ren, *vb.* serve.

Servier´platte, -n, *n.f.* platter.

Serviet´te, -n, *n.f.* napkin.

Sessel, -, *n.m.* easy-chair.

seßhaft, *adj.* settled, established.

setzen, *vb.* set, put, place; **(sich s.)** sit down.

Seuche, -n, *n.f.* plague, epidemic.

seufzen, *vb.* sigh.

Seufzer, -, *n.m.* sigh.

sexuell´, *adj.* sexual.

Siam, *n.nt.* Siam.

Siame´se, -n, -n, *n.m.* Siamese.z

siame´sisch, *adj.* Siamese.

Sibi´rien, *n.nt.* Siberia.

sich, *pron.* (him-, her-, it-, your-)self, (them-, your-)selves; each other, one another.

Sichel, -n, *n.f.* sickle; crescent.

sicher, *adj.* sure, certain, safe, secure.

Sicherheit, -en, *n.f.* safety, security, certainty.

Sicherheitsnadel, -n, *n.f.* safety-pin.

sicherlich, *adv.* surely.

sichern, *vb.* secure, safeguard.

Sicherung, -en, *n.f.* fuse.

Sicht, *n.f.* sight.

sichtbar, *adj.* visible.

sichten, *vb.* sift; sight.

sickern, *vb.* seep.

sie, *pron.* she; they.

Sie, *pron.* you (normal polite).

Sieb, -e, *n.nt.* sieve, strainer.

sieben, *vb.* sift, strain.

sieben, *num.* seven.

sieb(en)t-, *adj.* seventh.

Sieb(en)tel,-, *n.nt.* seventh part; **(ein s.)** one-seventh.

siebzig, *num.* seventy.

siebzigst-, *adj.* seventieth.

Siebzigstel, -, *n.nt.* seventieth part; **(ein s.)** one-seventieth.

siedeln, *vb.* settle.

sieden*, *vb.* boil.

Siedler, -, *n.m.* settler.

Siedlerin, -nen, *n.f.* settler.

Siedlung, -en, *n.f.* settlement.

Sieg, -e, *n.m.* victory.

Siegel, -, *n.nt.* seal.

siegeln, *vb.* seal.

siegen, *vb.* win, be victorious.

Sieger, -, *n.m.* winner, victor.

sieghaft, *adj.* triumphant.

siegreich, *adj.* victorious.

Signal´, -e, *n.nt.* signal.

Signal´horn, =er, *n.nt.* bugle.

Silbe, -n, *n.f.* syllable.

Silber, *n.nt.* silver.

silbern, *adj.* silver.

Silberwaren, *n.f.* silverware.

silbisch, *adj.* syllabic.

silbrig, *adj.* silvery.

Silves´ter, *n.nt.* New Year's Eve.

Sims, -e, *n.m.* cornice; ledge, sill, mantelpiece.

singen*, *vb.* sing.

Singular, -e, *n.m.* singular.

sinken*, *vb.* sink, decline, fall.

Sinn, -e, *n.m.* sense, mind, meaning, taste.

Sinnbild, -er, *n.nt.* symbol.

sinnen*, *vb.* think, meditate, plot.

sinnig, *adj.* thoughtful, appropriate.

sinnlich, *adj.* sensual.

sinnlos, *adj.* senseless.

Sintflut, *n.f.* flood, deluge.

Sippe, -n, *n.f.* kin; clan, tribe.

Sire´ne, -n, *n.f.* siren.

Sirup, -e, *n.m.* molasses; syrup.

Sitte, -n, *n.f.* custom; (*pl.*) mores, manners, morals.

Sittenlehre, -n, *n.f.* ethics.

sittenlos, *adj.* immoral.

sittig, *adj.* chaste, well-bred.

sittlich, *adj.* moral.

Situation´, -en, *n.f.* situation.

Sitz, -e, *n.m.* seat, residence.

sitzen*, *vb.* sit, be seated; fit; be in jail.

sitzen•bleiben*, *vb.* remain seated; get stuck (with); not be promoted.

sitzen•lassen*, *vb.* jilt.

Sitzplatz, =e, *n.m.* seat.

Sitzung, -en, *n.f.* session.

Sizilia´ner, -, *n.m.* Sicilian.

Sizilia´nerin, -nen, *n.f.* Sicilian.

sizilia´nisch, *adj.* Sicilian.

Sizi´lien, *n.nt.* Sicily.

Skala, -len, *n.f.* scale.

Skandal´, -e, *n.m.* scandal.

Skandina´vien, *n.nt.* Scandinavia.

Skandina´vier, -, *n.m.* Scandinavian.

Skandina´vierin, -nen, *n.f.* Scandinavian.

skandina´visch, *adj.* Scandinavian.

Skelett´, -e, *n.nt.* skeleton.

Skepsis, *n.f.* skepticism.

Skeptiker, -, *n.m.* skeptic.

skeptisch, *adj.* skeptic(al).

Ski, -er, *n.m.* ski.

ski•laufen*, *vb.* ski.

Skilehrer, -, *n.m.* ski instructor.

Skilehrerin, -nen, *n.f.* ski instructor.

Skilift, -s, *n.m.* ski lift.

Skizze, -n, *n.f.* sketch.

skizzie´ren, *vb.* sketch.

Sklave, -n, -n, *n.m.* slave.

Sklaverei´, *n.f.* slavery.

Sklavin, -nen, *n.f.* slave.

Skrupel, -, *n.m.* scruple.

skrupellos, *adj.* unscrupulous.

Slang, *n.m.* slang.

Slawe, -n, -n, *n.m.* Slav.

slawisch, *adj.* Slavic.

Slowa´ke, -n, -n, *n.m.* Slovak.

Slowakei´, *n.f.* Slovakia.

Slowa´kin, -nen, *n.f.* Slovak.

slowa´kisch, *adj.* Slovakian.

Smaragd´, -e, *n.m.* emerald.

Smoking, -s, *n.m.* dinner jacket, tuxedo.

Snob, -s, *n.m.* snob.

so, *adv.* so, thus; **(s. groß wie)** as big as.

Socke, -n, *n.f.* sock.

Sockenhalter, -, *n.m.* garter.

Soda, *n.nt.* soda.

Sodbrennen, *n.nt.* heartburn.

soe´ben, *adv.* just now.

Sofa, -s, *n.nt.* sofa.

sofort´, *adv.* immediately.

sofor´tig, *adj.* instantaneous.

Software, *n.f.* software.

Sog, *n.m.* suction; undertow.

sogar´, *adv.* yet, even.

sogenannt, *adj.* so-called.

Sohle, -n, *n.f.* sole.

Sohn, ⸚e, *n.m.* son.

solch(er, -es, -e), *adj.* such.

solcherlei, *adj.* of such a kind.

solchermaßen, *adv.* in such a way.

Sold, -e, *n.m.* pay.

Soldat´, -en, -en, *n.m.* soldier.

solid´, *adj.* solid.

Solidarität´, *n.f.* solidarity.

Solist´, -en, -en, *n.m.* soloist.

Solis´tin, -nen, *n.f.* soloist.

Soll, *n.nt.* debit; quota.

sollen*, *vb.* be supposed to, be said to; shall; **(er sollte gehen*)** he should, ought to go; **(er hätte gehen* sollen)** he should, ought to have gone.

Solo, -s, *n.nt.* solo.

Sommer, -, *n.m.* summer.

Sommersprosse, -n, *n.f.* freckle.

Sommerzeit, -en, *n.f.* summer time; daylight-saving time.

Sona´te, -n, *n.f.* sonata.

Sonde, -n, *n.f.* probe.

sonder, *prep.* without.

Sonder-, *cpds.* special.

Sonderangebot, -e, *n.nt.* bargain, special sale.

sonderbar, *adj.* strange, queer.

sonderbarerwei´se, *adv.* strange to say.

sonderglei´chen, *adv.* without equal, unparalleled.

sonderlich, *adj.* peculiar.

sondern, *vb.* separate.

sondern, *conj.* but (on the contrary).

sondie´ren, *vb.* sound, probe.

Sonett´, -e, *n.nt.* sonnet.

Sonnabend, -e, *n.m.* Saturday.

Sonne, -n, *n.f.* sun.

sonnen, *vb.* **(sich s.)** sun oneself, bask.

Sonnenbrand, ⸚e, *n.m.* sunburn.

Sonnenbräune, *n.f.* sun tan.

sonnenklar, *adj.* clear as daylight.

Sonnenschein, *n.m.* sunshine.

Sonnenstich, -e, *n.m.* sun stroke.

sonnenverbrannt, *adj.* sunburned.

sonnig, *adj.* sunny.

Sonntag, -e, *n.m.* Sunday.

sonst, *adv.* otherwise, else; formerly.

sonstig, *adj.* other; former.

sonstwie, *adv.* in some other way.

sonstwo, *adv.* somewhere else.

sonstwoher, *adv.* from some other place.

sonstwohin, *adv.* to some other place.

Sopran´, -e, *n.m.* soprano.

Sorbett´, -e, *n.nt.* sherbet.

Sorge, -n, *n.f.* sorrow; worry, anxiety, apprehension; care.

sorgen, *vb.* **(s. für)** care for, provide; **(sich s.)** worry, concern oneself.

sorgenfrei, *adj.* carefree.

sorgenvoll, *adj.* worried, care-worn.

Sorgfalt, *n.f.* care.

sorgfältig, *adj.* careful, meticulous.

sorglos, *adj.* carefree.

sorgsam, *adj.* careful, painstaking.

Sorte, -n, *n.f.* sort, kind.

sortie´ren, *vb.* sort, assort, classify.

Soße, -n, *n.f.* sauce, gravy.

souverän, *adj.* sovereign.

Souveränität´, *n.f.* sovereignty.

soviel, *adv.* so much, as much.

sowie´, *conj.* as well as; as soon as.

sowieso, *adv.* in any case.

Sowjet, -s, *n.m.* Soviet.

sowje´tisch, *adj.* Soviet.

Sowjetunion, *n.f.* Soviet Union.

sowohl, *adv.* as well; **(s. A als B, s. A wie B)** both A and B.

sozial´, *adj.* social.

sozialisie´ren, *vb.* socialize, nationalize.

Sozialis´mus, *n.m.* socialism.

Sozialist´, -en, -en, *n.m.* socialist.

Sozialis´tin, -nen, *n.f.* socialist.

sozialis´tisch, *adj.* socialistic.

Soziologie´, *n.f.* sociology.

sozusagen, *adv.* as it were, so to speak.

Spaghet´ti, *n.pl.* spaghetti.

Spalt, -e, *n.m.* crack, chink.

spaltbar, *adj.* fissionable.

Spalte, -n, *n.f.* crevice, gap; (newspaper) column.

spalten, *vb.* split.

Spaltung, -en, *n.f.* cleavage; fission.

Spange, -n, *n.f.* clasp, buckle.

Spanien, *n.nt.* Spain.

Spanier, -, *n.m.* Spaniard.

Spanierin, -nen, *n.f.* Spaniard.

spanisch, *adj.* Spanish.

Spann, -e, *n.m.* arch, instep.

Spanne, -n, *n.f.* span.

spannen, *vb.* stretch; tighten.

spannend, *adj.* exciting, gripping.

Spannkraft, *n.f.* elasticity; *(fig.)* energy.

Spannung, -en, *n.f.* tension; *(fig.)* close attention, suspense.

sparen, *vb.* save.

Spargel, -, *n.m.* asparagus.

Sparkasse, -n, *n.f.* savings bank.

spärlich, *adj.* sparse, meager.

Sparren, -, *n.m.* spar, rafter.

sparsam, *adj.* thrifty, economical.

Sparsamkeit, *n.f.* thrift.

Spaß, ⸚e, *n.m.* joke, fun.

spaßeshalber, *adv.* for the fun of it.

spaßig, *adj.* funny.

Spaßmacher, -, *n.m.* jester.

spät, *adj.* late.

Spaten, -, *n.m.* spade.

spätestens, *adv.* at the latest.

Spatz, -en, -en, *n.m.* sparrow.

spazie´ren•gehen*, *vb.* go for a walk, stroll.

Spazier´fahrt, -en, *n.f.* drive.

Spazier´gang, ≃, *n.m.* walk.

Specht, -e, *n.m.* woodpecker.

Speck, *n.m.* fat; bacon.

spedie´ren, *vb.* dispatch.

Spediteur´, -e, *n.m.* shipping agent.

Speer, -e, *n.m.* spear; javelin.

Speiche, -n, *n.f.* spoke.

Speichel, *n.m.* saliva.

Speicher, -, *n.m.* loft, storage place.

speien*, *vb.* spit.

Speise, -n, *n.f.* food, nourishment.

Speisekammer, -n, *n.f.* pantry.

Speisekarte, -n, *n.f.* bill of fare, menu.

speisen, *vb. (tr.)* feed; *(intr.)* eat.

Speiseröhre, -n, *n.f.* esophagus.

Speisewagen, -, *n.m.* diner, dining-car.

Speisezettel, -, *n.m.* menu.

Speisung, -en, *n.f.* feeding.

Spekta´kel, *n.m.* noise, racket.

spekulie´ren, *vb.* speculate.

spenda´bel, *adj.* free and easy with money; **(s. sein*)** splurge.

Spende, -n, *n.f.* donation.

spenden, *vb.* give; donate.

Sperling, -e, *n.m.* sparrow.

Sperre, -n, *n.f.* barrier, blockade; gate.

sperren, *vb.* block, obstruct, blockade; (money) freeze.

Sperrfeuer, -, *n.nt.* barrage.

Sperrstunde, -n, *n.f.* curfew.

Spesen, *n.pl.* charges, expenses, **(auf S.)** on an expense account.

spezialisie´ren, *vb.* specialize.

Spezialist´, -en, -en, *n.m.* specialist.

Spezialis´tin, -en, *n.f.* specialist.

Spezialität´, -en, *n.f.* specialty.

speziell´, *adj.* special, specific.

spezi´fisch, *adj.* specific.

spezifizie´ren, *vb.* specify.

Sphäre, -n, *n.f.* sphere.

Sphinx, -en, *n.f.* sphinx.

spicken, *vb.* lard, interlard.

Spiegel, -, *n.m.* mirror.

spiegeln, *vb.* mirror, reflect.

Spiegelung, -en, *n.f.* reflection.

Spiel, -e, *n.nt.* play, game; gambling; pack (of cards).

Spielbank, -en, *n.f.* gambling casino.

spielen, *vb.* play, act; **(um Geld s.)** gamble.

Spieler, -, *n.m.* player.

Spielerin, -nen, *n.f.* player.

spielerisch, *adj.* playful.

Spielgef ährte, -n, -n, *n.m.* playmate.

Spielgefährtin, -nen, *n.f.* playmate.

Spielplatz, ≃e, *n.m.* playground.

Spielraum, ≃, *n.m.* room for action, range; elbow room; margin.

Spielverderber, -, *n.m.* spoilsport.

Spielwaren, *n.pl.* toys.

Spielzeug, -e, *n.nt.* toy.

Spieß, -e, *n.m.* spear; top sergeant.

Spinat´, *n.m.* spinach.

Spindel, -n, *n.f.* spindle.

Spinett´, -e, *n.nt.* spinet, harpsichord.

Spinne, -n, *n.f.* spider.

spinnen*, *vb.* spin; be crazy.

Spinngewebe, -, *n.nt.* cobweb.

Spion´, -e, *n.m.* spy.

Spionag´e, *n.f.* espionage.

spionie´ren, *vb.* spy.

Spira´le, -n, *n.f.* spiral.

spiral´förmig, *adj.* spiral.

Spiritis´mus, *n.m.* spiritism.

Spiritualis´mus, *n.m.* spiritualism.

Spirituo´sen, *n.pl.* liquor, spirits.

spitz, *adj.* pointed, acute.

Spitzbart, ≃e, *n.m.* goatee.

Spitze, -n, *n.f.* point, tip, top; lace.

spitzenartig, *adj.* lacy.

spitzfindig, *adj.* shrewd; subtle.

Spitzhacke, -n, *n.f.* pick.

Spitzname(n), -, *n.m.* nickname.

spleißen*, *vb.* splice.

Splitter, -, *n.m.* splinter, chip.

splittern, *vb.* splinter, shatter.

spontan´, *adj.* spontaneous.

spora´disch, *adj.* sporadic.

Sporn, **Sporen**, *n.m.* spur.

Sport, -e, *n.m.* sport.

Sportler, -, *n.m.* sportsman; athlete.

Sportlerin, -nen, *n.f.* athlete.

sportlich, *adj.* athletic; sportsmanlike.

Sportplatz, ≃e, *n.m.* athletic field, stadium.

Spott, *n.m.* mockery, ridicule.

spottbillig, *adj.* dirt cheap.

spotten, *vb.* mock, scoff.

Spötter, -, *n.m.* scoffer.

spöttisch, *adj.* derisive.

Sprache, -n, *n.f.* speech; language.

spracheigen, *adj.* idiomatic.

Sprachfehler, -, *n.m.* speech impediment.

Sprachführer, -, *n.m.* phrase book.

sprachgewandt, *adj.* fluent.

sprachlos, *adj.* speechless.

Sprachschatz, *n.m.* vocabulary.

Sprachwissenschaft, -en, *n.f.* linguistics, philology.

sprechen*, *vb.* speak, talk.

Sprecher, -, *n.m.* speaker, spokesman.

Sprecherin, -nen, *n.f.* speaker, spokesperson.

Sprechstunde, -n, *n.f.* office hour.

spreizen, *vb.* spread apart.

sprengen, *vb.* explode, break; sprinkle.

Sprengstoff, -e, *n.m.* explosive.

Sprichwort, ≃er, *n.nt.* proverb, adage.

sprichwörtlich, *adj.* proverbial.

sprießen*, *vb.* sprout.

Springbrunnen, -, *n.m.* fountain.

springen*, *vb.* jump; crack.

Springer, -, *n.m.* (chess) knight.

Springquell, -e, *n.m.* fountain.

sprinten, *vb.* sprint.

Spritze, -n, *n.f.* spray; injection; hypodermic.

spritzen, *vb.* spray, squirt, splash, inject.

spröde, *adj.* brittle; chapped; reserved, prim.

Sproß, -sse, *n.m.* sprout.

Sprößling, -e, *n.m.* shoot; offspring.

Sprotte, -n, *n.f.* sprat.

Spruch, ⸚e, *n.m.* saying.

Sprudel, -, *n.m.* bubbling water; soda water.

sprudeln, *vb.* bubble.

Sprudeln, *n.nt.* effervescence.

sprühen, *vb.* spark, sparkle.

Sprühregen, *n.m.* drizzle.

Sprung, ⸚e, *n.m.* jump; fissure, crack.

Sprungbrett, -er, *n.nt.* diving board; (*fig.*) stepping stone.

sprunghaft, *adj.* jumpy; erratic.

Sprungschanze, -n, *n.f.* ski-jump.

Spucke, *n.f.* spit, saliva.

spucken, *vb.* spit.

Spuk, -e, *n.m.* spook, ghost.

Spule, -n, *n.f.* spool, reel; (*elec.*) coil; bobbin.

spulen, *vb.* reel, wind.

spülen, *vb.* rinse, wash; (toilet) flush.

Spülstein, -e, *n.m.* sink.

Spund, -e, *n.m.* spigot, tap.

Spur, -en, *n.f.* trace, track.

spuren, *vb.* follow the prescribed pattern.

spüren, *vb.* feel; trace.

spurlos, *adj.* without a trace.

Spurweite, -n, *n.f.* width of track, gauge.

sputen, *vb.* (**sich s.**) hurry up.

Staat, -en, *n.m.* state, government.

Staatenbund, ⸚e, *n.m.* federation.

staatlich, *adj.* national, governmental.

Staatsangehörig-, *n.m.& f.* national citizen.

Staatsangehörigkeit, -en, *n.f.* citizenship, nationality.

Stattsanwalt, ⸚e, *n.m.* district attorney.

Staatsanwältin, -nen, *n.f.* district attorney.

staatsfeindlich, *adj.* subversive.

Staatskunst, *n.f.* statesmanship.

Staatsmann, ⸚er, *n.m.* statesman.

Staatssekretär, -e, *n.m.* undersecretary of a ministry.

Staatsstreich, -e, *n.m.* coup d'état.

Stab, ⸚e, *n.m.* staff, rod.

stabil´, *adj.* stable.

stabilisie´ren, *vb.* stabilize.

Stabilität´, *n.f.* stability.

Stachel, -n, *n.m.* sting, thorn, spike.

Stachelbeere, -n, *n.f.* gooseberry.

Stachelschwein, -e, *n.nt.* porcupine.

Stadion, -dien, *n.nt.* stadium.

Stadium, -dien, *n.nt.* stage.

Stadt, ⸚e, *n.f.* town, city.

stadtbekannt, *adj.* known all over town, notorious.

städtisch, *adj.* municipal; urban.

Stadtplan, ⸚e, *n.m.* city map.

Stadtteil, -e, *n.m.* borough.

Staffel, -n, *n.f.* rung, step; (*mil.*) echelon, squadron.

staffeln, *vb.* graduate, stagger.

Stagflation´, *n.f.* stagflation.

stagnie´ren, *vb.* stagnate.

stagnie´rend, *adj.* stagnant.

Stahl, -e, *n.m.* steel.

Stahlhelm, -e, *n.m.* steel helmet.

Stahlwaren, *n.pl.* cutlery; hardware.

Stall, ⸚e, *n.m.* stall, stable, barn.

Stamm, ⸚e, *n.m.* (tree) trunk; (word) stem; tribe, clan.

Stammbaum, ⸚e, *n.m.* family tree; pedigree.

stammeln, *vb.* stammer.

stammen, *vb.* stem, originate, be descended.

Stammgast, ⸚e, *n.m.* habitué.

stämmig, *adj.* sturdy, burly.

stampfen, *vb.* stamp, trample.

Stand, ⸚e, *n.m.* stand(ing); position; level; status; class, estate.

Standard, -s, *n.m.* standard.

standardisie´ren, *vb.* standardize.

Ständchen, -, *n.nt.* serenade.

Ständer, -, *n.m.* rack, stand.

Standesamt, ⸚er, *n.nt.* marriage bureau; registrar.

standesbewußt, *adj.* class-conscious.

standesgemäß, *adj.* according to one's rank.

standhaft, *adj.* steadfast.

Standhaftigkeit, *n.f.* constancy.

stand·halten*, *vb.* hold one's ground, withstand.

Standpunkt, -e, *n.m.* standpoint, point of view.

Stange, -n, *n.f.* rod, bar, pole; carton (of cigarettes).

Stapel, -, *n.m.* pile; stock; (ship) slip; (**vom S. lassen***) launch.

stapeln, *vb.* pile up.

stapfen, *vb.* stamp, plod.

Star, -e, *n.m.* (eye) cataract; (bird) starling; (film) star.

stark (⸚), *adj.* strong.

Stärke, -n, *n.f.* strength; starch.

stärken, *vb.* strengthen; starch.

Stärkungsmittel, -, *n.nt.* tonic.

starr, *adj.* rigid.

starren, *vb.* stare.

Starrheit, *n.f.* rigidity.

starrköpfig, *adj.* stubborn, headstrong.

Starrsinn, *n.m.* obstinacy.

Start, -s, *n.m.* start.

Startbahn, -en, *n.f.* runway.

starten, *vb.* start.

Startklappe, -n, *n.f.* choke (auto).

Station´, -en, *n.f.* station.

stationär´, *adj.* stationary.

Stations´vorsteher, -, *n.m.* station master.

statisch, *adj.* static.

Statist´, -en, *n.m.* (theater) extra; (*fig.*) dummy.

Statis´tik, *n.f.* statistics.

Stativ´, -e, *n.nt.* (photo) tripod.

statt, *prep.* instead of.

Stätte, -n, *n.f.* place.
statt•finden*, *vb.* take place.
stattlich, *adj.* imposing.
Statue, -n, *n.f.* statue.
Staub, *n.m.* dust.
staubig, *adj.* dusty.
Staubsauger, -, *n.m.* vacuum cleaner.
Staudamm, ˝e, *n.m.* dam.
stauen, *vb.* dam up; **(sich s.)** be dammed up, get jammed up.
staunen, *vb.* be astonished, wonder.
Stausee, -n, *n.m.* reservoir.
Stauung, -en, *n.f.* congestion.
stechen*, *vb.* prick, sting; pierce, stab.
Stechschritt, *n.m.* goose step.
Steckdose, -n, *n.f. (elec.)* outlet, socket.
stecken(*), *vb. intr.* be located, be hidden; **(wo steckt er denn?)** where *is* he, anyhow?; **(s. bleiben*)** get stuck.
stecken, *vb. tr.* put, stick, pin, hide.
Steckenpferd, -e, *n.nt.* hobby-horse; hobby.
Stecknadel, -n, *n.f.* pin.
Steckrübe, -n, *n.f.* turnip.
Steg, -e, *n.m.* path; footbridge.
stehen*, *vb.* stand, be located; be becoming; **(sich gut s.)** be on good terms; **(es steht dahin´)** it has yet to be shown.
stehen•bleiben*, *vb.* stop.
stehen•lassen*, *vb.* leave standing; leave behind, forget.
stehlen*, *vb.* steal.
Stehplatz, ˝e, *n.m.* standing room.
steif, *adj.* stiff, rigid.
Steifheit, -en, *n.f.* stiffness, rigidity.
Steig, -e, *n.m.* path.
steigen*, *vb.* climb, rise.
steigern, *vb.* increase, boost; **(sich s.)** increase, *(fig.)* work oneself up.
Steigung, -en, *n.f.* rise, slope, ascent.
steil, *adj.* steep.
Stein, -e, *n.m.* stone, rock.

Steingut, *n.nt.* earthenware, crockery.
steinigen, *vb.* stone.
Stelldichein, *n.nt.* rendezvous.
Stelle, -n, *n.f.* place, spot, point.
stellen, *vb.* place, put, set.
Stellenangebot, -e, *n.nt.* position offered.
Stellenvermittlung, -en, *n.f.* employment agency.
stellenweise, *adv.* in parts; in places.
Stellung, -en, *n.f.* position, place, stand; job; **(S. nehmen)** comment.
Stellungnahme, -n, *n.f.* comment, attitude.
stellvertretend, *adj.* assistant, deputy.
Stellvertreter, -, *n.m.* representative, deputy, alternate.
Stellvertreterin, -nen, *n.f.* representative, deputy, alternate.
stemmen, *vb.* stem; **(sich s. gegen)** oppose, resist.
Stempel, -, *n.m.* stamp.
stempeln, *vb.* stamp; **(s. gehen)** be on the dole.
Stenographie´, -i´en, *n.f.* shorthand.
stenographie´ren, *vb.* take shorthand, write shorthand.
Stenotypis´tin, -nen, *n.f.* stenographer.
Steppdecke, -n, *n.f.* quilt comforter.
Steppe, -n, *n.f.* steppe.
steppen, *vb.* stitch.
sterben*, *vb.* die.
sterblich, *adj.* mortal.
stereophon´, *adj.* stereophonic, stereo.
steril´, *adj.* sterile.
sterilisie´ren, *vb.* sterilize.
Sterilität´, -, *n.f.* sterility.
Sterling, *n.nt.* pound sterling.
Stern, -e, *n.m.* star.
Sternbild, -er, *n.nt.* constellation.
Sternchen, -, *n.nt.* asterisk.
Sternkunde, *n.f.* astronomy.
Sternwarte, -n, *n.f.* observatory.

stet(ig), *adj.* steady.
stets, *adv.* always.
Steuer, -, *n.nt.* rudder, helm.
Steuer, -, *n.f.* tax.
Steuererklärung, -en, *n.f.* tax return.
steuerfrei, *adj.* tax-free; duty-free.
steuern, *vb.* steer, pilot, navigate.
Steuerruder, -, *n.nt.* rudder.
Steuerzahler, -, *n.m.* taxpayer.
Steward, -s, *n.m.* steward.
Stewardeß, -ssen, *n.f.* stewardess.
Stich, -e, *n.m.* stab; bite, sting; stitch.
stichhaltig, *adj.* valid, sound.
Stichwort, ˝er, *n.nt.* cue.
sticken, *vb.* embroider.
Stickerei´, -en, *n.f.* embroidery.
Stickstoff, *n.m.* nitrogen.
stieben*, *vb.* fly (about), scatter.
Stief-, *cpds.* step-; **(Stiefvater)** stepfather; etc.
Stiefel, -, *n.m.* boot.
Stiel, -e, *n.m.* handle; stalk, stem.
stier, *adj.* glassy (look).
Stier, -e, *n.m.* steer.
stieren, *vb.* stare.
Stift, -e, *n.m.* peg, pin, tack; crayon, pencil.
Stift, -e(r), *n.nt.* charitable institution.
stiften, *vb.* donate; found; endow.
Stiftung, -en, *n.f.* foundation; donation.
Stil, -e, *n.m.* style.
stilgerecht, *adj.* in good style, in good taste.
still, *adj.* still, quiet.
Stille, *n.f.* stillness, silence.
Stilleben, -, *n.nt.* still-life.
stillen, *vb.* still, quench; nurse (a baby).
stillos, *adj.* in bad taste.
stillschweigend, *adj.* silent; tacit, implicit.
Stillstand, *n.m.* halt.
Stimmabgabe, -n, *n.f.* vote; voting.
Stimmband, ˝er, *n.nt.* vocal cord.
Stimme, -n, *n.f.* voice; vote.

stimmen, *vb.* tune; vote; be correct.

Stimmengleichheit, *n.f.* tie vote.

Stimmenprüfung, -en, *n.f.* recounting of votes.

Stimmrecht, -e, *n.nt.* suffrage, franchise.

Stimmung, -en, *n.f.* mood; morale.

stimmungsvoll, *adj.* festive, moving; intimate.

Stimmzettel, -, *n.m.* ballot.

stinken*, *vb.* stink.

Stinktier, -e, *n.nt.* skunk.

Stint, -e, *n.m.* smelt.

Stipen´dium, -dien, *n.nt.* scholarship, grant.

Stirn, -en, *n.f.* forehead, brow.

Stirnhöhle, -n, *n.f.* sinus.

Stock, ¨e, *n.m.* stick, cane.

stockdunkel, *adj.* pitch-dark.

stocken, *vb.* stop, come to a halt; falter.

Stockung, -en, *n.f.* stop, standstill; deadlock.

Stockwerk, -e, *n.nt.* floor, story.

Stoff, -e, *n.m.* matter, substance; material; cloth.

stofflich, *adj.* material.

stöhnen, *vb.* groan.

Stoiker, -, *n.m.* stoic.

stoisch, *adj.* stoical.

Stola, -len, *n.f.* stole.

stolpern, *vb.* stumble, trip.

stolz, *adj.* proud.

Stolz, *n.m.* pride.

stolzie´ren, *vb.* strut.

stopfen, *vb.* stuff; (socks, etc.) darn.

stoppen, *vb.* stop.

Stöpsel, -, *n.m.* stopper; *(elec.)* plug.

Stör, -e, *n.m.* sturgeon.

Storch, ¨e, *n.m.* stork.

stören, *vb.* disturb, bother.

Störenfried, -e, *n.m.* intruder, troublemaker.

Störung, -en, *n.f.* disturbance; (radio) interference, static.

Stoß, ¨e, *n.m.* blow, hit, thrust.

stoßen*, *vb.* push, kick, hit, thrust.

Stoßstange, -n, *n.f.* bumper.

stottern, *vb.* stutter.

Strafanstalt, -en, *n.f.* penal intitution.

strafbar, *adj.* liable to punishment.

Strafe, -n, *n.f.* punishment; fine; sentence.

strafen, *vb.* punish.

straff, *adj.* taut, tight.

straffen, *vb.* tighten.

Strafgebühr, -en, *n.f.* fine.

Strafgericht, -e, *n.nt.* criminal court.

Strafkammer, -n, *n.f.* criminal court.

Sträfling, -e, *n.m.* convict.

Strafmandat, -e, *n.nt.* traffic ticket.

Strafporto, *n.nt.* postage due.

Strahl, -en, *n.m.* ray, beam; (water) spout.

strahlen, *vb.* beam, gleam, radiate.

Strahlen, *n.nt.* radiance.

strahlend, *adj.* radiant.

Strahlflugzeug, -e, *n.nt.* jet plane.

Strahlung, -en, *n.f.* radiation.

Strähne, -n, *n.f.* strand; streak.

stramm, *adj.* tight; *(fig.)* strapping.

strampeln, *vb.* kick.

Strand, -e, *n.m.* beach, shore.

stranden, *vb.* strand.

Strandgut, *n.nt.* jetsam.

Strang, ¨e, *n.m.* rope; **(über die Stränge schlagen*)** run riot.

Strapa´ze, -n, *n.f.* exertion, drudgery.

strapazier´fähig, *adj.* durable.

Straße, -n, *n.f.* street, road.

Straßenbahn, -en, *n.f.* streetcar, trolley.

Strategie´, *n.f.* strategy.

strate´gisch, *adj.* strategic.

Stratosphä´re, *n.f.* stratosphere.

sträuben, *vb.* **(sich s.)** bristle; *(fig.)* struggle against, resist.

Strauch, ¨er, *n.m.* shrub.

straucheln, *vb.* falter, stumble.

Strauß, ¨e, *n.m.* bouquet; ostrich.

streben, *vb.* strive, endeavor, aspire.

Streben, *n.nt.* pursuit.

Strebepfeiler, -, *n.m.* flying buttress.

Streber, -, *n.m.* (school) grind; (society) social climber.

strebsam, *adj.* zealous.

Strecke, -n, *n.f.* stretch, distance.

strecken, *vb.* stretch; **(die Waffen s.)** lay down one's arms.

Streich, -e, *n.m.* stroke, blow; prank.

streicheln, *vb.* stroke, caress.

streichen*, *vb.* scratch; paint.

Streichholz, ¨er, *n.nt.* match.

Streichorchester, -, *n.nt.* string orchestra.

Streichung, -en, *n.f.* deletion.

Streife, -n, *n.f.* patrol.

streifen, *vb.* touch lightly.

Streifen, -, *n.m.* strike.

Streik, -s, *n.m.* strike.

Streikposten, -, *n.m.* picket.

Streit, *n.m.* quarrel, dispute.

streiten*, *vb.* fight; **(sich s.)** quarrel.

Streitfrage, -n, *n.f.* controversy.

Streitpunkt, -e, *n.m.* point at issue.

streitsüchtig, *adj.* pugnacious.

streng, *adj.* strict, stern, severe.

strenggläubig, *adj.* orthodox.

streuen, *vb.* strew, scatter, sprinkle.

Strich, -e, *n.m.* stroke, line; **(nach S. und Faden)** thoroughly; **(gegen den S.)** against the grain.

Strick, -e, *n.m.* rope.

stricken, *vb.* knit.

strittig, *adj.* controversial.

Stroh, *n.nt.* straw.

Strolch, -e, *n.m.* vagabond.

Strom, ¨e, *n.m.* stream; *(elec.)* current.

strömen, *vb.* stream, flow.

Stromkreis, -e, *n.m.* circuit.

stromlinienförmig, *adj.* streamlined.

Stromspannung, -en, *n.f.* voltage.

Strömung, -en, *n.f.* current; trend, drift.

Strudel, -, *n.m.* whirlpool.

Struktur´, -en, *n.f.* structure.

Strumpf, ¨e, *n.m.* stocking.

Strumpfband, ¨er, *n.nt.* garter.

Strumpfbandgürtel, *n.m.* girdle.

Strumpfhose, -n, *n.f.* panty hose.

Strumpfwaren, *n.pl.* hosiery.

struppig, *adj.* shaggy.

Stube, -n, *n.f.* room.

Stuck, *n.m.* stucco.

Stück, -e, *n.nt.* piece; (theater) play.

stückeln, *vb.* patch, piece together.

stücken, *vb.* piece.

Student´, -en, -en, *n.m.* student.

Studen´tin, -nen, *n.f.* student.

Studie, -n, *n.f.* study.

Studiengeld, -er, *n.nt.* tuition.

studie´ren, *vb.* study (at a university), be a student.

Studium, -dien, *n.nt.* study.

Stufe, -n, *n.f.* step.

stufenweise, *adj.* gradual, step by step.

Stuhl, ⸗e, *n.m.* chair.

stumm, *adj.* mute, silent.

Stummel, -, *n.m.* stub, butt.

Stümper, -, *n.m.* beginner, amateur.

stumpf, *adj.* blunt; stupid; (angle) obtuse.

Stumpf, ⸗e, *n.m.* stump.

Stunde, -n, *n.f.* hour; (school) class.

Stundenplan, ⸗e, *n.m.* schedule.

stündlich, *adj.* hourly.

stupsen, *vb.* joggle.

stur, *adj.* stubborn; obtuse.

Sturm, ⸗e, *n.m.* storm.

stürmen, *vb.* storm.

stürmisch, *adj.* stormy.

Sturz, ⸗e, *n.m.* fall; overthrow.

stürzen, *vb.* plunge, hurl, overthrow; rush, crash.

Stute, -n, *n.f.* mare.

Stütze, -n, *n.f.* support, prop, help.

stutzen, *vb.* trim.

stützen, *vb.* support.

Stützpunkt, -e, *n.m.* base.

Subjekt´, -e, *n.nt.* subject.

subjektiv´, *adj.* subjective.

sublimie´ren, *vb.* sublimate.

Substantiv, -e, *n.nt.* noun.

Substanz´, -en, *n.f.* substance.

subtil´, *adj.* subtle.

subtrahie´ren, *vb.* subtract.

Subvention´, -en, *n.f.* subvention, subsidy.

Suche, *n.f.* search.

suchen, *vb.* search, seek, look for.

Sucht, *n.f.* addiction.

süchtig, *adj.* addicted.

Süd, Süden, *n.m.* south.

südlich, *adj.* southern; to the south.

Südos´ten, *n.m.* southeast.

südöst´lich, *adj.* southeast.

Südpol, *n.m.* South Pole.

Südwe´sten, *n.m.* southwest.

südwest´lich, *adj.* southwest.

suggerie´ren, *vb.* suggest.

Sühne, -n, *n.f.* atonement, expiation.

sühnen, *vb.* atone for, expiate.

Sülze, *n.f.* jellied meat.

summa´risch, *adj.* summary.

Summe, -n, *n.f.* sum.

summen, *vb.* hum, buzz.

Sumpf, ⸗e, *n.m.* swamp, mire.

Sünde, -n, *n.f.* sin.

Sündenbock, *n.m* scapegoat.

Sündenvergebung, *n.f.* absolution.

Sünder, -, *n.m.* sinner.

Sünderin, -nen, *n.f.* sinner.

Sündflut, *n.f.* the Flood; cataclysm.

sündhaft, *adj.* sinful.

sündigen, *vb.* sin.

super, *adj.* super.

Superstar, -s, *n.m.* superstar.

Suppe, -n, *n.f.* soup.

surren, *vb.* buzz.

suspendie´ren, *vb.* suspend.

süß, *adj.* sweet.

Süße, *n.f.* sweetness.

Süßigkeiten, *n.pl.* sweets.

Sylve´ster, *n.nt.* New Year's Eve.

Symbol´, -e, *n.nt.* symbol.

symbo´lisch, *adj.* symbolic.

Sympathie´, -i´en, *n.f.* sympathy.

sympa´tisch, *adj.* likable, congenial; (med.) sympathetic.

Symphonie´, -i´en, *n.f.* symphony.

sympho´nisch, *adj.* symphonic.

Symptom´, -e, *n.nt.* symptom.

symptoma´tisch, *adj.* symptomatic.

Synago´ge, -n, *n.f.* synagogue.

synchronisie´ren, *vb.* synchronize.

Syndrom´, -e, *n.nt.* syndrome.

Synonym´, -e, *n.nt.* synonym.

Synthe´se, -n, *n.f.* synthesis.

synthe´tisch, *adj.* synthetic.

Syphilis, *n.f.* syphilis.

System´, -e, *n.nt.* system.

systema´tisch, *adj.* systematic.

Szene, -n, *n.f.* scene.

T

Tabak, *n.m.* tobacco.

Tabel´le, -n, *n.f.* chart.

Tablett´, -e, *n.nt.* tray.

Tablet´te, -n, *n.f.* tablet.

Tadel, -, *n.m.* reproof, reprimand; (school) demerit.

tadeln, *vb.* reprove, find fault with.

tadelnswert, *adj.* reprehensible.

Tafel, -n, *n.f.* tablet; table; chart; blackboard; bar (of chocolate).

täfeln, *vb.* panel.

Tag, -e, *n.m.* day; (guten T.) how do you do.

Tagebuch, ⸗er, *n.nt.* diary.

Tagesanbruch, *n.m.* daybreak.

Tageslicht, *n.nt.* daylight.

Tageszeitung, -en, *n.f.* daily newspaper.

täglich, *adj.* daily.

Tagung, -en, *n.f.* convention, meeting.

Taille, -n, *n.f.* waist.

Takt, *n.m.* tact; rhythm.

taktisch, *adj.* tactical.

Tal, ⸗er, *n.nt.* valley.

Talent´, -e, *n.nt.* talent.

talentiert´, *adj.* talented.

tändeln, *vb.* dally.

Tango, -s, *n.m.* tango.

Tank, -s, *n.m.* tank.

Tankstelle, -n, *n.f.* filling station.

Tanne, -n, *n.f.* fir, spruce.

Tante, -n, *n.f.* aunt.

Tantie´me, -n, *n.f.* bonus.

Tanz, ⸚e, *n.m.* dance.

tänzeln, *vb.* flounce, caper.

tanzen, *vb.* dance.

Tänzer, -, *n.m.* dancer.

Tänzerin, -nen, *n.f.* dancer.

Tanzsaal, -säle, *n.m.* dance hall, ballroom.

Tape´te, -n, *n.f.* wallpaper.

Tapezie´rer, -, *n.m.* upholsterer.

tapfer, *adj.* brave, valiant.

Tapisserie, -i´en, *n.f.* tapestry.

tappen, *vb.* grope.

tapsig, *adj.* gawky.

tarnen, *vb.* screen, camouflage.

Tarnung, -en, *n.f.* screen, camouflage.

Tasche, -n, *n.f.* pocket; handbag.

Taschenausgabe, -n, *n.f.* paperback.

Taschendieb, -e, *n.m.* pickpocket.

Taschenformat, *n.nt.* pocket-size.

Tachengeld, -er, *n.nt.* allowance, pocket money.

Taschenlampe, -n, *n.f.* flashlight.

Taschenrechner, -, *n.m.* calculator.

Taschentuch, ⸚er, *n.nt.* handkerchief.

Tasse, -n, *n.f.* cup.

Tastatur´, -en, *n.f.* keyboard.

Taste, -n, *n.f.* key.

tasten, *vb.* feel; grope.

Tastentelefon, -e, *n.nt.* touch tone phone.

Tastsinn, *n.m.* sense of touch.

Tat, -en, *n.f.* act, deed; (**in der T.**) indeed.

Tatbestand, *n.m.* facts, findings.

Täter, -, *n.m.* culprit.

Täterin, -nen, *n.f.* culprit.

tätig, *adj.* active.

Tätigkeit, -en, *n.f.* activity.

Tatkraft, ⸚e, *n.f.* energy.

tatkräftig, *adj.* energetic.

tätlich, *adj.* violent.

Tätlichkeit, -en, *n.f.* violence.

Tatsache, -n, *n.f.* fact.

tatsächlich, *adj.* actual, real.

Tatze, -n, *n.f.* paw, claw.

Tau, *n.m.* dew.

Tau, -e, *n.nt.* rope.

taub, *adj.* deaf.

Taube, -n, *n.f.* pigeon, dove.

tauchen, *vb.* dive, plunge, dip.

Taucher, -, *n.m.* diver.

Taucherin, -nen, *n.f.* diver.

tauen, *vb.* melt, thaw.

Taufe, -n, *n.f.* baptism, christening.

taufen, *vb.* baptize, christen.

Taufkapelle, -n, *n.f.* baptistry.

taugen, *vb.* be worth; be of use.

Taugenichts, *n.m.* good-for-nothing.

tauglich, *adj.* useful, qualified.

taumeln, *vb.* stagger.

taumelnd, *adj.* groggy.

Tausch, *n.m.* exchange, trade.

tauschen, *vb.* exchange.

täuschen, *vb.* deceive, delude, fool.

täuschend, *adj.* deceptive.

Tauschhandel, *n.m.* barter.

Täuschung, -en, *n.f.* deception, delusion, fallacy.

tausend, *num.* a thousand.

Tausend, -e, *n.nt.* thousand.

tausendst-, *adj.* thousandth.

Tausendstel, -, *n.nt.* thousandth part; (**ein t.**) one one-thousandth.

Taxe, -n, *n.f.* tax; taxi.

taxie´ren, *vb.* appraise, estimate.

Technik, *n.f.* technique; technology.

technisch, *adj.* technical.

Tee, -s, *n.m.* tea.

Teekanne, -n, *n.f.* tea-pot.

Teelöffel, -, *n.m.* teaspoon.

Teer, *n.m.* tar.

Teich, -e, *n.m.* pond, pool.

Teig, -e, *n.m.* dough, batter.

Teil, -e, *n.m.* part, portion, section.

teilbar, *adj.* divisible.

teilen, *vb.* divide, share.

teil•haben*, *vb.* share.

Teilhaber, -, *n.m.* partner.

Teilhaberin, -nen, *n.f.* partner.

Teilnahme, *n.f.* participation; sympathy.

teilnahmslos, *adj.* lethargic.

teil•nehmen*, *vb.* participate, partake.

Teilnehmer, -, *n.m.* participant, partner.

Teilnehmerin, -nen, *n.f.* participant, partner.

teils, *adv.* partly.

Teilung, -en, *n.f.* partition, division.

teilweise, *adv.* partly.

Teint, -s, *n.m.* complexion.

Telefon´, -e, *n.nt.* telephone.

Telegramm´, -e, *n.nt.* telegram.

Telegraph´, -en, -en, *n.m.* telegraph.

telegraphie´ren, *vb.* telegraph.

Telephon´, -e, *n.nt.* telephone.

Telephon´buch, ⸚er, *n.nt.* telephone directory.

telephonie´ren, *vb.* telephone.

Telephonist´, -en, *n.m.* operator.

Telephonis´tin, -nen, *n.f.* operator.

Telephon´zelle, -n, *n.f.* telephone booth.

Teller, -, *n.m.* plate.

Temperament´, *n.nt.* temperament, disposition; vivacity.

temperament´voll, *adj.* temperamental; vivacious.

Temperatur´, -en, *n.f.* temperature.

Tempo, -s, *n.nt.* speed; tempo.

Tendenz´, -en, *n.f.* tendency, trend.

Tender, -, *n.m.* tender.

Tennis, *n.nt.* tennis.

Tennisschläger, -, *n.m.* tennis racket.

Tennisschuh, -e, *n.m.* sneaker.

Tenor´, -e, *n.m.* tenor.

Teppich, -e, *n.m.* rug, carpet.

Termin´, -e, *n.m.* deadline; appointment.

Terpentin´, *n.nt.* turpentine.

Terras´se, -n, *n.f.* terrace.

Terror, *n.m.* terror.

Terroranschlag, ⸗e, *n.m.* terrorist attack.

Terroris´mus, *n.m.* terrorism.

Testament´, -e, *n.nt.* testament, will.

testamenta´risch, *adj.* testamentary, noted in the will.

teuer, *adj.* expensive, dear.

Teuerung, *n.f.* rising cost of living.

Teufel, -, *n.m.* devil.

teuflisch, *adj.* diabolic.

Text, -e, *n.m.* text.

Texti´lien, *n.pl.* textiles.

Textil´ware, -n, *n.f.* textile.

Thea´ter, -, *n.nt.* theater; spectacle.

Thea´terkasse, -n, *n.f.* box office.

Thea´terstück, -e, *n.nt.* play.

Thea´terwissenschaft, -en, *n.f.* dramaturgy.

theatra´lisch, *adj.* theatrical.

Thema, -men, *n.nt.* theme, subject, topic.

Theolo´ge, -n, -n, *n.m.* theologian.

theore´tisch, *adj.* theoretical.

Theorie´, -i´en, *n.f.* theory.

Therapie´, -n, *n.f.* therapy.

Thermome´ter, -, *n.nt.* thermometer.

These, -n, *n.f.* thesis.

Thron, -e, *n.m.* throne.

Thunfisch, -e, *n.m.* tuna.

tief, *adj.* deep, low; profound.

Tiefe, -n, *n.f.* depth.

Tiefebene, -n, *n.f.* plain, lowland.

tiefgründig, *adj.* profound.

Tiefkühler, -, *n.m.* freezer.

Tiefkühltruhe, -n, *n.f.* deep freeze.

tiefsinnig, *adj.* profound; pensive.

tieftraurig, *adj.* heartbroken.

Tier, -e, *n.nt.* animal.

Tierarzt, ⸗e, *n.m.* veterinarian.

Tierärztin, -nen, *n.f.* veterinarian.

tierisch, *adj.* animal, bestial.

Tiger, -, *n.m.* tiger.

tilgen, *vb.* obliterate; delete; pay off, amortize.

Tilgung, -en, *n.f.* liquidation, amortization.

Tinte, -n, *n.f.* ink.

Tintenfisch, -e, *n.m.* octopus.

Tip, -s, *n.m.* hint, suggestion.

tippen, *vb.* type.

Tisch, -e, *n.m.* table.

Tischdecke, -n, *n.f.* tablecloth.

Tischler, -, *n.m.* carpenter.

Tischtuch, ⸗er, *n.nt.* tablecloth.

Titel, -, *n.m.* title.

Toast, -e, *n.m.* toast.

toben, *vb.* rave, rage.

Tochter, ⸗, *n.f.* daughter.

Tod, *n.m.* death.

Todesfall, ⸗e, *n.m.* (case of) death.

Todesstrafe, -n, *n.f.* capital punishment.

tödlich, *adj.* deadly, mortal; lethal.

Toilet´te, -n, *n.f.* toilet.

Toilet´tenartikel, *n.pl.* toilet articles.

tolerant´, *adj.* tolerant.

Toleranz´, -, *n.f.* tolerance.

toll, *adj.* mad, crazy.

tollkühn, *adj.* foolhardy.

Tollwut, *n.f.* rabies.

tölpelhaft, *adj.* clumsy.

Toma´te, -n, *n.f.* tomato.

Ton, ⸗e, *n.m.* tone, sound; clay.

tonangebend, *adj.* setting the style.

Tonart, -en, *n.f.* key.

Tonband, ⸗er, *n.nt.* magnetic tape.

Tonbandaufnahme, -n, *n.f.* tape recording.

Tonbandgerät, -e, *n.nt.* tape recorder.

tönen, *vb.* sound, resound, ring.

Tonfall, ⸗e, *n.m.* intonation, inflection.

Tonfilm, -e, *n.m.* sound movie.

Tonhöhe, -n, *n.f.* pitch.

Tonleiter, -n, *n.f.* scale.

Tonne, -n, *n.f.* ton; barrel.

Tonstufe, -n, *n.f.* (music) pitch.

Tonwaren, *n.pl.* earthenware.

Topf, ⸗e, *n.m.* pot.

Töpferware, -n, *n.f.* pottery.

Tor, -en, -en, *n.m.* fool.

Tor, -e, *n.nt.* gate, gateway; (sport) goal.

Torbogen, ⸗, *n.m.* archway.

Torheit, -en, *n.f.* folly.

töricht, *adj.* foolish.

torkeln, *vb.* lurch, stagger.

Torni´ster, -, *n.m.* knapsack, pack.

torpedie´ren, *vb.* torpedo.

Torpe´do, -s, *n.m.* torpedo.

Törtchen, -, *n.nt.* tart.

Torte, -n, *n.f.* tart, layer cake.

Tortur´, -en, *n.f.* torture.

Torwart, -e, *n.m.* goalie.

tosen, *vb.* rage, roar.

tot, *adj.* dead.

total´, *adj.* total.

totalitär, *adj.* totalitarian.

töten, *vb.* kill.

Totenwache, -n, *n.f.* wake.

Toto, *n.m.* lottery.

Totschlag, ⸗e, *n.m.* (case of) manslaughter.

Tour, -en, *n.f.* tour, excursion, trip.

Touris´mus, *n.m.* tourism.

Tourist´, -en, -en, *n.m.* tourist.

Touris´tin, -nen, *n.f.* tourist.

Trab, *n.m.* trot.

traben, *vb.* trot.

Tracht, -en, *n.f.* costume.

trachten, *vb.* seek, endeavor.

Tradition´, -en, *n.f.* tradition.

traditionell´, *adj.* traditional.

Tragbahre, -n, *n.f.* stretcher.

tragbar, *adj.* portable; bearable.

träge, *adj.* indolent, sluggish.

tragen*, *vb.* carry, bear; wear.

Träger, -, *n.m.* carrier; girder; (lingerie) straps.

Tragik, *n.f.* tragic art; calamity.

tragisch, *adj.* tragic.
Tragödie, -n, *n.f.* tragedy.
Tragweite, -n, *n.f.* range; significance, consequence.
Trainer, -, *n.m.* coach.
Trainerin, -nen, *n.f.* coach.
trainieren, *vb.* train, work out; coach.
Trambahn, -en, *n.f.* trolley.
trampeln, *vb.* trample.
Tranchiermesser, -, *n.nt.* carving-knife.
Träne, -n, *n.f.* tear.
tränen, *vb.* water (eye).
Trank, ²e, *n.m.* potion.
tränken, *vb.* water (animals).
Transaktion´, -en, *n.f.* transaction.
Transforma´tor, -o´ren, *n.m.* transformer, converter.
Transfusion´, -en, *n.f.* transfusion.
transpirie´ren, *vb.* perspire.
transponie´ren, *vb.* transpose.
Transport´, -e, *n.m.* transport.
transportie´ren, *vb.* transport.
transsexual´, *adj.* transsexual.
Transvestit´, -en, -en, *n.m.* transvestite.
Trapez´, -e, *n.nt.* trapeze.
Traube, -n, *n.f.* grape.
trauen, *vb. (intr.)* trust; *(tr.)* marry, join in marriage.
Trauer, *n.f.* grief; mourning.
trauern, *vb.* grieve, mourn.
trauervoll, *adj.* mournful.
Traufe, -n, *n.f.* gutter; **(vom Regen in die T.)** out of the frying pan into the fire.
Traum, ²e, *n.m.* dream; **(böser T.)** nightmare.
träumen, *vb.* dream; **(vor sich hin•t.)** daydream.
Träumer, -, *n.m.* dreamer.
Träumerei´, -en, *n.f.* daydream, reverie.
Träumerin, -nen, *n.f.* dreamer.
träumerisch, *adj.* fanciful, faraway.

traumhaft, *adj.* dreamlike; dreamy.
traurig, *adj.* sad.
Trauring, -e, *n.m.* wedding ring.
Travelerscheck, -s, *n.m.* traveler's check.
Trecker, -, *n.m.* tractor.
Treff, *n.nt.* clubs (cards).
treffen*, *vb.* hit; meet; **(sich t.)** meet.
treffend, *adj.* pertinent.
Treffer, -, *n.m.* hit.
trefflich, *adj.* excellent.
treiben*, *vb. (tr.)* drive; be engaged in; *(intr.)* drift, float.
Treibstoff, *n.m.* fuel.
Trend, -s, *n.m.* trend.
trennen, *vb.* separate, divide; hyphenate; **(sich t.)** part.
Trennung, -en, *n.f.* separation, division.
treppab´, *adv.* down the stairs.
treppauf´, *adv.* up the stairs.
Treppe, -n, *n.f.* staircase, stairs.
Tresor´, -e, *n.m.* vault.
treten*, *vb.* step, tread.
treu, *adj.* true, faithful, loyal.
Treue, *n.f.* faith, loyalty; allegiance.
Treueid, -e, *n.m.* oath of allegiance.
Treuhänder, -, *n.m.* trustee.
treuherzig, *adj.* trusting, guileless.
treulich, *adv.* faithfully.
treulos, *adj.* disloyal.
Treulosigkeit, -e, *n.f.* disloyalty.
Tribü´ne, -n, *n.f.* grandstand.
Trichter, -, *n.m.* funnel.
Trick, -s, *n.m.* trick.
Trickfilm, -e, *n.m.* animated cartoon.
Tricktrack, *n.nt.* backgammon.
Trieb, -e, *n.m.* sprout, shoot; urge.
Triebfeder, -n, *n.f.* mainspring.
triebhaft, *adj.* instinctive, unrestrained.
Triebwagen, -, *n.m.* railcar.
triefen*, *vb.* drip.
triftig, *adj.* weighty.

Trikot´, *n.nt.* knitted cloth.
trimmen, *vb.* trim.
trinkbar, *adj.* drinkable.
trinken*, *vb.* drink.
Trinker, -, *n.m.* drunkard.
Trinkerin, -nen, *n.f.* drinker.
Trinkgeld, -er, *n.nt.* tip.
Trinkspruch, ²e, *n.m.* toast.
Tripper, *n.m.* gonorrhea.
Tritt, -e, *n.m.* step; kick.
Trittleiter, -n, *n.f.* stepladder.
Triumph´, -e, *n.m.* triumph.
triumphie´ren, *vb.* triumph.
trivial´, *adj.* trivial.
trocken, *adj.* dry.
Trockenhaube, -n, *n.f.* hair drier.
trocken•legen, *vb.* (land) drain; (baby) change the diapers.
trocknen, *vb.* dry.
trödeln, *vb.* dawdle.
Trog, ²e, *n.m.* trough.
trollen, *vb.* **(sich t.)** toddle off.
Trommel, -n, *n.f.* drum.
Trommelfell, -e, *n.nt.* eardrum.
Trompe´te, -n, *n.f.* trumpet.
Tropen, *n.pl.* tropics.
Tropfen, -, *n.m.* drop.
tropfen, *vb.* drip.
Tropfer, -, *n.m.* dropper.
Trophä´e, -n, *n.f.* trophy.
tropisch, *adj.* tropical.
Trost, *n.m.* consolation, solace, comfort.
trösten, *vb.* console, comfort.
trostlos, *adj.* desolate, dreary.
trostreich, *adj.* comforting.
Trott, *n.m.* trot.
Trottel, -, *n.m.* idiot, dope.
Trotz, *n.m.* defiance, spite.
trotz, *prep.* in spite of, despite, notwithstanding.
trotzdem, 1. *conj.* although, despite the fact that. **2.** *adv.* nevertheless.
trotzen, *vb.* defy.
trotzig, *adj.* defiant.
trübe, *adj.* dim; muddy; cloudy.
Trubel, *n.m.* bustle, confusion.
trüben, *vb.* dim.

Trübsal, *n.f.* misery, sorrow.
trübselig, *adj.* sad, gloomy.
Trübsinn, *n.m.* dejection, gloom.
trübsinnig, *adj.* gloomy.
Trüffel, -n, *n.f.* truffle.
Trug, *n.m.* deceit; delusion.
trügen***, *vb. (tr.)* deceive; *(intr.)* be deceptive.
trügerisch, *adj.* deceptive; illusory; treacherous.
Trugschluß, =sse, *n.m.* fallacy.
Truhe, -n, *n.f.* chest.
Trümmer, *n.pl.* ruins, debris.
Trunk, =e, *n.m.* drink; draught.
Trunkenbold, -e, *n.m.* drunkard.
Trunkenheit, *n.f.* drunkenness.
Trupp, -s, *n.m.* troop, squad.
Truppe, -n, *n.f.* troops.
Truppeneinheit, -en, *n.f.* unit, outfit.
Trust, -s, *n.m.* trust.
Truthahn, =e, *n.m.* turkey.
Tscheche, -n, -n, *n.m.* Czech.
Tschechei´, *n.f.* Czechoslovakia.
Tschechin, -nen, *n.f.* Czech.
tschechisch, *adj.* Czech.
Tschechoslowa´ke, -n, -n, *n.m.* Czechoslovakian.
Tschechoslowa´kin, -nen, *n.f.* Czechoslovakian.
Tschechoslowakei´, *n.f.* Czechoslovakia.
tschechoslowa´kisch, *adj.* Czechoslovakian.
T-shirt, -s, *n.nt.* T-shirt.

Tube, -n, *n.f.* tube.
Tuberkulo´se, *n.f.* tuberculosis.
Tuch, =er, *n.nt.* cloth.
tüchtig, *adj.* able, efficient.
Tüchtigkeit, *n.f.* ability, efficiency.
Tücke, -n, *n.f.* malice, perfidy.
tückisch, *adj.* malicious, treacherous.
Tugend, -en, *n.f.* virtue.
tugendhaft, *adj.* virtuous.
tugendsam, *adj.* virtuous.
Tüll, *n.m.* tulle.
Tülle, -n, *n.f.* spout.
Tulpe, -n, *n.f.* tulip.
tummeln, *vb.* move about, romp.
Tummelplatz, =e, *n.m.* playground.
Tumor, -o´ren, *n.m.* tumor.
Tümpel, -, *n.m.* pool.
Tumult´, -e, *n.m.* tumult, uproar; hubbub.
tun***, *vb.* do.
Tünche, -n, *n.f.* whitewash; *(fig.)* veneer.
Tunichtgut, -e, *n.m.* ne'er-do-well.
Tunke, -n, *n.f.* sauce, gravy.
tunken, *vb.* dunk.
Tunnel, -, *n.m.* tunnel.
tupfen, *vb.* dab.
Tür, -en, *n.f.* door; **(mit der T. ins Haus fallen*)** blurt out.
Turbi´nenjäger, -, *n.m.* turbo-jet plane.
Turbi´nenpropellertriebwerk, -e, *n.nt.* turbo-prop.

Türeingang, =e, *n.m.* doorway.
Türke, -n, -n, *n.m.* Turk.
Türkei´, *n.f.* Turkey.
Türkin, -nen, *n.f.* Turk.
Türkis´, -e, *n.m.* turquoise.
türkisch, *adj.* Turkish.
Turm, =e, *n.m.* tower, spire, steeple; (chess) castle, rook; **(spitzer T.)** spire.
türmen, *vb. (tr.)* pile up; *(intr.)* beat it; **(sich t.)** rise high.
turnen, *vb.* do gymnastics.
Turner, -, *n.m.* gymnast.
Turnerin, -nen, *n.f.* gymnast.
Turnhalle, -n, *n.f.* gym(nasium).
Turnhose, -n, *n.f.* gym shorts.
Turnier´, -e, *n.nt.* tournament.
Turnschuh, -e, *n.m.* sneaker.
tuscheln, *vb.* whisper.
Tuschkasten, =, *n.m.* paint box.
Tüte, -n, *n.f.* (paper) bag, sack.
Tüttelchen, -, *n.nt.* dot.
TÜV, *n.m.* car inspection.
Typ, -en, *n.m.* type.
Type, -n, *n.f.* (printing) type.
Typhus, *n.m.* typhus, typhoid fever.
typisch, *adj.* typical.
Typographie´, *n.f.* typography.
Tyrann´, -en, -en, *n.m.* tyrant.
Tyrannei´, *n.f.* tyranny.
tyrannisie´ren, *vb.* tyrannize, oppress.

U

U-Bahn, -en, *n.f.* (= Untergrundbahn) subway.
übel, *adj.* bad; nasty; nauseated.
Übel, *n.nt.* evil; nuisance.
Übelkeit, *n.f.* nausea.
übel•nehmen***, *vb.* hold against, resent.
Übeltat, -en, *n.f.* offence.
Übeltäter, -, *n.m.* offender.
üben, *vb.* practice.

über, *prep.* over, about, above, across, beyond.
überall, *adv.* everywhere.
überar´beiten, *vb.* work over; **(sich ü.)** overwork.
überaus, *adv.* exceedingly.
überbelichten, *vb.* overexpose.
überbie´ten***, *vb.* outbid; surpass.
Überbleibsel, -, *n.nt.* rest, left-over.

Überblick, -e, *n.m.* survey; general view.
überbli´cken, *vb.* survey.
überbrin´gen***, *vb.* deliver.
Überbrin´ger, -, *n.m.* bearer.
Überbrin´gerin, -nen, *n.f.* bearer.
überbrü´cken, *vb.* bridge.
überdau´ern, *vb.* outlive, outlast.
überdies´, *adv.* furthermore.

Überdruß, *n.m.* boredom; **(bis zum Ü.)** ad nauseam.

überdrüssig, *adj.* tired of, sick of.

übereilt′, *adj.* rash, hasty.

übereinan′der, *adv.* one on top of the other.

überein′•kommen*, *vb.* agree.

Überein′kommen, -, *n.nt.* agreement.

Überein′kunft, ″e, *n.f.* agreement.

überein′stimmen, *vb.* agree.

Überein′stimmung, -en, *n.f.* agreement, accord.

überfah′ren*, *vb.* drive over, run over.

Überfahrt, -en, *n.f.* passage, crossing.

Überfall, ″e, *n.m.* raid; hold-up.

überfallen*, *vb.* attack suddenly, hold up.

überf′ällig, *adj.* overdue.

überflie′gen*, *vb.* fly over; *(fig.)* scan.

über•fließen*, *vb.* overflow.

überflü′geln, *vb.* surpass.

Überfluß, ″sse, *n.m.* abundance.

überflüssig, *adj.* superfluous.

überflu′ten, *vb.* overflow.

überfüh′ren, *vb.* transfer, transport; convict.

Überfüh′rung, -en, *n.f.* transport, transfer; (railroad) overpass.

überfüllt′, *adj.* overcrowded, jammed.

Übergabe, *n.f.* delivery; surrender.

Übergang, ″e, *n.m.* passage; transition.

überge′ben*, *vb.* hand over, deliver; **(sich ü.)** vomit.

über•gehen*, *vb.* go over to.

überge′hen*, *vb.* pass over, skip.

Übergewicht, *n.nt.* overweight, preponderance; **(das Ü. bekommen*)** get the upper hand.

über•greifen*, *vb.* spread; encroach.

Übergriff, -e, *n.m.* encroachment.

über•haben*, *vb.* be sick of, be fed up with.

überhand′nehmen*, *vb.* spread, become dominant.

überhäu′fen, *vb.* overwhelm.

überhaupt′, *adv.* in general; altogether, at all.

überheb′lich, *adj.* overbearing.

überho′len, *vb.* overhaul; drive past, pass.

überholt′, *adj.* out-of-date.

überhö′ren, *vb.* purposely not hear, ignore.

überla′den, *adj.* ornate.

überlas′sen*, *vb.* give to, yield, leave to.

über•laufen*, *vb.* defect, desert; boil over, run over.

überlau′fen, *adj.* overrun.

Überläufer, -, *n.m.* deserter.

überle′ben, *vb.* outlive, survive.

Überle′ben, *n.nt.* survival.

überle′gen, *vb.* reflect on, think over.

überle′gen, *adj.* superior.

überlegt′, *adj.* deliberate.

Überle′gung, -en, *n.f.* deliberation, consideration.

überlie′fern, *vb.* hand over.

Überlie′ferung, -en, *n.f.* tradition.

überlis′ten, *vb.* outwit.

Übermacht, *n.f.* superiority.

überman′nen, *vb.* overpower.

Übermaß, *n.nt.* excess.

übermäßig, *adj.* excessive.

Übermensch, -en, -en, *n.m.* superman.

übermit′teln, *vb.* transmit, convey.

übermorgen, *adv.* the day after tomorrow.

Übermü′dung, *n.f.* overfatigue, exhaustion.

Übermut, *n.m.* high spirits; arrogance.

übernächst, *adj.* next but one.

übernach′ten, *vb.* spend the night, stay overnight.

übernatürlich, *adj.* supernatural.

überneh′men*, *vb.* take over.

überparteilich, *adj.* nonpartisan.

überprü′fen, *vb.* examine, check.

Überprü′fung, -en, *n.f.* checking, check-up.

überque′ren, *vb.* cross.

überra′gen, *vb.* surpass.

überra′gend, *adj.* superior.

überra′schen, *vb.* surprise.

Überra′schung, -en, *n.f.* surprise.

überre′den, *vb.* persuade.

Überre′dung, -en, *n.f.* persuasion.

überreich, *adj.* abundant, profuse.

überrei′chen, *vb.* hand over, present.

Überrest, -e, *n.m.* remains, relics.

überrum′peln, *vb.* take by surprise.

Überschallgeschwindigkeit, -en, *n.f.* supersonic speed.

überschat′ten, *vb.* overshadow.

überschät′zen, *vb.* overestimate.

überschau′en, *vb.* survey, get the whole view of.

Überschlag, ″e, *n.m.* estimate.

überschla′gen*, *vb.* pass over, skip; **(sich ü.)** turn over.

Überschrift, -en, *n.f.* title, heading, headline.

Überschuhe, *n.pl.* galoshes.

Überschuß, ″sse, *n.m.* surplus.

überschüt′ten, *vb.* overwhelm.

überschwem′men, *vb.* inundate.

Überschwem′mung, -en, *n.f.* flood.

Übersee, *n.f.* oversea(s).

Überseedampfer, -, *n.m.* transoceanic liner.

überseh′bar, *adj.* capable of being taken in at a glance; foreseeable.

überse′hen*, *vb.* view; overlook, not notice, ignore.

Überse´hen, -, *n.nt.* oversight.

übersen´den*, *vb.* send, transmit; consign, remit.

überset´zen, *vb.* translate.

Überset´zer, -, *n.m.* translator.

Überset´zerin, -nen, *n.f.* translator.

Überset´zung, -en, *n.f.* translation.

Übersicht, -en, *n.f.* overview; summary, outline.

übersichtlich, *adj.* clear; easily understandable.

überspannt´, *adj.* eccentric.

übersprin´gen*, *vb.* skip.

übersprudelnd, *adj.* exuberant.

überste´hen*, *vb.* endure, survive.

überstei´gen*, *vb.* surpass.

überstim´men, *vb.* outvote, overrule.

Überstunde, -n, *n.f.* hour of overtime work; *(pl.)* overtime.

überstür´zen, *vb.* precipitate.

überstürzt´, *adj.* headlong, precipitate.

übertrag´bar, *adj.* transferable.

übertra´gen*, *vb.* transfer, transmit; translate; **(im Radio ü.)** broadcast; **(im Fernseh ü.)** televise.

Übertra´gung, -en, *n.f.* transfer; translation; broadcast.

übertref´fen*, *vb.* surpass, excel.

übertrei´ben*, *vb.* exaggerate.

Übertrei´bung, -en, *n.f.* exaggeration.

über•treten*, *vb.* pass; overflow; *(pol.)* go over; *(eccl.)* convert.

übertre´ten*, *vb.* trespass, violate, infringe.

Übertre´tung, -en, *n.f.* violation, infringement.

übertrie´ben, *adj.* exaggerated, extravagant.

übervor´teilen, *vb.* get the better of (someone).

überwa´chen, *vb.* watch over, keep under surveillance, control.

Überwa´chung, -en, *n.f.* surveillance, control.

überwäl´tigen, *vb.* overpower, overwhelm.

überwei´sen*, *vb.* transfer; remit.

Überwei´sung, -en, *n.f.* remittance.

überwer´fen*, *vb.* **(sich ü.)** have a falling-out with.

überwie´gen*, *vb.* outweigh; predominate.

überwie´gend, *adj.* preponderant.

überwin´den*, *vb.* conquer, overcome.

Überwin´dung, -en, *n.f.* conquest; effort, reluctance.

überwin´tern, *vb.* hibernate.

Überzahl, *n.f.* numerical superiority.

überzählig, *adj.* surplus.

überzeu´gen, *vb.* convince.

überzeu´gend, *adj.* convincing.

Überzeu´gung, -en, *n.f.* conviction.

Überzeu´gungskraft, *n.f.* forcefulness.

Überzieher, -, *n.m.* overcoat.

üblich, *adj.* customary, usual.

U-Boot, -e, *n.nt.* (= Unterseeboot) submarine.

übrig, *adj.* remaining, left over.

übrig•bleiben*, *vb.* be left over; **(es bleibt mir nichts anderes übrig)** I have no other choice.

übrigens, *adv.* incidentally, by the way.

übrig•haben*, *vb.* have left over; **(nichts ü. für)** have no use for.

Übung, -en, *n.f.* practice; exercise.

Übungsbeispiel, -e, *n.nt.* paradigm.

UdSSR, *abbr.* (= Union´ der Soziali´stischen Sowjetrepubliken) Union of Soviet Socialist Republics.

Ufer, -, *n.nt.* shore, bank.

Ufereinfassung, -en, *n.f.* embankment.

uferlos, *adj.* limitless.

Uhr, -en, *n.f.* watch, clock; **(wieviel U. ist es?)** what time is it?; **(sieben U.)** seven o'clock.

Uhrmacher, -, *n.m.* watchmaker.

Uhu, -s, *n.m.* owl.

Ulk, -e, *n.m.* fun.

ulkig, *adj.* funny.

Ultra-, *cpds.* ultra.

um, *prep.* around; at (clock time); **(um . . . zu)** in order to; **(u. so mehr)** the more, all the more so.

um•adressieren, *vb.* readdress.

um•arbeiten, *vb.* rework, revise.

umar´men, *vb.* embrace.

Umar´mung, -en, *n.f.* embrace.

um•bauen, *vb.* remodel.

um•biegen*, *vb.* turn, turn around.

um•bringen*, *vb.* kill.

um•drehen, *vb.* turn around, rotate, revolve.

Umdre´hen, -en, *n.f.* turn, revolution, rotation.

um•erziehen*, *vb.* reeducate.

umfah´ren*, *vb.* circumnavigate, circle.

um•fallen*, *vb.* fall over.

Umfang, -̈e, *n.m.* circumference; extent; volume.

umfangreich, *adj.* extensive; comprehensive; voluminous.

umfas´sen, *vb.* enclose, surround; comprise.

umfas´send, *adj.* comprehensive.

um•formen, *vb.* remodel, transform, convert.

Umfrage, -n, *n.f.* inquiry, poll.

Umgang, *n.m.* intercourse, association.

Umgangssprache, *n.f.* colloquial speech, vernacular.

umge´ben*, *vb.* surround.

Umge´bung, -en, *n.f.* surroundings, environment; vicinity.

um•gehen*, *vb.* go around, circulate; **(u. mit)** deal with, handle; **(mit dem**

Gedanken u.) contemplate, plan.

umge´hen*, *vb.* evade, circumvent.

Umge´hen, -, *n.nt.* evasion.

Umge´hung, -en, *n.f.* circumvention; *(mil.)* flanking movement.

Umge´hungsstraße, -n, *n.f.* by-pass.

umgekehrt, **1.** *adj.* reverse, inverse. **2.** *adv.* the other way round.

um•gestalten, *vb.* transform, alter, modify.

umgren´zen, *vb.* enclose; circumscribe.

um•gucken, *vb.* (**sich u.**) look around.

um•haben*, *vb.* have on.

Umhang, ≈e, *n.m.* wrap.

umher´, *adv.* around, about.

umher´gehen*, *vb.* walk around.

umher´wandern, *vb.* wander.

Umkehr, *n.f.* return; reversal.

um´kehren, *vb.* turn (back, round, inside out, upside down).

Umkehrung, -en, *n.f.* reversal, reversing.

um•kippen, *vb.* turn over, tip over.

um•kleiden, *vb.* (**sich u.**) change one's clothes.

Umkleideraum, ≈e, *n.m.* dressing-room.

um•kommen*, *vb.* perish.

Umkreis, -e, *n.m.* circumference; range, radius.

umkrei´sen, *vb.* circle around, rotate around.

Umlauf, *n.m.* circulation.

um•laufen*, *vb.* circulate.

um•legen, *vb.* put on; change the position, shift; change the date.

um•leiten, *vb.* divert.

Umleitung, -en, *n.f.* detour.

um•lernen, *vb.* learn anew, readjust one's views.

umliegend, *adj.* surrounding.

umrah´men, *vb.* frame.

umran´den, *vb.* edge.

um•rechnen, *vb.* convert.

umrei´ßen*, *vb.* outline.

umrin´gen, *vb.* surround.

Umriß, -sse, *n.m.* contour, outline.

um•rühren, *vb.* stir.

Umsatz, ≈e, *n.m.* turnover, sales.

Umsatzsteuer, -n, *n.f.* sales tax.

um•schalten, *vb.* switch.

Umschau, *n.f.* (**U. halten***) look around.

umschichtig, *adv.* in turns.

Umschlag, ≈e, *n.m.* envelope; (book) cover; turnover; compress.

umschlie´ßen*, *vb.* encircle, encompass.

umschlin´gen*, *vb.* embrace.

um•schreiben*, *vb.* rewrite.

umschrei´ben*, *vb.* circumscribe, paraphrase.

Umschrei´bung, -en, *n.f.* paraphrase.

Umschrift, -en, *n.f.* transcription.

Umschwung, ≈e, *n.m.* change, about-face.

um•sehen*, *vb.* (**sich u.**) look around.

um•setzen, *vb.* transpose; (goods) sell.

Umsicht, *n.f.* circumspection.

umsichtig, *adj.* circumspect, prudent.

umso, *adv.* (**u. besser**) so much the better; (**je mehr, u. besser**) the more the better.

umsonst´, *adv.* in vain; gratis, free of charge.

Umstand, ≈e, *n.m.* circumstance, condition; *(pl.)* formalities, fuss; (**in anderen Umständen**) pregnant.

umständlich, *adj.* complicated, fussy.

Umstandskleid, -er, *n.nt.* maternity dress.

Umstandswort, ≈er, *n.nt.* adverb.

Umstehend-, *n.m. & f.* bystander.

um•steigen*, *vb.* transfer, change.

Umsteiger, -, *n.m.* transfer (ticket).

um•stellen, *vb.* change the position of; (**sich u. auf**)

readjust, convert to; computerize.

umstel´len, *vb.* surround.

um•steuern, *vb.* reverse.

um•stimmen, *vb.* make someone change his mind.

um•stoßen*, *vb.* overturn, overthrow, upset.

umstri´cken, *vb.* ensnare.

Umsturz, ≈e, *n.m.* overthrow, revolution.

um•stürzen, *vb.* overturn.

Umtausch, -e, *n.m.* exchange; (**vom U. ausgeschlossen**) no exchange.

umtauschbar, *adj.* exchangeable.

um•tauschen, *vb.* exchange.

Umtrieb, -e, *n.m.* intrigue, machinations.

um•tun*, *vb.* (**sich nach etwas u.**) look for, apply for.

Umwälzung, -en, *n.f.* upheaval, revolution.

um•wandeln, *vb.* transform; change; convert.

um•wechseln, *vb.* change, convert.

Umweg, -e, *n.m.* detour.

Umwelt, *n.f.* environment.

Umweltschutz, *n.m.* environmental protection.

Umweltschtzer, -, *n.m.* environmentalist.

Umweltverschmutzung, *n.f.* pollution.

umwer´ben*, *vb.* woo, court.

Umwer´bung, *n.f.* courtship.

um•werfen*, *vb.* overthrow; upset.

um•ziehen*, *vb.* move; (**sich u.**) change one's clothes.

umzin´geln, *vb.* surround.

Umzug, ≈e, *n.m.* move; procession.

unabhängig, *adj.* independent.

Unabhängigkeit, *n.f.* independence.

unabkömmlich, *adj.* indispensable.

unabläs´sig, *adj.* incessant.

unabseh´bar, *adj.* unforeseeable.

unabwend´bar, *adj.* inevitable.

unachtsam, *adj.* inattentive; careless.

unähnlich, *adj.* dissimilar, unlike.

unangebracht, *adj.* out of place.

unangemessen, *adj.* unsuitable, improper.

unangenehm, *adj.* unpleasant, distasteful.

Unannehmlichkeit, -en, *n.f.* trouble.

unansehnlich, *adj.* plain, inconspicuous.

unanständig, *adj.* indecent, obscene.

unanwendbar, *adj.* inapplicable.

unappetitlich, *adj.* unappetizing; nasty.

Unart, -en, *n.f.* rudeness, bad manners.

unartig, *adj.* naughty.

unauffällig, *adj.* inconspicuous.

unaufhör'lich, *adj.* incessant.

unaufmerksam, *adj.* inattentive.

Unaufmerksamkeit, -en, *n.f.* inattentiveness; inadvertence.

unaufrichtig, *adj.* insincere.

Unaufrichtigkeit, -en, *n.f.* insincerity; lie.

unausbleib'lich, *adj.* inevitable.

unausgeglichen, *adj.* unbalanced, unstable.

unausgesetzt, *adj.* continual.

unaussteh'lich, *adj.* insufferable.

unbändig, *adj.* unruly; excessive.

unbarmherzig, *adj.* merciless.

unbeabsichtigt, *adj.* unintentional.

unbeachtet, *adj.* unnoticed; **(u. lassen*)** ignore.

unbedacht, *adj.* thoughtless.

unbedenklich, *adj.* harmless.

unbedeutend, *adj.* insignificant.

unbedingt', *adj.* absolute, unconditional.

unbefangen, *adj.* natural, naïve.

unbefleckt, *adj.* immaculate; **(unbefleckte Empf ängnis)** Immaculate Conception.

unbefriedigend, *adj.* unsatisfactory.

unbefriedigt, *adj.* dissatisfied.

unbefugt, *adj.* unauthorized.

unbegabt, *adj.* untalented.

unbegreif'lich, *adj.* incomprehensible.

unbegrenzt, *adj.* limitless.

unbegründet, *adj.* unfounded.

Unbehagen, *n.nt.* discomfort.

unbehaglich, *adj.* uneasy.

unbeherrscht, *adj.* uncontrolled.

unbeholfen, *adj.* awkward, clumsy.

unbekannt, *adj.* unknown, unfamiliar.

unbekümmert, *adj.* unconcerned.

unbeliebt, *adj.* unpopular.

unbemerkbar, *adj.* imperceptible.

unbemerkt, *adj.* unnoticed.

unbenommen, *adj.* **(es bleibt* Ihnen u.)** you are at liberty to.

unbequem, *adj.* inconvenient; uncomfortable.

unbere'chenbar, *adj.* incalculable; unreliable, erratic.

unberechtigt, *adj.* unauthorized; unjustified.

unberufen!, *interj.* touch wood!

unbeschädigt, *adj.* undamaged.

unbescheiden, *adj.* immodest; selfish.

Unbescholtenheit, *n.f.* integrity.

unbeschreiblich, *adj.* indescribable.

unbeschrieben, *adj.* blank.

unbesehen, *adj.* unseen.

unbesieg'bar, *adj.* invincible.

unbesonnen, *adj.* thoughtless.

unbesorgt, *adj.* carefree, unconcerned.

unbeständig, *adj.* changeable.

unbestellbar, *adj.* undeliverable.

unbestimmt, *adj.* indefinite, vague.

unbestritten, *adj.* undisputed.

unbeträchtlich, *adj.* inconsiderable.

unbeugsam, *adj.* inflexible; obstinate.

unbewandert, *adj.* inexperienced.

unbewiesen, *adj.* not proved.

unbewohnbar, *adj.* uninhabitable.

unbewohnt, *adj.* uninhabited.

unbewußt, *adj.* unconscious; unknown.

unbezahl'bar, *adj.* priceless.

unbrauchbar, *adj.* useless.

und, *conj.* and.

Undank, *n.m.* ingratitude.

undankbar, *adj.* ungrateful.

undefinier'bar, *adj.* indefinable.

undenk'lich, *adj.* inconceivable; **(seit u. en Zeiten)** since time out of mind.

undeutlich, *adj.* unclear, indistinct.

undicht, *adj.* leaky.

Unding, *n.nt.* absurdity, nonsense.

unduldsam, *adj.* intolerant.

undurchführ'bar, *adj.* not feasible.

undurchsichtig, *adj.* opaque.

uneben, *adj.* uneven.

unecht, *adj.* not genuine, false, counterfeit; artificial.

unehelich, *adj.* illegitimate.

unehrenhaft, *adj.* dishonorable.

unehrerbietig, *adj.* disrespectful.

unehrlich, *adj.* dishonest; insincere.

uneingeschränkt, *adj.* unlimited.

uneinig, *adj.* **(u. sein*)** disagree.

Uneinigkeit, -en, *n.f.* disagreement, dissension.

unempfindlich, *adj.* insensitive.

unend′lich, *adj.* infinite; **(u. klein)** infinitesimal.

Unend′lichkeit, -en, *n.f.* infinity.

unentbehrlich, *adj.* indispensable.

unentgeltlich, *adj.* gratuitous.

unentschieden, *adj.* undecided; **(das Spiel ist u.)** the game is a draw.

unentschlossen, *adj.* undecided.

unentwegt, *adj.* constant.

unerfahren, *adj.* inexperienced.

Unerfahrenheit, -en, *n.f.* inexperience.

unerfreulich, *adj.* unpleasant.

unerheblich, *adj.* insignificant, irrelevant.

unerhört′, *adj.* unheard of, outrageous.

unerkannt, *adj.* unrecognized.

unerkennbar, *adj.* unrecognizable.

unerklärlich, *adj.* inexplicable.

unerläßlich, *adj.* indispensable.

unerlaubt, *adj.* unlawful, illegal, illicit.

unermeß′lich, *adj.* immeasurable.

unermüdlich, *adj.* unpleasant.

unerquicklich, *adj.* unpleasant.

unersätt′lich, *adj.* insatiable.

unerschrocken, *adj.* intrepid.

unersetz′lich, *adj.* irreplaceable.

unersprieß′lich, *adj.* unpleasant.

unerträg′lich, *adj.* unbearable, insufferable.

unerwartet, *adj.* unexpected.

unerwünscht, *adj.* unwelcome.

unerzogen, *adj.* ill-bred, ill-mannered.

unf ähig, *adj.* unable, incapable, incompetent.

unfair, *adj.* unfair.

Unfall, ⸗e, *n.m.* accident.

unfaß′bar, *adj.* incomprehensible.

unfaß′lich, *adj.* incomprehensible.

unfehl′bar, *adj.* infallible.

Unfeinheit, -en, *n.f.* crudeness, crudity.

unförmig, *adj.* shapeless.

unfreiwillig, *adj.* involuntary.

unfreundlich, *adj.* unkind, unfriendly; rude.

unfruchtbar, *adj.* barren, sterile.

Unfug, *n.m.* mischief.

unfügsam, *adj.* unmanageable.

Ungar, -n, -n, *n.m.* Hungarian.

Ungarin, -nen, *n.f.* Hungarian.

ungarisch, *adj.* Hungarian.

Ungarn, *n.nt.* Hungary.

ungastlich, *adj.* inhospitable.

ungeachtet, *prep.* notwithstanding.

ungebildet, *adj.* uneducated.

ungebührlich, *adj.* improper.

ungebunden, *adj.* free.

Ungeduld, *n.f.* impatience.

ungeduldig, *adj.* impatient.

ungeeignet, *adj.* unqualified, unsuitable.

ungef ähr, 1. *adj.* approximate. **2.** *adv.* approximately, about.

ungef ährlich, *adj.* harmless.

ungef ällig, *adj.* unobliging, impolite.

ungeheuchelt, *adj.* sincere.

ungeheuer, *adj.* tremendous, huge.

Ungeheuer, -, *n.nt.* monster.

ungeheu′erlich, *adj.* monstrous.

ungehobelt, *adj.* uncouth.

ungehörig, *adj.* improper, rude.

ungehorsam, *adj.* disobedient.

Ungehorsam, *n.m.* disobedience.

ungekünstelt, *adj.* unaffected, natural.

ungeläufig, *adj.* unfamiliar.

ungelegen, *adj.* inconvenient.

ungelenk, *adj.* clumsy.

ungelernt, *adj.* unskilled.

ungemein, *adv.* uncommonly.

ungemütlich, *adj.* uncomfortable.

ungeneigt, *adj.* disinclined.

ungeniert, *adj.* free and easy.

ungenießbar, *adj.* inedible; unbearable.

ungenügend, *adj.* insufficient; unsatisfactory.

ungerade, *adj.* uneven; (numbers) odd.

ungerecht, *adj.* unjust, unfair.

ungerechtfertigt, *adj.* unwarranted.

Ungerechtigkeit, -en, *n.f.* injustice.

ungern, *adv.* unwillingly; reluctantly.

ungesalzen, *adj.* unsalted.

ungeschehen, *adj.* **(u. machen)** to undo.

Ungeschicklichkeit, -en, *n.f.* clumsiness.

ungeschickt, *adj.* clumsy, awkward.

ungeschlacht, *adj.* uncouth.

ungesetzlich, *adj.* illegal.

ungesittet, *adj.* unmannerly.

ungestört, *adj.* undisturbed.

ungestraft, 1. *adj.* unpunished. **2.** *adv.* with impunity.

ungestüm, *adj.* impetuous.

ungesund, *adj.* unhealthy; unsound.

Ungetüm, -e, *n.nt.* monster.

ungewandt, *adj.* awkward.

ungewiß, *adj.* uncertain.

Ungewißheit, -en, *n.f.* uncertainty.

Ungewitter, -, *n.nt.* thunderstorm.

ungewöhnlich, *adj.* unusual, abnormal.

ungewohnt, *adj.* unaccustomed, unfamiliar.

ungewollt, *adj.* unintentional.

ungezählt, *adj.* innumerable.

ungezügelt, *adj.* unrestrained.

ungezwungen, *adj.* easygoing.

Ungläubig-, *n.m.& f.* infidel.

unglaublich, *adj.* incredible.

unglaubwürdig, *adj.* unreliable.

ungleich, *adj.* unequal, uneven, unlike.

ungleichartig, *adj.* dissimilar.

Ungleichheit, -en, *n.f.* unequality, dissimilarity.

Unglück, -e, *n.nt.* misfortune, calamity, disaster, accident.

unglücklich, *adj.* unhappy; unfortunate.

unglücklicherweise, *adv.* unfortunately.

unglückselig, *adj.* disastrous; utterly miserable.

Ungnade, *n.f.* disfavor.

ungnädig, *n.f.* ungracious.

ungültig, *adj.* invalid, void; **(für u. erklären)** annul, declare null and void.

ungünstig, *adj.* unfavorable.

unhaltbar, *adj.* untenable.

unhandlich, *adj.* unwieldy.

Unheil, *n.nt.* harm, disaster.

unheilbar, *adj.* incurable.

unheilbringend, *adj.* fatal, ominous.

unheilvoll, *adj.* ominous.

unheimlich, *adj.* scary, sinister.

unhöflich, *adj.* impolite, rude.

unhygienisch, *adj.* unsanitary.

Uniform´, -en, *n.f.* uniform.

uninteressant, *adj.* uninteresting.

uninteressiert, *adj.* uninterested; disinterested.

unisex, *adj.* unisex.

universal´, *adj.* universal.

Universität´, -en, *n.f.* university.

Univer´sum, *n.nt.t* universe.

unkenntlich, *adj.* unrecognizable.

unklar, *adj.* unclear, obscure.

unkleidsam, *adj.* unbecoming.

unkompliziert, *adj.* uncomplicated.

Unkosten, *n.pl.* expenses, overhead.

Unkraut, *n.nt.* weeds.

unlängst, *adv.* recently.

unlauter, *adj.* impure; unfair.

unleserlich, *adj.* illegible.

unlieb, *adj.* disagreeable.

unliebenswürdig, *adj.* unfriendly, impolite.

unlogisch, *adj.* illogical.

unlustig, *adj.* listless.

unmanierlich, *adj.* unmannered.

unmaßgeblich, *adj.* irrelevant; unauthoritative.

unmäßig, *adj.* immoderate.

Unmenge, -n, *n.f.* enormous quantity.

Unmensch, -en, -en, *n.m.* brute.

unmenschlich, *adj.* inhuman.

unmerklich, *adj.* imperceptible.

unmittelbar, *adj.* immediate.

unmodern, *adj.* old-fashioned, out of style.

unmöglich, *adj.* impossible.

unmoralisch, *adj.* immoral.

unmündig, *adj.* underage.

unnachahmlich, *adj.* inimitable.

unnahbar, *adj.* inaccessible.

unnötig, *adj.* needless, unnecessary.

unnütz, *adj.* useless.

unordentlich, *adj.* disorderly, messy.

Unordnung, *n.f.* disorder.

unparteiisch, *adj.* impartial, neutral.

unpassend, *adj.* unsuitable; improper, off-color.

unpassierbar, *adj.* impassable.

unpäßlich, *adj.* unwell, indisposed.

unpersönlich, *adj.* impersonal.

unpolitisch, *adj.* nonpolitical.

unpraktisch, *adj.* impractical.

unpünktlich, *adj.* not on time.

unrecht, *adj.* wrong; **(u. haben*)** be wrong.

Unrecht, *n.nt.* wrong, harm, injustice.

unreell, *adj.* dishonest.

unregelmäßig, *adj.* irregular.

unreif, *adj.* immature.

unrein, *adj.* unclean; impure.

unrichtig, *adj.* incorrect.

Unruhe, -n, *n.f.* unrest, trouble, disturbance.

unruhig, *adj.* restless, troubled, uneasy.

unschädlich, *adj.* harmless.

unscheinbar, *adj.* insignificant.

unschicklich, *adj.* improper.

unschlüssig, *adj.* undecided.

Unschuld, *n.f.* innocence.

unschuldig, *adj.* innocent.

unselig, *adj.* unhappy, fatal.

unser, -, -e, *adj.* our.

uns(e)rer, -es, -e, *pron.* ours.

unsicher, *adj.* uncertain; unsafe.

Unsicherheit, -en, *n.f.* uncertainty, insecurity.

unsichtbar, *adj.* invisible.

Unsinn, *n.m.* nonsense.

unsinnig, *adj.* absurd, nonsensical.

Unsitte, -n, *n.f.* bad habit.

unsittlich, *adj.* immoral.

unsterblich, *adj.* immortal.

unstet, *adj.* unsteady.

Unstimmigkeit, -en, *n.f.* discrepancy, disagreement.

unsympatisch, *adj.* disagreeable.

untauglich, *adj.* unfit.

unteilbar, *adj.* indivisible.

unten, *adv.* below, down, downstairs.

unter, *prep.* under, beneath, below; among; **(u. uns)** just between you and me.

unter-, *adj.* under, lower.

Unterarm, -e, *n.m.* forearm.

unterbewußt, *adj.* subconscious.

Unterbewußtsein, *n.nt.* subconsciousness.

unterbie´ten*, *vb.* undercut; lower.

unterblei´ben*, *vb.* not get done.

unterbre´chen*, *vb.* interrupt.

Unterbre´chung, -en, *n.f.* interruption.

unterbrei´ten, *vb.* submit.

unter•bringen*, *vb.* lodge, accommodate.

unterdes´(sen), *adv.* meanwhile.

unterdrü'cken, *vb.* suppress, oppress, repress, stifle, subdue.

unterdrückt', *adj.* downtrodden.

Unterdrü'ckung, -en, *n.f.* suppression.

untereinan'der, *adv.* among them- (our-, your-) selves.

unterernährt, *adj.* undernourished.

Unterernährung, *n.f.* malnutrition.

Unterfüh'rung, -en, *n.f.* underpass.

Untergang, ⸚e, *n.m.* downfall, decline.

unterge'ben, *adj.* subordinate.

Unterge'ben-, -n.m.& f. subordinate.

unter•gehen*, *vb.* perish; set (sun).

untergeordnet, *adj.* subordinate.

untergra'ben*, *vb.* undermine, subvert.

Untergrundbahn, -en, *n.f.* subway.

unterhalb, *prep.* below.

Unterhalt, *n.m.* maintenance, keep.

unterhal'ten*, *vb.* maintain, support; entertain; **(sich u.)** converse.

Unterhal'tung, -en, *n.f.* maintenance; entertainment, conversation.

Unterhand'lung, -en, *n.f.* negotiation.

Unterhaus, *n.nt.* lower house (of parliament, congress).

Unterhemd, -en, *n.nt.* undershirt.

Unterhose, -n, *n.f.* underpants.

unterjo'chen, *vb.* subjugate.

Unterkunft, ⸚e, *n.f.* lodging.

Unterlage, -n, *n.f.* base, bed; evidence; bottom sheet.

unterlas'sen*, *vb.* omit, fail to do.

Unterlas'sung, -en, *n.f.* omission, default.

unterle'gen, *adj.* inferior.

Unterleib, -er, *n.m.* abdomen.

unterlie'gen*, *vb.* succumb to, be overcome by.

Untermieter, -, *n.m.* subtenant.

unterneh'men*, *vb.* undertake.

Unterneh'men, -, *n.nt.* enterprise.

unterneh'mend, *adj.* enterprising.

Unterneh'mer, -, *n.m.* entrepreneur, contractor.

Unterneh'merin, -nen, *n.f.* entrepreneur, contractor.

Unterneh'mung, -en, *n.f.* undertaking.

unterneh'mungslustig, *adj.* adventurous.

Unteroffizier, -e, *n.m.* noncommissioned officer, sergeant.

Unterpfand, *n.nt.* pledge, security.

Unterre'dung, -en, *n.f.* discussion, parley.

Unterricht, *n.m.* instruction.

unterrich'ten, *vb.* instruct.

Unterrich'tung, *n.f.* guidance.

Unterrock, ⸚e, *n.m.* slip, petticoat.

untersa'gen, *vb.* prohibit.

Untersatz, ⸚e, *n.m.* base; saucer.

unterschät'zen, *vb.* underestimate.

unterschei'den, *vb.* distinguish, differentiate; **(sich u.)** differ.

Unterschei'dung, -en, *n.f.* distinction.

Unterschied, -e, *n.m.* difference.

unterschiedslos, *adj.* indiscriminate.

unterschla'gen*, *vb.* embezzle, suppress.

unterschrei'ben*, *vb.* sign (one's name to).

Unterschrift, -en, *n.f.* signature.

Unterseeboot, -e, *n.nt.* submarine.

untersetzt', *adj.* chunky, thick-set.

Understand, ⸚e, *n.m.* dugout.

unterste'hen*, *vb.* **(sich u.)** dare.

Unterstel'lung, -en, *n.f.* innuendo, insinuation.

unterstrei'chen*, *vb.* underline, underscore.

unterstüt'zen, *vb.* support, back.

Unterstüt'zung, -en, *n.f.* support, backing.

untersu'chen, *vb.* investigate, examine.

Untersu'chung, -en, *n.f.* investigation, examination.

Untertan, (-en,) -en, *n.m.* subject.

Untertasse, -n, *n.f.* saucer.

unter•tauchen, *vb.* submerge.

Unterwäsche, *n.f.* underwear.

unterwegs', *adv.* on the way; bound for.

unterwei'sen*, *vb.* instruct.

Unterwei'sung, -en, *n.f.* instruction.

Unterwelt, *n.f.* underworld.

unterwer'fen*, *vb.* subjugate; subject to; **(sich u.)** submit (to).

Unterwer'fung, -en, *n.f.* submission.

unterwor'fen, *adj.* subject (to).

unterwür'fig, *adj.* subservient.

unterzeich'nen, *vb.* sign.

unterzie'hen*, *vb.* **(sich u.)** undergo.

untief, *adj.* shallow.

untreu, *adj.* unfaithful, disloyal.

Untreue, *n.f.* unfaithfulness, disloyalty.

untröstlich, *adj.* disconsolate.

unüberlegt, *adj.* inconsiderate, thoughtless.

unüberwind'lich, *adj.* insuperable.

unumgäng'lich, *adj.* unavoidable.

unverän'derlich, *adj.* invariable.

unverant'wortlich, *adj.* irresponsible.

unverbes'serlich, *adj.* incorrigible.

unverbindlich, *adj.* without obligation.

unverblümt, *adj.* blunt.

unverdaulich, *adj.* indigestible.

unverein'bar, *adj.* incompatible.

unvergeßlich, *adj.* unforgettable.

unvergleich'lich, *adj.* incomparable.

unverheiratet, *adj.* unmarried.

unverhohlen, *adj.* frank, aboveboard.

unverkenn'bar, *adj.* unmistakable.

unvermeidlich, *adj.* inevitable.

unvermittelt, *adj.* abrupt.

unvermutet, *adj.* unexpected.

unverschämt, *adj.* shameless, impudent, nervy.

Unverschämtheit, -en, *n.f.* impertinence, gall.

unversehens, *adv.* unexpectedly.

unverständlich, *adj.* incomprehensible.

unverzüglich, *adj.* speedy, without delay.

unvollendet, *adj.* incomplete, unfinished.

unvollkommen, *adj.* incomplete, imperfect.

unvoreingenommen, *adj.* unbiased.

unvorher'gesehen, *adj.* unforeseen.

unvorsichtig, *adj.* careless.

unvorstell'bar, *adj.* unimaginable.

unwäg'bar, *adj.* imponderable.

unwahr(haftig), *adj.* untrue.

Unwahrheit, -en, *n.f.* untruth.

unwahrnehmbar, *adj.* imperceptible.

unwahrscheinlich, *adj.* improbable.

unweigerlich, *adj.* unhesitating; without fail.

unwesentlich, *adj.* immaterial, nonessential.

unwiderleg'bar, *adj.* irrefutable.

unwidersteh'lich, *adj.* irresistible.

unwillkürlich, *adj.* involuntary.

unwirksam, *adj.* ineffectual.

unwissend, *adj.* ignorant.

unwürdig, *adj.* unworthy.

Unzahl, *n.f.* tremendous number.

unzählig, *adj.* countless.

Unze, -n, *n.f.* ounce.

unzertrenn'lich, *adj.* inseparable.

Unzucht, *n.f.* lewdness.

unzüchtig, *adj.* lewd.

unzufrieden, *adj.* dissatisfied.

Unzufriedenheit, -en, *n.f.* dissatisfaction.

unzulänglich, *adj.* insufficient, inadequate.

unzurechnungsfähig, *adj.* insane.

unzureichend, *adj.* insufficient.

unzuverlässig, *adj.* unreliable.

Ur-, *cpds.* original; very old; tremendously.

uralt, *adj.* very old, ancient.

Uraufführung, -en, *n.f.* première.

Urenkel, -, *n.m.* greatgrandson.

Urenkelin, -nen, *n.f.* greatgranddaughter.

Urgroßeltern, *n.pl.* greatgrandparents.

Urgroßmutter, ⸚, *n.f.* greatgrandmother.

Urgroßvater, ⸚, *n.m.* greatgrandfather.

Urheber, -, *n.m.* author, originator.

Urheberrecht, -e, *n.nt.* copyright.

Urin', **-e**, *n.nt.* urine.

urinie'ren, *vb.* urinate.

Urkunde, -n, *n.f.* document.

Urlaub, -e, *n.m.* leave, furlough.

Urlauber, -, *n.m.* vacationer.

Urlauberin, -nen, *n.f.* vacationer.

Urne, -n, *n.f.* urn; ballot box.

Urquell, -e, *n.m.* fountainhead.

Ursache, -n, *n.f.* cause; **(keine U.)** don't mention it.

Ursprung, ⸚e, *n.m.* origin.

ursprünglich, *adj.* original.

Urteil, -e, *n.nt.* judgment, sentence.

urteilen, *vb.* judge.

Urteilsspruch, ⸚e, *n.m.* verdict.

usurpie'ren, *vb.* usurp.

usw., *abbr.* (= und so weiter) etc., and so forth.

uto'pisch, *adj.* utopian.

V

Vagabund', **-en, -en**, *n.m.* tramp.

vage, *adj.* vague.

Vagi'na, (-nen), *n.f.* vagina.

Valu'ta, -ten, *n.f.* value; (foreign) currency.

Vanil'le, *n.f.* vanilla.

Variation', **-en**, *n.f.* variation.

Varieté', *n.nt.* variety show, vaudeville.

variie'ren, *vb.* vary.

Vase, -n, *n.f.* vase.

Vater, ⸚, *n.m.* father.

Vaterland, *n.nt.* fatherland.

väterlich, *adj.* fatherly, paternal.

vaterlos, *adj.* fatherless.

Vaterschaft, -en, *n.f.* fatherhood, paternity.

Vaterun'ser, *n.nt.* Lord's Prayer.

Veilchen, -, *n.nt.* violet.

Vene, -n, *n.f.* vein.

vene'risch, *adj.* venereal.

Ventil', **-e**, *n.nt.* valve.

Ventilation', *n.f.* ventilation.

Ventila'tor, -o'ren, *n.m.* ventilator, fan.

ventilie'ren, *vb.* ventilate.

verab'reden, *vb.* agree upon; **(sich v.)** make an appointment, date.

Verab'redung, -en, *n.f.* appointment, engagement, date.

verab'scheuen, *vb.* abhor, detest.

verab′schieden, *vb.* dismiss; pass (a bill); **(sich v.)** take one's leave.

verach′ten, *vb.* scorn, despise.

verach′tenswert, *adj.* despicable.

veräch′tlich, *adj.* contemptuous.

Verach′tung, -en, *n.f.* contempt.

verallgemei′nern, *vb.* generalize.

Verallgemei′nerung, -en, *n.f.* generalization.

veral′tet, *adj.* obsolete.

Veran′da, -den, *n.f.* porch.

verän′derlich, *adj.* changeable.

verän′dern, *vb.* change.

Verän′derung, -en, *n.f.* change.

veran′kern, *vb.* anchor, moor.

veran′lassen*, *vb.* cause, motivate.

Veran′lassung, -en, *n.f.* cause, motivation.

veran′schaulichen, *vb.* illustrate.

veran′stalten, *vb.* arrange, put on.

Veran′staltung, -en, *n.f.* arrangement, performance.

verant′wortlich, *adj.* responsible.

Verant′wortlichkeit, -en, *n.f.* responsibility.

Verant′wortung, -en, *n.f.* responsibility; accounting, justification.

verant′wortungslos, *adj.* irresponsible.

verant′wortungsvoll, *adj.* carrying responsibility.

verar′beiten, *vb.* process.

verär′gern, *vb.* exasperate.

verar′men, *vb.* become poor.

Verb, -en, *n.nt.* verb.

verbal′, *adj.* verbal.

Verband′, ̈e, *n.m.* association; bandage, dressing.

verban′nen, *vb.* banish, exile.

Verban′nung, -en, *n.f.* banishment, exile.

verbau′en, *vb.* build badly; obstruct.

verber′gen*, *vb.* hide.

verbes′sern, *vb.* improve, correct.

Verbes′serung, -en, *n.f.* improvement, correction.

verbeu′gen, *vb.* **(sich v.)** bow.

Verbeu′gung, -en, *n.f.* bow.

verbeu′len, *vb.* dent, batter.

verbie′gen*, *vb.* bend (out of shape).

verbie′ten*, *vb.* forbid, prohibit, ban.

verbie′terisch, *adj.* prohibitive.

verbin′den*, *vb.* connect, join, combine; bandage.

verbind′lich, *adj.* binding, obligatory.

Verbin′dung, -en, *n.f.* connection, combination; (chemical) compound; (student) fraternity; **(in V. stehen* mit)** be in touch with; **(sich in V. setzen mit)** get in touch with.

verbis′sen, *adj.* suppressed; dogged.

verbit′ten*, *vb.* **(sich v.)** decline; not stand for.

verbit′tern, *vb.* embitter.

verblas′sen, *vb.* turn pale, fade.

Verbleib′, *n.m.* whereabouts.

verblei′chen*, *vb.* grow pale, fade.

verblüf′fen, *vb.* dumbfound, flabbergast.

verbo′gen, *adj.* bent.

verbor′gen, *adj.* hidden.

Verbot′, -e, *n.nt.* prohibition.

Verbrauch′, *n.m.* consumption.

verbrau′chen, *vb.* consume, use up, wear out.

Verbrau′cher, -, *n.m.* consumer.

Verbrauchs′steuer, -n, *n.f.* excise tax.

Verbre′chen, -, *n.nt.* crime.

Verbre′cher, -, *n.m.* criminal.

Verbre′cherin, -nen, *n.f.* criminal.

verbre′cherisch, *adj.* criminal.

verbrei′ten, *vb.* disseminate, propagate, diffuse.

verbrenn′bar, *adj.* combustible.

verbren′nen*, *vb.* burn; cremate.

Verbren′nung, *n.f.* burning; cremation; combustion.

verbrin′gen*, *vb.* spend (time).

verbrü′hen, *vb.* scald.

verbun′den, *adj.* indebted, obliged.

verbün′den, *vb.* ally.

Verbün′det-, *n.m. & f.* ally, confederate.

verbür′gen, *vb.* guarantee.

Verdacht′, *n.m.* suspicion.

verdäch′tig, *adj.* suspicious, suspected.

verdam′men, *vb.* damn, condemn.

verdam′menswert, *adj.* damnable.

Verdamm′nis, *n.f.* (eternal) damnation.

verdammt′, *adj.* damned; damn it!

Verdam′mung, -en, *n.f.* damnation.

verdamp′fen, *vb.* evaporate.

verdau′en, *vb.* digest.

verdau′lich, *adj.* digestible.

Verdau′ung, *n.f.* digestion.

Verdau′ungsstörung, -en, *n.f.* indigestion.

Verdeck′, -e, *n.nt.* deck covering; top (of an auto).

verden′ken*, *vb.* take amiss.

verder′ben*, *vb.* perish, spoil, ruin.

Verder′ben, *n.nt.* perdition, ruin, doom.

verderb′lich, *adj.* ruinous; perishable.

verderbt′, *adj.* corrupt.

verdeut′lichen, *vb.* make clear.

verdich′ten, *vb.* thicken, solidify.

verdie′nen, *vb.* earn, deserve.

Verdienst′, -e, *n.m.* earnings.

Verdienst′, -e, *n.nt.* merit.

verdienst′lich, *adj.* meritorious.

verdient′, *adj.* deserving, deserved.

verdol′metschen, *vb.* interpret, translate.

verdop′peln, *vb.* double.

Verdop′pelung, -en, *n.f.* doubling.

verdor´ren, *vb.* wither.

verdrängen, *vb.* push out, displace; suppress, inhibit.

Verdrän´gung, -en, *n.f.* displacement; repression, inhibition.

verdre´hen, *vb.* twist, distort, pervert.

verdrie´ßen*, *vb.* grieve, vex, annoy.

verdrieß´lich, *adj.* morose, sulky.

Verdruß´, *n.m.* vexation, irritation.

verdun´keln, *vb.* darken.

Verdun´kelung, -en, *n.f.* blackout.

verdün´nen, *vb.* thin, dilute, rarefy.

verdut´zen, *vb.* bewilder.

vereh´ren, *vb.* adore, respect, revere.

Vereh´rer, -, *n.m.* admirer.

Vereh´rerin, -nen, *n.f.* admirer.

Vereh´rung, *n.f.* adoration, reverence.

verei´digen, *vb.* administer an oath to.

Verei´digung, -en, *n.f.* swearing-in.

Verein´, -e, *n.m.* association.

verein´bar, *adj.* compatible.

verein´baren, *vb.* come to an agreement, reconcile.

Verein´barkeit, *n.f.* compatibility.

Verein´barung, -en, *n.f.* agreement.

verein´fachen, *vb.* simplify.

verein´heitlichen, *vb.* standardize, make uniform.

verei´nigen, *vb.* unite.

Verei´nigte Staaten von Ame´rika, *n.pl.* United States of America.

Verei´nigung, -en, *n.f.* union, alliance, association, merger.

Verein´te Natio´nen, *n.pl.* United Nations.

verein´zelt, *adj.* isolated, individual; scattered, stray.

verei´teln, *vb.* thwart, foil.

verer´ben, *vb.* bequeath.

vererb´lich, *adj.* hereditary.

Verer´bung, -en, *n.f.* heredity.

verfah´ren*, *vb.* act, proceed, deal; (sich v.) lose one's way.

Verfah´ren, -, *n.nt.* procedure, process.

Verfall´, *n.m.* decay, decline, disrepair.

verfal´len*, *vb.* decay, decline, deteriorate; fall due, lapse.

verf äl´schen, *vb.* falsify, adulterate.

Verf äl´schung, -en, *n.f.* falsification, adulteration.

verf äng´lich, *adj.* captious, insidious.

verfas´sen, *vb.* compose, write.

Verfas´ser, -, *n.m.* author.

Verfas´serin, -nen, *n.f.* author.

Verfas´sung, -en, *n.f.* composition; state, condition; constitution.

verfas´sungsmäßig, *adj.* constitutional.

verfas´sungswidrig, *adj.* unconstitutional.

verfau´len, *vb.* rot.

verfault´, *adj.* putrid.

verfecht´bar, *adj.* defensible.

verfeh´len, *vb.* miss.

verfei´nern, *vb.* refine.

Verfei´nerung, -en, *n.f.* refinement.

verfer´tigen, *vb.* manufacture.

verfil´men, *vb.* film, make a movie of.

verflie´ßen*, *vb.* flow away, lapse.

verflu´chen, *vb.* curse, damn.

verflucht´, *adj.* cursed, damned; damn it!

verfol´gen, *vb.* pursue, haunt, persecute.

Verfol´gung, -en, *n.f.* pursuit, persecution.

Verfrach´ter, -, *n.m.* shipper.

verfrüht´, *adj.* premature.

verfüg´bar, *adj.* available.

verfü´gen, *vb.* enact, order; (v. über) have at one's disposal.

Verfü´gung, -en, *n.f.* disposition, instruction, enactment; (mir zur V. stehen*) be at my disposal;

(mir zur V. stellen) place at my disposal.

verfüh´ren, *vb.* lead astray, entice, pervert, seduce.

verführ´rerisch, *adj.* seductive.

vergan´gen, *adj.* past, last.

Vergan´genheit, *n.f.* past.

vergäng´lich, *adj.* ephemeral, transitory.

Verga´ser, -, *n.m.* carburetor.

verge´ben*, *vb.* forgive; (sich v.) misdeal (at cards); (sich etwas v.) compromise oneself.

verge´bens, *adv.* in vain.

vergeb´lich, *adj.* vain, futile.

Verge´bung, *n.f.* forgiveness.

vergegenwär´tigen, *vb.* envisage, picture to oneself.

verge´hen*, *vb.* pass, elapse; (sich v.) err, sin, commit a crime.

Verge´hen, -, *n.nt.* misdemeanor.

vergel´ten*, *vb.* repay; retaliate.

Vergel´tung, -en, *n.f.* recompense; retaliation.

Vergel´tungsmaßnahme, -n, *n.f.* reprisal.

verges´sen*, *vb.* forget.

Verges´senheit, *n.f.* oblivion.

vergeß´lich, *adj.* forgetful.

vergeu´den, *vb.* squander.

vergewal´tigen, *vb.* use force on, rape.

Vergewal´tigung, -en, *n.f.* rape.

vergewis´sern, *vb.* confirm; reassure.

vergie´ßen*, *vb.* shed.

vergif´ten, *vb.* poison.

Vergiß´meinnicht, -e, *n.nt.* forget-me-not.

Vergleich´, -e, *n.m.* comparison.

vergleich´bar, *adj.* comparable.

verglei´chen*, *vb.* compare.

vergnü´gen, *vb.* amuse.

Vergnü´gen, -, *n.nt.* fun; (viel V.) have a good time.

vergnügt´, *adj.* in good spirits, gay.

Vergnü´gung, -en, *n.f.* pleasure, amusement, diversion.

vergöt´tern, vb. idolize.

vergrei´fen*, vb. (sich v.) do the wrong thing; (sich an etwas v.) attack, misappropriate.

vergrö´ßern, vb. enlarge, magnify.

Vergrö´ßerung, -en, n.f. enlargement.

Vergrö´ßerungsapparat, -e, n.m. enlarger.

Vergün´stigung, -en, n.f. favor; reduction.

vergü´ten, vb. pay back.

verhaf´ten, vb. arrest.

Verhaftung, -en, n.f. arrest.

verhal´ten*, vb. hold back; (sich v.) be, behave.

verhal´ten, adj. suppressed.

Verhal´ten, n.nt. behavior.

Verhält´nis, -se, n.nt. relation(ship), proportion, ratio; love affair; (pl.) circumstances, conditions.

verhält´nismäßig, adj. relative, comparative.

verhan´deln, vb. negotiate.

Verhand´lung, -en, n.f. negotiation.

Verhand´lungsweise, n.f. procedure.

Verhäng´nis, -se, n.nt. fate, destiny.

verhäng´nisvoll, adj. fatal, fateful.

verharr´en, vb. remain, persist.

verhär´ten, vb. (sich v.) harden, stiffen.

verhaßt´, adj. hateful, odious.

verhau´en*, vb. beat up; make a mess of.

verhed´dern, vb. (sich v.) get snarled, caught.

verhee´ren, vb. desolate.

verhee´rend, adj. disastrous.

verheim´lichen, vb. conceal.

verhei´raten, vb. marry off; (sich v.) get married.

verherr´lichen, vb. glorify.

verhin´dern, vb. prevent, hinder.

Verhin´derung, n.f. prevention, hindrance.

verhoh´len, adj. hidden, clandestine.

verhöh´nen, vb. mock, diride.

Verhör´, -e, n.nt. interrogation, hearing.

verhö´ren, vb. interrogate.

verhun´gern, vb. starve to death.

verhü´ten, vb. prevent.

Verhü´tung, -en, n.f. prevention.

Verhü´tungsmittel, -, n.nt. contraceptive device.

verir´ren, vb. (sich v.) lose one's way, go astray.

Verkauf´, -¨e, n.m. sale.

verkau´fen, vb. sell.

Verkäu´fer, -, n.m. clerk, salesman.

Verkäu´ferin, -nen, n.f. clerk, salesperson.

verkäuf´lich, adj. saleable.

Verkehr´, n.m. trade, traffic; relations, intercourse.

verkeh´ren, vb. (tr.) change; (intr.) run, go; associate, consort, frequent.

Verkehrs´ampel, -n, n.f. traffic light.

Verkehrs´flugzeug, -e, n.nt. air liner.

Verkehrs´licht, -er, n.nt. traffic light.

Verkehrs´mittel, n.nt. means of transporation.

verkehrt´, adj. reversed, wrong, backwards.

verken´nen*, vb. mistake, misunderstand.

verket´ten, vb. link.

verkla´gen, vb. sue, accuse.

Verklagt´-, n.m. & f. defendant.

verklärt´, adj. transfigured, radiant.

verklei´den, vb. disguise; panel.

verklei´nern, vb. make smaller; belittle.

Verklei´nerung, -en, n.f. diminution; disparagement.

verknüp´fen, vb. connect, relate.

verkom´men*, vb. decay, come down in the world, die.

verkom´men, adj. squalid, dissolute.

verkör´pern, vb. embody.

verkör´pert, adj. incarnate.

Verkör´perung, -en, n.f. embodiment, epitome.

verkrü´ppelt, adj. crippled.

verküm´mern, vb. wither.

verkün´d(ig)en, vb. announce, proclaim.

Verkün´d(ig)ung, -en, n.f. announcement, Annunciation.

verkür´zen, vb. shorten.

verla´den*, vb. load, ship.

Verla´der, -, n.m. shipper.

Verlag´, -¨e, n.m. publishing house.

verla´gern, vb. shift, displace.

verlan´gen, vb. demand, require, ask; (v. nach) desire, long for.

Verlan´gen, n.nt. demand, request, craving.

verlän´gern, vb. lengthen, prolong, extend, renew.

Verlän´gerung, -en, n.f. prolongation, extension, renewal.

verlang´samen, vb. slow down.

verlas´sen*, vb. leave, abandon, forsake; (sich v. auf) depend on, rely on.

verlas´sen, adj. abandoned, deserted, forlorn.

verläß´lich, adj. dependable.

Verlauf´, n.m. course, lapse.

verlau´fen*, vb. pass, elapse; (sich v.) get lost.

verle´ben, vb. pass.

verlebt´, adj. dissipated.

verle´gen, vb. move, shift; block; misplace; publish.

verle´gen, adj. embarrassed.

Verle´ger, -, n.m. publisher.

Verle´gerin, -nen, n.f. publisher.

Verle´gung, -en, n.f. transfer, removal.

verlei´hen*, vb. lend; confer, bestow.

Verlei´hung, -en, n.f. bestowal.

verlei´ten, vb. lead astray, inveigle.

verler´nen, vb. forget.

verletz´bar, adj. vulnerable.

verlet´zen, vb. hurt, offend; violate, infringe.

Verlet´zung, -en, *n.f.* injury; violation.

verleug´nen, *vb.* deny, disown.

verleum´den, *vb.* slander.

verleum´derisch, *adj.* libelous.

Verleum´dung, -en, *n.f.* libel, slander.

verlie´ben, *vb.* **(sich v.)** fall in love.

verliebt´, *adj.* in love.

verlie´ren*, *vb.* lose.

verlo´ben, *vb.* affiance, betroth; **(sich v.)** get engaged.

verlobt´, *adj.* engaged.

Verlobt´-, *n.m.* fiancé.

Verlobt´-, *n.f.* fiancée.

Verlo´bung, -en, *n.f.* engagement.

verlo´cken, *vb.* entice, lure.

verlö´schen*, *vb.* go out, be extinguished.

Verlust´, -e, *n.m.* loss; *(pl.)* casualties.

verma´chen, *vb.* bequeath.

Vermächt´nis, -se, *n.nt.* bequest, legacy.

vermäh´len, *vb.* espouse.

Vermäh´lung, -en, *n.f.* espousal.

vermeh´ren, *vb.* augment, multiply, increase.

vermeid´bar, *adj.* avoidable.

vermei´den*, *vb.* avoid.

vermeint´lich, *adj.* supposed.

vermen´gen, *vb.* blend; mix up.

Vermerk´, -e, *n.m.* note; entry.

vermer´ken, *vb.* note down.

vermes´sen*, *vb.* measure, survey; **(sich v.)** have the audacity.

Vermes´senheit, *n.f.* presumptuousness.

Vermes´sung, -en, *n.f.* survey.

vermie´ten, *vb.* rent (to someone).

vermin´dern, *vb.* diminish; **(sich v.)** decrease.

vermis´sen, *vb.* miss.

vermit´teln, *vb.* mediate, negotiate, arrange.

Vermitt´ler, -, *n.m.* mediator.

Vermitt´lerin, -nen, *n.f.* mediator.

Vermitt´lung, -en, *n.f.* mediation.

vermö´ge, *prep.* by virtue of.

vermö´gen*, *vb.* be able.

Vermö´gen, -, *n.nt.* fortune, wealth, estate; ability, power.

vermö´gend, *adj.* wealthy, well-to-do.

vermuten, *vb.* presume.

vermut´lich, *adj.* presumable.

Vermu´tung, -en, *n.f.* surmise.

vernach´lässigen, *vb.* neglect.

Vernach´lässigung, -en, *n.f.* neglect.

verneh´men*, *vb.* perceive, hear, learn; examine.

vernehm´lich, *adj.* perceptible.

Verneh´mung, -en, *n.f.* hearing.

vernei´gen, *vb.* **(sich v.)** bow.

vernei´nen, *vb.* deny.

vernei´nend, *adj.* negative.

Vernei´nung, -en, *n.f.* denial.

vernich´ten, *vb.* annihilate, destroy.

vernich´tend, *adj.* devastating.

Vernich´tung, -en, *n.f.* annihilation, destruction.

Vernunft´, *n.f.* reason.

vernunft´gemäß, *adj.* rational, according to reason.

vernünf´tig, *adj.* reasonable, sensible.

veröf´fentlichen, *vb.* publish.

Veröf´fentlichung, -en, *n.f.* publication.

verord´nen, *vb.* decree, order.

Verord´nung, -en, *n.f.* decree, ordinance, edict.

verpa´cken, *vb.* pack up, wrap up.

Verpa´ckung, *n.f.* packaging, wrapping.

verpas´sen, *vb.* miss.

verpes´ten, *vb.* infect.

verpfän´den, *vb.* pawn, pledge.

verpfle´gen, *vb.* care for; feed.

Verpfle´gung, -en, *n.f.* food, board.

verpflich´ten, *vb.* oblige; **(sich v.)** commit oneself.

Verpflich´tung, -en, *n.f.* obligation.

Verrat´, *n.m.* treason, betrayal.

verra´ten*, *vb.* betray.

Verrä´ter, -, *n.m.* traitor.

Verrä´terin, -nen, *n.f.* traitor.

verrä´terisch, *adj.* treacherous.

verrech´nen, *vb.* reckon up; **(sich v.)** make a mistake in figuring, miscalculate.

verrei´sen, *vb.* go away on a trip.

verreist´, *adj.* away on a trip.

verren´ken, *vb.* sprain.

verrich´ten, *vb.* do, perform, carry out.

verrin´gern, *vb.* decrease.

verros´ten, *vb.* rust.

verrucht´, *adj.* infamous, wicked.

verrückt´, *adj.* mad, crazy.

Verrückt´heit, -en, *n.f.* madness; folly.

Verruf´, *n.m.* disrepute, notoriety.

verru´fen, *adj.* disreputable, notorious.

Vers, -e, *n.m.* verse.

versa´gen, *vb.* refuse; fail.

Versa´gen, *n.nt.* failure.

Versa´ger, -, *n.m.* failure, flop.

Versa´gerin, -nen, *n.f.* failure, flop.

versam´meln, *vb.* assemble.

Versamm´lung, -en, *n.f.* assembly, gathering, meeting.

Versand´, *n.m.* dispatch.

versäu´men, *vb.* neglect, miss.

Versäum´nis, -se, *n.nt.* omission.

verschaf´fen, *vb.* procure.

verschämt´, *adj.* bashful, coy.

verschan´zen, *vb.* entrench.

verschär´fen, *adj.* intensify.

verschei´den*, *vb.* expire.

verschen´ken, *vb.* give away.

verscher´zen, *vb.* throw away, lose frivolously.

verscheu´chen, *vb.* scare away.

verschi´cken, *vb.* send off.

verschie´ben*, *vb.* shift, displace; postpone.

Verschie´bung, -en, *n.f.* shift; postponement.

verschie´den, *adj.* different, distinct; various, assorted, separate.

verschie´denartig, *adj.* various; heterogeneous.

verschie´ßen*, *vb.* fire off; fade.

verschla´fen*, **1.** *vb.* miss by sleeping too long; sleep off; (**sich v.**) oversleep. **2.** *adj.* sleepy.

Verschlag´, ⸗e, *n.m.* partition, compartment.

verschla´gen*, **1.** *vb.* drive away; (**es verschlägt´ mir den Atem**) it takes my breath away. **2.** *adj.* sly.

verschlech´tern, *vb.* make worse, impair; (**sich v.**) become worse, deteriorate.

Verschlech´terung, -en, *n.f.* deterioration.

verschlei´ern, *vb.* veil.

verschlep´pen, *vb.* delay; abduct.

verschleu´dern, *vb.* squander.

verschlie´ßen*, *vb.* close, lock.

verschlim´mern, *vb.* make worse, aggravate; (**sich v.**) become worse, deteriorate.

verschlin´gen*, *vb.* devour.

verschlis´sen, *adj.* worn out, frayed.

verschlos´sen, *adj.* closed, locked; reserved, taciturn.

verschlu´cken, *vb.* swallow; (**sich v.**) swallow the wrong way, choke.

Verschluß´, ⸗sse, *n.m.* closure; lock, plug, stopper; fastening, fastener; (camera) shutter.

verschmach´ten, *vb.* languish.

verschmel´zen*, *vb.* fuse, merge.

Verschmel´zung, -en, *n.f.* fusion.

verschneit´, *adj.* covered with snow.

Verschnitt´, *n.m.* adulteration; watered spirits.

verschnupft´, *adj.* having a cold.

verschol´len, *adj.* missing, never heard of again.

verscho´nen, *vb.* spare.

verschö´nern, *vb.* beautify.

verschrei´ben*, *vb.* prescribe.

verschü´chtern, *vb.* intimidate.

verschul´det, *adj.* indebted.

verschüt´ten, *vb.* spill.

verschwei´gen*, *vb.* keep quiet about.

verschwen´den, *vb.* squander, waste, dissipate.

Verschwen´der, -, *n.m.* spendthrift.

Verschwen´derin, -nen, *n.f.* spendthrift.

verschwen´derisch, *adj.* wasteful, extravagant, prodigal.

Verschwen´dung, -en, *n.f.* extravagance, wastefulness.

verschwie´gen, *adj.* silent, discreet, reticent.

verschwin´den*, *vb.* disappear.

Verschwin´den, *n.nt.* disappearance.

verschwommen, *adj.* blurred.

verschwö´ren*, *vb.* renounce; (**sich v.**) conspire.

Verschwö´rer, -, *n.m.* conspirator.

Verschwörerin, -nen, *n.f.* conspirator.

Verschwö´rung, -en, *n.f.* conspiracy.

verse´hen*, *vb.* provide; perform; (**sich v.**) make a mistake.

Verse´hen, -, *n.nt.* oversight, error; (**aus V.**) by mistake.

versen´den*, *vb.* send off.

versen´gen, *vb.* singe, scorch.

versen´ken, *vb.* sink.

verset´zen, *vb.* move, transfer; (school) promote; pawn, hock; reply.

versi´chern, *vb.* insure, assure; affirm, assert.

Versi´cherung, -en, *n.f.* insurance, assurance.

versie´geln, *vb.* seal.

versie´gen, *vb.* dry up.

versin´ken*, *vb.* sink.

versinn´bildlichen, *vb.* symbolize.

Version´, -en, *n.f.* version.

versöh´nen, *vb.* reconcile.

versöh´nend, *adj.* conciliation.

versöhn´lich, *adj.* conciliatory.

Versöh´nung, -en, *n.f.* reconciliation.

versor´gen, *vb.* provide, supply.

Versor´gung, *n.f.* supply, maintenance.

verspä´ten, *vb.* (**sich v.**) be late.

verspä´tet, *adj.* late.

Verspä´tung, -en, *n.f.* lateness.

versper´ren, *vb.* bar, obstruct.

verspie´len, *vb.* gamble away; (**sich v.**) misplay.

verspielt´, *adj.* playful.

verspot´ten, *vb.* mock, deride.

verspre´chen*, *vb.* promise; (**sich v.**) make a slip of the tongue.

Verspre´chen, -, *n.nt.* promise.

verstaat´lichen, *vb.* nationalize.

Verstand´, *n.m.* mind, intellect, brains.

verstän´dig, *adj.* sensible, intelligent.

verstän´digen, *vb.* inform; (**sich v.**) make oneself understood, make an agreement.

Verstän´digung, -en, *n.f.* agreement, understanding.

verständ´lich, *adj.* understandable.

Verständ´nis, *n.nt.* understanding.

verständ´nisvoll, *adj.* understanding.

verstär´ken, *vb.* strengthen, reinforce, intensify, amplify.

Verstär´ker, -, *n.m.* amplifier.

Verstär´kung, -en, *n.f.* reinforcement.

verstau´ben, *vb.* get covered with dust.

verstäu´ben, *vb.* atomize.

verstau´chen, *vb.* sprain.

Versteck´, -e, *n.nt.* hiding place; ambush; **(V. spielen)** play hide-and-go-seek.

verste´cken, *vb.* hide.

versteckt´, *adj.* hidden; veiled, oblique, ulterior.

verste´hen*, *vb.* understand.

Verstei´gerung, -en, *n.f.* auction.

verstell´bar, *adj.* adjustable.

verstel´len, *vb.* adjust; change, disguise; **(sich v.)** pretend.

Verstel´lung, -en, *n.f.* adjustment; disguise, sham, hypocrisy.

versteu´ern, *vb.* pay tax on.

verstim´men, *vb.* annoy, upset.

verstimmt´, *adj.* annoyed, cross; *(music)* out of tune.

verstockt´, *adj.* obdurate; impenitent.

verstoh´len, *adj.* stealthy, surreptitious.

verstop´fen, *vb.* stop up, clog.

Verstop´fung, -en, *n.f.* obstruction, jam; *(med.)* constipation.

verstor´ben, *adj.* deceased.

verstört´, *adj.* distracted, bewildered.

Verstoß, ̈e, *n.m.* violation, offence.

versto´ßen*, *vb.* expel, disown; **(v. gegen)** infringe on, offend.

verstrei´chen*, *vb.* elapse.

verstri´cken, *vb.* ensnare, enmesh.

verstüm´meln, *vb.* mutilate.

Verstüm´melung, -en, *n.f.* mutilation.

verstum´men, *vb.* become silent.

Versuch´, -e, *n.m.* attempt; test, trial, experiment; effort.

versu´chen, *vb.* attempt, try, test; strive; entice, tempt.

versuchs´weise, *adv.* experimentally.

Versu´chung, -en, *n.f.* temptation.

versün´digen, *vb.* **(sich v.)** sin against.

versun´ken, *adj.* sunken; **(v. sein*)** be absorbed, be lost.

versü´ßen, *vb.* sweeten.

verta´gen, *vb.* adjourn.

Verta´gung, -en, *n.f.* adjournment.

vertau´schen, *vb.* exchange for; mistake for; substitute.

vertei´digen, *vb.* defend, advocate.

Vertei´diger, -, *n.m.* defender; *(jur.)* counsel for the defense.

Vertei´digerin, -nen, *n.f.* defender; *(jur.)* counsel for the defense.

Vertei´digung, -en, *n.f.* defense.

vertei´len, *vb.* distribute, disperse, divide.

Vertei´ler, -, *n.m.* distributor.

Vertei´lung, -en, *n.f.* distribution; dispersal, division.

vertie´fen, *vb.* deepen; **(sich v.)** deepen, become engrossed.

vertieft´, *adj.* absorbed.

vertil´gen, *vb.* consume; exterminate.

Vertrag´, ̈e, *n.m.* contract, treaty, pact.

vertra´gen*, *vb.* endure, tolerate, stand; **(sich v.)** agree, get along.

vertrag´lich, *adj.* contractual.

verträg´lich, *adj.* compatible, good-natured.

vertrau´en, *vb.* trust; confide in; rely on.

Vertrau´en, *n.nt.* trust, confidence, faith.

vertrau´ensvoll, *adj.* confident, reliant.

Vertrau´ensvotum, *n.nt.* vote of confidence.

vertrau´lich, *adj.* confidential.

Vertrau´lichkeit, -en, *n.f.* familiarity, intimacy; **(in aller V.)** in strict confidence.

vertraut´, *adj.* acquainted, familiar; intimate.

Vertraut´, -, *n.m. & f.* confidant(e).

Vertraut´heit, -en, *n.f.* familiarity; intimacy.

vertrei´ben*, *vb.* drive away, expel.

Vertrei´bung, -en, *n.f.* expulsion.

vertre´ten*, *vb.* represent; act as substitute; advocate.

Vertre´ter, -, *n.m.* representative, agent; deputy; substitute.

Vertre´terin, -nen, *n.f.* representative, agent; deputy, substitute.

Vertre´tung, -en, *n.f.* representation, agency; substitution.

Vertrieb´, -e, *n.m.* sale, market.

Vertrie´ben-, *n.m. & f.* expellee, refugee.

Vertriebs´stelle, -n, *n.f.* distributor.

vertu´schen, *vb.* hush up.

verü´beln, *vb.* take amiss.

verü´ben, *vb.* commit.

verun´glücken, *vb.* meet with an accident; fail.

verun´reinigen, *vb.* pollute.

verun´stalten, *vb.* disfigure.

verun´zieren, *vb.* mar.

verur´sachen, *vb.* cause, bring about; result in.

verur´teilen, *vb.* condemn; *(jur.)* sentence.

Verur´teilung, *n.f.* condemnation; *(jur.)* sentence.

verviel´fachen, *vb.* multiply.

verviel´f ältigen, *vb.* multiply; mimeograph; **(sich v.)** multiply.

vervoll´kommnen, *vb.* perfect.

Vervoll´kommnung, *n.f.* perfection.

vervoll´ständigen, *vb.* complete.

verwach´sen*, *vb.* grow together; become deformed.

Verwach´sung, -en, *n.f.* deformity.

verwah´ren, *vb.* keep, hold in safe-keeping.

verwahr´losen, *vb.* neglect.

verwahr´lost, *adj.* neglected.

Verwah´rung, *n.f.* custody.

verwal´ten, *vb.* administer, manage.

Verwal´ter, -, *n.m.* administrator.

Verwal′terin, -nen, *n.f.* administrator.

Verwal′tung, -en, *n.f.* administration, management.

verwan′deln, *vb.* change, transform; **(sich v.)** metamorphose.

Verwand′lung, -en, *n.f.* change, transformation; metamorphosis.

verwandt′, *adj.* related.

Verwandt′-, *n.m. & f.* relation, relative.

Verwandt′schaft, -en, *n.f.* relationship, affinity.

verwech′seln, *vb.* mistake for, confuse.

Verwechs′lung, -en, *n.f.* mistake, mix-up.

verwe′gen, *adj.* daring, bold.

verweh′ren, *vb.* prevent from; refuse.

verwei′gern, *vb.* refuse.

Verwei′gerung, -en, *n.f.* refusal.

verwei′len, *vb.* linger.

Verweis′, -e, *n.m.* reprimand; **(einen V. erteilen)** reprimand.

verwei′sen*, *vb.* banish; **(v. auf)** refer to.

verwend′bar, *adj.* usable, applicable.

Verwend′barkeit, *n.f.* usability, applicability.

verwen′den(*), *vb.* use, supply; expend.

Verwen′dung, -en, *n.f.* use, application.

verwer′fen*, *vb.* reject.

verwe′sen, *vb.* putrify, decay.

verwi′ckeln, *vb.* entangle, involve, implicate.

verwi′ckelt, *adj.* involved, intricate, complicated.

Verwick′lung, -en, *n.f.* entanglement, implication; complication.

verwin′den*, *vb.* get over, overcome.

verwir′ken, *vb.* forfeit.

verwirk′lichen, *vb.* realize, materialize.

Verwirk′lichung, -en, *n.f.* realization.

verwir′ren, *vb.* confuse, bewilder, confound, puzzle, mystify.

Verwir′rung, -en, *n.f.* confusion, bewilderment, perplexity.

verwi′schen, *vb.* wipe out; smudge.

verwit′wet, *adj.* widowed.

verwor′fen, *adj.* depraved.

verwor′ren, *adj.* confused.

verwun′den, *vb.* wound.

verwun′dern, *vb.* astonish.

Verwun′dung, -en, *n.f.* wound, injury.

verwun′schen, *adj.* enchanted.

verwün′schen, *vb.* curse; bewitch.

verwüs′ten, *vb.* devastate.

verza′gen, *vb.* despair.

verzagt′, *adj.* despondent.

verzäh′len, *vb.* **(sich v.)** miscount.

verzär′teln, *vb.* pamper.

verzau′bern, *vb.* bewitch.

verzeh′ren, *vb.* consume.

verzeich′nen, *vb.* register, list.

Verzeich′nis, -se, *n.nt.* list, index.

verzei′hen*, *vb.* pardon, forgive.

Verzei′hung, -en, *n.f.* pardon, forgiveness; **(ich bitte um V.)** I beg your pardon.

verzer′ren, *vb.* distort.

Verzicht′, -e, *n.m.* renunciation; **(V. leisten)** renounce.

verzich′ten, *vb.* renounce, forego, waive.

verzie′hen*, *vb.* pull out of shape; (child) spoil; **(sich v.)** withdraw; vanish, disperse; (wood) warp.

verzie′ren, *vb.* embellish.

Verzie′rung, -en, *n.f.* ornament, embellishment.

verzin′sen, *vb.* pay interest; **(sich v.)** bear interest.

Verzin′sung, -en, *n.f.* interest return; payment of interest; interest rate.

verzo′gen, *adj.* moved away; (child) spoiled.

verzö′gern, *vb.* delay.

Verzö′gerung, -en, *n.f.* delay.

verzol′len, *vb.* pay duty on.

verzückt′, *adj.* enraptured.

Verzug′, =e, *n.m.* delay; default.

verzwei′feln, *vb.* despair.

verzwei′felt, *adj.* desperate.

Verzweif′lung, -en, *n.f.* desperation.

verzwickt′, *adj.* complicated.

Vesper, -n, *n.f.* vespers.

Veterinär′, -e, *n.m.* veterinarian.

Veterinärin, -nen, *n.f.* veterinarian.

Vetter, -n, *n.m.* cousin.

Viadukt′, -e, *n.m.* viaduct.

Vibration′, -en, *n.f.* vibration.

vibrie′ren, *vb.* vibrate.

Video, -s, *n.nt.* video.

Vieh, *n.nt.* cattle.

viehisch, *adj.* brutal.

Viehzucht, *n.f.* cattle breeding.

viel, *adj.* much; *(pl.)* many.

vielbedeutend, *adj.* significant.

vieldeutig, *adj.* ambiguous.

Vieleck, -e, *n.nt.* polygon.

vielerlei, *adj.* various, many.

vielfach, *adj.* manifold.

Vielfalt, *n.f.* variety.

vielf′ältig, *adj.* multiple.

Vielf′ältigkeit, *n.f.* multiplicity.

vielfarbig, *adj.* multicolored.

Vielfraß, -e, *n.m.* glutton.

Vielheit, -en, *n.f.* multiplicity.

vielleicht′, *adv.* perhaps.

vielmals, *adv.* many times.

vielmehr, *adv.* rather.

vielsagend, *adj.* significant, highly suggestive.

vielseitig, *adj.* many-sided; versatile.

vielverheißend, *adj.* very promising.

vielversprechend, *adj.* very promising.

vier, *num.* four.

Viereck, -e, *n.nt.* square.

viereckig, *adj.* square.

vierfach, *adj.* fourfold.

Vierfüßler, -, *n.m.* quadruped.

vierschrötig, *adj.* thick-set.

viert-, *adj.* fourth.

vierteilen, *vb.* quarter.

Viertel, -, *n.nt.* fourth part, quarter; **(ein v.)** one-fourth.

vierzehn, *num.* fourteen.

vierzig, *num.* forty.

vierzigst-, *adj.* fortieth.

Vierzigstel, -, *n.nt.* fortieth part; **(ein v.)** one-fortieth.

violett´, *adj.* violet.

Violi´ne, -n, *n.f.* violin.

Violinist´, -en, -en, *n.m.* violinist.

Violini´stin, -nen, *n.f.* violinist.

Virtuo´se, -n, -n, *n.m.* virtuoso.

Visier´, -e, *n.nt.* visor; (gun) sight.

visuell´, *adj.* visual.

Visum, -sa, *n.nt.* visa.

Vitalität´, *n.f.* vitality.

Vize-, *cpds.* vice-.

Vogel, =, *n.m.* bird.

vogelartig, *adj.* birdlike.

Vogelbauer, -, *n.nt.* bird cage.

Vogelscheuche, -n, *n.f.* scarecrow.

Vogt, =e, *n.m.* overseer.

Vokal´, -e, *n.m.* vowel.

Volant´, -s, *n.m.* flounce.

Volk, =er, *n.nt.* people, nation.

Völkerbund, *n.m.* League of Nations.

Völkerkunde, *n.f.* ethnology; (school) social studies.

Völkermord, *n.m.* genocide.

Völkerrecht, *n.nt.* international law.

Volksabstimmung, -en, *n.f.* plebiscite, referendum.

Volkscharakter, *n.m.* national character.

Volksentscheid, *n.m.* plebiscite, referendum.

Volksgenosse, -n, -n, *n.m.* fellow countryman.

Volkskunde, *n.f.* folklore.

Volkslied, -er, *n.nt.* folksong.

Volksmenge, *n.f.* crowd, mob.

Volksschule, -n, *n.f.* elementary school.

Volkstanz, =e, *n.m.* folkdance.

volkstümlich, *adj.* popular.

Volkszählung, -en, *n.f.* census.

voll, *adj.* full.

Vollblut, *n.nt.* thoroughbred.

vollblütig, *adj.* full-blooded.

vollbrin´gen*, *vb.* accomplish, fulfill.

vollen´den, *vb.* finish, complete.

vollen´det, *adj.* accomplished.

vollends, *adv.* completely.

Völlerei´, *n.f.* gluttony.

vollfüh´ren, *vb.* accomplish.

Vollgas, *n.nt.* full throttle.

völlig, *adj.* complete, entire.

volljährig, *adj.* of age.

vollkom´men, *adj.* perfect.

Vollkom´menheit, *n.f.* perfection.

Vollmacht, =e, *n.f.* authority, warrant, proxy, power of attorney.

vollständig, *adj.* complete.

voll•stopfen, *vb.* cram, stuff.

vollstre´cken, *vb.* execute, carry out.

Vollversammlung, *n.f.* (U.N.) General Assembly.

vollzählig, *adj.* complete.

vollzie´hen*, *vb.* execute, carry out; consummate; **(sich v.)** take place.

Volontär, -e, *n.m.* volunteer.

Volontär´arzt, =e, *n.m.* intern.

Volontär´ärztin, -nen, *n.f.* intern.

Volt, -, *n.nt.* volt.

Volu´men, -, *n.nt.* volume.

von, *prep.* before; in front of; ago.

vor, *prep.* before; in front of; ago.

Vorabend, -e, *n.m.* eve.

Vorahnung, -en, *n.f.* premonition, foreboding.

voran´, *adv.* in front of, ahead; onward.

voran´•gehen*, *vb.* precede.

voran´•kommen*, *vb.* get ahead.

Voranmeldung, -en, *n.f.* (telephone) **(mit V.)** person-to-person call.

Voranschlag, =e, *n.m.* estimate.

Vorarbeit, -en, *n.f.* preparatory work.

Vorarbeiter, -, *n.m.* foreman.

vorauf´, *adv.* before, ahead.

voraus´, *adv.* in advance, ahead; **(im v.)** in advance.

voraus´•bedingen*, *vb.* precede.

voraus´•bestellen, *vb.* order ahead, make reservations.

voraus´•gehen*, *vb.* precede.

voraus´gesetz, *adv.* **(v. daß)** provided that.

voraus´nehmen*, *vb.* state now, anticipate.

Voraus´sage, -n, *n.f.* prediction, forecast.

voraus´•sagen, *vb.* predict, forecast.

voraus´setzen, *vb.* presume, presuppose.

Voraus´setzung, -en, *n.f.* supposition, assumption; prerequisite.

Voraus´sicht, *n.f.* foresight.

voraus´sichtlich, 1. *adj.* probable, prospective. **2.** *adv.* presumably.

voraus´•zahlen, *vb.* pay in advance, advance.

Vorbedacht, *n.m.* forethought.

Vorbedeutung, -en, *n.f.* omen.

Vorbedingung, -en, *n.f.* prerequisite.

Vorbehalt, *n.m.* reservation.

vor•behalten*, *vb.* reserve.

vorbei´, *adv.* over, past.

vorbelastet, *adj.* having a questionable record; *(jur.)* having a criminal record.

vor•bereiten, *vb.* prepare.

vor•bestellen, *vb.* order in advance, make reservations.

vor•beugen, *vb.* prevent.

vorbeugend, *adj.* preventive.

Vorbild, -er, *n.nt.* model.

vorbildlich, *adj.* exemplary.

vor•bringen*, *vb.* state; propose.

vorder-, *adj.* front, anterior.

Vorderfront, -en, *n.f.* frontage; *(fig.)* forefront.

Vordergrund, *n.m.* foreground.

vorderhand, *adv.* for the time being; right now.

Vordermann, =er, *n.m.* person ahead of one.

Vorderseite, -n, *n.f.* front.

Vorderteil, -e, *n.nt.* front part.

vor•drängen, *vb.* **(sich v.)** elbow one's way forward.

vor•dringen*, *vb.* press forward, advance.

Vordruck, ¨-e, *n.m.* form, blank.

voreilig, *adj.* rash, hasty.

voreingenommen, *adj.* prejudiced.

Voreingenommenheit, *n.f.* partiality.

vor•enthalten*, *vb.* withhold.

vorerst, *adv.* first of all.

Vorfahr, -en, -en, *n.m.* ancestor.

vor•fahren*, *vb.* drive up; (**v. lassen***) let pass.

Vorfahrtsrecht, -e, *n.nt.* right of way.

Vorfall, ¨-e, *n.m.* incident.

vor•fallen*, *vb.* occur.

vor•finden*, *vb.* find.

vor•führen, *vb.* show, demonstrate, produce.

Vorführung, -en, *n.f.* demonstration, show, production.

Vorgang, ¨-e, *n.m.* occurrence, process, procedure.

Vorgänger, -, *n.m.* predecessor.

Vorgängerin, -nen, *n.f.* predecessor.

vor•geben*, *vb.* pretend, feign.

Vorgefühl, -e, *n.nt.* presentiment, hunch.

vor•gehen*, *vb.* advance; come first, precede.

Vorgehen, *n.nt.* procedure, policy.

Vorgericht, -e, *n.nt.* appetizer; first course.

Vorgeschichte, *n.f.* prehistory; history, background.

vorgeschrieben, *adj.* prescribed.

vorgesehen, *adj.* planned, scheduled.

Vorgesetzt-, *n.m. & f.* superior.

vorgestern, *adv.* the day before yesterday.

vorgetäuscht, *adj.* make-believe.

vor•greifen*, *vb.* anticipate.

vor•haben*, *vb.* plan, intention.

Vorhaben, *n.nt.* plan, intention.

Vorhalle, -n, *n.f.* lounge.

vor•halten*, *vb.* (*fig.*) reproach.

Vorhand, *n.f.* forehand.

vorhan´den, *adj.* existing, present, available.

Vorhang, ¨-e, *n.m.* curtain, drapery.

vorher, *adv.* before, beforehand, previously.

vorher´gehend, *adj.* previous.

vor•herrschen, *vb.* prevail.

Vorherrschaft, *n.f.* predominance.

vorherrschend, *adj.* prevalent, predominant.

Vorher´sage, -n, *n.f.* prediction.

vorher´sagen, *vb.* foretell.

vorher´sehen*, *vb.* foresee.

Vorhut, *n.f.* vanguard.

vorig, *adj.* previous, last.

Vorjahr, -e, *n.nt.* preceding year.

Vorkämpfer, -, *n.m.* pioneer, champion.

Vorkenntnis, -se, *n.f.* preliminary knowledge; rudiments.

Vorkommen, *n.nt.* occurrence.

vor•kommen*, *vb.* occur.

Vorkommnis, -se, *n.nt.* occurrence.

Vorkriegs-, *cpds.* prewar.

vor•laden*, *vb.* summon.

Vorladung, -en, *n.f.* summons.

vor•lassen*, *vb.* let pass; admit.

Vorlassung, -en, *n.f.* admittance.

vorläufig, **1.** *adj.* preliminary, tentative; temporary. **2.** *adv.* for the time being.

vorlaut, *adj.* flippant, fresh.

vor•legen*, *vb.* show, submit, produce.

vor•lesen*, *vb.* read out loud.

Vorlesung, -en, *n.f.* reading; lecture.

Vorlesungsverzeichnis, -se, *n.nt.* university catalogue.

vorletzt, *adj.* last but one.

Vorliebe, *n.f.* preference, fondness.

vorlieb•nehmen*, *vb.* be satisfied with.

vor•liegen*, *vb.* exist.

vorliegend, *adj.* present, at hand, in question.

vor•machen, *vb.* show how to do; (**einem etwas v.**) deceive, fool.

Vormachtstellung, -en, *n.f.* predominance.

vormalig, *adj.* former.

vormals, *adv.* heretofore.

Vormann, ¨-er, *n.m.* foreman.

Vormarsch, ¨-e, *n.m.* advance.

vor•merken, *vb.* make a note of; reserve.

Vormittag, -e, *n.m.* forenoon.

Vormund, -e, *n.m.* guardian.

vorn, *adv.* in front.

Vorname(n), -, *n.m.* first name.

vornehm, *adj.* noble, distinguished.

vor•nehmen*, *vb.* (**sich v.**) undertake, consider, take up, resolve.

vornehmlich, *adv.* chiefly.

Vorort, -e, *n.m.* suburb.

Vorortzug, ¨-, *n.m.* local (train).

Vorplatz, ¨-e, *n.m.* hall; court.

Vorrang, *n.m.* priority, precedence.

Vorrat, ¨-e, *n.m.* supply, provision, stock, stockpile.

vorrätig, *adj.* in stock.

Vorratskammer, -n, *n.f.* storeroom; pantry.

Vorrecht, -e, *n.nt.* privilege, prerogative.

Vorrede, -n, *n.f.* preface.

Vorrichtung, -en, *n.f.* arrangement; contrivance, device, fixture.

vor•rücken, *vb.* move forward, advance.

Vorsatz, ¨-e, *n.m.* purpose, intention; (*jur.*) premeditation.

vorsätzlich, *adj.* willful, intentional; (*jur.*) premeditated.

Vorschein, *n.m.* (**zum V. kommen***) appear.

Vorschlag, ¨-e, *n.m.* proposal, proposition, suggestion.

vor•schlagen*, *vb.* propose, suggest.

vorschnell, *adj.* rash.

vor•schreiben*, *vb.* prescribe.

Vorschrift, -en, *n.f.* regulation.

vorschriftsmäßig, *adj.* as prescribed, regulation.

Vorschub, *n.m.* assistance.

Vorschule, -n, *n.f.* elementary school.

Vorschuß, ⁼sse, *n.m.* advance payment.

vor•schützen, *vb.* pretend, plead.

vor•sehen*, *vb.* earmark, plan, schedule; **(sich v.)** be careful.

Vorsehung, *n.f.* providence.

Vorsicht, -en, *n.f.* caution.

vorsichtig, *adj.* careful, cautious.

vorsichtshalber, *adv.* as a precaution.

Vorsichtsmaßregel, -n, *n.f.* precaution.

Vorsilbe, -n, *n.f.* prefix.

Vorsitz, -e, *n.m.* chairmanship, presidency; **(den V. führen)** preside.

Vorsitzend-, *n.m. & f.* chairperson.

Vorsitzende(r), -n, *n.m. & f.* chairman; chairwoman.

Vorsorge, *n.f.* providence, foresight; **(V. treffen*)** take precautions.

vorsorglich, *adv.* as a precaution.

Vorspeise, -n, *n.f.* appetizer.

vor•spiegeln, *vb.* deceive, delude.

Vorspiel, -e, *n.nt.* prelude.

vor•springen*, *vb.* project.

Vorsprung, ⁼e, *n.m.* advantage; head start; *(arch.)* ledge.

Vorstadt, ⁼e, *n.f.* suburb, outskirts.

Vorstand, *n.m.* board; committee.

vorstellbar, *adj.* conceivable.

vor•stellen, *vb.* present, introduce; (clock) set ahead; **(sich v.)** imagine, picture.

Vorstellung, -en, *n.f.* presentation, introduction; imagination, idea, notion; (theater) performance, show.

Vorstellungsgespräch, -e, *n.nt.* interview.

Vorstoß, ⁼e, *n.m.* attack.

vor•stoßen*, *vb.* push forward.

vor•strecken, *vb.* stretch forward; (money) advance.

vor•täuschen, *vb.* make-believe, simulate.

Vorteil, -e, *n.m.* advantage.

vorteilhaft, *adj.* advantageous, profitable.

Vortrag, ⁼e, *n.m.* lecture, talk.

vor•tragen*, *vb.* lecture, recite, report.

Vortragend-, *n.m. & f.* lecturer.

vortreff´lich, *adj.* excellent.

Vortritt, *n.m.* precedence.

vorü´ber, *adv.* past, gone.

vorü´ber•gehen*, *vb.* pass.

vorü´bergehend, *adj.* temporary.

Vorurteil, -e, *n.nt.* prejudice.

Vorväter, *n.pl.* forefathers.

Vorwahl, -en, *n.f.* primary election.

Vorwahlnummer, -n, *n.f.* area code (telephone).

Vorwand, ⁼e, *n.m.* pretense, pretext.

Vorwarnung, -en, *n.f.* forewarning.

vorwärts, *adv.* forward.

vorwärts•kommen*, *vb.* get ahead, make headway.

vorweg´nehmen*, *vb.* anticipate; forestall.

vor•werfen*, *vb.* reproach.

vorwiegend, *adv.* predominantly, mainly, chiefly.

Vorwort, -e, *n.nt.* preface.

Vorwurf, ⁼e, *n.m.* reproach.

vor•zeigen, *vb.* show, produce.

vorzeitig, *adj.* premature.

vor•ziehen*, *vb.* prefer.

Vorzimmer, -, *n.nt.* antechamber, anteroom.

Vorzug, ⁼e, *n.m.* preference; advantage.

vorzüg´lich, 1. *adj.* excellent, exquisite. **2.** *adv.* especially.

Vorzüg´lichkeit, -en, *n.f.* excellence.

vorzugsweise, *adv.* preferably.

vulgär, *adj.* vulgar.

Vulkan´, -e, *n.m.* volcano.

W

Waage, -n, *n.f.* scales.

waagerecht, *adj.* horizontal.

Waagschale, -n, *n.f.* scale.

Wabe, -n, *n.f.* honeycomb.

wach, *adj.* awake.

Wache, -n, *n.f.* watch, guard.

wachen, *vb.* be awake, stay awake; watch over.

wachhabend, *adj.* on duty.

Wachlokal, -e, *n.nt.* guardhouse, police station.

Wachposten, -, *n.m.* sentry.

Wachs, -e, *n.nt.* wax.

wachsam, *adj.* watchful, vigilant.

Wachsamkeit, *n.f.* vigilance.

wachsen*, *vb.* grow, increase.

wachsen, *vb.* wax.

Wachskerze, -n, *n.f.* candle.

Wachstum, *n.nt.* growth.

Wacht, *n.f.* guard, watch.

Wächter, -, *n.m.* watchman; keeper.

Wachtmeister, -, *n.m.* (police) sergeant.

wackelig, *adj.* shaky, wobbly.

wackeln, *vb.* shake, wobble.

wacker, *adj.* staunch, brave, stouthearted.

Wade, -n, *n.f.* calf (of the leg).

Waffe, -n, *n.f.* weapon, arm.

Waffel, -n, *n.f.* waffle.

Waffenfabrik, -en, *n.f.* arms factory.

Waffengattung, -en, *n.f.* arm; branch of the army.

waffenlos, *adj.* unarmed, defenseless.

Waffenstill´stand, ⁼e, *n.m.* armistice, truce.

waffnen, *vb.* arm.

wagemutig, *adj.* venturesome.

wagen, *vb.* dare, risk, venture.

Wagen, -, *n.m.* carriage, coach, wagon, car.

wägen(*), *vb.* consider.

Wagenheber, -, *n.m.* auto jack.

Waggon´, -s, *n.m.* railroad car.

Waggon´ladung, -en, *n.f.* carload.

waghalsig, *adj.* rash, risky.

Wagnis, -se, *n.nt.* venture.

Wahl, -en, *n.f.* choice, election, vote, ballot.

wählbar, *adj.* eligible; (nicht w.) ineligible.

wahlberechtigt, *adj.* eligible to vote.

Wahlbezirk, -e, *n.m.* constituency.

wählen, *vb.* choose; elect, vote; (telephone) dial.

Wähler, -, *n.m.* constituent, voter.

Wählerin -nen, *n.f.* constituent, voter.

wählerisch, *adj.* choosy, fastidious.

Wählerschaft, *n.f.* electorate.

Wahlgang, ¨e, *n.m.* ballot.

Wahlkampf, ¨e, *n.m.* election campaign.

Wahlliste, -n, *n.f.* ticket, slate.

Wahlrecht, -e, *n.nt.* franchise, suffrage; (W. erteilen) enfranchise; (W. entziehen*) disenfranchise.

Wählscheibe, -n, *n.f.* dial (on a telephone).

Wahlspruch, ¨e, *n.m.* slogan, motto.

Wahlstimme, -n, *n.f.* vote.

Wahn, *n.m.* delusion.

Wahnsinn, *n.m.* insanity.

wahnsinnig, *adj.* insane, delirious.

wahr, *adj.* true, truthful, real; (nicht w.?) isn't that so?

wahren, *vb.* keep, preserve.

währen, *vb.* continue, last.

während, 1. *prep.* during. 2. *conj.* while.

wahrhaftig, *adj.* true, sincere.

Wahrheit, -en, *n.f.* truth.

wahrnehmbar, *adj.* perceptible.

wahr•nehmen*, *vb.* perceive.

Wahrnehmung, -en, *n.f.* perception.

wahr•sagen, *vb.* prophesy, tell fortunes.

Wahrsager, -, *n.m.* fortuneteller.

Wahrsagerin, -nen, *n.f.* fortune-teller.

wahrschein´lich, *adj.* probable, likely.

Wahrschein´lichkeit, *n.f.* probability, likelihood.

Währung, -en, *n.f.* currency.

Wahrzeichen, -, *n.nt.* distinctive mark, landmark.

Waise, -n, *n.f.* orphan.

Waisenhaus, ¨er, *n.nt.* orphanage.

Wald, ¨er, *n.m.* wood, forest.

Walfisch, -e, *n.m.* whale.

Wall, ¨e, *n.m.* rampart.

wallen, *vb.* undulate; bubble.

Wallfahrer, -, *n.m.* pilgrim.

Wallfahrerin, -nen, *n.f.* pilgrim.

Wallfahrt, -en, *n.f.* pilgrimage.

Walnuß, ¨sse, *n.f.* walnut.

Walroß, ¨sse, *n.nt.* walrus.

walten, *vb.* rule.

Walze, -n, *n.f.* roll, roller.

walzen, *vb.* roll, roll out; waltz.

wälzen, *vb.* roll, revolve.

Walzer, -, *n.m.* waltz.

Wand, ¨e, *n.f.* wall.

Wandel, *n.m.* change.

wandelbar, *adj.* changeable.

Wandelhalle, -n, *n.f.* lobby.

wandeln, *vb.* go, wander; (sich w.) change.

wandern, *vb.* hike, wander, roam.

Wanderschaft, *n.f.* travels.

Wanderung, -en, *n.f.* hike, wandering; migration.

Wandgemälde, -, *n.nt.* mural.

Wandlung, -en, *n.f.* change, transformation.

Wandschrank, ¨e, *n.m.* (eingebauter W.) closet.

Wandtafel, -n, *n.f.* blackboard.

Wandteppich, -e, *n.m.* tapestry.

Wandverkleidung, -en, *n.f.* wallcovering.

Wange, -n, *n.f.* cheek.

wankelmütig, *adj.* fickle.

wanken, *vb.* stagger, sway.

wann, 1. *conj.* when. 2. *adv.* when.

Wanne, -n, *n.f.* tub.

Wanze, -n, *n.f.* bedbug.

Wappen, -, *n.nt.* coat of arms.

Ware, -n, *n.f.* article, commodity, merchandise, ware; (pl.) goods.

Warenhandel, *n.m.* trade, commerce.

Warenhaus, ¨er, *n.nt.* department store.

Warenrechnung, -en, *n.f.* invoice.

warm (¨), *adj.* warm.

Wärme, *n.f.* warmth, heat.

wärmen, *vb.* warm.

Wärmflasche, -n, *n.f.* hot water bottle.

warnen, *vb.* warn, caution.

Warnung, -en, *n.f.* warning.

Warte, -n, *n.f.* watch-tower, lookout.

warten, *vb.* wait.

Wärter, -, *n.m.* keeper, guard.

Wärterin, -nen, *n.f.* keeper, guard.

Warteraum, ¨e, *n.m.* waiting room.

Wartezeit, -en, *n.f.* wait.

Wartezimmer, -, *n.nt.* waiting room.

warum´, *adv.& conj.* why.

Warze, -n, *n.f.* wart.

was, *pron.* what.

Waschanstalt, -en, *n.f.* laundry.

waschbar, *adj.* washable.

Waschbecken, -, *n.nt.* washbasin.

Wäsche, *n.f.* laundry, linen.

waschecht, *adj.* colorfast; (fig.) dyed in the wool.

waschen*, *vb.* wash, launder.

Wäscherei´, -en, *n.f.* laundry.

Wäscheschrank, ¨e, *n.m.* linen closet.

Waschfrau, -en, *n.f.* laundress.

Waschlappen, -, *n.m.* face cloth.

Waschleder, *n.nt.* chamois.

Waschmaschine, -n, *n.f.* washing machine.

Waschpulver, *n.nt.* soap powder.

Waschraum, ⸚e, *n.m.* washroom.

Waschseife, -n, *n.f.* laundry soap.

Waschtisch, -e, *n.m.* washstand, washbowl.

Waschzettel, -, *n.m.* laundry list; (book) blurb; memo.

Wasser, -, *n.nt.* water.

wasserdicht, *adj.* watertight, waterproof.

Wasserfall, ⸚e, *n.m.* waterfall.

Wasserflugzeug, -e, *n.nt.* hydroplane.

Wasserhahn, ⸚e, *n.m.* faucet.

wässerig, *adj.* watery, aqueous.

Wasserleitung, -en, *n.f.* water main; aqueduct.

wässern, *vb.* water.

Wasserrinne, -n, *n.f.* gully, gutter.

Wasserstoff, *n.m.* hydrogen.

Wasserstoffbombe, -n, *n.f.* hydrogen bomb.

Wasserstoffsu'peroxyd, *n.nt.* hydrogen peroxide.

Wassersucht, *n.f.* dropsy.

Wasserverschmutzung, *n.f.* water pollution.

waten, *vb.* wade.

watscheln, *vb.* waddle.

Watte, *n.f.* cotton.

weben(*), *vb.* weave.

Webeschiffchen, -, *n.nt.* shuttle.

Webstuhl, ⸚e, *n.m.* loom.

Wechsel, -, *n.m.* change, shift, rotation; *(comm.)* draft.

Wechselgeld, *n.nt.* change.

Wechseljahre, *n.pl.* menopause.

Wechselkurs, -e, *n.m.* rate of exchange.

wechseln, *vb.* change, exchange.

wechselnd, *adj.* intermittent.

Wechselstrom, ⸚e, *n.m.* alternating current.

wecken, *vb.* wake, awaken.

Wecker, -, *n.m.* alarm clock.

wedeln, *vb.* wag.

weder, adj. (w. . . . noch) neither . . . nor.

weg, *adv.* away; gone.

Weg, -e, *n.m.* way, path, route.

wegen, *prep.* because of.

weg•fahren*, *vb.* drive away, leave.

weg•fallen*, *vb.* be omitted; not take place.

weg•gehen*, *vb.* go away, leave.

weg•kommen*, *vb.* get away; get off.

weg•lassen*, *vb.* leave out.

weg•nehmen*, *vb.* take away.

weg•räumen, *vb.* remove.

weg•schicken, *vb.* send off.

weg•schnappen, *vb.* snatch.

Wegweiser, -, *n.m.* guidepost, signpost.

Wegzehrung, -en, *n.f.* provisions for a journey.

Weh, *n.nt.* woe, pain, ache.

weh, *adj.* sore; **(w. tun*)** hurt, be sore.

wehen, *vb.* (wind) blow; (flag) wave.

Wehen, *n.pl.* labor pains.

Wehklage, -n, *n.f.* lament, lamentation.

wehklagen, *vb.* wail, lament.

Wehmut, *n.f.* sadness.

wehmütig, *adj.* sad, melancholy.

Wehr, -e, *n.nt.* dam.

Wehr, -en, *n.f.* defense, resistance.

Wehrdienst, *n.m.* military service.

wehren, *vb.* **(sich w.)** defend oneself, fight.

wehrfähig, *adj.* fit to serve (in the army).

wehrlos, *adj.* defenseless.

Wehrmacht, *n.f.* armed forces; (specifically, German army to 1945).

Wehrpflicht, *n.f.* duty to serve in armed forces; **(allgemeine W.)** compulsory military service.

weh•tun*, *vb.* hurt, be sore.

Weib, -er, *n.nt.* woman.

Weibchen, -, *n.nt. (zool.)* female.

Weibersache, -n, *n.f.* women's affair.

weiblich, *adj.* female, feminine.

weich, *adj.* soft.

Weiche, -n, *n.f.* switch.

weichen*, *vb.* give way, yield.

weichen, *vb.* soften.

weichlich, *adj.* soft; effeminate.

Weide, -n, *n.f.* pasture; willow.

weiden, *vb.* graze; **(sich w.)** feast one's eyes, gloat.

weidlich, *adv.* thoroughly.

weigern, *vb.* **(sich w.)** refuse.

Weihe, -n, *n.f.* consecration.

weihen, *vb.* consecrate.

Weiher, -, *n.m.* pond.

weihevoll, *adj.* solemn.

Weihnachten, -, *n.nt.* Christmas.

Weihnachtslied, -er, *n.nt.* Christmas carol.

Weihnachtsmann, ⸚er, *n.m.* Santa Claus.

Weihrauch, *n.m.* incense.

Weihung, -en, *n.f.* consecration.

weil, *conj.* because, since.

Weile, *n.f.* while.

weilen, *vb.* stay.

Weiler, -, *n.m.* hamlet.

Wein, -e, *n.m.* wine.

Weinbauer, -, *n.m.* wine grower.

Weinberg, -e, *n.m.* vineyard.

Weinbrand, -e, *n.m.* brandy.

weinen, *vb.* cry, weep.

Weingarten, ⸚, *n.m.* vineyard.

Weinlese, *n.f.* vintage.

Weinrebe, -n, *n.f.* grapevine.

Weinstock, ⸚e, *n.m.* grapevine.

Weinstube, -n, *n.f.* tap room.

Weintraube, -n, *n.f.* grape.

weise, *adj.* wise.

Weise, -n, *n.f.* manner, way, method.

weisen*, *vb.* show; **(von sich w.)** reject.

Weisheit, -en, *n.f.* wisdom.

weis•machen, *vb.* make someone believe, fool.

weiß, *adj.* white.

weissagen, *vb.* prophesy, tell fortunes.

Weissager, -, *n.m.* fortune teller.

Weissagerin, -nen, *n.f.* fortune teller.

Weißwaren, *n.pl.* linen goods.

Weisung, -en, *n.f.* order, direction.

weit, *adj.* far; wide, large.

weitab´, *adv.* far away.

weitaus´, *adv.* by far.

Weite, -n, *n.f.* width, largeness, expanse; size.

weiter, *adv.* farther, further; (und so w.) and so forth.

weiterhin, *adv.* furthermore.

weitgehend, *adj.* far-reaching.

weither´, *adv.* from afar.

weitläufig, *adj.* lengthy, elaborate, complex.

weitreichend, *adj.* far-reaching.

weitsichtig, *adj.* far-sighted.

weittragend, *adj.* far-reaching.

weitverbreitet, *adj.* widespread.

weitverstreut, *adj.* far-flung.

Weizen, *n.m.* wheat.

welcher, -es, -e, *pron.& adj.* which, what.

welchergestalt, *adv.* in what manner.

welk, *adj.* wilted.

welken, *vb.* wilt.

Welle, -n, *n.f.* wave; (tech.) shaft.

wellen, *vb.* wave; (tech.) corrugate.

Wellenlänge, -n, *n.f.* wave length.

wellig, *adj.* wavy.

Welt, -en, *n.f.* world.

Weltall, *n.nt.* universe.

Weltanschauung, -en, *n.f.* philosophy of life.

Weltbürger, -, *n.m.* cosmopolite.

Weltbürgerin, -nen, *n.f.* cosmopolite.

weltgeschichtlich, *adj.* historical.

weltgewandt, *adj.* sophisticated.

weltklug (=), *adj.* worldly-wise.

Weltkrieg, -e, *n.m.* world war.

Weltkugel, -n, *n.f.* globe.

weltlich, *adj.* worldly, secular.

Weltmeister, -, *n.m.* world's champion.

Weltmeisterin, -nen, *n.f.* world's champion.

Weltmeisterschaft, -en, *n.f.* world's championship.

weltnah, *adj.* worldly, realistic.

Weltraum, *n.m.* outer space.

Weltreich, -e, *n.nt.* empire.

Weltschmerz, *n.m.* world-weariness.

Weltstadt, ⸚e, *n.f.* metropolis.

weltweit, *adj.* world-wide.

Wende, -n, *n.f.* turn, bend.

Wendekreis, -e, *n.m.* tropic; (W. des Krebses) tropic of Cancer; (W. des Steinbocks) tropic of Capricorn.

wenden*, *vb.* turn; (sich w. an) appeal to.

Wendepunkt, *n.m.* turning point.

wendig, *adj.* versatile, resourceful.

Wendung, -en, *n.f.* turn.

wenig, *adj.* few, little.

weniger, *adj.* fewer; less; minus.

Wenigkeit, -e, *n.f.* trifle; (meine W.) yours truly.

wenigstens, *adv.* at least.

wenn, *conj.* when, if.

wer, *pron.* who.

werben*, *vb.* recruit, enlist, advertise; woo.

Werbeplakat, -e, *n.nt.* poster.

Werber, -, *n.m.* suitor.

Werbung, -en, *n.f.* recruiting, advertising; courting.

Werdegang, ⸚e, *n.m.* development; career.

werden*, *vb.* become, get, grow.

werfen*, *vb.* throw; cast; (über den Haufen w.) upset.

Werft, -en, *n.f.* dockyard, shipyard.

Werk, -e, *n.nt.* work, labor, deed; factory, plant.

werken, *vb.* work, operate.

Werkstatt, ⸚en, *n.f.* plant, shop.

Werktag, -e, *n.m.* work day, weekday.

werktags, *adv.* weekdays.

Werkzeug, -e, *n.nt.* tool, instrument.

Wermut, *n.m.* vermouth.

Wert, -e, *n.m.* value, worth, merit.

wert, *adj.* worth, valued, esteemed.

Wertarbeit, -en, *n.f.* workmanship.

Wertbrief, -e, *n.m.* registered insured letter.

wertlos, *adj.* worthless, useless.

Wertlosigkeit, -en, *n.f.* worthlessness, uselessness.

Wertpapier, -e, *n.nt.* security, bond, stock.

Wertschätzung, -en, *n.f.* esteem, value.

Werturteil, -e, *n.nt.* value judgement.

Wertverminderung, -en, *n.f.* depreciation.

wertvoll, *adj.* valuable.

Wesen, -, *n.nt.* being, creature; nature, character; essence, substance.

Wesenheit, *n.f.* entity.

wesenlos, *adj.* unreal.

Wesenszug, ⸚e, *n.m.* characteristic.

wesentlich, *adj.* essential; material; substantial; vital.

weshalb, 1. *conj.* for which reason. 2. *adv.* why.

Wespe, -n, *n.f.* wasp.

wessen, *pron.* whose.

West, Westen, *n.m.* west.

Weste, -n, *n.f.* vest, waistcoat.

westlich, *adj.* western; to the west.

westwärts, *adv.* westward.

Wettbewerb, -e, *n.m.* competition.

Wettbewerber, -, *n.m.* competitor, contestant.

Wettbewerberin, -nen, *n.f.* competitor, contestant.

Wette, -n, *n.f.* wager, bet.

wetteifern, *vb.* compete, rival.

wetten, *vb.* wager, bet.

Wetter, *n.nt.* weather.

Wetterfahne, -n, *n.f.* weather vane.

Wettermeldung, -en, *n.f.* weather report.

Wetterverhältnisse, *n.pl.* weather conditions.

Wettervorhersage, *n.f.* weather forecast.

Wettkampf, ≃e, *n.m.* match, contest; competition.

Wettlauf, ≃e, *n.m.* race (on foot).

Wettläufer, -, *n.m.* runner.

Wettläuferin, -nen, *n.f.* runner.

Wettrennen, -, *n.nt.* race.

Wettrüsten, *n.nt.* armament race.

Wettspiel, -e, *n.nt.* match, tournament.

Wettstreit, -e, *n.m.* contest, competition; match, race.

wetzen, *vb.* hone, sharpen.

Whisky, -s, *n.m.* whiskey.

wichsen, *vb.* polish; thrash.

Wicht, -e, *n.m.* little fellow.

wichtig, *adj.* important.

Wichtigkeit, *n.f.* importance.

Wichtigtuer, -, *n.m.* busy-body, pompous fellow.

Wickel, -, *n.m.* wrapping, compress; curler.

wickeln, *vb.* wind, reel; wrap; curl.

wider, *prep.* against, contrary to.

widerfah´ren*, *vb.* happen to.

Widerhall, -e, *n.m.* reverberation.

wider•hallen, *vb.* resound, reverberate.

Widerhalt, *n.m.* support.

widerle´gen, *vb.* refute, disprove.

Widerle´gung, -en, *n.f.* refutation, disproof, rebuttal.

widerlich, *adj.* distasteful, repulsive.

widernatürlich, *adj.* perverse.

widerra´ten*, *vb.* dissuade.

widerrechtlich, *adj.* illegal.

Widerrede, -n, *n.f.* contradiction.

Widerruf, -e, *n.m.* revocation; cancellation.

widerru´fen*, *vb.* revoke, repeal; retract; cancel.

Widersacher, -, *n.m.* antagonist.

Widerschein, *n.m.* reflection.

widerset´zen, *vb.* **(sich w.)** oppose.

Widersinn, *n.m.* absurdity.

widersinnig, *adj.* absurd, preposterous.

widerspenstig, *adj.* recalcitrant, contrary.

wider•spiegeln, *vb.* reflect.

widerspre´chen*, *vb.* contradict.

widerspre´chend, *adj.* contradictory.

Widerspruch, ≃e, *n.m.* contradiction, disagreement.

Widerstand, ≃e, *n.m.* resistance.

widerstandsf ähig, *adj.* resistant, tough.

Widerstandskraft, ≃e, *n.f.* power of resistance, resilience.

widerstandslos, *adj.* without resistance.

widerste´hen*, *vb.* resist, withstand.

widerstre´ben, *vb.* resist, be repugnant.

Widerstre´ben, *n.nt.* reluctance.

widerstre´bend, *adj.* reluctant.

Widerstreit, -e, *n.m.* antagonism, confict.

widerstrei´ten*, *vb.* resist, conflict with.

widerwärtig, *adj.* repugnant, repulsive.

Widerwille(n), *n.m.* distaste.

widerwillig, *adj.* unwilling, reluctant.

widmen, *vb.* dedicate, devote.

Widmung, -en, *n.f.* dedication.

widrig, *adj.* contrary.

widrigenfalls, *adv.* failing which, otherwise.

wie, 1. *conj.* how; as. **2.** *adv.* how.

wieder, *adv.* again; back, in return.

Wiederauf´bau, *n.m.* reconstruction.

wiederauf•bereiten, *vb.* recycle.

Wiederauf´erstehung, *n.f.* resurrection.

Wiederauf´rüstung, -en, *n.f.* rearmament.

Wiederauf´wertung, -en, *n.f.* revaluation.

Wiederbelebung, -en, *n.f.* revival.

wiederein´•setzen, *vb.* reinstate.

wiederein´•stellen, *vb.* reinstate.

wieder•erkennen*, *vb.* recognize.

Wiedererkennung, -en, *n.f.* recognition.

wieder•erlangen, *vb.* retrieve.

wieder•erstatten, *vb.* reimburse, refund.

wieder•finden*, *vb.* recover.

Wiedergabe, -n, *n.f.* return; rendition, reproduction.

wieder•geben*, *vb.* return, restore.

wiedergeboren, *adj.* born-again.

Wiedergeburt, *n.f.* rebirth.

wieder•gewinnen*, *vb.* recover, regain.

Wiedergewinnung, -en, *n.f.* recovery.

wiedergut´•machen, *vb.* redress, make amends for.

Wiedergut´machung, -en, *n.f.* restitution, redress.

wiederher´•stellen, *vb.* restore.

Wiederher´stellung, -en, *n.f.* restoration.

wiederho´len, *vb.* repeat; review.

Wiederho´lung, -en, *n.f.* repetition; review.

Wiederhören, *n.nt.* hearing again; **(auf W.)** good-bye (at the end of a telephone call).

Wiederinstand´setzung, -en, *n.f.* reconditioning.

Wiederkehr, *n.f.* return, recurrence.

wieder•kehren, *vb.* return.

Wiedersehen, *n.nt.* seeing again; **(auf W.)** good-bye.

Wiedervereinigung, *n.f.* reunification.

wieder•verheiraten, *vb.* **(sich w.)** remarry.

wieder•versöhnen, *vb.* reconcile.

Wiederversöhnung, -en, *n.f.* reconciliation.

Wiege, -n, *n.f.* cradle.

wiegen, *vb.* rock.

wiegen*, *vb.* weigh.

Wiegenlied, -er, *n.nt.* lullaby.

wiehern, *vb.* neigh.

Wiese, -n, *n.f.* meadow.

wieso´, *adv.* how so, why.

wild, *adj.* wild, ferocious, savage.

Wild, *n.nt.* game.

Wild-, *n.m.* savage.

Wildbret, *n.nt.* game.

Wildfang, ¨e, *n.m.* tomboy.

Wildheit, *n.f.* ferocity, fierceness.

Wildleder, -, *n.nt.* chamois, suede.

Wildnis, -se, *n.f.* wilderness.

Wille(n), *n.m.* will.

willenlos, *adj.* irresolute, passive, shifting.

Willenskraft, *n.f.* willpower.

willensstark (¨), *adj.* strong-willed, resolute.

willfah´ren*, *vb.* comply with, gratify.

willfährig, *adj.* complaisant.

willig, *adj.* willing, ready.

Willkom´men, *n.nt.* welcome.

Willkür, *n.f.* arbitrariness, choice.

willkürlich, *adj.* arbitrary.

wimmeln, *vb.* swarm.

wimmern, *vb.* moan.

Wimper, -n, *n.f.* eyelash.

Wind, -e, *n.m.* wind.

Winde, -n, *n.f.* reel.

Windel, -n, *n.f.* diaper.

winden*, *vb.* wind, coil; **(sich w.)** squirm.

Windhund, -e, *n.m.* greyhound.

windig, *adj.* windy.

Windmühle, -n, *n.f.* windmill.

Windpocken, *n.pl.* chickenpox.

Windschutzscheibe, -n, *n.f.* windshield.

windstill, *adj.* calm.

Windstoß, ¨e, *n.m.* gust.

Windzug, *n.m.* draft.

Wink, -e, *n.m.* sign, wave; *(fig.)* hint, tip.

Winkel, -, *n.m.* angle, corner.

Winkelzug, ¨e, *n.m.* dodge, subterfuge.

winken, *vb.* wave, beckon.

winseln, *vb.* whimper, wail.

Winter, -, *n.m.* winter.

Winterfrische, *n.f.* winter resort.

Wintergarten, ¨, *n.m.* conservatory.

winterlich, *adj.* wintry.

Winterschlaf, *n.m.* hibernation.

Winzer, -, *n.m.* wine-grower.

winzig, *adj.* tiny, minute.

Wippe, -n, *n.f.* seesaw.

wir, *pron.* we.

Wirbel, -, *n.m.* whirl, whirlpool; cowlick; vertebra.

wirbeln, *vb.* whirl.

Wirbelsäule, -n, *n.f.* vertebral column, spine.

Wirbelsturm, ¨e, *n.m.* cyclone.

Wirbeltier, -e, *n.nt.* vertebrate.

wirken, *vb.* work, effect; **(w. auf)** effect.

wirklich, *adj.* real, actual.

Wirklichkeit, *n.f.* reality.

Wirlichkeitsflucht, *n.f.* escapism.

wirklichkeitsnah, *adj.* realistic.

wirksam, *adj.* effective.

Wirksamkeit, *n.f.* effectiveness, validity; **(in W. treten*)**, take effect.

Wirkung, -en, *n.f.* effect.

Wirkungskraft, *n.f.* effect, efficacy.

wirkungslos, *adj.* ineffectual.

wirkungsvoll, *adj.* effective.

wirr, *adj.* confused.

Wirrnis, -se, *n.f.* tangle, confusion.

Wirrwarr, *n.nt.* confusion, maze.

Wirt, -e, *n.m.* host; landlord; proprietor.

Wirtin, -nen, *n.f.* hostess; landlady.

Wirtschaft, -en, *n.f.* inn, tavern; household; economy.

wirtschaften, *vb.* manage; keep house.

Wirtschafterin, -nen, *n.f.* housekeeper.

wirtschaftlich, *adj.* economic(al).

Wirtschaftlichkeit, *n.f.* economy.

Wirtschaftsabkommen, -, *n.nt.* trade agreement.

Wirtschaftsprüfer, -, *n.m.* certified public accountant.

Wirtschaftswissenschaft, *n.f.* economics.

Wirtschaftswunder, *n.nt.* economic miracle.

Wirtshaus, ¨er, *n.nt.* inn.

Wisch, -e, *n.m.* scrap.

wischen, *vb.* wipe.

Wischlappen, -, *n.m.* cleaning rag.

wispern, *vb.* whisper.

Wißbegier, *n.f.* desire for knowledge; curiosity.

wissen*, *vb.* know.

Wissen, *n.nt.* learning, knowledge.

Wissenschaft, -en, *n.f.* learning, knowledge, science, scholarship.

wissenschaftlich, *adj.* scientific, scholarly.

wissenswert, *adj.* worth knowing.

wissentlich, *adv.* knowingly.

wittern, *vb.* smell; suspect.

Witterung, *n.f.* weather.

Witterungsverhältnisse, *n.pl.* weather conditions.

Witwe, -n, *n.f.* widow.

Witwer, -, *n.m.* widower.

Witz, -e, *n.m.* joke, pun, gag.

Witzbold, -e, *n.m.* joker, wise guy.

witzeln, *vb.* quip.

witzig, *adj.* witty, humorous.

witzlos, *adj.* pointless, fatuous.

wo, *adv.* where, in what place.

woan´ders, *adv.* elsewhere.

wobei´, *adv.* whereby.

Woche, -n, *n.f.* week.

Wochenblatt, ⸚er, *n.nt.* weekly paper.

Wochenende, -n, *n.nt.* weekend.

Wochenschau, *n.f.* newsreel.

Wochentag, -e, *n.m.* weekday.

wöchentlich, *adj.* weekly.

wodurch´, *adv.* through what; whereby.

wofern´, *conj.* in so far as.

Woge, -n, *n.f.* wave, billow.

wogen, *vb.* wave, heave.

woher´, *adv.* whence, from where.

wohl, *adv.* well; presumably, I suppose.

Wohl, *n.nt.* well-being, good health; **(zum W.)** here's to you.

wohlbedacht, *adj.* well-considered.

Wohlbehagen, *n.nt.* comfort.

Wohlergehen, *n.nt.* welfare.

wohlerzogen, *adj.* well brought up.

Wohlfahrt, *n.f.* welfare.

Wohlfahrtsstaat, -en, *n.m.* welfare state.

Wohlgefallen, *n.nt.* pleasure.

wohlgefällig, *adj.* pleasant, agreeable.

wohlgemerkt, *adv.* nota bene.

wohlgemut, *adj.* cheerful.

wohlgeneigt, *adj.* affectionate.

Wohlgeruch, ⸚e, *n.m.* fragrance.

wohlhabend, *adj.* prosperous, well-to-do.

wohlig, *adj.* comfortable.

wohlklingend, *adj.* melodious.

wohlriechend, *adj.* fragrant.

wohlschmeckend, *adj.* tasty.

Wohlsein, *n.nt.* good health; **(zum W.)** your health.

Wohlstand, *n.m.* prosperity.

Wohltat, -en, *n.f.* benefit; pleasure.

Wohltäter, -, *n.m.* benefactor.

Wohltäterin, -nen, *n.f.* benefactress.

wohltätig, *adj.* charitable.

Wohltätigkeit, -en, *n.f.* charity.

wohltuend, *adj.* beneficial, pleasant, soothing.

wohlweislich, *adv.* wisely, prudently.

Wohlwollen, *n.nt.* benevolence, good will.

wohlwollend, *adj.* benevolent.

wohnen, *vb.* reside, live, dwell.

wohnhaft, *adj.* resident.

wohnlich, *adj.* comfortable, cozy.

Wohnort, -e, *n.m.* domicile, place of residence.

Wohnsitz, -e, *n.m.* residence.

Wohnung, -en, *n.f.* apartment, place of living.

Wohnwagen, -, *n.m.* trailer.

wölben, *vb.* **(sich w.)** arch over.

Wolf, ⸚e, *n.m.* wolf.

Wolke, -n, *n.f.* cloud.

Wolkenbruch, ⸚e, *n.m.* cloudburst.

Wolkenkratzer, -, *n.m.* skyscraper.

wolkenlos, *adj.* cloudless.

Wolle, *n.f.* wool.

wollen, *adj.* woolen.

wollen*, *vb.* want, be willing, intend.

wollig, *adj.* fluffy, fleecy.

Wollust, *n.f.* voluptuousness, lust.

wollüstig, *adj.* lascivious.

womög´lich, *adv.* if possible.

Wonne, -n, *n.f.* delight.

wonnig, *adj.* charming, delightful.

Wort, -e or ⸚er, *n.nt.* word.

Wortart, -en, *n.f.* part of speech.

Wörterbuch, ⸚er, *n.nt.* dictionary.

Wörterverzeichnis, -se, *n.nt.* vocabulary.

Wortführer, -, *n.m.* spokesman.

wortgetreu, *adj.* literal, verbatim.

wortkarg, *adj.* taciturn.

Wortlaut, -e, *n.m.* wording, text.

wörtlich, *adj.* literal.

wortlos, *adj.* speechless.

wortreich, *adj.* wordy, verbose.

Wortschatz, ⸚e, *n.m.* vocabulary.

Wortspiel, -e, *n.nt.* pun.

Wortwechsel, -, *n.m.* altercation.

Wrack, -s, *n.nt.* wreck.

wringen*, *vb.* wring.

Wucher, *n.m.* usury.

wucherisch, *adj.* usurious.

Wuchs, *n.m.* growth, figure, height.

Wucht, *n.f.* weight; momentum.

wühlen, *vb.* burrow, rummage; *(fig.)* agitate.

wühlerisch, *adj.* inflammatory, subversive.

wulstig, *adj.* thick.

wund, *adj.* sore, wounded.

Wunde, -n, *n.f.* wound.

Wunder, -, *n.nt.* miracle, wonder.

wunderbar, *adj.* wonderful, miraculous.

Wunderdoktor, -en, *n.m.* quack.

Wunderkind, -er, *n.nt.* child prodigy.

wunderlich, *adj.* strange.

wundern, *vb.* surprise; **(sich w.)** be surprised.

wundersam, *adj.* wondrous.

wunderschön, *adj.* lovely, exquisite.

wundervoll, *adj.* wonderful.

Wundmal, -e, *n.nt.* scar; *(pl.)* stigmata.

Wundstarrkrampf, *n.m.* tetanus.

Wunsch, ⸚e, *n.m.* wish, desire.

wünschen, *vb.* wish, desire, want.

wünschenswert, *adj.* desirable.

Würde, *n.f.* dignity.

Würdenträger, -, *n.m.* dignitary.

würdig, *adj.* worthy, dignified.

würdigen, *vb.* honor, appreciate.

Wurf, ⁓e, *n.m.* throw; litter, brood.

Würfel, -, *n.m.* cube; *(pl.)* dice.

Würfelzucker, *n.m.* lump sugar.

Wurfpfeil, -e, *n.m.* dart.

würgen, *vb.* choke, retch; strangle.

Wurm, ⁓er, *n.m.* worm.

wurmen, *vb.* annoy, rankle.

wurmstichig, *adj.* wormy.

Wurst, ⁓e, *n.f.* sausage.

Würstchen, -, *n.nt.* (heißes W.) frankfurter.

Würze, -n, *n.f.* seasoning, flavor.

Wurzel, -n, *n.f.* root.

würzen, *vb.* season, spice.

würzig, *adj.* aromatic, spicy.

wüst, *adj.* waste, desolate; unkempt; wild; vulgar.

Wüste, -n, *n.f.* desert.

Wut, *n.f.* rage, fury.

Wutanfall, ⁓e, *n.m.* rage; tantrum.

wüten, *vb.* rage.

wütend, *adj.* furious.

X

X-beinig, *adj.* knock-kneed.

x-beliebig, *adj.* any old, any . . . at all; (jeder x-beliebige) every Tom, Dick, and Harry.

x-mal, *adv.* umpteen times.

X-Strahlen, *n.pl.* x-rays.

Xylophon´, -e, *n.nt.* xylophone.

Y

Yacht, -en, *n.f.* yacht.

Z

Zacke, -n, *n.f.* jag; spike; (fork) prong; (dress) edging.

zacken, *vb.* indent, notch.

zackig, *adj.* jagged; notched; snappy.

zag, *adj.* faint-hearted.

zagen, *vb.* hesitate.

zaghaft, *adj.* timid.

zäh, *adj.* tough, tenacious.

zähflüssig, *adj.* viscous.

Zähigkeit, *n.f.* tenacity, perseverance.

Zahl, -en, *n.f.* number, figure.

zahlen, *vb.* pay; (Bitte z.) the check, please.

zählen, *vb.* count.

Zahlenangaben, *n.pl.* figures.

zahlenmäßig, *adj.* numerical.

Zähler, -, *n.m.* meter.

Zahlkarte, -n, *n.f.* money order.

zahllos, *adj.* countless.

zahlreich, *adj.* numerous.

Zahltag, -e, *n.m.* payday.

Zahlung, -en, *n.f.* payment.

zahlungsfähig, *adj.* solvent.

Zahlungsmittel, -, *n.nt.* tender, currency.

zahlungsunfähig, *adj.* insolvent.

Zahlwort, ⁓er, *n.nt.* numeral.

zahm, *adj.* tame.

zähmen, *vb.* tame, domesticate.

Zahn, ⁓e, *n.m.* tooth; *(tech.)* cog.

Zahnarzt, ⁓e, *n.m.* dentist.

Zahnärztin, -nen, *n.f.* dentist.

Zahnbürste, -n, *n.f.* toothbrush.

zahnen, *vb.* teethe.

Zahnfleisch, *n.nt.* gum.

Zahnheilkunde, *n.f.* dentistry.

Zahnpasta, -ten, *n.f.* toothpaste.

Zahnplombe, -n, *n.f.* filling.

Zahnputzmittel, -, *n.nt.* dentifrice.

Zahnradbahn, -en, *n.f.* cog railroad.

Zahnschmerzen, *n.pl.* toothache.

Zahnseide, *n.f.* dental floss.

Zahnstein, *n.m.* tartar.

Zahnstocher, -, *n.m.* toothpick.

Zahnweh, *n.nt.* toothache.

Zange, -n, *n.f.* pliers; forceps.

Zank, *n.m.* quarrel.

zanken, *vb.* (sich z.) quarrel, bicker.

zapfen, *vb.* tap.

Zapfen, -, *n.m.* peg, plug.

Zapfenstreich, *n.m.* (mil.) retreat.

zappelig, *adj.* fidgety.

zappeln, *vb.* flounder, fidget.

Zar, -en, -en, *n.m.* czar.

zart, *adj.* tender, dainty.

Zartheit, -en, *n.f.* tenderness, daintiness.

zärtlich, *adj.* tender, affectionate.

Zauber, -, *n.m.* enchantment, spell, charm, fascination.

Zauberei´, *n.f.* sorcery, magic.

Zauberer, -, *n.m.* magician, wizard.

zauberhaft, *adj.* enchanting.

Zauberkraft, ⁓e, *n.f.* magic power.

Zauberkunst, ⁓e, *n.f.* magic.

Zauberspruch, ⁓e, *n.m.* incantation, charm.

zaudern, *vb.* hesitate.

Zaum, -e, *n.m.* bridle.

zäumen, *vb.* bridle.

Zaun, ⁓e, *n.m.* fence.

zausen, *vb.* tousle.

Zebra, -s, *n.nt.* zebra.

Zeche, -n, *n.f.* bill for drinks; mine, colliery.

zechen, *vb.* drink, carouse.

Zeder, -n, *n.f.* cedar.

Zeh, -en, *n.m.* toe.

Zehe, -n, *n.f.* toe.

Zehenspitze, -n, *n.f.* tip of the toe; **(auf Z.n gehen)** tiptoe.

zehn, *num.* ten.

zehnt-, *adj.* tenth.

Zehntel, -, *n.nt.* tenth part; **(ein z.)** one-tenth.

zehren, *vb.* **(z. an)** wear out, consume; **(z. von)** live on.

Zeichen, -, *n.nt.* sign, mark, token.

Zeichentrickfilm, -e, *n.m.* animated cartoon.

zeichnen, *vb.* draw; initial; *(comm.)* subscribe.

Zeichner, -, *n.m.* draftsman.

Zeichnerin, -nen, *n.f.* draftswoman.

Zeichnung, -en, *n.f.* drawing, *(comm.)* subscription.

Zeigefinger, -, *n.m.* forefinger.

zeigen, *vb.* show, indicate, point; demonstrate; exhibit.

Zeiger, -, *n.m.* (clock) hand.

Zeile, -n, *n.f.* line.

Zeit, -en, *n.f.* time.

Zeitalter, -, *n.nt.* age, era.

Zeitaufnahme, -n, *n.f.* time exposure.

Zeitdauer, *n.f.* period of time.

Zeitgeist, *n.m.* spirit of the times.

zeitgemäß, *adj.* timely.

Zeitgenosse, -n, -n, *n.m.* contemporary.

Zeitgenossin, -nen, *n.f.* contemporary.

zeitgenössisch, *adj.* contemporary.

zeitig, *adj.* early.

zeitlich, 1. *adj.* temporal. **2.** *adv.* in time.

zeitlos, *adj.* timeless, ageless.

Zeitmangel, *n.m.* lack of time.

Zeitpunkt, -e, *n.m.* time, moment.

zeitraubend, *adj.* time-consuming.

Zeitraum, -e, *n.m.* period.

Zeitschrift, -en, *n.f.* magazine, journal, periodical.

Zeitspanne, -n, *n.f.* period of time.

Zeitung, -en, *n.f.* newspaper.

Zeitungsanzeige, -n, *n.f.* ad, announcement.

Zeitungsausschnitt, -e, *n.m.* newspaper clipping.

Zeitungshändler, -, *n.m.* newsdealer.

Zeitungshändlerin, -nen, *n.f.* newsdealer.

Zeitungsjunge, -n, -n, *n.m.* paper-boy.

Zeitungsnotiz, -en, *n.f.* press item.

Zeitvertreib, *n.m.* pastime.

zeitweilig, *adj.* temporary.

Zeitwort, -er, *n.nt.* verb.

Zelle, -n, *n.f.* cell.

zellig, *adj.* cellular.

Zellophan', *n.nt.* cellophane.

Zellstoff, -e, *n.m.* cellulose.

Zelluloid', *n.nt.* celluloid.

Zellulo'se, -n, *n.f.* cellulose.

Zelt, -e, *n.nt.* tent.

zelten, *vb.* live in a tent, camp.

Zelter, -, *n.m.* camper.

Zelterin, -nen, *n.f.* camper.

Zeltplatz, -e, *n.m.* campsite.

Zement', -e, *n.m.* cement, concrete.

zensie'ren, *vb.* censor; (school) grade, mark.

Zensor, -'oren, *n.m.* censor.

Zensur', -en, *n.f.* censorship; (school) grade, mark.

Zensus, *n.m.* census.

Zentime'ter, -, *n.nt.* centimeter.

Zentner, -, *n.m.* 100 German pounds.

zentral', *adj.* central.

Zentral'heizung, *n.f.* central heating.

zentralisie'ren, *vb.* centralize.

Zentrum, -tren, *n.nt.* center.

zerbre'chen*, *vb.* break to pieces, shatter.

zerbrech'lich, *adj.* fragile, frail.

zerbrö'ckeln, *vb.* crumble.

zerdrü'cken, *vb.* crush.

Zeremonie', -i'en, *n.f.* ceremony.

zeremoniell', *adj.* ceremonial.

zerfah'ren, *adj.* absent-minded, scatter-brained.

Zerfall', *n.m.* ruin, decay.

zerfal'len*, *vb.* fall into ruin, disintegrate; **(in Teile z.)** be divided.

zerfet'zen, *vb.* tear into shreds.

zerflei'schen, *vb.* mangle.

zerfres'sen*, *vb.* erode, corrode.

zerge'hen*, *vb.* dissolve, melt.

zerglie'dern, *vb.* dismember, dissect.

zerklei'nern, *vb.* reduce to small pieces; crush; (wood) chop.

zerknaut'schen, *vb.* crumple.

zerknirscht', *adj.* contrite.

zerknül'len, *vb.* crumple.

zerlas'sen*, *vb.* dissolve, melt.

zerle'gen, *vb.* separate, cut up, carve.

zerlumpt', *adj.* ragged.

zermal'men, *vb.* crunch.

zermar'tern, *vb.* torture; **(den Kopf z.)** rack one's brain.

zermür'ben, *vb.* wear down.

Zermür'bung, -en, *n.f.* attrition.

zerpflü'cken, *vb.* pick to pieces.

zerquet'schen, *vb.* squash.

Zerrbild, -er, *n.nt.* distorted picture, caricature.

zerrei'ßen*, *vb.* tear up, rend.

zerren, *vb.* tug, pull.

zerrin'nen*, *vb.* disappear, melt away.

zerrüt'ten, *vb.* ruin.

Zerrüt'tung, -en, *n.f.* ruin.

zerschla'gen*, *vb.* smash, shatter.

zerschmei'ßen*, *vb.* smash.

zerset'zen, *vb.* decompose.

zerset'zend, *adj.* subversive.

Zerset'zung, -en, *n.f.* decomposition; subversion.

zersprin'gen*, *vb.* burst.

zerstäu'ben, *vb.* pulverize; atomize; scatter.

zerstö'ren, *vb.* destroy, demolish.

zerstö´rend, *adj.* destructive.

Zerstö´rung, -en, *n.f.* destruction, demolition.

zerstreu´en, *vb.* scatter; divert, amuse.

zerstreut´, *adj.* absent-minded.

Zerstreu´ung, -en, *n.f.* scattering; relaxation, amusement.

zertei´len, *vb.* cut up; separate, divide.

zertren´nen, *vb.* sever; (dress) cut up.

zertre´ten*, *vb.* trample.

zertrüm´mern, *vb.* wreck, demolish.

Zerwürf´nis, -se, *n.nt.* discord, quarrel.

zerzau´sen, *vb.* tousle, rumple.

Zettel, -, *n.m.* slip of paper, note, sticker, bill.

Zeug, -e, *n.nt.* stuff, material, cloth.

Zeuge, -n, -n, *n.m.* witness.

zeugen, *vb.* testify, give evidence; beget, create, produce.

Zeugenaussage, -n, *n.f.* testimony.

Zeugin, -nen, *n.f.* witness.

Zeugnis, -se, *n.nt.* testimony, evidence; reference (for a job); (school) report card.

Zicho´rie, -n, *n.f.* chickory.

Zickzack, -e, *n.m.* zigzag.

Ziege, -n, *n.f.* (she-)goat.

Ziegel, -, *n.m.* tile.

Ziegelstein, -e, *n.m.* brick.

Ziegenbock, ²e, *n.m.* billygoat.

Ziegenpeter, *n.m.* mumps.

ziehen*, *vb.* (intr.) move, go, draw, be drafty; (tr.) pull, drag, draw, tug; cultivate.

Ziehharmonika, -s, *n.f.* accordion.

Ziehung, -en, *n.f.* drawing.

Ziel, -e, *n.nt.* goal, target, end, objective.

zielbewußt, *adj.* with a clear goal, resolute.

zielen, *vb.* aim.

ziellos, *adj.* aimless, erratic.

Zielscheibe, -n, *n.f.* target.

ziemen, *vb.* be fitting for; **(sich z.)** be proper.

ziemlich, 1. *adj.* suitable, fitting; pretty much of. **2.** *adv.* pretty, rather, quite.

Zier, *n.f.* ornament(ation).

Zierat, -e, *n.m., or* **-en,** *n.f.* ornament, decoration.

Zierde, -n, *n.f.* ornament; honor.

zieren, *vb.* adorn, ornament.

zierlich, *adj.* dainty.

Ziffer, -n, *n.f.* figure, numeral.

Zifferblatt, ²er, *n.nt.* dial, face (of a clock).

Zigaret´te, -n, *n.f.* cigarette.

Zigar´re, -n, *n.f.* cigar.

Zigeu´ner, -, -, *n.m.* gypsy.

Zigeu´nerin, -nen, *n.f.* gypsy.

Zimbel, -n, *n.f.* cymbal.

Zimmer, -, *n.nt.* room.

Zimmerdecke, -n, *n.f.* ceiling.

Zimmermädchen, -, *n.nt.* chambermaid.

Zimmermann, -leute, *n.m.* carpenter.

zimperlich, *adj.* finicky, prim.

Zimt, *n.m.* cinnamon.

Zinke, -n, *n.f.* prong.

Zinn, *n.nt.* tin, pewter.

Zins, -en, *n.m.* interest.

Zinseszins, -en, *n.m.* compound interest.

Zinssatz, ²e, *n.m.* rate of interest.

Zipfel, -, *n.m.* tip.

Zirkel, -, *n.m.* compass (for making a circle).

zirkulie´ren, *vb.* circulate.

zirkulie´rend, *adj.* circulatory.

Zirkus, -se, *n.m.* circus.

zirpen, *vb.* chirp.

zischen, *vb.* hiss, sizzle; whiz.

ziselie´ren, *vb.* engrave, chase.

Zitadel´le, -n, *n.f.* citadel.

Zitat´, -e, *n.nt.* quotation.

zitie´ren, *vb.* quote, cite.

Zitro´ne, -n, *n.f.* lemon.

zittern, *vb.* quiver, shiver, tremble.

zivil´, *adj.* civil; reasonable.

Zivil´, *n.nt.* civilians; civilian clothes.

Zivil´bevölkerung, -en, *n.f.* civilian population.

Zivilisation´, -en, *n.f.* civilization.

zivilisie´ren, *vb.* civilize.

Zivilist´, -en, -en, *n.m.* civilian.

Zobel, *n.m.* sable.

zögern, *vb.* hesitate.

zögernd, *adj.* hesitant.

Zölibat´, *n.m. or nt.* celibacy.

Zoll, -, *n.m.* inch.

Zoll, ²e, *n.m.* tariff, duty, toll.

Zollamt, ²er, *n.nt.* custom house.

Zollbeamt-, *n.m.* customs officer.

Zollbeamtin, -nen, *n.f.* customs officer.

zollfrei, *adj.* duty free.

Zöllner, -, *n.m.* customs collector; (Bible) publican.

zollpflichtig, *adj.* subject to duty.

Zolltarif, -e, *n.m.* tariff.

Zollverein, -e, *n.m.* customs union.

Zollverschluß, *n.m.* customs seal; **(unter Z.)** under bond.

Zone, -, *n.f.* zone.

Zoo, -s, *n.m.* zoo.

Zoologie´, *n.f.* zoology.

zoolo´gisch, *adj.* zoological.

Zorn, *n.m.* ire, wrath, anger.

zornig, *adj.* angry.

zottig, *adj.* shaggy.

zu, *adv.* too; closed.

zu, *prep.* to.

Zubehör, *n.nt.* accessories, appurtenances, trimmings.

zu·bereiten, *vb.* prepare.

Zubereitung, -en, *n.f.* preparation.

zu·bringen*, *vb.* bring to; pass, spend.

Zuch, -en, *n.f.* breed(ing), rearing, education, training, decency.

züchten, *vb.* breed, raise.

Züchter, -, *n.m.* breeder.

Züchterin, -nen, *n.f.* breeder.

Zuchthaus, ²er, *n.nt.* penitentiary.

züchtig, *adj.* chaste, demure.

züchtigen, *vb.* chasten, chastise.

zucken, *vb.* twitch, jerk, flash.

Zucker, *n.m.* sugar.

Zuckerbäcker, -, *n.m.* confectioner.

Zuckerguß, ⁼sse, *n.m.* icing.

Zuckerkrankheit, *n.f.* diabetes.

Zuckerwerk, *n.nt.* confectionery.

Zuckung, -en, *n.f.* twitch, convulsion.

zu•decken, *vb.* cover up.

zudem´, *adv.* in addition.

zudringlich, *adj.* intruding, obtrusive.

Zueignung, -en, *n.f.* dedication.

zueinan´der, *adv.* to one another.

zu•erkennen*, *vb.* award.

zuerst´, *adv.* first, at first.

Zufall, ⁼e, *n.m.* chance, coincidence.

zuf ällig, 1. *adj.* chance, fortuitous. **2.** *adv.* by chance.

Zuflucht, *n.f.* refuge; recourse.

Zufluchtsort, -e, *n.m.* place of refuge.

Zufluß, ⁼sse, *n.m.* flowing in, influx.

zufol´ge, *prep.* as a result of; according to.

zufrie´den, *adj.* content, satisfied.

zufrie´den•stellen, *vb.* satisfy.

zu•frieren*, *vb.* freeze over, freeze up.

zu•fügen, *vb.* inflict.

Zufuhr, -en, *n.f.* bringing in, importation, supply.

zu•führen, *vb.* bring to, import, supply.

Zug, ⁼e, *n.m.* pull, drawing, draft; stroke; feature, trait; move; train; procession; trend; flight; *(mil.)* squad.

Zugabe, -n, *n.f.* bonus, premium, encore.

Zugang, ⁼e, *n.m.* access, approach.

zugänglich, *adj.* accessible, approachable.

zu•geben*, *vb.* give in addition; admit.

zugegebenerma´ßen, *adv.* admittedly.

zuge´gen, *adv.* present.

zugehörig, *adj.* belonging to, pertinent.

Zügel, -, *n.m.* rein; restraint.

zügellos, *adj.* unbridled, unrestrained.

zügeln, *vb.* bridle, curb, check.

zugestandenerma´ßen, *adv.* avowedly.

Zugeständnis, -se, *n.nt.* confession; concession.

zu•gestehen*, *vb.* confess, concede.

zugetan, *adj.* devoted to, fond of.

zugig, *adj.* drafty.

Zugkraft, *n.f.* pull, thrust.

zugleich´, *adv.* at the same time.

Zugluft, *n.f.* draft.

zu•greifen*, *vb.* lend a hand; help oneself.

zugrun´de, *adv.* at the bottom, as a basis; **(z. gehen*)** go to ruin, perish; **(z. richten)** ruin, destroy.

zugun´sten, *adv. & prep.* for the benefit of, in favor of.

zugu´te, *adv.* for the benefit of.

zu•haken, *vb.* hook.

zu•halten*, *vb.* keep shut.

zuhan´den, *adv.* at hand.

zu•hören, *vb.* listen to.

Zuhörer, -, *n.m.* listener, auditor; *(pl.)* audience.

Zuhörerin, -nen, *n.f.* listener.

Zuhörerraum, ⁼e, *n.m.* auditorium.

Zuhörerschaft, -en, *n.f.* audience.

zu•kleben, *vb.* paste together.

zu•knallen, *vb.* slam.

zu•knöpfen, *vb.* button up.

zu•knüpfen, *vb.* tie, knot, fasten.

zu•kommen*, *vb.* be one's due; be proper for.

Zukunft, *n.f.* future.

zukünftig, *adj.* future.

Zulage, -n, *n.f.* extra pay, pay raise.

zu•langen, *vb.* help oneself.

zulänglich, *adj.* adequate.

zu•lassen*, *vb.* leave closed; admit; permit.

zulässig, *adj.* permissible, admissible.

Zulauf, *n.m.* run; **(Z. haben*)** be popular.

zu•laufen*, *vb.* run up to.

zu•legen, *vb.* add; **(sich etwas z.)** acquire.

zulei´de, *adv.* **(z. tun*)** hurt, harm.

zu•leiten, *vb.* lead to, direct to.

zuletzt´, *adv.* at last, finally.

zulie´be, *adv.* for the sake of.

zu•machen, *vb.* shut.

zumal´, 1. *adv.* especially; together. **2.** *conj.* especially; because.

zu•mauern, *vb.* wall up.

zumeist´, *adv.* for the most part.

zu•messen*, *vb.* allot.

zumin´dest, *adv.* at least.

zumu´te, *adv.* **(z. sein*)** feel, be in a mood.

zu•muten, *vb.* expect, demand.

Zumutung, -en, *n.f.* imposition.

zunächst´, *adv.* first of all.

Zunahme, -n, *n.f.* increase.

Zuname(n), -, *n.m.* surname, last name.

zünden, *vb.* ignite; *(fig.)* inflame.

zündend, *adj.* inflammatory.

Zünder, -, *n.m.* fuse.

Zündholz, ⁼er, *n.nt.* match.

Zündkerze, -n, *n.f.* spark plug.

Zündschlüssel, -, *n.m.* ignition key.

Zündstoff, -e, *n.m.* fuel.

Zündung, *n.f.* ignition; detonation.

zu•nehmen*, *vb.* grow, increase; (moon) wax; put on weight.

zu•neigen, *vb.* incline.

Zuneigung, -en, *n.f.* inclination; affection.

Zunft, ⁼e, *n.f.* guild.

Zunge, -n, *n.f.* tongue.

zungenfertig, *adj.* glib.

zunich´te, *adv.* to nothing, ruined; **(z. machen)** ruin, frustrate.

zunut´ze, *adv.* **(z. machen)** profit by, utilize.

zuo´berst, *adv.* at the top.

zu´packen, *vb. (fig.)* get to work.

zupfen, *vb.* pull, (wool) pick.

zu•raten*, *vb.* advise in favor of.

zurechnungsf ähig, *adj.* accountable.

zurecht´, *adv.* right, in good order.

zurecht´•finden*, *vb.* **(sich z.)** find one's way.

zurecht´•machen, *vb.* prepare.

zu•reden, *vb.* urge, encourage.

zureichend, *adj.* sufficient.

zu•richten, *vb.* prepare; **(übel z.)** maul.

zürnen, *vb.* be angry.

Zurschau´stellung, -en, *n.f.* display.

zurück´, *adv.* back, behind.

zurück´•behalten*, *vb.* keep back.

zurück´•bleiben*, *vb.* lag behind.

zurück´•bringen*, *vb.* return.

zurück´•drängen, *vb.* drive back.

zurück´•erstatten, *vb.* reimburse.

zurück´•fahren*, *vb.* drive back; recoil.

zurück´•fallen*, *vb.* fall back; relapse.

zurück´•führen, *vb.* lead back; trace back, attribute.

zurück´•geben*, *vb.* return.

zurück´geblieben, *adj.* backward.

Zurück´gebliebenheit, *n.f.* backwardness.

zurück´•gehen*, *vb.* go back; decline.

zurück´gesetzt, *adj.* (prices) reduced.

zurück´gezogen, *adj.* secluded.

Zurück´gezogenheit, *n.f.* seclusion.

zurück´•halten*, *vb.* retain; restrain; withhold.

zurück´haltend, *adj.* reticent.

Zurück´haltung, *n.f.* restraint.

zurück´•kehren, *vb.* return, revert.

zurück´•kommen*, *vb.* return.

zurück´•lassen*, *vb.* leave behind.

zurück´•legen, *vb.* lay aside; accomplish.

zurück´•lehnen, *vb.* **(sich z.)** lean back, recline.

zurück´•liegen*, *vb.* lie in the past.

zurück´•nehmen*, *vb.* take back; retract.

zurück´•prallen, *vb.* recoil, rebound.

zurück´•rufen*, *vb.* recall.

zurück´•schauen, *vb.* look back.

zurück´•schlagen*, *vb.* hit back, repulse.

zurück´•schrecken, *vb.* be startled; shrink (from).

zurück´•sehen*, *vb.* look back on; reflect.

zurück´•sehnen, *vb.* **(sich z.)** long to return.

zurück´•setzen, *vb.* put back; set aside; reduce.

zurück´•stehen*, *vb.* stand back; *(fig.)* be inferior.

zurück´•stellen, *vb.* set back; set aside; *(mil.)* defer.

zurück´•stoßen*, *vb.* repulse.

zurück´•strahlen, *vb.* reflect.

zurück´•treiben*, *vb.* repel.

zurück´•treten*, *vb.* resign.

zurück´•verfolgen, *vb.* trace.

zurück´•versetzen, *vb.* put back; **(sich z.)** go back to a time.

zurück´•weichen*, *vb.* retreat.

zurück´•weisen*, *vb.* send back; reject.

Zurück´weisung, -en, *n.f.* rebuff.

zurück´•zahlen, *vb.* refund, repay.

zurück´•ziehen*, *vb.* pull back, withdraw; **(sich z.)** withdraw, back out.

Zuruf, -e, *n.m.* call, shout; acclamation.

Zusage, -n, *n.f.* acceptance.

zu•sagen, *vb.* accept; **(es sagt mir zu)** it agrees with me.

zusam´men, *adv.* together.

Zusam´menarbeit, *n.f.* cooperation, collaboration.

zusam´men•arbeiten, *vb.* cooperate, collaborate.

Zusam´menbau, *n.m.* assemblage.

zusam´men•brauen, *vb.* concoct.

zusam´men•brechen*, *vb.* collapse.

Zusam´menbruch, ⸗e, *n.m.* collapse.

zusam´men•drängen, *vb.* **(sich z.)** crowd together; huddle.

zusam´men•fahren*, *vb.* ride together; crash; be startled, wince.

zusam´men•fassen, *vb.* summarize, recapitulate.

zusam´menfassend, *adj.* comprehensive; summary.

Zusam´menfassung, -en, *n.f.* summary, condensation.

zusam´men•fügen, *vb.* join together.

zusam´men•gehören, *vb.* belong together.

zusam´men•geraten*, *vb.* collide.

zusam´mengesetzt, *adj.* composed; compound.

Zusam´menhang, ⸗e, *n.m.* connection, relation; context; association.

zusam´men•hängen*, *vb.* hang together, be connected, cohere.

zusam´menhängend, *adj.* coherent.

zusam´menhangslos, *adj.* disconnected, incoherent.

zusam´men•häufen, *vb.* pile up.

zusam´men•kauern, *vb.* huddle.

zusam´men•kommen*, *vb.* get together, convene.

Zusam´menkunft, ⸗e, *n.f.* meeting.

zusam´men•laufen*, *vb.* converge.

zusam´men•legen, *vb.* combine, pool, merge.

zusam´men•nehmen*, *vb.* **(sich z.)** pull oneself together.

zusam´men•passen, *vb.* go well together.

Zusam´menprall, -e, *n.m.* collision, impact.

zusam´men•pressen, *vb.* compress.

zusam´men•rechnen, *vb.* add up.

zusam´men•reißen*, *vb.* (sich z.) pull oneself together.

zusam´men•rotten, *vb.* (sich z.) band together.

zusam´men•rufen*, *vb.* summon, convene.

zusam´men•scharen, *vb.* scrape together; (sich z.) band together, cluster.

zusam´men•schließen*, *vb.* join together; (sich z.) close ranks.

Zusam´menschluß, ⸗sse, *n.m.* federation, merger.

zusam´men•schrumpfen, *vb.* shrink, dwindle.

zusam´men•setzen, *vb.* combine, compound; (sich z.) consist, be composed.

Zusam´mensetzung, -en, *n.f.* combination, composition.

zusam´men•stehen*, *vb.* stand together, stick together.

zusam´men•stellen, *vb.* make up, compile.

Zusam´menstellung, -en, *n.f.* composition, arrangement.

Zusam´menstoß, ⸗e, *n.m.* collision, clash.

zusam´men•stoßen*, *vb.* get together; collide, clash, crash.

zusam´men•strömen, *vb.* flow together, flock together.

zusam´men•stürzen, *vb.* collapse.

zusam´men•tragen*, *vb.* compile.

zusam´men•treffen*, *vb.* meet, encounter; coincide.

Zusam´mentreffen, -, *n.nt.* encounter; coincide.

zusam´men•treten*, *vb.* convene.

zusam´men•tun*, *vb.* put together; (sich z.) unite.

zusam´men•wirken, *vb.* act together, collaborate.

zusam´men•zählen, *vb.* sum up.

zusam´men•ziehen*, *vb.* draw together; (sich z.) contract, constrict.

Zusam´menziehung, -en, *n.f.* contraction.

Zusatz, ⸗e, *n.m.* addition.

zusätzlich, *adj.* additional, supplementary.

zuschan´den•machen, *vb.* ruin.

zu•schauen, *vb.* look on, watch.

Zuschauer, -, *n.m.* spectator.

Zuschauerin, -nen, *n.f.* spectator.

zu•schicken, *vb.* send to, forward.

zu•schieben*, *vb.* shove towards; (die Schuld z.) put the blame on.

zu•schießen*, *vb.* contribute.

Zuschlag, ⸗e, *n.m.* increase; additional charge.

zu•schlagen*, *vb.* strike; bang shut.

zu•schließen*, *vb.* lock.

zu•schneiden*, *vb.* cut out.

zu•schreiben*, *vb.* ascribe, attribute, impute.

Zuschrift, -en, *n.f.* communication.

Zuschuß, ⸗sse, *n.m.* subsidy.

zu•sehen*, *vb.* look on, watch.

zusehends, *adv.* visibly.

zu•senden*, *vb.* send, forward.

zu•sichern, *vb.* assure, promise.

Zustand, ⸗e, *n.m.* state, condition; situation.

zustan´de•bringen*, *vb.* bring about, achieve, accomplish.

zustan´de•kommen*, *vb.* come about, be accomplished.

zuständig, *adj.* competent, qualified.

Zuständigkeit, -en, *n.f.* competence; jurisdiction.

zustat´ten•kommen*, *vb.* be useful.

zu•stehen*, *vb.* be due to; become, suit; behoove.

zu•stellen, *vb.* deliver.

Zustellung, -en, *n.f.* delivery.

zu•stimmen, *vb.* agree, consent.

Zustimmung, -en, *n.f.* agreement, consent, approval.

zu•stopfen, *vb.* plug.

zu•stoßen*, *vb.* slam tight, meet with, befall.

Zustrom, *n.m.* influx.

Zutat, -en, *n.f.* ingredient.

zu•teilen, *vb.* allot, assign, allocate.

zu•trauen, *vb.* believe someone capable of doing.

Zutrauen, *n.nt.* confidence.

zutraulich, *adj.* trusting.

zu•treffen*, *vb.* prove right, apply.

zutreffend, *adj.* correct, applicable.

Zutritt, -e, *n.m.* admittance, admission.

Zutun, *n.nt.* assistance.

zuverlässig, *adj.* reliable, trustworthy.

Zuverlässigkeit, *n.f.* reliability.

Zuversicht, *n.f.* confidence, trust.

zuversichtlich, *adj.* confident, sure.

zuviel´, *adv.* too much.

zuvor´, *adv.* beforehand.

zuvor´derst, *adv.* up front.

zuvor´derst, *adv.* first of all.

zuvor´•kommen*, *vb.* anticipate, forestall.

zuvor´kommend, *adj.* obliging, polite.

Zuvor´kommenheit, *n.f.* civility.

Zuwachs, *n.m.* increase, rise, growth.

zu•wandern, *vb.* immigrate.

zuwe´ge•bringen*, *vb.* bring about, achieve.

zuwei´len*, *adv.* at times.

zu•weisen*, *vb.* assign, apportion, allot.

Zuweisung, -en, *n.f.* assignment, allocation.

zu•wenden*, *vb.* turn towards; bestow upon.

Zuwendung, -en, *n.f.* donation.

zuwi´der, 1. *adv.* abhorrent, repugnant. **2.** *prep.* contrary to.

zuwi´der•handeln, *vb.* act contrary to, disobey.

zu•zahlen, *vb.* pay extra.

zu•ziehen*, *vb.* pull closed; **(sich etwas z.)** contract, incur.

Zuzug, *n.m.* move, influx.

zuzüglich, *adv.* plus.

Zwang, *n.m.* compulsion, coercion, duress; constraint.

zwanglos, *adj.* unrestrained, informal, casual.

Zwangsarbeit, *n.f.* forced labor; hard labor.

zwangsläufig, *adv.* necessarily.

zwangsräumen, *vb.* evict.

Zwangsverschleppt-, *n.m.& f.* displaced person.

zwangsweise, *adv.* forcibly.

Zwangswirtschaft, *n.f.* controlled economy.

zwanzig, *num.* twenty.

zwanzigst-, *adj.* twentieth.

Zwanzigstel, -, *n.nt.* twentieth part; **(ein z.)** one-twentieth.

zwar, *adv.* to be sure (means that a *but* is coming); **(und z.)** namely, to give further details.

Zweck, -e, *n.m.* purpose, end, aim.

zweckdienlich, *adj.* expedient.

Zwecke, -n, *n.f.* tack.

zweckmäßig, *adj.* expedient.

zwecks, *prep.* for the purpose of.

zwei, *num.* two.

zweideutig, *adj.* ambiguous.

Zweideutigkeit, -en, *n.f.* ambiguity.

zweierlei, *adj.* of two kinds.

zweifach, *adj.* twofold.

zweif ältig, *adj.* twofold, double.

Zweifel, -, *n.m.* doubt.

zweifelhaft, *adj.* doubtful.

zweifellos, *adj.* doubtless.

zweifeln, *vb.* doubt.

Zweifler, -, *n.m.* doubter, sceptic.

Zweiflerin, -nen, *n.f.* doubter, sceptic.

Zweig, -e, *n.m.* branch, bough, twig.

Zweikampf, ⸚e, *n.m.* duel.

zweimal, *adv.* twice.

zweimalig, *adj.* repeated, done twice.

zweimonatlich, *adj.* bimonthly.

Zweirad, ⸚er, *n.nt.* bicycle.

zweiseitig, *adj.* two-sided, bilateral.

Zweisitzer, -, *n.m.* two-seater, roadster.

zweisprachig, *adj.* bilingual.

zweit-, *adj.* second.

zweitbest-, *adj.* second-best.

zweiteilig, *adj.* two-piece; bipartite.

zweitens, *adv.* in the second place, secondly.

zweitklassig, *adj.* second-class.

Zwerchfell, -e, *n.nt.* diaphragm.

Zwerg, -e, *n.m.* dwarf; midget.

zwergenhaft, *adj.* dwarfish, diminutive.

Zwetschge, -n, *n.f.* plum.

zwicken, *vb.* pinch.

Zwickmühle, -n, *n.f.* dilemma, jam.

Zwieback, ⸚e *or* **-e,** *n.m.* rusk.

Zwiebel, -n, *n.f.* onion.

zwiefach, *adj.* double.

Zwiegespräch, -e, *n.nt.* dialogue.

Zwielicht, *n.nt.* twilight.

zwielichtig, *adj.* shady.

Zwiespalt, -e, *n.m.* discrepancy; discord; schism.

zwiespältig, *adj.* discrepant, conflicting.

Zwilling, -e, *n.m.* twin.

zwingen*, *vb.* force, compel.

zwingend, *adj.* compelling.

Zwinger, -, *n.m.* cage; (dog) kennel.

zwinkern, *vb.* wink.

Zwirn, -e, *n.m.* thread; twine.

Zwirnfaden, ⸚, *n.m.* thread.

zwischen, *prep.* between, among.

Zwischenakt, -e, *n.m.* entr'acte; interval.

Zwischenbemerkung, -en, *n.f.* incidental remark, interruption.

Zwischendeck, -e, *n.nt.* steerage.

Zwischending, -e, *n.nt.* something halfway between, mixture, cross.

zwischendurch´, *adv.* in between; now and then.

Zwischenfall, ⸚e, *n.m.* incident.

Zwischenhändler, -, *n.m.* jobber.

Zwischenhändlerin, -nen, *n.f.* jobber.

Zwischenlandung, -en, *n.f.* stopover.

Zwischenraum, ⸚e, *n.m.* space in between; interval.

Zwischenruf, -e, *n.m.* interjection, interruption.

Zwischenspiel, -e, *n.nt.* interlude, intermezzo.

Zwischenstock, ⸚e, *n.m.* mezzanine.

Zwischenzeit, *n.f.* interval, interim.

Zwist, -e, *n.m.* quarrel, discord.

zwitschern, *vb.* twitter, chirp.

Zwitter, -, *n.m.* hybrid.

zwo, *num.* two (used especially on the telephone to avoid having *zwei* misunderstood as *drei*).

zwölf, *num.* twelve.

Zwölffin´gerdarm, ⸚e, *n.m.* duodenum.

zwölft-, *adj.* twelfth.

Zwölftel, -, *n.nt.* twelfth part; **(ein z.)** one-twelfth.

zwot-, *adj.* second.

Zyklamat´, -e, *n.nt.* cyclamate.

Zyklon´, -e, *n.m.* cyclone.

Zyklotron, -e, *n.nt.* cyclotron.

Zyklus, -klen, *n.m.* cycle.

Zylin´der, -, *n.m.* cylinder; top hat.

Zyniker, -, *n.m.* cynic.

Zynikerin, -nen, *n.f.* cynic.

zynisch, *adj.* cynical.

Zypres´se, -n, *n.f.* cypress.

Zyste, -n, *n.f.* cyst.

ENGLISH-GERMAN

A

a, *art.* ein, -, -e.

abandon, *vb.* verlas´sen*.

abandoned, *adj.* verlas´sen; *(depraved)* verwor´fen.

abandonment, *n.* Aufgeben *nt.*

abash, *vb.* beschä´men.

abate, *vb.* nach•lassen*.

abatement, *n.* Vermin´derung, -en *f.*

abbess, *n.* Äbtis´sin, -nen *f.*

abbey, *n.* Abtei´, -en *f.*, Kloster, = *nt.*

abbot, *n.* Abt. =e *m.*

abbreviate, *vb.* ab•kürzen.

abbreviation, *n.* Abkürzung, -en *f.*

abdicate, *vb.* ab•danken.

abdication, *n.* Abdankung, -en *f.*

abdomen, *n.* Unterleib, -er *m.*

abdominal, *adj.* Leib- *(cpds.).*

abduct, *vb.* entfüh´ren.

abduction, *n.* Entfüh´rung, -en *f.*

abductor, *n.* Entfüh´rer, - *m.*

aberration, *n.* Abweichung, -en *f.*

abet, *vb.* an•treiben*, helfen*.

abetment, *n.* Beistand, -e *m.*

abettor, *n.* Helfershelfer, - *m.*

abeyance, *n.* Schwebezustand, =e *m.*

abhor, *vb.* verab´scheuen.

abhorrence, *n.* Abscheu, -e *m.*

abhorrent, *adj.* zuwi´der.

abide, *vb. (dwell)* wohnen; *(remain)* bleiben*; *(tolerate)* leiden*.

abiding, *adj.* dauernd.

ability, *n.* Fähigkeit, -en *f.*

abject, *adj.* elend, niedrig, unterwür´fig.

abjure, *vb.* ab•schwören*, entsa´gen.

ablative, *n.* Ablativ, -e *m.*

ablaze, *adj.* in Flammen.

able, *adj.* fähig, tüchtig; **(to be a.)** können*.

able-bodied, *adj.* kräftig.

ablution, *n.* Abwaschung, -en *f.*

ably, *adv.* fähig, tüchtig.

abnormal, *adj.* ungewöhnlich, abnorm´.

abnormality, *n.* Mißbildung, -en *f.*, Abnormität´, -en *f.*

aboard, *adv.* an Bord.

abode, *n.* Wohnsitz, -e *m.*, Wohnung, -en *f.*

abolish, *vb.* ab•schaffen.

abolition, *n.* Aufhebung, -en *f.*

abominable, *adj.* abscheu´lich.

abominate, *vb.* verab´scheuen.

abomination, *n.* Abscheu, -e *m.*

aboriginal, *adj.* ursprüng´lich, Ur- *(cpds.).*

aborigine, *n.* Ureinwohner, - *m.*

abort, *vb.* fehl•gebären*, ab•treiben*.

abortion, *n.* Fehlgeburt, -en *f.*, Abtreibung, -en *f.*

abortive, *adj.* mißglückt´.

abound, *vb.* im Überfluß vorhanden sein.

about, **1.** *adv. (approximately)* etwa, ungefähr; *(around)* herum´, umher´; **(be a. to)** im Begriff sein*. **2.** *prep. (around)* um; *(concerning)* über.

about-face, *n.* Kehrtwendung *f.*

above, **1.** *adj.* obig. **2.** *adv.* oben. **3.** *prep.* über.

aboveboard, *adj.* offen, unverhoh´len.

abrasion, *n.* Abschaben *nt.*, Abschleifen *nt.*

abrasive, **1.** *n.* Schleifmittel, - *nt.* **2.** *adj.* abschaben, abschleifend.

abreast, *adv.* nebeneinan´der, Seite an Seite.

abridge, *vb.* ab•kürzen.

abridgment, *n.* Abkürzung, -en *f.*

abroad, *adv.* im Ausland.

abrupt, *adj.* schroff, abrupt´.

abruptness, *n.* Schroffheit, -en *f.*

abscess, *n.* Eitergeschwulst, -e *f.*

abscond, *vb.* durch•brennen*.

absence, *n.* Abwesenheit, -en *f.*

absent, *adj.* abwesend.

absentee, *n.* Abwesend- *m.& f.*

absent-minded, *adj.* zerstreut´.

absinthe, *n.* Absinth´, -e *m.*

absolute, *adj.* absolut´, unbedingt´.

absoluteness, *n.* Unbedingt´heit, -en *f.*

absolution, *n.* Absolution´, -en *f.*

absolve, *vb.* frei•sprechen*, entla´sten.

absorb, *vb.* auf•saugen, absorbie´ren.

absorbed, *adj. (fig.)* vertieft´.

absorbent, **1.** *n.* Absorbie´rungsmittel, - *nt.* **2.** *adj.* aufsaugend.

absorbing, *adj.* aufsaugend; *(interesting)* packend.

absorption, *n.* Absorption´, -en *f.*

abstain, *vb.* sich enthal´ten*.

abstemious, *adj.* enthalt´sam.

abstinence, *n.* Enthalt´samkeit, -en *f.*

abstract, **1.** *n. (book, article)* Auszug, -e *m.* **2.** *adj.* abstrakt´. **3.** *vb.* abstrahie´ren.

abstraction, *n.* Abstraktion´, -en *f.*

abstruse, *adj.* abstrus´.

absurd, *adj.* unsinnig.

absurdity, *n.* Unsinnigkeit, -en *f.*

abundance, *n.* Überfluß, =sse *m.*

abundant, *adj.* überreich.

abuse, **1.** *vb.* mißbrau´chen; **2.** *n.* Mißbrauch, =e *m.*

abusive, *adj.* mißbräuchlich, beschimp´fend.

abut, *vb.* an•grenzen.

abutment, *n.* Angrenzung, -en *f.*

abyss, *n.* Abgrund, ⸗e *m.*

academic, *adj.* akade´misch.

academy, *n.* Akademie´, - mi´en *f.,* Hochschule, -n *f.*

acanthus, *n.* Akan´thus, -se *m.*

accede, *vb.* ein•willigen.

accelerate, *vb.* beschleu´nigen.

acceleration, *n.* Beschleu´nigung, -en *f.*

accelerator, *n.* Gashebel, - *m.*

accent, 1. *n.* Akzent´, -e *m.* **2.** *vb.* beto´nen.

accept, *vb.* an•nehmen*.

acceptability, *n.* Annehmbarkeit, -en *f.*

acceptable, *adj.* annehmbar.

acceptance, *n.* Annahme, -n *f.*

access, *n.* Zugang, ⸗e *m.*

accessible, *adj.* zugänglich.

accessory, 1. *n.* *(person)* Mithelfer, - *m.,* Mithelferin, -nen *f.;* *(thing)* Zubehör *nt.* **2.** *adj.* zusätzlich.

accident, *n.* Unfall, ⸗e *m;* *(chance)* Zufall, ⸗e *m.*

accidental, *adj.* zufällig.

acclaim, 1. *n.* Beifall, ⸗e *m.* **2.** *vb.* Beifall rufen*.

acclamation, *n.* Zuruf, ⸗e *m,* Beifall, ⸗e *m.*

acclimate, *vb.* akklamatisie´ren.

accommodate, *vb.* an•passen, unter•bringen*.

accommodating, *adj.* entge´genkommend.

accommodation, *n.* Anpassung, -en *f., (lodging)* Unterkunft, ⸗e *f.*

accompaniment, *n.* Beglei´tung, -en *f.*

accompanist, *n.* Beglei´ter, - *m.,* Begle´terin, -nen *f.*

accompany, *vb.* beglei´ten.

accomplice, *n.* Mittäter, - *m.,* Mittäterin, -nen *f.*

accomplish, *vb.* leisten.

accomplished, *adj.* vollen´det.

accomplishment, *n.* Leistung, -en *f.*

accord, *n.* Einvernehmen, - *nt.*

accordance, *n.* Überein´stimmung, -en *f.*

accordingly, *adv.* demgemäß.

according to, *prep.* laut, gemäß´.

accordion, *n.* Ziehharmonika, -s *f.*

accost, *vb.* an•sprechen*.

account, *n. (comm.)* Konto, -ten *nt., (narrative)* Bericht´, -e *m.*

accountable, *adj.* verant´wortlich.

accountant, *n.* Buchhalter, - *m.,* Buchhalterin, -nen *f.*

accounting, *n.* Buchführung, -en *f.*

accredit, *vb.* akkreditie´ren, beglau´bigen.

accrual, *n.* Zuwachs *m.*

accrue, *vb.* an•wachsen*.

accumulate, *vb.* (sich) an•häufen.

accumulation, *n.* Anhäufung, -en *f.*

accumulator, *n.* Ansammler, - *m.,* Akkumula´tor, - to´ren *m.*

accuracy, *n.* Genau´igheit, - en *f.*

accurate, *adj.* genau´.

accursed, *adj.* verflucht´.

accusation, *n.* Anklage, -n *f.*

accusative, 1. *n.* Akkusativ, -e *m.* **2.** *adj.* anklagend.

accuse, *vb.* an•klagen.

accused, *n.* Angeklagt- *m.& f.*

accuser, *n.* Ankläger, - *m.,* Anklägerin, -nen *f.*

accustom, *vb.* gewöh´nen.

accustomed, *adj.* gewohnt´, gewöhnt´; **(become a. to)** sich gewöh´nen an.

ace, *n.* As, -se *nt.*

acetate, *n.* Acetat´, -e *nt.*

acetic, *adj.* ace´tisch.

acetylene, *n.* Acetylen´ *nt.*

ache, 1. *n.* Schmerz, -en *m.* **2.** *vb.* weh tun*, schmerzen.

achieve, *vb.* errei´chen.

achievement, *n.* Leistung, - en *f.*

acid, 1. *n.* Säure, -n *f.* **2.** *adj.* sauer.

acidify, *vb.* in Säure verwandeln.

acidity, *n.* Säuerlichkeit, - en *f.*

acknowledge, *vb.* an•erkennen*, bestä´tigen.

acme, *n.* Höhepunkt, -e *m.*

acne, *n.* Akne, -n *f.*

acolyte, *n.* Altar´diener, - *m.*

acorn, *n.* Eichel, -n *f.*

acoustics, *n.* Aku´stik *f.*

acquaint, *vb.* bekannt´machen.

acquaintance, *n.* Bekannt´schaft, -en *f.*

acquainted, *adj.* bekannt´, vertraut´.

acquiesce, *vb.* ein•willigen, ruhig hin•nehmen*.

acquiescence, *n.* Einwilligung, -en *f.*

acquire, *vb.* erwer´ben*.

acquisition, *n.* Erwer´bung, -en *f.*

acquisitive, *adj.* gewinn´süchtig.

acquit, *vb.* frei•sprechen*.

acquittal, *n.* Freispruch, ⸗e *m.*

acre, *n.* Morgen, - *m.*

acreage, *n.* Flächeninhalt nach Morgen; Land.

acrimonious, *adj.* scharf, bitter.

acrimony, *n.* Bitterkeit, -en *f.*

acrobat, *n.* Akrobat´, -en, - en *m.*

across, 1. *prep.* über. **2.** *adv.* hinü´ber, herü´ber.

act, 1. *n. (deed)* Tat, -en *f.; (drama)* Akt, -e *m.; (law)* Gesetz´, -e *nt.* **2.** *vb.* handeln; *(stage)* spielen; *(behave)* sich beneh´men*.

acting, 1. *n. (stage)* Schauspielkunst, ⸗e *f.* **2.** *adj.* stellvertretend.

action, *n.* Handlung, -en *f.*

activate, *vb.* aktivie´ren.

activation, *n.* Aktivie´rung, -en *f.*

active, *adj.* tätig, aktiv´.

activity, *n.* Tätigkeit, -en *f.*

actor, *n.* Schauspieler, - *m.*

actress, *n.* Schauspielerin, - nen *f.*

actual, *adj.* tatsächlich.

actuality, *n.* Wirklichkeit, - en *f.*

actually, *adv.* wirklich.

actuary, *n.* Gerichts´-schreiber, - *m.;* Versi´-cherungsmathema´tiker, - *m.*

acumen, *n.* Scharfsinn *m.*

acupuncture, *n.* Akupunktur´, -en *f.*

acute, *adj.* scharf, scharfsinnig, akut´; *(angle)* spitz.

acuteness, *n.* Schärfe, -n *f.,* Scharfsinnigkeit *f.*

adage, *n.* Sprichwort, ⸗er *nt.*

adamant, *adj.* hartnäckig.

adapt, *vb.* an•passen, bear´beiten.

adaptability, *n.* Anpassungsfähigkeit, -en *f.*

adaptable, *adj.* anpassungsfähig.

adaptation, *n.* Anwendung, -en *f.,* Bear´beitung, -en *f.*

adapter, *n.* Bear´beiter, - *m.;* Adap´ter, - *m.*

add, *vb.* hinzu´•fügen, addie´ren.

adder, *n.* Natter, -n *f.*

addict, *n.* **(drug a.)** Rauschgiftsüchtig- *m.& f.;* **(alcohol a.)** Alkoholsüchtig- *m.& f.*

addicted, *adj.* süchtig.

addition, *n.* Zusatz, ⸗e *m.*

additional, *adj.* zusätzlich.

address, 1. *n. (on letters, etc.)* Adres´se, -n *f.; (speech)* Ansprache, -n *f.* **2.** *vb. (a letter)* adressie´ren; *(a person)* an•sprechen*.

addressee, *n.* Empfäng´er, - *m.,* Empfäng´erin, -nen *f.*

adenoid, *n.* Nasen-wucherung *f.; (pl.)* Poly´pen *pl.*

adept, *adj.* erfah´ren, geschickt´.

adequacy, *n.* Angemessen-heit, -en *f.*

adequate, *adj.* angemessen.

adhere, *vb.* haften, fest•halten*.

adherence, *n.* Festhalten *nt.*

adherent, *n.* Anhänger, - *m.*

adhesive, 1. *adj.* Klebemittel, - *nt.* **2.** *adj.* anhaftend; **(a. tape)** Leukoplast´ *n.nt.*

adieu, *interj.* lebewohl´!, ade´!

adjacent, *adj.* angrenzend.

adjective, *n.* Eigen-schaftswort, ⸗er *nt.,* Adjektiv, -e *nt.*

adjoin, *vb.* an•grenzen.

adjourn, *vb.* verta´gen.

adjournment, *n.* Verta´gung, -en *f.*

adjunct, 1. *n.* Zusatz, ⸗e *m.* **2.** *adj.* zusätzlich.

adjust, *vb.* passend machen, berich´tigen, aus•gleichen*.

adjuster, *n.* Ausgleicher, - *m.*

adjustment, *n.* Ausgle-ichung, -en *f.*

adjutant, *n.* Adjutant´, -en, -en *m.*

administer, *vb.* verwal´ten; ertei´len.

administration, *n.* Verwal´tung, -en *f.*

administrative, *adj.* Verwal´tungs- *(cpds.).*

administrator, *n.* Verwal´ter, - *m.*

admirable, *adj.* bewun´dernswert.

admiral, *n.* Admiral´, -e *m.*

admiralty, *n.* Admiralität´, -en *f.*

admiration, *n.* Bewun´derung *f.*

admire, *vb.* bewun´dern.

admirer, *n.* Vereh´rer, - *m.,* Vereh´rerin, -nen *f.*

admissible, *adj.* zulässig.

admission, *n. (entrance)* Eintritt, -e *m.; (confession)* Zugeständnis, -se *nt.*

admit, *vb. (permit)* zu•lassen*; *(concede)* zu•gestehen*.

admittance, *n.* Zutritt, -e *m.*

admittedly, *adv.* zugegebenerma´ßen; allerdings´.

admixture, *n.* Beimischung, -en *f.*

admonish, *vb.* ermah´nen.

admonition, *n.* Ermah´nung, -en *f.*

adolescence, *n.* das heran´wachsende Alter, Jugendzeit, -en *f.*

adolescent, 1. *n.* der heran´wachsende Junge, das heran´wachsende

Mädchen. **2.** *adj.* jugendlich.

adopt, *vb.* adoptie´ren, an•nehmen*.

adoption, *n.* Adoption´, -en *f.*

adorable, *adj.* reizend, entzück´end.

adoration, *n.* Vereh´rung *f.,* Anbetung *f.*

adore, *vb.* vereh´ren, an•beten.

adorn, *vb.* schmücken, zieren.

adornment, *n.* Verzie´rung, -en *f.*

adrift, *adv.* treibend, Wind und Wellen preisgegeben.

adroit, *adj.* geschickt´.

adulation, *n.* Schmeichelei´, -en *f.*

adult, 1. *n.* Erwach´sen- *m.& f.* **2.** *adj.* erwach´sen.

adulterate, *vb.* verfäl´schen.

adultery, *n.* Ehebruch, ⸗e *m.*

advance, 1. *n.* Fortschritt, -e *m.; (mil.)* Vormarsch, ⸗e *m.; (pay)* Vorschuß, ⸗sse; **(in a.)** im voraus´. **2.** *vb.* Fortschritte machen; *(mil.)* vor•rücken; *(pay)* voraus´•zahlen; *(promote)* beför´dern.

advanced, *adj.* fortgeschritten, modern´.

advancement, *n.* Förderung, -en *f.,* Beför´derung, -en *f.*

advantage, *n.* Vorteil, -e *m.*

advantageous, *adj.* vorteilhaft.

advent, *n.* Ankunft, ⸗e *f.; (eccl.)* Advent´ *m.*

adventure, *n.* Abenteuer, - *nt.*

adventurer, *n.* Abenteurer, - *m.*

adventurous, *adj.* abenteuerlich; unterneh´mungslustig.

adverb, *n.* Adverb´, -en *nt.,* Umstandswort, ⸗er *nt.*

adverbial, *adj.* adverbial´.

adversary, *n.* Gegner, - *m.* Gegnerin, -nen *f.*

adverse, *adj.* ungünstig, nachteilig.

adversity, *n.* Mißgeschick, -e *nt.*

advertise, vb. an•zeigen, annoncie´ren, Rekla´me machen.

advertisement, n. Annon´ce, -n f., Inserat´, -e nt., Rekla´me, -n f.

advertiser, n. Inserent´, -en, -en m., Anzeiger, -m.

advertising, n. Rekla´me, -n f.

advice, n. Rat m.

advisability, n. Ratsamkeit f.

advisable, adj. ratsam.

advise, vb. raten*, bera´ten*.

advisedly, adv. absichtlich.

adviser, n. Bera´ter, - m. Bera´terin, -nen f.

advocacy, n. Befür´wortung f.

advocate, 1. n. Anwalt, ≈e m., Anwältin, -nen f. **2.** vb. vertei´digen, befür´worten.

aerate, vb. mit Luft vermen´gen.

aerial, 1. n. Anten´ne, -n f. **2.** adj. Luft- (cpds.).

aeronautics, n. Aeronau´tik f.

aesthetic, adj. ästhe´tisch.

aesthetics, n. Ästhe´tik f.

afar, adv. von ferne.

affability, n. Freundlichkeit f.

affable, adj. freundlich.

affair, n. Angelegenheit, -en f.; Affä´re, -n f.

affect, 1. n. Affekt´, -e m. **2.** vb. wirken auf.

affectation, n. Affektiert´heit, -en f.

affected, adj. betrof´fen; (unnatural) affektiert´; affig.

affection, n. Zuneigung, -en f., Liebe, -n f.

affectionately, adv. (letter) mit herzlichen Grüßen.

affidavit, n. eidesstattliche Erklä´rung, -en f.

affiliate, vb. an•gliedern.

affiliation, n. Angliederung, -en f.

affinity, n. Verwandt´schaft, -en f.

affirm, vb. (declare) erklä´ren; (confirm) bestä´tigen; (say yes to) beja´hen.

affirmation, n. Bestä´tigung, -en f.; Beja´hung, -en f.

affirmative, adj. beja´hend.

affix, 1. n. (gram.) Affix, -e nt. **2.** vb. an•heften; (add on) bei•fügen.

afflict, vb. plagen.

affliction, n. Plage, -n f., Leid nt.

affluence, n. Reichtum, ≈er m.

affluent, adj. reich.

afford, vb. gewäh´ren; (have the means to) sich leisten.

affront, 1. n. Belei´digung, -en f. **2.** vb. belei´digen.

afield, adv. (far a.) weit entfernt´.

afire, adv. in Flammen.

afraid, adj. bange; (be a. of) sich fürchten vor.

Africa, n. Afrika, nt.

African, 1. n. Afrika´ner, - m., Afrika´nerin, -nen f. **2.** adj. afrika´nisch.

aft, adv. achtern.

after, 1. prep. nach, hinter. **2.** conj. nachdem´.

aftermath, n. Nachernte, -n f.

afternoon, n. Nachmittag, -e m.

afterward(s), adv. hinterher´, nachher, anschließend.

again, adv. wieder, noch einmal.

against, prep. gegen.

age, 1. n. Alter, - nt.; (era) Zeitalter, - nt. **2.** vb. altern.

aged, adj. bejahrt´.

ageless, adj. zeitlos.

age limit, n. Altersgrenze f.

agency, n. Vertre´tung, -en f., Agentur´, -en f.

agenda, n. Tagesordnung, -en f.

agent, n. Vertre´ter, -m., Vertre´terin, -nen f.

aggrandizement, n. Machterweiterung, -en f.

aggravate, vb. verschlim´-mern, erschwe´ren.

aggravation, n. Verschlim´merung, -en f.

aggregate, 1. n. Aggregat´, -e nt. **2.** adj. Gesamt- (cpds.).

aggregation, n. Anhäufung, -en f.

aggression, n. Angriff, -e m., Aggression´, -en f.

aggressive, adj. aggresiv´.

aggressiveness, n. Angriffslust f.

aggressor, n. Angreifer, - m.

aghast, adj. entsetzt´.

agile, adj. flink, behen´d(e).

agility, n. Behen´digkeit f.

agitate, vb. bewe´gen, beun´ruhigen.

agitation, n. Bewe´gung, -en f., Beun´ruhigung, -en f.

agitator, n. Hetzredner, -m.

agnostic, 1. n. Agno´stiker, - m. **2.** adj. agno´stisch.

ago, adv. vor.

agony, n. Qual, -en f.

agree, vb. überein•stimmen.

agreeable, adj. angenehm.

agreement, n. Überein´stimmung, -en f.

agricultural, adj. landwirtschaftlich.

agriculture, n. Landwirtschaft f.

ahead, adv. voraus´; (straight a.) gera´de aus.

aid, 1. n. Hilfe, -n f.; Hilfsmittel, nt. **2.** vb. helfen*.

aide, n. Adjutant´, -en, -en m.

AIDS, n. Aids (no article).

ail, vb. kranken.

ailment, n. Krankheit, -en f.

aim, 1. n. (goal) Ziel, -e nt.; (purpose) Zweck, -e m. **2.** vb. zielen.

aimless, adj. ziellos.

air, 1. n. Luft, ≈e f. **2.** vb. lüften.

airbag, n. (automobile) Luftsack, ≈e, m.

air base, n. Luftstützpunkt, -e m.

airborne, adj. in der Luft; (a. troops) Luftlandetruppen pl.

air-condition, vb. klimatisie´ren, mit Klima-Anlage verse´hen*.

air-conditioned, adj. klimatisiert´, mit Klima-Anlage verse´hen.

air-conditioning, n. Klima-Anlage, -n f.

aircraft, *n.* Flugzeug, -e *nt.*

aircraft carrier, *n.* Flugzeugträger, -, *m.,* Flugzeugmut´terschiff, -e *nt.*

air line, *n.* Luftlinie, -n *f.*

air liner, *n.* Verkehrs´flugzeug, -e *nt.*

airmail, *n.* Luftpost *f.*

airplane, *n.* Flugzeug, -e *nt.*

air pollution, *n.* Luftverpestung *f.,* Luftverschmutzung *f.*

airport, *n.* Flughafen, ÷ *m.*

air pressure, *n.* Luftdruck, -e *m.*

air raid, *n.* Luftangriff, -e *m.*

airsick, *adj.* luftkrank (÷).

airtight, *adj.* luftdicht.

airy, *adj.* luftig.

aisle, *n.* Gang, ÷e *m.; (church)* Chorgang, ÷e *m.*

ajar, *adj.* angelehnt, halb offen.

akin, *adj.* verwandt´.

alarm, 1. *n.* Alarm´, -e *m.* **2.** *vb.* alarmie´ren, beun´ruhigen.

albino, *n.* Albi´no, -s *m.*

album, *n.* Album, -ben *nt.*

albumen, *n.* Eiweißstoff, -e *m.,* Albu´men *nt.*

alcohol, *n.* Alkohol, -e *m.*

alcoholic, 1. *n.* Alkoho´liker, - *m.* **2.** *adj.* alkoho´lisch.

alcove, *n.* Alko´ven, - *m.*

ale, *n.* englisches Bier, Ale *nt.*

alert, 1. *n.* Alarm´, -e *m.,* Vorwarnung, -en *f.* **2.** *adj.* aufmerksam. **3.** *vb.* alarmie´ren.

alfalfa, *n.* Alfal´fa *nt.*

algebra, *n.* Algebra *f.*

algebraic, *adj.* algebra´isch.

alias, *adv.* alias.

alibi, *n.* Alibi, -s *nt.*

alien, 1. *n.* Ausländer, - *m.,* Ausländerin, -nen *f.* **2.** *adj.* fremd, ausländisch.

alienate, *vb.* entfrem´den.

alight, *vb.* sich nieder•-lassen*; *(dismount)* ab•steigen*.

align, *vb.* aus•richten; *(ally)* zusam´men•tun*.

alike, *adj.* gleich.

alive, *adj.* leben´dig; **(be a.)** leben.

alkali, *n.* Alka´li *nt.*

alkaline, *adj.* alka´lisch.

all, *adj.* aller, -es, -e; **(above a.)** vor allem; **(a. at once)** auf einmal; **(a. the same)** gleich; **(a. of you)** Sie alle; **(not at a.)** gar nicht.

allay, *vb.* beru´higen, stillen.

allegation, *n.* Behaup´tung, -en *f.*

allege, *vb.* an•führen, behaup´ten.

allegiance, *n.* Treue *f.,* Gehor´sam *m.*

allegory, *n.* Allegorie´, -i´en *f.;* Sinnbild, -er *nt.*

allergy, *n.* Allergie´, -i´en *f.*

alleviate, *vb.* erleich´tern, lindern.

alley, *n.* Gasse, -n *f.;* Durchgang, ÷e *m.;* **(blind a.)** Sackgasse, -n *f.*

alliance, *n.* Bündnis, -se *nt.;* Allianz´, -en *f.*

allied, *adj.* verbün´det; *(related)* verwandt´.

alligator, *n.* Alliga´tor, -to´ren *m.*

allocate, *vb.* zu•teilen.

allot, *vb.* zu•weisen*; zu•teilen.

allotment, *n.* Zuweisung, -en *f.*

allow, *vb.* erlau´ben, gestat´ten.

allowance, *n. (money)* Taschengeld, -er *nt.; (permission)* Erlaub´nis, -se *f.;* **(make a.s for)** Rücksicht nehmen•auf*.

alloy, 1. *n.* Legie´rung, -en *f.* **2.** *vb.* legie´ren.

all right, *interj.* gut, schön, in Ordnung.

allude, *vb.* hin•weisen*, an•spielen.

allure, 1. *n.* Charme *m.* **2.** *vb.* verlock´en.

allusion, *n.* Anspielung, -en *f.*

ally, 1. *n.* Verbün´deter- *m.& f.,* Alliiert´- *m. & f.* **2.** *vb.* verbün´den.

almanac, *n.* Almanach, -e *m.*

almighty, *adj.* allmäch´tig.

almond, *n.* Mandel, -n *f.*

almost, *adv.* beinahe, fast.

alms, *n.* Almosen, - *nt.*

aloft, *adv.* hochoben; empor´.

alone, *adv.* allein´; **(leave a.)** in Ruhe lassen*.

along, 1. *adj.* entlang´; **(come a.)** mit•kommen*. **2.** *prep.* entlang´, längs.

alongside, *prep.* neben.

aloof, 1. *adj.* gleichgültig. **2.** *adv.* abseits.

aloud, *adv.* laut.

alpaca, *n.* Alpa´ka, -s *nt.*

alphabet, *n.* Alphabet´, -e *nt.*

alphabetical, *adj.* alphabe´-tisch.

alphabetize, *vb.* alphabetisie´ren.

Alps, *n.,pl.* Alpen *pl.*

already, *adv.* schon.

also, *adv.* auch.

altar, *n.* Altar´, ÷e *m.*

alter, *vb.* ändern.

alteration, *n.* Änderung, -en *f.*

alternate, 1. *n.* Stellvertreter, - *m.,* Stellvertreterin, -nen *f.* **2.** *adj.* alternativ´. **3.** *vb.* ab•wechseln.

alternating current, *n.* Wechselstrom, ÷e *m.*

alternative, 1. *n.* Alternati´ve, -n *f.* **2.** *adj.* alternativ´.

although, *conj.* obwohl´, obgleich´.

altitude, *n.* Höhe, -n *f.*

alto, *n.* Altstimme, -n *f.*

altogether, *adv.* völlig, ganz und gar; alles in allem.

altruism, *n.* Altruis´mus *m.*

alum, *n.* Alaun´, -e *m.*

aluminum, *n.* Alumi´nium *nt.*

always, *adv.* immer.

amalgamate, *vb.* amalgamie´ren.

amass, *vb.* an•sammeln.

amateur, *n.* Amateur´, -e *m.*

amaze, *vb.* erstau´nen.

amazement, *n.* Erstau´nen *nt.*

amazing, *adj.* erstaun´lich.

ambassador, *n.* Botschafter, - *m.,* Botschafterin, -nen *f.,* Gesandt´ - *m.& f.*

amber, *n.* Bernstein, -e *m.*

ambiguity, *n.* Zwei-
deutigkeit, -en *f.*

ambiguous, *adj.* zweideutig.

ambition, *n.* Ehrgeiz *m.*,
Ambition´, -en *f.*

ambitious, *adj.* ehrgeizig.

ambulance, *n.* Krankenwagen, - *m.*, Krankenauto, -
s *nt.*, Rettungswagen, - *m.*

ambush, 1. *n.* Hinterhalt *m.*
2. *vb.* aus dem Hinterhalt
überfallen*.

ameliorate, *vb.* verbes´sern.

amenable, *adj.* zugänglich.

amend, *vb.* verbes´sern,
ergän´zen.

amendment, *n.* Gesetz´abän-
derung, -en *f.*, Verfas´-
sungszusatz, ≃e *m.*

amenity, *n.* Annehm-
lichkeit, -en *f.*

America, *n.* Ame´rika *nt.*

American, 1. *n.* Amerika´-
ner, - *m.*, Amerika´nerin,
-nen *f.* **2.** *adj.* amerika´-
nisch.

amethyst, *n.* Amethyst´, -e
m.

amiable, *adj.*
liebenswürdig.

amicable, *adj.* freundschaftlich.

amid, *prep.* inmit´ten.

amidships, *adv.* mittschiffs.

amiss, *adj.* los, schief;
(take a.) übel•nehmen*.

amity, *n.* Freundschaft, -en
f.

ammonia, *n.* Ammoniak
nt.; **(household a.)**
Salmiak´geist *m.*

ammunition, *n.* Munition´,
-en *f.*

amnesia, *n.* Amnesie´ *f.*

amnesty, *n.* Amnestie´, -
i´en *f.*

amniocentesis, *n.* Amnio-
kente´se *f.*

amoeba, *n.* Amö´be, -n *f.*

among, *prep.* unter, zwischen, bei.

amorous, *adj.* verliebt´.

amortize, *vb.* tilgen, amor-
tisie´ren.

amount, 1. *n.* (sum)
Betrag´, ≃e *m.*; **(large a.)**
Menge, -n *f.* **2.** *vb.* **(a. to)**
betra´gen*.

ampere, *n.* Ampere, - (pron.
Ampär´) *nt.*

amphibian, 1. *n.* Amphi´bie,
-n *f.* **2.** *adj.* amphi´bisch.

amphibious, *adj.* amphi´-
bisch.

amphitheater, *n.*
Amphi´theater, - *nt.*

ample, *adj.* reichlich.

amplify, *vb.* (enlarge)
erwei´tern; (make louder)
verstär´ken; (state more
fully) ausführ´licher dar-
stellen.

amputate, *vb.* amputie´ren.

amuse, *vb.* belus´tigen,
amüsie´ren.

amusement, *n.* Unterhal´-
tung, -en *f.*; Belus´ti-
gung, -en *f.*

amusement park, *n.* Rummelplatz, *m.*

an, *art.* ein, -, -e.

anachronism, *n.* Anachro-
nis´mus, -men *m.*

analogical, *adj.* analo´gisch.

analogous, *adj.* analog´.

analogy, *n.* Analogie´, -i´en *f.*

analysis, *n.* Analy´se, -n *f.*

analyst, *n.* Analy´tiker, - *m.*

analytic, *adj.* analy´tisch.

analyze, *vb.* analysie´ren.

anarchy, *n.* Anarchie´, -i´en
f.

anatomy, *n.* Anatomie´, -
i´en *f.*

ancestor, *n.* Vorfahr, -en, -
en, *m.*, Vorfahrin, -nen *f.*

ancestral, *adj.* Stamm-
(cpds.).

ancestry, *n.* Abstammung, -
en *f.*

anchor, 1. *n.* Anker, - *m.* **2.**
vb. veran´kern.

anchovy, *n.* Sardel´le, -n *f.*

ancient, *adj.* alt, uralt.

and, *conj.* und.

anecdote, *n.* Anekdo´te, -n *f.*

anemia, *n.* Blutarmut *f.*

anemic, *adj.* blutarm.

anesthesia, *n.* Anästhesie´ *f.*

anesthetic, 1. *n.* Narko´se, -
n *f.*, Betäu´bungsmittel, -
nt. **2.** *adj.* betäu´bend,
narko´tisch.

anew, *adv.* aufs neue, von
neuem.

angel, *n.* Engel, - *m.*

anger, *n.* Zorn *m.*, Ärger *m.*

angle, 1. *n.* (geom.) Winkel,
- *m.*; (point of view)
Gesichtspunkt, -e *m.* **2.**
vb. (fish) angeln.

angry, *adj.* böse, ärgerlich;
(be a.) sich ärgern.

anguish, *n.* Qual, -en *f.*

angular, *adj.* eckig.

animal, 1. *n.* Tier, -e *nt.* **2.**
adj. tierisch.

animate, *vb.* bele´ben.

animated, *adj.* lebhaft.

animated cartoon, *n.* Zeichentrickfilm, -e *m.*

animation, *n.* Lebhaftigkeit,
-en *f.*

animosity, *n.* Erbit´terung, -
en *f.*

ankle, *n.* Fessel, -n *f.*; Fesselgelenk, -e *nt.*

annals, *n.pl.* Anna´len *pl.*

annex, 1. *n.* Anhang, ≃e *m.*;
(building) Nebenge-
bäude, - *nt.* **2.** *vb.* annek-
tie´ren.

annexation, *n.* Annektie´-
rung, -en *f.*

annihilate, *vb.* vernich´ten.

anniversary, *n.* Jahrestag, -
e *m.*

annotate, *vb.* mit An-
merkungen verse´hen*,
annotie´ren.

announce, *vb.* an•kündigen,
bekannt´•geben*.

announcement, *n.*
Bekannt´machung, -en *f.*

announcer, *n.* Ansager, - *m.*
Ansagerin, -nen *f.*

annoy, *vb.* beläs´tigen, ärgern.

annoyance, *n.* Ärger *m.*;
Beläs´tigung, -en *f.*

annual, 1. *n.* Jahrbuch, -≃er
nt. **2.** *adj.* jährlich.

annuity, *n.* jährliche Rente,
-n *f.*

annul, *vb.* annullie´ren.

anoint, *vb.* salben.

anomaly, *n.* Anomalie´, -
i´en *f.*

anonymous, *adj.* anonym´.

another, *adj.* (different) ein
ander-; (additional) noch
ein; **(one a.)** sich,
einan´der.

answer, 1. *n.* Antwort, -en *f.*
2. *vb.* antworten,
beant´worten.

answerable, *adj.* beant´wort-
bar; verant´wortlich.

answering machine, *n.* Anrufbeantworter *m.*

ant, *n.* Ameise, -n *f.*

antagonism, Widerstreit, -e
m.

antagonist, *n.* Widersacher,
- *m.*, Gegner, - *m.*

antagonistic, *adj.*
widerstrei´tend.

antagonize, *vb.* vor den
Kopf stoßen*.

antarctic, 1. *n.* Antark´tis, *f.*
2. *adj.* antark´tisch.

antecedent, 1. *n.* (*gram.*)
Bezie´hungswort, ⸚er *nt.*
2. *adj.* vorher´gehend.

antelope, *n.* Antilo´pe, -n *f.*

antenna, *n.* (*radio*)
Anten´ne, -n *f.*; (*insect*)
Fühler, - *m.*

anterior, *adj.* vorder-.

anteroom, *n.* Vorzimmer, -
nt.

anthem, Hymne, -n *f.*; (**national a.**)
National´hymne, -n *f.*

anthology, *n.* Anthologie´, -
i´en *f.*

anthracite, *n.* Anthrazit´ *nt.*

anthropologist, *n.* Anthro-
polo´ge, -n, -n *m.*

anthropology, *n.* Anthro-
pologie´, -i´en *f.*

antiaircraft, *adj.* Flak
(*cpds.*).

antibody, *n.* Antikörper, - *m.*

antic, *n.* Posse, -n *f.*;
Mätzchen, - *nt.*

anticipate, *vb.*
vorweg•´nehmen*;
erwar´ten.

anticipation, *n.* Erwar´tung,
-en *f.*

anticlimax, *n.* enttäu´-
schende Wendung, -en *f.*

antidote, *n.* Gegengift, -e *nt.*

antinuclear, *adj.* antinuk-
lear´.

antiquated, *adj.* veral´tet.

antique, *adj.* antik´.

antiques, *n.* Antiquitäten *pl.*

antiquity, *n.* Anti´ke *f.*; Altertum, ⸚er *nt.*

anti-Semitism, *n.* Antisemi-
tis´mus *m.*

antiseptic, 1. *n.* antisep´tis-
ches Mittel *nt.* **2.** *adj.* an-
tisep´tisch.

antisocial, *adj.* antisozial´.

antitoxin, *n.* Gegengift, -e *nt.*

antlers, *n.pl.* Geweih´, -e
nt.

anvil, *n.* Amboß, -sse *m.*

anxiety, *n.* Angst, ⸚e *f.*; Be-
sorg´nis, -se *f.*

anxious, *adj.* besorgt´;
ängstlich.

any, *adj.* irgendein, -, -e; irgendwelcher, -es, -e;
jeder, -es, -e; (**not a.**)
kein, -, -e.

anybody, *pron.* jemand, irgendjemand; (**not . . . a.**)
niemand.

anyhow, *adv.* sowieso´.

anyone, *pron.* jemand, irgendjemand; (**not . . .
a.**)niemand.

anything, *pron.* etwas, irgendetwas; (**not . . . a.**)
nichts.

anyway, *adv.* sowieso´.

anywhere, *adv* (*location*)
irgendwo; (*direction*) ir-
gendwohin;

apart, *adv.* abseits,
beisei´te; (**a. from**) abgesehen von; (**take a.**) au-
seinan´der•nehmen*.

apartheid, *n.* Apart´heid *f.*

apartment, *n.* Mietswohnung, -en *f.*

ape, 1. *n.* Affe, -n, -n *m.* **2.**
vb. nach•affen.

aperture, *n.* Öffnung, -en *f.*

apex, *n.* Gipfel, - *m.*

aphorism, *n.* Aphoris´mus,
-men *m.*

apiece, *adv.* (**ten dollars a.**)
je zehn Dollar.

apologetic, *adj.* entschul´di-
gend.

apologize, *vb.* sich
entschul´digen.

apology, *n.* Entschul´di-
gung, -en *f.*

apoplexy, *n.* Schlaganfall,
⸚e *m.*

apostle, *n.* Apos´tel, - *m.*

apostrophe, *n.* Apostroph *m.*

appall, *vb.* entset´zen.

apparatus, *n.* Apparat´, -e
m.; Ausrüstung, -en *f.*

apparel, *n.* Kleidung, -en *f.*

apparent, *adj.* (*visible*)
sichtbar; (*clear*) klar;
(*obvious*) offensichtlich;
(*probable*) scheinbar.

apparition, *n.* Erschei´nung,
-en *f.*; Gespenst´, -er, *nt.*

appeal, 1. *n.* (*request*) Bitte,
-n *f.*; (*charm*) Reiz, -e
m.; (*law*) Beru´fung, -en
f. **2.** *vb.* (*law*) Beru´fung
ein•legen, appellie´ren;
(**a. to, turn to**) sich wenden* an; (**a. to, please**)
gefal´len*.

appear, *vb.* (*seem*)
scheinen*; (*come into
view*) erschei´nen*.

appearance, *n.*
Erschei´nung, -en *f.*, Anschein, -e *m.*

appease, *vb.*
beschwich´tigen.

appeasement, *n.*
Beschwich´tigung, -en *f.*

appendage, *n.* Anhang, ⸚e *m.*

appendectomy, *n.* Blinddar-
moperation -en *f.*

appendicitis, *n.* Blinddarmentzündung, -en *f.*

appendix, *n.* Anhang, ⸚e *m.*;
(*med.*) Blinddarm, ⸚e *m.*

appetite, *n.* Appetit´ *m.*

appetizer, *n.* Vorgericht, -e
nt.

appetizing, *adj.*
appetit´lich; lecker.

applaud, *vb.* applaudie´ren,
Beifall klatschen.

applause, *n.* Beifall, ⸚e *m.*

apple, *n.* Apfel, ⸚ *m.*

applesauce, *n.* Apfelmus *nt.*

appliance, *n.* Gerät´, -e *nt.*

applicable, *adj.* anwendbar.

applicant, *n.* Bewer´ber, -
m., Bewer´berin, -nen *f.*

application, *n.* (*request*)
Bewer´bung, -en *f.*; (*use*)
Anwendung, -en *f.*

appliqué, *adj.* (**a. work**)
Applikations´stickerei, -
en *f.*

apply, *vb.* (*make use of*)
an•wenden*; (*request*)
sich bewer´ben*.

appoint, *vb.* ernen´nen*.

appointment, *n. (to a position)* Ernen´nung, -en *f.; (doctor's)* Anmeldung, -en *f.; (date)* Verab´redung, -en *f.*

apportion, *vb.* proportional´verteilen; zu•teilen.

appraisal, *n.* Abschätzung, -en *f.*

appraise, *vb.* ab•schätzen.

appreciable, *adj.* beträcht-lich.

appreciate, *vb.* schätzen; an•erkennen*.

appreciation, *n.* Anerkennung, -en *f.*

apprehend, *vb. (grasp)* erfas´sen; *(arrest)* verhaf´ten; *(fear)* befürch´ten.

apprehension, *n. (worry)* Besorg´nis, -se *f.; (arrest)* Verhaf´tung, -en *f.*

apprehensive, *adj.* besorgt´.

apprentice, *n.* Lehrling, -e *m.*

apprise, *vb.* benach´richtigen.

approach, **1.** *n. (nearing)* Annäherung, -en *f.; (access)* Zugang, ⁼e *m.; (military)* Anmarsch *m.* **2.** *vb. (come nearer)* sich nähern; *(turn to)* sich wenden* an.

approachable, *adj.* zugänglich.

approbation, *n.* Geneh´migung, -en *f.*

appropriate, **1.** *adj.* angemessen, passend. **2.** *vb. (seize)* sich an•eignen; *(vote funds)* bewilligen.

appropriation, *n. (seizure)* Aneignung, -en *f.; (approval)* Bewil´ligung, -en *f.*

approval, *n.* Zustimmung, -en *f.,* Einwilligung, -en *f.*

approve, *vb.* zu•stimmen, geneh´migen.

approximate, **1.** *vb.* sich nähern. **2.** *adj.* annähernd.

approximately, *adv.* ungefähr, etwa.

approximation, *n.* Annäherung, -en *f.*

apricot, *n.* Apriko´se, -n *f.*

April, *n.* April´ *m.*

apron, *n.* Schürze, -n *f.*

apropos, **1.** *adj.* treffend. **2.** *prep.* hinsichtlich.

apt, *adj. (fitting)* passend; *(likely)* geneigt´; *(able)* fähig.

aptitude, *n.* Fähigkeit, -en *f.*

aquarium, *n.* Aqua´rium, -ien *nt.*

aquatic, *adj.* Wasser-(*cpds.*).

aqueduct, *n.* Wasserleitung, -en *f.*

Arab, **1.** *n.* Araber, - *m.;* Araberin, -nen *f.* **2.** *adj.* ara´bisch.

Arabian, *adj.* ara´bisch.

Arabic, *adj.* ara´bisch.

arable, *adj.* bestell´bar.

arbiter, *n.* Schlichter, - *m.*

arbitrary, *adj.* willkürlich.

arbitrate, *vb.* schlichten.

arbitration, *n.* Schlichtung, -en *f.*

arbitrator, *n.* Schlichter, - *m.*

arbor, *n.* Laube, -n *f.*

arc, *n.* Bogen, -(⁼) *m.*

arcade, *n.* Arka´de, -n *f.*

arch, *n.* Bogen, -(⁼) *m.; (instep)* Spann, -e *m.*

archaeology, *n.* Altertumskunde *f.,* Archäologie´ *f.*

archaic, *adj.* archa´isch, altertümlich.

archbishop, *n.* Erzbischof, ⁼e *m.*

archdiocese, *n.* Erzdiözese, -n *f.*

archduke, *n.* Erzherzog, ⁼e *m.*

archer, *n.* Bogenschütze, -n, -n *m.*

archery, *n.* Bogenschießen *nt.*

architect, *n.* Architekt´, -en, -en *m.,* Architek´tin, -nen *f.*

architectural, *adj.* architekto´nisch.

architecture, *n.* Architektur´, -en *f.*

archives, *n.* Archiv´, e *nt.*

archway, *n.* Torbogen, ⁼m.

arctic, **1.** *n.* Arktis *f.* **2.** *adj.* arktisch.

ardent, *adj.* eifrig, inbrünstig.

ardor, *n.* Eifer *m.,* Inbrunst *f.*

arduous, *adj.* mühsam.

area, *n.* Fläche, -n *f.,* Gebiet´, -e *nt.*

area code, *n. (phone)* Vorwahlnummer, -n *f.*

arena, *n.* Are´na, -nen *f.*

Argentina, *n.* Argenti´nien *nt.*

argue, *vb.* argumentie´ren; *(quarrel)* sich streiten*.

argument, *n.* Argument´, -e *nt.*

argumentative, *adj.* streitsüchtig.

aria, *n.* Arie, -n *f.*

arid, *adj.* dürr, trocken.

arise, *vb.* auf•stehen*, sich erhe´ben*; *(come into being)* entste´hen*.

aristocracy, *n.* Aristokratie´, -i´en *f.*

aristocrat, *n.* Aristokrat´, -en, -en *m.,* Aristokra´tin, -nen *f.*

aristocratic, *adj.* aristokra´tisch.

arithmetic, *n.* Rechnen *nt.,* Arithmetik´ *f.*

ark, *n.* Arche, -n *f.; (Noah's a.)* Arche Noah.

arm, **1.** *n.* Arm, -e *m.; (weapon)* Waffe, -n *f.* **2.** *v.* bewaff´nen, rüsten.

armament, *n.* Bewaff´nung, -en *f.; (weapons)* Waffen *pl.*

armchair, *n.* Lehnstuhl, ⁼e *m.*

armful, *n.* Menge, -n *f.*

armhole, *n.* Armloch, ⁼er *nt.*

armistice, *n.* Waffenstill´stand *m.*

armor, Rüstung, -en *f.,* Panzer, - *m.*

armored, *adj.* gepan´zert; Panzer- (*cpds.*)

armory, *n.* Exerzier´halle, -n *f.;* Waffenfabrik, -en *f.*

armpit, *n.* Achselhöhle, -n *f.*

arms, *n.pl.* Waffen *pl.*

army, *n.* Heer, -e *nt.,* Armee´, -me´en *f.*

aroma, *n.* Aro´ma, -s *nt.*

aromatic, *adj.* würzig.

around, 1. *adv.* herum´; *(approximately)* etwa, ungefähr. **2.** *prep.* um.

arouse, *vb. (excite)* erre´gen; *(waken)* wecken.

arraign, *vb.* richterlich vor•führen.

arrange, *vb.* arrangie´ren, ab•sprechen´, ein•richten; *(agree)* verein´baren.

arrangement, *n.* Anordnung, -en *f.*

array, 1. *n.* Anordnung, -en *f.; (fig.)* Menge, -n *f.* **2.** *vb.* ordnen.

arrears, *n.pl.* Schulden *pl.; (in a.)* in Rückstand.

arrest, 1. *n. (law)* Verhaf´tung, -en *f.* **2.** *vb. (law)* verhaf´ten; *(stop)* an•halten.

arrival, *n.* Ankunft, ⸗e *f.*

arrive, *vb.* an•kommen*.

arrogance, *n.* Anmaßung, -en *f.,* Arroganz, -en *f.*

arrogant, *adj.* anmaßend, arrogant´.

arrow, *n.* Pfeil, -e *m.*

arsenal, *n.* Waffenlager, - *nt.*

arsenic, *n.* Arsen´ *nt.*

arson, *n.* Brandstiftung, -en *f.*

art, *n.* Kunst, ⸗e *f.*

arterial, *adj.* Arte´rien- *(cpds.); (a. highway)* Hauptverkehrs´straße, -n *f.*

arteriosclerosis, *n.* Arte´rienverkalkung, -en *f.*

artful, *adj.* kunstvoll; *(sly)* schlau.

arthritis, *n.* Arthri´tis *f.*

artichoke, *n.* Artischock´e, -n *f.*

article, *n.* Arti´kel, - *m.*

articulate, 1. *vb. (utter)* artikulie´ren; *(join)* zusam´men•fügen. **2.** *adj.* deutlich.

articulation, *n.* Artikulie´rung, -en *f.*

artifice, *n.* List, -en *f.*

artificial, *adj.* künstlich.

artificiality, *n.* Künstlichkeit, -en *f.*

artillery, *n.* Artillerie´, -i´en *f.*

artisan, *n.* Handwerker, - *m.,* Handwerkerin, -nen *f.*

artist, *n.* Künstler, - *m.,* Künstlerin, -nen *f.*

artistic, *adj.* künstlerisch.

artistry, *n.* Künstlertum *nt.*

artless, *adj.* kunstlos.

as, *conj.& adv. (when)* wie, als; *(because)* da; **(a. if)** als ob; **(with X a. Hamlet)** mit X als Hamlet; **(a. big a.)** so groß wie; **(just a. big a.)** ebenso groß wie; **(he a. well a. I)** er sowohl wie ich.

asbestos, *n.* Asbest´, -e *m.*

ascend, *vb. (intr.)* steigen*; *(tr.)* bestei´gen*.

ascent, *n.* Aufstieg, -e *m.*

ascertain, *vb.* fest•stellen.

ascetic, 1. *n.* Asket´, -en, -en *m.* **2.** *adj.* aske´tisch.

ascribe, *vb.* zu•schreiben*.

ash, *n.* Asche, -n *f.; (tree)* Esche, -n *f.*

ashamed, *adj.* beschämt´; **(be a.)** sich schämen.

ashen, *adj.* aschgrau.

ashes, *n.pl.* Asche *f.*

ashore, *adv.* an Land.

ashtray, *n.* Aschenbecher, - *m.,* Aschbecher, - *m.*

Asia, *n.* Asien *nt.*

Asian, 1. *n.* Asiat´, -en, -en *m.,* Asia´tin, -nen *f.* **2.** *adj.* asia´tisch.

aside, *adv.* beisei´te; **(a. from)** außer.

ask, *vb. (question)* fragen; *(request)* bitten*; *(demand)* verlangen.

asleep, *adj.* schlafend; **(be a.)** schlafen*.

asparagus, *n.* Spargel, - *m.*

aspect, *n.* Anblick, -e *m.; (fig.)* Gesichts´punkt, -e *m.*

aspersion, *n.* Verleum´dung, -en *f.*

asphalt, *n.* Asphalt´, -e *m.*

asphyxiate, *vb.* erstick´en.

aspirant, Anwärter, - *m.*

aspirate, 1. *n.* Hauchlaut, -e *m.,* **2.** *adj.* aspiriert´. **3.** *vb.* aspirie´ren.

aspiration, *n.* Aspiration´, -en *f.,* Bestre´bung, -en *f.*

aspire, *vb.* streben.

aspirin, *n.* Aspirin´ *nt.*

ass, *n.* Esel, - *m.*

assail, *vb.* an•greifen*.

assailable, *adj.* angreifbar.

assailant, *n.* Angreifer, - *m.,* Angreiferin, -nen *f.*

assassin, *n.* Attentä´ter, - *m.,* Attentä´terin, -nen *f.* Mörder, - *m.,* Mörderin, - nen *f.*

assassinate, *vb.* ermor´den.

assassination, *n.* Ermor´dung, -en *f.,* Attentat´, -e *nt.*

assault, 1. *n.* Angriff, -e *m.; (law)* tätliche Belei´digung, -en *f.* **2.** *vb.* an•greifen*.

assay, 1. *n.* Probe, -n *f.* **2.** *vb.* prüfen.

assemblage, *n.* Versamm´lung, -en *f.*

assemble, *vb.* versam´meln; *(tech.)* montie´ren.

assembly, *n.* Versamm´lung, -en *f.; (tech.)* Monta´ge, -n *f.*

assent, 1. *n.* Zustimmung, - en *f.* **2.** *vb.* zu•stimmen.

assert, *vb.* behaup´ten.

assertion, *n.* Behaup´tung, - en *f.*

assertive, *adj.* bestimmt´.

assess, *vb.* ein•schätzen.

assessor, *n.* Steuerabschätzer, - *m.*

asset, *n.* Vorzug, ⸗e *m.; (comm.)* Guthaben, - *nt.*

asseverate, *vb.* beteu´ern.

assiduous, *adj.* emsig.

assign, *vb.* zu•teilen, zu•weisen*; *(homework)* auf•geben*.

assignable, bestimm´bar.

assignation, *n.* Anweisung, -en *f.; (tryst)* Stelldichein, - *nt.*

assignment, *n.* Anweisung, -en *f.; (homework)* Aufgabe, -n *f.*

assimilate, *vb.* an•gleichen*, assimilie´ren.

assimilation, *n.* Angleichung, -en *f.,* Assimilie´rung, -en *f.*

assimilative, *adj.* angleichend.

assist, *vb.* unterstüt′zen, helfen*.

assistance, *n.* Unterstüt′-zung, -en *f.*, Hilfe, -n *f.*

assistant, 1. *n.* Gehil′fe, -n, -n *m.*, Gehil′fin, -nen *f.* Assistent′, -en, -en *m.*, Assisten′tin, -nen *f.* **2.** *adj.* Hilfs- (*cpds.*) stellvertretend.

associate, 1. *n.* Partner, - *m.*, Partnerin, -nen *f.* **2.** *vb.* verkeh′ren, assoziie′ren.

association, *n.* Verbin′dung, -en *f.*, Verei′nigung, -en *f.*

assonance, *n.* Assonanz′, -en *f.*

assort, *vb.* sortie′ren.

assorted, *adj.* verschie′den.

assortment, *n.* Auswahl, -en *f.*

assuage, *vb.* beschwich′tigen.

assume, *vb.* an•nehmen*; (*arrogate*) sich an•maßen.

assuming, *adj.* anmaßend; **(a. that)** angenommen, daß.

assumption, *n.* Annahme, -n *f.*; (*eccles.*) Himmelfahrt *f.*

assurance, *n.* Versi′cherung, -en *f.*, Zusicherung, -en *f.*

assure, *vb.* versi′chern, zu•sichern.

assured, *adj.* sicher, zuversichtlich.

aster, *n.* Aster, -n *f.*

asterisk, *n.* Sternchen, - *nt.*

asthma, *n.* Asthma *nt.*

astigmatism, *n.* Astigmatis′mus, -men *m.*

astonish, *vb.* erstau′nen; **(be astonished)** staunen.

astonishment, *n.* Erstau′nen, - *nt.*

astound, *vb.* erstau′nen.

astray, *adj.* irre; **(go a.)** sich verir′ren, auf Abwege gera′ten*.

astringent, *adj.* gefäß′spannend, hautstraffend, adstringie′rend.

astrology, *n.* Astrologie′, -i′en *f.*

astronaut, *n.* Astronaut′, -en, -en *m.*, Astronau′tin, -nen *f.*

astronomy, *n.* Astronomie′, -i′en *f.*

astute, *adj.* scharf (÷), schlau.

asylum, *n.* (*refuge*) Asyl′, -e *nt.*; (*institution*) Anstalt, -en *f.*

at, *prep.* an; **(at home)** zu Hause.

atheist, *n.* Atheist′, -en, -en *m.*, Atheis′tin, -nen *f.*

athlete, *n.* Athlet′, -en, -en *m.*, Sportler, - *m.*, Sportlerin, -nen *f.*

athletic, *adj.* athle′tisch, sportlich.

athletics, *n.* Sport, -e *m.*

Atlantic, 1. *n.* Atlan′tik *m.* **2.** *adj.* atlan′tisch.

Atlantic Ocean, *n.* Atlan′tik *m.*

atlas, *n.* Atlas, -lan′ten *m.*

atmosphere, *n.* Atmosphä′re, -n *f.*

atmospheric, *adj.* atmosphä′risch.

atoll, *n.* Atoll′, -e *nt.*

atom, *n.* Atom′, -e *nt.*

atomic, *adj.* atomar′; Atom′- (*cpds.*).

atomize, *vb.* atomisie′ren.

atone, *vb.* büßen, sühnen.

atonement, *n.* Buße, -n *f.*, Sühne, -n *f.*

atrocious, *adj.* entsetz′lich, grausam.

atrocity, *n.* Grausamkeit, -en *f.*

atrophy, *n.* Atrophie′, -i′en *f.*

attach, *vb.* an•heften, beifügen; (*attribute*) bei•messen*.

attaché, *n.* Attaché, -s *m.*

attachment, *n.* Beifügung, -en *f.*; (*device*) Vorrichtung, -en *f.*, Zubehör *nt.*; (*liking*) Zuniegung, -en *f.*

attack, 1. *n.* Angriff, -e *m.* **2.** *vb.* an•greifen*.

attain, *vb.* errei′chen.

attainable, *adj.* erreich′bar.

attainment, *n.* Errun′genschaft, -en *f.*

attempt, 1. *n.* Versuch′, -e *m.* **2.** *vb.* versu′chen.

attend, *vb.* (*meeting*) bei•wohnen; (*lecture*) besu′chen, hören; (*pa-*

tient) behan′deln; (*person*) beglei′ten.

attendance, *n.* Anwesenheit, -en *f.*, Besuch′, -e *m.*

attendant, 1. *n.* Beglei′ter, - *m.* **2.** *adj.* beglei′tend, anwesend.

attention, *n.* Aufmerksamkeit, -en *f.*; **(a.!)** Achtung!; **(pay a.)** auf•passen.

attentive, *adj.* aufmerksam.

attenuate, *vb.* verdün′nen, vermin′dern; (*jur.*) mildern.

attest, *vb.* bezeu′gen.

attic, *n.* Dachboden, ÷ *m.*, Boden, ÷ *m.*

attire, 1. *n.* Kleidung, -en *f.* **2.** *vb.* kleiden.

attitude, *n.* Haltung, -en *f.*

attorney, *n.* Anwalt, ÷e *m.*, Anwältin, -nen *f.*

attract, *vb.* an•ziehen*.

attraction, *n.* Anziehungskraft, ÷e *f.*

attractive, *adj.* anziehend.

attribute, 1. *n.* Eigenschaft, -en *f.* **2.** *vb.* zu•schreiben*.

attribution, *n.* Beimessung, -en *f.*

auction, *n.* Verstei′gerung, -en *f.*

auctioneer, *n.* Verstei′gerer, -*m.*, Auktiona′tor, -to′ren *m.*

audacious, *adj.* kühn.

audacity, *n.* Kühnheit, -en *f.*

audible, *adj.* hörbar.

audience, *n.* Zuhörerschaft, -en *f.*, Publikum, -ka *nt.*; (*of a king*) Audienz′, -en *f.*

audiovisual, *adj.* audiovisuell′.

audit, 1. *n.* Rechnungsprüfung, -en *f.* **2.** *vb.* prüfen.

audition, *n.* Vorführungsprobe, -n *f.*

auditor, *n.* Hörer, - *m*; (*comm.*) Rechnungsprüfer, - *m.*

auditorium, *n.* Zuhörerraum, ÷e *m.*, Auditorium, -rien *nt.*

augment, *vb.* vermeh′ren.

augur, 1. *n.* Augur′, -en, -en *m.* **2.** *vb.* weissagen.

August, *n.* August′ *m.*

aunt, n. Tante, -n f.

auspices, n.pl. Auspi´zien.

auspicious, adj. günstig.

austere, adj. streng.

austerity, n.
Enthalt´samkeit, -en f.

Australia, n. Austra´lien nt.

Australian, n. Austra´lier, -
m., Austra´lierin, -nen f.

Austria, n. Österreich nt.

Austrian, 1. n. Österreicher,
- m., Österreicherin, -nen
f. **2.** adj. österreichisch.

authentic, adj. authen´tisch.

authenticate, vb.
beglau´bigen.

authenticity, n. Echtheit, -
en f.

author, n. Verfas´ser - m.,
Verfas´serin, -nen f.

authoritarian, adj. autoritär´.

authoritative, adj.
maßgebend.

authority, n. Autorität´, -en f.

authorization, n. Vollmacht, ¨e f.

authorize, vb. bevoll´-
mächtigen.

auto, n. Auto, -s nt.

autobiography, n. Autobi-
ographie´, -i´en f.

autocracy, n. Autokratie´, -
i´en f.

autocrat, n. Autokrat´, -en,
-en m.

autograph, n. Autogramm´,
-e nt.

automatic, adj. automa´tisch.

automation, n. Automation´
f.

automaton, n. Automat´, -
en, -en m.

automobile, n. Kraftwagen,
- m.

automotive, adj. Auto (cpds.).

autonomous, adj. autonom´.

autonomy, n. Autonomie´, -
i´en f.

autopsy, n. Leichenöff-
nung, -en f.

autumn, n. Herbst, -e m.

auxiliary, adj. Hilfs-
(cpds.).

avail, 1. n. Nutzen m. **2.** vb.
nützen; **(a. oneself of)**
benut´zen.

available, adj. vorhan´den.

avalanche, n. Lawi´ne, -n f.

avarice, n. Geiz, -e m.

avaricious, adj. geizig.

avenge, vb. rächen.

avenue, n. Allee´, -e´en f.

average, 1. n. Durchschnitt,
-e m. **2.** adj. durchschnittlich; Durchschnitts-
(cpds.).

averse, adj. abgeneigt.

aversion, n. Abneigung, -en
f.

aviation, n. Luftfahrt f.

aviator, n. Flieger, - m.

aviatrix, n. Fliegerin, -nen f.

avid, adj. begie´rig.

avocation, n. Nebenberuf, -
e m.

avoid, vb. vermei´den*.

avoidable, adj. vermeid´lich.

avoidance, n. Vermei´dung,
-en f.

avow, vb. geste´hen*.

avowal, n. Geständ´nis, -se
nt.

await, vb. erwar´ten.

awake, adj. wach.

awaken, vb. (tr.) wecken,
(intr.) erwach´en.

award, 1. n. Preis, -e m.;
(jur.) Urteil, -e nt. **2.** vb.
zu•erkennen*.

aware, adj. bewußt´.

away, adv. weg, fort.

awe, n. Ehrfurcht f.

awful, adj. schrecklich.

awhile, adv. eine Weile.

awkward, adj. (clumsy)
ungeschickt; (embar-
rassing) peinlich.

awning, n. Marki´se, -n f.

awry, adj. schief.

axe, n. Axt, ¨e f.

axiom, n. Axiom´, -e nt.

axis, n. Achse, -n f.

axle, n. Achse, -n f.

ayatollah, n. Ajatol´lah, -s m.

azure, adj. azur´blau.

B

babble, 1. n. Geschwätz´ nt.
2. vb. schwatzen.

baboon, n. Pavian, -e m.

baby, n. Baby, -s nt.,
Säugling, -e m.

bachelor, n. Junggeselle, -n,
-n m.

back, 1. n. Rücken, - m.,
Kreuz, -e nt.; (chair)
Lehne, -n f. **2.** vb. rück-
wärts•fahren*; (support)
unterstüt´zen. **3.** adj. hin-
ter-. **4.** adv. zurück´.

backbone, n. Rückgrat, -e
nt.

backfire, n. Fehlzündung, -
en f.

background, n. Hintergrund, ¨e m.

backing, n. Unterstüt´zung,
-en f.

backlash, n. Rückprall m.;
Bewir´kung des Gegen-
teils f.

backpack, vb. mit Rucksack wandern.

backward, 1. adj. zurück´-
geblieben, rückständig.
2. adv. rückwärts.

backwards, adv. rückwärts;
(wrongly) verkehrt´.

bacon, n. Speck m.

bacterium, n. Bakte´rium, -
rien nt.

bad, adj. (not good)
schlecht; (serious)
schlimm; (too b.) schade.

bag, n. Sack, ¨e m.; (paper)
Tüte, -n f.; (luggage)
Koffer, - m.; (woman's
purse) Tasche, -n f.

baggage, n. Gepäck´ nt.

baggage cart, n. (airport)
Kofferkuli, -s m.

baggy, adj. bauschig.

bail, n. Kaution´, -en f.,
Bürgschaft, -en f.

bail out, vb (set free) Kau-
tion´ stellen für; (empty
out water) schöpfen,
aus•schöpfen; (make a
parachute jump)
ab•springen*.

bake, vb. backen*.

baking, n. Backen nt.

baking soda, *n.* Natriumbikarbonat´ *n.*

balance, 1. *n. (equilibrium)* Gleichgewicht *nt.; (remainder)* Rest, -e *m; (trade)* Bilanz´, -en *f.* **2.** *vb.* balancie´ren; *(make come out equal)* aus•gleichen*.

balcony, *n.* Balkon´, -s *or* -e *m.*

bald, *adj.* kahl; **(b. head)** Glatzkopf, ˵e *m.;* **(b. spot)** Glatze, -n *f.*

balk, *vb. (hinder)* verhin´dern; **(b. at nothing)** vor nichts zurück´•scheuen

ball, *n. (for throwing, game, dance)* Ball, ˵e *m.; (spherical object, bullet)* Kugel, -n *f.*

ballerina, *n.* Balleri´na, -nen *f.*

ballot, *n. (paper)* Stimmzettel, - *m.; (voting)* Wahl, -en *f.*

ballpoint, *n.* Kugelschreiber *m.*

ballroom, *n.* Tanzsaal, -säle *m.*

balm, *n.* Balsam, -e *m.*

balmy, *adj.* sanft.

balsam, *n.* Balsam, -e *m.*

Baltic Sea, *n.* Ostsee *f.*

bamboo, *n.* Bambus, -se *m.*

ban, 1. *n.* Bann, -e *m.* **2.** *vb.* bannen, verbie´ten*.

banal, *adj.* banal´.

banana, *n.* Bana´ne, -n *f.*

band, 1. *n.* Band, ˵er *m.; (gang)* Bande, -n *f.; (music)* Musik´kapelle, -n *f.*

bandage, 1. *n.* Verband´, ˵e *m.* **2.** *vb.* verbin´den*.

bandanna, *n.* Kopftuch, ˵er *nt.,* Halstuch, ˵er *nt.*

bandit, *n.* Bandit´, -en, -en *m.*

baneful, *adj.* giftig, verderb´lich.

bang, 1. *n.* Knall, -e *m.* **2.** *vb.* knallen.

banish, *vb.* verban´nen.

banishment, *n.* Verban´nung, -en

banister, *n.* Treppengeländer, - *nt.*

bank, *n.* Bank, -en *f.; (river)* Ufer, - *nt.; (slope)* Böschung, -en *f.*

bank account, *n.* Bankkonto *nt.*

bankbook, *n.* Kontobuch, ˵er *nt.*

banker, *n.* Bankier´, -s *m.*

banking, *n.* Bankgeschäft, - *nt.*

bank note, *n.* Banknote, -n, *f.*

bankrupt, *adj.* bankrott´.

bankruptcy, *n.* Konkurs´, -e *m.*

banner, *n.* Banner, - *nt.*

banquet, *n.* Festessen, - *nt.*

banter, 1. *n.* Scherz, -e *m.* **2.** *vb.* scherzen.

baptism, *n.* Taufe, -n *f.*

baptismal, *adj.* Tauf- *(cpds.).*

Baptist, *n.* Baptist´, -en, -en *m.*

baptistery, *n.* Taufkapelle, -n *f.,* Taufstein, -e *m.*

baptize, *vb.* taufen.

bar, 1. *n.* Stange, -n *f.; (for drinks)* Bar, -s *f.; (jur.)* Gericht´, -e *nt.* **2.** *vb.* aus•schließen*.

barb, *n.* Widerhaken, - *m.*

barbarian, 1. *n.* Barbar´, -en, -en *m.* **2.** *adj.* barba´risch.

barbarism, *n.* Barbarei´, -en *f.*

barbarous, *adj.* barba´risch.

barber, *n.* Herrenfriseur, -e *m.*

barbiturate, *n.* Barbitur´säurepräparat, -e *nt.*

bare, 1. *adj.* bloß, nackt. **2.** *vb.* entblö´ßen.

barefoot, *adj.* barfuß.

barely, *adv.* kaum.

bargain, 1. *n.* Gele´genheitskauf, ˵e *m.* **2.** *vb.* feilschen, handeln.

barge, 1. *n.* Schleppkahn, ˵e *m.,* Leichter, - *m.* **2.** *vb.* stürmen.

baritone, *n.* Bariton, -e *m.*

barium, *n.* Barium *nt.*

bark, 1. *n. (tree)* Rinde, -n *f.; (boat)* Barke, -n *f.; (dog)* Bellen *nt.* **2.** *vb.* bellen.

barley, *n.* Gerste, -n *f.,* Graupen *pl.*

barn, *n. (hay, grain)* Scheune, -n *f.; (animals)* Stall, ˵e *m.*

barnacle, *n.* Entenmuschel, -n *f.*

barnyard, *n.* Bauernhof, ˵e *m.*

barometer, *n.* Barome´ter, - *nt.*

barometric, *adj.* barome´trisch.

baron, *n.* Baron´, -e *m.*

baroness, *n.* Barones´se, -n *f.*

baroque, 1. *n.* Barock´ *nt.* **2.** *adj.* barock´.

barracks, *n.* Kaser´ne, -n *f.*

barrage, *n.* Sperre, -n *f.; (mil.)* Sperrfeuer, - *nt.*

barrel, *n.* Faß, ˵sser *nt.*

barren, *adj.* unfruchtbar, dürr.

barricade, 1. *n.* Barrika´de, -n *f.* **2.** *vb.* verbarrikadie´ren.

barrier, *n.* Schranke, -n *f.*

barroom, *n.* Schankstube, -n *f.*

bartender, *n.* Barmixer, - *m.*

barter, 1. *n.* Tauschhandel *m.* **2.** *vb.* tauschen.

base, 1. *n.* der unterste Teil, -e *m.; (geom.)* Grundlinie, -n *f.; (mil.)* Stützpunkt, -e *m.* **2.** *vb.* basie´ren. **3.** *adj.* niederträchtig.

baseball, *n.* Baseball, ˵e *m.*

baseboard, *n.* Waschleiste, -n *f.*

basement, *n.* Keller, - *m.*

baseness, *n.* Niederträchtigkeit, -en *f.*

bashful, *adj.* schüchtern.

bashfulness, *n.* Schüchternheit, -en *f.*

basic, *adj.* grundlegend.

basin, *n.* Becken, - *nt.*

basis, *n.* Grundlage, -n *f.,* Basis, -sen *f.*

basket, *n.* Korb, ˵e *m.*

bass, *n. (singer)* Baß, ˵sse *m.; (fish)* Barsch, -e *m.*

bassinet, *n.* Korbwiege, -n *f.*

bassoon, *n.* Fagott´, -e *nt.*

bastard, *n.* uneheliches Kind *nt.,* Bastard, -e *m.*

baste, *vb. (thread)* heften; *(roast)* begie´ßen*.

bat, *n.* Fledermaus, ⸚e, *f.;* *(sport)* Schlagholz, ⸚er *nt.*

batch, *n.* Schub, ⸚e *m.*

bath, *n.* Bad, ⸚er *nt.*

bathe, *vb.* baden; **(b.ing suit)** Badeanzug, ⸚e, *m.*

bather, *n.* Badend- *m. & f.*

bathrobe, *n.* Bademantel, ⸚ *m.*

bathroom, *n.* Badezimmer, - *nt.*

bathtub, *n.* Bedewanne, -n *f.*

baton, *n.* Taktstock, ⸚e *m.*

battalion, *n.* Bataillon´, -e *nt.*

batter, 1. *n. (one who bats)* Schläger, - *m.; (cooking)* Teig, -e *m.* **2.** *vb.* schlagen*.

battery, *n.* Batterie´, -i´en *f.*

battle, 1. *n.* Schlacht, -en *f.* **2.** *vb.* kämpfen.

battlefield, *n.* Schlachtfeld, -er *nt.*

battleship, *n.* Schlachtschiff, -e *nt.*

bawl, *vb.* brüllen.

bay, 1. *n. (geography)* Bucht, -en *f.; (plant)* Lorbeer, -en *m.; (at b.)* in Schach. **2.** *vb.,* bellen.

bayonet, *n.* Bajonett´, -e *nt.*

bazaar, *n.* Bazar´, -e *nt.*

be, *vb.* sein*.

beach, *n.* Strand, -e *m.*

beachhead, *n.* Landekopf, ⸚e *m.*

beacon, *n.* Leuchtfeuer, - *nt.*

bead, *n.* Perle, -n *f.; (drop)* Tropfen, - *m.*

beading, *n.* Perlstickerei, -en *f.*

beak, *n.* Schnabel, ⸚ *m.*

beaker, *n.* Becher, - *m.*

beam, 1. *n. (construction)* Balken, - *m.; (light)* Strahl, -en *m.* **2.** *vb.* strahlen, glänzen.

beaming, *adj.* strahlend.

bean, *n.* Bohne, -n *f.*

bear, 1. *n. (animal)* Bär, -en, -en *m.* **2.** *vb. (carry)* tragen*; *(endure)* ertra´gen*; *(give birth to)* gebä´ren*.

bearable, *adj.* erträg´lich.

beard, *n.* Bart, ⸚e *m.*

bearer, *n.* Überbrin´ger, - *m.,* Überbrin´gerin, -nen *f.*

bearing, *n. (behavior)* Haltung, -en *f.; (affect)* Bezug´, ⸚e *m.; (machinery)* Lager, - *nt.*

beast, *n.* Vieh *nt.,* Tier, -e *nt.,* Bestie, - *f.*

beat, 1. *n.* Schlag, ⸚e *m.; (music)* Takt, -e *m.* **2.** *vb.* schlagen*.

beaten, *adj.* geschla´gen.

beatify, *vb.* selig•sprechen*.

beating, *n. (punishment)* Prügel *pl.,* Schläge *pl.; (defeat)* Niederlage, -n *f.*

beatitudes, *n.pl. (biblical)* Seligpreisungen *pl.*

beau, *n.* Vereh´rer, - *m.*

beautiful, *adj.* schön.

beautify, *vb.* verschö´nern.

beauty, *n.* Schönheit, -en *f.*

beauty parlor, *n.* Schönheitssalon, -s *m.,* Frisier´salon, -s *m.*

beaver, *n.* Biber, - *m.*

because, *conj.* weil; **(b. of)** wegen.

beckon, *vb.* winken.

become, *vb.* werden*.

becoming, *adj.* kleidsam.

bed, *n.* Bett, -en *nt.; (garden)* Beet, -e *nt.*

bedbug, *n.* Wanze, -n *f.*

bedding, *n.* Bettzeug *nt.*

bedroom, *n.* Schlafzimmer, - *nt.*

bedspread, *n.* Bettdecke, -n *f.*

bee, *n.* Biene, -n *f.*

beef, *n.* Rindfleisch *nt.*

beefsteak, *n.* Beefsteak, -s *nt.*

beehive, *n.* Bienenstock, ⸚e *m.*

beer, *n.* Bier, -e *nt.*

beet, *n.* Bete, -n *f.,* Runkelrübe, -n *f.,* rote Rübe, -n *f.*

beetle, *n.* Käfer, - *m.*

befall, *vb.* zu•stoßen*.

befit, *vb.* gezie´men.

befitting, *adj.* schicklich; **(be b.)** sich schicken.

before, 1. *adv. (time)* vorher; *(place)* voran´. **2.** *prep.* vor. **3.** *conj.* ehe, bevor´.

beforehand, *adv.* vorher.

befriend, *vb.* sich an•freunden mit.

befuddle, *vb.* verwir´ren.

beg, *vb.* betteln; *(implore)* bitten*.

beggar, *n.* Bettler, - *m.,* Bettlerin, -nen *f.*

begin, *vb.* an•fangen*, begin´nen*.

beginner, *n.* Anfänger, - *m.* Anfängerin, -nen *f.*

beginning, *n.* Anfang, ⸚e *m.*

begrudge, *vb.* mißgön´nen.

beguile, *vb.* bestrick´en.

behalf, *n.* **(on b. of)** zugun´sten von, im Namen von.

behave, *vb.* sich beneh´men*.

behavior, *n.* Beneh´men, *nt.*

behead, *vb.* enthaup´ten.

behind, 1. *adv.* hinten, zurück´. **2.** *prep.* hinter.

behold, 1. *vb.* sehen*. **2.** *interj.* sieh(e) da.

beige, *adj.* beigefarben.

being, *n.* Sein *nt.,* Wesen, - *nt.*

belated, *adj.* verspä´tet; nachträglich.

belch, *vb.* rülpsen.

belfry, *n.* Glockenturm, ⸚e *m.*

Belgian, 1. *n.* Belgier, - *m.,* Belgierin, -nen *f.* **2.** *adj.* belgisch.

Belgium, *n.* Belgien *nt.*

belie, *vb.* Lügen strafen.

belief, *n.* Glaube(n), - *m.*

believable, *adj.* glaubhaft.

believe, *vb.* glauben.

believer, *n.* Gläubig- *m. & f.*

belittle, *vb.* bagatellisie´ren.

bell, *n. (small)* Klingel, -n *f.; (large)* Glocke, -n *f.*

bellboy, *n.* Hotel´boy, -s *m.*

belligerence, *n.* Kriegslust, ⸚e *f.;* Kriegszustand, ⸚e *m.*

belligerent, *adj.* kriegerisch, kriegsführend.

bellow, *vb.* brüllen.

bellows, *n.* Blasebalg, ⸚e *m.*

belly, *n.* Bauch, ⸚e *m.*

belong, *vb.* gehö´ren.

belongings, *n.pl.,* Habseligkeiten *pl.*

beloved, *adj.* geliebt´.

below, 1. *adv.* unten. **2.** *prep.* unter.

belt, *n.* Gürtel, - *m.*

bench, *n.* Bank, ⸚e *f.*

bend, *vb.* biegen*.

beneath, 1. *adv.* unten. **2.** *prep.* unter.

benediction, *n.* Segen, - *m.*

benefactor, *n.* Wohltäter, - *m.*

benefactress, *n.* Wohltäterin, -nen *f.*

beneficent, *adj.* wohltätig.

beneficial, *adj.* wohltuend, nützlich.

beneficiary, *n.* Begün´stigt- *m.* & *f.*; Nutzniesser, - *m.*

benefit, 1. *n.* Wohltat, -en *f.*; *(advantage)* Nutzen, - *m.*, Vorteil, -e *m.* **2.** *vb.* nützen; **(b. from)** Nutzen ziehen* aus.

benevolence, *n.* Wohlwollen *nt.*

benevolent, *adj.* wohlwollend.

benign, *adj.* gütig.

bent, *adj.* gebeugt´; *(out of shape)* verbo´gen.

benzine, *n.* Benzin´ *nt.*

bequeath, *vb.* verma´chen.

bequest, *n.* Vermächt´nis, -se *nt.* Legat´, -e *nt.*

berate, *vb.* aus•schelten*.

bereave, *vb.* berau´ben.

bereavement, *n.* Verlust durch Tod.

berry, *n.* Beere, -n *f.*

berth, *n.* Bettplatz, ⸗e *m.*

beseech, *vb.* an•flehen.

beset, *vb.* bedrän´gen.

beside, *prep.* neben; **(b. oneself)** außer sich.

besides, 1. *adv.* außerdem. **2.** *prep.* außer.

besiege, *vb.* bela´gern.

best, 1. *adj.* best-. **2.** *adv.* übertref´fen*.

bestial, *adj.* bestia´lisch, tierisch.

bestow, *vb.* verlei´hen*.

bestowal, *n.* Verlei´hung, -en *f.*

bet, 1. *n.* Wette, -n *f.* **2.** *vb.* wetten.

betake oneself, *vb.* sich auf•machen.

betoken, *vb.* bezeich´nen.

betray, *vb.* verra´ten*.

betrayal, *n.* Verrat´ *m.*

betroth, *vb.* verlo´ben; **(be b.ed)** sich verlo´ben.

betrothal, *n.* Verlo´bung, -en *f.*

better, 1. *adj.* besser. **2.** *vb.* verbes´sern.

between, *prep.* zwischen.

bevel, 1. *n.* schräger Anschnitt, -e *m.* **2.** *vb.* schräg ab•schneiden*.

beverage, *n.* Getränk´, -e *nt.*

bewail, *vb.* bekla´gen.

beware, *vb.* sich hüten.

bewilder, *vb.* verwir´ren.

bewilderment, *n.* Verwir´rung, -en *f.*

bewitch, *vb.* bezau´bern; verzau´bern.

beyond, 1. *adv.* jenseits. **2.** *prep.* jenseits, über.

biannual, *adj.* halbjährlich.

bias, *n.* Vorurteil, -e *nt.*

bib, *n.* Lätzchen, - *nt.*

Bible, *n.* Bibel, -n *f.*

Biblical, *adj.* biblisch.

bibliography, *n.* Bibliographie´, -i´en *f.*

bicarbonate, *n. (of soda)* doppelkohlensaures Natron *nt.*

biceps, *n.* Bizeps, -e *m.*

bicker, *vb.* sich zanken.

bicycle, *n.* Fahrrad, ⸗er *nt.*

bicyclist, *n.* Radfahrer, - *m.*, Radfahrerin, -nen *f.*

bid, 1. *n.* Angebot, -e *nt.* **2.** *vb.* bieten*.

bidder, *n.* Bieter, *m.*, Bieterin, -nen *f.*

bide, *vb.* ab•warten.

biennial, *adj.* zweijährlich.

bier, *n.* Bahre, -n *f.*

bifocal, *adj.* bifokal´.

big, *adj.* groß (größer, größt-).

bigamist, *n.* Bigamist´, -en, -en *m.*

bigamous, *adj.* biga´misch.

bigamy, *n.* Bigamie´, -i´en *f.*

bigot, *n.* Frömmler, - *m.*

bigoted, *adj.* bigott´.

bigotry, *n.* Frömmelei´, -en *f.*

bilateral, *adj.* zweiseitig.

bile, *n.* Galle, -n *f.*

bilingual, *adj.* zweisprachig.

bilious, *adj.* gallig.

bill, *n. (bird)* Schnabel ⸗ *m.*; *(banknote)* Geldschein, -e *m.*; *(sum owed)* Rechnung, -en *f.*; *(legislative)* Geset´zesvorlage, -n *f.*

billboard, *n.* Rekla´meschild, -er *nt.*

billet, 1. *n.* Quartier´, -e *nt.* **2.** *vb.* ein•quartieren.

billfold, *n.* Brieftasche, -n *f.*

billiards, *n.* Billard *nt.*

billion, *n.* Billion´, -en *f.*

bill of fare, *n.* Speisekarte, -n *f.*

bill of health, *n.* Gesund´heitsattest, -e *nt.*

bill of lading, *n.* Frachtbrief, -e *m.*

bill of sale, *n.* Kaufkontrakt, -e *m.*

billow, 1. *n.* Woge, -n *f.* **2.** *vb.* wogen.

bimonthly, *adj.* zweimo´natlich.

bin, *n.* Kasten, ⸗ *m.*

bind, *vb.* binden*; verbin´den*.

bindery, *n.* Buchbinderei´, -en *f.*

binding, 1. *n. (book)* Einband, ⸗e *m.*; *(ski)* Bindung, -en *f.* **2.** *adj.* bindend.

binocular, *n.* Fernglas, ⸗er *nt.*

biochemistry, *n.* Biochemie´ *f.*

biodegradable, *adj.* orga´nisch abbaubar.

biofeedback, *n.* Biosignalrück´gabe, -n *f.*

biographer, *n.* Biograph´, -en, -en *m.*

biographical, *adj.* biogra´phisch.

biography, *n.* Biographie´, -i´en *f.*

biological, *adj.* biolo´gisch.

biology, *n.* Biologie´, -i´en *f.*

bipartisan, *adj.* die Regierungs- und die Oppositionspartei vertretend.

bird, *n.* Vogel, ⸗ *m.*

birth, *n.* Geburt´, -en *f.*

birth control, *n.* Gebur´tenkontrolle *f.*, Empfäng´nisverhütung *f.*

birthday, *n.* Geburts´tag, -e *m.*

birthmark, *n.* Muttermal, - *e nt.*

birthplace, *n.* Geburts´ort, -e *m.*

birth rate, *n.* Gebur´tenziffer, -n *f.*

birthright, *n.* Erstgeburtsrecht, -e *nt.;* angestammtes Recht *nt.*

biscuit, 1. *n.* Biskuit´, -e *nt.;* Keks, -e *m.*

bisect, *vb.* halbie´ren.

bishop, *n.* Bischof, ˝e, *m.*

bismuth, *n.* Wismut *nt.*

bison, *n.* Bison, -s *m.*

bit, *n. (piece)* Bißchen, - *nt.;* **(a b. of)** ein bißchen; *(harness)* Gebiß, -sse *nt.;* *(computer)* Bit, - *nt.*

bitch, *n.* Hündin, -nen *f.*

bite, 1. *n.* Bissen, - *m.* 2. *vb.* beißen*.

biting, *adj.* beißend.

bitter, *adj.* bitter.

bitterness, *n.* Bitterkeit, -en *f.*

biweekly, *adj.* zweiwöchentlich.

black, 1. *adj.* schwarz (˝). 2. *n. (person)* Schwarz- *m.& f.*

blackberry, *n.* Brombeere, -n *f.*

blackbird, *n.* Amsel, -n *f.*

blackboard, *n.* Wandtafel, -n *f.*

blacken, *vb.* schwärzen.

blackmail, 1. *n.* Erpres´sung, -en *f.* 2. *vb.* erpres´sen.

black market, *n.* Schwarzmarkt, ˝e *m.*

blackout, *n.* Verdun´kelung, -en *f.*

blacksmith, *n.* Schmied, -e *m.*

bladder, *n.* Blase, -n *f.*

blade, *n. (knife)* Klinge, -n *f.;* *(grass)* Halm, -e *m.*

blame, 1. *n.* Schuld, -en *f.* 2. *vb.* beschul´digen.

blanch, *vb.* bleichen; bleich werden*.

bland, *adj.* mild.

blank, 1. *n. (form)* Formular´, -e *nt.* 2. *adj.* unbeschrieben, leer.

blanket, *n.* Decke, -n *f.,* Wolldecke, -n *f.*

blaspheme, *vb.* lästern.

blasphemer, *n.* Gotteslästerer, - *m.*

blasphemous, *adj.* gotteslästerlich.

blasphemy, *n.* Gotteslästerung, -en *f.,* Blasphemie´, -i´en *f.*

blast, 1. *n. (of wind)* Windstoß, ˝e *m.;* *(explosion)* Explosion´, -en *f.* 2. *vb.* sprengen.

blatant, *adj.* laut, aufdring´lich.

blaze, 1. *n.* Flamme, -n *f.* 2. *vb.* lodern, leuchten.

bleach, *vb.* bleichen.

bleak, *adj.* öde.

bleed, *vb.* bluten.

blemish, *n.* Makel, - *m.*

blend, 1. *n.* Mischung, -en *f.* 2. *vb.* mischen.

bless, *vb.* segnen.

blessed, *adj.* gese´gnet, selig.

blessing, *n.* Segen, - *m.*

blight, 1. *n. (bot.)* Brand, ˝e *m.* 2. *(fig.)* vernich´ten.

blind, 1. *adj.* blind. 2. *vb.* blenden.

blindfold, 1. *n.* Augenbinde -n *f.* 2. *vb.* die Augen verbin´den*.

blindness, *n.* Blindheit, -en *f.*

blink, *vb.* blinken, blinzeln.

blinker, *n.* Scheuklappe, -n *f.;* *(signal)* Blinklicht, -er *nt.*

bliss, *n.* Glückseligkeit, -en *f.*

blissful, *adj.* glückselig.

blister, *n.* Blase, -n *f.*

blithe, *adj.* fröhlich.

blizzard, *n.* Schneesturm, ˝e *m.*

bloat, *vb.* blähen.

bloated, *adj.* aufgedunsen.

bloc, *n.* Block, ˝e *m.*

block, 1. *n. (wood)* Holzblock, ˝e *m.;* *(city)* Häuserblock, ˝e *m.* 2. *vb.* sperren.

blockade, *n.* Blocka´de, -n *f.*

blond, *adj.* blond.

blood, *n.* Blut *nt.*

blood donor, *n.* Blutspender, - *m.,* Blutspenderin, -nen *f.*

bloodhound, *n.* Bluthund, -e *m.*

blood plasma, *n.* Plasma, -men *nt.*

blood poisoning, *n.* Blutvergiftung, -en *f.*

blood pressure, *n.* Blutdruck, *m.*

bloodshed, *n.* Blutvergießen, *nt.*

bloodshot, *adj.* blutunterlaufen.

bloody, *adj.* blutig.

bloom, 1. *n.* Blüte, -n *f.* 2. *vb.* blühen.

blossom, *n.* Blüte, -n *f.*

blot, 1. *n.* Fleck, -e *m.* 2. *vb.* beflecken, *(ink)* löschen.

blotter, *n.* Löschpapier, -e *nt.*

blouse, *n.* Bluse, -n *f.*

blow, 1. *n.* Schlag, ˝e *m.,* Stoß, ˝e, *m.* 2. *vb.* blasen*.

blowout, *n.* Reifenpanne, -n *f.*

blubber, 1. *n.* Walfischspeck *m.* 2. *vb.* flennen.

blue, *adj.* blau.

bluebird, *n.* Blaukehlchen, - *nt.*

blue jeans, *n.pl.* Bluejeans *pl.*

blueprint, *n.* Blaudruck, ˝e *m.;* *(fig.)* Plan, ˝e *m.*

bluff, 1. *n. (cliff)* Klippe, -n *f.,* schroffer Felsen, - *m.;* *(cards)* Bluff, -s *m.* 2. *adj.* schroff. 3. *vb.* bluffen.

bluffer, *n.* Bluffer, - *m.*

bluing, *n.* Waschblau *nt.*

blunder, 1. *n.* Fehler, - *m.* 2. *vb.* Fehler machen.

blunderer, *n.* Tölpel, - *m.*

blunt, *adj.* stumpf; *(fig.)* unverblümt.

blur, 1. *n.* Verschwom´menheit *f.* 2. *vb. (intr.)* verschwim´men*; *(tr.)* trüben.

blurred, *adj.* verschwommen.

blush, 1. *n.* Erro´ten *nt.* 2. *vb.* errö´ten.

bluster, *vb.* toben; *(swagger)* prahlen.

boar, *n.* Eber, - *m.*

board, 1. *n. (plank)* Brett, -er *nt.,* Bord, -e *nt.;* *(food)* Verpfle´gung, -en *f.;* *(committee)* Ausschuß, ˝sse *m.;* *(council)* Behör´de, -n *f.;* *(ship)*

Bord, -e *m.* **2.** *vb.* an Bord gehen*.

boarder, *n.* Kostgänger, - *m.*

boarding house, *n.* Pension´, -en

boarding pass, *n.* Bordkarte, -n *f.*

boarding school, *n.* Internat´, -e *nt.*

boast, 1. *n.* Angeberei´, -en *f.* **2.** *vb.* prahlen, an•geben*.

boaster, *n.* Angeber, - *m.* Angeberin, -nen *f.*

boastful, *adj.* angeberisch.

boastfulness, *n.* Angeberei´, -en *f.*

boat, *n.* Boot, -e *nt.*, Schiff, -e *nt.*

bob, 1. *n.* (hair) Bubikopf *m.* **2.** *vb.* baumeln; (hair) kurz schneiden*.

bobby pin, *n.* Haarklammer, -n *f.*

bodice, *n.* Oberteil, -e *nt.*

bodily, *adj.* leiblich.

body, *n.* Körper, - *m.*, Leib, -er *m.*

bodyguard, *n.* Leibwache, -n *f.*

bog, 1. *n.* Sumpf, ⁼e *m.* **2.** *vb.* (b. down) stecken bleiben*.

Bohemian, 1. *n.* Böhme, -n, -n *m.* **2.** *adj.* böhmisch.

boil, 1. *n.* (med.) Furun´kel, -n *f.* **2.** *vb.* kochen.

boiler, *n.* Kessel, - *m.*

boisterous, *adj.* ungestüm.

bold, *adj.* kühn.

boldface, *n.* Fettdruck, -e *m.*

boldness, *n.* Kühnheit, -en *f.*

Bolivian, 1. *n.* Bolivia´ner, - *m.*, Bolivia´nerin, -nen *f.* **2.** *adj.* bolivia´nisch.

bolster, 1. *n.* Polster, - *nt.* **2.** *vb.* (support) unterstüt´zen.

bolster up, *vb.* stärken.

bolt, 1. *n.* (lock) Riegel, - *m.*; (screw with nut) Schraube, -n *f.*; (lightning) Blitz, -e *m.* **2.** *vb.* (lock) verrie´geln; (dash, of persons) davon•stürzen, (of horses) durch•gehen*.

bomb, 1. *n.* Bombe, -n *f.* **2.** *vb.* bomben.

bombard, *vb.* bombardie´ren.

bombardier, *n.* Bombardier´, -e *m.*

bombardment, *n.* Beschie´ßung, -en *f.*

bomber, *n.* Bombenflugzeug, -e *nt.*

bombproof, *adj.* bombensicher.

bombshell, *n.* Bombe, -n *f.*

bombsight, *n.* Bombenziel´vorrichtung, -en *f.*

bonbon, *n.* Fondant´, -s *m.*

bond, *n.* Band, -e *nt.*, Fessel, -n *f.*; (law) Bürgschaft, -en *f.*; (stock exchange) Obligation´, -en *f.*

bondage, *n.* Knechtschaft, -en *f.*

bone, *n.* Knochen, - *m.*; (fish) Gräte, -n *f.*

bonfire, *n.* Freudenfeuer, -nt.

bonnet, *n.* Damenhut, ⁼e *m.*

bonus, *n.* Extrazahlung, -en *f.*; Tantie´me, -n *f.*

bony, *adj.* knochig.

book, 1. *n.* Buch, ⁼er *nt.* **2.** *vb.* buchen.

bookcase, *n.* Bücherschrank, ⁼e *m.*

bookkeeper, *n.* Buchhalter, - *m.*, Buchhalterin, -nen *f.*

bookkeeping, *n.* Buchführung, -en *f.*

booklet, *n.* Broschü´re, -n *f.*

bookseller, *n.* Buchhändler, - *m.*, Buchhändlerin, -nen *f.*

bookstore, *n.* Buchhandlung, -en *f.*

boom, 1. *n.* Baum, ⁼e *m.*; (econ.) Hochkonjunktur, -en *f.* **2.** *vb.* brummen, dröhnen.

boon, *n.* Geschenk´, -e *nt.*; (fig.) Segen, - *m.*

boor, *n.* Grobian, -e *m.*

boorish, *adj.* grob (÷).

boost, 1. *n.* (increase) Aufschwung, ⁼e *m.*; (push) Antrieb, -e *m.* **2.** *vb.* (increase) steigern; (push) nachhelfen*.

boot, *n.* Stiefel, - *m.*

bootblack, *n.* Schuhputzer, - *m.*

booth, *n.* Bude, -n *f.*; (telephone) Fernsprechzelle, -n *f.*

border, 1. *n.* Grenze, -n *f.* **2.** *vb.* grenzen an.

borderline, *n.* Grenze, -n *f.*

bore, 1. *n* (hole) Bohrloch, ⁼er *nt.*; (cylinder) Bohrung, -en *f.*; (person) langweiliger Mensch, -en, -en *m.* **2.** *vb.* bohren; (annoy) langweilen.

boredom, *n.* Langeweile *f.*

boric, *adj.* Bor- (cpds.).

boring, *adj.* langweilig.

born, *adj.* gebo´ren.

born-again, *adj.* wiedergeboren.

borough, *n.* Stadtteil, -e *m.*

borrow, *vb.* borgen, leihen*.

bosom, *n.* Busen, - *m.*

boss, *n.* Chef, -s *m.*, Chefin, -nen *f.*

bossy, *adj.* herrschsüchtig.

botanical, *adj.* bota´nisch.

botany, *n.* Bota´nik *f.*

both, *adj.* & *pron.* beide.

bother, 1. *n.* Verdruß´ *m.* **2.** *vb.* beläs´tigen; (disturb) stören.

bothersome, *adj.* lästig.

bottle, *n.* Flasche, -n *f.*

bottle opener, *n.* Flaschenöffner, - *m.*

bottom, *n.* Grund, ⁼e *m.*; Hintern *m.*

bottomless, *adj.* bodenlos.

boudoir, *n.* Boudoir´, -s *nt.*

bough, *n.* Ast, ⁼e *m.*, Zweig, -e *zm.*

bouillon, *n.* Kraftbrühe, -n *f.*

boulder, *n.* Felsblock, ⁼e *m.*

boulevard, *n.* Boulevard´, -s *m.*

bounce, *vb.* springen*.

bound, 1. *n.* (jump) Sprung. ⁼e *m.*; (b.s.) Grenzen *pl.* **2.** *vb.* (jump) springen*; (limit) begren´zen. **3.** *adj.* (tied) gebun´den; (duty b.) verpflich´tet; (b. for) unterwegs´ nach.

boundary, *n.* Grenze, -n *f.*

bound for, *adj.* unterwegs´ nach.

boundless, *adj.* grenzenlos.

bounty, *n.* Freigebigkeit, -en *f.*

bouquet, *n.* Blumenstrauß, ⁼e *m.*

bourgeois, *adj.* bürgerlich.

bout, *n. (boxing)* Boxkampf, -̈e *m.*

bovine, *adj.* Rinder- *(cpds.).*

bow, 1. *n. (for arrows, violin)* Bogen, - *m.; (greeting)* Verbeu´gung, -en *f.; (hair, dress)* Schleife, -n *f.; (of boats)* Bug, -̈e *m.* **2.** *vb.* sich verbeu´gen.

bowels, *n.pl.* Eingeweide *pl.*

bowl, 1. *n.* Schüssel -n *f.,* Schale, -n *f.* **2.** *vb.* kegeln.

bowlegged, *adj.* o-beinig.

bowler, *n.* Kegelspieler, - *m.,* Kegelspielerin, -nen *f.; (hat)* Melo´ne, -n *f.*

bowling, *n.* Kegeln *nt.*

box, 1. *n. (small)* Schachtel, -n *f.; (large)* Kasten, -̈ *m.; (theater)* Loge, -n *f.; (letter b.)* Briefkasten, -̈ *m.* **2.** *vb. (sport)* boxen.

boxcar, *n.* Güterwagen, - *m.*

boxer, *n.* Boxer, - *m.*

boxing, *n.* Boxen *nt.*

box office, *n.* Thea´terkasse, -n *f.*

boy, *n.* Junge, -n, -n *m.,* Bube, -n, -n *m.*

Boycott, 1. *n.* boykott´, -e *m.* **2.** *vb.* boykottie´ren.

boyhood, *n.* Jugend, -en *f.*

boyish, *adj.* jungenhaft, jung.

bra, *n.* BH, -s *m.*

brace, 1. *n.* Klammer, -n *f.,* Stütze, -n *f.* **2.** *vb.* absteifen.

bracelet, *n.* Armband, -̈er *nt.*

bracket, *n.* Klammer, -n *f.; (typography)* Klammer, - n *f.; (group)* Gruppe, -n *f.*

brag, *vb.* prahlen, an•geben*.

braggart, *n.* Angeber, - *m.*

braid, 1. *n.* Flechte, -n *f.* **2.** *vb.* flechten*.

brain, *n.* Gehirn´, -e *nt.*

brake, 1. *n.* Bremse, -n *f.* **2.** *vb.* bremsen.

bran, *n.* Kleie, -n *f.*

branch, *n.* Ast, -̈e *m.,* Zweig, -e *m.;* Filia´le, -n *f.*

brand, 1. *n. (sort)* Sorte, -n *f.; (mark)* Marke, -n *f.* **2.** *vb.* brandmarken.

brandish, *vb.* schwingen*.

brandy, *n.* Weinbrand, -e *m.,* Kognak, -s *m.*

brash, *adj.* dreist.

brass, *n.* Messing *nt.*

brassiere, *n.* Büstenhalter, - *m.*

brat, *n.* Balg, -̈e *m.*

bravado, *n.* Bravour´ *f.,* Schneid *m.*

brave, *adj.* tapfer.

bravery, *n.* Tapferkeit, -en *f.*

brawl, *n.* Rauferei´, -en *f.*

brawn, *n.* Muskelkraft, -̈e *f.*

bray, 1. *n.* Eselsgeschrei *nt.* **2.** *vb.* schreien*.

brazen, *adj.* ehern; *(insolent)* unverschämt.

Brazil, *n.* Brasi´lien *nt.*

Brazilian, 1. *n.* Brasilia´ner, - *m.,* Brasilia´nerin, -nen *f.* **2.** *adj.* brasilia´nisch.

breach, *n.* Bruch, -̈e *m.*

bread, *n.* Brot, -e *nt.*

breadth, *n.* Breite, -n *f.*

break, 1. *n.* Bruch, -̈e *m.;* Pause, -n *f.* **2.** *vb.* brechen*.

breakable, *adj.* zerbrech´lich.

breakfast, *n.* Frühstück, -e *nt.*

breakneck, *adj.* halsbrecherisch.

breakwater, *n.* Mole, -n *f.*

breast, *n.* Brust, -̈e *f.*

breath, *n.* Atem, - *m.*

breathe, *vb.* atmen.

breathing, *n.* Atmen *nt.*

breathless, *adj.* atemlos.

breeches, *n.* Kniehose -n *f.*

breed, 1. *n.* Zucht, -en *f.* **2.** *vb. (beget)* erzeu´gen; *(raise)* züchten; *(educate)* erzie´hen*.

breeder, *n.* Züchter, - *m.,* Züchterin, -nen *f.*

breeding, *n.* Erzie´hung, - *f.*

breeze, *n.* Brise, -n *f.*

breezy, *adj.* luftig.

brevity, *n.* Kürze, -n *f.*

brew, 1. *n.* Gebräu, -e *nt.* **2.** *vb.* brauen.

brewer, *n.* Brauer, - *m.*

brewery, *n.* Brauerei´, -en *f.*

briar, *n.* Dornbusch, -̈e *m.;* Bruyèreholz *nt.*

bribe, *vb.* beste´chen*.

briber, *n.* Beste´cher, - *m.,* Beste´cherin, -nen *f.*

bribery, *n.* Beste´chung, -en *f.*

brick, *n.* Backstein, -e *m.;* Ziegelstein, -e *m.*

bricklayer, *n.* Maurer, - *m.*

bridal, *adj.* Hochzeits- *(cpds.).*

bride, *n.* Braut, -̈e *f.*

bridegroom, *n.* Bräutigam, -e *m.*

bridesmaid, *n.* Brautjungfer, -n *f.*

bridge, 1. *n.* Brücke, -n *f.; (game)* Bridge *nt.* **2.** *vb.* überbrü´cken.

bridle, *n.* Zaum, -̈e *m.*

brief, *adj.* kurz (-̈).

brief case, *n.* Aktenmappe, -n *f.*

bright, *adj.* hell; *(smart)* gescheit´.

brighten, *vb.* erhel´len.

brightness, *n.* Klarheit, -en *f.*

brilliance, *n.* Glanz, -e *m.*

brilliant, *adj.* glänzend; *(smart)* hochbegabt.

brim, *n. (cup)* Rand, -̈er *m.; (hat)* Krempe, -n *f.*

brine, *n.* Salzwasser, - *nt.,* Sole, -n *f.*

bring, *vb.* bringen*.

brink, *n.* Rand, -̈er *m.*

briny, *adj.* salzig.

brisk, *adj.* lebhaft.

brisket, *n. (meat)* Bruststück, -e *nt.*

briskness, *n.* Lebhaftigkeit, -en *f.*

bristle, 1. *n.* Borste, -n *f.* **2.** *vb.* sich sträuben.

Britain, *n.* Britan´nien *nt.*

British, *adj.* britisch.

Briton, *n.* Brite, -n, -n *m.,* Britin, -nen *f.*

brittle, *adj.* brüchig, spröde.

broad, *adj.* breit, weit.

broadcast, 1. *n.* Rundfunksendung, -en *f.,* Übertra´gung, -en *f.* **2.** *vb.* senden, im Radio übertra´gen*.

broadcaster, *n.* Rundfunksprecher, - *m.,* Rundfunksprecherin, -nen *f.*

broadcloth, *n.* feiner Wäschestoff *m.*

broaden, *vb.* erwei´tern.

broadly, *adv.* allgemein´.

broadminded, *adj.* großzügig, tolerant´.

brocade, *n.* Brokat´, -e *m.*

broil, *vb.* grillen.

broiler, *n.* Bratrost, -e *m.*

broke, *adj.* pleite.

broken, *adj.* gebro´chen; kaputt´.

broker, *n.* Makler, - *m.*, Maklerin, -nen *f.*

brokerage, *n.* *(business)* Maklergeschäft, -e *nt.;* *(charge)* Maklergebühr, -en *f.*

bronchial, *adj.* bronchial´.

bronchitis, *n.* Bronchi´tis *f.*

bronze, *n.* Bronze, -n *f.*

brooch, *n.* Brosche, -n *f.*

brood, 1. *n.* Brut, -en *f.* **2.** *vb.* brüten.

brook, *n.* Bach, =e *m.*

broom, *n.* Besen, - *m.*

broomstick, *n.* Besenstiel, -e *m.*

broth, *n.* Brühe, -n *f.*

brothel, *n.* Bordell´, -e *nt.*

brother, *n.* Bruder, = *m.*

brotherhood, *n.* Brüder- schaft, -en *f.*

brother-in-law, *n.* Schwa- ger, = *m.*

brotherly, *adj.* brüderlich.

brow, *n.* Stirn, -en *f.*

brown, *adj.* braun.

browse, *vb.* schmökern.

bruise, 1. *n.* Quetschung, - en *f.;* **2.** *vb.* quetschen, stoßen*.

brunette, *n.* Brünet´te, -n *f.*

brunt, *n.* **(bear the b.)** die Hauptlast tragen*.

brush, 1, *n.* Bürste, -n *f.;* *(artist's)* Pinsel, - *m.* **2.** *vb.* bürsten.

brusque, *adj.* brüsk.

brutal, *adj.* brutal´.

brutality, *n.* Brutalität´, -en *f.*

brutalize, *vb.* verro´hen.

brute, *n.* Unmensch, -en, - en *m.*

bubble, 1. *n.* Luftblase, -n *f.* **2.** *vb.* sprudeln.

buck, 1. *n.* Bock, =e *m.* **2.** *vb.* bocken; *(fig.)* sich gegen etwas auf•bäumen.

bucket, *n.* Eimer, - *m.*

buckle, 1. *n.* Schnalle, - *f.* **2.** *vb.* *(fasten)* schnallen;

(bend) sich krümmen, sich biegen*.

buckwheat, *n.* Buchweizen *m.*

bud, 1. *n.* Knospe, -n *f.* **2.** *vb.* knospen.

budge, *vb.* sich rühren.

budget, *n.* Etat´, -s *m.*

buffalo, *n.* Büffel, - *m.*

buffer, *n.* Puffer, - *m.;* **(b. state)** Pufferstaat, -en *m.*

buffet, 1. *n.* Büfett´, -e, Buffet´, -s *nt.* **2.** *vb.* schlagen*.

bug, *n.* Käfer, - *m.*

bugle, *n.* Signal´horn, =er *nt.*

build, *vb.* bauen.

builder, *n.* Baumeister, - *m.*

building, *n.* Gebäu´de, - *nt.*

bulb, *n.* Knolle, -n *f.;* *(electric)* Glühbirne, -n *f.*

bulge, 1. *n.* Ausbuchtung, - en *f.* **2.** *vb.* sich aus•buchten.

bulk, *n.* Umfang *m.*, Haupt- teil, -e *m.*

bulky, *adj.* umfangreich.

bull, *n.* Bulle, -n, -n *m.*

bulldog, *n.* Bulldogge, -n *f.*

bullet, *n.* Kugel, -n *f.*

bulletin, *n.* Bericht´, -e *m.*

bully, 1. *n.* Kraftmeier, - *m.* **2.** *vb.* kraftmeiern.

bulwark, *n.* Bollwerk, -e *nt.*

bum, 1. *n.* *(fam.)* Lump, - en, -en *m.* **2.** *vb.* *(fam.)* pumpen.

bumblebee, *n.* Hummel, -n *f.*

bump, 1. *n.* Stoß, =e *m.* **2.** *vb.* stoßen*.

bumper, *n.* Stoßstange, -n *f.*

bun, *n.* Brötchen, - *nt.*

bunch, *n.* Büschel, - *nt.*

bundle, *n.* Bündel, - *nt.*

bungle, *vb.* pfuschen.

bunion, *n.* Entzün´dung am großen Zeh.

bunny, *n.* Kanin´chen, - *nt.*

buoy, *n.* Boje, -n *f.*

buoyant, *adj.* schwimmend, tragfähig; *(fig.)* lebhaft.

burden, 1. *n.* Last, -en *f.* **2.** *vb.* belas´ten.

burdensome, *adj.* beschwer´lich.

bureau, *n.* Büro´, -s *nt.;* *(furniture)* Kommo´de, - n *f.*

burglar, *n.* Einbrecher, - *m.*, Einbrecherin, -nen *f.*

burglary, *n.* Einbruch, =e *m.*

burial, *n.* Begräb´nis, -se *nt.*

burlap, *n.* grobe Leinwand *f.*

burly, *adj.* stämmig.

burn, 1. *n.* Verbren´nung, - en *f.* **2.** *vb.* *(intr.)* bren- nen*, *(tr.)* verbren´nen*.

burner, *n.* Brenner, - *m.*

burrow, 1. *n.* *(of an animal)* Bau, -e *m.* **2.** *vb.* sich ein•graben*.

burst, 1. *n.* Krach, -e *m.;* Explosion´, -en *f.* **2.** *vb.* *(intr.)* platzen; *(tr.)* spren- gen.

bury, *vb.* begra´ben*; ein- graben*.

bus, *n.* Bus, -se *m.*

bush, *n.* Busch, =e *m.*

bushel, *n.* Scheffel, - *m.*

bushy, *adj.* buschig.

business, *n.* Geschäft´, -e *nt.*

businesslike, *adj.* geschäfts´mäßig.

businessman, *n.* Geschäfts´- mann, =er *or* -leute *m.*

businesswoman, *n.* Geschäfts´frau, -en *f.*

bust, 1. *n.* Büste, -n *f.* **2.** *vb.* *(fam.)* kaputt´ machen.

bustle, *n.* Geschäf´tigkeit, - en *f.*

busy, *adj.* beschäf´tigt; geschäf´tig.

but, 1, *prep.* außer. **2.** *conj.* aber.

butcher, *n.* Fleischer, - *m.*, Metzger, - *m.*, Schlächter, - *m.*, Schlachter, - *m.*

butler, *n.* Diener, - *m.*

butt, 1, *n.* *(gun)* Kolben, - *m.;* *(aim)* Ziel, -e *nt.* **2.** *vb.* mit dem Kopf stoßen*.

butter, *n.* Butter *f.*

butterfly, *n.* Schmetterling, -e *m.*

buttermilk, *n.* Buttermilch *f.*

buttocks, *n.pl.* Gesäß´, -e *nt.*

button, *n.* Knopf, =e *m.*

buttonhole, *n.* Knopfloch, =er *nt.*

buttress, 1. *n.* Stütze, -n *f.;* *(arch.)* Strebepfeiler, - *m.* **2.** *vb.* stützen.

buxom, *adj.* drall.

buy, vb. kaufen.

buyer, n. Käufer, - m., Käuferin, -nen f.

buzz, vb. summen.

buzzard, n. Bussard, -e m.

buzzer, n. Klingel, -n f.

by, prep. von; (through) durch; (near) bei.

by-and-by, adv. später.

bygone, adj. vergan´gen.

by-pass, n. Umge´hungsstraße, -n f.

by-product, n. Nebenprodukt, -e nt.

bystander, n. Zuschauer, - m., Zuschauerin, -nen f.

byte, n. Byte, -s nt.

byway, n. Nebenweg, -e m.

C

cab, n. (taxi) Taxe, -n f., Taxi, -s nt.; (locomotive) Führerstand, -e m.

cabaret, n. Kabarett´, -e nt.

cabbage, n. Kohl m.

cabin, n. Kabi´ne, -n f.

cabinet, n. Kabinett´, -e nt.

cabinetmaker, n. Kunsttischler, - m.

cable, 1. n. Kabel, - nt. 2. vb. kabeln.

cablegram, n. Kabel, - nt.

cache, n. Versteck´, -e nt.

cackle, vb. gackern.

cactus, n. Kaktus, -te´en m.

cad, n. Schuft, -e m.

cadaver, n. Leichnam, -e m.

cadet, n. Kadett´, -en, -en m.

cadence, n. Tonfall, =e m.; Kadenz´, -en f.

cadmium, n. Kadmium nt.

café, n. Cafe´, -s nt.; Konditorei´, -en f.

cafeteria, n. Mensa, -sen f.

caffeine, n. Koffein´, -e nt.

cage, n. Käfig, -e m.

cajole, vb. beschwat´zen.

cake, n. Kuchen, - m.

calamity, n. Unglück, -e nt.

calcium, n. Kalzium nt.

calculable, adj. bere´chenbar.

calculate, vb. berech´nen.

calculating machine, n. Rechenmaschine, -n f.

calculation, n. Berech´nung, -en f.

calculator, n. Taschenrechner, - m.

calculus, n. Differential´rechnung, -en f.

caldron, n. Kessel, - m.

calendar, n. Kalen´der, - m.

calf, n. Kalb, =er nt.

calfskin, n. Kalbleder, - nt.

caliber, n. Kali´ber, - nt.

calico, n. Kattun´, -e m.

calipers, n.pl. Greifzirkel, - m.

calisthenics, n.pl. Leibesübungen pl.

call, 1. n. Ruf, -e m.; (telephone) Anruf, -e m. 2. vb. rufen*.

calling card, n. Visi´tenkarte, -n f.

callous, adj. schwielig; (unfeeling) gefühl´los.

callus, n. Schwiele, -n f.

calm, 1. adj. ruhig. 2. vb. beru´higen.

calmness, n. Ruhe f.

caloric, adj. kalo´risch.

calorie, n. Kalorie´, -i´en f.

Calvary, n. Kalva´rienberg m.

calve, vb. kalben.

cambric, n. Batist´, -e m.

camel, n. Kamel´, -e nt.

cameo, n. Kame´e, -n f.

camera, n. Kamera, -s f.; Photoapparat, -e m.

camouflage, 1. n. Tarnung, -en f; (natural c.) Mimikry f. Schutzfarbe, -n f. 2. vb. tarnen.

camp, 1. n. Lager, - nt. 2. vb. lagern.

campaign, 1. n. Feldzug, =e m.; Kampag´ne, -n f. 2. vb. (political) Wahlreden halten*.

camper, n. Zelter, - m., Zelterin, -nen f.

camphor, n. Kampfer m.

camping, n. Zelten nt.

campsite, n. Zeltplatz, =e m.

campus, n. Universitäts´gelände, - nt., College-Gelände, - nt.

can, 1. n. (tin) Büchse, -n f.; (large) Kanne, -n f. 2. vb. (preserve) ein•machen; (be able) können*.

Canada, n. Kanada nt.

Canadian, 1. n. Kana´dier, - m., Kana´dierin, -nen f. 2. adj. kana´disch.

canal, n. Kanal´, =e m.

canapé, n. Cocktailgebäck nt.

canary, n. Kana´rienvogel, = m.

cancel, vb. entwer´ten, rückgängig machen, auf•heben*.

cancellation, n. Aufhebung, -en f., Entwer´tung, -en f.

cancer, n. Krebs, -e m.

candelabrum, n. Armleuchter, - m.

candid, adj. offen, ehrlich.

candidacy, n. Kandidatur´, -en f.

candidate, n. Kandidat´, -en, -en m., Kandida´tin, -nen f.

candied, adj. kandiert´.

candle, n. Kerze, -n f.

candlestick, n. Leuchter, - m.

candor, n. Offenheit, -en f.

cane, n. Stock, =e m; (sugar) Rohr, -e nt.

canine, adj. Hunde- (cpds.).

canister, n. Blechbüchse, -n f.

canker, n. Krebs, -e m.

canned, adj. eingemacht; Büchsen- (cpds.).

cannibal, n. Kanniba´le, -n, -n m.

canning, n. Einmachen nt.

cannon, n. Kano´ne, -n f.

cannot, vb. nicht können*.

canny, adj. schlau, umsichtig.

canoe, n. Kanu´, -s nt.

canon, n. (rule, song) Kanon, -s m.; (person) Domherr, -n, -en m.

canonical, adj. kano´nisch.

canonize, vb. kanonisie´ren.

can opener, n. Büchsenöffner, - m.

canopy, *n.* Baldachin, -e *m.*

cant, *n.* Heuchelei´, -en *f.*

cantaloupe, *n.* Melo´ne, -n *f.*

canteen, *n.* Kanti´ne, -n *f.*

canvas, *n. (material)* Segeltuch *nt.; (painter's)* Leinwand *f.*

canvass, 1. *n.* Stimmenprüfung, -en *f.* **2.** *vb.* untersu´chen, prüfen.

canyon, *n.* Schlucht, -en *f.*

cap, *n.* Mütze, -n *f.*

capability, *n.* Fähigkeit, -en *f.*

capable, *adj.* fähig.

capacious, *adj.* geräu´mig.

capacity, *n. (content)* Inhalt *m.; (ability)* Fähigkeit, -en *f.; (quality)* Eigenschaft, -en *f.*

cape, *n. (clothing)* Umhang, ⁀e *m.; (geogr.)* Kap, -s *nt.*

caper, 1. *n.* Luftsprung, ⁀e *m.* **2.** *vb.* Luftsprünge machen.

capital, 1. *n. (money)* Kapital´, -ien *nt.; (city)* Hauptstadt, ⁀e *f.* **2.** *adj.* kapital´.

capitalism, *n.* Kapitalis´mus *m.*

capitalist, *n.* Kapitalist´, -en, -en *m.*

capitalistic, *adj.* kapitalistisch.

capitalization, *n.* Kapitalisie´rung, -en *f.*

capitalize, *vb.* kapitalisie´ren.

capitulate, *vb.* kapitulie´ren.

capon, *n.* Kapaun´, -e *m.*

caprice, *n.* Laune, -n *f.*

capricious, *adj.* launenhaft.

capsize, *vb.* kentern.

capsule, *n.* Kapsel, -n *f.*

captain, *n.* Kapitän´, -e *m.; (army)* Hauptmann, -leute *m.*

caption, *n.* Überschrift, -en *f.*

captious, *adj.* verfäng´lich.

captivate, *vb.* fesseln.

captive, 1. *n.* Gefan´gen, -*m.* & *f.* **2.** *adj.* gefan´gen.

captivity, *n.* Gefan´genschaft, -en *f.*

captor, *n.* Fänger, - *m.*

capture, 1. *n.* Gefan´gennahme, -n *f.* **2.** *vb. (person)* fangen*; *(city)* ero´bern.

car, *n.* Wagen, - *m.; Auto,* -s *nt.*

carafe, *n.* Karaf´fe, -n *f.*

caramel, *n.* Karamel´ *nt.*

carat, *n.* Karat´, -e *nt.*

caravan, *n.* Karawa´ne, -n *f.*

caraway, *n.* Kümmel *m.*

carbide, *n.* Karbid´ *nt.*

carbine, *n.* Karabi´ner, - *m.*

carbohydrate, *n.* Kohlehydrat, -e *nt.*

carbon, *n.* Kohlenstoff, -e *m.*

carbon dioxide, *n.* Kohlendioxyd *nt.*

carbon monoxide, *n.* Kohlenoxyd´ *nt.*

carbon paper, *n.* Kohlepapier, -e *nt.*

carbuncle, *n.* Karbun´kel, -*m.; (gem)* Karfun´kel, - *m.*

carburetor, *n.* Verga´ser, - *m.*

carcass, *n.* Kada´ver, - *m.*

carcinogenic, *adj.* krebserregend.

card, *n.* Karte, -n *f.*

cardboard, *n.* Pappe, -n *f.*

cardiac, *adj.* Herz- *(cpds.).*

cardinal, 1. *n.* Kardinal´, -e *m.* **2.** *adj.* hauptsächlich.

care, 1. *n. (worry)* Sorge, -n *f.; (prudence)* Vorsicht *f.; (accuracy)* Sorgfalt *f.;* **(take c. of)** sorgen für. **2.** *vb. (attend)* sorgen für; **(c. for, like)** gern mögen*; **(c. about)** sich kümmern um.

careen, *vb.* wild fahren*.

career, *n.* Karrie´re, -n *f.*

carefree, *adj.* sorglos.

careful, *adj. (prudent)* vorsichtig; *(accurate)* sorgfältig.

carefulness, *n. (prudence)* Vorsicht *f.; (accuracy)* Sorgfalt *f.*

careless, *adj. (imprudent)* unvorsichtig, leichtsinnig; *(inaccurate)* unsorgfältig, nachlässig.

carelessness, *n. (imprudence)* Unvorsichtigkeit, -en *f.; (inaccuracy)* Nachlässigkeit, -en *f.*

caress, 1. *n.* Liebkosung, -en *f.* **2.** *vb.* liebkosen, streicheln.

caretaker, *n.* Verwal´ter, - *m.*

cargo, *n.* Ladung, -en *f.;* Fracht, -en *f.*

caricature, 1. *n.* Karikatur´, -en *f.* **2.** *vb.* karikie´ren.

caries, *n.* Karies *f.*

carload, *n.* Waggon´ladung, -en *f.*

carnal, *adj.* fleischlich.

carnation, *n.* Nelke, -n *f.*

carnival, *n.* Karneval, -s *m.*

carnivorous, *adj.* fleischfressend.

carol, 1. *n.* Weihnachtslied, -er *nt.* **2.** *vb.* singen*.

carouse, *vb.* zechen.

carousel, *n.* Karussell´, -s *nt.*

carpenter, *n. (construction)* Zimmermann, -leute *m; (finer work)* Tischler, - *m.*

carpet, *n.* Teppich, -e *m.*

car pool, *n.* Fahrgemeinschaft, -en *f.*

car rental, *n.* Autovermietung *f.*

carriage, *n. (vehicle)* Wagen, - *m.; (posture)* Haltung, -en *f.*

carrier, *n.* Träger, - *m.*

carrot, *n.* Mohr´rübe, -n *f.*

carry, *vb.* tragen*; **(c. on,** *intr.)* fort•fahren*; **(c. on,** *tr.)* fort•setzen; **(c. out)** aus•führen; **(c. through)** durch•führen.

cart, *n.* Karren, - *m.*

cartage, *n.* Transport´, -e *m.*

cartel, *n.* Kartell´, -e *nt.*

cartilage, *n.* Knorpel, - *m.*

carton, *n.* Karton´, -s *m.*

cartoon, *n.* Karikatur´, -en *f.*

cartridge, *n.* Patro´ne, -n *f.*

carve, *vb.* schneiden*; *(wood)* schnitzen; *(meat)* zerle´gen, tranchie´ren.

carving, *n.* Schnitzwerk, -e *nt.*

car wash, Autowaschanlage, -n *f.*

case, *n.* Fall, ⁀e *m.*

cash, 1. *n.* Bargeld, -er *nt.* **2.** *vb.* ein•lösen. **3.** *adj.* bar.

cashier, *n.* Kassie´rer, - *m.,* Kassie´rerin, -nen *f.*

cashmere, *n.* Kaschmir, -e *m.*

casing, *n.* Hülle, -n *f.*

casino, *n.* Kasi´no, -s *nt.*

cask, *n.* Tonne, -n *f.,* Faß, ⁀sser *nt.*

casket, *n.* Sarg, ‼e *m.*

casserole, *n.* Schmorpfanne, -n *f.*

cassette, *n.* Kasset´te, -n *f.*

cast, 1. *n. (theater)* Rollen-verteilung, -en *f.* 2. *vb. (throw)* werfen*; *(metal)* gießen*.

caste, *n.* Kaste, -n *f.*

castigate, *vb.* züchtigen.

castle, *n.* Schloß, ‼sser, *nt.*

castoff, *adj.* abgelegt.

castor oil, *n.* Rizinusöl, -e *nt.*

casual, *adj. (accidental)* zufällig; *(nonchalant)* zwanglos.

casualness, *n.* Zwanglosigkeit, -en *f.*

casualty, *n.* Opfer, - *nt.; (casualties)* Verlus´te *pl.*

cat, *n.* Katze, -n *f.; (tomcat)* Kater, - *m.*

cataclysm, *n.* Sündflut, -en *f.*

catacomb, *n.* Katakom´be, -n *f.*

catalogue, *n.* Katalog´, -e *m.*

catapult, *n.* Katapult´, -e *m.*

cataract, *n. (eye)* Katarakt´, -e *m.,* grauer Star, -e *m.*

catarrh, *n.* Katarrh´, -e *m.*

catastrophe, *n.* Katastro´phe, -n *f.*

catch, *vb.* fangen*; *(sickness, train)* bekom´men*.

catcher, *n.* Fänger, - *m.*

catechism, *n.* Katechis´mus, -men *m.*

categorical, *adj.* katego´risch.

category, *n.* Kategorie´, -i´en *f.*

cater, *vb.* versor´gen.

caterpillar, *n.* Raupe, -n *f.*

cathartic, 1. *n.* Abführmittel, - *nt.* 2. *adj.* abführend.

cathedral, *n.* Kathedra´le, -n *f.;* Dom, -e *m.,* Münster *nt.*

cathode, *n.* Katho´de, -n *f.*

Catholic, 1. *n.* Katholik´, -en, -en *m.* 2. *adj.* katho´lisch.

Catholicism, *n.* Katholizis´mus, -men *m.*

catsup, *n.* Ketchup *nt.*

cattle, *n.* Vieh *nt.*

cauliflower, *n.* Blumenkohl, -e *m.*

cause, 1. *n. (origin)* Ursache, -n *f.; (idea)* Sache, -n *f.* 2. *vb.* verur´sachen.

caustic, *adj.* beißend.

cauterize, *vb.* aus•brennen*.

cautery, *n.* Ausbrennen *nt.*

caution, 1. *n.* Vorsicht, -en *f.* 2. *vb.* warnen.

cautious, *adj.* vorsichtig.

cavalcade, *n.* Kavalka´de, -n *f.*

cavalier, *n.* Kavalier´, -e *m.*

cavalry, *n.* Kavallerie´, -i´en *f.*

cave, *n.* Höhle, -n *f.*

cavern, *n.* Höhle, -n *f.*

caviar, *n.* Kaviar *m.*

cavity, *n.* Loch, ‼er *nt.,* Höhle, -n *f.*

cease, *vb. (intr.)* auf•hören, *(tr.)* ein•stellen.

cedar, *n.* Zeder, -n *f.*

cede, *vb.* ab•treten*.

ceiling, *n.* Zimmerdecke, -n *f.; (fig.)* Höchstgrenze, -n *f.*

celebrate, *vb.* feiern.

celebrated, *adj.* berühmt´.

celebration, *n.* Feier, -n *f.*

celebrity, *n.* Berühmt´heit, -en *f.*

celery, *n.* Sellerie *m.*

celestial, *adj.* himmlisch.

celibacy, *n.* Zölibat´ *nt.,* Ehelosigkeit *f.*

celibate, *adj.* ehelos.

cell, *n.* Zelle, -n *f.*

cellar, *n.* Keller, - *m.*

cellist, *n.* Cellist´, -en, -en *m.,* Cellis´tin, -nen *f.*

cello, *n.* Cello, -s *nt.*

cellophane, *n.* Zellophan´ *nt.*

celluloid, *n.* Zelluloid´ *nt.*

cellulose, *n.* Zellstoff, -e *m.*

Celtic, *adj.* keltisch.

cement, 1. *n.* Zement´, -e *m.* 2. *vb.* zementie´ren.

cemetery, *n.* Friedhof, ‼e *m.*

censor, 1. *n.* Zensor, -o´ren *m.* 2. *vb.* zensie´ren.

censorship, *n.* Zensur´, -en *f.*

censure, *n.* Tadel, - *m.,* Verweis´, -e *m.*

census, *n.* Volkszählung, -en *f.,* Zensus, - *m.*

cent, *n.* Cent, -s *m.*

centenary, *n.* Hundertjahr´feier, -n *f.*

centennial, 1. *n.* Hundertjahr´feier, -n *f.* 2. *adj.* hundertjährig.

center, *n.* Mitte, -n *f.;* Mittelpunkt, -e *m.;* Zentrum, -tren *nt.*

centerfold, *n.* Mittelfaltblatt, ‼er *nt.*

centigrade, *n.* (c. thermometer) Celsiusthermometer, - *nt.;* (10 degrees c.) 10 Grad Celsius.

central, *adj.* zentral´.

centralize, *vb.* zentralisie´ren.

century, *n.* Jahrhun´dert, -e *nt.*

ceramic, *adj.* kera´misch.

ceramics, *n.* Kera´mik, -en *f.*

cereal, *n.* Getrei´de, - *nt.,* Getrei´despeise, - *nt.*

cerebral, *adj.* Gehirn-*(cpds.).*

ceremonial, *adj.* zeremoniell´.

ceremonious, *adj.* feierlich.

ceremony, *n.* Zeremonie´, -i´en *f.;* Feierlichkeit, -en *f.*

certain, *adj.* sicher.

certainty, *n.* Gewißheit, -en *f.*

certificate, *n.* Beschei´nigung, -en *f.;* Urkunde, -n *f.*

certification, *n.* Beschei´nigung, -en *f.*

certify, *vb.* beschei´nigen, beglau´bigen, bezeu´gen.

cervix, *n.* Gebär´mutterhals *m.*

cessation, *n.* Aufhören *nt.*

cesspool, *n.* Senkgrube, -n *f.*

chafe, *vb.* reiben*.

chagrin, *n.* Kummer, - *m.*

chain, 1. *n.* Kette, -n *f.* 2. *vb.* an•ketten, fesseln.

chain reaction, *n.* Kettenreaktion, -en *f.*

chair, *n.* Stuhl, ‼e *m.*

chairman, *n.* Vorsitzend- *m.*

chairperson, *n.* Vorsitzend-*m. & f.*

chalice, *n.* Kelch, -e *m.*

chalk, *n.* Kreide, -n *f.*

chalky, *adj.* kreidig.

challenge, 1. *n.* Heraus´forderung, -en *f.*

2. vb. heraus•fordern, auf•fordern.

challenger, n. Heraus´forderer, - m.

chamber, n. Kammer, -n f.; (pol.) Haus, ⸗er nt.

chambermaid, n. Zimmermädchen, - nt.

chamber music, n. Kammermusik f.

chamois, n. (animal) Gemse, -n f.; (leather) Wildleder nt.

champagne, n. Sekt, -e m., Champag´ner, - m.

champion, n. Kämpfer, - m.; (sport) Meister, - m., Meisterin, -nen f.

championship, n. Meisterschaft, -en f.

chance, 1. n. Zufall, ⸗e m.; (expectation) Aussicht, -en f.; (occasion) Gele´genheit, -en f. **2.** vb. wagen. **3.** adj. zufällig.

chancel, n. Altar´platz, ⸗e m.

chancellery, n. Kanzlei´, -en f.

chancellor, n. Kanzler, - m.

chandelier, n. Kronleuchter, - m.

change, 1. n. Verän´derung, -en f.; (alteration) Änderung, -en f.; (variety) Abwechslung, -en f.; (small coins) Kleingeld nt.; (money due) Rest m. **2.** vb. verändern; (alter) ändern; (money) wechseln.

changeability, n. Unbeständigkeit, -en f.

changeable, adj. unbeständig.

channel, n. Fahrwasser nt., Kanal´, ⸗e m.; (radio) Frequenz´band, ⸗er nt.

chant, 1. n. Gesang´, ⸗e m. **2.** vb. singen*.

chaos, n. Chaos, nt.

chaotic, adj. chao´tisch.

chap, 1. n. Bursche, -n, -n m., Kerl, -e m. **2.** vb. (become chapped) auf•springen*.

chapel, n. Kapel´le, -n f.

chaplain, n. Geistlich- m.; (mil.) Feldgeistlich- m.

chapter, n. Kapi´tel, - nt.

char, vb. verkoh´len.

character, n. Charak´ter, - te´re m., Person´, -en f.

characteristic, adj. charakteri´stisch.

characterization, n. Charakterisie´rung, -en f.

characterize, vb. charakterisie´ren.

charcoal, n. Holzkohle, -n f.

charge, 1. n. (load) Ladung, -en f.; (attack) Angriff, -e m.; (price) Preis, -e m.; (custody) Obhut, -en f. **2.** vb. (load) laden*; (set a price) berech´nen; (put on one's account) an•schreiben* lassen*.

chariot, n. Wagen, - m.

charisma, n. Charis´ma nt.

charitable, adj. wohltätig, nachsichtig.

charity, n. Wohltätigkeit, -en f., Nächstenliebe f.

charlatan, n. Scharlatan, -e m.

charm, 1. n. Charme m.; Liebreiz, -e m.; (magic saying) Zauberspruch, ⸗e m. **2.** vb. bezau´bern.

charming, adj. bezau´bernd, reizend.

chart, n. (map) Karte, -n f.; (graph) Tabel´le, -n f.

charter, n. Urkunde, -n f.

charter flight, n. Charterflug, ⸗e m.

charwoman, n. Putzfrau, - en f.

chase, 1. n. Jagd, -en f. **2.** vb. jagen.

chasm, n. Abgrund, ⸗e m.

chassis, n. Fahrgestell, -e nt.

chaste, adj. züchtig, keusch.

chasten, vb. züchtigen.

chastise, vb. züchtigen.

chastity, n. Keuschheit f.

chat, 1. n. Plauderei´, -en f. **2.** vb. plaudern.

chateau, n. Château´, -s nt.

chatter, 1. n. Geschwätz´ nt. **2.** vb. schwatzen; (teeth) klappern.

chauffeur, n. Fahrer, - m., Chauffeur´, -e m.

cheap, adj. billig, (fig.) ordinär´.

cheapen, vb. im Wert herab´setzen.

cheapness, n. Billigkeit, -en f.

cheat, vb. betrü´gen*; (harmless) schummeln.

check, 1. n. (restraint) Hemmnis, -se nt.; (verification) Kontrol´le, -n f., Überprü´fung, -en f.; (clothes, luggage) Kontroll´marke, -n f.; (bank) Scheck, -s m.; (bill) Rechnung, -en f. **2.** vb. (verify) kontrollie´ren, überprü´fen; (luggage) auf•geben*, ab•geben*; (mark) ab•hacken.

checkerboard, n. Damebrett, -er nt.

checkers, n. Damespiel nt.

cheek, n. Backe, -n f., Wange, -n f.

cheer, 1. n. Beifallsruf, -e m. **2.** vb. Beifall rufen*; (c. up) auf•muntern.

cheerful, adj. fröhlich.

cheerfulness, n. Fröhlichkeit f.

cheery, adj. heiter.

cheese, n. Käse m.

cheesecloth, n. grobe Gaze, -n f.

chef, n. Küchenchef, -s m.

chemical, 1. chemisches Präparat´, -e nt.; (c. s) Chemikal´ien pl. **2.** adj. chemisch.

chemist, n. Chemiker, -m., Chemikerin, -nen f.

chemistry, n. Chemie´ f.

chemotherapy, n. Chemotherapie´ f.

chenille, n. Chenille´, -n f.

cherish, vb. schätzen.

cherry, n. Kirsche, -n f.

cherub, n. Cherub, -s or - im or -i´nen m.

chess, n. Schach nt., Schachspiel nt.

chessboard, n. Schachbrett, -er nt.

chessman, n. Schachfigur, - en f.

chest, n. (box) Kiste, -n f., Truhe, -n f.; (body) Brust f.

chestnut, n. Kasta´nie, -n f.

chevron, n. Dienstgradabzeichen, - nt.

chew, vb. kauen.

chic, adj. schick; elegant´.

chick, n. Küken, - nt.

chicken, n. Huhn, ⸗er nt.

chicken pox, n. Windpocken pl.

chicory, n. Zicho´rie, -n f.

chide, vb. schelten*.

chief, 1. n. Oberhaupt, ⸗er nt. 2. adj. hauptsächlich; Haupt- (cpds.).

chiefly, adv. vorwiegend.

chieftain, n. Häuptling, -e m.

chiffon, n. Chiffon´, -s m.

child, n. Kind, -er nt.

childbirth, n. Geburt´ f.

childhood, n. Kindheit, -en f.

childish, adj. kindisch.

childishness, n. Kindhaftigkeit, -en f.

childless, adj. kinderlos.

childlike, adj. kindlich.

chill, 1. n. Frost, ⸗e m.; (fever) Schauer, - m. 2. vb. auf Eis stellen.

chilliness, n. Kühle f.

chilly, adj. kühl.

chime, 1. n. (chimes) Glockenspiel, -e nt. 2. vb. läuten.

chimney, n. Schornstein, -e m.

chimpanzee, n. Schimpan´se, -n, -n m.

chin, n. Kinn, -e nt.

china, n. Porzellan´, -e nt.

China, n. China nt.

chinchilla, n. Chinchil´la, -s m.

Chinese, 1. n. Chine´se, -n, -n m.; Chine´sin, -nen f. 2. adj. chine´sisch.

chintz, n. Chintz, -e m.

chip, 1. n. Splitter, - m. 2. vb. ab•brechen*; ab•splittern.

chiropodist, n. Fußpfleger, - m.

chiropractor, n. Chiroprak´tiker, - m., Chiroprak´tikerin, -nen f.

chirp, 1. n. Gezirp´ nt. 2. vb. zirpen.

chisel, 1. n. (stone, metal) Meißel, - m.; (wood) Beitel, - m. 2. vb. meißeln.

chivalrous, adj. ritterlich.

chivalry, n. Ritterlichkeit, -en f.

chive, n. Schnittlauch, m.

chloride, n. Chlorid´, -e nt.

chlorine, n. Chlor, -s nt.

chloroform, n. Chloroform´ nt.

chocolate, n. Schokola´de, - n f.

choice, n. Wahl, -en f.; (selection) Auswahl, -en f.

choir, n. Chor, ⸗e m.

choke, vb. erwür´gen, erstick´en.

choker, n. Halsband, ⸗er nt.

cholera, n. Cholera f.

choose, vb. wählen.

chop, 1. n. (meat) Kotelett´, -s nt. 2. vb. hacken.

choppy, adj. (sea) unruhig.

chopsticks, n. Eßstäbchen pl.

choral, adj. Chor- (cpds.).

chord, n. (string) Saite, -n f.; (harmony) Akkord´, -e m.

chore, n. Alltagsarbeit, -en f.

choreographer, n. Choreograph´, -en, -en m.

choreography, n. Choreographie´, -i´en f.

chorus, n. Chor, ⸗e m.; Refrain´, -s m.

Christ, n. Christus m.

christen, vb. taufen.

Christendom, n. Christenheit f.

christening, n. Taufe, -n f.

Christian, 1. n. Christ, -en, -en m. 2. adj. christlich.

Christianity, n. Christentum nt.

Christmas, n. Weihnachten nt.

Christmas Eve, n. Heiligabend m.

chrome, chromium, n. Chrom nt.

chronic, adj. chronisch.

chronicle, n. Chronik, -en f.

chronological, adj. chronolo´gisch.

chronology, n. Chronologie´, -i´en f.

chrysanthemum, n. Chrysanthe´me, -n f.

chubby, adj. dicklich.

chuckle, vb. vergnügt´lachen.

chug, vb. daher´•keuchen.

chunk, n. Stück, -e nt.

church, n. Kirche, -n f.

churchyard, n. Kirchhof, ⸗e m.

churn, 1. n. Butterfaß, ⸗sser nt. 2. vb. buttern; (fig.) auf•wühlen.

chute, n. (mail) Postschacht, ⸗e m.; (laundry) Wäscheschacht, ⸗e m.

cider, n. Apfelwein, -e m.

cigar, n. Zigar´re, -n f.

cigarette, n. Zigaret´te, -n f.

cinch, n. Sattelgurt, -e m; (fam.) Kleinigkeit, -en f.

cinder, n. Asche, -n f.

cinema, n. Kino, -s nt.

cinnamon, n. Zimt m.

cipher, n. (number) Ziffer, - n f.; (zero) Null, -en f.; (code) Chiffre, -n f.

circle, n. Kreis, -en m.

circuit, n. (course) Umkreis, -e m.; (elec.) Stromkreis, -e m.; (short c.) Kurzschluß, ⸗sse m.

circuitous, adj. umwegig.

circular, 1. n. Rundschreiben, - nt. 2. adj. kreisförmig.

circulate, vb. zirkulie´ren.

circulation, n. (blood) Kreislauf, ⸗e m.; (paper) Auflage, -n f.; (money) Umlauf, ⸗e m.

circulatory, adj. zirkulie´rend.

circumcise, vb. beschnei´den*.

circumcision, n. Beschnei´dung, -en f.

circumference, n. Umfang, ⸗e m.

circumlocution, n. Umschrei´bung, -en f.

circumscribe, vb. (geom.) umschrei´ben*; (delimit) begren´zen.

circumspect, adj. umsichtig.

circumstance, n. Umstand, ⸗e m.; (pl.) Verhält´nisse pl.

circumstantial, adj. eingehend; (c. evidence) Indi´zienbeweis, -e m.

circumvent, vb. umge´hen*.

circumvention, n. Umge´hung, -en f.

circus, n. Zirkus, -se m.

cirrhosis, n. Zirrho´se, -n f.

cistern, *n.* Zister´ne, -n *f.*

citadel, *n.* Zitadel´le, -n *f.*

citation, *n.* Auszeichnung, -en *f.; (law)* Vorladung, -en *f.*

cite, *vb.* an•führen, zitie´ren; *(law)* vor•laden*.

citizen, *n.* Bürger, - *m.,* Bürgerin, -nen *f.*

citizenship, *n.* Staatsange-hörigkeit, -en *f.*

city, *n.* Stadt, ⸗e *f.*

city map, *n.* Stadtplan, ⸗e *m.*

civic, *adj.* Bürger- *(cpds.).*

civil, *adj.* bürgerlich; *(law)* zivil´rechtlich; *(polite)* höflich.

civilian, 1. *n.* Zivilist´, -en, -en *m.* **2.** *adj.* bürgerlich.

civility, *n.* Höflichkeit, -en *f.*

civilization, *n.* Zivilisation´, -en *f.*

civilize, *vb.* zivilisie´ren.

civilized, *adj.* zivilisiert´.

civil rights, *n.* Bürgerrechte *pl.*

clad, *adj.* geklei´det.

claim, 1. *n.* Anspruch, ⸗e *m.* **2.** *vb.* bean´spruchen, fordern.

claimant, *n.* Bean´spruchend- *m. & f.*

clairvoyance, *n.* Hellsehen *nt.*

clairvoyant, 1. *n.* Hellseher, - *m.,* Hellseherin, -nen *f.* **2.** *adj.* hellseherisch.

clammy, *adj.* feuchtkalt.

clamor, 1. *n.* Geschrei´ *nt.* **2.** *vb.* schreien*.

clamp, 1. *n.* Klammer, -n *f.* **2.** *vb.* fest•klammern.

clandestine, *adj.* heimlich.

clap, *vb.* klatschen.

claret, *n.* Rotwein, -e *m.*

clarification, *n.* Klarstel-lung, -en *f.*

clarify, *vb.* klar•stellen.

clarinet, *n.* Klarinet´te, -n *f.*

clarity, *n.* Klarheit, -en *f.*

clash, 1. *n.* Zusam´men-stoß, ⸗e *m.* **2.** *vb.* zusam´men•stoßen*; *(fig.)* sich nicht vertra´gen*.

clasp, 1. *n.* Schnalle, -n *f.; (hands)* Händedruck *m.* **2.** *vb.* fest•schnallen;

(grasp) umfas´sen; *(embrace)* umar´men.

class, *n.* Klasse, -n *f.; (period of instruction)* Stunde, -n *f.*

classic, classical, *adj.* klas-sisch.

classicism, *n.* Klassizis´mus, -men *m.*

classification, *n.* Klassifizie´rung, -en *f.*

classify, *vb.* klassifizie´ren.

classmate, *n.* Klassenkam-erad, -en, -en *m.,* Klassenkameradin, -nen *f.*

classroom, *n.* Klassenzim-mer, - *nt.*

clatter, 1. *n.* Geklap´per *nt.* **2.** *vb.* klappern.

clause, *n.* Satzteil, -e *m.; (main c.)* Hauptsatz, ⸗e *m.; (subordinate c.)* Nebensatz, ⸗e *m.; (law)* Klausel, -n *f.*

claw, 1. *n.* Kralle, -n *f.,* Klaue, -n *f.* **2.** *vb.* krallen.

clay, *n.* Ton, -e *m.,* Lehm, -e *m.*

clean, 1. *vb.* sauber machen, reinigen. **2.** *adj.* sauber.

clean-cut, *adj.* sauber.

cleaner, *n.* **(the c.s)** Reini-gung, -en *f.*

cleanliness, cleanness, *n.* Sauberkeit *f.*

cleanse, *vb.* reinigen.

clear, 1. *vb.* klären; *(profit)* rein verdie´nen; *(weather)* sich auf•klären. **2.** *adj.* klar.

clearance, *n. (enough space)* Raum *m.; (sale)* Räumung, -en *f.; (approval)* Gutheißung *f.*

clearing, *n.* Lichtung, -en *f.*

clearness, *n.* Klarheit, -en *f.*

cleat, *n. (naut.)* Klampe, -n *f.; (on boots)* Krampe, -n *f.*

cleavage, *n.* Spaltung, -en *f.*

cleave, *vb.* spalten*.

cleaver, *n.* Fleischerbeil, -e *nt.*

clef, *n.* Notenschlüssel, - *m.*

cleft, 1. *n.* Spalte, -n *f.* **2.** *adj.* gespal´ten.

clemency, *n.* Milde *f.*

clench, *vb.* zusam´men•pressen; *(fist)* ballen.

clergy, *n.* Geistlichkeit *f.*

clergyman, *n.* Geistlich-, - *m.*

clerical, *adj. (eccles.)* geistlich, klerikal´; *(writing)* Schreib- *(cpds.).*

clerk, *n.* Schreiber, - *m.,* Schreibkraft, ⸗e *f.;* **(salesc.)** Verkäu´fer, - *m.,* Verkäu´ferin, -nen *f.*

clever, *adj.* klug (⸚), geschickt´, schlau.

cleverness, *n.* Klugheit, -en *f.,* Geschick´lichkeit, -en *f.*

clew, *n. (object)* Knäuel, - *nt.*

cliché, *n.* Klischee´, -s *nt.*

click, 1. *n.* Klicken *nt.; (language)* Schnalzlaut, -e *m.* **2.** *vb.* klicken, knacken.

client, *n.* Kunde, -n, -n *m.,* Kundin, -nen *f.* Klient´, -en, -en *m.,* Klien´tin, -nen *f.*

clientele, *n.* Kundschaft, -en *f.*

cliff, *n.* Klippe, -n *f.*

climate, *n.* Klima, -s *or* a´te *nt.*

climatic, *adj.* klima´tisch.

climax, *n.* Höhepunkt, -e *m.*

climb, *vb. (intr.)* steigen*, klettern; *(tr.)* erstei´gen*.

climber, *n.* Kletterer, - *m.*

clinch, *vb.* fest•machen; *(fig.)* den Ausschlag geben*.

cling, *vb.* sich an•klammern.

clinic, *n.* Klinik, -en *f.*

clinical, *adj.* klinisch.

clip, 1. *n.* Klammer, -n *f.; (jewelry)* Schmucknadel, -n *f.* **2.** *vb.* beschnei´den*.

clippers, *n.pl. (barber)* Haarschneide-maschine, -n, *f.*

clipping, *n. (newspaper)* Zeitungsausschnitt, -e *m.*

clique, *n.* Clique, -n *f.*

cloak, *n.* Mantel, ⸚ *m.*

cloakroom, *n.* Gardero´be, -n *f.*

clock, *n.* Uhr, -en *f.*

clod, *n.* Klumpen, - *m.*

clog, 1. *n.* Holzschuh, -e *m.* **2.** *vb.* verstop´fen.

cloister, *n.* Kloster, ⸚ *nt.; (arch.)* Kreuzgang, ⸗e *m.*

clone, *n.* Klon, -s *nt.*

close, 1. *adj. (narrow)* eng. knapp; *(near)* nah (≐). **2.** *vb.* schließen*, zu•machen.

closeness, *n.* Enge, -n *f.,* Nähe, -n *f.*

closet, *n.* Wandschrank, ¨e *m.*

clot, 1. *n.* Klumpen, - *m.* **2.** *vb.* gerin´nen*.

cloth, *n.* Tuch, ¨er *nt.,* Stoff, -e *m.*

clothe, *vb.* kleiden.

clothes, *n.pl.* Kleider *pl.*

clothing, *n.* Kleidung, -en *f.*

cloud, *n.* Wolke, -n *f.*

cloudburst, *n.* Wolkenbruch, ¨e *m.*

cloudiness, *n.* Bewölkt´heit *f.*

cloudy, *adj.* bewölkt´, trübe.

clove, *n.* Gewürz´nelke, -n *f.*

clover, *n.* Klee *m.*

clown, *n.* Clown, -s *m.*

cloy, *vb.* übersät´tigen.

club, *n. (group)* Klub, -s *m.; (stick)* Keule, -n *f.*

clubs, *n. (cards)* Treff *nt.*

clue, *n.* Anhaltspunkt, -e *m.,* Schlüssel, - *m.*

clump, *n.* Klumpen, - *m.*

clumsiness, *n.* Ungeschicklichkeit, -en *f.*

clumsy, *adj.* ungeschickt.

cluster, 1. *n.* Büschel, - *m.* **2.** *vb.* sich zusam´men•scharen.

clutch, 1. *n. (auto)* Kuppelung, -en *f.* **2.** *vb.* packen.

clutter, *vb.* umher´•streuen.

coach, 1. *n.* Kutsche, -n *f.; (train)* Eisenbahnwagen, - *m.; (sports)* Trainer, - *m.,* Trainerin, -nen *f.; (tutor)* Privat´lehrer, - *m.* **2,** *vb. (sports)* trainie´ren; *(tutor)* Privat´stunden geben*.

coagulate, *vb.* gerin´nen*.

coagulation, *n.* Gerin´nen *nt.*

coal, *n.* Kohle, -n *f.*

coalesce, *vb.* verschmel´zen*.

coalition, *n.* Koalition´, -en *f.*

coarse, *adj.* grob (≐).

coarsen, *vb.* vergrö´bern.

coarseness, *n.* Grobheit, -en *f.*

coast, *n.* Küste, -n *f.*

coastal, *adj.* Küsten- *(cpds.).*

coaster, *n.* Küstenfahrer, - *m.*

coat, *n. (suit)* Jacke, -n *f.; (overcoat)* Mantel, ¨ *m.*

coating, *n.* Überzug, ¨e *m.*

coat of arms, *n.* Wappen, - *nt.*

coax, *vb.* überre´den.

cobalt, *n.* Kobalt *m.*

cobblestone, *n.* Kopfstein, - e *m.*

cobweb, *n.* Spinngewebe, - *nt.*

cocaine, *n.* Kokain´ *nt.*

cock, 1. *n.* Hahn, ¨e *m.* **2.** *vb. (gun)* spannen.

cockeyed, *adj.* schielend; *(crazy)* verrückt´.

cockpit, *n.* Führersitz, -e *m.*

cockroach, *n.* Küchenschabe, -n *f.*

cocktail, *n.* Cocktail, -s *m.*

cocky, *adj.* frech.

cocoa, *n.* Kaka´o, -s *m.*

coconut, *n.* Kokosnuß, ¨sse *f.*

cocoon, *n.* Kokon´, -s *m.*

cod, *n.* Kabeljau, -e *m.*

C. O. D., *adv.* per Nachnahme.

coddle, *vb.* verpäp´peln.

code, *n. (law)* Kodex, -dizes *m.; (secret)* Kode, -s *m.*

codeine, *n.* Kodein´ *nt.*

codfish, *n.* Kabeljau, -e *m.*

codify, *vb.* kodifizie´ren.

cod-liver oil, *n.* Lebertran *m.*

coeducation, *n.* Koeduka- tion´ *f.*

coerce, *vb.* zwingen*.

coercion, *n.* Zwang *m.*

coexist, *vb.* koexistie´ren.

coffee, *n.* Kaffee *m.*

coffin, *n.* Sarg, ¨e *m.*

cog, *n.* Zahn, ¨e *m.; (c. railway)* Zahnradbahn, -en *f.*

cogent, *adj.* zwingend.

cogitate, *vb.* nach•denken*.

cognizance, *n.* Kenntnis, -se *f.*

cognizant, *adj.* bewußt´.

cogwheel, *n.* Zahnrad, ¨er *nt.*

cohere, *vb.* zusam´men•hängen*.

coherent, *adj.* zusam´menhängend.

cohesion, *n.* Kohäsion´ *f.*

cohesive, *adj.* kohärent´.

cohort, *n.* Kohor´te, -n *f.*

coiffure, *n.* Frisur´, -en *f.*

coil, 1. *n.* Rolle, -n *f.; (elec.)* Spule, -n *f.* **2.** *vb.* auf•rollen; *(rope)* auf•schießen.

coin, 1. *n.* Münze, -n *f.* **2.** *vb.* prägen.

coinage, *n.* Prägung, -en *f.*

coincide, *vb.* zusam´men•treffen*.

coincidence, *n.* Zufall, ¨e *m.*

coincident, *adj.* gleichzeitig.

coincidental, *adj.* zufällig.

cold, 1. *n.* Kälte, -n *f.; (med.)* Erkäl´tung, -en *f.* **2.** *adj.* kalt (≐).

cold-blooded, *adj.* kaltblütig.

collaborate, *vb.* zusam´men•arbeiten, mit•arbeiten.

collaboration, *n.* Mitarbeit *f.*

collaborator, *n.* Mitarbeiter, - *m.,* Mitarbeiterin, -nen *f.*

collapse, 1. *n.* Zusam´menbruch ¨e *m.* **2.** *vb.* zusam´men•brechen*.

collar, *n.* Kragen, - *m.*

collarbone, *n.* Schlüsselbein, -e *nt.*

collate, *vb.* verglei´chen*.

collateral, 1. *n. (econ.)* Deckung *f.* **2.** *adj.* kollat- eral´.

colleague, *n.* Kolle´ge, -n, - n *m.,* Kolle´gin, -nen *f.*

collect, *vb.* sammeln; *(money)* ein•kassieren.

collection, *n.* Sammlung, - en *f.; (church)* Kollek´te, -n *f.*

collective, *adj.* kollektiv´.

collector, *n. (art.)* Sammler, - *m.,* Sammlerin, -nen *f.; (tickets)* Schaffner, - *m.; (tax)* Steuereinnehmer, - *m.*

college, *n.* College, -s *nt.*

collegiate, *adj.* College- *(cpds.).*

collide, *vb.* zusam´men•stoßen*.

collision, *n.* Zusam´menstoß, ¨e *m.*

colloquial, *adj.* umgangssprachlich.

colloquialism, *n.* umgangssprachlicher Ausdruck, ≈e *m.*

collusion, *n.* Kollusion´, -en *f.*

Cologne, *n.* Köln *nt.*

colon, *n.* *(typogr.)* Doppelpunkt, -e *m.;* Kolon, -s *or* Kola *nt.; (med.)* Dickdarm, ≈e *m.,* Kolon, -s *or* Kola *nt.*

colonel, *n.* Oberst, -en, -en *m.*

colonial, *adj.* kolonial´.

colonist, *n.* Siedler, - *m.,* Kolonist´, -en, -en *m.*

colonization, *n.* Kolonisation´, -en *f.*

colonize, *vb.* kolonisie´ren.

colony, *n.* Kolonie´, -i´en *f.*

color, **1.** *n.* Farbe, -n *f.* **2.** *vb.* färben.

colored, *adj.* farbig.

colorful, *adj.* farbenreich.

coloring, *n.* Färbung, -en *f.*

colorless, *adj.* farblos.

colossal, *adj.* kolossal´.

colt, *n.* Fohlen, - *nt.*

column, *n.* *(arch.)* Säule, -n *f.; (typogr.)* Spalte, -n *f.; (mil.)* Kolon´ne, -n *f.*

columnist, *n.* Zeitungsartikelschreiber, - *m.*

coma, *n.* Koma *nt.*

comb, **1.** *n.* Kamm, ≈e *m.* **2.** *vb.* kämmen.

combat, **1.** *n.* Kampf, ≈e *m.* **2.** *vb.* bekäm´pfen.

combatant, *n.* Kämpfer, - *m.*

combination, *n.* Kombination´, -en *f.*

combine, *vb.* verbin´den*, verei´nigen, zusam´men•setzen, kombinie´ren.

combustible, *adj.* (ver)brenn´bar.

combustion, *n.* Verbren´nung *f.*

come, *vb.* kommen*.

comedian, *n.* Komiker, - *m.*

comedienne, *n.* Komikerin, -nen *f.*

comedy, *n.* Komö´die, -n *f.*

come in, *interj.* herein´!

comely, *adj.* hübsch.

comet, *n.* Komet´, -en, -en *m.*

comfort, **1.** *n.* Behag´lichkeit, -en *f.,* Bequem´lichkeit, -en *f.* **2.** *vb.* trösten.

comfortable, *adj.* behag´lich, bequem´.

comforter, *n.* Steppdecke, -n *f.*

comic, comical, *adj.* komisch.

comma, *n.* Komma, -s *or* -ta *nt.*

command, **1.** *n.* Befehl´, -e *m.* **2.** *vb.* befeh´len*.

commandeer, *vb.* requirie´ren.

commander, *n.* Befehls´haber, - *m.; (navy)* Fregat´tenkapitän, -e *m.*

commander in chief, *n.* Oberbefehlshaber, - *m.*

commandment, *n.* Gebot´, -e *nt.*

commemorate, *vb.* geden´ken*.

commemoration, *n.* Gedächt´nisfeier, -n *f.*

commemorative, *adj.* Gedächt´nis- *(cpds.).*

commence, *vb.* begin´nen*.

commencement, *n.* Anfang, ≈e *m.; (college)* akade´mische Abschlußfeier, -n *f.*

commend, *vb.* *(praise)* loben; *(recommend)* empfeh´len*.

commendable, *adj.* lobenswert.

commendation, *n.* Lob *nt.,* Auszeichnung, -en *f.*

commensurate, *adj.* angemessen.

comment, **1.** *n.* Bemerkung, -en *f.* **2.** *vb.* bemer´ken.

commentary, *n.* Kommentar´, -e *m.*

commentator, *n.* Kommenta´tor, -o´ren *m.*

commerce, *n.* Handel *m.*

commercial, *adj.* kommerziell´, kaufmännisch; *(cpds.)* Handels-.

commercialism, *n.* Handelsgeist *m.*

commercialize, *vb.* in den Handel bringen*.

commiserate, *vb.* bemit´leiden.

commissary, *n.* Kommissar´, -e *m.,* Kommissa´rin, -nen *f.; (store)* Militärversor´gungsstelle, -n *f.*

commission, **1.** *n.* *(committee)* Kommissi´on, -en *f.; (percentage)* Provision´, -en *f.; (assignment)* Auftrag, ≈e *m.* **2.** *vb.* beauf´tragen; *(mil.)* das Offiziers´patent verlei´hen*.

commissioner, *n.* Beauf´tragt- *m.*

commit, *vb.* *(give over)* an•vertrauen; *(crime)* bege´hen*; *(oneself)* sich verpflich´ten.

commitment, *n.* Verpflich´tung, -en *f.*

committee, *n.* Ausschuß, ≈sse *m.*

commodity, *n.* Ware, -n *f.*

common, *adj.* allgemein´, gewöhn´lich; *(vulgar)* ordinär´.

commonness, *n.* Häufigkeit *f.*

commonplace, **1.** *n.* Gemein´platz, ≈e *m.* **2.** *adj.* abgedroschen.

commonwealth, *n.* Commonwealth *nt.*

commotion, *n.* Aufruhr *m.*

communal, *adj.* Gemein´de- *(cpds.).*

commune, **1.** *n.* Gemein´de, -n *f.* **2.** *vb.* kommunizie´ren.

communicable, *adj.* mitteilbar; *(med.)* ansteckbar.

communicant, *n.* Kommunikant´, -en, -en *m.*

communicate, *vb.* mit•teilen.

communication, *n.* Mitteilung, -en *f.*

communicative, *adj.* mitteilsam.

communion, *n.* Gemein´schaft *f.; (eccl.)* Abendmahl *nt.; (Catholic)* Kommunion´, -en *f.*

communiqué, *n.* Kommuniqué´ -s *nt.*

communism, *n.* Kommunis´mus *m.*

communist, **1.** *n.* Kommunist´, -en, -en *m.,* Kom-

munis´tin, -nen *f.* **2.** *adj.*
kommuni´stisch.

communistic, *adj.* kom-
muni´stisch.

community, *n.* Gemein´de, -
n *f.*, Gemein´schaft, -en *f.*

commutation, *n.* Austausch
m.; (law) Milderung *f.*

commute, *vb.* pendeln; *(jur)*
herab•setzen.

commuter, *n.* Pendler, - *m.*,
Pendlerin, -nen *f.*

compact, 1. *n. (cosmetics)*
Puderdose, -n *f.* **2.** *adj.*
kompakt´.

compactness, *n.* Kompakt´-
heit *f.*

companion, *n.* Beglei´ter
m., Beglei´terin, -nen *f.*

companionable, *adj.* gesel´-
lig.

companionship, *n.* Kam-
erad´schaft, -en *f.*

company, *n.* Gesell´schaft,
-en *f.*, Firma, -men *f.*

comparable, *adj.*
vergleich´bar.

comparative, 1. *n. (gram.)*
Komparativ, -e *m.* **2.** *adj.*
verhält´nismäßig.

compare, *vb.* verglei´chen*.

comparison, *n.* Vergleich´, -
e *m.*

compartment, *n.* Abtei´lung,
-en *f.*, Fach, ˝er *nt.; (train)*
Abteil, -e *nt.*

compass, *n. (naut.)* Kompaß, -sse *m.; (geom.)*
Zirkel, - *m.*

compassion, *n.* Mitleid *nt.*,
Erbar´men *nt.*

compassionate, *adj.* mitleidig.

compatible, *adj.*
verträg´lich.

compatriot, *n.* Landsmann,
-leute *m.*, Landsmännin,
-nen *f.*

compel, *vb.* zwingen*.

compensate, *vb.* entschä´-
digen, kompensie´ren.

compensation, *n.* Entschä´-
digung, -en *f.*, Kompen-
sation´, -en *f.*

compete, *vb.* wetteifern,
konkurrie´ren.

competence, *n. (ability)*
Fähigkeit, -en *f.; (field*

of responsibility)
Zuständigkeit, -en *f.*

competent, *adj. (able)* fähig;
(responsible) zuständig.

competition, *n.* Wettbewerb,
-e *m.*, Konkurrenz´, -en *f.*

competitive, *adj.* auf
Konkurrenz´ eingestellt.

competitor, *n.* Mitbewerber,
- *m.*, Mitbewerberin, -nen
f. Konkurrent´, -en, -en
m., Konkurren´tin, -nen *f.*

compile, *vb.*
zusam´men•tragen*.

complacency, *n.* Selbstzufriedenheit *f.*

complacent, *adj.* selbstzufrieden.

complain, *vb.* sich bekla´gen,
sich beschwe´ren.

complaint, *n.* Klage, -n *f.*,
Beschwer´de, -n *f.*

complement, 1. *n.*
Ergän´zung, -en *f.* **2.** *vb.*
ergän´zen.

complete, 1. *vb.* vollen´den.
2. *adj.* vollständig, fertig.

completely, *adv.* völlig.

completion, *n.* Vollen´dung,
-en *f.*

complex, 1. *n.* Komplex´, -e
m. **2.** *adj.* komplex´,
weitläufig.

complexion, *n. (type)* Natur´
f.; (skin) Teint, -s *m.*

complexity, *n.* Weitläu-
figkeit, -en *f.*

compliance, *n.*
Bereit´willigkeit *f.*, Ein-
willigen *nt.*

compliant, *adj.*
bereit´willig, nachgiebig.

complicate, *vb. (make more
complex)* verwi´ckeln;
(make harder)
erschwe´ren.

complicated, *adj.* kom-
pliziert´, verwi´ckelt.

complication, *n.* Komplika-
tion´, -en *f.*

compliment, 1. *n.* Kompli-
ment´, -e *nt.* **2.** *vb.*
beglück´wünschen.

complimentary, *adj.* schmeichelhaft; *(free)* Frei-
(cpds.).

comply, *vb.* ein•willigen,
sich fügen.

component, *n.* Bestand´teil,
-e *m.*

compose, *vb.*
zusam´men•setzen;
(music) komponie´ren.

composer, *n.* Komponist´, -
en, -en *m.*, Komponis´tin,
-nen *f.*

composite, *adj.* zusam´-
mengesetzt.

composition, *n.* Zusam´-
mensetzung, -en *f.;
(school)* Aufsatz, ˝e *m.;
(mus.)* Komposition´, -en
f.

composure, *n.* Fassung *f.*

compote, *n.* Kompott´, - *e nt.*

compound, 1. *n.* Mischung,
-en *f.; (gram.)*
Kompo´situm, -ta *nt.;
(chem.)* Verbin´dung, -en
f.; (mil.) eingezäunte
Lagerabteilung, -en *f.* **2.**
adj. zusam´mengesetzt;
(c. interest) Zinseszins
m. **3.** *vb.* zusam´men•set-
zen.

comprehend, *vb.* verste´-
hen*, begrei´fen*.

comprehensible, *adj.* ver-
ständ´lich.

comprehension, *n.* Fassungsvermögen, - *nt.*

comprehensive, *adj.*
umfas´send.

compress, 1. *n.*
Kompres´se, -n *f.* **2** *vb.*
zusam´men•pressen.

compressed, *adj.* Press-
(cpds.).

compression, *n.* Kompres-
sion´, -en *f.*

comprise, *vb.* umfas´sen,
enthal´ten*.

compromise, 1. *n.* Kompro-
miß´, -sse *m.* **2.** *vb.* einen
Kompromiß schließen*;
(embarrass)* kompromit-
tie´ren.

compulsion, *n.* Zwang *m.*

compulsive, *adj.* Zwangs-
(cpds.).

compulsory, *adj.* obligato´-
risch.

compunction, *n.*
Beden´ken, - *nt.*

computation, *n.* Berech´-
nung, -en *f.*

compute, *vb.* rechnen, berech´nen.

computer, *n.* Komputer, - *m.;* Elektro´nenrechner, - *m.*

computerize, *vb.* auf Komputer umstellen.

computer science, *n.* Kompu´terwissenschaft *f.*

comrade, *n.* Kamerad´, -en, - en *m.,* Kamera´din, -nen *f.*

concave, *adj.* konkav´.

conceal, *vb.* verste´cken, verheim´lichen.

concealment, *n.* Versteck´, -e *nt.,* Verheim´lichung, -en *f.*

concede, *vb.* zu•gestehen*.

conceit, *n.* Einbildung, -en *f.*

conceited, *adj.* eingebildet.

conceivable, *adj.* vorstellbar.

conceivably, *adv.* unter Umständen.

conceive, *vb.* begrei´fen*, sich vor•stellen; *(child)* empfan´gen*.

concentrate, *vb.* konzentrie´ren.

concentration camp, *n.* Konzentrations´lager, - *nt.*

concept, *n.* Begriff´, -e *m.*

concern, 1. *n. (affair)* Angelegenheit, -en *f.; (interest)* Interes´se, -n *nt.; (firm)* Konzern´, -e *m.; (worry)* Sorge, -n *f.* **2.** *vb.* an•gehen*.

concerning, *prep.* hinsichtlich.

concert, *n.* Konzert´, -e *nt.*

concession, *n.* Konzession´, -en *f.*

concierge, *n.* Portier´, -s *m.*

conciliate, *vb.* versöh´nen, schlichten.

conciliation, *n.* Versöh´nung, -en *f.,* Schlichtung, -en *f.*

conciliator, *n.* Schlichter, - *m.*

conciliatory, *adj.* versöh´nend.

concise, *adj.* knapp, gedrängt´.

conciseness, *n.* Gedrängt´heit *f.*

conclude, *vb.* schließen*.

conclusion, *n.* Abschluß, ¨sse *m.,* Schluß, ¨sse *m.*

conclusive, *adj.* entschei´dend.

concoct, *vb.* zusam´men•brauen.

concoction, *n.* Gebräu´, -e *nt.*

concomitant, *adj.* beglei´tend.

concord, *n.* Eintracht *f.*

concourse, *n.* Sammelplatz, ¨e *m.*

concrete, 1. *n.* Zement´ *m.* **2.** *adj.* konkret´.

concubine, *n.* Konkubi´ne, -n *f.*

concur, *vb.* überein´•stimmen.

concurrence, *n.* Zustimmung, -en *f.*

concurrent, *adj. (simultaneous)* gleichzeitig; *(agreeing)* überein´stimmend.

concussion, *n.* Erschüt´terung, -en *f.; (brain)* Gehirn´erschütterung, -en *f.*

condemn, *vb.* verur´teilen; *(disapprove)* mißbil´ligen.

condemnable, *adj.* strafbar; nichtswürdig.

condemnation, *n.* Verur´teilung *f.;* Mißbilligung *f.*

condensation, *n.* Kondensation´, -en *f.; (summary)* Zusam´menfassung, -en *f.*

condense, *vb.* kondensie´ren; *(summarize)* zusam´men•fassen.

condenser, *n.* Kondensa´tor, -o´ren *m.*

condescend, *vb.* sich herab´•lassen*.

condescending, *adj.* herab´lassend.

condescension, *n.* Herab´lassung, -en *f.*

condiment, *n.* Gewürz´, -e *nt.*

condition, 1. *n. (stipulation)* Bedin´gung, -en *f.; (state)* Zustand, ¨e *m.* **2.** *vb.* bedin´gen; *(training)* in Form bringen*.

conditional, *adj.* abhängig.

conditionally, *adv.* unter gewissen Bedingungen.

condolence, *n.* Beileid *nt.*

condom, *n.* Kondom, -s *m.*

condominium, *n.* Eigentumswohnung, -en *f.*

condone, *vb.* entschul´digen.

conducive, *adj.* förderlich.

conduct, 1. *n.* Betra´gen *nt.* **2.** *vb.* leiten; *(behave)* sich betra´gen*; *(music)* dirigie´ren.

conductor, *n.* Leiter, - *m.,* Leiterin, -nen *f.; (train)* Schaffner, - *m.,* Schaffnerin, -nen *f.; (music)* Dirigent´, -en, -en *m.,* Dirigen´tin, -nen *f.*

conduit, *n.* Leitungsrohr, -e *nt.*

cone, *n.* Kegel, - *m.; (pine)* Tannenzapfen, - *m.*

confection, *n.* Konfekt´, -e *nt.*

confectioner, *n.* Zuckerbäcker, - *m.*

confectionery, *n.* Zuckerwerk *nt.*

confederacy, *n.* Bündnis, -se *nt.; (conspiracy)* Verschwö´rung, -en *f.*

confederate, 1. *n.* Helfershelfer, - *m.* **2.** *adj.* verbün´det.

confederation, *n.* Staatenbund, ¨e *m.*

confer, *vb. (bestow)* verlei´hen*; *(counsel)* berat´schlagen.

conference, *n.* Bespre´chung, -en *f.,* Konferenz´, -en *f.*

confess, *vb.* zu•gestehen*; *(eccles.)* beichten.

confession, *n.* Geständ´nis, -se *nt.; (eccles.)* Beichte, -n *f.*

confessional, *n.* Beichtstuhl, ¨e *m.*

confessor, *n.* Beken´ner, - *m.; (father c.)* Beichtvater, ¨ *m.*

confidant, *n.* Vertraut´- *m.*

confidante, *n.* Vertraut´- *f.*

confide, *vb.* vertrau´en; sich an•vertrauen.

confidence, *n. (trust)* Vertrau´en *nt.; (assurance)* Zuversicht *f.*

confident, *adj.* zuversichtlich.

confidential, *adj.* vertrau´lich.

confidentially, *adv.* unter uns.

confine, *vb.* beschrän´ken; *(imprison)* ein•sperren.
confirm, *vb.* bestä´tigen; *(church)* konfirmie´ren.
confirmation, *n.* Bestä´tigung, -en *f.; (church)* Konfirmation´, -en *f.*
confiscate, *vb.* beschlag´nahmen, konfiszie´ren.
confiscation, *n.* Beschlag´nahme, -n *f.*
conflagration, *n.* Brand, ⸗e *m.,* Feuersbrunst *f.*
conflict, 1. *n.* Konflikt´, -e *m.* **2.** *vb.* in Widerspruch stehen*, nicht überein•stimmen.
conform, *vb.* sich an•passen.
conformation, *n.* Anpassung, -en *f.; (shape)* Gestal´tung, -en *f.*
conformer, conformist, *n.* Mitmacher, - *m.*
conformity, *n.* Überein´stimmung, -en *f.*
confound, *vb. (make confused)* verwir´ren; **(c. A with B)** A mit B verwech´seln; **(c. it!)** zum Donnerwetter!
confront, *vb.* gegenü´ber•stellen, konfrontie´ren.
confuse, *vb. (make confused)* verwir´ren; **(c. A with B)** A mit B verwech´seln.
confusion, *n.* Verwir´rung, -en *f.;* Durcheinan´der *nt.;* Verwechs´lung, -en *f.*
congeal, *vb.* erstar´ren.
congenial, *adj.* sympa´thisch.
congenital, *adj.* angeboren.
congestion, *n.* Stauung, -en *f.*
conglomerate, 1. *n.* Anhäufung, -en *f.* **2.** *vb.* zusam´men•ballen.
conglomeration, *n.* Anhäufung, -en *f.*
congratulate, *vb.* gratulie´ren, beglück´wünschen.
congratulation, *n.* Glückwunsch, ⸗e *m.*
congratulatory, *adj.* Glückwunsch- *(cpds.).*
congregate, *vb.* sich versam´meln.

congregation, *n. (church)* Gemein´de, -n *f.*
congress, *n.* Kongreß´, -sse *m.*
congressional, *adj.* Kongreß´- *(cpds.).*
conjecture, 1. *n.* Mutmaßung, -en *f.* **2.** *vb.* mutmaßen.
conjugal, *adj.* ehelich.
conjugate, *vb.* konjugie´ren.
conjugation, *n.* Konjugation´, -en *f.*
conjunction, *n.* Zusam´mentreffen, - *nt.; (gram.)* Bindewort, ⸗er *nt.,* Konjunktion´, -en *f.*
conjunctive, *adj.* verbin´dend.
conjunctivitis, *n.* Bindehautentzündung, -en *f.*
conjure, *vb.* zaubern.
connect, *vb.* verbin´den*.
connection, *n.* Verbin´dung, -en *f.*
connive, *vb.* in heimlichem Einverständnis stehen*.
connoisseur, *n.* Kenner, - *m.*
connotation, *n.* Nebenbedeutung, -en *f.,* Beiklang, ⸗e *m.*
connote, *vb.* in sich schließen*.
conquer, *vb.* ero´bern.
conqueror, *n.* Ero´berer, - *m.*
conquest, *n.* Ero´berung, -en *f.*
conscience, *n.* Gewis´sen, - *nt.*
conscientious, *adj.* gewis´senhaft.
conscious, *adj.* bewußt´, bei Bewußt´sein.
consciousness, *n.* Bewußt´sein *nt.*
conscript, *n.* Dienstpflichtig- *m.*
conscription, *n.* Militär´dienstpflicht *f.*
consecrate, *vb.* weihen.
consecration, *n.* Weihung, -en *f.*
consecutive, *adj.* aufeinan´derfolgend.
consensus, *n.* allgemeine Meinung, -en *f.*
consent, 1. *n.* Zustimmung, -en *f.* **2.** *vb.* zu•stimmen.

consequence, *n.* Folge, -n *f.*
consequent, *adj.* folgend.
consequential, *adj.* folgenreich.
consequently, *adv.* folglich.
conservation, *n.* Bewah´rung, -en *f.;* Konservie´rung, -en *f.*
conservatism, *n.* Konservatis´mus *m.*
conservative, *adj.* konservativ´.
conservatory, *n. (music)* Konservato´rium, -rien *nt.; (plants)* Treibhaus, ⸗er *nt.*
conserve, *vb.* bewah´ren.
consider, *vb.* betrach´ten; *(take into account)* berück´sichtigen.
considerable, *adj.* beträcht´lich.
considerate, *adj.* rücksichtsvoll.
consideration, *n. (thought)* Erwä´gung, -en *f.; (kindness)* Rücksicht, -en *f.;* **(in c. of)** in Anbetracht.
consign, *vb.* übersen´den*.
consignment, *n.* Übersen´dung, -en *f.*
consist, *vb.* beste´hen*.
consistency, *n.* Folgerichtigkeit *f.; (substance)* Konsistenz´ *f.*
consistent, *adj.* folgerichtig, konsequent´.
consolation, *n.* Trost *m.*
console, *vb.* trösten.
consolidate, *vb.* festigen, konsolidie´ren.
consommé, *n.* Bouillon´, -s *f.*
consonant, *n.* Konsonant´, -en, -en *m.*
consort, 1. *n.* Gemahl´, -e *m.;* Gemah´lin, -nen *f.* **2.** *vb.* verkeh´ren.
conspicuous, *adj.* auffällig.
conspiracy, *n.* Verschwö´rung, -en *f.*
conspirator, *n.* Verschwö´rer, - *m.,* Verschwö´rerin, -nen *f.*
conspire, *vb.* sich verschwö´ren*.
constancy, *n.* Standhaftigkeit *f.*

constant, *adj.* bestän´dig, konstant´.

constantly, *adv.* dauernd.

constellation, *n.* Konstellation´, -en *f.*

consternation, *n.* Bestür´zung, -en *f.*

constipated, *adj.* verstopft´.

constipation, *n.* Verstop´fung, -en *f.*

constituency, *n.* (people) Wählerschaft, -en *f.;* (place) Wahlbezirk, -e *m.*

constituent, *n.* Bestand´teil, -e *m.;* (voter) Wähler, - *m.,* Wählerin, -nen *f.*

constitute, *vb.* (make up) aus•machen; (found) gründen.

constitution, *n.* Konstitution´, -en *f.;* (government) Verfas´sung, -en *f.*

constitutional, *adj.* konstitutionell´.

constrain, *vb.* zwingen*.

constrict, *vb.* zusam´men•ziehen*.

construct, *vb.* konstruie´ren.

construction, *n.* Konstruktion´, -en *f.*

constructive, *adj.* positiv.

construe, *vb.* aus•legen.

consul, *n.* Konsul, -n, *m.*

consular, *adj.* konsula´risch.

consulate, *n.* Konsulat´, -e *nt.*

consult, *vb.* zu Rate ziehen*; konsultie´ren.

consultant, *n.* Bera´ter, - *m.,* Bera´terin, -nen *f.*

consultation, *n.* Konferenz´, -en *f.;* (med.) Konsultation´, -en *f.*

consume, *vb.* verzeh´ren, verbrau´chen.

consumer, *n.* Verbrau´cher, - *m.*

consummate, 1. *vb.* vollen´den. 2. *adj.* vollen´det.

consummation, *n.* Vollzie´hung, -en *f.*

consumption, *n.* Verbrauch´ *m.;* (med.) Schwindsucht *f.*

consumptive, *adj.* schwindsüchtig.

contact, 1. *n.* Kontakt´, -e *m.* 2. *vb.* sich in Verbin´dung setzen mit.

contagion, *n.* Ansteckung, -en *f.*

contagious, *adj.* ansteckend.

contain, *vb.* enthal´ten*.

container, *n.* Behäl´ter, - *m.*

contaminate, *vb.* verun´reinigen.

contemplate, *vb.* betrach´ten.

contemplation, *n.* Betrach´tung, -en *f.*

contemplative, *adj.* nachdenklich.

contemporary, 1. *n.* Zeitgenosse, -n, -n, *m.,* Zeitgenossin, -nen *f.* 2. *adj.* zeitgenössisch.

contempt, *n.* Verach´tung, -en *f.*

contemptible, *adj.* verach´tenswert.

contemptuous, *adj.* veräch´tlich.

contend, *vb.* (assert) behaup´ten; (fight) streiten*.

contender, *n.* Streiter, - *m.*

content, 1. *n.* Inhalt *m.* 2. *adj.* zufrie´den.

contented, *adj.* zufrie´den.

contention, *n.* (assertion) Behaup´tung, -en *f.;* (fight) Streit, -e *m.*

contentment, *n.* Zufrie´denheit *f.*

contest, 1. *n.* Wettstreit, -e *m.;* (advertising) Preisausschreiben, - *nt.* 2. *vb.* bestrei´ten*.

contestant, *n.* Bewer´ber, - *m.,* Bewer´berin, -nen *f.*

context, *n.* Zusam´menhang, =e *m.*

continent, 1. *n.* Kontinent, -e *m.* 2. *adj.* enthalt´sam.

continental, *adj.* kontinental´.

contingency, *n.* Eventualität´, -en *f.*

continual, *adj.* dauernd.

continuation, *n.* Fortsetzung, -en *f.*

continue, *vb.* (tr.) fort•setzen; (intr.) fort•fahren*.

continuity, *n.* Fortdauer *f.*

continuous, *adj.* fortdauernd.

contort, *vb.* verdre´hen.

contortion, *n.* Verdre´hung, -en *f.*

contour, *n.* Umriß, -sse *m.*

contraband, *n.* Schmuggelware, -n *f.*

contraception, *n.* Empfängnisverhütung *f.*

contraceptive device, *n.* Verhütungsmittel, - *nt.*

contract, 1. *n.* Vertrag´, =e *m.* 2. *vb.* vertrag´lich ab•schließen*; (disease) sich zu•ziehen*.

contraction, *n.* Zusam´menziehung, -en *f.*

contractor, *n.* Bauunternehmer, - *m.*

contradict, *vb.* widerspre´chen*.

contradiction, *n.* Widerspruch, =e *m.*

contradictory, *adj.* widerspre´chend.

contralto, *n.* Altstimme, -n *f.*

contraption, *n.* Vorrichtung, -en *f.*

contrary, 1. *n.* Gegenteil, -e *nt.* 2. *adj.* (opposite) entge´gengesetzt; (obstinate) widerspenstig.

contrast, 1. *n.* Gegensatz, =e *m.* 2. *vb.* entge´gen•setzen.

contribute, *vb.* bei•tragen*.

contribution, *n.* Beitrag, =e *m.,* Beiträgerin, -nen *f.*

contributor, *n.* Beiträger, - *m.,* Beiträgerin, -nen *f.*

contributory, *adj.* mitwirkend.

contrite, *adj.* zerknirscht´.

contrivance, *n.* Vorrichtung, -en *f.*

contrive, *vb.* fertig bringen*, erfin´den*.

control, 1. *n.* Kontrol´le, -n *f.* 2. *vb.* beherr´schen.

controllable, *adj.* kontrollier´bar.

controller, *n.* Überprü´fer, - *m.*

controversial, *adj.* strittig.

controversy, *n.* Streitfrage, -n *f.*

contusion, *n.* Quetschung, -en *f.*

convalesce, *vb.* gene´sen*.

convalescence, *n.* Konvaleszenz´ *f.*

convalescent, *adj.* gene´send.

convene, *vb.* zusam´men•kommen*.

convenience, *n.* Annehmlichkeit, -en *f.*

convenient, *adj.* bequem´, geeig´net.

convent, *n.* Nonnenkloster, ⁼ *nt.*

convention, *n.* Versamm´lung, -en *f.,* Tagung, -en *f.; (contract)* Abkommen, - *nt.; (tradition)* Konvention´, -en *f.*

conventional, *adj.* konventionell´.

converge, *vb.* zusam´men•laufen*.

convergence, *n.* Konvergenz´, -en *f.*

convergent, *adj.* konvergie´rend.

conversant with, *adj.* bewan´dert in.

conversational, *adj.* Gesprächs´- *(cpds.).*

converse, 1. *n.* Kehrseite, -n *f.* **2.** *vb.* sich unterhal´ten*. **3.** *adj.* umgekehrt.

convert, 1. *n.* Konvertit´, -en, -en *m.* **2.** *vb. (belief, goods, money)* konvertie´ren; *(missionary)* bekeh´ren.

converter, *n.* Bekeh´rer, - *m.; (elec.)* Transforma´tor, -o´ren *m.*

convertible, 1. *n. (auto)* Kabriolett´, -s *nt.* **2.** *adj.* konvertier´bar.

convex, *adj.* konvex´.

convey, *vb.* beför´dern, übermit´teln.

conveyance, *n. (vehicle)* Beför´derungsmittel, - *nt.;* Übermitt´lung, -en *f.*

conveyor, *n.* Beför´derer, - *m.*

convict, 1. *n.* Sträfling, -e *m.* **2.** *vb.* überfüh´ren.

conviction, *n.* Schuldigsprechung, -en *f.; (belief)* Überzeu´gung, -en *f.*

convince, *vb.* überzeu´gen.

convincing, *adj.* überzeu´gend.

convivial, *adj.* gesel´lig.

convocation, *n.* Versamm´lung, -en *f.*

convoy, 1. *n.* Geleit´zug, ⁼e *m.* **2.** *vb.* gelei´ten.

convulse, *vb.* in Zuckungen versetzen; **(be c.d)** sich krümmen.

convulsion, *n.* Krampf, ⁼e *m.*

convulsive, *adj.* krampfhaft.

cook, 1. *n.* Koch, ⁼e *m.;* Köchin, -nen *f.* **2.** *vb.* kochen.

cookbook, *n.* Kochbuch, ⁼er *nt.*

cookie, *n.* Keks, -e *m.*

cool, 1. *adj.* kühl. **2.** *vb.* ab•kühlen.

coolness, *n.* Kühle, *f.*

coop, *n.* Hühnerkorb, ⁼e *m.*

cooperate, *vb.* zusam´men•arbeiten.

cooperation, *n.* Zusam´menarbeit, -en *f.*

cooperative, 1. *n.* Konsum´verein, -e *m.* **2.** *adj.* hilfsbereit.

coordinate, 1. *adj.* beigeordnet, koordiniert´. **2.** *vb.* bei•orden, koordinie´ren.

coordination, *n.* Beiordnung, -en *f.;* Koordination´, -en *f.*

coordinator, *n.* Organisations´planer, - *m.*

cop, *n.* Schupo, -s *m.*

cope, *vb.* sich ab•mühen.

copier, *n.* Kopier´maschine, -n *f.*

copious, *adj.* reichlich.

copper, *n.* Kupfer *nt.*

copy, 1. *n.* Abschrift, -en *f.,* Kopie´, -i´en *f.; (book)* Exemplar´, -e *nt.* **2.** *vb.* ab•schreiben*, kopie´ren.

copyright, *n.* Urheberrecht, -e *nt.*

coquette, 1. *n.* Koket´te, -n *f.* **2.** *adj.* kokett´.

coral, *n.* Koral´le, -n *f.*

cord, *n.* Schnur, ⁼e *f.*

cordial, *adj.* herzlich.

cordiality, *n.* Herzlichkeit *f.*

cordovan, *n.* Korduanleder, - *nt.*

core, *n. (fruit)* Kernhaus, ⁼er *nt.; (heart)* Kern, -e *m.*

cork, *n. (material)* Kork *m.; (stopper)* Korken, - *m.*

corkscrew, *n.* Korkenzieher, - *m.*

corn, *n. (grain)* Getrei´de *nt.; (maize)* Mais *m.; (foot)* Hühnerauge, -n *nt.*

cornea, *n.* Hornhaut, ⁼e *f.*

corner, *n.* Ecke, -n *f.*

cornet, *n.* Kornett´, -e *nt.*

cornice, *n.* Gesims´, -e *nt.*

corn-plaster, *n.* Hühneraugenpflaster, - *nt.*

cornstarch, *n.* Maize´na *nt.*

coronation, *n.* Krönung, -en *f.*

coronet, *n.* Adelskrone, -n *f.*

corporal, 1. *n. (mil.)* Gefreit- *m.* **2.** *adj.* körperlich.

corporate, *adj.* körperschaftlich.

corporation, *n.* Körperschaft, -en *f.; (comm.)* Aktiengesellschaft, -en *f.*

corps, *n.* Korps, - *nt.*

corpse, *n.* Leichnam, -e *m.*

corpulent, *adj.* korpulent´.

corpuscle, *n.* Körperchen, - *nt.*

correct, 1. *adj.* richtig, korrekt´. **2.** *vb.* verbes´sern, berich´tigen, korrigie´ren.

correction, *n.* Verbes´serung, -en *f.,* Berich´tigung, -en *f.*

corrective, *adj.* korrektiv´.

correctness, *n.* Korrekt´heit, -en *f.*

correlate, *vb.* aufeinan´der bezie´hen*.

correlation, *n.* Korrelation´, -en *f.*

correspond, *vb.* entspre´chen*; *(agree)* überein´•stimmen; *(letters)* korrespondie´ren.

correspondence, *n.* Entspre´chung, -en *f.; (agreement)* Überein´stimmung, -en *f.; (letters)* Korrespondenz, -en *f.*

correspondent, *n.* Korrespondent´, -en, -en *m.,* Korresponden´tin, -nen *f.*

corridor, *n.* Korridor, -e *m.*

corroborate, *vb.* bestä´tigen.

corroboration, *n.* Bestä´tigung, -en *f.*

corrode, *vb.* korrodie´ren.

corrosion, n. Korrosion´, -en f.

corrugate, vb. wellen.

corrupt, 1. vb. korrumpie´-ren. **2.** adj. korrupt´.

corrupter, n. Verführ´rer, m. Verführ´rerin, -nen f.

corruptible, adj. verführ´bar.

corruption, n. Korruption´, -en f.

corsage, n. Ansteckblume, -n f.

corset, n. Korsett´, -s nt.

cortège, n. Leichenzug, ‑e m.

cosmetic, 1. n. kosme´tisches Mittel, - nt. **2.** adj. kosme´tisch.

cosmic, adj. kosmisch.

cosmopolitan, adj. kosmopoli´tisch.

cosmos, n. Kosmos m.

cost, 1. n. Preis, -e m.; Kosten pl. **2.** vb. kosten.

costliness, n. Kostspieligkeit, -en f.

costly, adj. kostspielig.

costume, n. (fancy) Kostüm, -e nt.; (native) Tracht, -en f.

cot, n. Feldbett, -en nt.

cottage, n. Häuschen, - nt.; Landhaus, ‑er nt.

cotton, n. Baumwolle f.; Watte f.

couch, n. Couch, -es f.

cough, 1. n. Husten m. **2.** vb. husten.

could, vb. (was able) konnte: (would be able) könnte.

council, n. Rat, ‑e m.

counsel, 1. n. Rat, ‑e m.; (lawyer) Anwalt, ‑e m., Anwältin, -nen f. **2.** vb. bera´ten*, raten*.

counselor, n. Bera´ter, - m., Bera´terin, -nen f.

count, 1. n. Gesamt´zahl, -en f.; (noble) Graf, -en, -en m. **2.** vb. zählen.

countenance, n. Gesicht´, -er nt.

counter, 1. n. Zähler, - m.; (store) Ladentisch, -e m. **2.** adv. (c. to) entge´gen.

counteract, vb. entge´gen•arbeiten.

counterattack, 1. n. Gegenangriff, -e m. **2.** vb. einen Gegenangriff machen.

counterbalance, 1. n. Gegengewicht, -e nt. **2.** vb. auf•wiegen*.

counterfeit, 1. n. Falschgeld, -er nt. **2.** adj. gefälscht´. **3.** vb. fälschen.

countermand, vb. widerru´-fen*.

counteroffensive, n. Gegenoffensive, -n f.

counterpart, n. Gegenstück, -e nt.

countess, n. Gräfin, -nen f.

countless, adj. zahllos.

country, n. Land, ‑er nt.

countryman, n. Landsmann, -leute m.

countryside, n. Landschaft, -en f.

county, n. Grafschaft, -en f.

coupé, n. geschlossenes Zweisitzer-Auto, -s nt.

couple, 1. n. Paar, -e nt. **2.** vb. koppeln.

coupon, n. Coupon´, -s m.

courage, n. Mut m.

courageous, adj. mutig.

courier, n. Kurier´, -e m.

course, n. Lauf, ‑e m.; (race) Rennbahn, -en f.; (nautical) Kurs, -e m.; (school) Kursus, Kurse m.; (food) Gang, ‑e m.; (of c.) natür´lich.

court, 1. n. Hof, ‑e m. **2.** vb. den Hof machen.

courteous, adj. höflich.

courtesan, n. Kurtisa´ne, -n f.

courtesy, n. Höflichkeit, -en f.

courthouse, n. Gerichts´-gebäude, - nt.

courtier, n. Höfling, -e m.

courtly, adj. höfisch.

court-martial, n. Kriegsgericht, -e nt.

courtroom, n. Gerichts´saal, -säle m.

courtship, n. Freien nt.

courtyard, n. Hof, ‑e m.

cousin, n. Vetter, -n m.; Cousi´ne, -n f.

covenant, n. Vertrag´, ‑e m.

cover, 1. n. Deckel, - m. **2.** vb. bede´cken; (c. up) zu•decken.

covering, n. Bede´ckung, -en f.

covet, vb. begeh´ren.

covetous, adj. begie´rig.

cow, n. Kuh, ‑e f.

coward, n. Feigling, -e m.

cowardice, n. Feigheit, -en f.

cowardly, adj. feige.

cowboy, n. Cowboy, -s m.

cower, vb. kauern.

cowhide, n. Rindsleder, - nt.

coy, adj. spröde.

cozy, adj. behag´lich.

crab, n. Taschenkrebs, -e m.

crack, 1. n. Spalt, -e m., Sprung, ‑e m., Riß, -sse m. **2.** vb. brechen*, springen*.

cracker, n. Salzkeks, -e m.

cradle, n. Wiege, -n f.

craft, n. Kunstfertigkeit, -en f.; (ship) Schiff, -e nt.

craftsman, n. Handwerker, - m.

craftsmanship, n. Kunstfertigkeit, -en f.

crafty, adj. gewiegt´.

cram, vb. voll•stopfen; (exam) pauken.

cramp, n. Krampf, ‑e m.

crane, n. Kran, ‑e m.; (bird) Kranich, -e m.

crank, 1. n. (handle) Kurbel, -n f.; (crackpot) Sonderling, -e m. **2.** vb. an•kurbeln.

cranky, adj. mißvergnügt, grantig.

cranny, n. Ritze, -n f.

crash, 1. n. Krach m.; (collision) Zusam´menstoß, ‑e m.; (plane) Absturz, ‑e m. **2.** vb. krachen; zusam´men•stoßen*; ab•stürzen.

crate, n. Kiste, -n f.

crater, n. Krater, - m.

crave, vb. verlan´gen nach.

craving, n. gieriges Verlan´gen, - nt.

crawl, vb. kriechen*; (swimming) kraulen.

crayon, n. Buntstift, -e m.

crazed, adj. wahnsinnig.

crazy, adj. verrückt´.

creak, vb. knarren.

cream, *n.* Sahne *f.,* Rahm *m; (cosmetic)* Creme, -s *f.,* Krem, -s *m.*

creamery, *n.* Molkerei´, -en *f.*

creamy, *adj.* sahnig.

crease, 1. *n.* Falte, -n *f.* **2.** *vb.* falten.

create, *vb.* schaffen*, erschaf´fen*; erzeu´gen.

creation, *n.* Erschaf´fung, -en *f.;* Schöpfung, -en *f.*

creative, *adj.* schöpferisch.

creator, *n.* Schöpfer, - *m.*

creature, *n.* Geschöpf´, -e *nt.;* Wesen, - *nt.*

credentials, *n.pl.* Beglau´bigungsschreiben, - *nt.*

credibility, *n.* Glaubwürdigkeit *f.*

credible, *adj.* glaubwürdig.

credit, 1. *n.* Verdienst´, *nt.; (comm.)* Kredit´, -e *m.* **2.** *vb.* gut•schreiben*.

creditable, *adj.* anerkennenswert.

credit card, *n.* Kredit´karte, -n *f.*

creditor, *n.* Gläubig - *m.*

credo, *n.* Glaubensbekenntnnis, -se *nt.*

credulity, *n.* Leichtgläubigkeit *f.*

credulous, *adj.* leichtgläubig.

creed, *n.* Glaubensbekenntnis, -se *nt.*

creek, *n.* Bach, ⸗e *m.*

creep, *vb.* kriechen*.

cremate, *vb.* ein•äschern.

cremation, *n.* Einäscherung, -en *f.*

crematory, *n.* Kremato´rium, -rien *nt.*

crepe, *n.* Krepp *m.*

crescent, *n.* Mondsichel, -n *f.*

crest, *n.* Kamm, ⸗e *m.*

crestfallen, *adj.* geknickt´.

cretonne, *n.* Kretonn´e, -s *m.*

crevasse, *n.* Gletscherspalte, -n *f.*

crevice, *n.* Riß, -sse *m.*

crew, *n.* Mannschaft, -en *f.*

crib, *n.* Krippe, -n *f.; (bed)* Kinderbett, -en *nt.*

cricket, *n.* Grille, -n *f.*

crime, *n.* Verbre´chen, - *nt.*

criminal, 1. *n.* Verbre´cher, - *m.,* Verbre´cherin, -nen *f.* **2.** *adj.* verbre´cherisch.

criminology, *n.* Kriminalis´tik *f.*

crimson, *adj.* karmin´rot.

cringe, *vb.* sich krümmen.

cripple, 1. *n.* Krüppel, - *m.* **2.** *vb.* zum Krüppel machen; lähmen.

crippled, *adj.* verkrüp´pelt, gelähmt´.

crisis, *n.* Krise, -n *f.*

crisp, *adj. (weather, vegetables)* frisch; *(bread, etc.)* knusprig.

criterion, *n.* Krite´rium, - rien *nt.*

critic, *n.* Kritiker, - *m.,* Kritikerin, -nen *f.*

critical, *adj.* kritisch.

criticism, *n.* Kritik´, -en *f.*

criticize, *vb.* kritisie´ren.

croak, *vb.* krächzen.

crochet, *vb.* häkeln.

crock, *n.* Steintopf, ⸗e *m.*

crockery, *n.* Steingut *nt.*

crocodile, *n.* Krokodil´, -e *nt.*

crook, *n. (bend)* Biegung, -en *f.; (cheater)* Schwindler, - *m.,* Schwindlerin, -nen *f.*

crooked, *adj. (not straight)* krumm, schief; *(dishonest)* unehrlich, betrü´gerisch.

croon, *vb.* summen; *(jazz)* Schlager singen*.

crop, *n.* Ernte, -n *f.; (riding)* Peitsche, -n *f.*

croquet, *n.* Kroket´spiel *nt.*

croquette, *n.* Kroket´te, -n *f.*

cross, 1. *n.* Kreuz, -e *nt.; (mixture)* Kreuzung, -en *f.* **2.** *vb.* kreuzen.

cross-eyed, *adj.* **(be c.)** schielen.

crossing, *n.* Kreuzung, -en *f.*

crossroads, *n.pl.* Scheideweg, -e *m.;* Kreuzung, -en *f.*

cross section, *n.* Querschnitt, -e *m.*

crossword puzzle, *n.* Kreuzworträtsel, - *nt.*

crotch, *n. (trousers)* Schritt, -e *m.; (tree)* Gabelung, - en *f.*

crouch, *vb.* kauern.

croup, *n.* Krupp *m.*

crouton, *n.* Crouton´, -s *m.*

crow, 1. *n.* Krähe, -n *f.* **2.** *vb.* krähen.

crowd, 1. *n.* Menge, -n *f.* **2.** *vb.* drängeln.

crown, 1. *n.* Krone, -n *f.* **2.** *vb.* krönen.

crucial, *adj.* entschei´dend.

crucible, *n.* Schmelztiegel, - *m.*

crucifix, *n.* Kruzifix, -e *nt.*

crucifixion, *n.* Kreuzigung, -en *f.*

crucify, *vb.* kreuzigen.

crude, *adj.* roh, grob (÷).

crudeness, *n.* Grobheit, -en *f.,* Unfeinheit, -en *f.*

crudity, *n.* Roheit, -en *f.,* Unfeinheit, -en *f.*

cruel, *adj.* grausam.

cruelty, *n.* Grausamkeit, -en *f.*

cruise, 1. *n.* Seereise, -n *f.* **2.** *vb.* kreuzen.

cruiser, *n.* Kreuzer, - *m.*

crumb, *n.* Krümel, - *m.*

crumble, *vb.* zerbrö´ckeln.

crumple, *vb.* zerknül´len.

crusade, *n.* Kreuzzug, ⸗e *m.*

crusader, *n.* Kreuzzügler, - *m.*

crush, 1. *n. (crowd)* Gedrän´ge *nt.* **2.** *vb.* zerdrü´cken.

crust, *n.* Kruste, -n *f.*

crustacean, *n.* Krustzzentier, -e *nt.*

crusty, *adj.* knusprig.

crutch, *n.* Krücke, -n *f.*

cry, 1. *n.* Schrei, -e *m.* **2.** *vb.* schreien*; *(weep)* weinen.

crying, *adj. (urgent)* dringend.

cryosurgery, *n.* Kryochirurgie´ *f.*

cryptic, *adj.* geheim´.

cryptography, *n.* Geheim´schrift, -en *f.*

crystal, 1. *n.* Kristall´, -e *nt.* **2.** *adj.* kristal´len.

crystalline, *adj.* kristal´len.

crystallize, *vb.* kristallisie´ren.

cub, *n.* Jung- *nt.*

cube, *n.* Würfel, - *m.*

cubic, *adj.* würfelförmig, kubisch; Kubik´- *(cpds.).*

cubicle, *n.* kleiner Schlafraum, ⸗e *m.*

cuckoo, *n.* Kuckuck, -e *m.*

cucumber, *n.* Gurke, -n *f.*

cud, *n.* Widergekäut- *nt.;* (chew the c.) wieder•käuen.

cuddle, *vb.* herzen.

cudgel, *n.* Keule, -n *f.*

cue, *n.* Stichwort, ≃er *nt.*

cuff, *n. (sleeve)* Manschet´te, -n *f.; (trousers)* Hoseaufschlag, ≃e *m.*

cuisine, *n.* Küche, -n *f.*

culinary, *adj.* kulina´risch.

cull, *vb.* pflücken.

culminate, *vb.* gipfeln.

culmination, *n.* Höhepunkt, -e *m.*

culpable, *adj.* schuldhaft.

culprit, *n.* Täter, - *m.,* Täterin, -nen *f.*

cult, *n.* Kult, -e *m.*

cultivate, *vb.* kultivie´ren.

cultivated, *adj.* kultiviert´.

cultivation, *n.* Kultivie´rung *f.*

cultural, *adj.* kulturell´.

culture, *n.* Kultur´, -ren *f.*

cultured, *adj.* kultiviert´.

cumbersome, *adj.* schwerfällig.

cumulative, *adj.* kumulativ´.

cunning, 1. *n.* List, -en *f.* **2.** *adj.* listig; *(sweet)* goldig.

cup, *n.* Tasse, -n *f.*

cupboard, *n.* Schrank, ≃e *m.*

cupidity, *n.* Begier´de, -n *f.*

cupola, *n.* Kuppel, -n *f.*

curable, *adj.* heilbar.

curator, *n.* Kura´tor, -o´ren *m.*

curb, 1. *n. (sidewalk)* Bordstein, -e *m., (harness)* Zügel, - *m.* **2.** *vb.* zügeln.

curdle, *vb.* gerin´nen*.

cure, 1. *n.* Kur, -en *f.; (medicine)* Heilmittel, - *nt.* **2.** *vb.* heilen.

curfew, *n.* Polizei´stunde, -n *f.*

curio, *n.* Kuriosität´, -en *f.*

curiosity, *n.* Neugierde *f.*

curious, *adj.* neugierig.

curl, 1. *n.* Locke, -n *f.* **2.** *vb.* locken, kräuseln.

curly, *adj.* lockig, kraus.

currant, *n.* Johan´nisbeere, -n *f.; (dried)* Korin´the, -n *f.*

currency, *n.* Währung, -en *f.*

current, 1. *n.* Strom, ≃e *m.* **2.** *adj.* laufend; aktuell´.

currently, *adv.* zur Zeit.

curriculum, *n.* Lehrplan, ≃e *m.*

curry, *n.* Curry *nt.*

curse, 1. *n.* Fluch, ≃e *m.* **2.** *vb. (intr.)* fluchen, *(tr.)* verflu´chen.

cursed, *adj.* verflucht´.

curse-word, *n.* Schimpfwort, ≃er *nt.*

cursory, *adj.* flüchtig.

curt, *adj.* kurz angebunden.

curtail, *vb.* ein•schränken.

curtain, *n.* Gardi´ne, -n *f.; (drapes)* Vorhang, ≃e *m.*

curtsy, *n.* Knicks, -e *m.*

curvature, *n.* Krümmung, -en *f.*

curve, *n.* Kurve, -n *f.*

cushion, *n.* Kissen, - *nt.*

custard, *n.* Eierpudding, -s *m.*

custodian, *n.* Hausmeister, - *m.*

custody, *n.* Verwah´rung *f.*

custom, *n.* Sitte, -n *f., (habit)* Brauch, ≃e *m.; (habit)* Gewohn´heit, -en *f.*

customary, *adj.* gebräuch´lich.

customer, *n.* Kunde, -n, - *m.,* Kundin, -nen *f.*

custom house, *n.* Zollamt, ≃er *nt.*

customs, *n.* Zoll, ≃e *m.*

customs officer, *n.* Zollbeamt- *m.,* Zollbeamtin, -nen, *f.*

cut, 1. *n.* Schnitt, -e *m.; (wound)* Schnittwunde, -n *f.; (salary)* Kürzung, -en *f.; (taxes)* Senkung, -en *f.* **2.** *vb.* schneiden*; kürzen; senken; *(class)* schwänzen.

cute, *adj.* niedlich, süß, goldig.

cut glass, *n.* geschlif´fenes Glas *nt.*

cuticle, *n.* Nagelhaut, ≃e *f.*

cutlery, *n.* Stahlwaren *pl.*

cutlet, *n.* Kotelett´, -s *nt.*

cutter, *n.* Zuschneider, - *m.; (boat)* Kutter, - *m.*

cyclamate, *n.* Zyklamat´, -e *nt.*

cycle, 1. *n.* Kreislauf, ≃e *m.;* Zyklus, -klen *m.* **2.** *vb.* radeln.

cyclist, *n.* Radfahrer, - *m.,* Radfahrerin, -nen *f.*

cyclone, *n.* Wirbelsturm, ≃e *m.*

cyclotron, *n.* Zyklotron, -e *nt.*

cylinder, *n.* Zylin´der, - *m.*

cylindrical, *adj.* zylin´drisch.

cymbal, *n.* Zimbel, -n *f.*

cynic, *n.* Zyniker, - *m.,* Zynikerin, -nen, *f.*

cynical, *adj.* zynisch.

cynicism, *n.* Zynis´mus, -men *m.*

cypress, *n.* Zypres´se, -n *f.*

cyst, *n.* Zyste, -n *f.*

D

dab, *vb.* tupfen.

dabble, *vb.* sich dilettan´tenhaft mit einer Sache ab•geben*.

daffodil, *n.* Narzis´se, -n *f.*

dagger, *n.* Dolch, -e *m.*

dahlia, *n.* Dahlie, -n *f.*

daily, 1. *n. (newspaper)* Tageszeitung, -en *f.* **2.** *adj.* täglich.

daintiness, *n.* Zartheit, -en *f.*

dainty, *adj.* zart, delikat´, zierlich.

dairy, *n.* Milchwirtschaft, -en *f.,* Molkerei´ -en *f.*

dairyman, *m.* Milchhändler, - *m.*

dais, *n.* Podium, -ien *nt.*

daisy, *n.* Margeri´te, -n *f.*

dale, *n.* Tal, ≃er *nt.*

dally, vb. tändeln; *(dawdle)* trödeln.

dam, 1. n. Damm, ⸗e m. **2.** vb. ein•dämmen.

damage, 1. n. Schaden, ⸗ m.; *(damages, law)* Schadenersatz m. **2.** vb. schädigen; beschä´digen.

damask, n. Damast, -e m.

damn, vb. verdam´men; *(curse)* verflu´chen.

damnation, n. Verdam´mung, -en f.

damp, adj. feucht.

dampen, vb. *(moisten)* ein•feuchten; *(quiet)* dämpfen; *(fig.)* nieder•schlagen*.

dampness, n. Feuchtigkeit, -en f.

dance, 1. n. Tanz, ⸗e m. **2.** vb. tanzen.

dancer, n. Tänzer, - m., Tänzerin, -nen f.

dancing, n. Tanzen nt.

dandelion, n. Löwenzahn m.

dandruff, n. Kopfschuppen pl.

dandy, 1. n. Geck, -en, -en m. **2.** adj. prima.

Dane, n. Däne, -n, -n m., Dänin, -nen f.

danger, n. Gefahr´, -en f.

dangerous, adj. gefähr´lich.

dangle, vb. baumeln; baumeln lassen*.

Danish, adj. dänisch.

dapper, adj. klein und elegant´.

dare, vb. wagen.

daredevil, n. Draufgänger, - m.

daring, adj. gewagt´.

dark, 1. n. Dunkel nt.; Dunkelheit, -en f. **2.** adj. dunkel.

darken, vb. verdun´keln.

darkness, n. Dunkel nt.; Dunkelheit, -en f.

darling, 1. n. Liebling, -e m. **2.** adj. goldig.

darn, vb. *(socks)* stopfen.

dart, 1. n. Wurfpfeil, -e m. **2.** vb. fliezen*.

dash, 1. n. *(pen)* Strich, -e m; *(sport)* Lauf, ⸗e m. **2.** vb. *(intr.)* sich stürzen; *(tr.)* stoßen*, schleudern.

dashboard, n. Armatu´renbrett, -er nt.

dashing, adj. schneidig.

data, n.pl. Angaben pl.

data processing, n. Datenverarbeitung, -en f.

date, 1. n. Datum, -ten nt.; *(appointment)* Verab´redung, -en f.; *(fruit)* Dattel, -n f. **2.** vb. datie´ren; aus•gehen* mit.

daub, vb. schmieren.

daughter, n. Tochter, ⸗ f.

daughter-in-law, n. Schwiegertochter, ⸗ f.

daunt, vb. entmu´tigen.

dauntless, adj. kühn.

dawdle, vb. trödeln.

dawn, 1. n. Morgendämmerung, -en f. **2.** vb. dämmern.

day, n. Tag, -e m.

daybreak, n. Tagesanbruch m.

daydream, 1. n. Träumerei´, -en f. **2.** vb. vor sich hin träumen; sinnie´ren.

daylight, n. Tageslicht nt.

daze, 1. n. Benom´menheit f. **2.** vb. betäu´ben.

dazzle, vb. blenden.

deacon, n. Diakon´, -e m.

dead, adj. tot.

deaden, vb. dämpfen.

dead end, n. Sackgasse, -n f.

deadline, n. Termin´, -e m., Frist, -en f.

deadlock, n. Stockung, -en f.

deadly, adj. tötlich.

deaf, adj. taub.

deafen, vb. betäu´ben.

deafness, n. Taubheit f.

deal, 1. n. Anzahl f.; *(business)* Geschäft´, -e nt. **2.** vb. *(cards)* geben*; **(d. with)** behan´deln; **(d. in)** handeln mit.

dealer, n. Händler, - m., Händlerin, -nen f.; *(cards)* Geber, - m.

dean, n. Dekan´, -e m.

dear, adj. lieb, teuer.

dearly, adv. sehr.

dearth, n. Mangel, ⸗ m.

death, n. Tod m.; Todesfall, ⸗e m.

deathless, adj. unsterblich.

debase, vb. ernie´drigen.

debatable, adj. bestreit´bar.

debate, 1. n. Debat´te, -n f. **2.** vb. debattie´ren.

debauch, 1. n. Orgie, -n f. **2.** vb. verfüh´ren.

debenture, n. Obligation´, -en f.

debilitate, vb. entkräf´ten.

debit, n. Debet, -s nt.

debonair, adj. zuvor´kommend; heiter und sorglos.

debris, n. Trümmer pl.

debt, n. Schuld, -en f.

debtor, n. Schuldner, - m., Schuldnerin, -nen f.

debunk, vb. mit etwas auf•räumen, den Nimbus rauben.

debut, n. Debüt´, -s nt.

debutante, n. Debütan´tin, -nen f.

decade, n. Jahrzehnt´, -e nt.

decadence, n. Dekadenz´ f.

decadent, adj. dekadent´.

decaffeinated, adj. koffein´-frei.

decanter, n. Karaf´fe, -n f.

decapitate, vb. enthaup´ten.

decay, 1. n. Verfall´ m.; Verwe´sung, -en f. **2.** vb. verfal´len*; verwe´sen.

deceased, adj. verstor´ben.

deceit, n. Täuschung, -en f.; Betrug´, ⸗e m.

deceitful, adj. falsch; betrü´gerisch.

deceive, vb. täuschen; betrü´gen*.

December, n. Dezem´ber m.

decency, n. Anständigkeit, -en f.

decent, adj. anständig.

decentralization, n. Dezentralisation´, -en f.

decentralize, vb. dezentralisie´ren.

deception, n. Täuschung, -en f.

deceptive, adj. irreführend, täuschend.

decibel, n. Dezi´bel, -n f.

decide, vb. entschei´den*; sich entschlie´ßen*.

decimal, 1. n. Dezimal´bruch, ⸗e m. **2.** adj. Dezimal´- *(cpds.)*.

decimate, vb. dezimie´ren.

decipher, vb. entzif´fern.

decision, *n.* Entschei´dung,
-en *f.;* Beschluß´, ̈sse
m.

decisive, *adj.* entschei´dend.

deck, *n. (ship)* Deck, -s *nt.;*
(cards) Spiel, -e *nt.*

declaration, *n.* Erklä´rung, -
en *f.*

declarative, *adj.* erklä´rend;
(d. sentence) Aussage-
satz, ̈e *m.*

declare, *vb.* erklä´ren, be-
haup´ten; *(customs)*
deklarie´ren.

declension, *n.* Deklination´,
-en *f.*

decline, 1. *n.* Niedergang *m.*
2. *vb.* neigen; *(refuse)*
ab•lehnen; *(gram.)* dek-
linie´ren.

décolleté, *n.* Dekolleté´, -s *nt.*

decompose, *vb. (tr.)*
zerset´zen; *(intr.)*
verwe´sen.

decomposition, *n.* Zerset´-
zung, -en *f.;* Verwe´sung,
-en *f.*

decongestant, *n.* schleim-
lösendes Mittel *nt.*

décor, *n.* Ausstattung, -en *f.*

decorate, *vb.* schmücken,
dekorie´ren.

decoration, *n.* Dekoration´,
-en *f.*

decorative, *adj.* dekorativ´.

decorator, *n.* Dekorateur´, -
e *m.,* Dekorateu´rin, -nen
f.; **(interior d.)** Innenar-
chitekt, -en, -en *m.,* In-
nenarchitektin, -nen *f.*

decorous, *adj.* schicklich.

decorum, *n.* Schicklichkeit
f.

decoy, 1. *n.* Lockvogel, ̈
m. **2.** *vb.* locken.

decrease, 1. *n.* Abnahme, -n
f. **2.** *vb. (tr.)* verrin´gern;
(intr.) ab•nehmen*.

decree, 1. *n.* Erlaß´, -sse *m.*
2. *vb.* verord´nen.

decrepit, *adj.* gebrech´lich,
klapprig.

decry, *vb.* mißbil´ligen,
tadeln.

dedicate, *vb.* widmen.

dedication, *n.* Widmung, -
en *f.*

deduce, *vb.* folgern.

deduct, *vb.* ab•ziehen*.

deduction, *n.* Abzug, ̈e *m.;*
(logic) Folgerung, -en *f.*

deductive, *adj.* deduktiv´.

deed, *n.* Tat, -en *f.; (document)* Urkunde, -n *f.*

deem, *vb.* denken*; halten*
für.

deep, *adj.* tief.

deepen, *vb.* vertie´fen.

deep freeze, *n.*
Tiefkühltruhe, -n *f.*

deer, *n.* Reh, -e *nt.;* Hirsch,
-e *m.*

deerskin, *n.* Rehleder, - *nt.;*
Hirschleder, - *nt.*

deface, *vb.* entstel´len.

defamation, *n.*
Verleum´dung, -en *f.*

defame, *vb.* in schlechten
Ruf bringen*.

default, 1. *n.* Versäum´nis, -
se *nt.;* Unterlas´sung, -en
f. **2.** *vb.* im Verzug´ sein*.

defeat, 1. *n.* Niederlage, -n
f. **2.** *vb.* besie´gen.

defect, 1. *n.* Fehler, - *m.,*
Defekt´, -e *m.* **2.** *vb.*
über•laufen*.

defection, *n.* Versa´gen *nt.;*
Treubruch, ̈e *m.*

defective, *adj.* fehlerhaft.

defend, *vb.* vertei´digen.

defendant, *n.* Angeklagt-
m.& f.

defender, *n.* Vertei´diger, -
m., Vertei´digerin, -nen
f., Beschüt´zer, - *m.,*
Beschüt´zerin, -nen *f.*

defense, *n.* Vertei´digung, -
en *f.*

defenseless, *adj.* wehrlos.

defensible, *adj.* verfecht´bar,
zu vertei´digen.

defensive, 1. *n.* Defensi´ve,
-n *f.* **2.** *adj.* defensiv´.

defer, *vb. (put off)* auf•-
schieben*; *(yield)* nach•-
geben*.

deference, *n.* Achtung *f.*

deferential, *adj.* ehrerbietig.

defiance, *n.* Heraus´-
forderung, -en *f.;* Trotz *m.*

defiant, *adj.* trotzig,
heraus´fordernd.

deficiency, *n.* Mangel, ̈ *m.*

deficient, *adj.* unzureichend.

deficit, *n.* Defizit, -e *nt.*

defile, 1. *n.* Engpaß, ̈sse *m.*
2. *vb. (march)* defilie´ren;
(soil) besu´deln.

definite, *adj.* bestimmt´.

definition, *n.* Definition´, -
en *f.*

definitive, *adj.* definitiv´.

deflate, *vb.* die Luft
heraus´lassen*.

deflation, *n.* Deflation´, -en *f.*

deflect, *vb.* ab•wenden*.

deform, *vb.* entstel´len.

deformity, *n.*
Verwachs´ung, -en *f.*

defraud, *vb.* betrü´gen*.

defray, *vb.* bestrei´ten*.

defrost, *vb.* entfros´ten.

deft, *adj.* geschickt´.

defy, *vb.* trotzen.

degenerate, 1. *adj.* degene-
riert´. **2.** *vb.* entar´ten.

degeneration, *n.* Degenera-
tion´ *f.*

degradation, *n.* Ernie´dri-
gung, -en *f.*

degrade, *vb.* ernie´drigen.

degree, *n.* Grad, -e *m.*

deify, *vb.* vergött´lichen.

deign, *vb.* geru´hen.

deity, *n.* Gottheit, -en *f.*

dejected, *adj.*
niedergeschlagen.

dejection, *n.* Trübsinn *m.*

delay, 1. *n.* Verzö´gerung, -
en *f.* **2.** *vb.* auf•schieben*,
verzö´gern.

delectable, *adj.* ergötz´lich.

delegate, 1. *n.* Delegiert´-
m.& f. **2.** *vb.* delegie´ren.

delegation, *n.* Abordnung, -
en *f.,* Delegation´, -en *f.*

delete, *vb.* aus•streichen*.

deletion, *n.* Streichung *f.*

deliberate, 1. *vb.* erwä´gen*.
2. *adj.* bedäch´tig; *(on
purpose)* absichtlich.

deliberation, *n.* Überle´gung,
-en *f.,* Erwä´gung, -en *f.*

delicacy, *n. (food)*
Delikates´se, -n *f.; (fig.)*
Feinheit, -en *f.*

delicate, *adj.* delikat´.

delicious, *adj.* köstlich.

delight, 1. *n.* Entzü´cken, -
nt. **2.** *vb.* entzü´cken.

delightful, *adj.*
entzü´ckend.

delineate, *vb.* dar•stellen*.

delinquency, *n.* Verge´hen, -
nt.; Unterlas´sung, -en *f.*

delinquent, 1. *n.* Kriminell´
- *m. & f.;* **(juvenile d.)**
Jugendverbrecher, - *m.* **2.**
adj. verbre´cherisch,
kriminell´; *(in default)*
säumig.

delirious, *adj.* im Fieberwahnsinn; wahnsinnig.

delirium, *n.* Deli´rium, -
rien *nt.*

deliver, *vb. (set free)*
erlö´sen; *(hand over)*
überge´ben*, ab•liefern.

deliverance, *n.* Erlö´sung, -
en *f.,* Befrei´ung, -en *f.*

delivery, *n.* Lieferung, -en
f.; (childbirth)
Entbin´dung, -en *f.*

delude, *vb.* täuschen,
verlei´ten.

deluge, 1. *n.*
Überschwem´mung, -en
f.; (Bible) Sintflut *f.* **2.**
vb. überflu´ten.

delusion, *n.* Täuschung, -en
f., Wahn *m.*

de luxe, *adj.* Luxus- *(cpds.).*

delve, *vb.* graben*; *(fig.)*
sich vertie´fen.

demand, 1. *n.* Forderung, -
en *f.; (claim)* Anspruch,
⸗e *m.; (econ.)* Nachfrage
f. **2.** *vb.* fordern,
verlan´gen; fragen.

demean (oneself), *vb.* sich
entwür´digen.

demeanor, *n.* Betra´gen *nt.*

demerit, *n. (school)* Tadel, -
m.

demilitarize, *vb.* entmili-
tarisie´ren.

demobilization, *n.* Demo-
bilisie´rung, -en *f.*

demobilize, *vb.*
demobilisie´ren.

democracy, *n.* Demokratie´,
-n *f.*

democrat, *n.* Demokrat´, -
en, -en *m.*

democratic, *adj.* demokra´-
tisch.

demolish, *vb.* ab•reißen*,
zerstö´ren.

demolition, *n.* Zerstö´rung,
-en *f.*

demon, *n.* Dämon, -o´nen *m.*

demonstrable, *adj.* nachweisbar.

demonstrate, *vb.* zeigen,
vor•führen,
demonstrie´ren.

demonstration, *n.* Beweis´ -
e *m.,* Darlegung, -en *f.;*
Kundgebung, -en *f.*

demonstrative, *adj.* demon-
strativ´.

demonstrator, *n.* Demon-
strie´rend- *m. & f.*

demoralize, *vb.*
demoralisie´ren.

demote, *vb.* degradie´ren.

demur, *vb.* Einwendungen
machen.

demure, *adj.* züchtig.

den, *n.* Höhle, -n *f.*

denaturalize, *vb.* denatural-
isie´ren.

denial, *n.* Vernei´nung, -en *f.*

denim, *n.* Jeansstoff, -e *m.*

Denmark, *n.* Dänemark *nt.*

denomination, *n. (money)*
Nennwert, -e *m.;*
(church) Sekte, -n *f.*

denominator, *n.* Nenner, - *m.*

denote, *vb.* kennzeichnen.

dense, *adj.* dicht.

density, *n.* Dichte *f.*

dent, *n.* Einbuchtung, -en *f.*

dental, *adj.* Zahn- *(cpds.).*

dental floss, *n.* Zahnseide *f.*

dentifrice, *n.* Zahnputzmittel, - *nt.*

dentist, *n.* Zahnarzt, ⸗e *m.,*
Zahnärztin, -nen, *f.*

dentistry, *n.* Zahnheilkunde
f.

denture, *n.* künstliches
Gebiß´, -sse *nt.*

denunciation, *n.*
Denunzie´rung, -en *f.*

deny, *vb.* leugnen, vernei´nen.

deodorant, *n.*
Desodorisie´rungsmittel,
- *nt.,* Deodorant´ *m.*

depart, *vb.* ab•fahren*; *(deviate)* ab•weichen*.

department, *n.* Abtei´lung,
-en *f.; (government)*
Ministe´rium, -rien *nt.*

departmental, *adj.*
Abtei´lungs- *(cpds.).*

departure, *n.* Abfahrt, -en
f.; (deviation) Abwe-
ichung, -en *f.*

depend, *vb.* ab•hängen*;
(rely) sich verlas´sen*.

dependability, *n.*
Verläß´lichkeit *f.*

dependable, *adj.* zuverlässig.

dependence, *n.* Ab-
hängigkeit *f.*

dependent, 1. *n.* Ange-
hörig- *m. & f.* **2.** *adj.* abhängig; angewiesen.

depict, *vb.* dar•stellen.

depiction, *n.* Darstellung, -
en *f.*

deplete, *vb.* erschöp´fen.

deplorable, *adj.*
bekla´genswert.

deplore, *vb.* bekla´gen.

deport, *vb.* deportie´ren.

deportation, *n.*
Deportation´, -en *f.*

deportment, *n.* Betra´gen
nt.

depose, *vb.* ab•setzen.

deposit, 1. *n.* Anzahlung, -
en *f.; (bank)* Einzahlung,
-en *f.; (ore, etc.)* Lager, -
nt. **2.** *vb.* ein•zahlen; hin-
terle´gen.

deposition, *n.* (eidesstattliche) schriftliche Aus-
sage, -n *f.*

depositor, *n.* Einzahler, -
m., Bankkunde, -n, -n *m.*

depot, *n.* Lager, ⸗ *nt.;*
Depot´, -s *nt.; (railroad)*
Kleinbahnhof, ⸗e *m.*

depravity, *n.* Verwor´fen-
heit *f.*

deprecate, *vb.* mißbilligen.

depreciate, *vb. (tr.)* entwer´-
ten, den Wert mindern;
(intr.) im Wert sinken*.

depreciation, *n.* Wertmin-
derung *f.*

depress, *vb.* deprimie´ren.

depression, *n.* Depression´,
-en *f.*

deprivation, *n.* Berau´bung,
-en *f.*

deprive, *vb.* berau´ben.

depth, *n.* Tiefe, -n *f.*

deputy, *n. (substitute)* Stellvertreter, - *m.,* Stel-
lvertreterin, -nen *f.; (parliament)* Abgeordnet-
m. & f.

derail, *vb.* entglei´sen lassen*; **(be d.ed)** entglei´sen.

deranged, *adj.* geistesgestört.

derelict, 1. *n.* Wrack, -s *or* -*e nt.* **2.** *adj.* nachlässig.

dereliction, *n.* Vernach´lässigung, -en *f.*

deride, *vb.* verspot´ten, verhöhnen.

derision, *n.* Hohn *m.*

derisive, *adj.* spöttisch.

derivation, *n.* Ableitung, -en *f.*

derivative, *adj.* abgeleitet.

derive, *vb.* ab•leiten.

derogatory, *adj.* abfällig.

derrick, *n.* Ladebaum, ⸗e *m.; (oil)* Bohrturm, ⸗e *m.*

descend, *vb.* herab•steigen*; *(ancestry)* ab•stammen.

descendant, *n.* Nachkomme, -n, -n *m.*

descent, *n.* Abstieg, -e *m.*

describe, *vb.* beschrei´ben*.

description, *n.* Beschrei´bung, -en *f.*

descriptive, *adj.* beschrei´bend.

desecrate, *vb.* entwei´hen.

desert, 1. *n.* Wüste, -n *f.; (merit)* Verdienst´, -e *nt.* **2.** *vb.* verlas´sen*.

deserter, *n.* Fahnenflüchtig-*m. & f.,* Deserteur´, -e *m.*

desertion, *n. (law)* böswilliges Verlas´sen *nt.; (army)* Desertion´, -en *f.,* Fahnenflucht *f.*

deserve, *vb.* verdie´nen.

deserving, *adj.* verdienst´voll.

design, 1. *n.* Entwurf´, ⸗e *m.,* Muster, - *nt.; (aim)* Absicht, -en *f.* **2.** *vb.* entwer´fen*; beab´sichtigen.

designate, *vb.* bezeich´nen, bestim´men.

designation, *n.* Bezeich´nung, -en *f.,* Bestim´mung, -en *f.*

designer, *n.* Konstrukteur´, -e *m.; (fashion)* Modeschöpfer, - *m.,* Modeschöpferin, -nen *f.*

desirability, *n.* Erwünscht´heit, -en *f.*

desirable, *adj.* wünschenswert.

desire, 1. *n.* Verlan´gen, -*nt.,* Wunsch, ⸗e *m.* **2.** *vb.* verlan´gen, wünschen.

desirous, *adj.* begie´rig.

desist, *vb.* ab•lassen*.

desk, *n.* Schreibtisch, -e *m.*

desolate, 1. *adj.* trostlos. **2.** *vb.* verhee´ren.

desolation, *n.* Verwüs´tung, -en *f.;* Trostlosigkeit *f.*

despair, 1. *n.* Verzweif´lung, -en *f.* **2.** *vb.* verzwei´feln.

despatch, 1. *n.* Absendung, -en *f.* **2.** *vb.* ab•senden*, eilig weg•schicken.

desperado, *n.* Bandit´, -en, -en *m.,* Despera´do, -s *m.*

desperate, *adj.* verzwei´felt.

desperation, *n.* Verzweif´lung, -en *f.*

despicable, *adj.* verach´tenswert, gemein´.

despise, *vb.* verach´ten.

despite, *prep.* trotz.

despondent, *adj.* verzagt´.

despot, *n.* Despot´, -en, -en *m.*

despotic, *adj.* despo´tisch.

despotism, *n.* Gewalt´herrschaft *f.*

dessert, *n.* Nachtisch, -e *m.*

destination, *n.* Bestim´mung *f.;* Bestim´mungsort, -e *m.*

destine, *vb.* bestim´men.

destiny, *n.* Schicksal, -e *nt.*

destitute, *adj.* mittellos.

destitution, *n.* Armut *f.,* Not, ⸗e *f.*

destroy, *vb.* zerstö´ren.

destroyer, *n.* Zerstö´rer, - *m.*

destruction, *n.* Zerstö´rung, -en *f.*

destructive, *adj.* zerstö´rend.

desultory, *adj.* flüchtig.

detach, *vb.* ab•trennen; *(mil.)* ab•kommandieren.

detachment, *n. (mil.)* Abtei´lung, -en *f.;* Objektivität´ *f.*

detail, *n.* Einzelheit, -en *f.*

detain, *vb.* ab•halten*; fest•halten*; auf•halten*.

detect, *vb.* entde´cken, ermit´teln.

detection, *n.* Entde´cken *nt.;* Ermitt´lung, -en *f.*

detective, *n.* Detektiv´ -e *m.*

détente, *n.* Entspan´nung *f.*

detention, *n.* Haft *f.*

deter, *v.* ab•halten*, hindern.

detergent, *n.* Waschmittel, -*nt,* Reinigungsmittel, -*nt.*

deteriorate, *vb.* sich verschlech´tern.

deterioration, *n.* Verschlech´terung, -en *f.*

determination, *n.* Bestim´mung, -en *f.; (resolve)* Entschlos´senheit *f.*

determine, *vb.* bestim´men.

determined, *adj.* entschlos´sen.

deterrence, *n.* Abschreckung *f.z*

detest, *vb.* verab´scheuen.

detonate, *vb.* explodie´ren.

detonation, *n.* Explosion´, -en *f.*

detour, *n.* Umweg, -e *m.; (traffic)* Umleitung, -en *f.*

detract, *vb.* ab•ziehen*; **(d. from)** schmälern.

detriment, *n.* Nachteil, -e *m.,* Schaden, ⸗ *m.*

detrimental, *adj.* nachteilig.

devaluate, *vb.* ab•werten.

devastate, *vb.* verwüs´ten.

devastation, *n.* Verwüs´tung, -en *f.*

develop, *vb.* entwi´ckeln.

developer, *n.* Entwick´ler, - *m.*

developing nation, *n.* Entwick´lungsland, ⸗er *nt.*

development, *n.* Entwick´lung, -en *f.*

deviate, *vb.* ab•weichen*.

deviation, *n.* Abweichung, -en *f.*

device, *n.* Vorrichtung, -en *f.*

devil, *n.* Teufel, - *m.*

devilish, *adj.* teuflisch.

devious, *adj.* abweichend.

devise, *vb.* ersin´nen*.

devoid, *adj.* **(d. of)** leer an, ohne.

devote, *vb.* widmen.

devoted, *adj.* erge´ben.

devotee, *n.* Verfech´ter, - *m.*

devotion, *n.* Hingebung *f.;* *(religious)* Andacht, -en *f.*

devour, *vb.* verschlin´gen*.

devout, *adj.* andächtig, fromm.

dew, *n.* Tau *m.*

dewy, *adj.* betaut´.

dexterity, *n.* Gewandt´heit, -en *f.*

dexterous, *adj.* gewandt´.

diabetes, *n.* Zuckererkrankheit *f.*

diabolic, *adj.* teuflisch.

diadem, *n.* Diadem´, -e *nt.*

diagnose, *vb.* diagnostizie´ren.

diagnosis, *n.* Diagno´se, -n *f.*

diagnostic, *adj.* diagnos´tisch.

diagonal, 1. *n.* Diagona´le, -n *f.* **2.** *adj.* diagonal´, schräg.

diagram, *n.* graphische Darstellung, -en *f.*

dial, 1. *n.* Zifferblatt, ⁼er *nt.; (telephone)* Wählscheibe, -n *f.* **2.** *vb. (telephone)* wählen.

dialect, *n.* Dialekt´, -e *m.,* Mundart, -en *f.*

dialogue, *n.* Dialog´, -e *m.*

diameter, *n.* Durchmesser, - *m.*

diametrical, *adj.* diametral´.

diamond, *n.* Diamant´, -en, -en *m.; (cards)* Karo *nt.*

diaper, *n.* Windel, -n *f.*

diaphragm, *n.* Zwerchfell, -e *nt.*

diarrhea, *n.* Durchfall *m.*

diary, *n.* Tagebuch, ⁼er *nt.*

diathermy, *n.* Diathermie´ *f.*

diatribe, *n.* Schmähschrift, -en *f.*

dice, *n.pl.* Würfel, - *m.*

dicker, *vb.* feilschen.

dictate, *vb.* diktie´ren.

dictation, *n.* Diktat´, -e *nt.*

dictator, *n.* Dikta´tor, -o´ren *m.*

dictatorial, *adj.* diktato´risch.

dictatorship, *n.* Diktatur´, -en *f.*

diction, *n.* Aussprache, -n *f.*

dictionary, *n.* Wörterbuch, ⁼er *nt.,* Lexikon, -ka *nt.*

didactic, *adj.* didak´tisch.

die, 1. *n. (gaming cube)* Würfel, - *m.; (stamper)* Prägestempel, - *m.* **2.** *vb.* sterben*.

diet, *n.* Diät´, -en *f.; (government)* Parlament´, -e *nt.*

dietary, *adj.* diät´gemäß.

dietetic, *adj.* diäte´tisch.

dietitian, *n.* Diät´planer, - *m.*

differ, *vb.* sich unterschei´den*, ab•weichen*, verschiedener Meinung sein*.

difference, *n.* Unterschied, -e *m.*

different, *adj.* verschie´den, ander-.

differential, 1. *n.* Unterschied, - *m.;* **(d. gear)** Differential´, -e *nt.,* Ausgleichsgetriebe, - *nt.* **2.** *adj.* differential´.

differentiate, *vb.* unterschei´den*.

difficult, *adj.* schwer, mühsam, schwierig.

difficulty, *n.* Schwierigkeit, -en *f.*

diffident, *adj.* zurück´haltend, schüchtern.

diffuse, 1. *adj.* weitverbreitet, diffus´. **2.** *vb.* verbrei´ten.

diffusion, *n.* Diffusion´, -en *f.*

dig, *vb.* graben*.

digest, *vb.* verdau´en.

digestible, *adj.* verdau´lich.

digestion, *n.* Verdau´ung *f.*

digestive, *adj.* Verdau´ungs*(cpds.).*

digital, *adj.* digital´.

digitalis, *n.* Digita´lis *nt.*

dignified, *adj.* würdig.

dignify, *vb.* ehren, aus•zeichnen.

dignitary, *n.* Würdenträger, - *m.*

dignity, *n.* Würde *f.*

digress, *vb.* ab•schweifen.

digression, *n.* Abschweifung, -en *f.*

dike, *n.* Deich, -e *m.*

dilapidated, *adj.* baufällig.

dilate, *vb.* aus•dehnen.

dilemma, *n.* Dilem´ma, -s *nt.*

dilettante, *n.* Dilettant´, -en, -en *m.*

diligence, *n.* Fleiß *m.*

diligent, *adj.* fleißig.

dill, *n.* Dill *m.*

dilute, *vb.* verdün´nen.

dilution, *n.* Verdün´nung, -en *f.*

dim, 1. *adj.* trübe, dunkel. **2,** *vb.* trüben; *(auto lights)* ab•blenden.

dimension, *n.* Ausmaß, -e *nt.,* Dimension´, -en *f.*

diminish, *vb.* vermin´dern.

diminution, *n.* Vermin´derung, *f.*

diminutive, 1. *n.* Diminutiv´, -e *nt.* **2.** *adj.* winzig.

dimness, *n.* Dunkelheit *f.*

dimple, *n.* Grübchen, - *nt.*

din, *n.* Lärm *m.*

dine, *vb.* speisen.

diner, dining-car, *n.* Speisewagen, - *m.*

dingy, *adj.* schäbig.

dining room, *n.* Eßzimmer, - *nt.; (in hotel)* Speiseraum, ⁼e *m.*

dinner, *n. (noon)* Mittagessen, - *nt.; (evening)* Abendessen, - *nt.*

dinosaur, *n.* Dinosau´rier, - *m.*

diocese, *n.* Diöze´se, -n *f.*

dip, *vb.* tauchen, ein•tauchen.

diphtheria, *n.* Diphtherie´ *f.*

diploma, *n.* Diplom´, -e *nt.*

diplomacy, *n.* Diplomatie´, -en *f.*

diplomat, *n.* Diplomat´, -en, -en *m.*

diplomatic, *adj.* diploma´tisch.

dipper, *n.* Schöpflöffel, - *m.,* Schöpfkelle, -n *f.;* **(Big D.)** Großer Bär *m.;* **(Little D.)** Kleiner Bär *m.*

dire, *adj.* gräßlich.

direct, 1. *adj.* direkt´. **2.** *vb.* führen; an•weisen*; leiten.

direct current, *n.* Gleichstrom, ⁼e *m.*

direction, *n. (leadership)* Leitung, -en *f.,* Führung, -en *f.; (instruction)* Anweisung, -en *f.; (course)* Richtung, -en *f.*

directional, *adj.* Leitungs-, Richtungs- *(cpds.).*

directive, 1. *adj.* leitend; Richtung gebend. **2.** *n.* Direkti´ve, -n *f.*

directness, *n.* Gerad´heit *f.,* Offenheit *f.*

director, *n.* Leiter, - *m.,* Leiterin, -nen *f.,* Direk´tor, -o´ren *m.,* Direkto´rin, -nen *f.*

directory, *n. (addresses)* Adreß´buch, ⸚er *nt.;* **(telephone d.)** Telephon´buch, ⸚er *nt.*

dirigible, *n.* Luftschiff, -e *nt.*

dirt, *n.* Schmutz *m.*

dirty, *adj.* schmutzig.

disability, *n.* Unfähigkeit *f.;* Körperbehinderung, -en *f.*

disable, *vb.* untauglich machen.

disabled, *adj.* untauglich; kriegsversehrt.

disadvantage, *n.* Nachteil, -e *m.*

disagree, *vb.* anderer Meinung sein*; *(food)* nicht bekom´men*.

disagreeable, *adj.* unangenehm, unsympathisch.

disagreement, *n.* Uneinigkeit, -en *f.,* Widerspruch, ⸚e *m.*

disappear, *vb.* verschwin´den*.

disappearance, *n.* Verschwin´den *nt.*

disappoint, *vb.* enttäu´schen.

disappointment, *n.* Enttäu´schung, -en *f.*

disapproval, *n.* Mißbilligung, -en *f.*

disapprove, *vb.* mißbilligen.

disarm, *vb.* entwaff´nen, ab•rüsten.

disarmament, *n.* Abrüstung, -en *f.*

disarray, *n.* Unordnung *f.*

disaster, *n.* Unglück, -e *nt.,* Katastro´phe, -n *f.*

disastrous, *adj.* verhee´rend.

disavow, *vb.* ab•leugnen.

disband, *vb.* auf•lösen.

disburse, *vb.* aus•zahlen.

discard, *vb.* ab•legen.

discern, *vb.* unterschei´den*.

discerning, *adj.* scharfsinnig.

discernment, *n.* Scharfsinn *m.,* Einsicht *f.*

discharge, 1. *n.* Entlas´sung, -en *f.; (medicine)* Ausscheidung, -en *f.* **2.** *vb.* entlas´sen*, aus•scheiden*; *(gun)* ab•feuern.

disciple, *n.* Jünger, - *m.*

disciplinary, *adj.* maßregelnd.

discipline, 1. *n.* Disziplin´ *f.* **2.** *vb.* schulen, disziplinie´ren.

disclaim, *vb.* ab•leugnen; verzich´ten.

disclose, *vb.* enthül´len.

disclosure, *n.* Enthül´lung, -en *f.*

discomfort, *n.* Unbehagen *nt.*

disconcert, *vb.* in Verwir´rung bringen*.

disconnect, *vb.* los•lösen; *(elec.)* aus•schalten.

discontent, 1. *n.* Unzufriedenheit *f.* **2.** *adj.* unzufrieden.

discontinue, *vb.* ein•stellen.

discord, *n.* Mißklang ⸚e *m.; (fig.)* Uneinigkeit, -en *f.*

discotheque, *n.* Diskothek´, -en *f.*

discount, 1. *n.* Rabatt´ *m.* **2.** *vb.* ab•ziehen*.

discourage, *vb.* entmu´tigen.

discouragement, *n.* Entmu´tigung, -en *f.*

discourse, 1. *n.* Gespräch´, -e *nt.;* Abhandlung, -en *f.* **2.** *vb.* sprechen*.

discourteous, *adj.* unhöflich.

discourtesy, *n.* Unhöflichkeit, -en *f.*

discover, *vb.* entde´cken.

discovery, *n.* Entde´ckung, -en *f.*

discredit, 1. *n.* Nichtachtung *f.* **2.** *vb.* nicht glauben; in schlechten Ruf bringen*.

discreet, *adj.* diskret´.

discrepancy, *n.* Zwiespalt, -e *m.*

discretion, *n.* Diskretion´ *f.;* Beson´nenheit *f.*

discriminate, *vb.* unterschei´den*; diskriminie´ren.

discrimination, *n.* Diskriminie´rung, -en *f.*

discuss, *vb.* diskutie´ren.

discussion, *n.* Diskussion´, -en *f.*

disdain, *vb.* verach´ten.

disdainful, *adj.* veräch´tlich.

disease, *n.* Krankheit, -en *f.*

disembark, *vb.* landen.

disembarkation, *n.* Landung, -en *f.*

disenchantment, *n.* Enttäu´schung, -en *f.,* Ernüch´terung *f.*

disengage, *vb.* los•lösen.

disentangle, *vb.* entwir´ren.

disfavor, *n.* Mißfallen *nt.;* Ungnade *f.*

disfigure, *vb.* entstel´len.

disgrace, 1. *n.* Schande, -n *f.,* Unehre *f.* **2.** *vb.* schänden, blamie´ren.

disgraceful, *adj.* schändlich.

disgruntled, *adj.* mürrisch.

disguise, 1. *n.* Verklei´dung, -en *f.* **2.** *vb.* verklei´den.

disgust, 1. *n.* Ekel *m.* **2.** *vb.* an•ekeln.

disgusting, *adj.* ekelhaft, widerlich.

dish, *n.* Schüssel, -n *f.; (food)* Gericht´, -e *nt.*

dishcloth, *n.* Abwaschtuch, ⸚er *nt.*

dishearten, *vb.* entmu´tigen.

dishonest, *adj.* unehrlich.

dishonzesty, *n.* Unehrlichkeit, -en *f.*

dishonor, 1. *n.* Schande, -n *f.* **2.** *vb.* enteh´ren.

dishonorable, *adj.* unehrenhaft.

dishtowel, *n.* Geschirr´handtuch, ⸚er *nt.*

disillusion, 1. *n.* Enttäu´schung, -en *f.* **2.** *vb.* enttäu´schen.

disinfect, *vb.* desinfizie´ren.

disinfectant, *n.* Desinfizie´rungsmittel, - *nt.*

disinherit, *vb.* enter´ben.

disintegrate, *vb.* zerfal´len*.

disinterested, *adj.* gleichgültig.

disjointed, *adj.* unzusammenhängend.

disk, *n.* Scheibe, -n *f.;* Diskette, -n *f.*

dislike, 1. *n.* Abneigung, -en *f.* **2.** *vb.* nicht mögen*.

dislocate, *vb.* aus•renken.

dislodge, *vb.* los•reißen*, vertrei´ben*.

disloyal, *adj.* treulos.

disloyalty, *n.* Untreue, -n *f.*

dismal, *adj.* jämmerlich.

dismantle, *vb.* demontie´ren.

dismay, 1. *n.* Bestür´zung, -en *f.* **2.** *vb.* erschre´cken.

dismember, *vb.* zerstü´ckeln.

dismiss, *vb.* entlas´sen*; fallen lassen*.

dismissal, *n.* Entlas´sung, -en *f.*

dismount, *vb.* ab•steigen*.

disobedience, *n.* Ungehorsam *m.*

disobedient, *adj.* ungehorsam.

disobey, *vb.* nicht gehor´-chen.

disorder, *n.* Unordnung *f.*

disorderly, *adj.* unordentlich, liederlich.

disorganize, *vb.* in Unordnung bringen*.

disown, *vb.* verleug´nen.

disparage, *vb.* herab•setzen.

disparity, *n.* Ungleichheit, -en *f.*

dispassionate, *adj.* leidenschaftslos.

dispatch, 1. *n.* Absendung, -en *f.* **2.** *vb.* ab•senden*, eilig weg•schicken.

dispatcher, *n.* Absender, - *m.*

dispel, *vb.* vertrei´ben*.

dispensable, *adj.* entbehr´-lich.

dispensary, *n.* Arznei´ausgabestelle, -n *f.*

dispensation, *n.* Befrei´ung, -en *f.*

dispense, *vb.* aus•geben*; (d. with) verzich´ten auf.

dispersal, *n.* Vertei´lung, -en *f.*

disperse, *vb.* vertei´len.

displace, *vb.* verdrän´gen.

displaced person, *n.* Zwangsverschleppt- *m. & f.*

display, 1. *n.* Aufwand *m.; (window)* Schaufensterauslage, -n *f.* **2.** *vb.* entfal´ten, zeigen.

displease, *vb.* mißfal´len*.

displeasure, *n.* Mißfallen *nt.*

disposable, *adj.* verfüg´bar.

disposal, *n.* Verfü´gung, -en *f.*

dispose, *vb.* bestim´men.

disposition, *n.* Verfü´gung, -en *f.; (character)* Anlage *f.*

dispossess, *vb.* enteig´nen.

disproof, *n.* Widerle´gung, -en *f.*

disproportion, *n.* Mißverhältnis, -se *nt.*

disproportionate, *adj.* unverhältnismäßig.

disprove, *vb.* widerle´gen.

disputable, *adj.* bestreit´bar.

dispute, 1. *n.* Streit, -e *m.* **2.** *vb.* bestrei´ten*.

disqualification, *n.* Disqualifizie´rung, -en *f.*

disqualify, *vb.* disqualifizie´ren.

disregard, 1. *n.* Nichtbeachtung *f.* **2.** *vb.* nicht beach´ten.

disrepair, *n.* Verfall´ *m.*

disreputable, *adj.* verru´fen.

disrespect, *n.* Nichtachtung *f.,* Mißachtung *f.*

disrespectful, *adj.* unehrerbietig, unhöflich.

disrobe, *vb.* entklei´den.

disrupt, *vb.* stören.

dissatisfaction, *n.* Unzufriedenheit, -en *f.*

dissatisfy, *vb.* nicht befrie´digen.

dissect, *vb.* zerglie´dern; (med.) sezie´ren.

disseminate, *vb.* verbrei´ten.

dissension, *n.* Uneinigkeit, -en *f.*

dissent, 1. *n.* Meinungsverschiedenheit, -en *f.* **2.** *vb.* anderer Meinung sein*.

dissertation, *n.* Dissertation´, -en *f.*

dissimilar, *adj.* unähnlich.

dissipated, *adj.* ausschweifend, verlebt´.

dissipation, *n.* Ausschweifung, -en *f.*

dissociate, *vb.* trennen.

dissolute, *adj.* verkom´men.

dissolution, *n.* Auflösung, -en *f.*

dissolve, *vb.* auf•lösen.

dissonance, *n.* Dissonanz´, -en *f.*

dissonant, *adj.* dissonant´.

dissuade, *vb.* ab•raten*.

distance, *n.* Entfer´nung, -en *f.,* Abstand, ⸗e *m.*

distant, *adj.* entfernt´; (fig.) zurück´haltend.

distaste, *n.* Widerwille(n), - *m.,* Abneigung, -en *f.*

distasteful, *adj.* widerwärtig, widerlich.

distemper, *n.* (dog) Staupe *f.*

distend, *vb.* aus•dehnen.

distill, *vb.* destillie´ren.

distillation, *n.* Destillation´, -en *f.*

distiller, *n.* Destillateur´, -e *m.*

distillery, *n.* Branntweinbrennerei, -en *f.*

distinct, *adj.* deutlich; (different) verschie´den.

distinction, *n.* (difference) Unterscheidung, -en *f.,* Unterschied, -e *m.; (elegance)* Vornehmheit *f.; (honor)* Auszeichnung, -en *f.*

distinctive, *adj.* kennzeichnend.

distinctness, *n.* Deutlichkeit *f.*

distinguish, *vb.* (differentiate) unterschei´den*; (honor) aus•zeichnen.

distinguished, *adj.* (famous) berühmt´; (elegant) vornehm.

distort, *vb.* verzer´ren.

distract, *vb.* ab•lenken.

distraction, *n.* Ablenkung, -en *f.*

distress, 1. *n.* Not, ⸗e *f.* **2.** *vb.* betrü´ben.

distribute, *vb.* vertei´len.

distribution, *n.* Vertei´lung, -en *f.*

distributor, *n.* Vertei´ler, - *m.; (agent)* Vertriebs´stelle, -n *f.*

district, *n.* Bezirk´, -e *m.*

distrust, 1. *n.* Mißtrauen *nt.* **2.** *vb.* mißtrau´en.

distrustful, *adj.* mißtrauisch.

disturb, *vb.* stören, beun´-ruhigen.

disturbance, *n.* Störung, -en *f.,* Unruhe, -n *f.*

ditch, *n.* Graben, ≈ *m.*

diva, *n.* Diva, -s *f.*

divan, *n.* Diwan, -e *m.*

dive, 1. *n.* Kopfsprung, ≈e *m.* **2.** *vb.* tauchen.

diver, *n.* Taucher, - *m.,* Taucherin, -nen *m.*

diverge, *vb.* auseinan'der•gehen*.

divergence, *n.* Divergenz', -en *f.*

divergent, *adj.* divergie'rend.

diverse, *adj.* verschie'den.

diversion, *n.* Ablenkung, -en *f.; (pastime)* Zeitvertreib, -e *m.*

diversity, *n.* Mannigfaltigkeit, -en *f.*

divert, *vb.* ab•lenken, um•leiten.

divest, *vb.* entle'digen, entklei'den.

divide, *vb.* teilen.

dividend, *n.* Dividen'de, -n *f.*

divine, *adj.* göttlich.

divinity, *n.* Gottheit, -en *f.; (study)* Theologie', -i'en *f.*

divisible, *adj.* teilbar.

division, *n.* Teilung, -en *f.; (mil.)* Division', -en *f.*

divorce, 1. *n.* Scheidung, -en *f.* **2.** *vb. (get d.d)* sich scheiden lassen*; **(d. a person)** sich von einem Menschen scheiden lassen*.

divorcée, *n.* geschie'dene Frau, -en *f.*

divulge, *vb.* enthül'len.

dizziness, *n.* Schwindel *m.*

dizzy, *adj.* schwindlig.

do, *vb.* tun*, machen.

docile, *adj.* fügsam.

dock, *n.* Dock, -s *nt.*

docket, *n.* Gerichts'kalender, - *m.;* Geschäfts'ordnung, -en *f.*

doctor, *n.* Doktor, -o'ren *m.; (physician)* Arzt, ≈e *m.,* Ärztin, -nen *f.*

doctorate, *n.* Doktorat', -e *nt.*

doctrine, *n.* Lehre, -n *f.;* Grundsatz, ≈e *m.*

document, *n.* Urkunde, -n *f.;* Dokument', -e *nt.*

documentary, *adj.* urkundlich, dokumenta'risch.

documentation, *n.* Dokumentation', -en *f.*

dodge, *vb.* aus•weichen*.

doe, *n.* Reh, -e *nt.*

doeskin, *n.* Rehleder *nt.*

dog, *n.* Hund, -e *m.*

dogma, *n.* Dogma, -men *nt.*

dogmatic, *adj.* dogma'tisch.

dogmatism, *n.* Dogma'tik *f.*

dole, *vb.* **(d. out)** vertei'len.

doleful, *adj.* kummervoll.

doll, *n.* Puppe, -n *f.*

dollar, *n.* Dollar, -s *m.*

domain, *n.* Bereich', -e *m.*

dome, *n.* Dom, -e *m.,* Kuppel, -n *f.*

domestic, *adj.* häuslich; **(d. policy)** Innenpolitik *f.*

domesticate, *vb.* zähmen.

domicile, *n.* Wohnort, -e *m.*

dominance, *n.* Herrschaft, -en *f.*

dominant, *adj.* vorherrschend.

dominate, *vb.* beherr'schen.

domination, *n.* Herrschaft, -en *f.*

domineer, *vb.* tyrannisie'ren.

dominion, *n.* Domi'nion, -s *nt.*

domino, *n.* Domino, -s *m.*

don, *vb.* an•ziehen*; *(hat)* auf•setzen.

donate, *vb.* stiften.

donation, *n.* Gabe, -n *f.,* Schenkung, -en *f.*

done, *adj. (food)* gar.

donkey, *n.* Esel, - *m.*

doom, *n.* Verder'ben *nt.*

door, *n.* Tür, -en *f.*

doorman, *n.* Portier', -s *m.*

doorway, *n.* Türeingang, ≈e *m.*

dope, *n. (drug)* Rauschgift, -e *nt.; (fool)* Trottel, - *m.*

dormant, *adj.* ruhend, latent'.

dormitory, *n. (room)* Schlafsaal, -säle *m.; (building)* Studentenheim, -e *nt.*

dosage, *n.* Dosie'rung, -en *f.*

dose, *n.* Dosis, -sen *f.*

dossier, *n.* Akte, -n *f.*

dot, *n.* Punkt, -e *m.*

double, 1. *n.* Doppelgänger, - *m.* **2.** *adj.* doppelt.

double-breasted, *adj.* zweireihig.

double-cross, *vb.* hinterge'hen*.

doubt, 1. *n.* Zweifel, - *m.* **2.** *vb.* zweifeln, bezwei'feln.

doubtful, *adj.* zweifelhaft.

doubtless, *adj.* zweifellos.

dough, *n.* Teig, -e *m.*

douse, *vb.* begie'ßen; *(fire)* löschen.

dove, *n.* Taube, -n *f.*

dowdy, *adj.* unschick.

down, 1. *n.* Flaum *m.; (material)* Daune, -n *f.* **2.** *vb.* nieder•werfen*, *(fig.)* besie'gen. **3.** *adv.* unten, nieder, ab; hin-, herun'ter; hin-, herab'.

downcast, *adj.* niedergeschlagen.

downfall, *n.* Untergang, ≈e *m.*

downhearted, *adj.* betrübt'.

downhill, *adv.* bergab'.

down payment, *n.* Anzahlung, -en *f.*

downpour, *n.* Regenguß, ≈sse *m.*

downstairs, *adv.* unten.

downtown, 1. *n.* Geschäfts'viertel, -*nt.* **2.** *adv. (direction)* in die Stadt; *(location)* in der Stadt.

downward, *adv.* nach unten.

dowry, *n.* Mitgift, -en *f.*

doze, *vb.* dösen.

dozen, *n.* Dutzend, -e *nt.*

drab, *adj. (color)* bräunlich gelb; *(dull)* farblos.

draft, 1. *n. (plan)* Entwurf', ≈e *m.; (money)* Wechsel, -*m.; (air)* Zug, ≈e *m.; (military service)* militä'rische Dienstpflicht *f.* **2.** *vb.* entwer'fen*; *(mil.)* ein•ziehen*.

draftee, *n.* Rekrut', -en, -en *m.*

draftsman, *n.* Zeichner, - *m.,* Zeichnerin, -nen *f.*

drafty, *adj.* zugig.

drag, *vb.* schleppen, schleifen.

dragon, *n.* Drache, -n, -n *m.*

drain, 1. *n.* Abfluß, ⹀sse *m.* **2.** *vb.* ab•laufen lassen*; entwäs´sern.

drainage, *n.* Abfluß, ⹀sse *m.;* Entwäs´serung, -en *f.*

dram, *n.* Drachme, -n *f.*

drama, *n.* Drama, -men *nt.;* Schauspiel, -e *nt.*

dramatic, *adj.* drama´tisch.

dramatist, *n.* Drama´tiker, - *m.*

dramatize, *vb.* dramatisie´ren.

dramaturgy, *n.* Thea´terwissenschaft, -en *f.*

drape, 1. *n.* Vorhang, ⹀e *m.* **2.** *vb.* drapie´ren.

drapery, *n.* Vorhang, ⹀e *m.;* Behang´, ⹀e *m.*

drastic, *adj.* drastisch.

draught, see draft.

draw, *vb.* *(pull)* ziehen*; *(picture)* zeichnen; **(d. up)** ab•fassen.

drawback, *n.* Nachteil, -e *m.;* Schattenseite, -n *f.*

drawbridge, *n.* Zugbrücke, -n *f.*

drawer, *n.* Schublade, -n *f.*

drawing, *n.* *(picture)* Zeichnung, -en *f.;* *(lottery)* Ziehung, -en *f.*

drawl, *vb.* langsam und ausgedehnt sprechen*.

dread, 1. *n.* Furcht *f.*, Angst, ⹀e *f.* **2.** *vb.* fürchten.

dreadful, *adj.* furchtbar.

dream, 1. *n.* Traum, ⹀e *m.* **2.** *vb.* träumen.

dreamy, *adj.* träumerisch, verträumt´.

dreary, *adj.* trostlos.

dredge, 1. *n.* Bagger, - *m.* **2.** *vb.* baggern.

dregs, *n.pl.* Bodensatz, ⹀e *m.;* *(fig.)* Abschaum, ⹀e *m.*

drench, *vb.* durchnäs´sen.

dress, 1. *n.* Kleid, -er *nt.* **2.** *vb.* an•ziehen*, kleiden.

dresser, *n.* Kommo´de, -n *f.*

dressing, *n.* *(food)* Soße, -n *f.;* *(med.)* Verband´, ⹀e *m.*

dressing gown, *n.* Schlafrock, ⹀e *m.*, Morgenrock, ⹀e *m.*

dressmaker, *n.* Schneiderin, -nen.

drier, *n.* *(hair)* Trockenhaube, -n *f.;* *(clothes)* Trockner, - *m.*

drift, 1. *n.* *(snow)* Schneewehe, -n *f.;* *(tendency)* Richtung, -en *f.*, Strömung, -en *f.* **2.** *vb.* treiben*.

drill, 1. *n.* *(tool)* Drillbohrer, - *m.;* *(practice)* Schulung, -en *f.;* *(mil.)* Exerzie´ren *nt.* **2.** *vb.* bohren; schulen; exerzie´ren.

drink, 1. *n.* Getränk´, -e *nt.* **2.** *vb.* trinken*.

drinkable, *adj.* trinkbar.

drip, *vb.* tropfen.

drive, 1. *n.* *(ride)* Spazier´fahrt, -en *f.;* *(energy)* Schwungkraft *f.* **2.** *vb.* treiben*; *(auto)* fahren*.

driver, *n.* Fahrer, - *m.*, Fahrerin, -nen *f.;* **(d.'s license)** Führerschein *m.*

driveway, *n.* Auffahrt, -en *f.*

drizzle, 1. *n.* Sprühregen, - *m.* **2.** *vb.* nieseln.

drone, 1. *n.* *(bee)* Drohne, -n *f.;* *(hum)* Gesum´me *nt.* **2.** *vb.* summen.

droop, *vb.* herab´•hängen*.

drop, 1. *n.* Tropfen, - *m.* **2.** *vb.* *(fall)* fallen*; *(let fall)* fallen* lassen*.

dropout, *n.* jemand, der absichtlich seine ordnungsgemäße Tätigkeit, Ausbildung, Lebensart, aufgibt.

dropper, *n.* Tropfer, - *m.*

dropsy, *n.* Wassersucht *f.*

drought, *n.* Dürre, -n *f.*, Trockenheit, -en *f.*

drown, *vb.* *(intr.)* ertrin´ken*; *(tr.)* erträn´ken.

drowsiness, *n.* Schläfrigkeit *f.*

drowsy, *adj.* schläfrig.

drudgery, *n.* Plackerei´, -en *f.*

drug, *n.* Droge, -n *f.*, Medikament´, -e *nt.*

druggist, *n.* Drogist´, -en, -en *m.*, Drogistin, -nen *f.*, Apothe´ker, - *m.*, Apothe´kerin, -nen *f.*

drug store, *n.* Drogerie´, -i´en *f.*, Apothe´ke, -n *f.*

drum, *n.* Trommel, -n *f.*

drummer, *n.* Trommler, *m.*

drumstick, *n.* Trommelschlegel, - *m.;* *(fowl)* Geflü´gelschlegel, - *m.*

drunk, *adj.* betrun´ken; **(get d.)** sich betrin´ken*.

drunkard, *n.* Trinker, - *m.;* Trunkenbold, -e *m.*

drunken, *adj.* betrun´ken.

drunkenness, *n.* Trunkenheit *f.*

dry, 1. *adj.* trocken. **2.** *vb.* trocknen.

dry cell, *n.* Trockenelement, -e *nt.*

dry-cleaner, *n.* Reinigung, -en *f.*

dry-cleaning, *n.* chemische Reinigung, -en *f.*

dry goods, *n.pl.* Texti´lien *pl.*

dryness, *n.* Trockenheit, -en *f.*

dual, *adj.* Doppel- *(cpds.).*

dubious, *adj.* zweifelhaft.

duchess, *n.* Herzogin, -nen *f.*

duchy, *n.* Herzogtum, ⹀er *nt.*

duck, 1. *n.* Ente, -n *f.* **2.** *vb.* sich ducken.

duct, *n.* Rohr, -e *nt.;* Kanal´, ⹀e *m.*

due, *adj.* schuldig; fällig.

duel, *n.* Duell´, -e *nt.*

dues, *n.pl.* Gebüh´ren *pl.*, Beitrag, ⹀e *m.*

duet, *n.* Duett´, -e *nt.*

duffle bag, *n.* Seesack, ⹀e *m.*

duke, *n.* Herzog, ⹀e *m.*

dull, *adj.* *(not sharp)* stumpf; *(boring)* langweilig.

dullness, *n.* Stumpfheit *f.;* Langweiligkeit *f.*

duly, *adv.* gebüh´rend.

dumb, *adj.* stumm; *(stupid)* dumm (⹀), blöde.

dumbwaiter, *n.* Drehaufzug, ⹀e *m.*

dumfound, *vb.* verblüf´fen.

dummy, *n.* *(posing as someone)* Strohmann, ⹀er *m.;* *(window-display)* Schaufensterpuppe, -n *f.;* *(bridge)* Tisch *m.;* *(theater)* Statist´, -en, -en *m.*

dump, 1. *n.* Abladeplatz, ⹀e *m.;* *(refuse)* Schuttablade, -n *f.* **2.** *vb.* ab•laden*.

dumpling, *n.* Kloß, ⹀e *m.*

dun, 1. *adj.* graubraun. **2.** *vb.* zur Zahlung mahnen.

dunce, *n.* Schafskopf, ≃e *m.,* Dummkopf, ≃e *m.*

dune, *n.* Düne, -n *f.*

dung, *n.* Dung *m.*

dungarees, *n.pl.* Arbeitshose, -n *f.*

dungeon, *n.* Kerker, - *m.*

dunk, *vb.* tunken.

dupe, 1. *vb.* düpie′ren. **2.** *n.* Düpiert′- *m.& f.*

duplex, *adj.* Doppel- *(cpds.).*

duplicate, *vb.* verdop′peln, kopie′ren.

duplication, *n.* Verdop′pelung, -en *f.*

duplicity, *n.* Duplizität′, -en *f.*

durability, *n.* Dauerhaftigkeit *f.*

durable, *adj.* dauerhaft; strapazierfähig.

duration, *n.* Dauer *f.*

duress, *n.* Zwang *m.*

during, *prep.* während.

dusk, *n.* Abenddämmerung, -en *f.*

dust, 1. *n.* Staub *m.* **2.** *vb.* ab•stauben.

dusty, *adj.* staubig.

Dutch, *adj.* holländisch.

Dutchman, *n.* Holländer, - *m.*

Dutchwoman, *n.* Holländerin, -nen *f.*

dutiful, *adj.* pflichtgetreu.

duty, *n.* Pflicht, -en *f.; (tax)* Zoll, ≃e *m.*

duty-free, *adj.* zollfrei.

dwarf, *n.* Zwerg, -e *m.*

dwell, *vb.* wohnen.

dweller, *n.* Bewoh′ner, - *m.*

dwelling, *n.* Wohnung, -en *f.; Wohnsitz, -e *m.*

dwindle, *vb.* schrumpfen.

dye, 1. *n.* Farbe, -n *f.;* Farbstoff, -e *m.* **2.** *vb.* färben.

dyer, *n.* Färber, - *m.*

dyestuff, *n.* Farbstoff, -e *m.*

dynamic, *adj.* dyna′misch.

dynamite, *n.* Dynamit′ *nt.*

dynamo, *n.* Dyna′mo, -s *m.*

dynasty, *n.* Dynastie′, -i′en *f.*

dysentery, *n.* Ruhr *f.*

dyslexia, *n.* Dyslexie′ *f.*

dyspepsia, *n.* Dyspepsie′ *f.*

E

each, *adj.* jeder, -es, -e.

each other, *pron.* einan′der.

eager, *adj.* eifrig.

eagerness, *n.* Eifer *m.*

eagle, *n.* Adler, - *m.*

ear, *n.* Ohr, -en *nt.*

earache, *n.* Ohrenschmerzen *pl.*

eardrum, *n.* Trommelfell, -e *nt.*

earl, *n.* Graf, -en, -en *m.*

early, *adj.* früh.

earmark, 1. *n.* Anzeichen, -*nt.* **2.** *vb.* bestim′men; **(be e.ed)** vorgesehen sein*.

earn, *vb.* verdie′nen.

earnest, *adj.* ernst.

earnestness, *n.* Ernst *m.*

earnings, *n.pl.* Einnahmen *pl.*

earring, *n.* Ohrring, -e *m.*

earth, *n.* Erde, -n *f.*

earthenware, *n.* Steingut *nt.*

earthly, *adj.* irdisch.

earthquake, *n.* Erdbeben, -*nt.*

earthy, *adj.* erdig; *(fig.)* derb.

ease, 1. *n.* Leichtigkeit, -en *f.; (comfort)* Behag′lichkeit, -en *f.* **2.** *vb.* erleich′tern, lindern.

easel, *n.* Staffelei′, -en *f.*

easiness, *n.* Leichtigkeit, -en *f.*

east, 1. *n.* Osten *m.,* Orient *m.* **2.** *adj.* östlich; Ost *(cpds.).*

Easter, *n.* Ostern *nt.*

easterly, *adj.* östlich.

eastern, *adj.* östlich.

eastward, *adv.* ostwärts.

easy, *adj.* leicht.

easygoing, *adj.* gutmütig, ungezwungen.

eat, *vb.* essen*.

eatable, *adj.* eßbar.

eaves, *n.pl.* Dachrinne, -n *f.*

ebb, 1. *n.* Ebbe, -n *f.* **2.** *vb.* ab•nehmen*.

ebony, *n.* Ebenholz, ≃er *nt.*

eccentric, *adj.* exzen′trisch.

eccentricity, *n.* Exzentrizität′, -en *f.*

ecclesiastic, *adj.* kirchlich, geistlich.

ecclesiastical, *adj.* kirchlich, geistlich.

echelon, *n.* Staffel, -n *f.*

echo, 1. *n.* Echo, -s *nt.* **2.** *vb.* wider•hallen.

eclipse, *n.* Finsternis, -se *f.*

ecological, *adj.* ökologisch.

ecology, *n.* Ökologie′ *f.*

economic, *adj.* wirtschaftlich.

economical, *adj.* sparsam.

economics, *n.* Volkswirtschaft *f.,* National′ökonomie *f.*

economist, *n.* Volkswirtschaftler, - *m.*

economize, *vb.* haus•halten*.

economy, *n.* Wirtschaft *f.;* Sparsamkeit *f.*

ecstasy, *n.* Verzü′ckung, -en *f.*

ecumenical, *adj.* ökume′nisch.

eczema, *n.* Ekzem′, -e *nt.*

eddy, *n.* Strudel, - *m.*

edge, *n.* Rand, ≃er *m.; (knife, etc.)* Schneide, -n *f.*

edible, *adj.* eßbar.

edict, *n.* Verord′nung, -en *f.,* Edikt′, -e *nt.*

edifice, *n.* Gebäu′de, - *nt.*

edify, *vb.* erbau′en.

edit, *vb.* heraus′•geben*.

edition, *n.* Ausgabe, -n *f.,* Auflage, -n *f.*

editor, *n.* Heraus′geber, - *m.,* Heraus′geberin, -nen *f.*

editorial, 1. *n.* Leitartikel, - *m.* **2.** *adj.* Redaktions′- *(cpds.).*

educate, *vb. (bring up)* erzie′hen*; *(train)* aus•bilden.

education, *n. (upbringing)* Erzie′hung *f.; (training)* Ausbildung *f.; (culture)* Bildung *f.*

educational, *adj.* erzie′herisch.

educator, *n.* Erzie′her, - *m.,* Erzie′herin, -nen *f.;* Pädago′ge, -n, -n *m.* Pädago′gin, -nen *f.*

eel, *n.* Aal, -e *m.*

effect, *n.* Wirkung, -en *f.*

effective, *adj.* wirkungsvoll.

effectiveness, *n.* Wirksamkeit *f.*

effectual, *adj.* wirksam.

effeminate, *adj.* verweichlicht.

effervescence, *n.* Sprudeln *nt.*

effete, *adj.* entkräftet.

efficiency, *n.* Leistungsfähigkeit *f.,* Tüchtigkeit *f.,* Wirksamkeit *f.*

efficient, *adj.* leistungsfähig, tüchtig, wirksam.

effigy, *n.* Abbild, -er *nt.*

effort, *n.* Mühe, -n *f.; (exertion)* Anstrengung, -en *f.; (attempt)* Versuch, -e *nt.*

effrontery, *n.* Frechheit, -en *f.*

effusive, *adj.* überschwenglich.

egg, *n.* Ei, -er *nt.*

eggplant, *n.* Aubergine, -n *f.*

ego, *n.* Ich *nt.*

egoism, *n.* Egoismus *m.*

egotism, *n.* Egotismus *m.*

egotist, *n.* Egoist´, -en, -en *m.*

Egypt, *n.* Ägypten *nt.*

Egyptian, 1. *n.* Ägypter, - *m.,* Ägypterin, -nen *f.* **2.** *adj.* ägyptisch.

eight, *num.* acht.

eighteen, *num.* achtzehn.

eighteenth, 1. *adj.* achtzehnt- **2.** *n.* Achzehntel, -*nt.*

eighth, 1. *adj.* acht-. **2.** *n.* Achtel, - *nt.*

eightieth, 1. *adj.* achtzigst-. **2.** *n.* Achtzigstel, - *nt.*

eighty, *num.* achtzig.

either, 1. *pron. & adj.* jeder, -es, -e; beides, *pl.* beide. **2.** *conj.* **(e. . . . or)** entweder . . . oder. **3.** *adv.* **(not . . . e.)** auch nicht, auch kein, -, -e.

ejaculation, *n.* Ausruf, -e *m.*

eject, *vb.* hinaus´•werfen*; vertrei´ben*.

ejection, *n.* Hinaus´werfen *nt.*

eke out, *vb.* sich durch•helfen*.

elaborate, 1. *adj.* weitläufig; kunstvoll. **2.** *vb.* ins einzelne gehen*.

elapse, *vb.* verge´hen*.

elastic, 1. *n.* Gummiband, ⸚er *nt.* **2.** *adj.* elas´tisch.

elasticity, *n.* Elastizität´ *f.*

elate, *vb.* erfreu´en.

elated, *adj.* hocherfreut.

elation, *n.* Freude, -n *f.*

elbow, *n.* Ellbogen, - *m.*

elder, 1. *n. (tree)* Holun´der, - *m.; (church)* Ältest- *m.* **2.** *adj.* älter.

elderly, *adj.* ältlich.

eldest, *adj.* ältest-.

elect, *vb.* wählen.

election, *n.* Wahl, -en *f.*

elective, *adj.* Wahl- *(cpds.).*

electorate, *n.* Wählerschaft, -en *f.*

electric, electrical, *adj.* elek´trisch.

electrician, *n.* Elek´triker, - *m.*

electricity, *n.* Elektrizität´ *f.*

electrocardiogram, *n.* EKG, -s *nt.;* Elektrokardiogramm´, -e *nt.*

electrocution, *n.* Tötung durch elektrischen Strom.

electrode, *n.* Elektro´de, -n *f.*

electrolysis, *n.* Elektroly´se *f.*

electron, *n.* Elektron, -o´nen *nt.*

electronic, *adj.* Elektro´nen- *(cpds.).*

electronics, *n.* Elektro´nenwissenschaft *f.*

elegance, *n.* Eleganz´ *f.*

elegant, *adj.* elegant´.

elegy, *n.* Elegie´, -i´en *f.*

element, *n.* Element´, -e *nt.*

elemental, elementary, *adj.* elementar´.

elephant, *n.* Elefant´, -en, - en *m.*

elephantine, *adj.* elefan´tenartig.

elevate, *vb.* erhö´hen.

elevation, *n.* Erhö´hung, -en *f.;* Höhe, -n *f.*

elevator, *n.* Fahrstuhl, ⸚e *m.*

eleven, *num.* elf.

eleventh, 1. *adj.* elft-. **2.** *n.* Elftel, - *nt.*

elf, *n.* Kobold, -e *m.*

elfin, *adj.* koboldartig.

elicit, *vb.* heraus´•holen.

eligibility, *n.* Qualifiziert´heit *f.*

eligible, *adj.* qualifiziert´.

eliminate, *vb.* besei´tigen, aus•scheiden*.

elimination, *n.* Besei´tigung, -en *f.;* Ausscheidung, -en *f.*

elixir, *n.* Elixier´, -e *nt.*

elk, *n.* Elch, -e *m.*

elm, *n.* Ulme, -n *f.*

elocution, *n.* Redekunst, ⸚e *f.*

elongate, *vb.* verlän´gern.

elope, *vb.* mit einem Mädchen oder einem Jungen durchbrennen*.

eloquence, *n.* Bered´samkeit *f.*

eloquent, *adj.* redegewandt.

else, *adv.* anders, sonst.

elsewhere, *adv.* anderswo.

elucidate, *vb.* erläu´tern.

elude, *vb.* entge´hen*.

elusive, *adj.* nicht greifbar; aalglatt.

emaciated, *adj.* abgezehrt.

emanate, *vb.* aus•strömen.

emancipate, *vb.* emanzipie´ren.

emancipation, *n.* Emanzipation´, -en *f.*

emancipator, *n.* Befrei´er, - *m.*

emasculate, *vb.* entman´nen.

embalm, *vb.* ein•balsamieren.

embankment, *n.* Uferanlage, -n *f.*

embargo, *n.* Embar´go, -s *nt.*

embark, *vb.* (sich) ein•schiffen.

embarrass, *vb.* in Verle´genheit bringen*.

embarrassed, *adj.* verle´gen.

embarrassment, *n.* Verle´genheit, -en *f.*

embassy, *n.* Botschaft, -en *f.*

embellish, *vb.* aus•schmücken.

embellishment, *n.* Ausschmückung, -en *f.*

embezzle, *vb.* unterschla´gen*.

embitter, *vb.* verbit´tern.

emblem, n. Wahrzeichen, -nt., Emblem´, -e nt.

embody, vb. verkör´pern.

embrace, vb. umar´men.

embroider, vb. sticken.

embroidery, n. Stickerei´, -en f.

embroil, vb. verwi´ckeln.

embryo, n. Embryo, -s m.

emerald, n. Smaragd´, -e m.

emerge, vb. hervor´•treten*, auf•tauchen.

emergency, n. Notfall, ´´e m. **(e. exit)** Notausgang m.

emery, n. Schmirgel m.

emetic, n. Brechmittel, - nt.

emigrant, n. Auswanderer, - m.

emigrate, vb. aus•wandern.

emigration, n. Auswanderung, -en f.

eminence, n. (hill) Anhöhe, -n f.; (distinction) Auszeichnung, -en f.; (title) Eminenz´, -en f.

eminent, adj. erha´ben.

emissary, n. Gesandt´ - m. & f.

emission controls, n.pl. Abgasbestimmungen f.pl.

emit, vb. von sich geben*.

emotion, n. Gefühl´, -e nt.; Erre´gung, -en f.

emotional, adj. gefühls´mäßig; erreg´bar.

emperor, n. Kaiser, - m.

emphasis, n. Nachdruck m., Schwerpunkt m.

emphasize, vb. beto´nen, hervor´•heben*.

emphatic, adj. nachdrücklich.

empire, n. Kaiserreich, -e nt.

empirical, adj. empi´risch.

employ, vb. an•stellen, beschäf´tigen.

employee, n. Arbeitnehmer, - m., Arbeitnehmerin, -nen f., Angestellt- m. & f.

employer, n. Arbeitgeber, - m., Arbeitgeberin, -nen f.

employment, n. Anstellung, -en f.; Beschäf´tigung, -en f.

employment office, n. Arbeitsamt nt.

empower, vb. ermäch´tigen.

empress, n. Kaiserin, -nen f.

emptiness, n. Leere f.

empty, 1. vb. leeren. **2.** adj. leer.

emulate, vb. nach•eifern.

emulsion, n. Emulsion´, -en f.

enable, vb. ermög´lichen; **(enabling act)** Ermäch´tigungsgesetz, -e nt.

enact, vb. (law) erlas´sen; (role) spielen.

enactment, n. Verord´nung, -en f.

enamel, n. Emai´lle f.

enamor, vb. **(be e.ed of)** in jemand verliebt´ sein*; **(become e.ed of)** sich in jemand verlie´ben.

encamp, vb. sich lagern.

encampment, n. Lager, - nt.

encephalitis, n. Gehirn´entzündung, -en f.

enchant, vb. entzü´cken; bezau´bern.

enchantment, n. Bezau´berung f.; Zauber m.

encircle, vb. umrin´gen.

enclose, vb. ein•schließen*; (letter) bei•fügen.

enclosure, n. Einzäunung, - en f.; (letter) Beilage, -n f.

encompass, vb. umschlie´ßen*, ein•schließen*.

encounter, vb. treffen*, begeg´nen.

encourage, vb. ermu´tigen.

encouragement, n. Ermu´tigung, -en f.

encroach upon, vb. sich ein•drängen.

encyclical, n. Enzy´klika, - ken f.

encyclopedia, n. Konversations´lexikon, -ka nt.; Enzyklopädie´, -i´en f.

end, 1. n. Ende, -n nt.; (purpose) Zweck, -e m.; (goal) Ziel, -e nt. **2.** vb. been´den, vollen´den, been´digen.

endanger, vb. gefähr´den.

endear, vb. lieb, teuer, wert machen.

endearment, n. Zärtlichkeit, -en f.

endeavor, vb. sich bemü´hen, streben.

ending, n. Ende, -n nt., Schluß, ´´sse m.

endless, adj. endlos.

endocrine, adj. endokrin´.

endorse, vb. gut•heißen*; (check) girie´ren.

endorsement, n. Billigung, -en f.; (check) Giro nt.

endow, vb. aus•statten; stiften.

endowment, n. Ausstattung, -en f.; Stiftung, -en f.

endurance, n. Ausdauer f.

endure, vb. (last) dauern; (bear) ertra´gen*.

enema, n. Klistier´, -e nt.

enemy, n. Feind, -e m., Feindin, -nen f.

energetic, adj. ener´gisch, tatkräftig.

energy, n. Tatkraft, ´´e f., Energie´, -n f.

enfold, vb. ein•hüllen.

enforce, vb. durch•setzen.

enforcement, n. Durchführung -en f., Durchsetzung, -en f.

engage, vb. (hire) an•stellen; (affiance) verlo´ben; (rent) mieten.

engaged, adj. (busy) beschäf´tigt; (affianced) verlobt´.

engagement, n. (date) Verab´redung, -en f.; (betrothal) Verlo´bung, -en f.

engaging, adj. anziehend.

engender, vb. hervor´•bringen*.

engine, n. Maschi´ne, - f.; Motor, -o´ren, m.; Lokomoti´ve, -n f.

engineer, n. Ingenieur´, -e m., Ingenie´rin, -nen f.; (locomotive) Lokomotiv´führer, - m.; (mil.) Pionier´, -e m.

engineering, n. Ingenieur´wesen nt.

England, n. England nt.

English, adj. englisch.

Englishman, n. Engländer, - m.

Englishwoman, n. Engländerin, -en f.

engrave, vb. gravie´ren.

engraver, n. Graveur´, -e m. Graveu´rin, -nen f.

engraving, *n.* Kupferstich, -e *m.*

engross, *vb.* in Anspruch nehmen*.

enhance, *vb.* erhö′hen.

enigma, *n.* Rätsel, - *nt.*

enigmatic, *adj.* rätselhaft, dunkel.

enjoin, *vb.* (*command*) befeh′len*; (*forbid*) verbie′ten*.

enjoy, *vb.* genie′ßen*, sich erfreu′en.

enjoyable, *adj.* erfreu′lich, angenehm, nett.

enjoyment, *n.* Freude, -n *f.*, Genuß′, ∺sse *m.*

enlarge, *vb.* vergrö′ßern.

enlargement, *n.* Vergrö′-ßerung, -en *f.*

enlarger, *n.* Vergrö′-ßerungsapparat, -e *m.*

enlighten, *vb.* auf•klären.

enlightenment, *n.* Aufklärung *f.*

enlist, *vb.* ein•spannen; (*mil.*) sich freiwillig melden.

enlisted man, *n.* Soldat′, -en, -en *m.*

enlistment, *n.* freiwillige Meldung zum Militärdienst.

enliven, *vb.* bele′ben.

enmity, *n.* Feindschaft, -en *f.*

ennui, *n.* Langeweile *f.*

enormity, *n.* Ungeheuerlichkeit, -en *f.*

enormous, *adj.* ungeheuer, enorm′.

enough, *adv.* genug′, genü′gend.

enrage, *vb.* rasend machen.

enrapture, *vb.* entzü′cken.

enrich, *vb.* berei′chern.

enroll, *vb.* als Mitglied ein•tragen.*

enrollment, *n.* Eintragung (*f.*) als Mitglied; Mitgliederzahl, -en *f.*

ensemble, *n.* Ensem′ble, -s *nt.*

enshrine, *vb.* als Heiligtum verwah′ren.

ensign, *n.* (*rank*) Fähnrich, -e *m.*; (*flag*) Fahne, -n *f.*

enslave, *vb.* verskla′ven, knechten.

enslavement, *n.* Versklavung *f.*

ensnare, *vb.* verstri′cken.

ensue, *vb.* folgen.

entail, *vb.* ein•schließen*.

entangle, *vb.* verwi′ckeln.

enter, *vb.* ein•treten*, ein•dringen*.

enterprise, *n.* Unterneh′-men, - *nt.*

enterprising, *adj.* unterneh′mend.

entertain, *vb.* unterhal′ten*.

entertainer, *n.* Unterhal′ter, - *m.*, Unterhal′terin, - nen *f.*

entertainment, *n.* Unterhal′tung, -en *f.*

enthrall, *vb.* bezau′bern.

enthuse, *vb.* schwärmen.

enthusiasm, *n.* Begeis′terung, *f.*

enthusiastic, *adj.* begeis′tert, enthusiastisch.

entice, *vb.* verlo′cken.

entire, *adj.* ganz, gesamt′.

entirety, *n.* Ganz- *nt.*, Ganzheit *f.*, Gesamt′heit *f.*

entitle, *vb.* berech′tigen; (*name*) beti′teln.

entity, *n.* Wesenheit *f.*

entrails, *n.pl.* Eingeweide *pl.*

entrain, *vb.* den Zug bestei′gen*.

entrance, *n.* Eingang, ∺e *m.*

entrant, *n.* Teilnehmer, - *m.*, Teilnehmerin, -nen *f.*

entrap, *vb.* in einer Falle fangen*; verstri′cken.

entreat, *n.* an•flehen.

entreaty, *n.* Gesuch′, -e *nt.*

entree, *n.* Haupgericht, -e *nt.*

entrench, *vb.* verschan′zen.

entrepreneur, *n.* Unterneh′mer, - *m.*, Unterneh′merin, -nen *f.*

entrust, *vb.* an•vertrauen.

entry, *n.* Eintritt, -e *m.*; (*writing*) Eintragung, -en *f.*

enumerate, *vb.* auf•zählen.

enumeration, *n.* Aufzählung, -en *f.*

enunciate, *vb.* aus•sprechen*.

enunciation, *n.* Aussprache, -n *f.*

envelop, *vb.* ein•hüllen.

envelope, *n.* Umschlag, ∺e *m.*, Kuvert′, -s *nt.*

enviable, *adj.* benei′denswert.

envious, *adj.* neidisch.

environment, *n.* Umge′-bung, -en *f.*, Umwelt *f.*

environmentalist, *n.* Umweltschützer, - *m.*

environmental protection, *n.* Umweltschutz *m.*

environs, *n.* Umge′bung, -en *f.*

envisage, *vb.* vergegenwär′-tigen.

envoy, *n.* Gesandt′- *m& f.*

envy, *n.* Neid *m.*

eon, *n.* Äon′, -en *m.*

ephemeral, *adj.* vergäng′-lich.

epic, **1.** *n.* Epos, -pen *nt.* **2.** *adj.* episch.

epicure, *n.* Feinschmecker, - *m.*

epidemic, **1.** *n.* Epidemie′, -i′en *f.* **2.** *adj.* epide′misch.

epidermis, *n.* Epider′mis *f.*

epigram, *n.* Epigramm′, -e *nt.*

epilepsy, *n.* Epilepsie′ *f.*

epilogue, *n.* Epilog, -e *m.*

episode, *n.* Episo′de, -n *f.*

epistle, *n.* Schreiben, - *nt.*

epitaph, *n.* Epitaph′, -e *nt.*

epithet, *n.* Beiwort, ∺er *nt.*

epitome, *n.* Kurzfassung, -en *f.*; (*fig.*) Verkör′pe-rung, -en *f.*

epitomize, *vb.* zusam′men•fassen; bezeich′nend sein* für.

epoch, *n.* Epo′che, -n *f.*

equal, **1.** *adj.* gleich. **2.** *vb.* gleichen*.

equality, *n.* Gleichheit *f.*

equalize, *vb.* gleich•machen; aus•gleichen*.

equanimity, *n.* Gleichmut *m.*

equate, *vb.* gleich•setzen.

equation, *n.* Gleichung, -en *f.*

equator, *n.* Äqua′tor *m.*

equatorial, *adj.* äquatorial′.

equestrian, *n.* Reiter, - *m.*

equilateral, *adj.* gleichseitig.

equilibrium, *n.* Gleichgewicht *nt.*

equinox, n. Tag- und Nacht- gleiche, -n f.

equip, vb. aus•rüsten.

equipment, n. Ausrüstung, -en f.

equitable, adj. gerecht´, billig.

equity, n. Billigkeit f.; Billigkeitsrecht nt.; (mortgage, etc.) Rückkaufswert, -e m.

equivalent, adj. gleichwertig.

equivocal, adj. zweideutig.

equivocate, vb. zweideutig sein*.

era, n. Zeitalter, - nt.

eradicate, vb. aus•rotten.

erase, vb. aus•radieren.

erasure, n. Ausradierung, -en f.

erect, 1. adj. gera´de. 2. vb. errich´ten.

erection, n. Errich´tung, -en f.

erectness, n. Gerad´heit f.

ermine, n. Hermelin´ m.

erode, vb. erodie´ren, zerfres´sen*.

erosion, n. Erosion´, -en f.

erotic, adj. ero´tisch.

err, vb. irren.

errand, n. Besor´gung, -en f.

errant, adj. wandernd; abwegig.

erratic, adj. verirrt´; ziellos.

erroneous, adj. irrtümlich.

error, n. Fehler, - m.; Irrtum, ¨er m.

erudite, adj. gelehrt´.

erudition, n. Gelehr´samkeit f.

erupt, vb. hervor´•brechen*, aus•brechen*.

eruption, n. Ausbruch, ¨e m.

escalate, vb. steigern.

escalator, n. Rolltreppe, -n f.

escapade, n. Streich, -e m.

escape, 1. n. Flucht f. 2. vb. entkom´men*, entge´hen*.

escapism, n. Wirklichkeitsflucht f.

escort, 1. n. Beglei´ter, - m., Beglei´terin, -nen f. 2. vb. beglei´ten.

escutcheon, n. Wappenschild, -er nt.

esophagus, n. Speiseröhre, -n f.

esoteric, adj. esote´risch.

especial, adj. beson´der-.

especially, adv. beson´ders.

espionage, n. Spiona´ge f.

espousal, n. Vermäh´lung, -en f.; (e. of) Eintreten für nt.

espouse, vb. vermäh´len; (e. a cause) ein•treten* für.

essay, 1. n. Essay, -s m. 2. vb. versu´chen.

essence, n. Wesen nt., Wesentlich- nt.

essential, adj. wesentlich.

establish, vb. fest•setzen; errich´ten; ein•richten.

establishment, n. Einrichtung, -en f.; Betrieb´, -e m.

estate, n. (inheritance) Nachlaß, ¨sse m.; (possessions) Vermö´gen nt.; (condition) Zustand, ¨e m., Stand, ¨e m.

esteem, 1. n. Achtung f. 2. vb. achten, schätzen.

estimable, adj. schätzenswert.

estimate, 1. n. Kostenanschlag, ¨e m. 2. vb. schätzen.

estimation, n. Achtung f.; (view) Ansicht, -en f.

Estonia, n. Estland nt.

estrange, vb. entfrem´den.

etch, vb. ätzen.

etching, n. Radie´rung, -en f.

eternal, adj. ewig.

eternity, n. Ewigkeit, -en f.

ether, n. Äther m.

ethereal, adj. äthe´risch.

ethical, adj. ethisch, sittlich, mora´lisch.

ethics, n. Ethik f.

ethnic, adj. ethnisch.

etiquette, n. Etiket´te f.

etymology, n. Etymologie´, -i´en f.

eucalyptus, n. Eukalyp´tus, -ten m.

eugenic, adj. euge´nisch.

eugenics, n. Eugene´tik f.

eulogize, vb. lobprei·sen*.

eulogy, n. Lobrede, -n f.

eunuch, n. Eunuch´, -en, -en m.

euphonious, adj. wohlklingend.

Europe, n. Euro´pa nt.

European, 1. n. Europä´er, - m. Europä´erin, -nen f. 2. adj. europä´isch.

European Community, n. Europäische Gemeinschaft f.

euthanasia, n. Gnadentod m., Euthanasie´ f.

evacuate, vb. evakuie´ren, den Wert berech´nen.

evade, vb. aus•weichen*, vermei´den*.

evaluate, vb. ab•schätzen, den Wert berech´nen.

evaluation, n. Abschätzung, -en f., Wertbestimmung, -en f.

evangelist, n. Evangelist´, -en, -en m.

evaporate, vb. verdam´pfen.

evaporation, n. Verdam´-pfung f.

evasion, n. Umge´hen, - nt.

evasive, adj. ausweichend.

eve, n. Vorabend, -e m.

even, 1. adj. gleich, gera´de, eben. 2. adv. eben, sogar´, selbst.

evening, n. Abend, -e m.

evenness, n. Ebenheit, -en f.; Gleichheit, -en f.; Gleichmut m.

event, n. Ereig´nis, -se nt.

eventful, adj. ereig´nisreich.

eventual, adj. (approximate) etwaig; (final) schließlich.

ever, adv. je, jemals.

evergreen, adj. immergrün.

everlasting, adj. ewig.

every, adj. jeder, -es, -e.

everybody, pron. jeder m.; alle pl.

everyday, adj. Alltags-(cpds.).

everyone, pron. jeder m.; alle pl.

everything, pron. alles.

everywhere, adv. überall´.

evict, vb. aus•weisen*; zwangsräumen.

eviction, n. Ausweisung, -en f.; Zwangsräumung, -en f.

evidence, n. Beweis´, -e m.; Augenschein, m.; (law) Beweis´material, -ien nt.; (give e.) aus•sagen.

evident, *adj.* klar, deutlich.

evidently, *adv.* offenbar.

evil, 1. *n.* Bös- *nt.* **2.** *adj.* böse, übel.

evince, *vb.* offenba´ren.

evoke, *vb.* hervor´•rufen*.

evolution, *n.* Evolution´, -en *f.*

evolve, *vb.* entwi´ckeln.

ewe, *n.* Mutterschaf, -e *nt.*

exact, 1. *adj.* genau´. **2.** *vb.* erzwin´gen*.

exaggerate, *vb.* übertrei´-ben*.

exaggeration, *n.* Übertrei´-bung, -en *f.*

exalt, *vb.* erhö´hen, verherr´lichen.

exaltation, *n.* Erhö´hung *f.;* Erre´gung, -en *f.*

examination, *n.* Prüfung, -en *f.,* Exa´men, - *nt.;* Untersu´chung, -en *f.*

examine, *vb.* prüfen; untersu´chen.

example, *n.* Beispiel, -e *nt.*

exasperate, *vb.* reizen, verär´gern.

exasperation, *n.* Gereizt´heit *f.*

excavate, *vb.* aus•graben*.

excavation, *n.* Ausgrabung, -en *f.;* Aushöhlung, -en *f.*

exceed, *vb.* übertref´fen*.

exceedingly, *adv.* außerordentlich.

excel, *vb.* sich aus•zeichnen.

excellence, *n.* Vorzüg´lichkeit, -en *f.*

Excellency, *n.* Excellenz´, -en *f.*

excellent, *adj.* ausgezeich´-net.

except, 1. *vb.* aus•-schließen*. **2.** *prep.* außer, ausgenommen; **(e. for)** außer.

exception, *n.* Ausnahme, -n *f.*

exceptional, *adj.* außergewöhnlich.

excerpt, *n.* Auszug, ⸗e *m.*

excess, *n.* Übermaß *nt.*

excessive, *adj.* übermäßig.

exchange, 1. *n.* Tausch *m.;* **(rate of e.)** Wechselkurs *m.;* **(foreign e.)** Valu´ta *f.;* **(student)** Austausch *m.;* **(stock e.)** Börse, -n *f.*

2. *vb.* tauschen; wechseln; aus•tauschen; *(goods)* um•tauschen.

exchangeable, *adj.* austauschbar; umtauschbar.

excise, 1. *n.* Verbrauchs´steuer, -n *f.* **2.** *vb.* heraus´schneiden*.

excite, *vb.* auf•regen, erre´gen; **(get e.d)** sich auf•regen.

excitement, *n.* Erre´gung, -en *f.;* Aufregung, -en *f.*

exclaim, *vb.* aus•rufen*.

exclamation, *n.* Ausruf, -e *m.*

exclamation point *or* **mark,** *n.* Ausrufungszeichen, - *nt.*

exclude, *vb.* aus•schließen*.

exclusion, *n.* Ausschluß, ⸗sse *m.*

exclusive, *adj.* ausschließlich; **(e. of)** abgesehen von; *(select)* exklusiv´.

excommunicate, *vb.* exkommunizie´ren.

excommunication, *n.* Exkommunikation´, -en *f.*

excrement, *n.* Exkrement´, -e *nt.*

excruciating, *adj.* qualvoll.

excursion, *n.* Ausflug, ⸗e *m.*

excusable, *adj.* entschuld´-bar.

excuse, *vb.* entschul´digen, verzei´hen*.

execute, *vb.* aus•führen; *(legal killing)* hin•richten.

execution, *n.* Ausführung, -en *f.; (legal killing)* Hinrichtung, -en *f.*

executioner, *n.* Scharfrichter, - *m.*

executive, 1. *n.* leitender Angestellter *m.,* leitende Angestellte *f. (gov't.)* Exekuti´ve *f.* **2.** *adj.* vollzie´hend, ausübend.

executor, *n.* Testaments´vollstrecker, - *m.*

exemplary, *adj.* musterhaft.

exemplify, *vb.* als Beispiel dienen.

exempt, 1. *adj.* befreit´. **2.** *vb.* befrei´en.

exercise, 1. *n.* Übung, -en *f.; (carrying out)*

Ausübung, -en *f.; (physical)* Bewe´gung, -en *f.* **2.** *vb.* üben; aus•üben; bewe´gen.

exert, *vb.* aus•üben; *(e. oneself)* sich an•strengen.

exertion, *n.* Anstrengung, -en *f.*

exhale, *vb.* aus•atmen.

exhaust, 1. *n. (auto.)* Auspuff, -e *m.* **2.** *vb.* erschöp´fen.

exhaustion, *n.* Erschöp´fung, -en *f.*

exhaustive, *adj.* erschöp´-fend.

exhibit, 1. *n.* Ausstellung, -en *f.* **2.** *vb.* aus•stellen; zeigen.

exhibition, *n.* Ausstellung, -en *f.*

exhibitionism, *n.* Exhibitio´nis´mus *m.*

exhilarate, *vb.* auf•heitern.

exhort, *vb.* ermah´nen.

exhortation, *n.* Ermah´nung, -en *f.*

exhume, *vb.* aus•graben*.

exigency, *n.* Dringlichkeit, -en *f.*

exile, 1. *n.* Verban´nung, -en *f.* **2.** *vb.* verban´nen.

exist, *vb.* beste´hen*, exi-stie´ren.

exodus, *n.* Auszug, ⸗e *m.;* Auswanderung, -en *f.*

exonerate, *vb.* entlas´ten.

exorbitant, *adj.* übermäßig.

exotic, *adj.* exo´tisch.

expand, *vb.* aus•dehnen, aus•breiten, erwei´tern.

expanse, *n.* Ausdehnung, -en *f.,* Weite, -n *f.*

expansion, *n.* Ausdehnung, -en *f.,* Ausbreitung, -en *f.;* Expansion´ *f.*

expansive, *adj.* umfas´send.

expatriate, *n.* Emigrant´, -en, -en *m.*

expect, *vb.* erwar´ten.

expectancy, *n.* Erwar´tung, -en *f.*

expectation, *n.* Erwar´tung, -en *f.*

expectorate, *vb.* (aus•)-spucken.

expediency, *n.* Zweckmäßigkeit, -en *f.*

expedient, *adj.* zweckmäßig.

expedite, *vb.* beschleu´-nigen.

expedition, *n.* Expedition´, -en *f.*

expel, *vb.* vertrei´ben*.

expend, *vb. (money)* aus•geben*; *(energy)* auf•wenden*.

expenditure, *n.* Ausgabe, -n *f.*, Aufwand *m.*

expense, *n.* Ausgabe, -n *f.;* Kosten *pl.,* Unkosten *pl.;* **(on an e. account)** auf Spesen.

expensive, *adj.* teuer, kost-spielig.

experience, 1. *n.* Erfah´rung, -en *f.* **2.** *vb.* erfah´ren*.

experienced, *adj.* erfah´ren.

experiment, 1. *n.* Versuch´ -e *m.,* Experiment´, -e *nt.* **2.** *vb.* experimentie´ren.

experimental, *adj.* Versuchs´- *(cpds.).*

experimentally, *adv.* ver-suchs´weise.

expert, 1. *n.* Sachver-ständig- *m&* *f.,* Exper´te, -n, -n *m.,* Exper´tin, -nen *f.* **2.** *adj.* erfah´ren.

expiate, *vb.* büßen.

expiration, *n. (breath)* Ausatmung, -en *f.; (end)* Ablauf *m.*

expire, *vb. (breathe out)* aus•atmen; *(die)* verschei´den; *(end)* ab•-laufen*.

explain, *vb.* erklä´ren.

explanation, *n.* Erklä´rung, -en *f.*

explanatory, *adj.* erklä´rend.

expletive, 1. *n.* Füllwort, *=er nt.;* Ausruf, -e *m.* **2.** *adj.* ausfüllend.

explicit, *adj.* ausdrücklich.

explode, *vb.* explodie´ren.

exploit, *vb.* aus•beuten, aus•nutzen.

exploitation, *n.* Ausbeutung, -en *f.,* Ausnutzung, -en *f.*

exploration, *n.* Erfor´schung, -en *f.*

exploratory, *adj.* untersu´-chend, erkun´dend.

explore, *vb.* erfor´schen, untersu´chen.

explorer, *n.* Forscher, - *m.,* Forschungsreisend- *m.*

explosion, *n.* Explosion´, -en *f.*

explosive, 1. *n.* Sprengstoff, -e *m.* **2.** *adj.* explosiv´.

exponent, *n.* Exponent´, -en, -en *m.*

export, 1. *n.* Export´, -e *m.,* Ausfuhr *f.* **2.** *vb.* exportie´-ren, aus•führen.

exportation, *n.* Ausfuhr *f.*

expose, *vb.* aus•setzen; *(photo)* belich´ten; *(dis-close)* enthül´len.

exposé, *n.* Darlegung, -en *f.; (disclosure)* Enthül´lung, -en *f.*

exposition, *n.* Darlegung, -en *f.; (exhibit)* Ausstel-lung, -en *f.*

expository, *adj.* erklä´rend.

exposure, *n.* Aussetzung, -en *f.; (photo)* Belich´tung, -en *f.;* Bloßstellung, -en *f.*

expound, *vb.* aus•legen, erklä´ren.

express, 1. *n. (train)* Schnellzug, *=e m.* **2.** *vb.* aus•drücken. **3.** *adj.* aus-drücklich.

expression, *n.* Ausdruck, *=e m.*

expressive, *adj.* aus-drucksvoll.

expropriate, *vb.* enteig´nen.

expulsion, *n.* Vertrei´bung, -en *f.,* Entlas´sung, -en *f.*

expurgate, *vb.* reinigen.

exquisite, *adj.* vorzüg´lich.

extant, *adj.* vorhan´den.

extemporaneous, *adj.* aus dem Stegreif.

extend, *vb. (intr.)* sich erstre´cken, reichen; *(tr.)* aus•dehnen.

extension, *n.* Ausdehnung, -en *f.;* Verlän´gerung, -en *f.*

extensive, *adj.* umfangre-ich.

extent, *n.* Umfang, *=e m.*

exterior, *adj.* äußer-, äußer-lich.

exterminate, *vb.* aus•rotten. vernich´ten.

extermination, *n.* Ausrot-tung, -en *f.,* Vernich´tung, -en *f.*

external, *adj.* äußer-; auswärtig.

extinct, *adj.* ausgestorben.

extinction, *n.* Aussterben *nt.*

extinguish, *vb.* aus•löschen.

extol, *vb.* loben, preisen*.

extort, *vb.* ab•zwingen*.

extortion, *n.* Erpres´sung, -en *f.*

extra, *adj.* extra, beson´der-.

extra-, *(cpds.)* außer-.

extract, 1. *n.* Auszug, *=e m.,* Extrakt´, -e *m.* **2.** *vb.* her-aus´•ziehen*, heraus´•holen.

extraction, *n.* Ausziehen *nt.; (ethnic)* Herkunft, *=e f.,* Abstammung, -en *f.*

extradite, *vb.* aus•liefern.

extradition, *n.* Ausliefer-ung, -en *f.*

extraneous, *adj.* fremd.

extraordinary, *adj.* außergewöhnlich.

extravagance, *n.* Verschwen´dung, -en *f.,* Extravaganz´, -en *f.*

extravagant, *adj.* verschwen´derisch; übertrie´ben.

extravaganza, *n.* phantas´tische, überspann´te Komposi-tion´, -en *f.*

extreme, *adj.* äußerst-.

extremely, *adv.* äußerst, höchst.

extremity, *n.* Äußerst- *nt.; (limbs)* Gliedmaßen *pl.*

extricate, *vb.* heraus•winden*.

exuberant, *adj.* über-schwenglich.

exult, *vb.* frohlo´cken.

exultant, *adj.* frohlo´ckend.

eye, *n.* Auge, -n *nt.*

eyeball, *n.* Augapfel, *= m.*

eyebrow, *n.* Augenbraue, -n *f.*

eyeglasses, *n.pl.* Brille, -n *f.*

eyelash, *n.* Augenwimper, -n *f.*

eyelet, *n.* Öse, -n *f.*

eyelid, *n.* Augenlid -er *nt.*

eyesight, *n.* Augensicht *f.;* Augen *pl.*

F

fable, *n.* Fabel, -n *f.*

fabric, *n.* Stoff, -e *m.*

fabricate, *vb.* her•stellen; *(lie)* erdich´ten.

fabrication, *n.* Herstellung, -en *f.; (lie)* Erdich´tung, -en *f.*

fabulous, *adj.* sagenhaft.

façade, *n.* Fassa´de, -n *f.*

face, 1. *n.* Gesicht´, -er *nt.; (surface)* Oberfläche, -n *f.* **2.** *vb.* ins Gesicht´ sehen*; *(be opposite)* gegen•ber•liegen*.

facet, *n.* Facet´te, -n *f.*

facetious, *adj.* scherzhaft.

face value, *n.* Nennwert, -e *m.*

facial, 1. *n.* Gesichts´massage, -n *f.* **2.** *adj.* Gesichts´- *(cpds.).*

facile, *adj.* gewandt´.

facilitate, *vb.* erleich´tern.

facility, *n. (ease)* Leichtigkeit *f.; (skill)* Geschick´lichkeit *f.; (possibility)* Möglichkeit, -en *f.*

facing, *n. (clothing)* Besatz´ *m.*

facsimile, *n.* Faksi´mile, -s *nt.*

fact, *n.* Tatsache, -n *f.*

faction, *n.* Gruppe, -n *f.*

factor, *n.* Faktor, -o´ren *m.*

factory, *n.* Fabrik´, -en *f.*

factual, *adj.* auf Tatsachen beschränkt´; Tatsachen- *(cpds.).*

faculty, *n.* Fähigkeit, -en *f.,* Gabe, -n *f.; (college)* Fakultät´, -en *f.*

fad, *n.* Mode, -n *f.*

fade, *vb.* verblas´sen.

fail, *vb.* versa´gen; *(school)* durch•fallen*; **(f. to do)** nicht tun*.

failure, *n.* Versa´gen *nt.,* Mißerfolg, -e *m.; (bankruptcy)* Bankrott´, -e *m.*

faint, 1. *adj.* schwach. **2.** *vb.* in Ohnmacht fallen*.

fair, 1. *n.* Messe, -n *f.,* Jahrmarkt, -e *m.,* Rummelplatz, -e *m.* **2.** *adj.*

(weather) heiter; *(blond)* blond; *(just)* gerecht´.

fairness, *n.* Gerech´tigkeit, -en *f.*

fairy, *n.* Fee, Fe´en *f.*

fairy tale, *n.* Märchen, - *nt.*

faith, *n. (trust)* Vertrau´en *nt.; (belief)* Glaube(n), - *m.*

faithful, *adj.* treu.

faithfulness, *n.* Treue *f.*

faithless, *adj.* treulos.

fake, 1. *adj.* falsch. **2.** *vb.* vor•täuschen.

faker, *n.* Schwindler, - *m.,* Schwindlerin, -nen *f.*

falcon, *n.* Falke, -n, -n *m.*

fall, 1. *n.* Fall, -e *m.,* Sturz -e *m.; (autumn)* Herbst, -e *m.* **2.** *vb.* fallen*.

fallacious, *adj.* trügerisch.

fallacy, *n.* Trugschluß, -sse *m.*

fallible, *adj.* fehlbar.

fallout, *n.* (radioaktiver) Niederschlag, -e *m.*

fallow, *adj.* brach.

false, *adj.* falsch.

falsehood, *n.* Lüge, -n *f.*

falseness, *n.* Falschheit, -en *f.*

falsetto, *n.* Falsett´, -e *nt.*

falsification, *n.* Verfäl´schung, -en *f.*

falsify, *vb.* verfäl´schen.

falter, *vb.* straucheln, stocken.

fame, *n.* Ruhm *m.*

famed, *adj.* berühmt´.

familiar, *adj.* vertraut´.

familiarity, *n.* Vertraut´heit, -en *f.;* Vertrau´lichkeit, -en *f.*

familiarize, *vb.* vertraut´machen.

family, *n.* Fami´lie, -n *f.*

famine, *n.* Hungersnot, -e *f.*

famished, *adj.* ausgehungert.

famous, *adj.* berühmt´.

fan, 1. *n.* Fächer, - *m.;* Ventila´tor, -o´ren *m.; (enthusiast)* Vereh´rer, - *m.,* Vereh´rerin, -nen *f.,* Anhänger, - *m.,* Anhängerin, -nen *f.* **2.** *vb.* fächern.

fanatic, 1. *n.* Fana´tiker, - *m.,* Fana´tikerin, -nen *f.* **2.** *adj.* fana´tisch.

fanatical, *adj.* fana´tisch.

fanaticism, *n.* Fanatis´mus *m.*

fanciful, *adj.* phantas´tisch.

fancy, 1. *n. (imagination)* Einbildung, -en *f.; (mood)* Laune, -n *f.; (liking)* Vorliebe *f.* **2.** *adj.* apart´, ausgefallen; Luxus- *(cpds.).* **3.** *vb.* sich ein•bilden.

fanfare, *n.* Fanfa´re, -n *f.; (fig.)* Getu´e *nt.*

fang, *n.* Fang, -e *m.*

fantastic, *adj.* phantas´tisch.

fantasy, *n.* Phantasie´, -i´en *f.*

far, *adj.* weit, fern.

faraway, *adj.* entfernt´; *(fig.)* träumerisch.

farce, *n.* Farce, -n *f.*

fare, 1. *n. (passenger)* Fahrgeld, -er *nt.; (price)* Fahrpreis, -e *m.; (food)* Kost *f.* **2.** *vb.* gehen*.

farewell, 1. *n.* Abschied, -e *m.;* Abschieds- *(cpds.).* **2.** *interj.* lebe wohl! leben Sie wohl!

far-fetched, *adj.* gesucht´.

farina, *n.* Grießmehl *nt.*

farm, 1. *n.* landwirtschaftlicher Betrieb´, -e *m.,* Farm, -en *f.* **2.** *vb.* Landwirtschaft betrei´ben*, Landwirt sein*.

farmer, *n.* Landwirt, -e *m.,* Landwirtin, -nen *f.* Farmer, - *m.,* Bauer, (-n) -n *m.*

farmhouse, *n.* Farmhaus, -er *nt.;* Bauernhaus, -er *nt.*

farming, *n.* Landwirtschaft *f.;* Ackerbau *m.*

farmyard, *n.* Bauernhof, -e *m.*

far-sighted, *adj.* weitsichtig.

farther, *adj.* weiter.

farthest, *adj.* weitest-.

fascinate, *vb.* faszinie´ren, bezau´bern.

fascination, *n.* Faszination *f.,* Zauber *m.*

fascism, *n.* Faschis´mus *m.*

fascist, 1. *n.* Faschist´, -en, -en *m.* **2.** *adj.* faschis´tisch.

fashion, *n.* Mode, -n *f.;* (*manner*) Art, -en *f.*

fashionable, *adj.* modern´, schick.

fast, 1. *n.* Fasten *nt.* **2.** *adj.* (*speedy*) schnell; (**be f.,** of a clock) vor•gehen*; (*firm*) fest. **3.** *vb.* fasten.

fasten, *vb.* fest•machen.

fastener, fastening, *n.* Verschluß´, ¨sse *m.*

fastidious, *adj.* wählerisch; eigen.

fat, 1. *n.* Fett, -e *nt.* **2.** *adj.* fett, dick.

fatal, *adj.* tötlich; verhäng´nisvoll.

fatality, *n.* Verhäng´nis, -se *nt.;* Todesfall, ¨e *m.*

fate, *n.* Schicksal, -e *nt.*

fateful, *adj.* schicksalsschwer; verhäng´nisvoll.

father, *n.* Vater, ¨ *m.*

fatherhood, *n.* Vaterschaft, -en *f.*

father-in-law, *n.* Schwiegervater, ¨ *m.*

fatherland, *n.* Vaterland *nt.*

fatherless, *adj.* vaterlos.

fatherly, *adj.* väterlich.

fathom, 1. *n.* Klafter, -n *f.* **2.** *vb.* loten; (*fig.*) ergrün´den.

fatigue, 1. *n.* Ermü´dung *f.* **2.** *vb.* ermü´den.

fatten, *vb.* mästen.

fatty, *adj.* fettig.

faucet, *n.* Wasserhahn, ¨e *m.*

fault, *n.* Fehler, - *m.;* (**it's my f.**) es ist meine Schuld.

faultless, *adj.* fehlerlos, makellos.

faulty, *adj.* fehlerhaft.

favor, 1. *n.* Gunst, -en *f.;* (**do a f.**) einen Gefallen tun*. **2.** *vb.* begün´stigen, bevor´zugen; (*a sore limb*) schonen.

favorable, *adj.* günstig.

favorite, 1. *n.* Liebling, -e *m.;* (*sport*) Favorit´, -en, -en *m.,* Favori´tin, -nen *f.* **2.** *adj.* Lieblings- (*cpds.*).

favoritism, *n.* Begün´stigung *f.*

fawn, *n.* Rehkalb, -er *nt.*

fax, *vb.* faxen.

faze, *vb.* in Verle´genheit bringen*.

fear, 1. *n.* Furcht *f.,* Angst, ¨e *f.* **2.** *vb.* fürchten.

fearful, *adj.* (*afraid*) furchtsam; (*terrible*) furchtbar.

fearless, *adj.* furchtlos.

fearlessness, *n.* Furchtlosigkeit *f.*

feasible, *adj.* durchführbar, machbar.

feast, *n.* Fest, -e *nt.,* Festmahl, -e *nt.*

feat, *n.* Tat, -en *f.;* Kunststück, -e *nt.*

feather, *n.* Feder, -n *f.*

feature, *n.* (*quality*) Eigenschaft, -en *f.;* (*face*) Gesichtszug, ¨e *m.;* (*distinguishing mark*) Kennzeichen, - *nt.*

February, *n.* Februar *m.*

feces, *n.pl.* Exkremen´te *pl.*

federal, *adj.* bundesstaatlich; Bundes- (*cpds.*).

federation, *n.* Staatenbund, -e *m.,* Föderation´, -en *f.;* Bundesstaat, -en *m.*

fee, *n.* Gebühr´, -en *f.*

feeble, *adj.* schwach (¨).

feeble-minded, *adj.* schwachsinnig.

feebleness, *n.* Schwäche, -n *f.*

feed, 1. *n.* Futter, - *nt.* **2.** *vb.* füttern.

feedback, *n.* Feedback *m.,* Rückkopplung *f.*

feel, *vb.* fühlen.

feeling, *n.* Gefühl´, -e *nt.*

feign, *vb.* vor•geben*, heucheln.

felicitate, *vb.* beglück´wünschen.

felicity, *n.* Glück *nt.*

fell, *vb.* fällen.

fellow, *n.* Kerl, -e *m.,* Bursche, -n, -n *m.;* (*member*) Mitglied, -er *nt.*

fellowship, *n.* Gemein´schaft, -en *f.*

felony, *n.* Gewalt´verbrechen, - *nt.*

felt, *n.* Filz, -e *m.*

female, 1. *n.* (*human*) Frau, -en *f.;* (*animal*) Weibchen, - *nt.* **2.** *adj.* weiblich.

feminine, *adj.* weiblich, feminin´.

femininity, *n.* Weiblichkeit *f.*

feminist, *n.* Frauenrechtlerin, -nen *f.,* Frauenrechtler, -*m.;* Feminist´, -en, -en *m.,* Feminist´tin, -nen *f.*

fence, 1. *n.* Zaun, ¨e *m.* **2.** *vb.* ein•zäunen; (*sport*) fechten*.

fencing, *n.* Fechten *nt.*

fender, *n.* (*auto*) Kotflügel, - *m.*

ferment, *vb.* gären*.

fermentation, *n.* Gärung, -en *f.*

fern, *n.* Farnkraut, ¨er *nt.*

ferocious, *adj.* wild.

ferocity, *n.* Wildheit *f.*

ferry, *n.* Fähre, -n *f.*

fertile, *adj.* fruchtbar.

fertility, *n.* Fruchtbarkeit *f.*

fertilization, *n.* Befruch´tung, -en *f.*

fertilize, *vb.* befruch´ten; düngen.

fertilizer, *n.* Dünger *m.,* Kunstdünger *m.*

fervent, *adj.* inbrünstig.

fervid, *adj.* brennend.

fervor, *n.* Inbrunst *f.,* Eifer *m.*

fester, *vb.* eitern.

festival, *n.* Fest, -e *nt.*

festive, *adj.* festlich.

festivity, *n.* Festlichkeit, -en *f.*

festoon, *n.* Girlan´de, -n *f.*

fetch, *vb.* holen.

fetching, *adj.* reizend.

fête, *n.* Fest, -e *nt.*

fetid, *adj.* stinkend.

fetish, *n.* Fetisch, -e *m.*

fetters, *n.pl.* Fesseln *pl.*

fetus, *n.* Foetus, -se *m.*

feud, *n.* Feindschaft, -en *f.;* (*historical*) Fehde, -n *f.*

feudal, *adj.* feudal´.

feudalism, *n.* Feudalis´mus *m.*

fever, *n.* Fieber, - *nt.*

feverish, *adj.* fieberhaft.

few, *adj.* wenig; (**a f.**) ein paar.

fiancé, *n.* Verlobt´- *m.*

fiancée, *n.* Verlobt´- *f.*

fiasco, *n.* Fias´ko, -s *nt.*

fib, *n.* Lüge, -n *f.*

fiber, *n.* Faser, -n *f.*

fickle, *adj.* wankelmütig.

fickleness, *n.* Wankelmütigkeit *f.*

fiction, *n.* Erdich´tung, *f.;* *(novel writing)* Prosadichtung, -en *f.*

fictional, *adj.* erdich´tet.

fictitious, *adj.* fingiert´.

fiddle, 1. *n.* Geige, -n *f.* **2.** *vb.* geigen.

fidelity, *n.* Treue *f.*

fidget, *vb.* zappeln.

field, *n.* Feld, -er *nt.*

fiend, *n.* Teufel, - *m.*

fiendish, *adj.* teuflisch.

fierce, *adj.* wild.

fiery, *adj.* feurig.

fife, *n.* Querpfeife, -n *f.*

fifteen, *num.* fünfzehn.

fifteenth, 1. *adj.* fünfzehnt-. **2.** *n.* Fünfzehntel, - *nt.*

fifth, 1. *adj.* fünft-. **2.** *n.* Fünftel, - *nt.*

fiftieth, 1. *adj.* fünfzigst-. **2.** *n.* Fünfzigstel, - *nt.*

fifty, *num.* fünfzig.

fig, *n.* Feige, -n *f.*

fight, 1. *n.* Kampf, ‗e *m.;* *(brawl)* Schlägerei´, -en *f.;* *(quarrel)* Streit, -e *m.* **2.** *vb.* kämpfen; bekämp´fen.

fighter, *n.* Kämpfer, - *m.*

figment, *n.* Fiktion´, -en *f.*

figurative, *adj.* bildlich; **(f. meaning)** übertra´gene Bedeu´tung, -en *f.*

figure, 1. *n.* Figur´, -en *f.,* Gestalt´, -en *f.; (number)* Zahl, -en *f.* **2.** *vb.* rechnen; berech´nen.

figurehead, *n.* Galionsfigur, -en *f.; (fig.)* Repräsentations´figur, -en *f.*

figure of speech, *n.* Redewendung, -en *f.*

figurine, *n.* Porzellan´figur, -en *f.*

filament, *n.* Faser, -n *f.,* Faden, ‗ *m.*

file, 1. *n. (tool)* Feile, -n *f.; (row)* Reihe, -n *f.; (papers, etc.)* Akte, -n *f.; (cards)* Kartothek´, -en *f.* **2.** *vb. (tool)* feilen; *(papers)* ein•ordnen.

filigree, *n.* Filigran´, -e *nt.*

fill, *vb.* füllen.

fillet, *n.* Filet´, -s *nt.*

filling, *n. (tooth)* Plombe, -n *f.*

filling station, *n.* Tankstelle, -n *f.*

film, 1. *n.* Film, -e *m.* **2.** *vb.* filmen.

filmy, *adj.* mit einem Häutchen bedeckt; duftig.

filter, 1. *n.* Filter, - *m.* **2.** *vb.* filtrie´ren.

filth, *n.* Dreck *m.*

filthy, *adj.* dreckig; *(fig.)* unanständig.

fin, *n.* Flosse, -n *f.*

final, *adj.* endgültig.

finale, *n.* Fina´le, -s *nt.*

finalist, *n.* Teilnehmer (-, *m.),* Teilnehmerin (-nen, *f.*) in der Schlußrunde.

finality, *n.* Endgültigkeit *f.*

finance, 1. *n.* Finanz´, -en *f.; (study)* Finanz´wesen *nt.; (f.s.)* Finan´zen *pl.* **2.** *vb.* financie´ren.

financial, *adj.* finanziell´.

financier, *n.* Finanz´mann, ‗er *m.*

find, *vb.* finden*.

findings, *n.pl.* Tatbestand, ‗e *m.*

fine, 1. *n.* Geldstrafe, -n *f.* **2.** *adj.* fein. **3.** *vb.* zu einer Geldstrafe verur´teilen.

fine arts, *n.* Kunstwissenschaft *f.*

finery, *n.* Putz *m.*

finesse, *n.* Fines´se, -n *f.*

finger, *n.* Finger, - *m.*

fingernail, *n.* Fingernagel, *m.*

fingerprint, *n.* Fingerabdruck, ‗e *m.*

finicky, *adj.* zimperlich.

finish, 1. *n.* Ende, -n *nt.;* Abschluß. ‗sse *m.* **2.** *vb.* been´den, vollen´den.

finite, *adj.* endlich.

fir, *n.* Fichte, -n *f.*

fire, 1. *n.* Feuer, - *nt.* **2.** *vb. (shoot)* feuern; *(dismiss)* entlas´sen*.

fire alarm, *n.* Feueralarm, -e *m.*

fire-alarm box, *n.* Feuermelder, - *m.*

firearm, *n.* Feuerwaffe, -n *f.*

fire engine, *n.* Feuerspritze, -n *f.*

fire escape, *n.* Feuerleiter, -n *f.*

fire extinguisher, *n.* Feuerlöscher, - *m.*

fireman, *n.* Feuerwehrmann, ‗er *m.*

fireplace, *n.* Kamin´, -e *m.*

fireproof, *adj.* feuerfest.

fireworks, *n.* Feuerwerk, -e *nt.*

firm, 1. *n.* Firma, -men *f.* **2.** *adj.* fest.

firmness, *n.* Festigkeit *f.*

first, 1. *adj.* erst. **2.** *adv.* zuerst´.

first aid, *n.* erste Hilfe *f.*

first-class, *adj.* erstklassig, erster Klasse.

fiscal, *adj.* fiska´lisch.

fish, 1. *n.* Fisch. -e *m.* **2.** *vb.* fischen, angeln.

fisherman, *n.* Fischer, - *m.,* Angler, - *m.*

fishing, *n.* Angeln *nt.*

fission, *n.* Spaltung, -en *f.;* **(nuclear f.)** Kernspaltung *f.*

fissure, *n.* Spalt, -e *m.*

fist, *n.* Faust, ‗e *f.*

fit, 1. *(attack)* Anfall, ‗e *m.* **2.** *adj.* in Form. **3.** *vb.* passen; *(adapt)* an•passen.

fitful, *adj.* unregelmäßig.

fitness, *n.* Tauglichkeit *f.;* Gesund´heit *f.*

fitting, 1. *n.* Anprobe, -n *f.* **2.** *adj.* passend.

five, *num.* fünf.

fix, 1. *n. (predicament)* Verle´genheit, -en *f.* **2.** *vb.* fest•setzen; *(prepare)* zubereiten; *(repair)* reparie´ren.

fixation, *n.* Fixie´rung, -en *f.*

fixed, *adj. (repaired)* heil; *(set)* fest.

fixture, *n.* Vorrichtung, -en *f.;* Zubehör *nt.*

flabby, *adj.* schlaff.

flag, *n.* Fahne, -n *f.,* Flagge, -n *f.*

flagpole, *n.* Fahnenstange, -n *f.*

flagrant, *adj.* schreiend.

flagship, *n.* Flaggschiff, -e *nt.*

flair, *n.* Flair *nt.*

flake, *n.* Flocke, -n *f.*

flamboyant, *adj.* flammend; *(fig.)* überla´den.

flame, 1. *n.* Flamme, -n *f.* **2.** *vb.* flammen.

flank, 1. *n.* Flanke, -n *f.* **2.** *vb.* flankie´ren.

flannel, *n.* Flanell´, -e *m.*

flap, 1. *n.* Klappe, -n *f.; (wings)* Flügelschlag, ⸗e *m.* **2.** *vb.* flattern.

flare, 1. *n.* Leuchtsignal, -e *nt.* **2.** *vb.* flackern.

flash, 1. *n.* Lichtstrahl, -en *m.* **2.** *vb.* auf•flammen.

flashcube, *n.* Blitzwürfel, - *m.*

flashlight, *n.* Taschenlampe, -n *f.*

flashy, *adj.* auffällig; *(clothes, etc.)* laut.

flask, *n.* Flasche, -n *f.*

flat, 1. *n.* Mietswohnung, - en *f.* **2.** *adj.* flach, platt.

flatcar, *n.* offener Güterwagen, - *m.*

flatness, *n.* Flachheit, -en *f.*

flatten, *vb.* flach machen.

flatter, *vb.* schmeicheln.

flattering, *adj.* schmeichelhaft.

flattery, *n.* Schmeichelei´, - en *f.*

flaunt, *vb.* zur Schau stellen.

flavor, 1. *n. (taste)* Geschmack´, ⸗e *m.; (odor)* Geruch´, ⸗e *m.* **2.** *vb.* würzen.

flavoring, *n.* Geschmack´, ⸗e *m.;* Essenz´, -en *f.*

flavorless, *adj.* fade.

flaw, *n.* Fehler, - *m.,* Makel, - *m.*

flawless, *adj.* fehlerfrei, makellos.

flax, *n.* Flachs *m.*

flay, *vb.* schinden*.

flea, *n.* Floh, ⸗e *m.*

fleck, *n.* Fleck, -e *m.*

flee, *vb.* fliehen*, flüchten.

fleece, *n.* Vlies, -e *nt.*

fleecy, *adj.* wollig.

fleet, *n.* Flotte, -n *f.*

fleeting, *adj.* flüchtig.

Fleming, *n.* Flame, -n, -n *m.*

Flemish, *adj.* flämisch.

flesh, *n.* Fleisch *nt.*

fleshy, *adj.* fleischig.

flex, *vb.* biegen*; beugen.

flexibility, *n.* Biegsamkeit *f.*

flexible, *adj.* biegsam, flexi´bel.

flicker, *vb.* flackern.

flier, *n.* Flieger, - *m.*

flight, *n.* Flug, ⸗e *m.; (escape)* Flucht, -en *f.*

flight attendants, *n.pl.* Flugpersonal *nt.*

flimsy, *adj.* dünn; lose.

flinch, *vb.* zurück•zucken.

fling, *vb.* schleudern.

flint, *n.* Feuerstein, -e *m.*

flip, *vb.* schnellen.

flippant, *adj.* vorlaut.

flirt, 1. *n.* Flirt, -s *m.* **2.** *vb.* flirten, kokettie´ren.

flirtation, *n.* Flirt, -s *m.*

float, 1. *n.* Floß, ⸗e *nt.* **2.** *vb.* treiben*, schwimmen*.

flock, *n.* Herde, - *f.,* Schar, - en *f.*

flog, *vb.* peitschen.

flood, 1. *n.* Flut, -en *f.;* Überschwem´mung, -en *f.* **2.** *vb.* überschwem´men.

floodlight, *n.* Scheinwerfer, - *m.*

floor, *n.* Fußboden, ⸗ *m.; (story)* Stockwerk, -e *nt.*

floorwalker, *n.* Abteilungsaufseher (, - *m.*) in einem Warenhaus.

flop, 1. *n. (thud)* Plumps *m.; (failure)* Reinfall, ⸗e *m.* **2.** *vb.* plumpsen: rein•gallen*.

floral, *adj.* Blumen- *(cpds.).*

florid, *adj.* gerö´tet.

florist, *n.* Blumenhändler, - *m.,* Blumenhändlerin, - nen *f.*

flounce, 1. *n.* Volant´, -s *m.* **2.** *vb.* tänzeln.

flounder, 1. *n.* Flunder, -n *f.* **2.** *vb.* taumeln.

flour, *n.* Mehl *nt.*

flourish, *vb. (grow)* gedei´hen*, blühen; *(shake)* schwenken.

flow, *vb.* fließen*.

flower, 1. *n.* Blume, -n *f.* **2.** *vb.* blühen.

flowerpot, *n.* Blumentopf, ⸗e *m.*

flowery, *adj.* blumig.

fluctuate, *vb.* schwanken.

fluctuation, *n.* Schwankung, -en *f.*

flue, *n.* Rauchfang, ⸗e *m.*

fluency, *n.* Geläu´figkeit *f.*

fluent, *adj.* fließend.

fluffy, *adj.* flaumig, wollig.

fluid, 1. *n.* Flüssigkeit, -en *f.* **2.** *adj.* flüssig.

fluidity, *n.* flüssiger Aggregat´zustand *m.;* Flüssigsein *nt.*

fluorescent, *adj.* fluoreszie´rend.

fluoroscope, *n.* Leuchtschirm, -e *m.,* Fluroskop´, -e *nt.*

flurry, *n.* Wirbel, - *m.*

flush, 1. *n.* Röte *f.; (fig.)* Flut *f.* **2.** *vb.* errö´ten; *(wash out)* aus•spülen; *(toilet)* aufziehen*.

flute, *n.* Flöte, -n *f.*

flutter, *vb.* flattern.

flux, *n.* Fluß *m.;* Strömen *nt.*

fly, 1. *n.* Fliege, -n *f.* **2.** *vb.* fliegen*.

foam, 1. *n.* Schaum, ⸗e *m.* **2.** *vb.* schäumen.

focal, *adj.* fokal´.

focus, 1. *n.* Brennpunkt, -e *m.* **2.** *vb.* (scharf, richtig) ein•stellen.

fodder, *n.* Futter *nt.*

foe, *n.* Feind, -e *m.*

fog, *n.* Nebel *m.*

foggy, *adj.* neblig.

foil, 1. *n.* Rapier´, -e *nt.* **2.** *vb.* verei´teln.

foist, *vb.* unterschie´ben*.

fold, 1. *n.* Falte, -n *f.* **2.** *vb.* falten.

folder, *n. (for papers)* Mappe, -n *f.,* Hefter, - *m.; (brochure)* Broschü´re, -n *f.,* Prospekt´, -e *m.*

foliage, *n.* Laub *nt.*

folio, *n.* Folio, -lien *nt.*

folk, *n.* Volk, ⸗er *nt.*

folklore, *n.* Volkskunde *f.*

folks, *n.pl.* Leute *pl.*

follow, *vb.* folgen.

follower, *n.* Anhänger, - *m.,* Anhängerin, -nen *f.*

folly, *n.* Torheit, -en *f.*, Verrückt´heit, -en *f.*

foment, *vb.* schüren.

fond, *adj.* **(be f. of)** gern haben*.

fondle, *vb.* liebkosen.

fondness, *n.* Vorliebe *f.*

food, *n.* Nahrung, *f.*, Essen *nt.*

foodstuffs, *n.* Nahrungsmittel *pl.*

fool, 1. *n.* Narr, -en, -en *m.* **2.** *vb.* täuschen, zum Narren halten*.

foolhardiness, *n.* Tollkühnheit, -en *f.*

foolhardy, *adj.* tollkühn.

foolish, *adj.* dumm, närrisch.

foolproof, *adj.* narrensicher.

foot, *n.* Fuß, ⸚e *m.*

footage, *n.* Länge in Fuß gemessen.

football, *n.* Fußball, ⸚e *m.*

foothills, *n.pl.* Vorgebirge *nt.*

foothold, *n.* Halt *m.*

footing, *n.* Stand *m.;* Boden *m.*

footlights, *n.pl.* Rampenlicht, -er *nt.*

footnote, *n.* Fußnote, -n *f.*

footprint, *n.* Fußstapfe, -n *f.*

footstep, *n.* Fußstapfe, -n *f.*

for, 1. *prep.* für **2.** *conj.* denn.

forage, 1. *n.* Futter *nt.* **2.** *vb.* furagie´ren.

foray, *n.* Überfall, ⸚e *m.*

forbearance, *n.* Enthal´tung *f.;* Nachsicht *f.*

forbid, *vb.* verbie´ten*.

forbidding, *adj.* abschreckend.

force, 1. *n.* Kraft, ⸚e *f.*, Gewalt´, -en *f.* **2.** *vb.* zwingen*.

forceful, *adj.* kräftig, wirkungsvoll.

forcefulness, *n.* Überzeu´gungskraft *f.*

forceps, *n.* Zange, -n *f.*

forcible, *adj.* kräftig, heftig, mit Gewalt´.

ford, *n.* Furt, -en *f.*

fore, *adv.* vorn.

forearm, *n.* Unterarm, -e *m.*

forebears, *n.pl.* Vorfahren *pl.*

foreboding, *n.* Vorahnung, -en *f.*

forecast, 1. *n.* Voraus´sage, -n *f.* **2.** *vb.* voraus´•sagen.

forecaster, *n.* Wetterprophet, -en, -en *m.*

foreclosure, *n.* Zwangsvollstreckung, -en *f.*

forefather, *n.* Vorfahr, -en, -en *m.*

forefinger, *n.* Zeigefinger, - *m.*

forefront, *n.* Vorderseite *f.*

foreground, *n.* Vordergrund *m.*

forehead, *n.* Stirn, -en *f.*

foreign, *adj.* fremd, ausländisch.

foreign aid, *n.* Entwick´lungshilfe *f.*

foreigner, *n.* Ausländer, - *m.*, Ausländerin, -nen *f.*

foreman, *n.* Vorarbeiter, - *m.*

foremost, *adj.* vorderst-.

forenoon, *n.* Vormittag, -e *m.*

forerunner, *n.* Vorläufer, - *m.*

foresee, *vb.* vorher´•sehen*.

foreshadow, *vb.* ahnen lassen*.

foresight, *n.* Voraus´sicht *f.*

forest, *n.* Wald, ⸚er *m.*

forestall, *vb.* verhin´dern, vorweg´•nehmen*.

forester, *n.* Förster, - *m.*

forestry, *n.* Forstwirtschaft *f.*

foretaste, *n.* Vorgeschmack, ⸚e *m.*

foretell, *vb.* vorher´•sagen, prophezei´en.

forever, *adv.* ewig.

forevermore, *adv.* für, auf immer und ewig.

forewarn, *vb.* vorher warnen.

foreword, *n.* Vorwort, -e *nt.*

forfeit, *vb.* verwir´ken, ein•büßen.

forfeiture, *n.* Verwir´kung *f.*, Einbuße *f.*

forgather, *vb.* sich versam´meln.

forge, 1. *n.* Schmiede, -n *f.* **2.** *vb.* schmieden; *(falsify)* fälschen.

forger, *n.* Fälscher, - *m.*, Fälscherin, -nen *f.*

forgery, *n.* Fälschung, -en *f.*

forget, *vb.* verges´sen*.

forgetful, *adj.* vergeß´lich.

forgive, *vb.* verge´ben*, verzei´hen*.

forgiveness, *n.* Verge´bung *f.*

forgo, *vb.* verzich´ten auf.

forlorn, *adj.* verlas´sen.

form, 1. *n.* Form, -en *f.; (blank)* Formular´, -e *nt.* **2.** *vb.* bilden, formen.

formal, *adj.* formell´; offiziell´.

formaldehyde, *n.* Formaldehyd´, -e *nt.*

formality, *n.* Formalität´, -en *f.;* Förmlichkeit, -en *f.*

format, *n.* Format´, -e *nt.*

formation, *n.* Gestal´tung, -en *f.; (mil.)* Formation´, -en *f.*

former, *adj.* ehemalig, früher; **(the f.)** jener, -es, -e.

formerly, *adv.* früher.

formidable, *adj.* beacht´lich.

formless, *adj.* formlos.

formula, *n.* Formel, -n *f.*

formulate, *vb.* formulie´ren.

formulation, *n.* Formulie´rung, -en *f.*

forsake, *vb.* verlas´sen*.

fort, *n.* Feste, -n *f.*

forte, *n.* Stärke, -n *f.*

forth, *adv.* fort; **(and so f.)** und so weiter.

forthcoming, *adj.* angekündigt.

forthright, *adj.* offen, ehrlich.

fortieth, 1. *adj.* vierzigst-. **2.** *n.* Vierzigstel, -nt.

fortification, *n.* Befes´tigungswerk, -e *nt.*

fortify, *vb.* stärken, befes´tigen.

fortissimo, *adj.* fortis´simo.

fortitude, *n.* seelische Stärke *f.*, Mut *m.*

fortnight, *n.* vierzehn Tage *pl.*

fortress, *n.* Festung, -en *f.*

fortuitous, *adj.* zufällig.

fortunate, *adj.* glücklich.

fortune, *n.* Glück *nt.; (money)* Vermö´gen, - *nt.*

fortune-teller, *n.* Wahrsager, - *m.*, Wahrsagerin, -nen *f.*

forty, *adj.* vierzig.

forum, *n.* Forum, -ra *nt.*

forward, *adv.* vorwärts.

forwardness, *n.* Dreistigkeit *f.*

fossil, *n.* Fossil´, -ien *nt.*

foster, *vb. (nourish)* nähren; *(raise)* auf´ziehen*; Pflege- *(cpds.).*

foul, *adj.* schmutzig.

found, *vb.* gründen.

foundation, *n. (building)* Fundament´, -e *nt.; (fund)* Stiftung, -en *f.*

founder, *n.* Gründer, - *m.*

foundling, *n.* Findling, -e *m.*

foundry, *n.* Gießerei´, -en *f.*

fountain, *n.* Springbrunnen, - *m.*

fountainhead, *n.* Urquell, -e *m.*

fountain pen, *n.* Füllfederhalter, - *m.*

four, *num.* vier.

fourteen, *num.* vierzehn.

fourteenth, 1. *adj.* vierzehnt-. **2.** *n.* Vierzehntel, - *nt.*

fourth, 1. *adj.* viert-. **2.** *n.* Viertel, - *nt.*

fowl, *n.* Geflü´gel *nt.;* Huhn, ∺er *nt.*

fox, *n.* Fuchs, ∺e *m.*

foxglove, *n.* Fingerhut, ∺e *m.*

foxhole, *n.* Schüt´zenloch, ∺er *nt.*

foxy, *adj.* schlau.

foyer, *n.* Foyer´, -s *nt.*

fracas, *n.* Keilerei´, -en *f.*

fraction, *n. (number)* Bruchstück, -e *nt.; (part)* Bruchteil, -e *m.;* **(f.s.)** Bruchrechnung *f.*

fracture, 1. *n.* Bruch, ∺e *nt.* **2.** *vb.* brechen*.

fragile, *adj.* zerbrech´lich.

fragment, *n.* Bruchstück, -e *nt.*

fragmentary, *adj.* fragmenta´risch.

fragrance, *n.* Duft, ∺e *m.*

fragrant, *adj.* wohlriechend.

frail, *adj.* zerbrech´lich, schwach (∺).

frailty, *n.* Schwachheit, -en *f.*

frame, 1. *n.* Rahmen, - *m.* **2.** *vb. (shape)* formen; *(enclose)* ein∙rahmen.

framework, *n.* Rahmen, - *m.*

France, *n.* Frankreich *nt.*

franchise, *n.* Wahlrecht, -e *nt.*

frank, *adj.* frei, offen.

frankfurter, *n.* Frankfurter Würstchen, - *nt.*

frankly, *adv.* ehrlich gesagt.

frankness, *n.* Offenheit *f.*

frantic, *adj.* wahnsinnig.

fraternal, *adj.* brüderlich.

fraternity, *n.* Brüderlichkeit *f.; (students)* Studen´tenverbindung, -en *f.*

fraternize, *vb.* fraternisie´ren.

fraud, *n.* Betrug´ *m.*

fraudulent, *adj.* betrügerisch.

fraught, *adj.* voll.

fray, *n.* Tumult´, -e *m.;* Schlägerei´, -en *f.*

freak, 1. *n.* Mißgeburt, -en *f.; Kurio´sum, -sa *nt.* **2.** *adj.* monströs´, bizarr´.

freckle, *n.* Sommersprosse, -n *f.*

freckled, *adj.* sommersprossig.

free, 1. *adj.* frei; kostenlos. **2.** *vb.* befrei´en; frei∙lassen*.

freedom, *n.* Freiheit, -en *f.*

freeze, *vb. (be cold)* frieren*; *(turn to ice) (intr.)* gefrie´ren*, *(tr.)* gefrie´ren lassen*; *(food)* tief kühlen; *(wages)* stoppen (Löhne).

freezer, *n.* Tiefkühler, - *m.; (in refrigerator)* Gefrier´fach, ∺er *nt.*

freezing, *adj.* eisig.

freight, *n.* Fracht, -en *f.;* Frachtgut *nt.*

freightage, *n.* Frachtspesen *pl.*

freighter, *n.* Frachter, - *m.*

French, *adj.* franzö´sisch.

Frenchman, *n.* Franzo´se, -n, -n *m.*

Frenchwoman, *n.* Franzö´sin, -nen *f.*

frenzied, *adj.* rasend.

frenzy, *n.* Raserei´, -en *f.*

frequency, *n.* Häufigkeit, -en *f.; (physics)* Frequenz´, -en *f.*

frequent, *adj.* häufig.

fresh, *adj.* frisch; *(impudent)* frech.

freshen, *vb.* erfri´schen.

freshman, *n.* Student´ im ersten College-Jahr.

freshness, *n.* Frische *f.*

fresh water, *n.* Süßwasser *nt.*

fret, *vb.* nervös´ sein*, nervös´ werden*.

fretful, *adj.* nervös´, unruhig.

fretfulness, *n.* Reizbarkeit, *f.*

friar, *n.* Bettelmönch, -e *m.*

fricassee, *n.* Frikassee´, -s *nt.*

friction, *n.* Reibung, -en *f.*

Friday, *n.* Freitag, -e *m.*

friend, *n.* Freund, -e *m.;* Freundin, -nen *f.*

friendless, *adj.* freundlos.

friendliness, *n.* Freundlichkeit, -en *f.*

friendly, *adj.* freundlich.

friendship, *n.* Freundschaft, -en *f.*

frigate, *n.* Fregat´te, -n *f.*

fright, *n.* Angst, ∺e *f.,* Schreck *m.*

frighten, *vb.* ängstigen, erschre´cken; **(be f.ed)** erschre´cken*.

frightful, *adj.* schrecklich.

frigid, *adj.* kalt (∺); *(sexual)* frigid´.

frill, *n.* Krause, -n *f.*

fringe, *n.* Franse, -n *f.;* Rand, ∺er *m.*

frisky, *adj.* lebhaft.

fritter, *n.* eine Art Pfannkuchen.

frivolity, *n.* Frivolität´, -en *f.*

frivolous, *adj.* leichtsinnig, frivol´.

frivolousness, *n.* Leichtsinnigkeit, -en *f.*

frock, *n.* Kleid, -er *nt.; (monk)* Kutte, -n *f.*

frog, *n.* Frosch, ∺e *m.*

frolic, *vb.* ausgelassen sein*.

from, *prep.* von, aus.

front, *n.* Vorderseite, -n *f.; (mil.)* Front, -en *f.;* **(in f.)** vorn; **(in f. of)** vor.

frontage, *n.* Vorderfront, -en *f.*

frontal, *adj.* frontal´.

frontier, *n.* Grenze, -n *f.*

frost, *n.* Frost, ∺e *m.*

frostbite, *n.* Frostbeule, -n *f.*

frosting, *n.* Kuchenglasur, - en *f.*

frosty, *adj.* frostig.

froth, *n.* Schaum, ⸗e *m.*

frown, *vb.* die Stirn runzeln.

frugal, *adv.* sparsam, frugal´.

frugality, *n.* Sparsamkeit *f.*

fruit, *n.* Frucht, ⸗e *f.,* Obst *nt.*

fruitful, *adj.* fruchtbar.

fruition, *n.* Reife *f.*

fruitless, *adj.* unfruchtbar; *(fig.)* vergeb´lich.

frustrate, *vb.* verdrän´gen; *(nullify)* verei´teln.

frustration, *n.* Verdrän´gung, -en *f.;* Verei´telung, -en *f.*

fry, *vb.* braten*.

fryer, *n.* junges Brathuhn, ⸗er *nt.*

frying pan, *n.* Bratpfanne, - n *f.*

fuchsia, *n.* Fuchsie, -n *f.*

fuel, *n.* Brennstoff, -e *m;* Treibstoff *m.*

fugitive, *n.* Flüchtling, -e *m.*

fugue, *n.* Fuge, -n *f.*

fulcrum, *n.* Drehpunkt, -e *m.*

fulfill, *vb.* erfül´len.

fulfillment, *n.* Erfül´lung, - en *f.*

full, *adj.* voll.

full dress, *n.* Frack, ⸗e *m.;* Gala-Uniform, -en *f.*

fullness, *n.* Fülle *f.*

fully, *adv.* völlig.

fumble, *vb.* umher•tappen.

fume, 1. *n.* Dampf, ⸗e *m.,* Dunst, ⸗e *m.* **2.** *vb.* dampfen, dunsten; *(fig.)* wüten.

fumigate, *vb.* aus•räuchern.

fumigator, *n.* Räucherapparat, -e *m.*

fun, *n.* Vergnü´gen *nt.,* Spaß *m.,* Jux *m.*

function, 1. *n.* Funktion´, - en *f.* **2.** *vb.* funktionie´ren.

functional, *adj.* sachlich.

fund, *n.* Fond, -s *m.*

fundamental, *adj.* grundlegend.

funeral, *n.* Begräb´nis, -se *nt.,* Beer´digung, -en *f.*

funereal, *adj.* düster.

fungicide, *n.* Pilzvernichtungsmittel, - *nt.*

fungus, *n.* Fungus, - *m.*

funnel, *n.* Trichter, - *m.; (smoke-stack)* Schornstein, -e *m.*

funny, *adj.* komisch, drollig.

fur, *n.* Pelz, -e *m.*

furious, *adj.* wütend.

furlough, *n.* Urlaub, -e *m.*

furnace, *n.* Ofen, ⸗ *m.*

furnish, *vb.* möblie´ren.

furnishings, *n.pl.* Ausstattung, -en *f.*

furniture, *n.* Möbel *pl.*

furor, *n.* Aufsehen *nt.*

furrier, *n.* Pelzhändler, - *m.*

furrow, *n.* Furche, -n *f.*

furry, *adj.* pelzartig.

further, 1. *vb.* fördern. **2.** *adj.* weiter, ferner.

furtherance, *n.* Förderung, -en *f.*

furthermore, *adv.* außerdem, überdies´.

fury, *n.* Wut *f.;* Zorn *m.; (mythology)* Furie, -n *f.*

fuse, 1. *n. (elec.)* Sicherung, -en *f.; (explosives)* Zünder, -e *m.* **2.** *vb.* verschmel´zen*.

fuselage, *n.* Rumpf, ⸗e *m.*

fusillade, *n.* Gewehr´feuer *nt.*

fusion, *n.* Verschmel´zung, -en *f.;* Fusion´, -en *f.*

fuss, *n.* Aufheben *nt,* Umstand, ⸗e *m.*

fussy, *adj.* umständlich, genau´, betu´lich.

futile, *adj.* vergeb´lich, nutzlos.

futility, *n.* Nutzlosigkeit *f.*

future, 1. *n.* Zukunft *f.* **2.** *adj.* zukünftig.

futurity, *n.* Zukunft *f.*

futurology, *n.* Futurologie´ *f.*

fuzz, *n.* Flaum *m.*

fuzzy, *adj.* flaumig.

G

gab, *vb.* schwatzen.

gabardine, *n.* Gabardine *m.*

gable, *n.* Giebel, - *m.*

gadget, *n.* Vorrichtung, -en *f.*

gag, 1. *n.* Knebel, - *m.; (joke)* Witz, -e *m.* **2.** *vb.* knebeln.

gaiety, *n.* Ausgelassenheit *f.*

gain, 1. *n.* Gewinn´, -e *m.* **2.** *vb.* gewin´nen*.

gainful, *adj.* einträglich.

gait, *n.* Gang, ⸗e *m.*

gala, *adj.* festlich.

galaxy, *n.* Milchstraße, -n *f.*

gale, *n.* Sturm, ⸗e *m.*

gall, 1. *n. (bile)* Galle, -n *f.; (insolence)* Unverschämtheit, -en *f.* **2.** *vb.* ärgern.

gallant, *adj.* aufmerksam, galant´.

gallantry, *n.* Höflichkeit, - en *f.,* Galanterie´, -i´en *f.*

gall bladder, *n.* Gallenblase, -n *f.*

gallery, *n.* Galerie´, -i´en *f.*

galley, *n. (ship)* Galee´re, -n *f.; (kitchen)* Kombü´se, - n *f.; (typogr.)* Setzschiff, -e *nt.*

Gallic, *adj.* gallisch.

gallivant, *vb.* bummeln.

gallon, *n.* Gallo´ne, -n *f.*

gallop, 1. *n.* Galopp´, -s *m.* **2.** *vb.* galoppie´ren.

gallows, *n.pl.* Galgen, - *m.*

gallstone, *n.* Gallenstein, -e *m.*

galore, *adv.* in Hülle und Fülle.

galosh, *n.* Überschuh, -e *m.*

gamble, 1. *n. (game)* Glücksspiel, -e *nt.; (risk)* Risiko, -s *nt.* **2.** *vb.* um Geld spielen; riskie´ren.

gambler, *n.* Glücksspieler,- *m.,* Glücksspielerin, -nen *f.*

gambling, *n.* Glücksspiel, -e *nt.*

game, 1. *n.* Spiel, -e *nt.; (hunting)* Wild *nt.,* Wildbret *nt.* **2.** *adj.* beherzt´; *(lame)* lahm.

gander, *n.* Gänserich, -e *m.*

gang, *n.* Bande, -n *f.*

gangplank, n. Laufplanke, -n f.

gangrene, n. Gangrän´, -e nt.

gangrenous, adj. gangränös´, brandig.

gangster, n. Gangster, - m.

gangway, n. Laufplanke, -n f.

gap, n. Lücke, -n f.; Spalte, -n f.

gape, vb. gaffen.

garage, n. Gara´ge, -n f.

garb, n. Gewand´, ≃er nt.

garbage, n. Abfall, ≃e m., Müll m.

garble, vb. entstel´len, verzer´ren.

garden, n. Garten, ≃ m.

gardener, n. Gärtner, - m., Gärtnerin, -nen f.

gardenia, n. Garde´nia, -ien f.

gargle, vb. gurgeln.

gargoyle, n. Wasserspeier, - m.

garish, adj. grell.

garland, n. Girlan´de, -n f.

garlic, n. Knoblauch m.

garment, n. Klei- dungsstück, -e nt.

garner, vb. auf•speichern.

garnet, n. Granat´, -e m.

garnish, vb. garnie´ren.

garret, n. Dachstube, -n f.

garrison, n. Garnison´, -en f.

garrulous, adj. schwatzhaft.

garter, n. Strumpfband, ≃er nt.; Hosenband, ≃er nt.; Sockenhalter, - m.

gas, n. Gas, -e nt.; (gaso-line) Benzin´ nt; (g. sta-tion) Tankstelle, -n f.

gaseous, adj. gasförmig.

gash, 1. n. klaffende Wunde, -n f. 2. vb. eine tiefe Wunde schlagen*.

gasket, n. Dichtung f.

gas mask, n. Gasmaske, -n f.

gasohol, n. Benzin-Alko-hol-Gech´ nt.

gasoline, n. Benzin´ nt.

gasp, vb. keuchen; nach Luft schnappen.

gastric, adj. gastrisch.

gastritis, n. Magen-schleimhautentzündung, -en f.

gastronomical, adj. gas-trono´misch.

gate, n. Tor, -e nt., Pforte, - n f.

gateway, n. Einfahrt, -en f., Tor, -e nt.

gather, vb. sammeln, pflücken; (infer) schließen*.

gathering, n. Versamm´lung, -en

gaudiness, n. auffälliger Protz m.

gaudy, adj. protzig.

gauge, 1. n. (measurement) Maß, -e nt.; (instrument) Messer, - m., Zeiger, - m.; (railway) Spurweite, -n f. 2. vb. ab•messen*.

gaunt, adj. hager.

gauntlet, n. Handschuh, -e m.

gauze, n. Gaze, -n f.

gavel, n. Hammer, ≃ m.

gawky, adj. linkisch.

gay, adj. fröhlich, heiter; (homosexual) homosex-uell, schwul.

gaze, vb. starren.

gazelle, n. Gazel´le, -n f.

gazette, n. Zeitung, -en f.

gazetteer, n. geogra´phis-ches Namenverzeichnis, -se nt.

gear, n. Zahnrad, ≃er nt.; (auto) Gang, ≃e m.; (equipment) Zeug nt.

gearing, n. Getrie´be, - nt.

gearshift, n. Schalthebel, m.

gelatin, n. Gelati´ne, -n f.

gelatinous, adj. gallertartig.

geld, vb. kastrie´ren.

gelding, n. Wallach, -e m.

gem, n. Edelstein, -e m.

gender, n. Geschlecht´, -er nt., Genus, -nera nt.

gene, n. Gen, -e nt.

genealogical, adj. genealo´gisch.

genealogy, n. Genealogie´, - i´en f.

general, 1. n. General´, ≃e m. 2. adj. allgemein.

generality, n. Allgemein´heit, -en f.

generalization, n. Verallge-mei´nerung, -en f.

generalize, vb. verallgemei´nern.

generally, adv. (in general) im allgemei´nen; (usu-ally) gewöhn´lich, meis-tens.

generate, vb. erzeu´gen.

generation, n. Generation´, -en f.

generator, n. Genera´tor, - o´ren m.

generic, adj. Gattungs- (cpds.).

generosity, n. Großzügigkeit f.

generous, adj. großzügig, freigebig.

genetic, adj. gene´tisch.

genetics, n. Verer´bungslehre f.

Geneva, n. Genf nt.

genial, adj. freundlich, froh.

geniality, n. Freundlichkeit f.

genital, adj. genital´.

genitals, n. Geschlechts´or-gane pl.

genitive, n. Genitiv, -e m.

genius, n. Genie´, -s nt.

genocide, n. Völkermord m.

genre, n. Genre, -s nt.

genteel, adj. vornehm.

gentile, 1. n. Nichtjude, -n, - n m. 2. adj. nichtjüdisch.

gentility, n. Vornehmheit f.

gentle, adj. sanft, mild.

gentleman, n. Herr, -n, -en m.

gentleness, n. Sanftheit f.

gentry, n. niederer Adel m.

genuflect, vb. das Knie beu-gen.

genuine, adj. echt.

genuineness, n. Echtheit f.

genus, n. Geschlecht´, -er nt., Gattung, -en f.

geographer, n. Geograph´, - en, -en m.

geographical, adj. geogra´-phisch.

geography, n. Geographie´ f., Erdkunde f.

geometric, adj. geome´-trisch.

geometry, n. Geometrie´ f.

geopolitics, n. Geopolitik´ f.

geranium, n. Gera´nie, -n f.

germ, n. Keim, -e m.; Bakte´rie, -n f.

German, 1. n. Deutsch-m.& f. 2. adj. deutsch.

germane, *adj.* zur Sache gehö´rig.

Germanic, *adj.* germa´nisch.

German measles, *n.* Röteln *pl.*

Germany, *n.* Deutschland *nt.; Bundesrepublik´ f.;* **(former East G.)** Deutsche Demokratische Republik *f.;* Ostdeutschland *nt.*

germicide, *n.* keimtötendes Mittel, - *nt.*

germinal, *adj.* Keim- *(cpds.).*

germinate, *vb.* keimen.

gestate, *vb.* aus•tragen*.

gestation, *n.* Gestation´, -en *f.*

gesticulate, *vb.* gestikulie´ren.

gesticulation, *n.* Gebär´de, - *n f.*

gesture, *n.* Gebär´de, -n *f.,* Geste, -n *f.*

get, *vb. (receive)* bekom´men*, kriegen; *(fetch)* holen; *(become)* werden*; *(arrive)* ankommen*; **(g. to)** hin•kommen*; **(g. up)** auf•stehen*; **(g. in)** ein•steigen*; **(g. out)** aus•steigen*.

geyser, *n.* Geiser, - *m.*

ghastly, *adj.* grauenhaft.

ghost, *n.* Geist, -er *m.,* Gespenst´, -er *nt.*

giant, **1.** *n.* Riese, -n, -n *m.* **2.** *adj.* riesenhaft.

gibberish, *n.* Kauderwelsch *nt.z*

gibbon, *n.* Gibbon, -s *m.*

giblets, *n.* Geflü´gelklein *nt.*

giddy, *adj.* schwindlig.

gift, *n.* Gabe, -n *f.,* Geschenk´, -e *nt.*

gifted, *adj.* begabt´.

gigantic, *adj.* riesenhaft.

giggle, *vb.* kichern.

gigolo, *n.* Gigolo, -s *m.*

gild, *vb.* vergol´den.

gill, *n.* Kieme, -n *f.*

gilt, *n.* Vergol´dung, -en *f.*

gimlet, *n.* Handbohrer, - *m.*

gin, *n.* Gin, -s *m.; (cotton)* Entker´nungsmaschine, - *n f.*

ginger, *n.* Ingwer *m.*

gingerly, *adv.* sachte.

gingham, *n.* Kattun´, -e *m.*

giraffe, *n.* Giraf´fe, -n *f.*

gird, *vb.* gürten.

girder, *n.* Träger, - *m.*

girdle, *n.* Gürtel, - *m.;* Strumpfbandgürtel, - *m.*

girl, *n.* Mädchen, - *nt.*

girlish, *adj.* mädchenhaft.

girth, *n.* Umfang, ≃e *m.*

gist, *n.* Kern, -e *m.*

give, *vb.* geben*.

given name, *n.* Vorname(n), - *m.*

gizzard, *n.* Geflü´gelmagen, ≃ *m.*

glacé, *adj.* glaciert´.

glacial, *adj.* Eis- *(cpds.).*

glad, *adj.* froh.

gladden, *vb.* erfreu´en.

gladiolus, *n.* Schwertlilie, - *n f.*

gladly, *adv.* gern.

gladness, *n.* Freude, -n *f.*

glamor, *n.* äußerer Glanz *m.;* beste´chende Schönheit *f.*

glamorous, *adj.* äußerst beste´chend, blendend.

glance, **1.** *n.* Blick, -e *m.* **2.** *vb.* blicken.

gland, *n.* Drüse, -n *f.*

glandular, *adj.* Drüsen- *(cpds.).*

glare, **1.** *n.* blendendes Licht *nt.* **2.** *vb.* blenden: *(look)* starren; **(g. at)** an•starren.

glaring, *adj.* grell.

glass, *n.* Glas, ≃er *nt.*

glasses, *n.pl.* Brille, -n *f.*

glassware, *n.* Glasware, -n *f.*

glassy, *adj.* glasig.

glaucoma, *n.* Glaukom´, -e *nt.*

glaze, **1.** *n.* Glasur´, -en *f.* **2.** *vb.* glasie´ren.

glazier, *n.* Glaser, - *m.*

gleam, **1.** *n.* Lichtstrahl, -en *m.* **2.** *vb.* strahlen, glänzen.

glee, *n.* Freude, -n *f.*

gleeful, *adj.* fröhlich.

glen, *n.* enges Tal, ≃er *nt.*

glib, *adj.* zungenfertig.

glide, **1.** *n.* Gleitflug, ≃e *m.* **2.** *vb.* gleiten*.

glider, *n.* Segelflugzeug, -e *nt.*

glimmer, **1.** *n.* Schimmer, - *m.* **2.** *vb.* schimmern.

glimpse, *n.* flüchtiger Blick, -e *m.*

glint, *n.* Lichtschimmer, - *m.*

glisten, *vb.* glänzen.

glitter, **1.** *n.* Glanz *m.* **2.** *vb.* glitzern.

gloat, *vb.* sich weiden; schadenfroh sein*.

global, *adj.* global´.

globe, *n.* Erdkugel, -n *f.;* Globus, -se *m.*

globular, *adj.* kugelförmig.

globule, *n.* Kügelchen, - *nt.*

gloom, *n.* Düsterheit *f.; (fig.)* Trübsinn *m.*

gloomy, *adj.* düster; trübsinnig.

glorification, *n.* Verherr´lichung *f.*

glorify, *vb.* verherr´lichen.

glorious, *adj.* ruhmvoll, glorreich.

glory, *n.* Ruhm *m.;* Herrlichkeit *f.*

gloss, *n.* Glanz *m.*

glossary, *n.* Glossar´, -e *nt.*

glossy, *adj.* glänzend.

glove, *n.* Handschuh, -e *m.*

glow, **1.** *n.* Glühen *nt.* **2.** *vb.* glühen.

glucose, *n.* Traubenzucker *m.*

glue, **1.** *n.* Leim *m.,* Klebstoff, -e *m.* **2.** *vb.* leimen, kleben.

glum, *adj.* mürrisch.

glumness, *n.* Mürrischkeit *f.*

glut, **1.** *n.* Überfluß *m.* **2.** *vb.* übersät´tigen.

glutinous, *adj.* leimig.

glutton, *n.* Vielfraß, -e *m.*

gluttonous, *adj.* gefrä´ßig.

glycerine, *n.* Glyzerin´ *nt.*

gnarled, *adj.* knorrig.

gnash, *vb.* knirschen.

gnat, *n.* Schnake, -n *f.*

gnaw, *vb.* knabbern.

go, *vb.* gehen*; *(become)* werden*; **(g. without)** entbeh´ren.

goad, **1.** *n.* Treibstock, ≃e *m.* **2.** *vb.* an•stacheln.

goal, *n.* Ziel, -e *nt.; (soccer)* Tor, -e *nt.*

goal-keeper, *n.* Torwart, ≃er *m.*

goat, *n.* Ziege, -n *f.; * Geiß, -en *f.; * **(billy g.)** Ziegenbock, ⸗e *m.*

goatee, *n.* Spitzbart, ⸗e *m.*

goatskin, *n.* Ziegenleder *nt.*

gobble, *vb.* verschlin´gen*.

go-between, *n.* Vermitt´ler, - *m.,* Vermitt´lerin, -nen *f.*

goblet, *n.* Kelchglas, ⸗er *nt.*

goblin, *n.* Kobold, -e *m.*

god, *n.* Gott, ⸗er *m.*

godchild, *n.* Patenkind, -er *nt.*

goddess, *n.* Göttin, -nen *f.*

godfather, *n.* Patenonkel *m.*

godless, *adj.* gottlos.

godlike, *adj.* gottähnlich.

godly, *adj.* göttlich.

godmother, *n.* Patentante, - n *f.*

godsend, *n.* Gottesgabe, -n *f.*

Godspeed, *n.* Lebewohl´ *nt.*

go-getter, *n.* Draufgänger, - m.

goiter, *n.* Kropf, ⸗e *m.*

gold, *n.* Gold *nt.*

golden, *adj.* golden.

goldfinch, *n.* Stieglitz, -e *m.*

goldfish, *n.* Goldfisch, -e *m.*

goldsmith, *n.* Goldschmied, -e *m.*

golf, *n.* Golf *nt.*

gondola, *n.* Gondel, -n *f.*

gondolier, *n.* Gondelführer, - *m.*

gone, *adv.* weg.

gong, *n.* Gong, -s *m.*

gonorrhea, *n.* Tripper *m.*

good, *adj.* gut (besser, best-).

good-by, *interj.* auf Wiedersehen.

Good Friday, *n.* Karfrei´tag *m.*

good-hearted, *adj.* gutherzig.

good-humored, *adj.* gutmütig.

good-looking, *adj.* gutaussehend.

good-natured, *adj.* gutmütig.

goodness, *n.* Güte *f.*

goods, *n.pl.* Waren *pl.*

good will, *n.* Wohlwollen *nt.*

goose, *n.* Gans, ⸗e *f.*

gooseberry, *n.* Stachelbeere, -n *f.*

gooseneck, *n.* Gänsehals, ⸗e *m.*

goose step, *n.* Stechschritt *m.*

gore, **1.** *n.* Blut *nt.* **2.** *vb.* auf•spießen.

gorge, *n.* *(anatomical)* Gurgel, -n *f.; (ravine)* Schlucht, -en *f.*

gorgeous, *adj.* prachtvoll.

gorilla, *n.* Goril´la, -s *m.*

gory, *adj.* blutig.

gospel, *n.* Evange´lium, -ien *nt.*

gossamer, **1.** *n.* hauchdünner Stoff *m.* **2.** *adj.* hauchdünn.

gossip, **1.** *n.* Klatsch *m.* **2.** *vb.* klatschen.

Gothic, **1.** *n.* Gotik *f.* **2.** *adj.* gotisch.

gouge, **1.** *n.* Hohleisen, - *nt.* **2.** *vb.* aus•höhlen.

gourd, *n.* Kürbis, -se *m.*

gourmand, *n.* Schlemmer, - *m.,* Schlemmerin, -nen *f.*

gourmet, *n.* Feinschmecker, - *m.,* Feinschmeckerin, -nen *f.*

govern, *vb.* regie´ren.

governess, *n.* Erzie´herin, -nen *f.*

government, *n.* Regie´rung, -en *f.*

governmental, *adj.* Regie´rungs- *(cpds.).*

governor, *n.* Gouverneur´, -e *m.,* Gouverneu´rin, -nen *f.*

governorship, *n.* Gouverneurs´amt, ⸗er *nt.*

gown, *n.* Kleid, -er *nt.*

grab, *vb.* greifen*.

grace, *n.* Anmut *f.; (mercy)* Gnade *f.*

graceful, *adj.* anmutig.

graceless, *adj.* unbeholfen.

gracious, *adj.* gnädig, gütig.

grade, **1.** *n.* Grad, -e *m.,* Rang, ⸗e *m.; (mark)* Zensur´, -en *f.; (class)* Klasse, -n *f.; (rise)* Steigung, -en *f.* **2.** *vb.* bewer´ten; *(smooth)* ebnen.

grade crossing, *n.* Bahnübergang, ⸗e *m.*

gradual, *adj.* allmäh´lich.

graduate, *vb.* gradui´eren.

graft, **1.** *n.* Beste´chung, -en *f.,* Korruption´ *f.* **2.** *vb. (bot.)* propfen.

grail, *n.* Gral *m.*

grain, *n.* Körnchen, - *nt.; (wheat, etc.)* Getrei´de *nt.; (wood)* Maserung, -en *f.*

gram, *n.* Gramm, - *nt.*

grammar, *n.* Gramma´tik, -en *f.*

grammar school, *n.* Grundschule, -n *f.*

grammatical, *adj.* gramma´tisch.

gramophone, *n.* Grammophon´, -e *nt.*

granary, *n.* Kornspeicher, - *m.*

grand, *adj.* großartig.

grandchild, *n.* Enkelkind, -er *nt.*

granddaughter, *n.* Enkelin, -nen *f.*

grandeur, *n.* Erha´benheit *f.*

grandfather, *n.* Großvater, ⸗ *m.*

grandiloquent, *adj.* schwülstig.

grandiose, *adj.* grandios´.

grandmother, *n.* Großmutter, ⸗ *f.*

grandparents, *n.pl.* Großeltern *pl.*

grandson, *n.* Enkel, - *m.*

grandstand, *n.* Tribü´ne, -n *f.*

granite, *n.* Granit´ *m.*

grant, **1.** *n.* finanziel´le Beihilfe, -n *f.; * Stipen´dium, -en *nt.* **2.** *vb.* gewäh´ren.

granular, *adj.* körnig.

granulated sugar, *n.* Streuzucker *m.*

granulation, *n.* Körnung *f.*

granule, *n.* Körnchen, - *nt.*

grape, *n.* Weintraube, -n *f.*

grapefruit, *n.* Pampelmu´se, -n *f.*

grapevine, *n.* Weinstock, ⸗e *m.; (rumor)* Gerücht *nt.*

graph, *n.* graphische Darstellung, -en *f.,* Diagramm´, -e *nt.*

graphic, *adj.* graphisch.

graphite, *n.* Graphit´, -e *m.*

graphology, *n.* Graphologie´ *f.*

grapple, **1.** *n.* Enterhaken, - *m.* **2.** *vb.* packen; ringen*.

grasp, **1.** *n.* Griff, -e *m.; (mental)* Fassungsvermögen *nt.* **2.** *vb.* ergrei´fen*.

grasping, *adj.* habgierig.

grass, *n.* Gras, ⸚er *nt.; (lawn)* Rasen, - *m.; (marijuana)* Hasch *m.*

grasshopper, *n.* Heuschrecke, -n *f.*

grassy, *adj.* grasartig.

grate, 1. *n.* Rost *m.* **2.** *vb. (cheese, etc.)* reiben*, *(irritate)* irritie'ren.

grateful, *adj.* dankbar.

grater, *n.* Reibe, -n *f.*

gratify, *vb.* befrie'digen.

grating, *n.* Gitter, - *nt.*

gratis, *adj.* gratis.

gratitude, *n.* Dankbarkeit, -en *f.*

gratuitous, *adj.* unentgeltlich.

gratuity, *n.* Geschenk', -e *nt.; (tip)* Trinkgeld, -er *nt.*

grave, 1. *n.* Grab, ⸚er *nt.* **2.** *adj.* schwerwiegend.

gravel, *n.* Kies *m.*

graveyard, *n.* Friedhof, ⸚e *m.*

gravitate, *vb.* angezogen werden*; gravitie'ren.

gravity, *n.* Schwerkraft *f.;* Ernst *m.*

gravure, *n.* Gravü're, -n *f.*

gravy, *n.* Soße, -n *f.*

gray, *adj.* grau.

graze, *vb.* grasen, weiden.

grease, 1. *n.* Fett, -e *nt.* **2.** *vb.* fetten; schmieren.

greasy, *adj.* fettig, schmierig.

great, *adj.* groß (größer, größt-).

greatness, *n.* Größe, -n *f.*

Greece, *n.* Griechenland *nt.*

greed, *n.* Gier *f.,* Habsucht *f.*

greediness, *n.* Gier *f.,* Habsucht *f.*

greedy, *adj.* gierig, habsüchtig.

Greek, 1. *n.* Grieche, -n, -n *m.,* Griechin, -nen *f.* **2.** *adj.* griechisch.

green, *adj.* grün.

greenery, *n.* Grün *nt.*

greenhouse, *n.* Gewächs'-haus, ⸚er *nt.,* Treibhaus, ⸚er *nt.*

greet, *vb.* begrü'ßen.

greeting, *n.* Gruß, ⸚e *m.*

gregarious, *adj.* gesel'lig.

grenade, *n.* Grana'te, -n *f.*

grenadine, *n.* Granat'apfel-likör *m.*

greyhound, *n.* Windhund, -e *m.*

grid, *n.* Gitter, - *nt.; (elec.)* Stromnetz, -e *nt.*

griddle, *n.* Bratpfanne, -n *f.*

grief, *n.* Kummer *m.*

grievance, *n.* Beschwer'de, -n *f.*

grieve, *vb. (intr.)* trauern; *(tr.)* betrü'ben.

grievous, *adj.* schmerzlich; *(serious)* schwerwiegend.

grill, *n.* Grill, -s *m.*

grim, *adj.* grimmig.

grimace, *n.* Grimas'se, -n *f.,* Fratze, -n *f.*

grime, *n.* Ruß *m.*

grimy, *adj.* schmutzig.

grin, 1. *n.* Grinsen *nt.* **2.** *vb.* grinsen.

grind, *vb.* mahlen*.

grindstone, *n.* Schleifstein, -e *m.*

grip, 1. *n.* Griff, -e *m.; (suitcase)* Koffer, - *m.* **2.** *vb.* fassen.

gripe, 1. *n. (complaint)* Ärgernis, -se *nt.* **2.** *vb. (complain)* nörgeln.

grippe, *n.* Grippe, -n *f.*

gristle, *n.* Knorpel, - *m.*

grit, 1. *n.* Kies *m.; (courage)* Mut *m.* **2.** *vb. (g. one's teeth)* die Zähne zusam'men•beißen*.

grizzled, *adj.* grau.

groan, 1. *n.* Stöhnen *nt.* **2.** *vb.* stöhnen.

grocer, *n.* Kolonial'waren-händler, - *m.*

groceries, *n.pl.* Kolonial'waren *pl.*

grocery store, *n.* Kolonial'warengeschäft, -e *nt.,* Lebensmit-telgeschäft, -e *nt.*

grog, *n.* Grog, -s *m.*

groggy, *adj.* benom'men; (be g.) taumeln.

groin, *n.* Leistengegend *f.*

groom, *n.* Reitknecht, -e *m.; (footman)* Diener, - *m.; (bridegroom)* Bräutigam -e *m.*

groove, *n.* Rinne, -n *f.*

grope, *vb.* tappen.

gross, 1. *n.* Gros, -se *nt.* **2.** *adj.* grob (⸚); *(weight)* brutto.

grossness, *n.* Kraßheit, -en *f.*

grotesque, *adj.* grotesk'.

grotto, *n.* Grotte, -n *f.*

grouch, 1. *n.* Griesgram, -e *m.* **2.** *vb.* verdrieß'lich sein*.

ground, 1. *n.* Grund, ⸚e *m.,* Boden *m.;* Gebiet', -e *nt.* **2.** *vb. (elec.)* erden.

groundless, *adj.* grundlos.

groundwork, *n.* Grundlage, -n *f.*

group, 1. *n.* Gruppe, -n *f.* **2.** *vb.* gruppie'ren.

groupie, *n.* Mitläufer im Gefolge Prominenter, besonders Rockmusik-stars.

grouse, *n.* schottisches Schneehuhn, ⸚er *nt.*

grove, *n.* Hain, -e *m.*

grovel, *vb.* kriechen*, spe-ichelleckerisch sein*.

grow, *vb.* wachsen*.

grow up, *vb.* auf•wachsen*, heran•wachsen*.

growl, *vb.* knurren.

grown, *adj.* erwach'sen.

grown-up, 1. *n.* Erwach'sen-*m.& f.* **2.** *adj.* erwach'sen.

growth, *n.* Wachstum *nt.; (med.)* Gewächs', -e *nt.*

grub, 1. *n.* Larve, -n *f.; (food)* Fressa'lien *pl.* **2.** *vb.* wühlen.

grudge, *n.* Groll *m.*

gruel, *n.* dünne Hafergrütze *f.*

gruesome, *adj.* schauerlich.

gruff, *adj.* bärbeißig.

grumble, *vb.* murren.

grumpy, *adj.* mürrisch.

grunt, 1. *n.* Grunzen, - *nt.* **2.** *vb.* grunzen.

guarantee, 1. *n.* Garantie', -i'en *f.* **2.** *vb.* garantie'ren.

guarantor, *n.* Bürge, -n, -n *m.*

guaranty, *n.* Sicherheit, -en *f.;* Bürgschaft, -en *f.*

guard, 1. *n.* Wache, -n *f.;* **2.** *vb.* bewa'chen.

guarded, *adj.* vorsichtig.

guardian, *n.* Vormund, -e *m.*

guerrilla, *n.* Partisan´, (-en,) -en *m.*

guess, *vb.* raten*.

guesswork, *n.* Raterei´ *f.*

guest, *n.* Gast, ⸗e *m.*

guidance, *n.* Leitung *f.*, Führung *f.*

guide, 1. *n.* Führer, - *m.*, Führerin, -nen *f.* **2.** *vb.* führen, leiten.

guidebook, *n.* Reiseführer, - *m.*

guidepost, *n.* Wegweiser, - *m.*

guild, *n.* Gilde, -n *f.*

guile, *n.* Arglist *f.*

guillotine, *n.* Guilloti´ne, -n *f.*

guilt, *n.* Schuld *f.*

guiltless, *adj.* schuldlos.

guilty, *adj.* schuldig.

guinea fowl, *n.* Perlhuhn, ⸗er *nt.*

guinea pig, *n.* Meerschweinchen, - *nt.*

guise, *n.* Art, -en *f.*; *(clothes)* Aussehen *nt.*

guitar, *n.* Gitar´re, -n *f.*

gulf, *n.* Golf, -e *m.*

gull, *n.* Möwe, -n *f.*

gullet, *n.* Kehle, -n *f.*

gullible, *adj.* leichtgläubig.

gully, *n.* Wasserrinne, -n *f.*

gulp, *vb.* schlucken.

gum, *n.* Gummi, -s *nt.*; *(teeth)* Zahnfleisch *nt.*; **(chewing g.)** Kaugummi, -s *m.*

gummy, *adj.* gummiartig, klebrig.

gun, *n.* (small) Gewehr´, -e *nt.*; *(large)* Geschütz´, -e *nt.*

gunboat, *n.* Kano´nenboot, -e *nt.*

gunner, *n.* Kanonier´, -e *m.*

gunpowder, *n.* Schießpulver *nt.*

gunshot, *n.* Schuß, ⸗sse *m.*

gurgle, *vb.* gluckern.

guru, *n.* Guru, -s *m.*

gush, *vb.* hervor´quellen*.

gusher, *n.* sprudelnde Petroleumquelle, -n *f.*

gusset, *n.* Zwickel, - *m.*

gust, *n.* Windstoß, ⸗e *m.*

gustatory, *adj.* Geschmacks´- *(cpds.)*.

gusto, *n.* Schwung *m.*

gusty, *adj.* windig.

guts, *n.* Eingeweide *pl.*; *(courage)* Mumm *m.*

gutter, *n.* *(street)* Rinnstein, -e *m.*, Gosse, -n *f.*; *(house)* Dachtraufe, -n *f.*

guttural, *adj.* guttural´.

guy, *n.* Kerl, -e *m.*

guzzle, *vb.* saufen*.

gymnasium, *n.* Turnhalle, -n *f.*

gymnast, *n.* Turner, - *m.*, Turnerin, -nen *f.*

gymnastic, *adj.* gymnas´-tisch.

gymnastics, *n.* Gymnas´tik *f.*

gynecologist, *n.* Frauenarzt, ⸗e *m.*, Frauenärztin, -nen *f.* Gynäkolo´ge, -n, -n *m.*, Gynäkolo´gin, -nen *f.*

gynecology, *n.* Gynäkologie´ *f.*

gypsum, *n.* Gips *m.*

gypsy, *n.* Zigeu´ner, - *m.*, Zigeu´nerin, -nen *f.*

gyrate, *vb.* kreiseln.

gyroscope, *n.* Kreiselkompaß, -sse *m.*

H

haberdashery, *n.* Geschäft´ für Herrenartikel.

habit, *n.* Gewohn´heit, -en *f.*; Kleidung, -en *f.*

habitable, *adj.* bewohn´bar.

habitat, *n.* Wohnbereich, -e *m.*

habitual, *adj.* gewöhn´lich; Gewohn´heits- *(cpds.).*

habitué, *n.* Stammgast, ⸗e *m.*

hack, 1. *n.* Droschke, -n *f.*; *(horse)* Klepper, - *m.* **2.** *vb.* hacken.

hacksaw, *n.* Metall´säge, -n *f.*

hag, *n.* Vettel, -n *f.*

haggard, *adj.* abgehärmt.

haggle, *vb.* feilschen.

Hague, *n.* Den Haag *m.*

hail, 1. *n.* Hagel *m.* **2.** *vb.* hageln; *(greet)* begrü´ßen. **3.** *interj.* heil!

hailstone, *n.* Hagelkorn, ⸗er *nt.*

hailstorm, *n.* Hagelwetter, - *nt.*

hair, *n.* Haar, -e *nt.*

haircut, *n.* Haarschnitt, -e *m.*; **(get a h.)** sich die Haare schneiden lassen*.

hairdo, *n.* Frisur´, -en *f.*

hairdresser, *n.* Friseur´, - *m.*, Friseu´se, -n *f.*

hair drier, *n.* Fön *m.*, Haartrockner *m.*

hairline, *n.* Haaransatz, ⸗e *m.*; Haarstrich, -e *m.*

hairpin, *n.* Haarnadel, -n *f.*

hair-raising, *adj.* haarsträubend.

hairspray, *n.* Haarspray *m.*

hairy, *adj.* haarig.

hale, *adj.* kräftig.

half, 1. *n.* Hälfte, -n *f.* **2.** *adj.* halb.

half-breed, *n.* Mischling, -e *m.*

half-brother, *n.* Stiefbruder, ⸗ *m.*

half-hearted, *adj.* lauwarm.

half-mast, *n.* Halbmast *m.*

halfway, *adv.* halbwegs.

half-wit, *n.* Narr, -en, -en *m.*

halibut, *n.* Heilbutt, -e *m.*

hall, *n.* *(auditorium)* Halle, -n *f.*; *(large room)* Saal, Säle *m.*; *(corridor)* Gang, ⸗e *m.*, Korridor, -e *m.*; **(front h.)** Diele, -n *f.*

hallmark, *n.* Stempel der Echtheit *m.*

hallow, *vb.* heiligen.

Halloween, *n.* Abend *(m.)* vor Allerhei´ligen.

hallucination, *n.* Wahnvorstellung, -en *f.*, Halluzination´, -en *f.*

hallway, *n.* Gang, ⸗e *m.*, Korridor, -e *m.*

halo, *n.* Heiligenschein, -e *m.*

halt, 1. *n.* Halt, -e *m.*; *(fig.)* Stillstand *m.* **2.** *vb.* an•halten*. **3.** *interj.* halt!

halter, n. (horse) Halfter, -nt.; (female clothing) Oberteil eines Bade- oder Luftanzuges.

halve, vb. halbie´ren.

ham, n. Schinken, - m.

Hamburg, n. Hamburg nt.

hamlet, n. Flecken, - m.

hammer, 1. n. Hammer, ⸗ m. **2.** vb. hämmern.

hammock, n. Hängematte, -n f.

hamper, 1. n. Korb, ⸗e m. **2.** vb. hemmen.

hamstring, vb. lähmen.

hand, 1. n. Hand, ⸗e f. **2.** vb. reichen.

handbag, n. Handtasche, -n f.

handbook, n. Handbuch, ⸗er nt.

handcuffs, n.pl. Handschellen pl.

handful, n. Handvoll f.

handicap 1. n. Handikap, -s nt.; Hindernis, -se nt. **2.** vb. hemmen.

handicraft, n. Handwerk nt.

handiwork, n. Handarbeit, -en f., Handwerk nt.

handkerchief, n. Taschentuch, ⸗er nt.

handle, 1. n. Henkel, - m., Griff, -e m. **2.** vb. handhaben.

hand-made, adj. handgearbeitet.

handout, n. Almosen, - nt.

hand-rail, n. Gelän´der, - nt.

handsome, adj. gutaussehend; ansehnlich.

handwriting, n. Handschrift, -en f.

handy, adj. handlich; (skilled) geschickt´.

handyman, n. Fakto´tum, -s nt.

hangar, n. Schuppen, - m.

hanger, n. Aufhänger, - m.; (clothes) Kleiderbügel, - m.

hanger-on, n. Schmarot´zer, - m.

hang glider, n. Drachenflieger, - m.

hanging, n. Hinrichtung (-en f.) durch Hängen.

hangman, n. Henker, - m.

hangnail, n. Niednagel, ⸗ m.

hangout, n. Stammlokal, -e nt.

hangover, n. Kater, - m., Katzenjammer m.

hangup, n. (to have a h.) einen Komplex haben, verklemmt sein.

haphazardly, adv. aufs Geratewohl´.

happen, vb. sich ereig´nen, gesche´hen*, passie´ren.

happening, n. Ereig´nis, -se nt.

happiness, n. Glück nt.

happy, adj. glücklich.

happy-go-lucky, adj. sorglos.

harangue, 1. n. marktschreierische Ansprache, -n f. **2.** vb. eine marktschreierische Ansprache halten*.

harass, vb. plagen.

harbinger, n. Vorbote, -n, - n m.

harbor, n. Hafen, ⸗ m.

hard, adj. (not soft) hart (⸗); (not easy) schwer, schwierig.

hard-boiled, adj. hartgekocht; (fig.) abgebrüht.

hard coal, n. Anthrazit´, -e m.

harden, vb. (intr.) hart werden*; (tr.) ab´härten.

hard-headed, adj. praktisch, realis´tisch.

hard-hearted, adj. hartherzig.

hardiness, n. Rüstigkeit f.

hardly, adv. kaum.

hardness, n. Härte, -n f.

hardship, n. Not, ⸗e f.; (exertion) Anstrengung, -en f.

hardware, n. Eisenwaren pl.

hardwood, n. Hartholz nt.

hardy, adj. rüstig.

hare, n. Hase, -n, -n m.

harem, n. Harem, -s m.

hark, vb. horchen.

Harlequin, n. Harlekin, -e m.

harm, 1. n. Schaden, ⸗ m.; Unrecht, -e nt. **2.** vb. schaden; Unrecht zu•fügen.

harmful, adj. schädlich.

harmless, adj. harmlos.

harmonic, adj. harmo´nisch.

harmonica, n. Harmo´nika, -s f.

harmonious, adj. harmo´nisch.

harmonize, vb. harmonisie´ren.

harmony, n. Harmonie´, -i´en f.; (fig.) Eintracht f.

harness, 1. n. Geschirr´, -e nt. **2.** vb. ein•spannen.

harp, n. Harfe, -n f.

harpoon, 1. n. Harpu´ne, -n f. **2.** vb. harpunie´ren.

harpsichord, n. Spinett´, -e nt.

harrow, 1. n. Egge, -n f. **2.** vb. eggen.

harry, vb. plündern; plagen.

harsh, adj. rauh; streng.

harshness, n. Rauheit f.; Strenge f.

harvest, 1. n. Ernte, -n f. **2.** vb. ernten.

hassle, n. Hetze f.

hassock, n. gepolsterter Hocker, - m.

haste, n. Eile f.

hasten, vb. eilen; sich beei´len.

hat, n. Hut, ⸗e m.; Mütze, -n f.

hatch, 1. n. Luke, -n f. **2.** vb. aus•brüten.

hatchet, n. Beil, -e nt.

hate, 1. n. Haß m. **2.** vb. hassen.

hateful, adj. verhaßt´; widerlich.

hatred, n. Haß m.

haughtiness, n. Hochmut m.

haughty, adj. hochmütig.

haul, vb. schleppen.

haunch, n. Keule, -n f.

haunt, vb. verfol´gen.

have, vb. haben*; (I h. it made) ich lasse* es machen; (I h. him make it) ich lasse* ihn es machen.

haven, n. Hafen, ⸗ m.; Zufluchts- ort, -e m.

havoc, n. Verwüs´tung, -en f.

hawk, n. Habicht, -e m.

hawser, n. Trosse, -n f.

hay, n. Heu nt.

hay fever, n. Heuschnupfen, - m.

hayloft, n. Heuboden, ≃ m.

haystack, n. Heuhaufen, - m.

hazard, 1. n. Risiko, -s or -en nt. 2. vb. riskie´ren.

hazardous, adj. gewagt´.

haze, n. Dunst, ≃e m.

hazel, adj. haselnußbraun.

hazelnut, n. Haselnuß, ≃sse f.

hazy, adj. dunstig, unklar.

he, pron. er.

head, n. Kopf, ≃e m., Haupt, ≃er nt.

headache, n. Kopfschmerzen pl.

headfirst, adv. Hals über Kopf.

headgear, n. Kopfbedeckung, -en f.

heading, n. Überschrift, -en f., Rubrik´, -en f.

headlight, n. Scheinwerfer, - m.

headline, n. Überschrift, -en f.; (newspaper) Schlagzeile, -n f.

headlong, adj. überstürzt´.

headmaster, n. Schuldirektor, -en m.

headmistress, n. Schuldirektorin, -nen f.

head-on, adv. direkt von vorn.

headquarters, n.pl. Hauptquartier, -e nt.

headstone, n. (grave) Grabstein, -e m.; (arch.) Eckstein, -e m.

headstrong, adj. dickköpfig.

headwaters, n.pl. Quelle, -n f.

headway, n. (make h.) vorwärts kommen*.

heal, vb. heilen.

health, n. Gesund´heit, -en f.

healthful, adj. gesund´ (≃).

health insurance, -nen, n. Krankenkasse f.

healthy, adj. gesund´(≃).

heap, 1. n. Haufen, - m. 2. vb. häufen.

hear, vb. hören.

hearing, n. Gehör´ nt.; (jur.) Verhör´, -e nt.

hearsay, n. Hörensagen nt.

hearse, n. Leichenwagen, - m.

heart, n. Herz(en), - nt.

heartache, n. Herzenskummer m.

heartbreaking, adj. herzzerbrechend.

heartbroken, adv. tieftraurig.

heartburn, n. Sodbrennen, - nt.

heartfelt, adj. aufrichtig.

hearth, n. Kamin´, -e m.

heartless, adj. herzlos.

heartrending, adj. herzzerreißend.

heartsick, adj. niedergeschlagen.

heart-to-heart, adj. freimütig.

hearty, adj. herzhaft.

heat, 1. n. Hitze f., Wärme f.; (house) Heizung f. 2. vb. heiß machen, erhit´zen; (house) heizen.

heated, adj. geheizt´; (fig.) hitzig.

heater, n. Heizvorrichtung, -en f.

heathen, 1. n. Heide, -n, -n m. 2. adj. heidnisch.

heather, n. Heidekraut nt.

heat-stroke, n. Hitzschlag, ≃e m.

heat up, vb. auf•wärmen.

heat wave, n. Hitzewelle, -n f.z

heave, vb. heben*; wogen; (utter) aus•stoßen*.

heaven, n. Himmel, - m.

heavenly, adj. himmlisch.

heavy, adj. schwer; (fig.) heftig.

heavyweight, n. Schwergewicht nt.

Hebrew, 1. n. Hebrä´er, - m. Hebrä´erin, -nen f. 2. adj. hebrä´isch.

heckle, vb. hecheln.

hectic, adj. hektisch.

hedge, n. Hecke, -n f.

hedgehog, n. Igel, - m.

hedge-hop, vb. (mil.) im Tiefflug an•fliegen*.

hedgerow, n. Baumhecke, - n f.

hedonism, n. Hedonis´mus m.

heed, vb. beach´ten.

heedless, adj. achtlos.

heel, n. (shoes) Absatz, ≃e m.; (foot) Ferse, -n f.; (scoundrel) Schuft, -e m.

heifer, n. junge Kuh, ≃e f.

height, n. Höhe, -n f.; (person) Größe -n f.

heighten, vb. erhö´hen.

heinous, adj. abscheu´lich, verrucht´.

heir, n. Erbe, -n, -n m.

heiress, n. Erbin, -nen f.

heirloom, n. Erbstück, -e nt.

helicopter, n. Hubschrauber, - m.

heliotrope, n. Heliotrop´, -e nt.

helium, n. Helium nt.

hell, n. Hölle, -n f.

Hellenic, adj. helle´nisch.

Hellenism, n. Hellenis´mus m.

hello, interj. guten Tag (Morgen, Abend); (call for attention) hallo.

helm, n. Steuerruder, - nt.

helmet, n. Helm, -e m.

helmsman, n. Steuermann, ≃er m.

help, 1. n. Hilfe f. 2. vb. zhelfen*.

helper, n. Helfer, - m., Helferin, -nen f.

helpful, adj. hilfreich, hilfsbereit.

helpfulness, n. Hilfsbereitschaft f.

helping, n. Portion´, -en f.

helpless, adj. hilflos.

helter-skelter, adv. hol´terdiepol´ter.

hem, 1. n. Saum, ≃e m. 2. vb. säumen.

hematite, n. Hematit´, -e m.

hemisphere, n. Halbkugel, - n f.

hemlock, n. Schierling m.

hemoglobin, zn. Hämoglobin´ nt.

hemophilia, zn. Bluterkrankheit f.

hemorrhage, n. Bluterguß, ≃sse m.

hemorrhoid, n. Hämorrhoi´de, -n f.

hemp, n. Hanf m.

hemstitch, n. Hohlsaum, ≃e m.

hen, n. Henne, -n f.

hence, *adv. (time)* von nun an; *(place)* von hier aus; *(therefore)* daher, deshalb, deswegen, also.

henceforth, *adv.* von nun an.

henchman, *n.* Trabant´, -en *m.*

henna, *n.* Henna *f.*

henpecked, *adj.* unter dem Pantof´fel stehend.

hepatic, *adj.* Leber- *(cpds.)*.

hepatica, *n.* Hepa´tika, -ken *f.*

her, 1. *pron.* sie, ihr. **2.** *adj.* ihr, -, -e.

heraldic, *adj.* heral´disch.

heraldry, *n.* Wappenkunde *f.*

herb, *n.* Kraut, ⸚er *nt.,* Gewürz´kraut, ⸚er *nt.*

herculean, *adj.* herku´lisch.

herd, *n.* Herde, -n *f.*

here, *adv. (in this place)* hier; *(to this place)* hier-her´; *(from h.)* hierhin´.

hereabout, *adv.* hier.

hereafter, 1. *n.* Leben *(nt.)* nach dem Tode. **2.** *adv.* in Zukunft.

hereby, *adv.* hiermit.

hereditary, *adj.* erblich.

heredity, *n.* Erblichkeit *f.;* Verer´bung, -en *f.*

herein, *adv.* hierbei, hiermit.

heresy, *n.* Ketzerei´, -en *f.*

heretic, 1. *n.* Ketzer, - *m.* **2.** *adj.* ketzerisch.

heritage, *n.* Erbe *nt.*

hermetic, *adj.* herme´tisch.

hermit, *n.* Einsiedler, - *m.*

hernia, *n.* Bruch, ⸚e *m.*

hero, *n.* Held, -en, -en *m.*

heroic, *adj.* heldenhaft.

heroin, *n.* Heroin´ *nt.*

heroine, *n.* Heldin, -nen *f.*

heroism, *n.* Heldenmut *m.*

heron, *n.* Reiher, - *m.*

herring, *n.* Hering, -e *m.*

herringbone, *n.* Heringsgräte, -n *f.*

hers, *pron.* ihrer, -es, -e.

hertz, *n.* Hertz *nt.*

hesitancy, *n.* Zögern *nt.*

hesitant, *adj.* zögernd.

hesitate, *vb.* zögern.

hesitation, *n.* Zögern *nt.*

heterodox, *adj.* heterodox´.

heterogeneous, *adj.* heterogen´. ·

heterosexual, *adj.* heterosexuell.

hew, *vb.* hauen*.

hexagon, *n.* Sechseck, -e *nt.*

heyday, *n.* Blütezeit, -en *f.*

hi, *interj.* hallo.

hibernate, *vb.* überwin´tern.

hibernation, *n.* Überwin´terung, -en *f.*

hibiscus, *n.* Hibis´kus, -ken *m.*

hiccup, *n.* Schluckauf *m.*

hickory, *n.* Hickoryholz, ⸚er *nt.*

hide, 1. *n.* Haut, ⸚e *f.;* Fell, -e *nt.* **2.** *vb.* verber´gen*, verste´cken; verheim´lichen.

hideous, *adj.* gräßlich.

hide-out, *n.* Schlupfwinkel, - *m.*

hierarchy, *n.* Rangordnung, -en *f.,* Hierarchie´, -i´en *f.*

hieroglyphic, *adj.* hierogly´phisch.

high, *adj.* hoch, hoh- (höher, höchst); *(tipsy)* beschwipst´.

highbrow, *adj.* intellektuell´.

high fidelity, *n.* Hifi *nt.*

high-handed, *adj.* anmaßend.

highland, *n.* Hochland, ⸚er *nt.*

highlight, *n.* Höhepunkt, -e *m.*

highly, *adv.* höchst.

high-minded, *adj.* edelmütig.

Highness, *n.* Hoheit, -en *f.*

high school, *n.* höhere Schule, -n *f.*

high seas, *n.* hohe See *f.*

high-strung, *adj.* nervös, kribbelig.

high tide, *n.* Flut, -en *f.*

highway, *n.* Landstraße, -n *f.,* Chaussee´, -n *f.*

hijacker, *n.* Flugzeugentführer, - *m.;* Luftpirat, -en, -en *m.*

hike, 1. *n.* Wanderung, -en *f.* **2.** *vb.* wandern.

hilarious, *adj.* ausgelassen.

hilarity, *n.* Ausgelassenheit *f.*

hill, *n.* Hügel, - *m.*

hilt, *n.* Heft, -e *nt.*

him, *pron.* ihn; ihm.

hind, *adj.* hinter-.

hinder, *vb.* hindern; verhin´dern.

hindmost, *adj.* letzt-, hinterst-.

hindrance, *n.* Hindernis, -se *nt.; (disadvantage)* Nachteil, -e *m.*

hinge, *n.* Scharnier, -e *nt.*

hint, 1. *n.* Wink, -e *m.* **2.** *vb.* an•deuten.

hinterland, *n.* Hinterland *nt.*

hip, *n.* Hüfte, -n *f.*

hippopotamus, *n.* Nilpferd, -e *nt.*

hire, *vb.* mieten; *(persons)* an•stellen.

his, 1. *adj.* sein, -, -e. **2.** *pron.* seiner, -es, -e.

Hispanic, *n.* erste oder zweite Generation Amerikaner spanisch sprechender Herkunft.

hiss, *vb.* zischen.

historian, *n.* Histo´riker, - *m.,* Histo´rikerin, -nen *f.*

historic, historical, *adj.* histo´risch.

history, *n.* Geschich´te, -en *f.*

hit, 1. *n.* Stoß, ⸚e *m.,* Schlag, ⸚e *m.; (success)* Treffer, - *m.* **2.** *vb.* stoßen*, schlagen*, treffen*.

hitch, 1. *n. (knot)* Knoten, - *m.; (obstacle)* Hindernis, -se *nt.* **2.** *vb.* fest•machen.

hitchhike, *vb.* per Anhalter fahren*.

hive, *n.* Bienenstock, ⸚e *m.*

hives, *n.* Nesselsucht *f.*

hoard, 1. *n.* Vorrat, ⸚e *m.* **2.** *vb.* hamstern.

hoarse, *adj.* heiser.

hoax, *n.* Schabernack, -e *m.*

hobble, *vb.* humpeln.

hobby, *n.* Hobby, -s *nt.,* Liebhaberei´, -en *f.*

hobgoblin, *n.* Kobold, -e *m.*

hobnob with, *vb.* mit jemand auf vertrau´tem Füße stehen*.

hobo, *n.* Landstreicher, - *m.*

hockey, *n.* Hockey *nt.*

hocus-pocus, *n.* Ho´kuspo´kus *m.*

hod, *n.* Traggestell, -e *nt.*

hodgepodge, *n.* Mischmasch, -e *m.*

hoe, 1. *n.* Hacke, -n *f.* **2.** *vb.* hacken.

hog, *n.* Schwein, -e *nt.*

hoist, *vb.* hoch•ziehen*, hissen.

hold, 1. *n.* Halt *m.*; *(ship)* Laderaum, ⸗e *m.* **2.** *vb.* halten*; *(contain)* enthalten*; **(h. up)** auf•halten*.

holder, *n.* Halter, - *m.*

holdup, *n.* Überfall, ⸗e *m.*

hole, *n.* Loch, ⸗er *nt.*

holiday, *n.* Feiertag, -e *m.,* Festtag, -e *m.*

holiness, *n.* Heiligkeit *f.*

Holland, *n.* Holland *nt.*

hollow, *adj.* hohl.

holly, *n.* Stechpalme, -n *f.*

hollyhock, *n.* Malve, -n *f.*

holocaust, *n.* Brandopfer, - *nt.,* Großfeuer, - *nt.*

hologram, *n.* Hologramm´, -e *nt.*

holography, *n.* Holografie´ *f.*

holster, *n.* Pisto´lenhalter, - *m.*

holy, *adj.* heilig.

holy day, *n.* Kirchenfeiertag, -e *m.*

Holy Spirit, *n.* der Heilige Geist *m.*

Holy Week, *n.* Karwoche *f.*

homage, *n.* Huldigung, -en *f.*

home, 1. *n.* Heim, -e *nt.*; **(h. town)** Heimat, -en *f.*; *(place of residence)* Wohnort, -e *m.*; *(house)* Haus, ⸗er *nt.*; *(institution)* Heim, -e *nt.* **2.** *adv. (location)* zu Hause, daheim´; *(direction)* nach Hause, heim.

homeland, *n.* Heimatland, ⸗er *nt.*

homeless, *adj.* heimatlos; obdachlos.

homelike, *adj.* behag´lich.

homely, *adj.* häßlich.

home-made, *adj.* selbstgefertigt.

home rule, *n.* Selbstverwaltung *f.*

homesick, be, *vb.* Heimweh haben*.

homesickness, *n.* Heimweh *nt.*

homestead, *n.* Fami´liensitz, -e *m.*

homeward, *adv.* heimwärts.

homework, *n.* Hausaufgabe, -n *f.,* Schularbeiten *pl.*

homicide, *n.* Mord, -e *m.*

homogeneous, *adj.* homogen´.

homogenize, *vb.* homogenisie´ren.

homonym, *n.* Homonym´, -e *nt.*

homosexual, *adj.* homosexuell´.

hone, *n.* Wetzstein, -e *m.*

honest, *adj.* ehrlich, aufrichtig.

honesty, *n.* Ehrlichkeit, -en *f.*

honey, *n.* Honig *m.*

honey-bee, *n.* Honigbiene, -n *f.*

honeycomb, *n.* Honigwabe, -n *f.z*

honeymoon, *n.* Hochzeitsreise, -n *f.,* Flitterwochen *pl.*

honeysuckle, *n.* Geißblatt *nt.*

honor, 1. *n.* Ehre, -n *f.* **2.** *vb.* ehren; honorie´ren.

honorable, *adj.* ehrbar, ehrenvoll.

honorary, *adj.* Ehren- *(cpdsz.).*

honored, *adj* geehrt´.

hood, *n.* Haube, -n *f.,* *(monk)* Kapu´ze, -n *f.*

hoodlum, *n.* Rowdy, -s *m.*

hoodwink, *vb.* übertöl´peln.

hoof, *n.* Huf, -e *nt.*

hook, 1. *n.* Haken, - *m.* **2.** *vb.* zu•haken; *(catch)* fangen*.

hoop, *n.* Reifen, - *m.*

hoot, *vb.* schreien*.

hop, 1. *n. (plant)* Hopfen *m.*; *(jump)* Sprung, ⸗e *m.* **2.** *vb.* hüpfen, springen*.

hope, 1. *n.* Hoffnung, -en *f.* **2.** *vb.* hoffen.

hopeful, *adj.* hoffnungsvoll.

hopeless, *adj.* hoffnungslos.

hopelessness, *n.* Hoffnungslosigkeit *f.*

horde, *n.* Horde, -n *f.*

horizon, *n.* Horizont´, -e *m.*

horizontzal, *adj.* waagerecht, horizontal´.

hormone, *n.* Hormon´, -e *nt.*

horn, *n.* Horn, ⸗er *nt.*

hornet, *n.* Hornis´se, -n *f.*

horny, *adj.* hornig, hörnern.

horoscope, *n.* Horoskop´, -e *nt.*

horrible, *adj.* grauenhaft.

horrid, *adj.* gräßlich.

horrify, *vb.* entset´zen.

horror, *n.* Grauen *nt.*

horse, *n.* Pferd, -e *nt.*

horseback, on, *adv.* zu Pferde.

horsehair, *n.* Roßhaar, -e *nt.*

horseman, *n.* Reiter, - *m.*

horsemanship, *n.* Reitkunst *f.*

horse-power, *n.* Pferdestärke, -n *f.*

horseradish, *n.* Meerrettich, -e *m.*

horseshoe, *n.* Hufeisen, - *nt.*

horticulture, *n.* Gartenbau *m.*

hose, *n. (tube)* Schlauch, ⸗e *m.*; *(stocking)* Strumpf, ⸗e *m.*

hosiery, *n.* Strumpfwaren *pl.*

hospitable, *adj.* gastfreundlich, gastfrei.

hospital, *n.* Krankenhaus, ⸗er *nt.*

hospitality, *n.* Gastfreundschaft, Gastfreiheit *f.*

hospitalization, *n.* Krankenhausaufenthalt *m.*

hospitalize, *vb.* ins Krankenhaus einweisen; **(be h.d)** im Krankenhaus liegen müssen*.

host, *n.* Gastgeber, - *m.*; *(innkeeper)* Wirt, -e *m.*; *(crowd)* Menge, -n *f.*; *(Eucharist)* Hostie *f.*

hostage, *n.* Geisel, -n *m.*

hostel, *n.* Herberge, -n *f.*; **(youth h.)** Jugendherberge, -n *f.*

hostess, *n.* Gastgeberin, -nen *f.*

hostile, *adj.* feindlich.

hostility, *n.* Feindseligkeit, -en *f.,* Krieg, -e *m.*

hot, *adj.* heiß.

hotbed, *n.* Mistbeet, -e *nt.*; *(fig.)* Brutstätte, -n *f.*

hot dog, *n.* Bockwurst, ⸗e *f.*

hotel, *n.* Hotel´, -s *nt.*

hothouse, *n*. Treibhaus, ≈er *nt*.

hound, *n*. Hund, -e *m*.

hour, *n*. Stunde, -n *f*.

hourglass, *n*. Stundenglas, ≈er *nt*.

hourly, *adj*. stündlich.

house, *n*. Haus, ≈er *nt*.

housefly, *n*. Stubenfliege, -n *f.z*

household, *n*. Haushalt, -e *m*.

housekeeper, *n*. Haushälterin, -nen *f*.

housekeeping, *n*. Haushaltung *f*.

housemaid, *n*. Hausmädchen, - *nt*.

housewife, *n*. Hausfrau, -en *f*.

housework, *n*. Hausarbeit, -en *f*.

hovel, *n*. Hütte, -n *f*.

hover, *vb*. schweben.

hovercraft, *n*. Hovercraft *m. & nt.;* Luftkissenboot, -e *nt*.

how, *adv*. wie.

however, **1.** *conj*. aber, doch, jedoch´. **2.** *adv*. wie . . . auch.

howitzer, *n*. Haubit´ze, -n *f*.

howl, **1.** *n*. Gebrüll´ *nt*. **2.** *vb*. brüllen.

hub, *n*. Nabe, -n *f.; (fig.)* Mittelpunkt, -e *m*.

hubbub, *n*. Tumult´, -e *m*.

huckleberry, *n*. Heidelbeere, -n *f*.

huddle, *vb*. zusam´men•kauern, sich zusam•drängen.

hue, *n*. Färbung, -en *f*.

hug, **1.** *n*. Umar´mung, -en *f*. **2.** *vb*. umar´men.

huge, *adj*. sehr groß, ungeheuer.

hull, *n*. Hülse, -n *f.; (fruit)* Schale, -n *f.; (ship)* Rumpf, ≈e *m*.

hum, **1.** *n. (people)* Gemur´mel *nt.; (insects)* Summen *nt*. **2.** *vb*. murmeln; summen.

human, *adj*. menschlich.

humane, *adj*. human´, menschlich.

humanism, *n*. Humanis´mus *m*.

humanitarian, *adj*. menschenfreundlich.

humanity, *n. (mankind)* Menschheit *f.; (humaneness)* Menschlichkeit *f*.

humble, *adj*. demütig, beschei´den.

humbug, *n*. Schwindel *m.,* Quatsch *m*.

humdrum, *adj*. langweilig, eintönig.

humid, *adj*. feucht.

humidity, *n*. Feuchtigkeit *f*.

humidor, *n*. Tabakstopf, ≈e *m*.

humiliate, *vb*. demütigen.

humiliation, *n*. Demütigung, -en *f*.

humility, *n*. Demut *f*.

humor, *n*. Humor´ *m.; (mood)* Laune, -n *f*.

humorist, *n*. zHumorist´, -en, -en *m*.

humorous, *adj*. humor´voll, witzig.

hump, *n*. Buckel, - *m.,* Höcker, - *m.z*

hunch, **1.** *n*. Höcker, - *m.,* Buckel, - *m.; (suspicion)* Ahnung, -en *f.,* Riecher, - *m*. **2.** *vb*. krümmen.

hunchback, **1.** *n*. Buckel, - *m.; (person)* zBuckligm.& *f*. **2.** *adj*. bucklig.

hundred, *num*. hundert.

hundredth, **1.** *adj*. hundertst-. **2.** *n*. Hundertstel, - *nt*.

Hungarian, **1.** *n*. Ungar, -n, -n *m.,* Ungarin, -nen *f.* **2.** *adj*. ungarisch.

Hungary, *n*. Ungarn *nt*.

hunger, *n*. Hunger *m*.

hungry, *adj*. hungrig.

hunt, **1.** *n*. Jagd, -en *f*. **2.** *vb*. jagen.

hunter, *n*. Jäger, - *m*.

hunting, *n*. Jagd, -en *f*.

hurdle, **1.** *n*. Hürde, -n *f*. **2.** *vb*. hinü´ber•springen*.

hurl, *vb*. schleudern.

hurrah, *interj*. hurra! (h. for him) er lebe hoch!

hurricane, *n*. Orkan´, -e *m*.

hurry, *vb*. eilen, sich beei´len.

hurt, *vb*. weh tun*, verlet´zen.

hurtful, *adj*. schädlich.

husband, *n*. Mann, ≈er *m.,* Gatte, -n, -n *m*.

husbandry, *n*. Landwirtschaft *f.; (management)* Wirtschaften *nt*.

hush, **1.** *n*. Stille *f*. **2.** *vb*. zum Schweigen bringen*. **3.** *interj*. still!

husk, **1.** *n*. Hülse, -n *f*. **2.** *vb*. enthül´sen.

husky, *adj. (hoarse)* rauh; *(strong)* stark (≈).

hustle, *vb*. rührig sein*.

hut, *n*. Hütte, -n *f*.

hyacinth, *n*. Hyazin´the, -n *f*.

hybrid, *adj*. hybrid´.

hydrangea, *n*. Horten´sie, -n *f*.

hydrant, *n*. Hydrant´, -en, -en *m*.

hydraulic, *adj*. hydrau´lisch.

hydrochloric acid, *n*. Salzsäure *f*.

hydroelectric, *adj*. hydroelek´trisch.

hydrogen, *n*. Wasserstoff *m*.

hydrogen bomb, *n*. Wasserstoffbombe, -n *f*.

hydrophobia, *n*. krankhafte Wasserscheu *f*.

hydroplane, *n*. Wasserflugzeug, -e *nt*.

hydrotherapy, *n*. Hydrotherapize´ *f*.

hyena, *n*. Hyä´ne, -n *f*.

hygiene, *n*. Hygie´ne *f.,* Körperpflege *f*.

hygienic, *adj*. hygie´nisch.

hymn, *n*. Hymne, -n *f.,* Chozral´, ≈e *m.,* Kirchenlied, -er *nt*.

hymnal,z *n*. Gesang´buch, ≈er *nt*.

hyperacizdity, *n*. Hyperacidität´, *f*.

hyperbole, *n*. Hyper´bel, -n *f*.

hypercritical, *adj*. überkritisch.

hypersenszitive, *adj*. überempfindlich.

hypertension, *n*. übernormaler Blutdruck *m*.

hyphen, *n*. Bindestrich, -e *m*.

hyphenate, *vb*. trennen.

hypnosis, *n*. Hypno´se, -n *f*.

hypnotic, *adj*. hypno´-tisch.

hypnotism, *n*. Hypnotis´mus *m*.

hypnotize, *vb*. hypnotisie´ren.

hypochondria, *n.* Schwermut *f.*

hypochondriac, 1. *n.* Hypochon´der, - *m.* **2.** *adj.* schwermütig.

hypocrisy, *n.* Heuchelei´, -en *f.*

hypocrite, *n.* Heuchler, - *m.*, Heuchlerin, -nen *f.*

hypocritical, *adj.* heuchlerisch.

hypodermic, *n.* Spritze, -n *f.*

hypothesis, *n.* Hypothe´se, -n *f.*

hypothetical, *adj.* hypothe´tisch.

hysterectomy, *n.* Hysterek´tomie *f.*

hysteria, hysterics, *n.* Hysterie´ *f.*

hysterical, *adj.* hyste´risch.

I

I, *pron.* ich.

ice, *n.* Eis *nt.*

iceberg, *n.* Eisberg, -e *m.*

ice-box, *n.* Eisschrank, ‑̈e *m.*

ice cream, *n.* Eis *nt.*, Sahneneis *nt.*

ice cream parlor, *n.* Eisdiele, -n *f.*

ice skate, 1. *n.* Schlittschuh, -e *m.* **2.** *vb.* Schlittschuh laufen*.

icing, *n.* Zuckerguß, ‑̈sse *m.*

icon, *n.* Iko´ne, -n *f.*

icy, *adj.* eisig.

idea, *n.* Idee´, -de´en *f.*, Gedan´ke(n), - *m.*

ideal, 1. *n.* Ideal´, -e *nt.* **2.** *adj.* ideal´.

idealism, *n.* Idealis´mus *m.*

idealist, *n.* Idealist´, -en, -en *m.*

idealistic, *adj.* idealis´tisch.

idealize, *vb.* idealisie´ren.

identical, *adj.* iden´tisch.

identifiable, *adj.* identifizier´bar.

identification, *n.* Identifizie´rung, -en *f.*; *(card)* Ausweis, -e *m.*

identify, *vb.* identifizie´ren.

identity, *n.* Identität´, -en *f.*

ideology, *n.* Ideologie´, -i´en *f.*

idiocy, *n.* Blödsinn *m.*

idiom, *n.* Idiom´, -e *nt.*, Redewendung, -en *f.*

idiot, *n.* Idiot´, -en, -en *m.*

idiotic, *adj.* idio´tisch, blödsinnig.

idle, *adj.* müßig; arbeitslos; untätig.

idleness, *n.* Müßigkeit *f.*

idol, *n.* Götzenbild, -er *nt.*

idolatry, *n.* Abgötterrei´, -en *f.*

idolize, *vb.* vergöt´tern.

if, *conj.* wenn; **(as if)** als ob.

ignite, *vb.* an•zünden.

ignition, *n.* Zündung *f.*

ignition key, *n.* Zündschlüssel, - *m.*

ignominious, *adj.* schmachvoll.

ignoramus, *n.* Nichtswisser, - *m.*

ignorance, *n.* Unwissenheit *f.*

ignorant, *adj.* unwissend.

ignore, *vb.* überse´hen*, unbeachtet lassen*.

ill, *adj.* krank (‑̈).

illegal, *adj.* illegal, ungesetzlich.

illegible, *adj.* unleserlich.

illegitimate, *adj.* ungesetzlich; *(unmarried)* unehelich.

illicit, *adj.* unerlaubt.

illiteracy, *n.* Analphabe´tentum, *nt.*

illiterate, 1. *n.* Analphabet´, -en, -en *m.* **2.** *adj.* des Lesens und Schreibens unkundig.

illness, *n.* Krankheit, -en *f.*

illogical, *adj.* unlogisch.

illuminate, *vb.* beleuch´ten, erleuch´ten.

illumination, *n.* Beleuch´ztung, -en *f.*

illusion, *n.* Illusion´, -en *f.*

illusive, illusory, *adj.* trügerisch, illuso´risch.

illustrate, *vb.* erläu´tern; *(with pictures)* illustrie´ren.

illustration, *n.* Erläu´terung, -en *f.*; *(picture)* Illustration´, -en *f.*

illustrative, *adj.* erläu´ternd.

illustrious, *adj.* berühmt´.

image, *n.* Abbild, -er *nt.*

imaginable, *adj.* denkbar.

imaginary, *adj.* scheinbar, imaginär´.

imagination, *n.* Einbildung, -en *f.*, Vorstellung, -en *f.*

imaginative, *adj.* phantasievoll.

imagine, *vb.* sich ein•bilden, sich vor•stellen.

imam, *n.* Imam, -e *m.*

imbecile, *adj.* schwachsinnig.

imitate, *vb.* nach•ahmen, imitie´ren.

imitation, *n.* Nachahmung, -en *f.*, Imitation´, -en *f.*

immaculate, *adj.* unbefleckt, makellos, blitzsauber; **(i. conception)** unbefleckte Empfäng´nis *f.*

immaterial, *adj.* unwesentlich.

immature, *adj.* unreif.

immediate, *adj.* unmittelzbar.

immediately, *adv.* sofort´.

immense, *adj.* unermeßlich.

immerse, *vb.* unter•tauchen, versen´ken.

immigrant, *n.* Einwanderer, - *m.*, Einwanderin, -nen *f.*

immigrate, *vb.* ein•wandern.

imminent, *adj.* bevor´stehend.

immobile, *adj.* unbeweglich.

immobilize, *vb.* unbeweglich machen.

immoderate, *adj.* maßlos, unmäßige.

immodest, *adj.* unbescheiden, anstößig.

immoral, *adj.* unsittlich, unmoralisch.

immorality, *n.* Unsittlichkeit, -en *f.*

immortal, *adj.* unsterblich.

immortality, *n.* Unsterblichkeit *f.*

immortalize, *vb.* unsterblich machen.

immune, *adj.* immun´.

immune system, *n.* Abwehrsystem, *nt.*

immunity, *n.* Immunität´, -en *f.*

immunize, *vb.* immunisie´ren.

impact, *n.* Zusam´menprall *m.; (fig.)* Auswirkung, -en *f.*

impair, *vb.* verrin´gern, verschlechtern.

impart, *vb.* zu•kommen lassen*.

impartial, *adj.* umparteiisch.

impatience, *n.* Ungeduld *f.*

impatient, *adj.* ungeduldig.

impeach, *vb.* an•klagen, beschul´digen.

impeachment, *n.* Anklage, -n *f.;* Beschul´digung, -en *f.*

impede, *vb.* behin´dern.

impediment, *n.* Behin´derung, -en *f.; (speech i.)* Sprachfehler, - *m.*

impel, *vb.* an•treiben*, zwingen*.

impenetrable, *adj.* undurchdringlich.

imperative, 1. *n.* Imperativ, -e *m.* **2.** *adj.* zwingend.

imperceptible, *adj.* unmerklich, unwahrnehmbar.

imperfect, 1. *n.* Imperfekt, -e *nt.* **2.** *adj.* unvollkommen, fehlerhaft.

imperfection, *n.* Unvollkommenheit, -en *f.,* Fehler, - *m.*

imperial, *adj.* kaiserlich.

imperialism, *n.* Imperialis´mus *m.*

impersonal, *adj.* unpersönlich.

impersonate, *vb.* verkör´pern; *(theater)* dar•stellen.

impersonation, *n.* Verkör´perung, -en *f.; (theater)* Darstellung, -en *f.*

impersonator, *n.* Imita´tor, -o´ren *m.; (swindler)* Hochstapler, - *m.*

impertinence, *n.* Frechheit, -en *f.,* Unverschämtheit, -en *f.*

impertinent, *adj.* frech, unverschämt.

impervious, *adj.* unzugänglich; *(fig.)* gefühl´los.

impetuous, *adj.* ungestüm.

impetus, *n.* Anstoß *m.,* Antrieb *m.*

implement, 1. *n.* Werkzeug, -e *nt.* **2.** *vb.* durch•führen.

implicate, *vb.* verwi´ckeln.

implication, *n.* implizier´ter Gedan´ke(n), - *m.;* Verwick´lung, -en *f.;* **(by i.)** impli´zite.

implicit, *adj.* inbegriffen, stillschweigend.

implied, *adj.* miteinbegriffen.

implore, *vb.* an•flehen.

imply, *vb.* in sich schliessen*, impli´zite sagen, an•deuten.

impolite, *adj.* unhöflich.

import, 1. *n.* Einfuhr *f.,* Import´, -e *m.; (meaning)* Bedeu´tung, -en *f.* **2.** *vb.* ein•führen, importie´ren.

importance, *n.* Wichtigkeit *f.*

important, *adj.* wichtig, bedeu´tend.

importation, *n.* Einfuhr *f.*

impose, *vb.* auf•erlegen.

imposition, *n.* Belas´tung, -en *f.*

impossibility, *n.* Unmöglichkeit, -en *f.*

impossible, *adj.* unmöglich.

impotence, *n.* Unfähigkeit, -en *f.; (med.)* Impotenz, -en *f.*

impotent, *adj.* unfähig; *(med.)* impotent.

impoverish, *vb.* arm machen; *(fig.)* aus•saugen.

impregnable, *adj.* uneinnehmbar.

impregnate, *vb.* durchdrin´gen*; *(make pregnant)* schwängern.

impresario, *n.* Impresa´rio, -s *m.*

impress, *vb. (imprint)* prägen, ein•prägen; *(affect)* beein´drucken, imponie´ren.

impression, *n.* Druck, -e *m.; (copy)* Abdruck, -e *m.; (fig.)* Eindruck, ‑e *m.*

impressive, *adj.* eindrucksvoll.

imprison, *vb.* ein•sperren.

imprisonment, *n.* Haft *f.*

improbable, *adj.* unwahrscheinlich.

impromptu, *adv.* aus dem Stegreif.

improper, *adj.* unrichtig; unschicklich.

improve, *vb.* verbes´sern.

improvement, *n.* Verbes´serung, -en *f.;* Besserung *f.*

improvise, *vb.* improvisie´ren.

impudent, *adj.* frech.

impulse, *n.* Impuls´, -e *m.*

impulsive, *adj.* impulsiv´.

impunity, *n.* **(with i.)** ungestraft.

impure, *adj.* unrein.

impurity, *n.* Unreinheit, -en *f.*

in, *prep.* in.

inadvertent, *adj.* achtlos, unaufmerksam.

inalienable, *adj.* unveräußerlich.

inane, *adj.* leer, geistlos.

inaugural, *adj.* Antritts- *(cpds.).*

inaugurate, *vb.* ins Amt ein•führen.

inauguration, *n.* Einweihung, -en *f.;* Amtseinführung, -en *f.*

incandescence, *n.* Glühen *nt.*

incandescent, *adj.* glühend; Glüh- *(cpds.).*

incantation, *n.* Beschwö´rung *f.,* Zauberspruch, ‑e *m.*

incapacitate, *vb.* unfähig machen.

incapacity, *n.* Unfähigkeit, -en *f.*

incarcerate, *vb.* ein•kerkern.

incarnate, *adj.* verkör´pert, fleischgeworden.

incarnation, n. Verkör´pe-
rung, -en f., Fleischwer-
dung f.

incendiary, adj. Brand-
(cpds.); aufwieglerisch.

incense, n. Weihrauch m.

incentive, n. Anreiz, -e m.,
Antrieb, -e m.

inception, n. Begin´nen nt.

incessant, adj. unaufhörlich.

incest, n. Blutschande f.

inch, n. Zoll, - m.

incidence, n. Vorkommen nt.

incident, n. Vorfall, ⸗e m.

incidental, adj. zufällig.

incidentally, adv. übrigens.

incision, n. Einschnitt, -e m.

incisor, n. Schneidezahn, ⸗e
m.

incite, vb. an•regen,
an•stacheln.

inclination, n. Neigung, -en
f.

incline, vb. neigen; **(be i.d)**
geneigt sein*.

include, vb. ein•schließen*.

including, prep. ein-
schließlich.

inclusive, adj. einschließlich.

incognito, adv. inkog´nito.

income, n. Einkommen, - nt.

incomparable, adj. unver-
gleichlich.

inconsiderate, adj. unüberlegt, rücksichtslos.

inconvenience, n. Mühe, -n
f., Belas´tung, -en f.

inconvenient, adj. mühsam,
ungelegen.

incorporate, vb. verei´nigen;
auf•nehmen*.

incorrigible, adj. un-
verbesserlich.

increase, 1. n. Zunahme, -n
f. **2.** vb. zu•nehmen*,
wachsen*.

incredible, adj. unglaublich.

incredulity, n. Zweifel, - m.

incredulous, adj. zweifelnd.

increment, n. Zunahme, -n f.

incriminate, vb. belas´ten,
beschul´digen.

incrimination, n.
Beschul´digung, -en f.,
Belas´tung, -en f.

incrust, vb. überkrus´ten.

incubator, n. Brutapparat, -
e m.

incumbent, 1. n. Amtsin-
haber, - m. **2.** adj.
verpflich´tend.

incur, vb. auf sich laden*.

incurable, adj. unheilbar.

indebted, adj. verschul´det.

indeed, adv. in der Tat.

indefatigable, adj. unermüdlich.

indefinite, adj. unbestimmt.

indefinitely, adv. endlos.

indelible, adj. unaus-
löschlich.

indemnify, vb. sicher•stellen;
entschä´digen.

indemnity, n. Sicherstel-
lung, -en f.; Entschä´di-
gung, -en f.

indent, vb. zacken; (paragraph) ein´rücken;
(damage) verbeu´len.

indentation, n. Einkerbung,
-en f.; (paragraph) Ein-
rückung, -en f.; (dam-
age) Verbeu´lung, -en f.

independence, n. Unabhängigkeit f.

independent, adj. unabhän-
gizg.

in-depth, adj. gründlich,
Tiefen- (cpds.).

index, n. Verzeich´nis, -se
nt., Regis´ter, - nt.; (i.
finger) Zeigefinger, - m.

India, n. Indien nt.

Indian, 1. n. Inder, - m., Inderin, -nen f.; **(Ameri-
can I.)** India´ner, - m.,
India´nerin, -nen f. **2.**
adj. indisch; india´nisch.

indicazte, vb. zeigen,
an•deuten.

indicatizon, n. Hinweis, -e
m., Anzeichen, - nt.

indicative, 1. n. Indikativ, -e
m. **2.** adj. bezeich´nend.

indicator, n. Zeiger, - m.,
Indika´tor, -o´ren m.;
(sign) Zeichen, - nt.

indict, vb. an•klagen.

indictment, n. Anklage, -n f.

indifference, n. Gle-
ichgültigkeit.

indifferent, adj. gleichgültig.

indigent, adj. bedürftig.

indigestible, adj. unverdaulich.

indigestion, n. Verdau´-
ungsstörung, -en f.

indignant, adj. entrüs´tet.

indignation, n. Entrüs´tung,
-en f.

indignity, n. Unwürdigkeit,
-en f.; (insult) Belei´di-
gung, -en f.

indirect, adj. indirekt.

indiscreet, adj. indiskret.

indiscretion, n.
Indiskretion´, -en f.

indispensable, adj. unabkömmlich.

indisposed, adj. unpäßlich;
(disinclined) abgeneigt.

indisposition, n. Un-
päßlichkeit, -en f.; Ab-
neigung, -en f.

individual, 1. n. Einzeln- m.,
Indivi´duum, -duen nt. **2.**
adj. einzeln, individuell´.

individuality, n. Individual-
ität´, -en f.

indivisible, adj. unteilbar.

indoctrinate, vb. schulen.

indolent, adj. träge.

Indonesia, n. Indone´sien nt.

indoor, adj. Haus-, Zim-
mer- (cpds.).

indoors, adv. zu Hause,
drinnen.

induce, vb. veran´lassen;
(elec.) induzie´ren.

induct, vb. ein•führen;
(physics) induzie´ren;
(mil.) verei´digen.

induction, n. Einführung, -
en f.; (physics)
Induktion´, -en f.; (mil.)
Verei´digung, -en f.

inductive, adj. induktiv´.

indulge, vb. nach•sehen*;
fröznen.

indulgence, n. Nachsicht, -en
f., Langmut m., Frönen nt.;
(eccles.) Ablaß, ⸗sse m.

indulgent, adj. nachsichtig,
langmütig.

industrial, adj. industriell´,
Industrie´- (cpds.).

industrialist, n. Industriell´-
m.

industrious, adj. fleißig.

industry, n. Industrie´, -i´en
f.; (hard work) Fleiß m.

ineligible, adj. unwählbar;
nicht in Frage kommend.

inept, *adj.* ungeschickt, unfähig.

inert, *adj.* träge.

inertia, *n.* Trägheit, -en *f.*

inevitable, *adj.* unvermeidlich.

infallible, *adj.* unfehlbar.

infamous, *adj.* berüch´tigt.

infamy, *n.* Niedertracht, -en *f.*, Schande, -n *f.*

infancy, *n.* Kindheit, -en *f.*; *(fig.)* Anfang, ˦e *m.*

infant, *n.* Säugling, -e *m.*

infantile, *adj.* kindlich, kindisch.

infantry, *n.* Infanterie´, -i´en *f.*

infantryman, *n.* Infantorist´, -en, -en *m.*

infatuate, *vb.* betö´ren, hin•reißen*.

infect, *vb.* an•stecken.

infected, *adj.* entzün´det.

infection, *n.* Entzün´dung, -en *f.*

infectious, *adj.* ansteckend.

infer, *vb.* folgern, an•nehmen*.

inference, *n.* Folgerung, -en *f.*, Annahme, -n *f.*

inferior, *adj.* minderwertig, uznterle´gen

inferiority, *n.* Minderwertigkeit, -en *f.*, Unterle´genheit *f.*

infernal, *adj.* höllisch.

inferno, *n.* Hölle *f.*; Fegefeuerz *nt.*

infest, *vb.* heim•suchen.

infidel, *n.* Ungläubig- *m.& f.*

infidelity, *n.* Untreue *f.*

infiltrate, *vb.* ein•dringen*, infiltrie´ren.

infinite, *adj.* unendlich.

infinitesimal, *adj.* unendlich klein; winzig.

infinitive, *n.* Infinitiv, -e *m.*

infinity, *n.* Unendlichkeit, -en *f.*

infirm, *adj.* schwach (˦).

infirmary, *n.* Schul- oder Studen´tenkrankenhaus, ˦er *nt.*

infirmity, *n.* Schwachheit, -en *f.*

inflame, *vb.* entzün´den.

inflammable, *adj.* entzünd´bar, feuergefährlich.

inflammation, *n.* Entzün´dung, -en *f.*

inflate, *vb.* auf•blasen*; *(tires)* auf•pumpen.

inflation, *n.* Inflation´, -en *f.*

inflection, *n.* Biegung, -en *f.*; *(voice)* Tonfall, ˦e *m.*; *(gram.)* Beugung, -en *f.*

inflict, *vb.* zu•fügen.

infliction, *n.* Last, -en *f.*

influence, 1. *n.* Einfluß, ˦sse *m.* **2.** *vb.* beein´flussen.

influential, *adj.* einflußreich.

influenza, *n.* Grippe, -n *f.*

inform, *vb.* benach´richtigen, mit•teilen; **(i. on)** denunzie´ren.

informal, *adj.* zwanglos, nicht formell´.

information, *n.* Auskunft, ˦e *f.*, Information´, *f.*

infringe, *vb.* übertre´ten*; *(jur.)* verlet´zen.

infuriate, *vb.* wütend machen, rasend machen, erbo´sen.

ingenious, *adj.* erfin´derisch, genial´.

ingenuity, *n.* Findigkeit *f.*, Genialität´ *f.*

ingredient, *n.* Bestand´teil, -e *m.*; *(cooking)* Zutat, -en *f.*

inhabit, *vb.* bewoh´nen.

inhabitant, *n.* Bewoh´ner, -m., Bewoh´nerin, -nen *f.*, Einwohner, - *m.* Einwohnerin, -nen *f.*

inhale, *vb.* ein•atmen.

inherent, *adzj.* angeboren, eigen.

inherit, *vb.* erben.

inheritance, *n.* Erbe *nt.*; Erbschaft, -zen *f.*

inhibit, *vb.* hindern, ab•halten*.

inhibited, *adj.* gehemmt´.

inhibition, *n.* Hemmung, -en *f.*

inhuman, *adj.* unmenschlich.

inimitable, *adj.* unnachahmlich.

iniquity, *n.* Ungerechtigkeit, -en *f.*; Schändlichkeit, -en *f.*

initial, 1. *n.* Anfangsbuchstabe, -n, -n *m.* **2.** *adj.* anfänglich; Anfangs- *(cpds.).*

initiate, *vb.* ein•führen, ein•weihen.

initiation, *n.* Einführung, -en *f.*, Einweihung, -en *f.*

initiative, *n.* Initiati´ve, -n *f.*

inject, *vb.* ein•spritzen.

injection, *n.* Einspritzung, -en *f.*

injunction, *n.* gerichtlicher Unterlas´sungsbefehl, -e *m.*

injure, *vb.* verlet´zen.

injurious, *adj.* schädlich; *(fig.)* nachteilig.

injury, *n.* Verlet´zung, -en *f.*; Schaden, ˦ *m.*

injustice, *n.* Ungerechtigkeit, -en *f.*

ink, *n.* Tinte, -n *f.*

inland, 1. *n.* Binnenland, ˦er *nt.* **2.** *adj.* inländisch.

inlet, *n.* kleine Bucht, -en *f.*

inmate, *n.* Insasse, -n, -n *m.*, Insassin, -nen *f.*

inn, *n.* Gasthaus, ˦er *nt.*, Wirtshaus, ˦er *nt.*

inner, *adj.* inner-.

innermost, *adj.* innerst-.

innocence, *n.* Unschuld *f.*

innocent, *adj.* unschuldig.

innovation, *n.* Neuerung, -en *f.*

innuendo, *n.* Unterstel´lung, -en *f.*

innumerable, *adj.* zahllos.

inoculate, *vb.* ein•impfen.

inoculation, *n.* Einimpfung, -en *f.*

input, *n.* Input, -s *m.*; Eingabe, -n *f.*

inquest, *n.* gerichtliche Untersuchung, -en *f.*

inquire, *vb.* fragen, sich erkun´digen.

inquiry, *n.* Nachfrage, -n *f.*, Erkun´digung, -en *f.*

inquisition, *n.* Untersu´chung, -en *f.*; *(eccles.)* Inquisition´, -en *f.*

inquisitive, *adj.* neugierig.

insane, *adj.* wahnsinnig, unzurechnungsfähig.

insanity, *n.* Wahnsinn *m.*

insatiable, *adj.* unersättlich.

inscribe, *vb.* ein´zeichnen, ein•schreiben*.

inscription, *n.* Inschrift, -en *f.*

insect, *n.* Insekt´, -en *nt.*

insecticide, *n.* Insek´tenpulver, - *nt.*

insensible, *adj.* gefühl´los.

insensitive, *adj.* unempfindlich.

inseparable, *adj.* unzertrennlich.

insert, 1. *n.* Beilage, -n *f.* **2.** *vb.* ein•fügen, ein•setzen.

insertion, *n.* Einsatz, ⸗e *m.*

inside, 1. *n.* Innenseite, -n *f.*, Inner- *nt.* **2.** *adj.* inner- . **3.** *adv.* innen, drinnen.

insidious, *adj.* hinterlistig.

insight, *n.* Einsicht, -en *f.*

insignia, *n.pl.* Abzeichen, - *nt.;* Insig´nien *pl.*

insignificance, *n.* Bedeutungslosigkeit *f.*

insignificant, *adj.* bedeu´tungslos.

insinuate, *vb.* an•spielen auf; **(i. oneself)** sich ein•schmeicheln.

insinuation, *n.* Anspielung, -en *f.*

insipid, *adj.* fade.

insist, *vb.* beste´hen*, behar´ren.

insistence, *n.* Beste´hen *nt.,* Behar´ren *nt.*

insistent, *adj.* beharr´lich, hartnäckig.

insolence, *n.* Unverschämtheit, -en *f.*

insolent, *adj.* unverschämt.

insomnia, *n.* Schlaflosigkeit *f.*

inspect, *vb.* besich´tigen.

inspection, *n.* Besich´tigung, -en *f.*

inspector, *n.* Inspek´tor, -o´ren *m.,* Inspekto´rin, -nen *f.*

inspiration, *n.* Eingebung, -en *f.,* Inspiration´, -en *f.*

inspire, *vb.* an•feuern, begei´stern.

install, *vb.* ein•bauen; *(fig.)* ein•führen.

installation, *n.* Installation´, -en *f.*

installment, *n.* Rate, -n *f.;* **(i. plan)** Ratenzahlung, -en *f.*

instance, *n. (case)* Fall, ⸗e *m.; (example)* Beispiel, -e *nt.;* **(law)** Instanz´, -en *f.;* **(for i.)** zum Beispiel.

instant, 1. *n.* Augenblick, -e *m.* **2.** *adj.* augenblicklich.

instantaneous, *adj.* sofor´tig.

instantly, *adv.* sofort´, auf der Stelle.

instead, *adv.* statt dessen, dafür; **(i. of)** statt, anstatt´.

instigate, *vb.* veran´lassen, an•stacheln.

instill, *vb.* ein•flößen.

instinct, *n.* Instinkt´, -e *m.*

instinctive, *adj.* unwillkürlich, instinktiv´.

institute, 1. *n.* Institut´, -e *nt.* **2.** *vb.* ein•leiten, an•ordnen.

institution, *n.* Einrichtung, -en *f.;* Institut´, -e *nt.,* Anstalt, -en *f.*

instruct, *vb.* unterrich´ten, an•weisen*.

instruction, *n.* Anweisung, -en *f.; (school)* Unterricht *m.*

instructive, *adj.* lehrreich.

instructor, *n.* Lehrer, - *m.*

instructress, *n.* Lehrerin, -nen *f.*

instrument, *n.* Werkzeug, -e *nt.,* Instrument´, -e *nt.*

instrumental, *adj.* behilf´lich; *(music)* Instrumental´- *(cpds.).*

insufferable, *adj.* unerträglich.

insufficient, *adj.* ungenügend.

insulate, *vb.* insolie´ren.

insulation, *n.* Isolie´rung, -en *f.*

insulator, *n.* Isola´tor, -o´ren *m.*

insulin, *n.* Insulin´ *nt.*

insult, 1. *n.* Belei´digung, -en *f.* **2.** *vb.* belei´digen.

insurance, *n.* Versi´cherung, -en *f.*

insure, *vb.* versi´chern.

insurgent, 1. *n.* Aufständisch - *m.* **2.** *adj.* aufständisch.

insurrection, *n.* Aufstand, ⸗e *m.*

intact, *adj.* intakt´.

intangible, *adj.* nicht greifbar.

integral, 1. *n. (math.)* Integral´, -e *nt.* **2.** *adj.* unerläßlich.

integrate, *vb.* integrie´ren.

integrity, *n.* Unbescholtenheit *f.*

intellect, *n.* Verstand´ *m.,* Intellekt´ *m.*

intellectual, **1.** *n.* Intellektuell- *m.& f.* **2.** *adj.* intellektuell´.

intelligence, *n.* Intelligenz´ *f.*

intelligent, *adj.* intelligent´.

intelligentsia, *n.* geistige Oberschicht *f.*

intelligible, *adj.* verständ´lich.

intend, *vb.* beab´sichtigen.

intense, *adj.* angespannt, intensiv´.

intensify, *vb.* verstär´ken.

intensive, *adj.* intensiv´.

intent, 1. *n.* Absicht, -en *f.* **2.** *adj.* erpicht´.

intention, *n.* Absicht, -en *f.*

intentional, *adj.* absichtlich.

inter, *vb.* beer´digen.

intercede, *vb.* dazwi´schen•treten*.

intercept, *vb.* ab•fangen*.

intercourse, *n.* Verkehr´ *m.,* Umgang *m.*

interest, 1. *n.* Interes´se, -n *nt.; (comm.)* Zins, -en *m.* **2.** *vb.* interessie´ren.

interesting, *adj.* interessant´.

interface, *n.* Schnittstelle, -n *f.*

interfere, *vb.* sich ein•mischen; ein•greifen*.

interference, *n.* Einmischung, -ezn *f.; (radio)* Störung, -en *f.*

interim, 1. *n.* Zwischenzeit, -en *f.* **2.** *adj.* Interims- *(cpds.).*

interior, 1. *n.* Inner- *nt.* **2.** *adj.* inner-; Innen- *(cpds.).*

interject, *vb.* dazwi´schen•werfen*.

interjection, *n.* Ausruf, -e *m.; (gram.)* Interjektion´, -en *f.*

interlude, *n.* Zwischenspiel, -e *nt.*

intermarry, *vb.* untereinander heiraten.

intermediary, 1. *n.* Vermitt´ler, - *m.,* Vermitt´lerin, -nen *f.* **2.** *adj.* Zwischen- *(cpds.).*

intermediate, *adj.* Zwischen- *(cpds.).*

interment, *n.* Begräb´nis, -se *nt.*

intermission, *n.* Unterbre´chung, -en *f.; (theater)* Pause, -n *f.*

intermittent, *adj.* wechselnd, perio´disch.

intern, *vb.* internie´ren.

intern, *n.* Volontär´arzt, ¨e *m.,* Volontär´ärztin, -nen *f.*

internal, *adj.* inner-, innerlich.

international, *adj.* international´.

internationalism, *n.* Internationalis´mus *m.*

interne, *n.* Volontär´arzt, ¨e *m.*

interpose, *vb.* ein•fügen.

interpret, *vb.* interpretie´ren; *(language)* dolmetschen.

interpretation, *n.* Interpretation´, -en *f.,* Auslegung, -en *f.*

interpreter, *n.* Dolmetscher, - *m.,* Dolmetscherin, -nen *f.*

interrogate, *vb.* aus•fragen; *(law)* verneh´men*, verhö´ren.

interrogation, *n.* Verhör´, -e *nt.*

interrogative, 1. *n.* Fragewort, ¨er *nt.* **2.** *adj.* fragend, Frage- *(cpds.).*

interrupt, *vb.* zunterbre´chen*.

interruption, *n.* Unterbre´chung, -en *f.*

intersect, *vb. (intr.)* sich schneiden*, sich kreuzen; *(tr.)* durchschnei´den, durchkreu´zen.

intersection, *n.* Kreuzung, - en *f.*

intersperse, *vb.* durchset´zen.

interval, *n.* Abstand, ¨e *m.*

intervene, *vb.* dazwi´schen•kommen*, sich ein•mischen.

intervention, *n.* Dazwi´schentreten *nt.,* Einmischung, -en *f.*

interview, 1. *n.* Interview´ -s *nt.,* Vorstellungsgespräch, *nt.* **2.** *vb.* interview´en.

intestine, *n.* Darm, ¨e *m.*

intimacy, *n.* Vertrau´lichkeit, -en *f.*

intimate, *adj.* vertraut´, innig.

intimidate, *vb.* ein•schüchtern.

intimidation, *n.* Einschüchterung, -en *f.*

into, *prep.* in.

intolerant, *adj.* intolerant.

intonation, *n.* Tonfall, ¨e *m.*

intoxicate, *vb.* berau´schen.

intoxication, *n.* Rausch, ¨e *m.*

intravenous, *adj.* intravenös´.

intrepid, *adj.* furchtlos.

intricacy, *n.* Kompliziert´heit, -en *f.*

intricate, *adj.* verwi´ckelt, kompliziert´.

intrigue, 1. *n.* Intri´ge, -n *f.* **2.** *vb.* intrigie´ren.

intrinsic, *adj.* innerlich; wahr.

introduce, *vb.* ein•führen, ein•leiten; *(persons)* vor•stellen.

introduction, *n.* Einführung, -en *f.,* Einleitung, -en *f.;* Vorstellung, -en *f.*

introductory, *adj.* einleitend.

introvert, *n.* nach innen gekehr´ter Mensch, -en, - en *m.*

intrude, *vb.* ein•dringen*.

intruder, *n.* Eindringling, -e *m.*

intuition, *n.* Intuition´, -en *f.*

inundate, *vb.* überschwem´men.

invade, *vb.* ein•dringen*, ein•fallen*.

invader, *n.* Angreifer, - *m.*

invalid, 1. *n.* Invali´de, -n, - n *m.* **2.** *adj.* ungültig.

invariable, *adj.* unveränderlich.

invasion, *n.* Invasion´, -en *f.*

inveigle, *vb.* verlei´ten.

invent, *vb.* erfin´den*.

invention, *n.* Erfin´dung, - en *f.*

inventive, *adj.* erfin´derisch.

inventor, *n.* Erfin´der, - *m.,* Erfin´derin, -nen *f.*

inventory, *n.* Inventar´, -e *nt.;* Inventur´, -en *f.*

inverse, *adj.* umgekehrt.

invertebrate, *adj.* ohne Wirbelsäule.

invest, *vb.* investie´ren, an•legen.

investigate, *vb.* untersu´chen.

investigation, *n.* Untersu´chung, -en *f.*

investment, *n.* Kapitals´anlage,z -n *f.*

inveterate, *adj.* eingefleischt.z

invigorate, *vb.* bele´ben, erfri´schen.

invincible, *adj.* unbesiegbar.

invisible, *adj.* unsichtbar.

invitation, *n.* Einladung, -en *f.,* Aufforderung, -en *f.*

invite, *vb.* ein•laden*, auf•fordern.

invocation, *n.* Anrufung, -en *f.z; (eccles.)* Bittgebet, -e *nt.z*

invoice, *n.* Warenrechnung, -en *f.*

invoke, *vb.* an•rufen*; erbit´ten.

involuntary, *adj.* unfreiwizllig.

involve, *vb.* ein•schließen*; verwi´ckeln.

involved, *adj.* verwi´ckelt.

invulnerable, *adj.* unverletzlich; uneinnehmbar.

inward, *adj.* inner-, innerlich.

inwardly, *adv.* innerlich.

iodine, *n.* Jod *nt.*

Iran, *n.* Iran´ *nt.*

Iraq, *n.* Irak´ *nt.*

irate, *adj.* zornig.

Ireland, *n.* Irland *nt.*

iridium, *n.* Iri´dium *nt.*

iris, *n.* Iris *f.; (flower)* Schwertlilie, -n *f.*

Irish, *adj.* irisch.

Irishman, *n.* Irländer,- *m.,* Ire, -n, -n *m.*

Irishwoman, *n.* Irländerin, - nen *f.*

irk, *vb.* ärgern.

iron, 1. *n.* Eisen *nt.; (flati.)* Bügeleisen, - *nt.* **2.** *adj.* eisern. **3.** *vb.* bügeln.

ironical, *adj.* spöttisch, iro´nisch.

irony, *n.* Spott *m.,* Ironie´ *f.*

irrational, *adj.* irrational´.

irrefutable, *adj.* unwiderlegbar.

irregular, *adj.* unregelmäßig.

irregularity, *n.* Unregelmäßigkeit, -en *f.*

irrelevant, *adj.* belang´los; unanwendbar.

irresistible, *adj.* unwiderstehlich.

irresponsible, *adj.* unverantwortlich.

irreverent, *adj.* unehrerbietig.

irrevocable, *adj.* unwiderruflich.

irrigate, *vb.* bewäs´sern.

irrigation, *n.* Bewäs´serung, -en *f.*

irritability, *n.* Reizbarkeit *f.*

irritable, *adj.* reizbar.

irritant, *n.* Reizfaktor, -en *m.*

irritate, *vb.* reizen, irritie´ren.

irritation, *n.* Reizung, -en *f.;* Ärger *m.*

island, *n.* Insel, -n *f.*

isolate, *vb.* isolie´ren.

isolation, *n.* Isolie´rung, -en *f.*

isolationist, *n.* Isolationist´, -en, -en *m.*

Israel, *n.* Israel *nt.*

Israeli, 1. *n.* Israe´li, -s *m&f.* **2.** *adj.* israe´lisch.

Israelite, 1. *n.* Israelit´, -en, -en *m.* **2.** *adj.* israeli´tisch.

issuance, *n.* Ausgabe, -n *f.*

issue, 1. *n.* Ausgabe, -n *f.; Problem´,* -e *nt.; (result)* Ergeb´nis, -se *nt.* **2.** *vb.* aus•geben*, aus•stellen.

isthmus, *n.* Isthmus, -men *m.*

it, *pron.* es.

Italian, 1. *n.* Italie´ner, - *m.,* Italie´nerin, -nen *f.* **2.** *adj.* italie´nisch.

Italic, *adj.* ita´lisch.

italics, *n.* Kursiv´schrift *f.*

Italy, *n.* Ita´lien *nt.*

itch, 1. *n.* Jucken *nt.* **2.** *vb.* jucken.

item, *n.* Arti´kel, - *m.,* Posten, - *m.*

itemize, *vb.* auf•zählen.

itinerary, *n.* Reiseroute, -n *f.*

ivory, *n.* Elfenbein *nt.*

ivy, *n.* Efeu *m.*

J

jab, 1. *n.* Stoß, ⸚e *m.,* Stich, -e *m.* **2.** *vb.* stoßen*, stechen*.

jack, *n. (auto)* Wagenheber, - *m.; (card)* Bube, -n, -n *m.*

jackal, *n.* Schakal´, -e *m.*

jackass, *n.* Esel, - *m.*

jacket, *n.* Jacke, -n *f.*

jack-knife, *n.* Klappmesser, - *nt.*

jack-of-all-trades, *n.* Hansdampf in allen Gassen *m.*

jade, *n.* Jade *m.*

jaded, *adj.* ermat´tet.

jagged, *adj.* zackig.

jail, *n.* Gefäng´nis, -se *nt.*

jailer, *n.* Gefäng´niswärter, - *m.,* Gefäng´niswärterin, -nen *f.*

jam, 1. *n.* Marmela´de, -n *f.,* Konfitüre, -n *f.; (trouble)* Klemme, -n *f.* **2.** *vb.* klemmen.

jangle, *vb.* rasseln.

janitor, *n.* Pförtner, - *m.,* Hausmeister, - *m.*

January, *n.* Januar *m.*

Japan, *n.* Japan *nt.*

Japanese, 1. *n.* Japa´ner, - *m.,* Japa´nerin, -nen *f.* **2.** *adj.* japa´nisch.

jar, 1. *n.* Krug, ⸚e *m.,* Glas, ⸚er *nt.* **2.** *vb.* rütteln.

jargon, *n.* Jargon´, -s *m.*

jasmine, *n.* Jasmin´, -e *m.*

jaundice, *n.* Gelbsucht *f.*

jaunt, *n.* kurze Reise, -n *f.*

javelin, *n.* Speer, -e *m.*

jaw, *n.* Kiefer, - *m.*

jay, *n.* Eichelhäher, - *m.*

jaywalk, *vb.* quer über eine Straßenkreuzung gehen*.

jazz, *n.* Jazz *m.*

jealous, *adj.* eifersüchtig.

jealousy, *n.* Eifersucht *f.*

jeans, *n.* Jeans *pl.*

jeer, *vb.* spotten.

jelly, *n.* Gelee´, -s *nt.*

jeopardize, *vb.* gefähr´den.

jeopardy, *n.* Gefahr´, -en *f.*

jerk, 1. *n.* Ruck, -e *m.* **2.** *vb.* ruckartig bewe´gen.

jerky, *adj.* ruckartig.

jersey, *n.* Jersey, -s *nt.*

Jerusalem, *n.* Jeru´salem *nt.*

jest, 1. *n.* Scherz, -e *m.* **2.** *vb.* scherzen.

jester, *n.* Spaßmacher, - *m.; (court j.)* Hofnarr, -en, - en *m.*

Jesuit, 1. *n.* Jesuit´, -en, -en *m.* **2.** *adj.* jesui´tisch; Jesui´ten- *(cpds.)*

Jesus Christ, *n.* Jesus Christus *m.*

jet, *n.* Strahl, -en *m.; (tech.)* Düse, -n *f.; (plane)* Düsenflugzeug, -e *nt.; (mineral)* Pechkohle, -n *f.*

jet lag, *n.* Jet-lag *m.;* körperliches Unbehagen durch Zeitverschiebung.

jetsam, *n.* Strandgut *nt.;* über Bord gewor´fenes Gut *nt.*

jetty, *n.* Mole, -n *f.*

Jew, *n.* Jude, -n, -n *m.,* Jüdin, -nen *f.*

jewel, *n.* Juwel´, -en *nt.,* Edelstein, -e *m.*

jeweler, *n.* Juwelier´, -e *m.,* Juwelie´rin, -nen *f.*

jewelry, *n.* Schmucksachen *pl.,* Schmuck *m.*

Jewish, *adj.* jüdisch.

jib, *n.* Klüver, - *m.*

jibe, *vb. (sailing)* halsen; *(agree)* sich decken.

jiffy, *n.* Nu *m.*

jig, *n.* Gigue *f.*

jilt, *vb.* sitzen lassen*.

jingle, *vb.* klingeln.

job, *n.* Stellung, -en *f.;* Aufgabe, -n *f.*

jobber, *n.* Zwischenhändler, - *m.,* Zwischenhändlerin, -nen *f.*

jockey, *n.* Jockey, -s *m.*

jocular, *adj.* scherzhaft.

jog, *vb. (push)* schubsen; *(run)* joggen.

joggle, *vb. (tr.)* stubsen; *(intr.)* wackeln.

join, *vb.* verbin´den*; *(club, etc.)* bei•treten*.

joint, 1. *n.* Gelenk´, -e *nt.* **2.** *adj.* gemein´sam.

joist, *n.* Querbalken, - *m.*

joke, 1. *n.* Witz, -e *m.,* Scherz, -e *m.,* Spaß, ⁼e *m.* **2.** *vb.* einen Witz machen, scherzen.

joker, *n.* Witzbold, -e *m.;* *(cards)* Joker, - *m.*

jolly, *adj.* heiter.

jolt, 1. *n.* Stoß, ⁼e *m.* **2.** *vb.* rütteln.

jonquil, *n.* gelbe Narzis´se, -n *f.*

jostle, *vb.* stoßen*.

journal, *n.* Journal´, -e *nt.;* *(diary)* Tagebuch, ⁼er *nt.;* *(newspaper)* Zeitung, -en *f.;* *(periodical)* Zeitschrift, -en *f.*

journalism, *n.* Zeitungswesen *nt.*

journalist, *n.* Journalist´, -en, -en *m.,* Journalis´tin, -nen *f.*

journey, *n.* Reise, -n *f.*

journeyman, *n.* Gesel´le, -n, -n *m.*

jovial, *adj.* jovial´.

jowl, *n.* Backe, -n *f.*

joy, *n.* Freude, -n *f.*

joyful, *adj.* freudig.

joyous, *adj.* freudig.

jubilant, *adj.* frohlockend.

jubilee, *nz.* Jubiläum, -ä´en *nt.*

Judaism, *n.* Judentum *nt.*

judge, 1. *n.* Kenner, - *m.;* *(law)* Richter, - *m.,* Richterin, -nen *f.* **2.** *vb.* beur´teilen; *(law)* richten, Recht sprechen*.

judgment, *n.* Urteil, -e *nt.;* *(law also:)* Rechtsspruch, ⁼e *m.*

judicial, *adj.* richterlich; Gerichts´- *(cpds.).*

judiciary, 1. *n.* Justiz´gewalt *f.;* Richterstand *m.* **2.** *adj.* richterlich.

judicious, *adj.* weise, klug.

jug, *n.* Krug, ⁼e *m.*

juggle, *vb.* jonglie´ren.

juggler, *n.* Jongleur´, -e *m.*

juice, *n.* Saft, ⁼e *m.*

juicy, *adj.* saftig.

July, *n.* Juli *m.*

jumble, *n.* Durcheinan´der *nt.*

jump, 1. *n.* Sprung, ⁼e *m.* **2.** *vb.* springen*.

junction, *n.* Verbin´dung, -en *f.;* *(railroad)* Knotenpunkt, -e *m.*

juncture, *n.* Zusam´mentreffen, - *nt.*

June, *n.* Juni *m.*

jungle, *n.* Dschungel, - *m.* *or nt. (or* -n *f.).*

junior, *adj.* jünger.

juniper, *n.* Wachol´der, - *m.*

junk, *n.* Altwaren *pl.;* *(fig.)* Kram *m.*

junket, *n. (food)* Milchpudding *m.;* *(trip)* Reise, -n *f.*

jurisdiction, *n.* Rechtsprechung, -en *f.;* Gerichts´barkeit *f.;* Zuständigkeit *f.*

jurisprudence, *n.* Rechtswissenschaft *f.*

jurist, *n.* Rechtsgelehrt- *m. & f.*

juror, *n.* Geschwo´ren- *m. & f.*

jury, *n.* Geschwo´ren- *pl.*

just, 1. *adj.* gerecht´. **2.** *adv.* gera´de, eben.

justice, *n.* Gerech´tigkeit *f.*

justifiable, *adj.* berech´tigt.

justification, *n.* Rechtfertigung, -en *f.,* Berech´tigung, -en *f.*

justify, *vb.* rechtfertigen.

jut, *vb.* hervor•stehen*.

jute, *n.* Jute *f.*

juvenile, *adj.* jugendlich.

K

kale, *n.* Grünkohl *m.*

kaleidoscope, *n.* Kaleidoskop´, -e *nt.*

kangaroo, *n.* Känguruh´, -s *nt.*

karat, *n.* Karat´, -e *nt.*

karate, *n.* Kara´te *nt.*

keel, *n.* Kiel, -e *m.*

keen, *adj.* scharf; *(fig.)* eifrig.

keep, 1. *n. (lodging)* Unterhalt *m.* **2.** *vb.* behal´ten*, bewah´ren; *(animals, etc.)* halten*; **(k. doing something)** etwas immer wieder tun*; **(k. on doing something)** etwas weiter tun*.

keeper, *n.* Wärter, - *m.,* Wärterin, -nen *f.,* Wächter, - *m.,* Wächterin, -nen *f.*

keepsake, *n.* Andenken, - *nt.*

keg, *n.* Faß, ⁼sser *nt.*

kennel, *n.* Hundezwinger, - *m.*

kerchief, *n.* Halstuch, ⁼er *nt.;* Kopftuch, ⁼er *nt.*

kernel, *n.* Kern, -e *m.;* *(grain)* Korn, ⁼er *nt.*

kerosene, *n.* Kerosin´ *nt.*

ketchup, *n.* Ketchup *nt.*

kettle, *n.* Kessel, - *m.*

kettledrum, *n.* Kesselpauke, -n *f.*

key, *n.* Schlüssel, - *m.;* *(piano)* Taste, -n *f.;* *(musical structure)* Tonart, -en *f.*

keyhole, *n.* Schlüsselloch, ⁼er *nt.*

khaki, *n.* Khaki *nt.*

kick, 1. *n.* Stoß, ⁼e *m.,* Tritt, -e *m.* **2.** *vb.* stoßen*, treten*.

kid, 1. *n. (goat)* Zicklein, - *nt.;* *(child)* Kind, -er *nt.* **2.** *vb.* necken, rein•legen.

kidnap, vb. gewalt´sam ent-
füh´ren.
kidnaper, n. Kinderräuber, -
m., Kinderräuberin, -nen f.
kidnaping, n. Kinderraub m.
kidney, n. Niere, -n f.
kidney bean, n.
Schminkbohne, -n f.
kill, vb. töten, um•brin-
gen*.
killer, n. Mörder, - m.
kiln, n. Brennofen, - m.
kilocycle, n. Kilohertz, - nt.
kilogram, n. Kilo, - nt.
kilohertz, n. Kilohertz nt.
kilometer, n. Kilome´ter, - m.
kilowatt, n. Kilowatt, - nt.
kilt, n. Kilt, -s m.
kimono, n. Kimo´no, -s m.
kin, n. Verwandt´schaft, -en f.
kind, 1. n. Art, -en f., Sorte,
-n f. **2.** adj. gütig, freundlich.

kindergarten, n. Kindergarten, - m.
kindle, vb. an•zünden,
entzün´den.
kindly, adj. freundlich.
kindness, n. Güte f., Freundlichkeit f.
kindred, adj. verwandt´.
king, n. König, -e m.
kingdom, n. Königreich, -e nt.
kink, n. Knoten, - m.
kiosk, n. Kiosk, -e m.
kiss, 1. n. Kuß, ⸚sse m. **2.**
vb. küssen.
kitchen, n. Küche, -n f.
kite, n. Drachen, - m.;
(bird) Milan, -e m.
kitten, n. Kätzchen, - nt.
kleptomaniac, n.
Kleptoma´ne, -n, -n m.
knack, n. Talent´, -e nt.
knapsack, n. Rucksack, ⸚e m.
knead, vb. kneten.

knee, n. Knie, Kni´e nt.
kneel, vb. knien.
knickers, n.pl. Kniehose, -n
f.
knife, n. Messer, - nt.
knight, nn. Ritter, - m.;
(chess) Springer, - m.
knit, vb. stricken; (fig.)
verknüp´fen.
knock, 1. n. Klopfen nt. **2.**
vb. klopfen.
knot, 1. n. Knoten, - m.;
(wood) Knorren, - m. **2.**
vb. knoten.
knotty, adj. knotig; (wood)
knorrig; (fig.) schwierig.
know, vb. (facts) wissen*;
(people, places, things)
kennen*.
knowledge, n. Kenntnis, -se
f.; Wissen nt.
knuckle, n. Knöchel, - m.
Korea, n. Kore´a nt.

L

label, n. Etiket´te, -n f.
labor, 1. n. Arbeit, -en f.;
(workers) Arbeiterschaft
f.; (birth) Wehen pl. **2.**
vb. arbeiten.
laboratory, n. Laborato´-
rium, -rien nt.
laborer, n. Arbeiter, - m.
laborious, adj. arbeitsam,
mühselig.
labor union, n. Gewerk´-
schaft, -en f.
labyrinth, n. Labyrinth´, -e nt.
lace, n. Spitze, -n f.
lacerate, vb. auf•reißen*.
laceration, n. Riß, -sse m.
lack, 1. n. Mangel, ⸚ m. **2.**
vb. Mangel leiden* an; (I
l. something) es fehlt,
mangelt mir an etwas.
lackadaisical, adj. schwunglos, unlustig.
laconic, adj. lako´nisch.
lacquer, 1. n. Lack, -e m. **2.**
vb. lackie´ren.
lacy, adj. spitzenartig;
Spitzen- (cpds.).
lad, n. Knabe, -n, -n m.
ladder, n. Leiter, -n f.
ladle, n. Schöpflöffel, - m.
lady, n. Dame, -n f.

ladybug, n. Mari´enkäfer, -
m.
lag, n. Verzö´gerung, -en f.
lag behind, vb. zurück´•-
bleiben*.
lagoon, n. Lagu´ne, -n f.
laid-back, adj. entspannt,
unverkrampft.
lair, n. Lagerstätte, -n f.;
Höhle, -n f.
laity, n. Laienstand m.,
Laien pl.
lake, n. See, Se´en m.
lamb, n. Lamm, ⸚er nt.
lame, adj. lahm.
lament, 1. n. Wehklage, -n
f. **2.** vb. bekla´gen.
lamentable, adj. bekla´-
genswert.
lamentation, n. Wehklage, -
n f.
laminate, vb. (metal) aus•-
walzen, plattie´ren; (l.d
wood) Furnier´holz nt.
lamp, n. Lampe, -n f.
lance, 1. n. Lanze, -n f. **2.** vb.
durchsto´ßen*; (med.) mit
der Lanzet´te öffnen.
land, 1. n. (country) Land, ⸚er
nt.; (ground) Grund und
Boden m. **2.** vb. landen.

landing, n. Landung, -en f.;
(stairs) Treppenabsatz,
⸚e m.
landlady, n. Wirtin, -nen f.;
Hausbesitzerin, -nen f.
landlord, n. Wirt, -e m.;
Hausbesitzer, - m.
landmark, n. Markstein, -e
m.
landscape, n. Landschaft, -
en f.
landslide, n. Erdrutsch, -e
m.; (election) überwäl´-
tigender Wahlsieg, -e m.
lane, n. Pfad, -e m.; (boat)
Fahrrinne, -n f.; (auto)
Fahrbahn, -en f.
language, n. Sprache, -n f.
languid, adj. energie´los,
schlaff.
languish, vb. schmachten.
lanky, adj. baumlang.
lanolin, n. Lanolin´ nt.
lantern, n. Later´ne, -n f.
lap, 1. n. Schoß, ⸚e m.;
(sport) Runde, -n f. **2.** vb.
übereinan´der•legen.
lapel, n. Revers´, - m.
lapin, n. Kanin´chenpelz m.
lapse, n. (error) Lapsus,
- m., Verse´hen, - nt.;

(time) Zwischenzeit, -en f. **2.** *vb.* verstrei´chen*.

larceny, n. Diebstahl, ˝e m.

lard, n. Schweinefett nt.

large, adj. groß (größer, größt-); weit; umfangreich.

largely, adv. größtenteils.

largo, n. Largo, -s nt.

lariat, n. Lasso, -s nt.

lark, n. Lerche, -n f.; *(fun)* Vergnü´gen nt.

larkspur, n. Rittersporn m.

larva, n. Larve, -n f.

laryngitis, n. Kehl- kopfentzündung, -en f.

larynx, n. Kehlkopf, ˝e m.

lascivious, adj. wollüstig.

laser, n. Laser m.

lash, 1. n. Peitsche, -n f.; Peitschenhieb, -e m.; *(eye)* Wimper, -n f. **2.** vb. peitschen.

lass, n. Mädchen, - nt.

lasso, n. Lasso, -s nt.

last, 1. n. Leisten, - m. **2.** adj. letzt-. **3.** vb. dauern.

lasting, adj. dauernd, anhal- tend, bestän´dig.

latch, 1. n. Klinke, -n f. **2.** vb. ein•klinken.

late, adj. spät, verspä´tet; *(dead)* verstor´ben.

lately, adv. in letzter Zeit.

latent, adj. latent.

lateral, adj. seitlich.

lath, n. Latte, -n f.

lathe, n. Drehbank, ˝e f.

lather, n. Schaum m.

Latin, 1. n. *(language)* Latein´ nt.; *(person)* Roma´ne, -n, -n m. **2.** adj. latei´nisch; roma´nisch.

latitude, n. Breite, -n f.

latrine, n. Latri´ne, -n f.

latter, 1. adj. letzter-. **2.** pron. *(the l.)* dieser, -es, -e.

lattice, n. Gitterwerk nt.

laud, vb. loben, preisen*.

laudable, adj. lobenswert.

laudanum, n. Laudanum nt.

laudatory, adj. Lob- *(cpds.).*

laugh, 1. n. Lachen nt. **2.** vb. lachen.

laughable, adj. lächerlich.

laughter, n. Gelächter nt.

launch, 1. n. Barkas´se, -n f. **2.** vb. *(throw)* schleudern; *(boat)* vom Stapel lassen*.

launching, n. Stapellauf, ˝e m.

launder, vb. waschen*.

laundress, n. Waschfrau, - en f.

laundry, n. *(clothes)* Wäsche f.; *(establish- ment)* Wäscherei´, -en f.

laundryman, n. Wäscherei´angestellt- m.

laurel, n. Lorbeer, -en m.

lava, n. Lava f.

lavatory, n. Waschraum, ˝e m. z

lavender, n. Laven´del m.

lavish, adj. üppig.

law, n. *(individual)* Gesetz´ -e nt.; *(system)* Recht nt.

lawful, adj. gesetz´lich, rechtmäßig.

lawless, adj. gesetz´los; *(fig.)* zügellos.

lawn, n. Rasen m.

lawsuit, n. Prozeß´, -sse m.

lawyer, n. Rechtsanwalt, ˝e m., Rechtsanwältin, -nen f.; Jzurist´, -en, -en m., Juris´tin, -nen f.

lax, adj. lax.

laxative, n. Abführmittel, - nt.

laxity, n. Laxheit f.

lay, 1. adj. Laien- *(cpds.).* **2.** vb. z legen.

layer, n. Schicht, -en f.

layman, n. Laie, -n, -n m.

lazy, adj. faul.

lead, 1. n. Führung f.; Leitzung f.; *(metal)* Blei nt. **2.** vb. führen, leiten.

leaden, adj. bleiern.

leader, zn. Führer, - m., Führerin, -nen f., Leiter, - m., Leiterin, -nen f.

leadership, n. Führung f.

lead pencil, n. Bleistift, -e m.

leaf, n. Blatt, ˝er nt.

leaflet, n. Broschü´re, -n f.; Flugblatt, ˝er nt.

league, n. Bund, ˝e m., Bündnis, -se nt.

League of Nations, n. Völkerbund m.

leak, 1. n. Leck, -e nt. **2.** vb. lecken.

leakage, n. Durchsickern nt.

leaky, adj. leck, undicht.

lean, 1. adj. mager. **2.** vb. lehnen.

leap, 1. n. Sprung, ˝e m. **2.** vb. springen*.

leap year, n. Schaltjahr, -e nt.

learn, vb. lernen; erfah´ren*.

learned, adj. gelehrt´.

learning, n. Wissen nt., Bil- dung f.

lease, 1. n. Mietvertrag, ˝e m., Pacht, -en f. **2.** vb. mieten, pachten.

leash, n. Leine, -n f.

least, adj. *(slightest)* ger- ingst´-; *(smallest)* kle- inst-; *(at l.,* in any case*)* wenigstens; *(at l.,* surely this much*)* mindestens, zum mindesten.

leather, 1. n. Leder, - nt. **2.** adj. ledern.

leathery, adj. ledern.

leave, 1. n. *(farewell)* Ab- schied, -e m.; *(permis- sion)* Erlaub´nis, -e f.; *(furlough)* Urlaub, -e m. **2.** vb. *(depart)* ab•fahren*; *(go away)* fort•gehen*; *(abandon)* verlas´sen*; *(let)* lassen*.

leaven, n. Sauerteig, -e m.

lecherous, adj. lüstern.

lecture, 1. n. Vortrag, ˝e m.; *(acazdemic)* Vorlesung, - en f. **2.** vb. einen Vortrag halten*; eine Vorlesung halten*.

lecturerz, n. Vortragend- m. & f.

ledge, n. Felsvorsprung, ˝e m.; Sims, -e m.

ledger, n. Hauptbuch, ˝er nt.

lee, n. Lee f.

leech, n. Blutegel, - m.

leek, n. Lauch, -e m.

leer, vb. begehr´lich schie- len.

leeward, adv. leewärts.

left, 1. n. z *(pol.)* Link- f. **2.** adj. link-; *(l.* over*)* übriggeblieben. **3.** adv. links.

leftist, adj. links orientiert´.

left-over, nz. Überbleibsel, - nt., Rest, -e m.

leg, n. Bein, -e nt.

legacy, n. Vermächt´nis, -se nt., Erbschaft, -en f.

legal, *adj.* gesetz´lich, gesetz´mäßig.
legalize, *vb.* legalisie´ren.
legation, *n.* Gesandt´schaft, -en *f.*
legend, *n.* Legen´de, -n *f.*
legendary, *adj.* legendär´.
legible, *adj.* leserlich.
legion, *n.* Legion´, -e *f.*
legislate, *vb.* Gesetze geben*.
legislation, *n.* Gesetz´gebung *f.*
legislator, *n.* Gesetz´geber, - *m.*, Gesetz´geberin, -nen *f.*
legislature, *n.* gesetz´gebende Gewalt´ *f.*; gesetz´gebende Versamm´lung, -en *f.*
legitimate, *adj.* legitim´.
leisure, *n.* Muße *f.*
leisurely, *adj.* gemäch´lich.
lemon, *n.* Zitro´ne, -n *f.*
lemonade, *n.* Limona´de, -n *f.*
lend, *vb.* leihen*.
length, *n.* Länge, -n *f.*; *(time)* Dauer *f.*
lengthen, *vb.* verlän´gern.
lengthwise, *adv.* der Länge nach.
lengthy, *adj.* langwierig.
lenient, *adj.* mild, nachsichtig.
lens, *n.* Linse, -n *f.*; *(photo)* Objektiv´, -e *nt.*
Lent, *n.* Fastenzeit *f.*
Lenten, *adj.* Fasten- *(cpds.)*.
lentil, *n.* Linse, -n *f.*
leopard, *n.* Leopard´, -en, -en *m.*
leper, *n.* Aussätzig- *m.& f.*
leprosy, *n.* Aussatz *m.*
lesbian, *adj.* lesbisch.
lesion, *n.* Verlet´zung, -en *f.*
less, *adj.* weniger.
lessen, *vb. (tr.)* vermin´dern; *(intr.)* nach•lassen*.
lesser, *adj. (size)* kleiner; *(degree)* gerin´ger.
lesson, *n.* Lehre, -n *f.*; *(school)* Lehrstunde, -n *f.*; *(assignment)* Aufgabe, -n *f.*
lest, *conj.* damit´ . . . nicht.
let, *vb. (allow)* lassen*; *(lease)* vermie´ten.

letdown, *n.* Enttäu´schung, -en *f.*
lethal, *adj.* tödlich.
lethargic, *adj.* teilnahmslos, lethar´gisch.
lethargy, *n.* Teilnahmslosigkeit *f.*, Lethargie´ *f.*
letter, *n. (alphabet)* Buchstabe(n)-, - *(or -n, -n) m.*; *(communication)* Brief, -e *m.*
letterhead, *n.* Briefkopf, ⸗e *m.*
lettuce, *n.* Kopfsalat, -e *m.*
leukemia, *n.* Leukämie´ *f.*
levee, *n.* Damm, ⸗e *m.*
level, 1. *n.* Stand, ⸗e *m.*, Niveau´, -s *nt.* **2.** *adj.* eben, gera´de; flach. **3.** *vb.* ebnen; gleich•machen.
lever, *n.* Hebel, - *m.*
levity, *n.* Leichtsinn *m.*
levy, 1. *n.* Abgabe, -n *f.*, Steuer, -n *f.* **2.** *vb.* erheben*.
lewd, *adj.* unzüchtig.
lexicon, *n.* Lexikon, -ka *nt.*
liability, *n.* Verant´wortlichkeit, -en *f.*; Verpflich´tung, -en *f.*
liable, *adj.* verant´wortlich; *(law)* haftbar.
liaison, *n.* Verbin´dung, -en *f.*; Liaison´, -s *f.*
liar, *n.* Lügner, - *m.*, Lügnerin, -nen *f.*
libel, *n.* Verleum´dung, -en *f.*
libelous, *adj.* verleum´derisch.
liberal, 1. *n.* Liberal´- *m.* **2.** *adj.* liberal´.
liberalism, *n.* Liberalis´mus *m.*
liberality, *n.* Freigebigkeit *f.*; Freisinnigkeit *f.*
liberate, *vb.* befrei´en.
liberation, *n.* Befrei´ung, -en *f.*
libertine, *n.* Lüstling, -e *m.*
liberty, *n.* Freiheit, -en *f.*
libido, *n.* Libido *f.*
librarian, *n.* Bibliothekar´, -e *m.*; Bibliotheka´rin, -nen *f.*
library, *n.* Bibliothek´, -en *f.*, Bücherei´, -en *f.*
libretto, *n.* Libret´to, -s *nt.*
license, *n.* Erlaub´nis, -se *f.*; Geneh´migung,

-en *f.* **(driver's l.)** Führerschein, -e *m.*
lick, *n.* lecken.
licorice, *n.* Lakrit´ze, -n *f.*
lid, *n.* Deckel, - *m.*; *(eye)* Lid, -er *nt.*
lie, 1. *n.* Lüge, -n *f.* **2.** *vb.* *(tell untruths)* lügen*; *(recline)* liegen*; **(l. down)** sich (hin•)legen.
lien, *n.* dinglich gesi´chertes Anrecht *nt.*
lieutenant, *n.* Leutnant, -s *m.*
life, *n.* Leben, - *nt.*
lifeboat, *n.* Rettungsboot, -e *nt.*
lifeguard, *n.* Bademeister, - *m.*, Bademeisterin, -nen *f.*
life insurance, *n.* Lebensversicherung, -en *f.*
lifeless, *adj.* leblos.
life preserver, *n.* Rettzungsring, -e *m.*; *(vest)* Schwimmweste, -n *f.*
life style, *n.* Lebensstil *m.*
lifetime, *n.* Lebenszeit, -en *f.*
lift, 1. *n.* Fahrstuhl, ⸗e *m.* **2.** *vb.* heben*.
ligament, *n.* Sehne, -n *f.*
ligature, *n.* Ligatur´, -en *f.*
light, 1. *n.* Licht, -er *nt.* **2.** *adj. (color)* hell; *(weight)* leicht. **3.** *vb.* *(fire)* an´zünden; *(illuminate)* beleuch´ten.
lighten, *vb.* leichter machen; *(fig.)* erleich´tern; *(lightning)* blitzen.
lighter, *n. (cigar, cigarette)* Feuerzeug, -e *nt.*
lighthouse, *n.* Leuchtturm, ⸗e *m.*
lightness, *n. (color)* Helligkeit *f.*; *(ease)* Leichtfertigkeit *f.*
lightning, *n.* Blitz, -e *m.*
like, 1. *adj.* gleich. **2.** *vb.* gern haben*, *(gern)* mögen*; **(I l. it)** es gefällt* mir; **(I l. to do it)** ich tue(*) es gern. **3.** *prep.* wie; **(l. this, l. that)** so.
likeable, *adj.* angenehm, liebenswert.
likelihood, *n.* Wahrschein´lichkeit, -en *f.*
likely, *adj.* wahrschein´lich.
liken, *vb.* verglei´chen*.

likeness, *n.* Ähnlichkeit, -en *f.*

likewise, *adv.* ebenso.

lilac, *n.* Flieder *m.*

lilt, *n.* wiegender Rhythmus *m.*

lily, *n.* Lilie, -n *f.*

lily of the valley, *n.* Maiglöckchen, - *nt.*

limb, *n.* Glied, -er *nt.*

limber, *adj.* biegsam.

limbo, *n.* Vorhölle *f.*

lime, *n.* Kalk *m.; (fruit)* Limo′ne, -n *f.*

limelight, *n.* Rampenlicht, - er *nt.*

limestone, *n.* Kalkstein *m.*

limit, 1. *n.* Grenze, -n *f.;* Höchstgrenze, -n *f.* **2.** *vb.* begren′zen, beschrän′ken.

limitation, *n.* Begren′zung, -en *f.,* Beschrän′kung, - en *f.*

limited, *adj.* begrenzt′, beschränkt′.

limitless, *adj.* unbegrenzt.

limousine, *n.* Limousi′ne -n *f.*

limp, 1. *adj.* schlaff. **2.** *vb.* hinken.

linden, *n.* Linde, -n *f.*

line, *n.* Linie, -n *f.; (mark)* Strich, -e *m.; (row)* Reihe, -n *f.; (writing)* Zeile, -n *f.; (rope)* Leine, -n *f.*

lineage, *n.* Geschlecht′, - er *nt.*

lineal, *adj.* in gerader Linie.

linear, *adj.* linear′.

linen, 1. *n.* Leinen - *nt.; (household)* Wäsche *f.* **2.** *adj.* leinen.

liner, *n. (boat)* Ozean-dampfer, - *m.*

linger, *vb.* verwei′len.

lingerie, *n.* Damenunter-wäsche *f.*

linguist, *n.* Sprachwissenschaftler, - *m.,* Sprachwissenschaftlerin, -nen *f.* Linguist′, -en, -en *m.,* Linguis′tin, -nen *f.*

linguistic, *adj.* sprachlich; sprachwissenschaftlich, lingui′stisch.

linguistics, *n.* Sprachwissenschaft, -en *f.,* Linguis′tik *f.*

liniment, *n.* Einreibemittel, - *nt.*

lining, *n.* Futter, - *nt.*

link, 1. *n. (bond)* Band, -e *nt.; (chain)* Glied, -er *nt.* **2.** *vb.* verbin′den*; verket′ten.

linoleum, *n.* Lino′leum *nt.*

linseed oil, *n.* Leinöl *nt.*

lint, *n.* Fussel, -n *f.*

lion, *n.* Löwe, -n, -n *m.*

lip, *n.* Lippe, -n *f.*

lip-stick, *n.* Lippenstift, -e *m.*

liquefy, *vb.* flüssig machen.

liqueur, *n.* Likör′, -e *m.*

liquid, 1. *n.* Flüssigkeit, -en *f.* **2.** *adj.* flüssig.

liquidate, *vb.* liquidie′ren.

liquidation, *n.* Liquidation′, -en *f.*

liquor, *n.* Alkohol *m.,* Spiri-tuo′sen *pl.*

lira, *n.* Lira, -re *f.*

lisp, *vb.* lispeln.

lisle, *n.* Baumwollfaden *m.*

list, 1. *n.* Liste, -n *f.,* Verzeich′nis, -se *nt.; (ship)* Schlagseite *f.* **2.** *vb.* verzeich′nen.

listen, *vb.* zu•hören, horchen.

listless, *adj.* lustlos.

litany, *n.* Litanei′ *f.*

liter, *n.* Liter, - *nt.*

literacy, *n.* Lesen und Schreiben Können *nt.*

literal, *adj.* buchstäblich, wörtlich.

literary, *adj.* litera′risch.

literate, *adj.* des Lesens und Schreibens kundig.

literature, *n.* Literatur′, -en *f.*

lithe, *adj.* geschmei′dig.

lithograph, 1. *n.* Lithographie′, -i′en *f.* **2.** *vb.* litho-graphie′ren.

litigant, *n.* Rechtsstreit-führer, - *m.*

litigation, *n.* Rechtsstreit, -e *m.*

litter, 1. *n. (rubbish)* Abfall, -e *m.; (stretcher)* Trag-bahre, -n *f.; (puppies, kittens, etc.)* Wurf, -e *m.* **2.** *vb.* Sachen herum′•liegen lassen*.

little, *adj. (size)* klein; *(amount)* wenig; **(a l.)** ein bißchen, ein wenig.

liturgical, *adj.* litur′gisch.

liturgy, *n.* Liturgie′, -i′en *f.*

live, 1. *adj.* leben′dig. **2.** *vb. (be alive)* leben; *(dwell)* wohnen.

livelihood, *n.* Lebensunter-halt *m.*

lively, *adj.* lebhaft.

liver, *n.* Leber, -n *f.*

livery, *n.* Livree′, -n *f.*

livestock, *n.* Viehbestand *m.*

livid, *adj.* aschfahl.

living, 1. *n.* Leben *nt.;* Lebensweise *f.* **2.** *adj.* lebend.

lizard, *n.* Eidechse, -n *f.*

lo, *interj.* siehe!

load, 1. *n.* Ladung, -en *f.,* *(burden)* Last, -en *f.* **2.** *vb.* laden*.

loaf, 1. *n.* Laib, -e *m.* **2.** *vb.* faulenzen.

loafer, *n.* Faulenzer, - *m.* Faulenzerin, -nen *f.*

loam, *n.* Lehm *m.*

loan, 1. *n.* Anleihe, -n *f.* **2.** *vb.* leihen*.

loath, *adj.* abgeneigt.

loathe, *vb.* verab′scheuen.

loathing, *n.* Abscheu *f.*

loathsome, *adj.* widerlich, ekelhaft.

lobby, *n.* Wandelhalle, -n *f.; (political)* Interes′sen-gruppe, -n *f.*

lobe, *n.* Lappen, - *m.*

lobster, *n.* Hummer, - *m.*

local, 1. *n. (train)* Vorortzug, -e *m.* **2.** *adj.* örtlich, lokal′.

locale, *n.* Schauplatz, -e *m.*

locality, *n.* Ort, -e *m.*

localize, *vb.* lokalisie′ren.

locate, *vb.* finden*; **(be l.d)** liegen*.

location, *n.* Lage, -n *f.*

lock, 1. *n.* Schloß, -sser *nt.; (canal)* Schleuse, -n *f.; (hair)* Locke, -n *f.* **2.** *vb.* ab•schließen*.

locker, *n.* Schrank, -e *m.; (baggage)* Schließfach, -er *nt.*

locket, *n.* Medaillon′, -s *nt.*

lockjaw, *n.* Kieferkrampf.

locksmith, *n.* Schlosser, - *m.*

locomotion, *n.* Fortbewegung, -en *f.*

locomotive, *n.* Lokomoti´ve, -n *f.*

locust, *n.* Heuschrecke, -n *f.*

lode, *n.* Erzader, -n *f.*

lodge, 1. *n.* Häuschen, - *nt.; (fraternal)* Loge, -n *f.* **2.** *vb. (intr.)* logie´ren; *(tr.)* beherbergen.

lodger, *n.* Untermieter, - *m.,* Untermieterin, -nen *f.*

lodging, *n.* Unterkunft, ⸗e *f.*

loft, *n.* Boden, ⸗ *m.; (warehouse)* Speicher, - *m.*

lofty, *adj.* erha´ben.

log, *n.* Holzklotz, ⸗e *m.; (tree trunk)* Baumstamm, ⸗e *m.; (ship's l.)* Logbuch, ⸗er *nt.*

loge, *n.* Loge, -n *f.*

logic, *n.* Logik *f.*

logical, *adj.* logisch.

loin, *n.* Lende, -n *f.*

loiter, *vb.* herum´•stehen*.

London, *n.* London *nt.*

lone, lonely, lonesome, *adj.* einsam.

loneliness, *n.* Einsamkeit *f.*

long, 1. *adj.* lang (⸗). **2.** *vb.* sich sehnen.

longevity, *n.* Langlebigkeit *f.*

longing, 1. *n.* Sehnsucht *f.* **2.** *adj.* sehnsüchtig.

longitude, *n.* Länge *f.*

longitudinal, *adj.* Längen- *(cpds.).*

long-lived, *adj.* langlebig.

long playing record, *n.* Langspielplatte, -n *f.*

look, 1. *n.* Blick, -e *m.; (appearance,* **l.s)** Aussehen *nt.* **2.** *vb.* sehen*, schauen, blicken, gucken; **(l. at)** an•sehen*, •schauen, •blicken, •gucken; **(l. good, etc.)** gut *(etc.)* aus•sehen*; **(l. out,** *be careful)* auf•passen.

looking glass, *n.* Spiegel, - *m.*

loom, *n.* Webstuhl, ⸗e *m.*

loop, *n.* Schlaufe, -n *f.*

loophole, *n.* Schlupfloch, ⸗er *nt.*

loose, *adj.* lose, locker.

loosen, *vb.* lockern.

loot, 1. *n.* Beute *f.* **2.** *vb.* plündern.

lop off, *vb.* ab•schlagen*.

lopsided, *adj.* schief.

loquacious, *adj.* schwatzhaft.

lord, *n.* Herr, -n, -en *m.; (title)* Lord, -s *m.*

lordship, *n.* Herrschaft, -en *f.*

lose, *vb.* verlie´ren*.

loss, *n.* Verlust´, -e *m.*

lot, *n.* Los, -e *nt.; (quantity)* Menge, -n *f.; (ground)* Grundstück, -e *nt.*

lotion, *n.* Lotion´, -en *f.*

lottery, *n.* Lotterie´, -i´en *f.*

lotus, *n.* Lotosblume, -n *f.*

loud, *adj.* laut; *(color)* grell.

loudspeaker, *n.* Lautsprecher, - *m.*

lounge, 1. *n.* Vorhalle, -n *f.* **2.** *vb.* herum´•lungern.

louse, *n.* Laus, ⸗e *f.*

lout, *n.* Lümmel, - *m.*

louver, *n.* Lattenfenster, - *nt.*

lovable, *adj.* liebenswert.

love, 1. *n.* Liebe, -n *f.* **2.** *vb.* lieben; **(fall in l.)** sich verlie´ben.

lovely, *adj.* lieblich, reizend.

lover, *n.* Liebhaber, - *m.,* Liebhaberin, -nen *f.*

low, *adj.* niedrig, tief; *(nasty)* gemein´.

lowbrow, *adj.* unintellektuell, ungeistig.

lower, 1. *adj.* tiefer, niedriger; gemei´ner. **2.** *vb.* herun´ter•lassen*; herab´•setzen, senken.

lowly, *adj.* beschei´den.

loyal, *adj.* treu.

loyalist, *n.* Loyalist´, -en *m.*

loyalty, *n.* Treue *f.,* Loyalität´ *f.*

lozenge, *n.* Pastil´le, -n *f.*

lubricant, *n.* Schmiermittel, - *nt.*

lubricate, *vb.* schmieren.

lucid, *adj.* klar.

luck, *n.* Glück *nt.,* Zufall, ⸗e *m.*

lucky, *adj.* glücklich; **(be l.)** Glück haben*.

lucrative, *adj.* gewinn´bringend.

ludicrous, *adj.* lächerlich.

lug, *vb.* schleppen.

luggage, *n.* Gepäck´ *nt.*

lukewarm, *adj.* lauwarm.

lull, 1. *n.* Pause, -n *f.* **2.** *vb.* beru´higen; **(l. to sleep)** ein•schläfern.

lullaby, *n.* Wiegenlied, -er *nt.*

lumbago, *n.* Hexenschuß *m.*

lumber, *n.* Holz *nt.*

luminous, *adj.* leuchtend.

lump, *n.* Klumpen, - *m., (skin)* Beule, -n *f.*

lumpy, *adj.* klumpig.

lunacy, *n.* Irrsinn *m.*

lunar, *adj.* Mond- *(cpds.).*

lunatic, 1. *n.* Irrsinnig- *m.* **2.** *adj.* irrsinnig.

lunch, 1. *n.* leichtes Mittagessen, - *nt.* **2.** *vb.* zu Mittag essen*.

luncheon, *n.* leichtes Mittagessen, - *nt.*

lung, *n.* Lunge, -n *f.*

lunge, *vb.* vor•stoßen*.

lurch, *n.* torkeln; **(leave in the l.)** sitzen lassen*.

lure, *vb.* locken.

lurid, *adj.* grell; *(fig.)* grausig.

lurk, *vb.* lauern.

luscious, *adj.* saftig, lecker.

lush, *adj.* saftig, üppig.

lust, 1. *n.* Wollust *f.* **2.** *vb.* gelü´sten.

luster, *n.* Glanz *m.*

lustful, *adj.* lüstern.

lustrous, *adj.* glänzend.

lusty, *adj.* munter; kräftig.

lute, *n.* Laute, -n *f.*

Lutheran, 1. *n.* Luthera´ner, - *m.* **2.** *adj.* luthe´risch.

luxuriant, *adj.* üppig.

luxurious, *adj.* verschwen´derisch, luxuriös.

luxury, *n.* Luxus *m.*

lying, *adn.* lügnerisch.

lymph, *n.* Lymphe, -n *f.*

lynch, *vb.* lynchen.

lyre, *n.* Leier, -n *f.*

lyric, *adj.* lyrisch.

lyricism, *n.* Lyrik *f.*

M

macabre, *adj.* maka´ber.

macaroni, *n.* Makkaro´ni *pl.*

machine, *n.* Maschi´ne, -n *f.*

machine gun, *n.* Maschi´-nengewehr, -e *nt.*

machinery, *n.* Mechanis´-mus *m.;* Maschi´nen *pl.*

machinist, *n.* Maschinist´, -en, -en *m.*

machismo, *n.* Männlichkeit, Virilität´ *f.*

macho, *adj.* protzig männlich.

mackerel, *n.* Makre´le, -n *f.*

mackinaw, *n.* kurzer wollener Mantel, = *m.*

mad, *adj.* verrückt´; *(angry)* böse.

madam, *n.* gnädige Frau *f.*

madden, *vb.* verrückt´ machen.

mafia, *n.* Mafia *f.*

magazine, *n.* Magazin´, -e *nt.,* Zeitschrift, -en *f.*

magic, 1. *n.* Zauberkunst, =e *f.* **2.** *adj.* magisch.

magician, *n.* Zauberer, - *m.*

magistrate, *n.* Polizei´richter, - *m.*

magnanimous, *zadj.* großzügig.

magnate, *n.* Magnat´, -en, -en *m.*

magnesium, *n.* Magne´sium *nt.*

magnet, *n.* Magnet´, (-en,) -en *m.*

magnetic, *adj.* magne´tisch.

magnificence, *n.* Herrlichkeit *f.,* Pracht *f.*

magnificent, *adj.* großartig, prächtig.

magnify, *vb.* vergrö´ßern.

magnitude, *n.* Größe, -n *f.*

mahogany, *n.* Mahago´ni *nt.*

maid, *n.* Dienstmädchen, - *nt.;* (old m.) alte Jungzfer, -n *f.*

maiden, *adj.* Jungfern-*(cpds.);* **(m. name)** Mädchenname(n), - *m.*

mail, 1. *n.* Post *f.* **2.** *vb.* mit der Post schicken; zur Post bringen*.

mailbox, *n.* Briefkasten, =*m.*

mail carrier, *n.* Postbote, -n, -n *m.;* Postbotin, -nen *f.;* Briefträger, - *m.,* Briefträgerin, -nen *f.*

maim, *vb.* verstüm´meln.

main, *adj.* hauptsächlich.

mainframe, *n.* Großrechenanlage, -n *f.*

mainland, *n.* Festland *nt.*

mainspring, *n.* Triebfeder, -n *f.*

maintain, *vb.* aufrecht•erhalten*; *(assert)* behaup´ten.

maintenance, *n.* Aufrechterhaltung *f.,* Instand´haltung *f.*

maize, *n.* Mais *m.*

majestic, *adj.* majestä´tisch.

majesty, *n.* Majestät´, -en *f.*

major, 1. *n.* Major´, -e *m.* **2.** *adj.* größer; Haupt- *(cpds.);* (music) Dur *nt.,* **(A-major)** A-dur.

majority, *n.* Mehrzahl, -en *f.,* Mehrheit, -en *f.,* Majorität, -en *f.*

make, *vb.* machen; *(manufacture)* her•stellen; *(compel)* zwingen*.

make-believe, 1. *n.* Vorspiegelung, -en *f.* **2.** *adj.* vorgetäuscht. **3.** *vb.* vor•täuschen.

maker, *n.* Hersteller, - *m.*

makeshift, *n.* Notbehelf *m.*

makeup, *n.* Struktur´, -en *f.;* Aufmachung, -en *f.;* *(face)* Schminke *f.,* Make-up *nt.*

malady, *n.* Krankheit, -en *f.*

malaria, *n.* Mala´ria *f.*

male, 1. *n.* (human) Mann, =er *m.;* (animal) Männchen, - *nt.* **2.** *adj.* männlich.

malevolent, *adj.* böswillig.

malice, *n.* Bosheit, -en *f.*

malicious, *adj.* boshaft.

malignant, *adj.* bösartig.

malnutrition, *n.* Unterernährung *f.*

malt, *n.* Malz *nt.*

maltreat, *vb.* mißhan´deln.

mammal, *1. n.* Säugetier, -e *nt.*

man, *n.* Mann, =er *m.;* (human being) Mensch, -en, -en *m.*

manage, *n.* handhaben; *(administer)* verwal´ten; *(direct)* leiten.

management, *n.* Verwal´tung, -en *f.;* Leitung, -en *f.*

manager, *n.* Leiter, - *m.* Leiterin, -nen *f.;* Unterneh´mer, - *m.* Unterneh´merin, -nen *f.*

mandate, *n.* Mandat´, -e *nt.*

mandatory, *adj.* unerläßlich.

mandolin, *n.z* Mandoli´ne, -n *f.*

mane, *n.* Mähne, -n *f.*

maneuver, 1. *n.* Manö´ver, -e *nt.* **2.** *vb.* manövrie´ren.

manganese, *n.* Mangan´ *nt.*

manger, *n.* Krippe, -n *f.*

mangle, *vb.* zerflei´schen; *(laundry)* mangeln.

manhood, *n.* Mannesalter *nt.;* Mannhaftigkeit *f.*

mania, *n.* Manie´, -i´en *f.*

maniac, *n.* Wahnsinnig- *m.*

manicure, 1. *n.* Manikü´re, -n *f.* **2.** *vb.* manikü´ren.

manifest, 1. *adj.* offenkundig. **2.** *vb.* bekun´den.

manifesto, *n.* Manifest´, -e *nt.*

manifold, *adj.* mannigfaltig.

manipulate, *vb.* manipulie´-ren.

mankind, *n.* Menschheit *f.*

manly, *adj.* mannhaft.

manner, *n.* Art, -en *f.,* Weise, -n *f.;* Manier´, -en *f.*

mannerism, *n.* Manieris´-mus *m.*

mansion, *n.* Haus, =er *nt.*

manslaughter, *n.* Totschlag, =e *m.*

mantelpiece, *n.* Kamin´sims, -e *m.*

mantle, *n.* Mantel, = *m.*

manual, 1. *n.* Handbuch, =er *nt.* **2.** *adj.* Hand- *(cpds.).*

manufacture, 1. *n.* Herstellung, -en *f.* **2.** *vb.* her•stellen.

manufacturer, *n.* Fabrikant´, -en, -en *m.*

manure, *n.* Mist *m.*

manuscript, *n.* Handschrift, -en *f.,* Manuskript´, -e *nt.*

many, *adj. pl.* viele.

map, *n.* Landkarte, -n *f.; (of a small area)* Plan, ⸗e *m.*

maple, *n.* Ahorn, -e *m.*

mar, *vb.* verun´zieren.

marble, *n.* Marmor, -e *m.*

march, 1. *n.* Marsch, ⸗e *m.* **2.** *vb.* marschie´ren.

March, *n.* März *m.*

mare, *n.* Stute, -n *f.*

margarine, *n.* Margari´ne *f.*

margin, *n. (edge)* Rand, ⸗er *m.; (latitude)* Spielraum, ⸗e *m.*

marginal, *adj.* Rand- *(cpds.).*

marijuana, *n.* Marihua´na *nt.*

marinate, *vb.* marinie´ren.

marine, *adj.* Meeres-, See- *(cpds.).*

mariner, *n.* Seemann, -leute *m.*

marionette, *n.* Marionet´te, -n *f.*

marital, *adj.* ehelich.

maritime, *adj.* Schiffahrts-, Seemanns- *(cpds.).*

mark, 1. *n.* Zeichen, - *nt.; (school)* Zensur´, -en *f.,* Note, -n *f.* **2.** *vb.* kennze-ichnen.

market, *n.* Markt, ⸗e *m.*

market place, Marktplatz, -e *m.*

marmalade, *n.* Marmelade, -n *f.*

maroon, 1. *adj.* rotbraun. **2.** *vb.* aus•setzen.

marquee, *n.* Überda´chung, -en *f.*

marquis, *n.* Marquis´, - *m.*

marriage, *n.* Heirat, -en *f.; (ceremony)* Trauung, -en *f.; (institution)* Ehe, -n *f., (matrimony)* Ehestand *f.*

marrow, *n.* Mark *nt.*

marry, *vb.* heiraten; *(join in marriage)* trauen; **(get married)** heiraten, sich verhei´raten; **(m. off)** verhei´raten.

marsh, *n.* Marsch, -en *f.*

marshal, *n.* Marschall, ⸗e *m.*

martial, *adj.* kriegerisch; Kriegs- *(cpds.).*

martyr, *n.* Märtyrer, - *m.* Märtyrerin, -nen

martyrdom, *n.* Märtyr-ertum *nt.*

marvel, 1. *n.* Wunder, - *nt.* **2.** *vb.* **(m. at)** bewun´dern.

marvelous, *adj.* wunderbar.

mascara, *n.* Augenwim-perntusche *f.*

mascot, *n.* Maskot´te, -n *f.*

masculine, *adj.* männlich, maskulin.

mash, 1. *n.* Brei, -e *m.* **2.** *vb.* zersto´ßen*.

mask, 1. *n.* Maske, -n *f.* **2.** *vb.* maskie´ren.

mason, *n.* Maurer, - *m.*

masquerade, *n.* Maskera´de, -n *f.*

mass, 1. *n.* Masse, -n *f., (church)* Messe, -n *f.*

massacre, 1. *n.* Gemet´zel, -nt. **2.** *vb.* nieder•metzeln.

massage, 1. *n.* Massa´ge, -n *f.* **2.** *vb.* massie´ren.

masseur, *n.* Masseur´, -e *m.*

masseuse, *n.* Masseuse, -n *f.*

massive, *adj.* massiv´.

mass meeting, *n.* Massen-versammlung, -en *f.*

mast, *n.* Mast, -en *m.*

master, 1. *n.* Meister, - *m.;* Herr, -n, -en *m.* **2.** *vb.* be-herr´schen.

masterpiece, *n.* Meister-stück, -e *nt.*

mastery, *n.* Beherr´schung *f.;* Herrschaft *f.*

mat, *n.* Matte, -n *f.*

match, 1. *n. (light)* Streich-holz, ⸗er *nt.; (contest)* Wettkampf, ⸗e *m.; (marriage)* Heirat, -en *f.,* Partie´, -i´en *f.* **2.** *vb.* passen zu; sich messen* mit.

mate, 1. *n. (spouse)* Ehe-mann, ⸗er *m.;* Ehefrau, -en *f.; (naut.)* Maat, -e *m.* **2.** *vb.* sich paaren.

material, 1. *n.* Material´, -ien *nt.; (cloth)* Stoff, -e *m.* **2.** *adj.* materiell´; wesentlich.

materialism, *n.* Materialis´mus *m.*

materialize, *vb.* sich ver-wirk´lichen.

maternal, *adj.* mütterlich.

maternity, *n.* Mutterschaft *f.*

mathematical, *adj.* mathema´tisch.

mathematics, *n.* Mathe-matik´ *f.*

matinée, *n.* Nachmit-tagsvorstellung, -en *f.*

matrimony, *n.* Ehestand *m.*

matron, *n.* Matro´ne, -n *f.*

matter, 1. *n.* Stoff, -e *m.,* Mate´rie, -n *f.; (fig.)* Sache, -n *f.,* Angelegen-heit, -en *f.* **2.** *vb.* von Bedeu´tung sein*; aus•machen; **(it doesn't m.)** es macht nichts.

mattress, *n.* Matrat´ze, -n *f.*

mature, 1. *adj.* reif. **2.** *vb.* reifen; *(fall due)* fällig werden*.

maturity, *n.* Reife *f.;* Fäl-ligkeit *f.*

maul, *vb.* übel zu•richten.

mausoleum, *n.* Mausole´um, -le´en *nt.*

maxim, *n.* Grundsatz, ⸗e *m.*

maximum, 1. *n.* Maximum, -ma *nt.* **2.** *adj.* höchst- *(cpds.).*

may, *vb.* **(be permitted)** dürfen*; **(he m. come)** er wird vielleicht kom-men*; **(that m. be)** das kann *or* mag sein*.

May, *n.* Mai *m.*

maybe, *adv.* vielleicht´.

mayhem, *n.* Mord *und* Totschlag *m.*

mayonnaise, *n.* Mayonnai´-se, -n *f.*

mayor, *n.* Bürgermeister, - *m.,* Bürgermeisterin, -nen *f.*

maze, *n.* Wirrwarr *nt.*

me, *pron.* mir; mich.

meadow, *n.* Wiese, -n *f.*

meager, *adj.* dürftig.

meal, *n.* Mahlzeit, -en *f.; (flour)* Mehl *nt.*

mean, 1. *n. (average)* Durchschnitt, -e *m.* **2.** *adj.* mittler-, durch-schnittlich; Mittel-, Durchschnitts- *(cpds.); (nasty)* gemein´. **3.** *vb. (signify)* bedeu´ten; *(intend to say)* meinen.

meaning, *n.* Bedeu'tung, -en *f.*, *(sense)* Sinn, -e *m.*

means, *n.* Mittel *pl.*

meantime, meanwhile, *n.* Zwischenzeit *f.*; **(in the m.)** inzwi'schen, unterdes'sen.

measles, *n.* Masern *pl.*

measure, 1. *n.* Maß -e *nt.*; *(fig.)* Maßnahme, -n *f.* **2.** *vb.* messen*.

measurement, *n.* Maß, -e *nt.*

measuring, *n.* Messen *nt.*

meat, *n.* Fleisch *nt.*

mechanic, *n.* Mecha'niker, - *m.*, Mecha'nikerin, -nen *f.*

mechanical, *adj.* mecha'nisch.

mechanism, *n.* Mechanis'mus, -men *m.*

mechanize, *vb.* mechanisie'ren.

medal, *n.* Orden, - *m.*

meddle, *vb.* sich ein•mischen.

mediaeval, *adj.* mittelalterlich.

median, *n.* Mittelwert, -e *m.*

mediate, *vb.* vermit'teln.

mediator, *n.* Vermitt'ler, - *m.*, Vermitt'lerin, -nen *f.*

medical, *adj.* ärztlich, medizi'nisch.

medicate, *vb.* medizi'nisch behan'deln.

medicine, *n.* Medizin', -en *f.*

mediocre, *adj.* mittelmäßig.

mediocrity, *n.* Mittelmäßigkeit *f.*

meditate, *vb.* nach•denken*.

meditation, *n.* Nachdenken *nt.*

Mediterranean, *adj.* Mittelmeer- *(cpds.).*

Mediterranean Sea, *n.* Mittelmeer *nt.*

medium, 1. *n.* Mittel, - *nt.*; Medium, -ien *nt.* **2.** *adj.* mittler-.

medley, *n. (music)* Potpourri, -s *nt.*

meek, *adj.* sanft.

meekness, *n.* Sanftmut *f.*

meet, *vb.* treffen*; sich treffen*; begeg'nen.

meeting, *n.* Versamm'lung, -en *f.*, Zusam'menkunft, -ᵉe *f.*, Tagung, -en *f.*; *(en-*

counter) Begeg'nung, -en *f.*

melancholy, 1. *n.* Schwermut *f.*, Melancholie' *f.* **2.** *adj.* schwermütig, melancho'lisch.

megahertz, *n.* Megahertz *nt.*

mellow, *adj.* gereift'.

melodious, *adj.* wohlklingend, melo'disch.

melodrama, *n.* Melodrama, -men *nt.*

melody, *n.* Melodie', -i'en *f.*

melon, *n.* Melo'ne, -n *f.*

melt, *vb.* schmelzen*.

meltdown, *n. (atomic power plant)* Zerschmel'zen *nt.*

member, *n.* Mitglied, -er *nt.*

membership, *n.* Mitgliedschaft *f.*

membrane, *n.* Membra'ne, -n *f.*

memento, *n.* Andenken, - *nt.*

memoirs, *n.pl.* Memoi'ren *pl.*

memorable, *adj.* denkwürdig.

memorandum, *n.* Memoran'dum, -den *nt.*

memorial, 1. *n.* Denkmal, -ᵉer *nt.*; Andenken, - *nt.* **2.** *adj.* Gedenk- *(cpds.).*

memorize, *vb.* auswendig lernen.

memory, *n. (retentiveness)* Gedächt'nis, -se *nt.*; *(remembrance)* Erin'nerung, -en *f.*

menace, 1. *n.* drohende Gefahr', -en *f.* **2.** *vb.* drohen, bedro'hen.

menagerie, *n.* Menagerie', -i'en *f.*

mend, *vb.* aus•bessern.

menial, *adj.* niedrig.

menopause, *n.* Wechseljahre *pl.*

menstruation, *n.* Regel *f.*, Menstruation' *f.*

menswear, *n.* Herrenbekleidung *f.*

mental, *adj.* geistig.

mentality, *n.* Mentalität', -en *f.*

menthol, *n.* Menthol' *nt.*

mention, 1. *n.* Erwäh'nung, -en *f.* **2.** *vb.* erwäh'nen.

menu, *n.* Menü', -s *nt.*; Speisekarte, -n *f.*

mercantile, *adj.* kaufmännisch.

mercenary, *adj.* gewinnsüchtig.

merchandise, *n.* Ware, -n *f.*

merchant, *n.* Kaufmann, -leute *m.*; Geschäfts'mann, -leute *m.*

merchant marine, *n.* Handelsmarine, -n *f.*

merciful, *adj.* barmher'zig, gütig, gnädig.

merciless, *adj.* unbarmherzig, schonungslos.

mercury, *n.* Quecksilber *nt.*

mercy, *n.* Gnade *f.*, Mitleid *nt.* Erbar'men *nt.*

mere, *adj.* bloß, nichts als.

merely, *adv.* nur, bloß.

merge, *vb.* verschmel'zen*.

merger, *n.* Zusam'menschluß, -ᵉsse *m.*; Fusion', -en *f.*

meringue, *n.* Baiser', -s *nt.*

merit, 1. *n.* Verdienst', -e *nt.*; Wert, -e *m.*; Vorzug, -ᵉe *m.* **2.** *vb.* verdie'nen.

meritorious, *adj.* verdienst'lich.

mermaid, *n.* Nixe, -n *f.*

merriment, *n.* Fröhlichkeit, -en *f.*

merry, *adj.* fröhlich, lustig.

merry-go-round, *n.* Karussell', -s *nt.*

mesh, *n.* Netz, -e *nt.*

mess, *n.* Durcheinan'der *nt.*; Unordnung *f.*; Schlamas'sel *nt.*; *(mil.)* Eßsaal, -säle *m.*

message, *n.* Botschaft, -en *f.*, Nachricht, -en *f.*

messenger, *n.* Bote, -n, -n *m.*, Botin, -nen *f.*

messy, *adj.* unordentlich, schlampig.

metabolism, *n.* Stoffwechsel *m.*

metal, *n.* Metall', -e *nt.*

metallic, *adj.* metal'len.

metamorphosis, *n.* Metamorpho'se, -n *f.*

metaphysics, *n.* Metaphysik' *f.*

meteor, *n.* Meteor', -e *m.*

meteorite, *n.* Meteorit´, -e *m.*

meteorology, *n.* Meteorologie´ *f.*

meter, *n. (unit of measure)* Meter, - *nt. or m.; (recording device)* Zähler, - *m.*

method, *n.* Metho´de, -n *f.*

meticulous, *adj.* sorgfältig.

metric, *adj.* metrisch.

metropolis, *n.* Großstadt, ⸗e *f.*

metropolitan, *adj.* zur Großstadt gehö´rend.

mettle, *n.* Mut *m.*

Mexican, 1. *n.* Mexika´ner, - *m.,* Mexika´nerin, -nen *f.* **2.** *adj.* mexika´nisch.

Mexico, *n.* Mexiko *nt.*

mezzanine, *n.* Zwischenstock *m.*

microbe, *n.* Mikro´be, -n *f.*

microfiche, *n.* Mikrofiche *m.*

microfilm, *n.* Mikrofilm, -e *m.*

microform, *n.* Mikroform *f.*

microphone, *n.* Mikrophon´, -e *nt.*

microscope, *n.* Mikroskop´, -e *nt.*

mid, *adj.* Mittel- *(cpds.);* **(in m. air)** mitten in der Luft.

middle, 1. *n.* Mitte, -n *f.* **2.** *adj.* mittler-.

middle-aged, *adj.* in mittlerem Alter.

Middle Ages, *n.* Mittelalter *nt.z*

middle class, *n.* Mittelstand, ⸗e *m.*

Middle East, *n.* Mittlerer Ostezn *m.;* Nahost- *(cpds.).*

midget, *n.* Lilliputa´ner, - *m.*

midnight, *n.* Mitternacht *f.*

midwife, *n.* Hebamme, -n *f.*

mien, *n.* Miene, -n *f.*

might, *n.* Macht, ⸗e *f.*

mighty, *adj.* mächtig.

migraine, *n.* Migrä´ne *f.*

migrate, *vb.* wandern.

migration, *n.* Wanderung *f.*

migratory, *adj.* wandernd, Zug- *(cpds.).*

mildew, *n.* Schimmel *m.*

mildness, *n.* Milde *f.*

mile, *n.* Meile, -n *f.*

mileage, *n.* Meilenzahl *f.*

militant, *adj.* kriegerisch.

militarism, *n.* Militaris´mus *m.*

military, 1. *n.* Militär´, -s *nt.* **2.** *adj.* militä´risch.

militia, *n.* Miliz´, -en *f.*

milk, 1. *n.* Milch *f.* **2.** *vb.* melken*.

milkman, *n.* Milchmann, ⸗er *m.*

milky, *adj.* milchig.

mill, 1. *n.* Mühle, -n *f.; (factory)* Fabrik´, -en *f.* **2.** *vb.* mahlen*.

miller, *n.* Müller, - *m.,* Müllerin, -nen *f.*

millimeter, *n.* Millime´ter, - *nt.*

millinery, *n.* Putzwaren *pl.*

million, *n.* Million´, -en *f.*

millionaire, *n.* Millionär´, - *m.& f.* **2.** *adj.* Millionärin, -nen *f.*

mimic, 1. *n.* Schauspieler, - *m.* **2.** *vb.* nach•ahmen.

mince, *vb.* klein schneiden*; **(he doesn't m. his words)** er nimmt kein Blatt vor den Mund.

mind, 1. *n.* Geist *m.,* Verstand´ *m.,* Sinn *m.* **2.** *vb. (obey)* gehor´chen; *(watch over)* auf•passen auf; **(never m.)** das macht nichts.

mindful, *adj.* eingedenk.

mine, 1. *n.* Bergwerk, -e *nt.; (mil.)* Mine, -n *f.* **2.** *pron.* meiner, -es, -e. **3.** *vb.* ab•bauen; *(mil.)* Minen legen.

miner, *n.* Bergarbeiter, - *m.*

mineral, 1. *n.* Mineral´, -e *nt.* **2.** *adj.* minera´lisch.

mingle, *vb.* mischen.

miniature, *n.* Miniatur´, -en *f.*

miniaturize, *vb.* miniaturisie´ren.

minimal, *adj.* minimal´; Mindest-, Minimal´- *(cpds.).*

minimize, *vb.* herab´•setzen.

minimum, *n.* Minimum, - ma *nt.*

mining, *n.* Bergbau *m.*

minister, *n. (government)* Mini´ster, - *m.,* Mini´sterin, -nen *f.; (church)*

Pfarrer, - *m.,* Pastor, - o´ren *m.,* Geistlich- *m.*

ministry, *n. (government)* Ministe´rium, -rien *nt.; (church)* Geistlicher Stand *m.*

mink, *n.* Nerz, -e *m.*

minnow, *n.* Elritze, -n *f.*

minor, 1. *n.* Minderjährige *m.& f.* **2.** *adj.* gering´; minderjährig; *(music)* Moll *nt.,* **(A-minor)** a-Moll.

minority, *n.* Minderzahl, - en *f.,* Minderheit, -en *f.,* Minorität´, -en *f.*

minstrel, *n.* Spielmann, -leute *m.*

mint, 1. *n. (plant)* Minze, -n *f.; (coin factory)* Münze, - n *f.* **2.** *vb.* münzen.

minus, *prep.* minus, weniger.

minute, 1. *n.* Minu´te, -n *f.* **2.** *adj.* winzig.

miracle, *n.* Wunder, - *nt.*

miraculous, *adj.* wie ein Wunder.

mirage, *n.* Luftspiegelung, -en *f.*

mire, *n.* Sumpf, ⸗e *m.;* Schlamm *m.*

mirror, *n.* Spiegel, - *m.*

mirth, *n.* Fröhlichkeit *f.*

misappropriate, *vb.* verun´treuen.

misbehave, *vb.* sich schlecht beneh´men*.

miscellaneous, *adj.* divers´.

mischief, *n.* Unfug *m.*

mischievous, *adj.* schelmisch.

misconstrue, *vb.* mißdeu´ten.

misdemeanor, *n.* Verge´hen, - *nt.*

miser, *n.* Geizhals, ⸗e *m.*

miserable, *adj.* jämmerlich, kläglich.

miserly, *adj.* geizig.

misery, *n.* Elend *nt.,* Jammer *m.*

misfit, *n.* Blindgänger, - *m.*

misfortune, *n.* Unglück, -e *nt.,* Pech *nt.*

misgiving, *n.* Beden´ken, - *nt.*

mishap, *n.* Unglück, -e *nt.*

mislay, *vb.* verle´gen.

mislead, vb. irre•führen.

misplace, vb. verle´gen.

mispronounce, vb. falsch aus•sprechen*.

miss, 1. n. Fehlschlag, ⸗e m. 2. vb. verfeh´len; (feel the lack of) vermis´sen; (fail to obtain) verpas´sen.

Miss, n. Fräulein, - nt.

missile, n. Wurfgeschoß, -sse nt.; (guided m.) ferngesteuertes Rake´tengeschoß, -sse nt.

mission, n. Mission´, -en f.

missionary, 1. n. Missionar´, -e m., Missiona´rin, -nen f. 2. adj. Missionars´- (cpds.).

misspell, vb. falsch buchstabie´ren.

mist, n. (fog) Nebel, - m.; (haze) Dunst, ⸗e m.

mistake, 1. n. Fehler, - m., Irrtum, ⸗er m. 2. vb. verken´nen*.

mistaken, adj. falsch; irrig; (be m.) sich irren.

mister, n. Herr, -n, -en m.

mistletoe, n. Mistel, -n f.

mistreat, vb. mißhan´deln.

mistress, n. Herrin, -nen f.; (of the house) Hausfrau, -en f.; (of a pet) Frauchen, - nt.; (lover) Geliebt´- f.

mistrust, 1. n. Mißtrauen nt. 2. vb. mißtrau´en.

misty, adj. neblig; dunstig.

misunderstand, vb. mißverstehen*.

misuse, 1. n. Mißbrauch, ⸗e m. 2. vb. mißbrau´chen.

mite, n. Bißchen nt.; (bug) Milbe, -n f.

mitigate, vb. mildern.

mitten, n. Fausthandschuh, -e m.

mix, vb. mischen.

mixture, n. Mischung, -en f.

mix-up, n. Verwir´rung, -en f.; Verwechs´lung, -en f.

moan, n. stöhnen.

mob, n. Menschenmenge, -n f.; Pöbel m.

mobile, adj. beweg´lich; mobilisiert´.

mobilization, n. Mobil´-machung, -en f.

mobilize, vb. mobilisie´ren.

mock, vb. (tr.) verspot´ten; (intr.) spotten.

mockery, n. Spott m., Hohn m.

mod, adj. auffällig modern in Kleidung, Benehmen.

mode, n. (way) Art und Weise f.; (fashion) Mode, -n f.

model, 1. n. Vorbild, -er nt., Muster, - nt.; Modell´, -e nt. 2. vb. modellie´ren.

moderate, 1. adj. mäßig, gemä´Bigt. 2. vb. mäßigen; vermit´teln.

moderation, n. Mäßigung f.

modern, adj. modern´.

modernize, vb. modernisie´ren.

modest, adj. beschei´den.

modesty, n. Beschei´denheit f.

modify, vb. modifizie´ren.

modish, adj. modisch.

modulate, vb. modulie´ren.

moist, adj. feucht.

moisten, vb. befeuch´ten.

moisture, n. Feuchtigkeit f.

molar, n. Backenzahn ⸗e m.

molasses, n. Melas´se f.; Sirup m.

mold, 1. n. Form, -en f.; (mildew) Schimmel m. 2. vb. formen; schimmelig werden*.

moldy, adj. schimmelig.

mole, n. (animal) Maulwurf, ⸗e m.; (mark) Muttermal, -e nt.

molecule, n. Molekül´, -e nt.

molest, vb. beläs´tigen.

molten, adj. flüssig.

moment, n. Augenblick, -e m., Moment´, -e m.; (factor) Moment´, -e nt.

momentary, adj. augenblick´lich, momentan´.

momentous, adj. folgenschwer.

monarch, n. Monarch´, -en, -en m.

monarchy, n. Monarchie´, -i´en f.

monastery, n. Kloster, ⸗ nt.

Monday, n. Montag, -e m.

monetary, adj. Geld- (cpds.).

money, n. Geld, -er nt.

money changer, n. Geldwechsler, - m.

money order, n. Postanweisung, -en f.

mongrel, n. Bastard, -e m.

monitor, n. (man) Abhörer, - m.; (apparatus) Kontroll´gerät, -e nt.

monk, n. Mönch, -e m.

monkey, n. Affe, -n, -n m.

monocle, n. Mono´kel, - nt.

monologue, n. Monolog´, -e m.

monopolize, vb. monopolizie´ren.

monopoly, n. Monopol´, -e nt.

monotone, n. einförmiger Ton, ⸗e m.

monotonous, adj. eintönig, monoton´.

monotony, n. Eintönigkeit f., Monotonie´ f.

monster, n. Ungeheuer, - nt.

monstrosity, n. Ungeheuerlichkeit, -en f.

monstrous, adj. ungeheuerlich, haarsträubend.

month, n. Monat, -e m.

monthly, 1. n. Monatschrift, -en f. 2. adj. monatlich.

monument, n. Denkmal, ⸗er nt.

monumental, adj. monumental´.

mood, n. Stimmung, -en f.; Laune, -n f.

moody, adj. launisch; schwermütig.

moon, n. Mond, -e m.

moonlight, n. Mondschein m.

moor, 1. n. Moor, -e nt. 2. vb. veran´kern.

mooring, n. Ankerplatz, ⸗e m.

moot, adj. strittig.

mop, n. Mop, -s m.

moped, n. Mofa, -s nt.

moral, 1. n. Moral´, -en f. 2. adj. sittlich, mora´lisch.

morale, n. Stimmung, -en f., Moral´ f.

moralist, n. Moralist´, -en, -en m.

morality, n. Sittlichkeit f., Moral´ f.; Sittenlehre f.

morbid, adj. morbid´.

more, *adv.* mehr.

moreover, *adv.* außerdem.

morgue, *n.* Leichenhaus, ≈er *nt.*

morning, *n.* Morgen, - *m.,* Vormittag, -e *m.*

moron, *n.* Schwachsinnig- *m.& f.*

morose, *adj.* verdrieß'lich.

morphine, *n.* Morphium *nt.*

morsel, *n.* Bissen, - *m.*

mortal, *adj.* sterblich; tödlich.

mortality, *n.* Sterblichkeit *f.*

mortar, *n.* (*vessel*) Mörser, - *m.;* (*building material*) Mörtel *m.*

mortgage, *n.* Hypothek', -en *f.*

mortician, *n.* Le- ichenbestatter, - *m.*

mortify, *vb.* kastei'en; demütigen.

mortuary, *n.* Leichenhalle, -n *f.*

mosaic, *n.* Mosaik', -e *nt.*

Moscow, *n.* Moskau *nt.*

Moslem, *n.* Moslem *m.*

mosque, *n.* Moschee' *f.*

mosquito, *n.* Mücke, -n *f.*

moss, *n.* Moos, -e *nt.*

most, *adj.* meist-.

mostly, *adv.* meistens, hauptsächlich.

moth, *n.* Motte, -n *f.*

mother, *n.* Mutter, ≈ *f.*

mother-in-law, *n.* Schwiegermutter, ≈ *f.*

motif, *n.* Motiv', -e *nt.*

motion, *n.* Bewe'gung, -en *f.;* (*parliament*) Antrag, ≈e *m.*

motionless, *adj.* bewe'- gungslos.

motion picture, *n.* Film, -e *m.*

motivate, *vb.* veran'lassen, motivie'ren.

motivation, *n.* Motivie'rung, -en *f.*

motive, *n.* Beweg'grund, ≈e *m.*

motor, *n.* Motor, -o'ren *m.*

motorboat, *n.* Motorboot, -e *nt.*

motorcycle, *n.* Motorrad, ≈er *nt.*

motorist, *n.* Kraftfahrer, - *m.,* Kraftfahrerin, -nen *f.*

motto, *n.* Motto, -s *nt.*

mound, *n.* Erdhügel, - *m.*

mount, *vb.* (*get on*) bestei'gen*; (*put on*) montie'ren.

mountain, *n.* Berg, -e *m.*

mountaineer, *n.* Bergbe- wohner, - *m.;* Berg- steiger, - *m.* Berg- steigerin, -nen *f.*

mountainous, *adj.* bergig, gebir'gig.

mourn, *vb.* (*intr.*) trauern; (*tr.*) betrau'ern.

mournful, *adj.* trauervoll.

mourning, *n.* Trauer *f.*

mouse, *n.* Maus, ≈e *f.*

mouth, *n.* Mund, ≈er *m.;* (*river*) Mündung, -en *f.*

mouthpiece, *n.* (*instrument*) Mundstück, -e *nt.;* (*spokesman*) Wortführer, - *m.*

movable, *adj.* beweg'lich.

move, 1. *n.* (*household goods*) Umzug, ≈e *m.;* (*motion*) Bewe'gung, -en *f.;* (*games*) Zug, ≈e *m.* **2.** *vb.* um•ziehen*; bewe'- gen, sich bewe'gen; ziehen*; (*parliamentary*) bean'tragen.

movement, *n.* Bewe'gung, -en *f.;* (*music*) Satz, ≈e *m.*

movie, *n.* Kino, -s *nt;* Film, -e *m.*

moving, 1. *n.* Umzug, ≈e *m.* **2.** *adj.* ergrei'fend.

mow, *vb.* mähen.

Mr., *n.* Herr *m.*

Mrs., *n.* Frau *f.*

much, *adj.* viel.

mucilage, *n.* Klebstoff, -e *m.*

muck, *n.* Schlamm *m.*

mucous, *adj.* schleimig.

mucus, *n.* Nasenschleim *m.*

mud, *n.* Schlamm *m.,* Dreck *m.*

muddy, *adj.* schlammig, trübe.

muff, 1. *n.* Muff, -e *m.* **2.** *vb.* vermas'seln.

muffle, *vb.* (*wrap up*) ein•hüllen; (*silence*) dämpfen.

muffler, *n.* (*scarf*) Schal, -s *m.;* (*auto*) Auspufftopf, ≈e *m.*

mug, *n.* Krug, ≈e *m.*

mulatto, *n.* Mulat'te, -n, -n *m.*

mule, *n.* Esel, - *m.*

mullah, *n.* Mullah, -s *m.*

multinational, *adj.* multina- tional'.

multiple, *adj.* vielfältig.

multiplication, *n.* Multipli- kation', -en *f.*

multiply, *vb.* (*math.*) multi- plizie'ren; (*increase*) verviel'fältigen.

multitude, *n.* Menge, -n *f.*

mummy, *n.* Mumie, -n *f.*

mumps, *n.* Ziegenpeter *m.*

Munich, *n.* München *nt.*

municipal, *adj.* städtisch.

munificent, *adj.* freigebig.

munition, *n.* Munition', -en *f.*

mural, *n.* Wandgemälde, - *nt.*

murder, 1. *n.* Mord, -e *m.* **2.** *vb.* morden, ermor'den.

murderer, *n.* Mörder, - *m.,* Mörderin, -nen *f.*

murmur, 1. *n.* Gemur'mel, - *nt.* **2.** *vb.* murmeln.

muscle, *n.* Muskel, -n *m.*

muscular, *adj.* muskulös; Muskel- (*cpds.*).

muse, 1. *n.* Muse, -n *f.* **2.** *vb.* nach•denken*.

museum, *n.* Muse'um, - se'en *nt.*

mushroom, *n.* Pilz, -e *m.*

music, *n.* Musik' *f.*

musical, *adj.* musika'lisch.

musical comedy, *n.* Operet'te, -n *f.*

musician, *n.* Musiker, - *m.,* Musikerin, -nen *f.*

muslin, *n.* Musselin', -e *m.*

must, *vb.* müssen*.

mustache, *n.* Schnurrbart, ≈e *m.*

mustard, *n.* Senf *m.,* Mostrich *m.*

muster, 1. *n.* Musterung, - en *f.* **2.** *vb.* mustern.

musty, *adj.* muffig.

mutation, *n.* Mutation', -en *f.*

mute, *adj.* stumm.

mutilate, *vb.* verstüm'meln.

mutiny, 1. *n.* Meuterei´, -en *f.* **2.** *vb.* meutern.

mutter, *vb.* murmeln.

mutton, *n.* Hammelfleisch *nt.*

mutual, *adj.* gegenseitig, gemein´sam.

muzzle, *n. (gun)* Mündung, -en *f.; (animal's mouth)* Maul, ˮer *nt.; (mouth covering)* Maulkorb, ˮe *m.*

my, *adj.* mein, -, -e.

myopia, *n.* Kurzsichtigkeit *f.*

myriad, 1. *n.* Myria´de, -n *f.; (fig.)* Unzahl, -en *f.* **2.** *adj.* unzählig.

myrtle, *n.* Myrte, -n *f.*

mysterious, *adj.* geheim´nisvoll.

mystery, *n.* Geheim´nis, -se *nt.;* Rätsel, - *nt.*

mystic, 1. *n.* Mystiker, - *m.* **2.** *adj.* mystisch; Geheim´- *(cpds.).*

mystify, *vb.* verwir´ren; verdun´keln.

myth, *n.* Sage, -n *f.;* Mythus, -then *m.*

mythical, *adj.* sagenhaft, mythisch.

mythology, *n.* Mythologie´, -i´en *f.*

N

nag, 1. *n.* Gaul, ˮe *m.* **2.** *vb.* herum•nörgeln; keifen.

nail, 1. *n.* Nagel, ˮ *m.; (n. polish)* Nagellack *m.* **2.** *vb.* nageln.

naïve, *adj.* naiv´, unbefangen.

naked, *adj.* nackt.

name, 1. *n.* Name(n), - *m.* **2.** *vb.* nennen*.

namely, *adv.* nämlich.

namesake, *n.* Namensvetter, -n *m.*

nap, 1. *n. (sleep)* Nickerchen, - *nt.,* Nachmittagsschläfchen, - *nt.; (cloth)* Noppe, -n *f.* **2.** *vb.* ein•nicken.

naphtha, *n.* Naphtha *nt.*

napkin, *n.* Serviet´te, -n *f.; (sanitary n.)* Binde, -n *f.*

narcissus, *n.* Narzis´se, -n *f.*

narcotic, 1. *n.* Rauschgift, -e *nt.* **2.** *adj.* narko´tisch.

narrate, *vb.* erzäh´len.

narration, *n.* Erzäh´lung, -en *f.*

narrative, 1. *n.* Erzäh´lung, -en *f.* **2.** *adj.* erzäh´lend.

narrow, *adj. (tight, confined)* eng; *(not broad)* schmal (ˮ, -).

nasal, *adj.* nasal´.

nasty, *adj.* häßlich.

natal, *adj.* Geburts´- *(cpds.).*

nation, *n.* Nation´, -en *f.,* Volk, ˮer *nt.*

national, 1. *n.* Staatsangehörig- *m. & f.* **2.** *adj.* national´.

nationalism, *n.* Nationalis´mus *m.*

nationality, *n.* Staatsangehörigkeit, -en *f.,* Nationalität´, -en *f.*

nationalization, *n.* Verstaat´lichung, -en *f.*

nationalize, *vb.* verstaat´lichen.

native, 1. *n.* Eingeboren- *m. & f.,* Einheimisch- *m. & f.* **2.** *adj.* gebür´tig, einheimisch.

Native American, *n.* India´ner, -*m.,* Indian´nerin, -nen *f.*

nativity, *n.* Geburt´, -en *f.*

natural, *adj.* natür´lich.

naturalist, *n.* Natur´forscher, - *m.,* Natur´forscherin, -nen *f.,* Naturalist´, -en, -en *m.*

naturalize, *vb.* naturalisie´ren.

naturalness, *n.* Natür´lichkeit *f.*

nature, *n.* Natur´, -en *f.; (essence)* Wesen *nt.*

naughty, *adj.* unartig.

nausea, *n.* Übelkeit *f.*

nauseating, *adj.* ekelerregend.

nautical, *adj.* nautisch.

naval, *adj.* See-, Schiffs-, Mari´ne- *(cpds.).*

nave, *n.* Kirchenschiff, -e *nt.*

navel, *n.* Nabel, - *m.*

navigable, *adj.* schiffbar.

navigate, *vb.* schiffen, steuern.

navigation, *n.* Schiffahrt *f.,* Navigation´ *f.*

navigator, *n.* Seefahrer, - *m.; (airplane)* Orter, - *m.*

navy, *n.* Mari´ne *f.;* Flotte, -n *f.*

navy yard, *n.* Mari´newerft, -en *f.*

near, 1. *prep.* in der Nähe von. **2.** *adj.* nahe (näher, nächst-).

nearby, 1. *adj.* naheliegend, nahe gele´gen. **2.** *adv.* in der Nähe.

nearly, *adv.* beinahe, fast.

near-sighted, *adj.* kurzsichtig.

neat, *adj.* ordentlich, sauber.

neatness, *n.* Sauberkeit *f.*

nebula, *n.* Nebelfleck, -e *m.*

nebulous, *adj.* nebelhaft.

necessary, *adj.* nötig, notwendig.

necessity, *n.* Notwendigkeit, -en *f.*

neck, *n.* Hals, ˮe *m.*

necklace, *n.* Halskette, -n *f.*

necktie, *n.* Schlips, -e *m.,* Krawat´te, -n *f.*

nectar, *n.* Nektar *m.*

need, 1. *n.* Not, ˮe *f.;* Bedürf´nis, -se *nt.* **2.** *vb.* benö´tigen, brauchen.

needful, *adj.* notwendig.

needle, *n.* Nadel, -n *f.*

needless, *adj.* unnötig.

needy, *adj.* notleidend.

negative, 1. *n. (photo)* Negativ, -e *nt.* **2.** *adj.* vernei´nend, negativ.

neglect, 1. *n.* Vernach´lässigung, -en *f.* **2.** *vb.* vernach´lässigen.

negligee, *n.* Negligé´, -s *nt.*

negligent, *adj.* nachlässig, fahrlässig.

negligible, *adj.* gering´fügig.

negotiate, *vb.* verhan´deln.

negotiation, *n.* Verhand´-lung, -en *f.*

neighbor, *n.* Nachbar, (-n,) -n *m.*, Nachbarin, -nen *f.*

neighborhood, *n.* Nach-barschaft, -en *f.*

neither, 1. *pron.* keiner, -es, -e (von beiden). **2.** *conj.* **(n. . . . nor)** weder . . . noch.

neon, *n.* Neon *nt.*

nephew, *n.* Neffe, -n, -n *m.*

nepotism, *n.* Nepotis´mus *m.*

nerve, *n.* Nerv, -en *m.*; (*ef-frontery*) Dreistigkeit *f.*

nervous, *adj.* nervös´.

nest, *n.* Nest, -er *nt.*

nestle, *vb.* nisten; (*fig.*) sich an•schmiegen.

net, 1. *n.* Netz, -e *nt.* **2.** *adj.* netto.

network, *n.* Netz, -e *nt.*

neuralgia, *n.* Neuralgie´ *f.*

neurology, *n.* Neurologie´ *f.*

neurotic, *adj.* neuro´tisch.

neutral, *adj.* neutral´, un-parteiisch.

neutrality, *n.* Neutralität´ *f.*

neutron, *n.* Neutron, -o´nen *nt.*

neutron bomb, *n.* Neutro´-nenbombe, -n *f.*

never, *adv.* nie, niemals.

nevertheless, *adv.* dennoch, trotzdem.

new, *adj.* neu.

news, *n.* Nachrichten *pl.*; (*item of n.*) Nachricht, -en *f.*

newsboy, *n.* Zeitungsjunge, -n, -n *m.*

newscast, *n.* Nachricht-ensendung, -en *f.*

newspaper, *n.* Zeitung, -en *f.*

newsreel, *n.* Wochenschau *f.*

next, *adj.* nächst-.

nibble, *vb.* knabbern.

nice, *adj.* nett, hübsch.

nick, *n.* Kerbe, -n *f.*

nickel, *n.* Nickel *nt.*

nickname, *n.* Spitzname(n), - *m.*

nicotine, *n.* Nikotin´ *nt.*

niece, *n.* Nichte, -n *f.*

niggardly, *adj.* knauserig.

night, *n.* Nacht, ⸗e *f.*

night club, *n.* Nachtlokal, -e *nt.*

nightgown, *n.* Nachthemd, -en *nt.*

nightingale, *n.* Nachtigall, -en *f.*

nightly, *adj.* nächtlich, jede Nacht.

nightmare, *n.* Alptraum, ⸗e *m.*, böser Traum, ⸗e *m.*, Alpdruck *m.*

nimble, *adj.* flink.

nine, *num.* neun.

nineteen, *num.* neunzehn.

nineteenth, 1. *adj.* neun-zehnt-. **2.** *n.* Neunzehn-tel, - *nt.*

ninetieth, 1. *adj.* neunzigst-. **2.** *n.* Neunzigstel, - *nt.*

ninety, *num.* neunzig.

ninth, 2. *adj.* neunt-. **2.** *n.* Neuntel, - *nt.*

nip, 1. *n.* Zwick, -e *m.*; (*drink*) Schlückchen, - *nt.* **2.** *vb.* zwicken.

nipple, *n.* Brustwarze, -n *f.*; (*baby's bottle*) Sauger, - *m.*

nitrate, *n.* Nitrat´, -e *nt.*

nitrogen, *n.* Stickstoff *m.*

no, 1. *adj.* kein, -, -e. **2.** *in-terj.* nein.

nobility, *n.* Adel *m.*

noble, *adj.* (*rank*) adlig; (*character*) edel.

nobleman, *n.* Adlig-, -en *m.*

nobody, *pron.* niemand, keiner.

nocturnal, *adj.* nächtlich.

nocturne, *n.* Noktur´ne, -n *f.*

nod, *vb.* nicken.

no-frills, *adj.* einfach, ohne Verschönerung.

noise, *n.* Geräusch´, -e *nt.*; Lärm *m.*

noiseless, *adj.* geräusch´los.

noisy, *adj.* laut.

nomad, *n.* Noma´de, -n, -n *m.*

nominal, *adj.* nominal´.

nominate, *vb.* ernen´nen*; (*candidate*) auf•stellen.

nomination, *n.* Ernen´nung, -en *f.*; Kandidatur´, -en *f.*

nominee, *n.* Kandidat´, -en, -en *m.*

non-aligned, *adj.* blockfrei.

nonchalant, *adj.* zwanglos, nonchalant´.

noncombatant, *n.* Nicht-kämpfer, - *m.*

non-commissioned officer, *n.* Unteroffizier, -e *m.*

noncommittal, *adj.* nichtverpflich´tend.

nondescript, *adj.* unbes-timmbar.

none, *pron.* keiner, -es, -e.

nonpartisan, *adj.* unpartei-isch.

nonsense, *n.* Unsinn *m.*

nonstop, *adj.* durchgehend.

noodle, *n.* Nudel, -n *f.*

nook, *n.* Ecke, -n *f.*, Winkel, - *m.*

noon, *n.* Mittag *m.*

noose, *n.* Schlinge, -n *f.*

nor, *conj.* noch.

normal, *adj.* normal´, gewöhn´lich.

north, 1. *n.* Norden *m.* **2.** *adj.* nördlich; Nord- (*cpds.*).

northeast, 1. *n.* Nordos´ten *m.* **2.** *adj.* nordöst´lich; Nordost- (*cpds.*).

northeastern, *adj.* nordöst´-lich.

northern, *adj.* nördlich.

North Pole, *n.* Nordpol *m.*

North Sea, *n.* Nordsee *f.*

northwest, 1. *n.* Nordwes´-ten *m.* **2.** *adj.* nordwest´-lich; Nordwest- (*cpds.*).

Norway, *n.* Norwegen *nt.*

Norwegian, 1. *n.* Norweger, - *m.*, Norwegerin, -nen *f.* **2.** *adj.* norwegisch.

nose, *n.* Nase, -n *f.*

nosebleed, *n.* Nasenbluten *nt.*

nose dive, *n.* Sturz, ⸗e *m.*; (*airplane*) Sturzflug, ⸗e *m.*

nostalgia, *n.* Heimweh *nt.*; Sehnsucht *f.*

nostril, *n.* Nasenloch, ⸗er *nt.*, Nüster, -n *f.*

not, *adv.* nicht; **(n. a, n. any)** kein, -, -e.

notable, *adj.* bemer´-kenswert.

notary, *n.* Notar´, -e *m.*

notation, *n.* Aufzeichnung, -en *f.*

notch, 1. n. Kerbe, -n f. **2.**
vb. ein•kerben.
note, 1. n. Notiz´, -en f.;
(comment) Anmerkung, -
en f.; (music) Note, -n f.;
(letter) kurzer Brief, -e
m. **2.** vb. bemer´ken.
note-book, n. Notiz´buch,
=er nt., Heft, -e nt.
noted, adj. bekannt´.
notepaper, n. Notiz´block,
=e m.; Schreibblock, =e m.
noteworthy, adj. beach´-
tenswert.
nothing, pron. nichts.
notice, 1. n. (attention)
Beach´tung, -en f.;
(poster) Bekannt´-
machung, -en f.; (an-
nouncement) Anzeige, -n
f.; (give n.) kündigen. **2.**
vb. beach´ten; bemer´ken.
noticeable, adj. bemer´-
kenswert; (conspicuous)
auffällig.
notification, n.
Benach´richtigung, -en f.
notify, vb. benach´richtigen.
notion, n. Vorstellung, -en
f., Idee´, -de´en f.; (n.s,
articles) Kurzwaren pl.
notoriety, n. Verruf´ m.,
Verru´fenheit f.
notorious, adj. berüch´tigt.
notwithstanding, 1. prep.
ungeachtet, trotz. **2.** adv.
nichtsdestoweniger.

noun, n. Hauptwort, =er nt.,
Substantiv, -e nt.
nourish, vb. nähren;
ernäh´ren.
nourishment, n. Nahrung, -
en f.
novel, 1. n. Roman´, -e m.
2. adj. neu.
novelist, n. Roman´schrift-
steller, - m., Roman
´schriftstellerin, -nen f.
novelty, n. Neuheit, -en f.
November, n. Novem´ber
m.
novena, n. Nove´ne, -n f.
novice, n. Neuling, -e m.
novocaine, n. Novocain´
nt.
now, adv. jetzt, nun.
nowadays, adv. heutzutage.
nowhere, adv. nirgends.
nozzle, n. Düse, -n f.; (gun)
Mündung, -en f.
nuance, n. Nuan´ce, -n f.
nuclear, adj. Kern- (cpds.);
nuklear´.
nuclear power plant, n.
Kernkraftwerk, -e nt.
nuclear warhead, n.
nuklea´rer Sprengkopf
m.
nuclear waste, n.
Atom´müll m.
nucleus, n. Kern, -e m.
nude, adj. nackt.
nugget, n. Klumpen, - m.

nuisance, n. Ärgernis, -se
nt.; (be a n.) ärgerlich,
lästig sein*.
nuke, n. Rakete mit nuk-
learem Sprengkopf.
nullify, vb. annullie´ren,
auf•heben*.
number, 1. n. Zahl, -en f.;
(figure) Ziffer, -n f.; (magazine, telephone, house)
Nummer, -n f.; (amount)
Anzahl, -en f. **2.** vb. nu-
merie´ren; (amount to)
sich belau´fen auf.
numerical, adj. zahlenmäßig.
numerous, adj. zahlreich.
nun, n. Nonne, -n f.
nuptial, adj. Hochzeits-,
Ehe- (cpds.).
nurse, 1. n. Kranken-
schwester, -n f. **2.** vb.
pflegen; (suckle) stillen.
nursery, n. Kinderzimmer,
- nt.; (plants)
Pflanzschule, -n f.
nursing home, n. Altersheim, -e nt.
nurture, vb. ernäh´ren,
nähren; (fig.) hegen.
nut, n. Nuß, =sse f.
nutcracker, n. Nußknacker,
m.
nutrition, n. Ernäh´rung f.
nutritious, adj. nahrhaft.
nylon, n. Nylon nt.
nymph, n. Nymphe, -n f.

O

oak, n. Eiche, -n f.
oar, n. Ruder, - nt.
oasis, n. Oa´se, -n f.
oath, n. (pledge) Eid, -e m.,
Schwur, =e m.; (curse)
Fluch, =e m.
oatmeal, n. Hafergrütze f.
oats, n. Hafer m.; Hafer-
flocken pl.
obedience, n. Gehor´sam m.
obedient, adj. gehor´sam.
obeisance, n. Ehrerbietung,
-en f.
obese, adj. fettleibig.
obey, vb. gehor´chen,
befol´gen.
obituary, n. Nachruf, -e m.

object, 1. n. Gegenstand, =e
m.; (aim) Ziel, -e nt.;
(purpose) Zweck, -e m.;
(gram.) Objekt´, -e nt. **2.**
vb. ein•wenden*, Ein-
spruch erhe´ben*.
objection, n. Einwand, =e
m., Einspruch, =e m.
objectionable, adj. widerwärtig.
objective, 1. n. Ziel, -e nt.;
(photo) Objektiv´, -e nt. **2.**
adj. sachlich, objektiv´.
obligation, n.
Verpflich´tung, -en f.
obligatory, adj. obligato´-
risch.

oblige, vb. verpflich´ten; jemandem gefäl´lig sein*.
obliging, adj. gefäl´lig.
oblique, adj. schief, schräg.
obliterate, vb. aus•radieren,
vernich´ten.
oblivion, n. Verges´senheit f.
oblong, adj. länglich;
rechteckig.
obnoxious, adj. widerlich.
obscene, adj. unanständig,
obszön´.
obscure, adj. dunkel.
obsequious, adj. unterwür-
fig.
observance, n. Beach´tung, -
en f.; (celebration) Feier f.

observation, *n.* Beob´-
achtung, -en *f.*

observatory, *n.* Sternwarte,
-n *f.*

observe, *vb.* beob´achten;
befol´gen.

observer, *n.* Beo´bachter, -
m., Beo´bachterin, -nen *f.*

obsession, *n.* fixe Idee´, -
de´en *f.*

obsolete, *adj.* veral´tet,
überholt´.

obstacle, *n.* Hindernis, -se *nt.*

obstetrical, *adj.* geburts´hilf-
lich.

obstetrician, *n.* Geburts´-
helfer, - *m.*, Geburts´-
helferin, -nen *f.*

obstinate, *adj.* hartnäckig.

obstreperous, *adj.* laut-
mäulig.

obstruct, *vb.* versper´ren,
hindern.

obstruction, *n.* Hindernis, -
se *nt.*

obtain, *vb.* erhal´ten*,
bekom´men*.

obviate, *vb.* besei´tigen.

obvious, *adj.* selbstverständlich, offensichtlich.

occasion, *n.* Gele´genheit, -
en *f.*

occasional, *adj.* gele´gent-
lich.

Occident, *n.* Abendland *nt.*

occidental, *adj.*
abendländisch.

occult, *adj.* verbor´gen,
okkult´.

occupant, *n.* Inhaber, - *m.*,
Inhaberin, -nen *f.*, In-
sasse, -n, -n *m.*, Insassin,
-nen *f.*, Bewoh´ner, - *m.*
Bewoh´nerin, -nen *f.*

occupation, *n.* *(profession)*
Beruf´, -e *m.*; *(mil.)*
Beset´zung, -en *f.*; *(o.
forces)* Besat´zung, -en *f.*

occupy, *vb.* *(take up)*
ein•nehmen*; *(keep
busy)* beschäf´tigen;
(mil.) beset´zen.

occur, *vb.* vor´kommen*,
gesche´hen*, passie´ren.

occurrence, *n.* Ereig´nis, -
se *nt.*

ocean, *n.* Ozean, -e *m.*

o'clock, *n.* Uhr *f.*

octagon, *n.* Achteck, -e *nt.*

octave, *n.* Okta´ve, -n *f.*

October, *n.* Okto´ber *m.*

octopus, *n.* Tintenfisch, -e *m.*

ocular, *adj.* Augen- *(cpds.).*

oculist, *n.* Augenarzt, ¨-e *m.*,
Augenärztin, -nen *f.*

odd, *adj.* *(numbers)* ungerade; *(queer)* merk-
würdig.

oddity, *n.* Merkwürdigkeit,
-en *f.*

odds, *n.pl.* Chance, -n *f.*;
(probability)
Wahrschein´lichkeit, -en
f.; *(advantage)* Vorteil, -
e *m.*

odious, *adj.* verhaßt.

odor, *n.* Geruch´, ¨-e *m.*

of, *prep.* von.

off, *adv.* ab.

offend, *vb.* verlet´zen,
belei´digen.

offender, *n.* Missetäter, -
m., Missetäterin, -nen *f.*

offense, *n.* *(crime)* Verge´-
hen, - *nt.*; *(offensive)* Of-
fensi´ve, -n *f.*; *(insult)*
Kränkung, -en *f.*

offensive, **1.** *n.* Offensi´ve, -
n *f.* **2.** *adj.* anstößig.

offer, **1.** *n.* Angebot, -e *nt.*
2. *vb.* an•bieten*.

offering, *n.* Opfer, - *nt.*,
Spende, -n *f.*

offhand, *adj.* beiläufig.

office, *n.* Amt, ¨-er *nt.*; *(room)*
Büro´, -s *nt.*; *(doctor's,
dentist's o.)* Praxis *f.*

officer, *n.* Offizier, -e *m.*;
(police) Polizist´, -en, -
en *m.* Polizis´tin, -nen *f.*

official, **1.** *n.* Beamt´- *m.*,
Beam´tin, -nen *f.* **2.** *adj.*
amtlich, offiziell´.

officiate, *vb.* amtie´ren.

offspring, *n.* Abkömmling,
-e *m.*

often, *adv.* oft, häufig.

oil, **1.** Öl, -e *nt.*; Petro´leum
nt. **2.** *vb.* ölen.

oily, *adj.* ölig, fettig.

ointment, *n.* Salbe, -n *f.*

okay, *adv.* okay.

old, *adj.* alt (¨=).

old-fashioned, *adj.* altmodisch.

olive, *n.* Oli´ve, -n *f.*

ombudsman, *n.* Ombudsmann, ¨-er *m.*

omelet, *n.* Omelett´, -e *nt.*

omen, *n.* Omen *nt.*

ominous, *adj.* unheilvoll.

omission, *n.* Versäum´nis, -
se *nt.*, Überse´hen, - *nt.*

omit, *vb.* aus•lassen*, un-
terlas´sen*.

omnibus, *n.* Omnibus, -se *m.*

omnipotent, *adj.*
allmäch´tig.

on, *prep.* auf, an.

once, *adv.* einmal.

one, **1.** *pron.* man; einer, -
es, -e. **2.** *adj.* ein, -, -e. **3.**
num. eins.

one-sided, *adj.* einseitig.

one-way, *adj.* Einbahn-
(cpds.).

onion, *n.* Zwiebel, -n *f.*

only, **1.** *adj.* einzig. **2.** *adv.*
nur.

onslaught, *n.* Angriff, -e *m.*

onward, *adv.* vorwärts.

ooze, *vb.* hervor•quellen*.

opacity, *n.* Undurch-
sichtigkeit *f.*

opal, *n.* Opal´, -e *m.*

opaque, *adj.* undurchsichtig.

open, **1.** *adj.* offen. **2.** *adv.*
offen, auf. **3.** *vb.* öffnen,
auf•machen; *(inaugu-
rate)* eröff´nen.

opening, **1.** *n.* *(hole)* Öffnung, -en *f.*; *(inaugura-
tion)* Eröff´nung, -en *f.* **2.**
adj. eröff´nend.

opera, *n.* Oper, -n *f.*

opera-glasses, *n.-pl.* Opernglas, ¨-er *nt.*

operate, *vb.* operie´ren.

operatic, *adj.* Opern-
(cpds.).

operation, *n.* Verfah´ren, -
nt.; Unterneh´men, - *nt.*;
(med.) Operation´, -en *f.*

operator, *n.* *(of a machine)*
Bedie´ner, - *m.*; *(telephone)* Telefonist´, -en
m., Telephonis´tin, -en *f.*,
Vermitt´lung *f.*; *(man-
ager)* Manager, - *m.*

operetta, *n.* Operet´te, -n *f.*

ophthalmic, *adj.* Augen-
(cpds.).

opinion, *n.* Meinung, -en *f.*,
Ansicht, -en *f.*

opponent, *n.* Gegner, - *m.,* Gegnerin, -nen *f.*

opportunism, *n.* Opportunis´mus *m.*

opportunity, *n.* günstige Gele´genheit, -en *f.,* Chance, -n *f.*

oppose, *vb.* sich widerset´zen.

opposite, 1. *n.* Gegenteil, -e *nt.; (contrast)* Gegensatz, ≃e *m.* **2.** *adj.* entge´gengesetzt. **3.** *adv.* gegenü´ber.

opposition, *n.* Opposition´, -en *f.*

oppress, *vb.* unterdrü´cken.

oppression, *n.* Unterdrü´ckung, -en *f.*

oppressive, *adj.* tyran´nisch; bedrü´ckend, drü´ckend.

oppressor, *n.* Unterdrü´cker, - *m.*

optic, *adj.* optisch.

optician, *n.* Optiker, - *m.,* Optikerin, -nen *f.*

optics, *n.* Optik *f.*

optimism, *n.* Optimis´mus *m.*

optimistic, *adj.* optimis´tisch.

option, *n.* Wahl, -en *f.; (privilege of buying)* Vorkaufsrecht, -e *nt.*

optional, *adj.* freigestellt, fakultativ´.

optometry, *n.* praktische Augenheilkunde *f.*

opulence, *n.* Üppigkeit *f.*

opulent, *adj.* üppig.

or, *conj.* oder.

oracle, *n.* Ora´kel, - *nt.*

oral, *adj.* mündlich.

orange, 1. *n.* Apfelsi´ne, -n *f.,* Oran´ge, -n *f.* **2.** *adj.* orange´farbig; *(pred. adj. only)* orange´.

oration, *n.* Rede, -n *f.*

orator, *n.* Redner, - *m.,* Rednerin, -nen *f.*

oratory, *n.* Redekunst *f.*

orbit, *n.* Bahn, -en *f.;* Gestirns´-, Plane´tenbahn, -en *f.*

orchard, *n.* Obstgarten, ≃ *m.*

orchestra, *n. (large)* Orches´ter, - *nt.; (small)* Kapel´le, -n *f.*

orchid, *n.* Orchide´e, -n *f.*

ordain, *vb.* bestimm´en, *(eccles.)* ordinier´en.

ordeal, *n.* Qual, -en *f.*

order, 1. *n. (command)* Befehl´, -e *m.; (neatness)* Ordnung *f.; (decree)* Erlaß, -sse *m.,* Verord´nung, -en *f.; (fraternity, medal)* Orden, - *m.* **2.** *vb. (command)* befeh´len*; *(put in o.)* ordnen; *(decree)* verord´nen.

orderly, *adj.* ordentlich; geord´net.

ordinance, *n.* Verord´nung, -en *f.*

ordinary, *adj.* gewöhn´lich.

ore, *n.* Erz, -e *nt.*

organ, *n.* Organ´, -e *nt.; (music)* Orgel, -n *f.*

organdy, *n.* Organ´dy *m.*

organic, *adj.* orga´nisch.

organism, *n.* Organis´mus, -men *m.*

organist, *n.* Organist´, -en, -en *m.,* Organis´tin, -nen *f.*

organization, *n.* Organisation´, -en *f.*

organize, *vb.* organisie´ren.

orgy, *n.* Orgie, -n *f.*

orient, *vb.* orientie´ren.

Orient, *n.* Orient *m.*

Oriental, *adj.* orienta´lisch.

orientation, *n.* Orientie´rung, -en *f.*

origin, *n.* Ursprung, ≃e *m.*

original, *adj.* ursprünglich; *(novel)* originell´.

originality, *n.* Originalität´, -en *f.*

ornament, 1. *n.* Verzie´rung, -en *f.,* Schmuck *m.* **2.** *vb.* verzie´ren, schmücken.

ornamental, *adj.* dekorativ´.

ornate, *adj.* überla´den.

ornithology, *n.* Vogelkunde *f.*

orphan, *n.* Waise, -n *f.*

orphanage, *n.* Waisenhaus, ≃er *nt.*

orthodox, *adj.* orthodox´.

orthography, *n.* Rechtschreibung, -en *f.,* Orthographie´, -i´en *f.*

orthopedic, *adj.* orthopä´disch.

oscillate, *vb.* schwingen*.

osmosis, *n.* Osmo´se *f.*

ostensible, *adj.* augenscheinlich.

ostentation, *n.* Schaustellung *f.*

ostentatious, *adj.* ostentativ´.

ostracize, *vb.* ächten.

ostrich, *n.* Strauß, -e *m.*

other, *adj.* ander-.

otherwise, *adv.* sonst.

ouch, *interj.* au!

ought, *vb.* sollte; *(o. to have)* hätte . . . sollen.

ounce, *n.* Unze, -n *f.*

our, *adj.* unser, -, -e.

ours, *pron.* unserer, -es, -e.

oust, *vb.* enthe´ben* (eines Amtes).

out, *adv.* aus, hin-, heraus´.

outbreak, *n.* Ausbruch, ≃e *m.*

outburst, *n.* Ausbruch, ≃e *m.*

outcast, *n.* Ausgestoßen- *m.& f.*

outcome, *n.* Ergeb´nis, -se *nt.*

outdoors, *adv.* draußen, im Freien.

outer, *adj.* äußer-.

outfit, 1. *n.* Ausrüstung, -en *f.; (mil.)* Einheit, -en *f.* **2.** *vb.* aus•rüsten.

outgrowth, *n.* Folge, -n *f.*

outing, *n.* Ausflug, ≃e *m.*

outlandish, *adj.* bizarr´.

outlaw, 1. *n.* Gesetz´los- *m.* **2.** *vb.* verbie´ten*.

outlet, *n.* Abfluß, ≃sse *m.; (fig.)* Ventil´, -e *nt.; (elec.)* Steckdose, -n *f.*

outline, 1. *n.* Umriß, -sse *m.,* Kontur´, -en *f.; (summary)* Übersicht, -en *f.* **2.** *vb.* umrei´ßen*.

outlive, *vb.* überle´ben, überdau´ern.

out of, *prep.* aus.

out-of-date, *adj.* veral´tet, überholt´.

outpost, *n.* Vorposten, - *m.*

output, *n.* Leistung, -en *f.,* Produktion´, -en *f.; (computer)* Output, -s *m.;* Ausgabe, -n *f.*

outrage, *n.* Frevel, - *m.*

outrageous, *adj.* unerhört´.

outrank, *vb.* einen höheren Rang bekleiden.

outright, *adj.* uneingeschränkt.

outrun, *vb.* hinter sich lassen*.

outside, 1. *n.* Außenseite, -n *f.;* Außenwelt *f.* **2.** *adj.* äußer-. **3.** *adv.* draußen. **4.** *prep.* außer, außerhalb.

outskirts, *n.* Außenbezirke *pl.*

outward, *adj.* äußerlich.

oval, *adj.* oval´.

ovary, *n.* Eierstock, ⸗e *m.*

ovation, *n.* Huldigung, -en *f.*

oven, *n.* Ofen, ⸗ *m.*

over, 1. *prep.* über. **2.** *adv.* über; hin-, herü´ber; *(past)* vorbei´.

overbearing, *adj.* anmaßend.

overcoat, *n.* Mantel, ⸗ *m.,* Überzieher, - *m.*

overcome, *vb.* überwin´den*.

overdue, *adj.* überfällig.

overflow, 1. *n.* Überfluß, ⸗sse *m.* **2.** *vb.* über•fließen*.

overhaul, *vb.* überho´len.

overhead, 1. *n.* laufende Unkosten *pl.* **2.** *adv.* oben.

overkill, *n.* Overkill *nt.;* übertriebenes Vernichtungsvermögen *nt.*

overlook, *vb.* überse´hen*.

overnight, *adv.* über Nacht.

overpass, *n.* Unterfüh´rung, -en *f.*

overpower, *vb.* überwäl´tigen.

overrule, *vb.* überstim´men.

overrun, *vb.* überlau´fen*, *(flood)* überflu´ten.

oversee, *vb.* beauf´sichtigen.

oversight, *n.* Überse´hen, - *nt.*

overt, *adj.* offen.

overtake, *vb.* ein•holen.

overthrow, 1. *n.* Sturz *m.* **2.** *vb.* stürzen; um•werfen*.

overtime, *n.* Überstunden *pl.*

overture, *n. (music)* Ouvertü´re, -n *f.;* Annäherung, -en *f.*

overturn, *vb.* um•stürzen.

overview, *n.* Übersicht *f.*

overweight, *n.* Übergewicht *nt.*

overwhelm, *vb.* überwäl´tigen.

overwork, *vb.* überar´beiten.

owe, *vb.* schulden.

owing, *adj.* schuldig; **(o. to)** dank.

owl, *n.* Eule, -n *f.*

own, 1. *adj.* eigen. **2.** *vb.* besit´zen*.

owner, *n.* Besit´zer, - *m.,* Besit´zerin, -nen *f.;* Eigentümer, - *m.,* Eigentümerin, -nen *f.;* Inhaber, - *m.* Inhaberin, -nen *f.*

ox, *n.* Ochse, -n, -n *m.*

oxygen, *n.* Sauerstoff *m.*

oyster, *n.* Auster, -n *f.*

P

pace, *n.* Schritt, -e *m.; (fig.)* Tempo, -pi *nt.*

pacific, *adj.* friedlich.

Pacific Ocean, *n.* Pazi´fischer Ozean *m.*

pacifier, *n. (baby's)* Schnuller, - *m.*

pacifism, *n.* Pazifis´mus *m.*

pacifist, *n.* Pazifist´, -en, - en *m.*

pacify, *vb.* beschwich´tigen.

pack, 1. *n.* Bündel, - *nt.; (gang)* Bande, -n *f.; (cards)* Kartenspiel, -e *nt.; (animals)* Rudel, - *nt.* **2.** *vb.* packen.

package, *n.* Paket´, -e *nt.*

packing, *n.* Dichtung, -en *f.*

pact, *n.* Pakt, -e *m.*

pad, 1. *n.* Polster, - *nt.; (paper)* Block, -s *m.* **2.** *vb.* polstern.

padding, *n.* Polsterung, -en *f.*

paddle, 1. *n.* Paddel, - *nt.* **2.** *vb.* paddeln.

padlock, *n.* Vorlegeschloß, ⸗sser *nt.*

pagan, *adj.* heidnisch.

page, 1. *n. (book)* Seite, -n *f.; (servant)* Page, -n, -n *m.* **2.** *vb.* suchen lassen.

pageant, *n.* prunkvoller Aufzug, ⸗e *m.*

pail, *n.* Eimer, - *m.*

pain, 1. *n.* Schmerz, -en *m.* **2.** *vb.* schmerzen.

painful, *adj.* schmerzlich, schmerzhaft.

painless, *adj.* schmerzlos.

painstaking, *adj.* sorgfältig.

paint, 1. *n.* Farbe, -n *f.* **2.** *vb.* malen.

painter, *n.* Maler, - *m.,* Malerin, -nen *f.*

painting, *n.* Bild, -er *nt.,* Malerei´, -en *f.*

pair, *n.* Paar, -e *nt.*

palace, *n.* Schloß, ⸗sser *nt.,* Palast´, ⸗e *m.*

palatable, *adj.* schmackhaft.

palate, *n.* Gaumen, - *m.*

palatial, *adj.* palast´artig.

pale, *adj.* blaß (⸗, -).

paleness, *n.* Blässe *f.*

palette, *n.* Palet´te, -n *f.*

pall, *vb.* schal werden*.

pallbearer, *n.* Sargträger, - *m.*

palm, *n. (tree)* Palme, -n *f.; (hand)* Handfläche, -n *f.*

palpitate, *vb.* klopfen.

paltry, *adj.* armselig.

pamper, *vb.* verzär´teln.

pamphlet, *n.* Broschü´re, -n *f.*

pan, 1. *n.* Pfanne, -n *f.* **2.** *vb.* herun´ter•machen.

panacea, *n.* Universal´mittel, - *nt.*

pancake, *n.* Pfannkuchen, - *m.*

pane, *n.* Glasscheibe, -n *f.*

panel, *n. (wood)* Einsatzstück, -e *nt.,* Täfelung *f.; (group of men)* Diskussionsgruppe, -n *f.; (dashboard)* Armatu´renbrett, -er *nt.*

pang, *n.* plötzlicher Schmerz, -en *m.*

panic, *n.* Panik *f.*

panorama, *n.* Panora´ma, - men *nt.*

pant, *vb.* keuchen, schnaufen.

panther, *n.* Panther, - *m.*

pantomime, *n.* Pantomi´me, -n *f.*

pantry, *n.* Speisekammer, - n *f.*

pants, *n.* Hose, -n *f.*

panty hose, *n.* Strumpfhose, -n *f.*

papal, *adj.* päpstlich.

paper, 1. *n.* Papier´, -e *nt.;* *(news)* Zeitung, -en *f.* **2.** *adj.* papieren; Papier´- *(cpds.)*

paperback, *n.* Taschenausgabe, -n *f.*

paper-hanger, *n.* Tapezie´rer, - *m.*

par, *n.* Pari *nt.*

parachute, *n.* Fallschrim, -e *m.*

parade, *n.* Para´de, -n *f.*

paradise, *n.* Paradies´ *nt.*

paradox, *n.* Paradox´, -e *m.*

paraffin, *n.* Paraffin´, -e *nt.*

paragraph, *n.* Paragraph´, -en, -en *m.; (typing)* Absatz, ⸗e *m.*

parallel, 1. *n.* Paralle´le, -n *f.* **2.** *adj.* parallel´.

paralysis, *n.* Lähmung, -en *f.*

paralyze, *vb.* lähmen.

paramedic, *n.* jemand, der Erste Hilfe bei Unglücksfällen leistet.

parameter, *n.* Para´meter, - *m.*

paramount, *adj.* oberst-.

paraphrase, *vb.* umschrei´ben*.

parasite, *n.* Schmarot´zer, - *m.*

parcel, *n.* Päckchen, - *nt.;* Paket´, -e *nt.*

parch, *vb.* dörren.

parchment, *n.* Pergament´, -e *nt.*

pardon, 1. *n.* Verzei´hung, - en *f.; (legal)* Begna´digung, -en *f.* **2.** *vb.* verzei´hen*; begna´digen.

pare, *vb.* schälen.

parentage, *n.* Herkunft. ⸗e *f.*

parenthesis, *n.* Klammer, -n *f.*

parents, *n.pl.* Eltern *pl.*

Paris, *n.* Paris´ *nt.*

parish, *n.* Kirchspiel, -e *nt.,* Gemein´de, -n *f.*

Parisian, 1. *n.* Pari´ser, - *m.,* Pari´serin, -nen *f.* **2.** *adj.* pari´sisch.

park, 1. *n.* Park, -s *m.* **2.** *vb.* parken.

parking meter, *n.* Parkuhr, - en *f.*

parkway, *n.* Ausfallstrasse, -n *f.*

parliament, *n.* Parlament´, - e *nt.*

parliamentary, *adj.* parlamenta´risch.

parlor, *n.* gute Stube, -n *f.,* Salon´, -s *m.*

parochial, *adj.* Pfarr-, Gemein´de- *(cpds.); (fig.)* beschränkt´.

parody, *n.* Parodie´, -i´en *f.*

parrot, *n.* Papagei´, -en *m.*

parsimony, *n.* Geiz *m.*

parsley, *n.* Petersi´lie *f.*

parson, *n.* Geistlich- *m.*

part, 1. *n.* Teil, -e *m.; (hair)* Scheitel, - *m.; (theater)* Rolle -n *f.* **2.** *vb.* trennen.

partake, *vb.* teil•nehmen*.

partial, *adj.* Teil- *(cpds.);* partei´isch.

partiality, *n.* Voreingenommenheit *f.*

participant, *n.* Teilnehmer, - *m.,* Teilnehmerin, -nen *f.*

participate, *vb.* teil•nehmen*.

participation, *n.* Teilnahme *f.*

participle, *n.* Partizip´, -ien *nt.*

particle, *n.* Teilchen, - *nt.*

particular, *adj.* beson´der-.

parting, *n.* Abschied, -e *m.*

partisan, 1. *n.* Anhänger, - *m.,* Partisan´, (-en,) -en *m.* **2.** *adj.* partei´isch.

partition, *n.* Teilung, -en *f.; (wall)* Scheidewand, ⸗e *f.*

partly, *adv.* teilweise, teils.

partner, *n.* Teilhaber, - *m.,* Teilhaberin, -nen *f.; (games)* Partner, - *m.,* Partnerin, -nen *f.*

part of speech, *n.* Redeteil, -e *m.,* Wortart, -en *f.*

party, 1. *n. (pol.)* Partei´, -en *f.; (social)* Gesell´schaft, -en *f.*

pass, 1. *n. (mountain)* Paß, ⸗sse *m.; (identification)* Ausweis, -e *m.* **2.** *vb.* vorü´ber•gehen*; *(car)* überho´len; *(exam)* beste´hen*; *(to hand)* reichen.

passable, *adj. (roads)* befahr´bar; *(fig.)* erträg´lich, passa´bel.

passage, *n.* Durchgang, ⸗e *m.,* Durchfahrt, -en *f.; (steamer)* Überfahrt, -en *f.; (law)* Annahme, -n *f.*

passenger, *n.* Passagier´, -e *m.*

passer-by, *n.* Passant´, -en, -en *m.*

passion, *n.* Leidenschaft, - en *f.; (Christ)* Passion´ *f.*

passionate, *adj.* leidenschaftlich.

passive, 1. *n.* Passiv *nt.* **2.** *adj.* passiv.

passport, *n.* Paß, ⸗sse *m.*

past, 1. *n.* Vergan´genheit *f.* **2.** *adj.* vergan´gen, früher. **3.** *adv.* vorbei´, vorü´ber.

paste, 1. *n.* Paste, -n *f.; (mucilage)* Klebstoff, -e *m.* **2.** *vb.* kleben.

pasteurize, *vb.* pasteurisie´ren.

pastime, *n.* Zeitvertreib *m.*

pastor, *n.* Pfarrer, - *m.*

pastry, *n.* Gebäck´ *nt.*

pastry shop, *n.* Bäckerei´, - en *f.,* Konditorei´, -en *f.*

pasture, *n.* Weide, -n *f.*

pat, 1. *n.* Klaps, -e *m.* **2.** *vb.* einen leichten Schlag geben*.

patch, 1. *n.* Flicken, - *m.* **2.** *vb.* flicken.

patchwork, *n.* Flickwerk *nt.*

patent, *n.* Patent´, -e *nt.*

patent leather, *n.* Lackleder *nt.*

paternal, *adj.* väterlich.

path, *n.* Weg, -e *m.,* Pfad, - e *m.*

pathetic, *adj.* rührend, armselig.

pathology, *n.* Pathologie´ *f.*

patience, *n.* Geduld´ *f.*

patient, 1. *n.* Patient´, -en, -en *m.,* Patien´tin, -nen *f.* **2.** *adj.* gedul´dig.

patio, *n.* Patio, -s *m.*

patriarch, *n.* Patriarch´, -en, -en *m.*

patriot, *n.* Patriot´, -en, -en *m.*

patriotic, *adj.* patrio´tisch.

patriotism, *n.* Patriotis´mus *m.*

patrol, 1. *n.* Streife, -n *f.* 2. *vb.* patrouillie´ren.

patrolman, *n.* Polizist´, -en, -en *m.*

patron, *n.* Schutzherr, -n, -en *m.; (client)* Kunde, -n, -n *m.*

patronage, *n.* Schirmherrschaft *f.*

patronize, *vb.* begün´stigen.

pattern, *n.* Muster, - *nt.; (sewing)* Schnittmuster, - *nt.*

pauper, *n.* Arm- *m.& f.*

pause, *n.* Pause, -n *f.*

pave, *vb.* pflastern.

pavement, *n.* Pflaster, - *nt.*

pavillion, *n.* Pavillon, -s *m.*

paw, *n.* Pfote, -n *f.*

pawn, 1. *n.* Pfand, ⸚er *m.; (chess)* Bauer, (-n,) -n *m.* 2. *vb.* pfänden.

pay, 1. *n.* Bezah´lung *f.,* Gehalt´, ⸚er *nt.* 2. *vb.* bezah´len.

payment, *n.* Bezah´lung *f.; (installment)* Rate, -n *f.*

pea, *n.* Erbse, -n *f.*

peace, *n.* Friede(n), - *m.*

peaceful, *adj.* friedlich.

peach, *n.* Pfirsich, -e *m.*

peacock, *n.* Pfau, -e *m.*

peak, *n.* Gipfel, - *m.*

peal, *vb.* läuten, dröhnen.

peanut, *n.* Erdnuß, ⸚sse *f.*

pear, *n.* Birne, -n *f.*

pearl, *n.* Perle, -n *f.*

peasant, *n.* Bauer, (-n,) -n *m.,* Bäuerin, -nen *f.*

pebble, *n.* Kieselstein, -e *m.*

peck, *vb.* picken.

peculiar, *adj.* merkwürdig, beson´der-.

peculiarity, *n.* Beson´derheit, -en *f.*

pedal, *n.* Pedal´, -e *nt.*

pedant, *n.* Pedant´, -en, -en *m.*

peddler, *n.* Hausie´rer, - *m.*

pedestal, *n.* Sockel, - *m.*

pedestrian, *n.* Fußgänger, - *m.*

pediatrician, *n.* Kinderarzt, ⸚e *m.,* Kinderärztin, -nen *f.*

pedigree, *n.* Stammbaum, ⸚e *m.*

peek, *vb.* gucken.

peel, 1. *n.* Schale, -n *f.* 2. *vb.* schälen.

peep, *vb. (look)* lugen; *(chirp)* piepsen.

peer, *n.* Ebenbürtig- *m.& f.*

peg, *n.* Pflock, ⸚e *m.;* Stift, -e *m.*

pelt, 1. *n.* Fell, -e *nt.* 2. *vb.* bewer´fen*; nieder•prasseln.

pelvis, *n.* Becken, - *nt.*

pen, 1. *n.* Feder, -n *f.; (sty)* Stall, ⸚e *m.* 2. *vb.* schreiben*.

penalty, *n.* Strafe, -n *f.*

penchant, *n.* Hang *m.*

pencil, *n.* Bleistift, -e *m.*

pendant, *n.* Anhänger, - *m.*

penetrate, *vb. (tr.)* durchdrin´gen*; *(intr.)* ein•dringen*.

penetration, *n.* Eindringen *nt.,* Durchdrin´gung *f.*

penicillin, *n.* Penicillin´ *nt.*

peninsula, *n.* Halbinsel, -n *f.*

penis, *n.* Penis, -se *m.*

penitent, *adj.* reuig.

penitentiary, *n.* Zuchthaus, ⸚er *nt.*

penknife, *n.* Federmesser, - *nt.*

penniless, *adj.* mittellos.

penny, *n.* Pfennig, -e *m.*

pension, *n.* Pension´, -en *f.*

pensive, *adj.* nachdenklich.

people, *n.* Leute *pl.,* Menschen *pl.; (nation)* Volk, ⸚er *nt.*

pepper, *n.* Pfeffer *m.*

per, *prep.* pro.

perambulator, *n.* Kinderwagen, - *m.*

perceive, *vb.* wahr•nehmen*.

percent, *n.* Prozent´, -e *nt.*

percentage, *n.* Prozent´satz, ⸚e *m.;* Provision´, -en *f.*

perceptible, *adj.* wahrnehmbar.

perception, *n.* Wahrnehmung, -en *f.*

perch, 1. *n. (fish)* Barsch, -e *m.; (pole)* Stange, -n *f.* 2. *vb.* sich nieder•setzen.

peremptory, *adj.* endgültig, diktato´risch.

perennial, 1. *n. (plant)* Staude, -n *f.* 2. *adj.* alljähr´lich.

perfect, 1. *n. (gram.)* Perfekt, -e *nt.* 2. *adj.* vollkom´men, perfekt´. 3. *vb.* vervoll´kommnen.

perfection, *n.* Vollkom´menheit *f.*

perforate, *vb.* durchlö´chern.

perforation, *n.* Durchlö´cherung, -en *f.*

perform, *vb.* aus•führen; *(drama)* auf•führen.

performance, *n.* Ausführung, -en *f.; (accomplishment)* Leistung, -en *f.; (drama)* Aufführung, -en *f.,* Vorstellung, -en *f.*

perfume, *n.* Parfüm´, -s *nt.*

perfunctory, *adj.* oberflächlich, mecha´nisch.

perhaps, *adv.* vielleicht´.

peril, *n.* Gefahr´, -en *f.*

perimeter, *n.* Umfang, ⸚e *m.*

period, *n.* Zeitraum, ⸚e *m.,* Perio´de, -n *f.; (punctuation)* Punkt, -e *m.*

periodic, *adj.* perio´disch.

periphery, *n.* Umkreis, -e *m.,* Peripherie´, -i´en *f.*

perish, *vb.* unter•gehen*; verder´ben*.

perishable, *adj.* verderb´lich.

perjure oneself, *vb.* Meineid bege´hen*.

perjury, *n.* Meineid, -e *m.*

permanent, 1. *n. (hair)* Dauerwelle, -n *f.* 2. *adj.* bestän´dig.

permissible, *adj.* zulässig.

permission, *n.* Erlaub´nis, -se *f.*

permit, 1. *n.* Erlaub´nisschein, -e *m.* 2. *vb.* erlau´ben, zu•lassen*.

perpendicular, *adj.* senkrecht.

perpetrate, *vb.* bege´hen*.

perpetual, *adj.* ewig.

perplex, *vb.* verwir´ren.

perplexity, *n.* Verwir´rung, -en *f.*

persecute, vb. verfol´gen.

persecution, n. Verfol´gung, -en f.

perseverance, n. Beharr´lichkeit f.

persevere, vb. behar´ren.

persist, n. behar´ren, beste´hen*.

persistent, adj. beharr´lich.

person, n. Mensch, -en, -en m., Person´, -en f.

personal, adj. persön´lich.

personality, n. Persön´lichkeit, -en f.

personnel, n. Personal´ nt.

perspective, n. Perspekti´ve, -n f.

perspiration, n. Schweiß m.

perspire, vb. schwitzen.

persuade, vb. überre´den.

persuasive, adj. überzeu´gend.

pertain, vb. betref´fen*.

pertinent, adj. zugehörig.

perturb, vb. beun´ruhigen.

perverse, adj. verkehrt´, widernatürlich; pervers´.

perversion, n. Verdre´hung, -en f.

pervert, 1. n. perver´ser Mensch, -en, -en m. 2. vb. verdre´hen; verfüh´ren.

pessimism, n. Pessimis´mus m.

pestilence, n. Pest f.

pet, 1. n. Liebling, -e m.; (animal) Haustier, -e nt. 2. vb. streicheln.

petal, n. Blütenblatt, ⸚er nt.

petition, n. Eingabe, -n f., Antrag, ⸚e m.

petrify, vb. verstei´nern; (be petrified) wie gelähmt´ sein*.

petrol, n. Benzin´ nt.

petroleum, n. Petro´leum nt.

petticoat, n. steifer Unterrock, ⸚e m.

petty, adj. gering´fügig; kleinlich.

petulant, adj. mürrisch.

pew, n. Kirchenstuhl, ⸚e m.

phantom, n. Phantom´, -e nt.

pharmacist, n. Apothe´ker, - m., Apothe´kerin, -nen f.

pharmacy, n. Apothe´ke, -n f.

phase, n. Phase, -n f.

pheasant, n. Fasan´, -e(n) m.

phenomenal, adj. erstaun´lich.

phenomenon, n. Erschei´nung, -en f., Phänomen´, -e nt.

philanthropy, n. Menschenliebe f., Wohltätigkeit, -en f.

philately, n. Briefmarkenkunde f.

philosopher, n. Philosoph´, -en, -en m., Philoso´phin, -nen f.

philosophical, adj. philoso´phisch.

philosophy, n. Philosophie´, -i´en f.

phlegm, n. Phlegma nt.; (med.) Schleim m.

phlegmatic, adj. phlegma´tisch.

phobia, n. krankhafte Angst f., Phobie´, -i´en f.

phonetic, n. phone´tisch.

phonetics, n. Phone´tik f.

phonograph, n. Grammophon´, -e nt.

phosphorus, n. Phosphor m.

photocopier, n. Photokopier´maschine, -n f.

photocopy, n. Photokopie´, -i´en f.; Ablichtung, -en f.

photocopy, vb. photokopie´ren.

photogenic, adj. photogen´.

photograph, n. Photographie´, -i´en f., Lichtbild, -er nt.

photographer, n. Photograph´, -en, -en m., Photogra´phin, -nen f.

photography, n. Photographie´ f.

photostat, 1. n. Photokopie´, -i´en f. 2. vb. photokopie´ren.

phrase, 1. n. Satz, ⸚e m.; Redewendung, -en f. 2. vb. aus•drücken.

physical, adj. körperlich, physisch.

physician, n. Arzt, ⸚e m., Ärztin, -nen f.

physicist, n. Physiker, - m., Physikerin, -nen f.

physics, n. Physik´ f.

physiology, n. Physiologie´ f.

physiotherapy, n. Physiotherapie´ f.

physique, n. Körperbau m.

pianist, n. Klavier´spieler, - m., Klavier´spielerin, -nen f., Pianist´, -en, -en m., Pianis´tin, -nen f.

piano, n. Klavier´, -e nt.

piccolo, n. Piccoloflöte, -n f.

pick, 1. n. Spitzhacke, -n f. 2. vb. (gather) pflücken; (select) aus•wählen.

picket, 1. n. Holzpfahl, ⸚e m.; (striker) Streikposten, - m. 2. vb. Streikposten stehen*.

pickle, n. saure Gurke f.

pickpocket, n. Taschendieb, -e m.

picnic, n. Picknick, -s nt.

picture, 1. n. Bild, -er nt.; (fig.) Vorstellung, -en f. 2. vb. dar•stellen; sich vor•stellen.

picturesque, adj. malerisch.

pie, n. eine Art Backwerk.

piece, n. Stück, -e nt.

pier, n. Pier, -s m.

pierce, vb. durchboh´ren.

piety, n. Frömmigkeit f.

pig, n. Schwein, -e nt.; (young) Ferkel, -e nt.

pigeon, n. Taube, -n f.

pigment, n. Pigment´, -e nt.

pile, 1. n. (heap) Haufen, m.; (post) Pfahl, ⸚e m. 2. vb. auf•häufen.

pilfer, vb. stehlen*.

pilgrim, n. Pilger, - m., Pilgerin, -nen, f.

pilgrimage, n. Wallfahrt, -en f.

pill, n. Pille, -n f.

pillage, 1. n. Plünderung, -en f. 2. vb. plündern.

pillar, n. Säule, -n f.

pillow, n. Kissen, - nt.

pillowcase, n. Kissenbezug, ⸚e m.

pilot, n. Pilot´, -en, -en m., Pilo´tin, -nen f.; (ship) Lotse, -n, -n m.

pimple, n. Pickel, - m.

pin, 1. n. Stecknadel, -n f. 2. vb. stecken.

pinch, 1. n. (of salt, etc.) Prise, -n f. 2. vb. kneifen*, zwicken.

pine, 1. *n.* Fichte, -n *f.;* Keifer, -n *f.* **2.** *vb.* sich sehnen.

pineapple, *n.* Ananas, -se *f.*

ping-pong, *n.* Tischtennis *nt.*

pink, *adj.* rosa.

pinnacle, *n.* Gipfel, - *m.*

pint, *n.* etwa ein halber Liter.

pioneer, *n.* Pionier´, -e *m.*

pious, *adj.* fromm(=, -).

pipe, *n.* Rohr, -e *nt.;* Röhre, -n *f.; (smoking)* Pfeife, - n *f.*

piquant, *adj.* pikant´.

pirate, *n.* Seeräuber, - *m.*

pistol, *n.* Pisto´le, -n *f.*

piston, *n.* Kolben, - *m.*

pit, *n. (stone)* Kern, -e *m; (hole)* Grube, -n *f.*

pitch, 1. *n. (tar)* Pech *nt.; (resin)* Harz, -e *nt.; (throw)* Wurf, =e *m.; (music)* Tonhöhe, -n *f.* **2.** *vb. (throw)* werfen*; *(a tent)* auf•schlagen*.

pitcher, *n. (jug)* Krug, =e *m.; (thrower)* Ballwerfer beim Baseball *m.*

pitchfork, *n.* Heugabel, -n *f.,* Mistgabel, -n *f.; (music)* Stimmgabel, -n *f.*

pitfall, *n.* Falle, -n *f.*

pitiful, *adj.* erbärm´lich.

pitiless, *adj.* erbar´mungslos.

pity, *n.* Mitleid *nt.,* Erbar´men *nt.*

pivot, *n.* Drehpunkt, -e *m.*

pizza, *n.* Pizza, -s *f.*

placard, *n.* Plakat´, -e *nt.*

placate, *vb.* beschwich´- tigen.

place, 1. *n.* Platz, =e *m.,* Ort, -e *m.* **2.** *vb.* setzen, stellen, legen; unter•bringen*.

placid, *adj.* gelas´sen.

plagiarism, *n.* Plagiat´ *nt.*

plague, 1. *n.* Seuche, -n *f.* **2.** *vb.* plagen.

plain, 1. *n.* Ebene, -n *f.* **2.** *adj.* eben; *(fig.)* einfach, schlicht.

plaintiff, *n.* Kläger, - *m.,* Klägerin, -nen *f.*

plan, 1. *n.* Plan, =e *m.* **2.** *vb.* planen.

plane, 1. *n. (geom.)* Fläche, -n *f.; (tool)* Hobel, - *m.;*

(airplane) Flugzeug, -e *nt.* **2.** *vb.* hobeln.

planet, *n.* Planet´, -en, -en *m.*

planetarium, Planeta´rium, -ien *nt.*

plank, *n.* Brett, -er *nt.,* Planke, -n *f.*

plant, 1. *n.* Pflanze, -n *f.; (factory)* Fabrik´, -en *f.; (installation)* Werk, -e *nt.* **2.** *vb.* pflanzen.

planter, *n.* Pflanzer, - *m.*

plasma, *n.* Plasma, -men *nt.*

plaster, *n.* Gips *m.; (med.)* Pflaster, - *nt.; (walls)* Verputz´ *m.*

plastic, 1. *n.* Kunststoff, -e *m.* **2.** *adj.* plastisch.

plate, *n.* Platte, -n *f.; (dish)* Teller, - *m.*

plateau, *n.* Hochebene, -n *f.,* Plateau´, -s *nt.*

platform, *n.* Plattform, -en *f.; (train)* Bahnsteig, -e *m.*

platinum, *n.* Platin *nt.*

platitude, *n.* Plattheit, -en *f.*

platoon, *n.* Zug, =e *m.*

platter, *n.* Servier´platte, -n *f.*

plausible, *adj.* einleuchtend.

play, 1. *n.* Spiel, -e *nt.; (theater)* Thea´terstück, - e *nt.* **2.** *vb.* spielen.

player, *n. (game)* Mitspieler, - *m.,* Mitspielerin, -nen *f.; (theater)* Schauspieler, - *m.,* Schauspielerin, -nen *m.; (music)* Spieler, - *m.,* Spielerin, -nen *f.*

playful, *adj.* spielerisch.

playground, *n.* Spielplatz, =e *m.*

playmate, *n.* Spielgefährte, -n, -n *m.,* Spielgefährtin, -nen *f.*

playwright, *n.* Drama´tiker, - *m.*

plea, *n.* Bitte, -n *f.; (excuse)* Vorwand, =e *m.; (jur.)* Plädoyer´, -s *nt.*

plead, *vb.* bitten*, plädie´ren.

pleasant, *adj.* angenehm.

please, 1. *vb.* gefal´len*. **2.** *interj.* bitte.

pleasing, *adj.* angenehm.

pleasure, *n.* Vergnü´gen *nt.,* Freude, -n *f.*

pleat, *n.* Falte, -n *f.*

plebiscite, *n.* Volksabstim- mung, -en *f.*

pledge, 1. *n.* Gelüb´de, - *nt.* **2.** *vb.* gelo´ben.

plentiful, *adj.* reichlich.

plenty, *n.* Fülle *f.;* **(p. of)** reichlich, genug´.

pleurisy, *n.* Rippenfell- entzündung, -en *f.*

pliable, pliant, *adj.* biegsam.

pliers, *n.* Zange, -n *f.,* Kneifzange, -n *f.*

plight, *n.* schwierige Lage, -n *f.*

plot, 1. *n.* Stück Land *nt.; (story)* Handlung, -en *f.; (intrigue)* Komplott´, -e *nt.* **2.** *vb.* intrigie´ren; *(plan)* entwer´fen*.

plow, 1. *n.* Pflug, =e *m.* **2.** *vb.* pflügen.

pluck, 1. *n.* Mut *m.* **2.** *vb.* rupfen.

plug, 1. *n.* Stöpsel, - *m.,* Pfropfen, - *m.; (spark p.)* Zündkerze, -n *f.;* **(fire p.)** Feuerhydrant, -en, -en *m.* **2.** *vb.* zu•stopfen.

plum, *n.* Pflaume, -n *f.*

plumage, *n.* Gefie´der *nt.*

plumber, *n.* Klempner, - *m.*

plume, *n.* Feder, -n *f.*

plump, *adj.* dicklich.

plunder, 1. *n.* Beute *f.,* Raub *m.* **2.** *vb.* plündern.

plunge, *vb.* rauchen, stürzen.

plural, *n.* Mehrzahl, -en *f.,* Plural, -e *m.*

plus, *prep.* plus.

plutocrat, *n.* Plutokrat´, - en, -en *m.*

pneumatic, *adj.* pneuma´- tisch.

pneumonia, *n.* Lun- genentzündung, -en *f.*

poach, *vb. (hunt illegally)* wildern; *(eggs)* pochie´ren.

pocket, *n.* Tasche, -n *f.*

pocketbook, *n.* Handtasche, -n *f.*

pod, *n.* Schote, -n *f.*

podiatry, *n.* Fußheilkunde *f.*

poem, *n.* Gedicht´, -e *nt.*

poet, *n.* Dichter, - *m.,* Dich- terin, -nen *f.*

poetic, *adj.* dichterisch, poe´tisch.

poetry, *n.* Dichtung, -en *f.,* Poesie´ *f.*

poignant, *adj.* treffend.

point, 1. *n.* Punkt, -e *m.* **2.** *vb.* zeigen, hin•weisen*.

pointed, *adj.* spitz.

pointless, *adj.* sinnlos, witzlos.

poise, *n.* Schwebe *f.; (assuredness)* sicheres Auftreten *nt.*

poison, 1. *n.* Gift, -e *nt.* **2.** *vb.* vergif´ten.

poisonous, *adj.* giftig.

poke, *vb.* stoßen*.

Poland, *n.* Polen *nt.*

polar, *adj.* polar´.

pole, *n. (post)* Pfahl, ¨e *m.; (rod)* Stange, -n *f.; (electrical, geographic)* Pol, -e *m.*

Pole, *n.* Pole, -n, -n *m.,* Polin, -nen *f.*

police, *n.* Polizei´ *f.*

police officer, *n.* Polizist´, -en, -en *m.,* Polizis´tin, -nen *f.*

policy, *n.* Politik´ *f.; (insurance)* Poli´ce, -n *f.*

polish, 1. *n.* Politur´, -en *f.; (shoe p.)* Schuhkrem, -s *f.* **2.** *vb.* polie´ren, putzen.

Polish, *adj.* polnisch.

polite, *adj.* höflich.

politeness, *n.* Höflichkeit, -en *f.*

politic, political, *adj.* poli´tisch.

politician, *n.* Poli´tiker, -m., Poli´tikerin, -nen *f.*

politics, *n.* Politik´ *f.*

poll, 1. *n.* Wahl, -en *f.,* Abstimmung, -en *f.;* Meinungsumfrage, -n *f.* **2.** *vb.* befra´gen.

pollen, *n.* Blütenstaub *m.*

pollute, *vb.* verun´reinigen.

pollution, *n.* Umweltverschmutzung *f.*

polonaise, *n.* Poloña´se, -n *f.*

polygamy, *n.* Polygamie´ *f.*

pomp, *n.* Pomp *m.*

pompous, *adj.* prunkvoll; *(fig.)* hochtrabend.

poncho, *n.* Poncho, -s *m.*

pond, *n.* Teich, -e *m.*

ponder, *vb. (tr.)* erwä´gen; *(intr.)* nach•denken*.

ponderous, *adj.* schwerfällig.

pontiff, *n.* Papst, ¨e *m.*

pontoon, *n.* Schwimmer, - *m.*

pony, *n.* Pony, -s *nt.*

pool, 1. *n. (pond)* Tümpel, -m.; **(swimming p.)** Schwimmbad, ¨er, *nt.; (group)* Interes´sengemeinschaft, -en *f.* **2.** *vb.* zusam´men•legen.

poor, *adj.* arm (¨).

pop, 1. *n.* Knall, -e *m.; (father)* Papi, -s *m.* **2.** *vb.* knallen.

pope, *n.* Pabst, ¨e *m.*

popular, *adj.* volkstümlich; beliebt´.

popularity, *n.* Beliebt´heit *f.*

population, *n.* Bevöl´kerung, -en *f.*

porcelain, *n.* Porzellan´, -e *nt.*

porch, *n.* Veran´da, -den *f.*

pore, *n.* Pore, -n *f.*

pork, *n.* Schweinefleisch *nt.*

pornography, *n.* Pornographie´ *f.*

porous, *adj.* porös´.

port, *n.* Hafen, ¨ *m.; (wine)* Port *m.*

portable, *adj.* tragbar.

portal, *n.* Portal´, -e *nt.*

portend, *vb.* Unheil verkün´den.

porter, *n.* Gepäck´träger, -m.

portfolio, *n.* Mappe, -n *f.;* Portefeuille´ *nt.*

porthole, *n.* Luke, -n *f.*

portion, *n.* Teil, -e *m.; (serving)* Portion´, -en *f.*

portrait, *n.* Porträt´, -s *nt.*

portray, *vb.* schildern.

Portugal, *n.* Portugal *nt.*

Portuguese, 1. *n.* Portugie´se, -n, -n *m.,* Portugie´sin, -nen *f.* **2.** *adj.* portugie´sisch.

pose, 1. *n.* Haltung, -en *f.,* Pose, -n *f.* **2.** *vb.* stellen; **(p. as)** sich aus•geben* für.

position, *n.* Stellung, -en *f.*

positive, *adj.* positiv.

possess, *vb.* besit´zen*.

possession, *n.* Besitz, -e *m.,* Eigentum, ¨er *nt.*

possessive, *adj.* besitz´gierig.

possessor, *n.* Besit´zer, -m., Besit´zerin, -nen *f.,* Eigentümer, -m., Eigentümerin, -nen *f.*

possibility, *n.* Möglichkeit, -en *f.*

possible, *adj.* möglich.

possibly, *adv.* möglicherweise.

post, 1. *n. (pole)* Pfahl, ¨e *m.; (place)* Posten, -m.; *(mail)* Post *f.* **2.** *vb.* auf•stellen; zur Post geben*.

postage, *n.* Porto *nt.*

postal, *adj.* Post- *(cpds.).*

postcard, *n.* Postkarte, -n *f.*

poster, *n.* Plakat´, -e *nt.*

posterior, *adj.* hinter-; Hinter- *(cpds.).*

posterity, *n.* Nachwelt *f.*

postmark, *n.* Poststempel, -m.

postman, *n.* Postbote, -n, -n *m.,* Briefträger, -m.

post office, *n.* Post *f.,* Postamt, ¨er *nt.*

postpone, *vb.* auf•schieben*, verschie´ben*.

postscript, *n.* Nachschrift, -en *f.*

posture, *n.* Haltung, -en *f.*

pot, *n.* Topf, ¨e *m.; (marijuana)* Hasch *m.*

potassium, *n.* Kalium *nt.*

potato, *n.* Kartof´fel, -n *f.*

potent, *adj.* stark (¨).

potential, 1. *n.* Möglichkeit, -en *f.* **2.** *adj.* möglich.

potion, *n.* Trank, ¨e *m.*

pottery, *n.* Töpferware, -n *f.*

pouch, *n.* Tasche, -n *f.,* Beutel, -m.

poultry, *n.* Geflü´gel *nt.*

pound, 1. *n.* Pfund, -e *nt.* **2.** *vb.* hämmern, schlagen*.

pour, *vb.* gießen*.

poverty, *n.* Armut *f.*

powder, 1. *n.* Pulver, -nt.; *(cosmetic)* Puder, -m. **2.** *vb.* pudern.

power, *n.* Macht, ¨e *f.*

powerful, *adj.* mächtig.

powerless, *adj.* machtlos.

practicable, *adj.* durch-führbar.

practical, *adj.* praktisch.

practice, 1. *n.* Übung, -en *f.; (carrying out)* Ausübung *f.; (custom)* Gewohn'heit, -en *f.; (doctor)* Praxis, -xen *f.* **2.** *vb.* üben; *(carry out)* aus•üben.

practitioner, *n.* Vertre'ter, -m., Vertre'terin, -nen *f.; (med.)* praktischer Arzt, -̈e *m.*

prairie, *n.* Prairie', -i'en *f.*

praise, 1. *n.* Lob, -e *nt.* **2.** *vb.* loben.

prank, *n.* Streich, -e *m.*

pray, *vb.* beten.

prayer, *n.* Gebet', -e *nt.*

preach, *n.* predigen.

preacher, *n.* Prediger, - *m.*

precarious, *adj.* heikel.

precaution, *n.* Vorsichts-maßregel, -n *f.*

precede, *vb.* voran'•gehen*.

precedence, *n.* Vorrang *m.*

precedent, *n.* Präzedenz'fall, -̈e *m.*

precept, *n.* Vorschrift, -en *f.*

precinct, *n.* Bezirk', -e *m.*

precious, *adj.* kostbar.

precipice, *n.* Abgrund, -̈e *m.*

precipitate, 1. *adj.* über-stürzt'. **2.** *vb.* überstür'zen.

precise, *adj.* genau.

precision, *n.* Genau'igkeit *f.,* Präzision' *f.*

preclude, *vb.* aus•schließen*.

precocious, *adj.* frühreif, altklug (-̈).

predecessor, *n.* Vorgänger, -m., Vorgängerin, -nen *f.*

predestination, *n.* Prädesti-nation' *f.*

predicament, *n.* Dilem'ma, -s *nt.*

predicate, 1. *n.* Prädikat', -e *nt.* **2.** *vb.* begrün'den.

predict, *vb.* voraus'•sagen.

predisposed, *adj.* geneigt'; *(med.)* anfällig.

predominant, *adj.* vorherrschend.

prefabricated, *adj.* Fertig- *(cpds.).*

preface, *n.* Vorwort, -e *nt.*

prefer, *vb.* vor•ziehen*.

preferable, *adj.* vorzuziehend; **(is p.)** ist vorzuziehen.

preferably, *adv.* vorzugsweise.

preference, *n.* Vorzug *m.,* Vorliebe *f.*

prefix, *n.* Vorsilbe, -n *f.,* Präfix, -e *nt.*

pregnancy, *n.* Schwanger-schaft, -en *f.*

pregnant, *adj.* schwanger.

prehistoric, *adj.* vorgeschichtlich, prähisto'risch.

prejudice, *n.* Vorurteil, -e *nt.*

prejudiced, *adj.* vorein-genommen.

preliminary, *adj.* einleitend.

prelude, *n.* Einleitung, -en *f.,* Vorspiel, -e *nt.*

premature, *adj.* vorzeitig.

premeditate, *vb.* vorher überle'gen.

premeditated, *adj.* vorbe-dacht; mit Vorbedacht.

premier, *n.* Minis'terpräsi-dent, -en, -en *m.*

première, *n.* Uraufführung, -en *f.*

premise, *n.* Prämis'se, -n *f.*

premium, *n.* Prämie, -n *f.*

premonition, *n.* Vorahnung, -en *f.*

prenatal, *adj.* vorgeburtlich.

preparation, *n.* Vorbere-itung, -en *f.; (of food)* Zubereitung *f.*

preparatory, *adj.* vorbereit-end; Vorbereitungs-*(cpds.).*

prepare, *vb.* vor•bereiten; *(food)* zu•bereiten.

preponderant, *adj.* überwie'gend.

preposition, *n.* Präposition', -en *f.*

preposterous, *adj.* wider-sinnig.

prerequisite, *n.* Vorbedin-gung, -en *f.*

prerogative, *n.* Vorrecht, -e *nt.*

prescribe, *vb.* vor•schreiben*; *(med.)* verschrei'ben*.

prescription, *n.* Rezept', -e *nt.*

presence, *n.* Anwesenheit *f.,* Gegenwart *f.*

present, 1. *n. (time)* Gegen-wart *f.; (gram.)* Präsens *nt.; (gift)* Geschenk', -e *nt.* **2.** *adj.* anwesend, gegenwärtig. **3.** *vb.* dar•bieten*; *(introduce)* vor•stellen; *(arms)* präsentie'ren.

presentable, *adj.* präsenta'-bel.

presentation, *n.* Darstellung, -en *f.;* Vorstellung, -en *f.*

presently, *adv.* gleich.

preservation, *n.* Erhal'tung *f.*

preservative, *n.* Konservie'-rungsmittel, - *nt.*

preserve, *vb.* bewah'ren, erhal'ten*; *(food)* kon-servie'ren, ein•machen.

preside, *vb.* den Vorsitz führen.

presidency, *n.* Vorsitz, -e *m.;* Präsident'schaft *f.*

president, *n.* Präsident', -en, -en *m.,* Präsiden'tin, -nen *f.*

press, 1. *n.* Presse *f.* **2.** *vb.* pressen, drücken; *(iron)* bügeln.

pressing, *adj.* dringend.

pressure, *n.* Druck *m.*

pressure cooker, *n.* Dampfkochtopf, -̈e *m.*

prestige, *n.* Prestige' *nt.*

presume, *vb.* an•nehmen*; voraus'•setzen.

presumptuous, *adj.* an-maßend.

presuppose, *vb.* voraus'•setzen.

pretend, *vb.* vor•geben*.

pretense, *n.* Vorwand, -̈e *m.*

pretentious, *adj.* prätentiös'.

pretext, *n.* Vorwand, -̈e *m.*

pretty, 1. *adj.* hübsch, niedlich. **2.** *adv.* ziemlich.

prevail, *vb.* vor•herrschen; *(win)* siegen; **(p. upon)** überre'den.

prevalent, *adj.* vorherrschend.

prevent, *vb.* verhin'dern, verhü'ten.

prevention, *n.* Verhin´derung *f.*, Verhü´tung, -en *f.*

preventive, *adj.* Verhü´tungs-, Präventiv´- *(cpds.).*

preview, *n.* Vorschau *f.*, Voranzeige, -n *f.*

previous, *adj.* vorher´gehend.

prey, *n.* Raub *m.*, Beute *f.*

price, *n.* Preis, -e *m.*

priceless, *adj.* unbezahl´bar.

prick, *vb.* stechen*.

pride, *n.* Stolz *m.*, Hochmut *m.*

priest, *n.* Priester, - *m.*, Pfarrer, - *m.*

prim, *adj.* spröde, prüde.

primary, *adj.* primär´.

prime, 1. *n.* Blüte *f.* 2. *adj.* Haupt- *(cpds.)*; erstklassig; **(p. number)** Primzahl, -en *f.*

prime minister, *n.* Premier´minister, - *m.*, Premier´ministerin, -nen *f.*

primitive, *adj.* primitiv´.

prince, *n. (king's son)* Prinz, -en, -en *m.*; *(other ruler)* Fürst, -en, -en *m.*

princess, *n.* Prinzes´sin, -nen *f.*

principal, 1. *n. (school)* Schuldirektor, -o´ren *m.*, Schuldirektorin, -nen *f.* 2. *adj.* hauptsächlich, Haupt- *(cpds.).*

principle, *n.* Prinzip´, -ien *nt.*, Grundsatz, ⁺e *m.*

print, 1. *n.* Druck, -e *m.* 2. *vb.* drucken.

printing, *n.* Buchdruck *m.*

printing press, *n.* Druckerpresse, -n *f.*

printout, *n.* Printout, -s *m.*

priority, *n.* Vorrang *m.*, Priorität´, -en *f.*

prism, *n.* Prisma, -men *nt.*

prison, *n.* Gefäng´nis, -se *nt.*

prisoner, *n.* Gefan´genm.& *f.*

privacy, *n.* ungestörtes Allein´sein *nt.*

private, 1. *n. (mil.)* Soldat´, -en, -en *m.* 2. *adj.* privat´.

privation, *n.* Berau´bung, -en *f.*; Not, ⁺e *f.*

privilege, *n.* Vorrecht, -e *nt.*, Privileg´, -ien *nt.*

privy, 1. *n.* Abort, -e *m.* 2. *adj.* geheim´.

prize, 1. *n.* Preis, -e *m.* 2. *vb.* schätzen.

probability, *n.* Wahrschein´lichkeit, -en *f.*

probable, *adj.* wahrschein´lich.

probation, *n.* Probezeit, -en *f.*; *(jur.)* Bewäh´rungsfrist *f.*

probe, *vb.* sondie´ren.

problem, *n.* Problem´, -e *nt.*

procedure, *n.* Verfah´ren *nt.*

proceed, *vb. (go on)* fort•fahren*; *(act)* verfah´ren*.

process, *n.* Verfah´ren, - *nt.*

procession, *n.* Prozession´, -en *f.*

proclaim, *vb.* aus•rufen*, verkün´den.

proclamation, *n.* Bekannt´machung, -en *f.*, Proklamation´, -en *f.*

procrastinate, *vb.* zögern.

procure, *vb.* besor´gen, verschaf´fen.

prodigy, *n.* Wunder, - *nt.*; **(infant p.)** Wunderkind, -er *nt.*

produce, *vb. (show)* vor•legen, vor•führen; *(create)* erzeu´gen, her•stellen, produzie´ren.

product, *n.* Erzeug´nis, -se *nt.*, Produkt´, -e *nt.*

production, *n.* Herstellung, -en *f.*, Produktion´, -en *f.*

productive, *adj.* produktiv´.

profane, *adj.* profan´.

profanity, *n.* Fluchen *nt.*

profess, *vb.* beken´nen*; *(pretend)* vor•geben*.

profession, *n.* Bekennt´nis, -se *nt.*; *(calling)* Beruf´, -e *m.*

professional, *adj.* berufs´mäßig.

professor, *n.* Profes´sor, -o´ren *m.*, Professo´rin, -nen *f.*

proficient, *adj.* erfah´ren, beschla´gen.

profile, *n.* Profil´, -e *nt.*

profit, 1. *n.* Gewinn´ *m.* 2. *vb.* profitie´ren.

profitable, *adj.* einträglich; *(fig.)* vorteilhaft.

profiteer, *n.* Schieber, - *m.*

profound, *adj.* tief, tiefsinnig.

profundity, *n.* Tiefe *f.*; Tiefgründigkeit *f.*

profuse, *adj.* überreich.

program, *n.* Programm´, -e *nt.*

progress, 1. *n.* Fortschritt, -e *m.* 2. *vb.* fort•schreiten*.

progressive, *adj.* fortschrittlich.

prohibit, *vb.* verbie´ten*; verhin´dern.

prohibition, *n.* Verbot´, -e *nt.*

prohibitive, *adj.* verbie´terisch.

project, 1. *n.* Projekt´, -e *nt.* 2. *vb.(plan)* projizie´ren; *(stick out)* vor•springen*.

projectile, *n.* Geschoß´, -sse *nt.*

projection, *n.* Projektion´, -en *f.*

projector, *n.* Projek´tor, -o´ren *m.*

proliferation, *n.* Verbreitung *f.*

prolific, *adj.* fruchtbar.

prologue, *n.* Prolog´, -e *m.*

prolong, *vb.* verlän´gern, aus•dehnen.

prominent, *adj.* prominent´.

promiscuous, *adj.* unterschiedslos; sexuell´ zügellos.

promise, 1. *n.* Verspre´chen, - *nt.* 2. *vb.* verspre´chen*.

promote, *vb.* fördern; *(in rank)* beför´dern.

promotion, *n.* Förderung *f.*; Beför´derung, -en *f.*

prompt, *adj.* prompt.

promulgate, *vb.* verkün´den.

pronoun, *n.* Fürwort, ⁺er *nt.*, Prono´men, -mina *nt.*

pronounce, *vb.* aus•sprechen*.

pronunciation, *n.* Aussprache, -n *f.*

proof, *n.* Beweis, -e *m.*; *(printing)* Korrektur´bogen, ⁺ *m.*; *(photo)* Abzug, ⁺e *m.*

prop, 1. *n.* Stütze, -n *f.* **2.** *vb.* stützen.

propaganda, *n.* Propagan'da *f.*

propagate, *vb.* fort•pflanzen; verbrei'ten.

propel, *vb.* an•treiben*.

propeller, *n.* Propel'ler, - *m.*

proper, *adj.* passend, angebracht.

property, *n.* Besitz' *m.*, Eigentum *nt.*

prophecy, *n.* Prophezei'ung, -en *f.*

prophesy, *vb.* prophezei'en.

prophet, *n.* Prophet', -en, -en *m.*

prophetic, *adj.* prophe'tisch.

propitious, *adj.* günstig.

proponent, *n.* Verfech'ter, - *m.*

proportion, *n.* Verhält'nis, -se *nt.*, Proportion', -en *f.*, Ausmaß, -e *nt.*

proportionate, *adj.* angemessen.

proposal, *n.* Vorschlag, -̈e *m.*; *(marriage)* Heiratsantrag, -̈e *m.*

propose, *vb.* vor•schlagen*; *(intend)* beab'sichtigen; einen Heiratsantrag machen.

proposition, *n.* Vorschlag, -̈e *m.*; *(logic)* Lehrsatz, -̈e *m.*

proprietor, *n.* Inhaber, - *m.*, Inhaberin, -nen *f.*, Eigentümer, - *m.*, Eigentümerin, -nen *f.*

propriety, *n.* Anstand *m.*

prosaic, *adj.* prosa'isch.

prose, *n.* Prosa *f.*

prosecute, *vb.* verfol'gen; *(jur.)* an•klagen.

prospect, *n.* Aussicht, -en *f.*

prospective, *adj.* voraus'sichtlich.

prosper, *vb.* gedei'hen*.

prosperity, *n.* Wohlstand *m.*

prosperous, *adj.* blühend, wohlhabend.

prostitute, *n.* Prostituiert'- *f.*

prostrate, 1. *adj.* hingestreckt. **2.** *vb.* zu Boden werfen*.

protect, *vb.* schützen, beschüt'zen.

protection, *n.* Schutz *m.*

protective, *adj.* Schutz- *(cpds.).*

protector, *n.* Beschüt'zer, - *m.*

protégé, *n.* Protegé', -s *m.*

protein, *n.* Protein' *nt.*

protest, 1. *n.* Einspruch, -̈e *m.*, Protest', -e *m.* **2.** *vb.* Einspruch erhe'ben*, protestie'ren.

Protestant, 1. *n.* Protestant', -en, -en *m.* **2.** *adj.* protestan'tisch.

Protestantism, *n.* Protestantis'mus *m.*

protocol, *n.* Protokoll', -e *nt.*

proton, *n.* Proton, -o'nen *nt.*

protrude, *vb.* hervor'•stehen*.

protuberance, *n.* Auswuchs, -̈e *m.*, Buckel, - *m.*

proud, *adj.* stolz.

prove, *vb.* bewei'sen*.

proverb, *n.* Sprichwort, -̈er *nt.*

proverbial, *adj.* sprichwörtlich.

provide, *vb.* **(p. for)** sorgen für; **(p. with)** versor'gen mit, verse'hen* mit.

provided, *adv.* voraus'gesetzt daß.

providence, *n.* Vorsehung *f.*; Vorsorge *f.*

province, *n.* Provinz', -en *f.*

provincial, *adj.* provinziell'.

provision, *n.* *(stipulation)* Bestim'mung, -en *f.*; *(food)* Proviant' *m.*; *(stock)* Vorrat, -̈e *m.*

provocation, *n.* Provokation', -en *f.*

provoke, *vb.* provozie'ren; *(call forth)* hervor'•rufen*.

prowess, *n.* Tüchtigkeit *f.*

prowl, *vb.* umher'•schleichen*.

proximity, *n.* Nähe *f.*

proxy, *n.* *(thing)* Vollmacht, -en *f.*; *(person)* Stellvertreter, - *m.*

prudence, *n.* Vorsicht *f.*; Klugheit *f.*

prudent, *adj.* klug (-̈); umsichtig.

prune, *n.* Backpflaume, -n *f.*

Prussia, *n.* Preußen *nt.*

pry, *vb.* *(break open)* auf•brechen*; *(peer about)* herum'•schnüffeln.

psalm, *n.* Psalm, -en *m.*

pseudonym, *n.* Pseudonym', -e *nt.*

psychedelic, *adj.* psychede'lisch, halluzinie'rend.

psychiatrist, *n.* Psychia'ter, - *m.*, Psychia'terin, -nen *f.*

psychiatry, *n.* Psychiatrie' *f.*

psychoanalysis, *n.* Psychoanaly'se, -n *f.*

psychological, *adj.* psychzolo'gisch.

psychology, *n.* Psychologie' *f.z*

psychosis, *n.* Psycho'se, -n *f.*

ptomaine, *n.* Ptomain', -e *nt.*

puberty, *n.* Pubertät *f.*

public, 1. *n.* Öffentlichkeit *f.* **2.** *adj.* öffentlich.

publication, *n.* Veröf'fentlichung, -en *f.*, Publikation', -en *f.*

publicity, *n.* Rekla'me *f.*, Propagan'da *f.*

publish, *vb.* veröf'fentlichen, publizie'ren; *(make known)* bekannt'•machen.

publisher, *n.* Heraus'geber, - *m.*, Heraus'geberin, -nen *f.*, Verle'ger, - *m.*, Verle'gerin, -nen *f.*

pudding, *n.* Pudding, -s *m.*

puddle, *n.* Pfütze, -n *f.*

puff, 1. *n.* *(wind)* Windstoß, -̈e *m.*; *(smoke)* Rauchwolke, -n *f.*; *(powder)* Puderquaste, -n *f.* **2.** *vb.* blasen*; paffen.

pull, 1. *n.* Zugkraft *f.*, Anziehungskraft *f.*; *(influence)* Bezie'hung, -en *f.* **2.** *vb.* ziehen*.

pulley, *n.* Flaschenzug, -̈e *m.*

pulmonary, *adj.* Lungen- *(cpds.).*

pulp, *n.* Brei *m.*; *(fruit)* Fruchtfleisch *nt.*

pulpit, *n.* Kanzel, -n *f.*

pulsar, *n.* Pulsar *m.*

pulsate, *vb.* pulsie'ren.

pulse, *n.* Puls, -e *m.*

pump, 1. *n.* Pumpe, -n *f.*; *(shoe)* Pump -s *m.* **2.** *vb.* pumpen.

pumpkin, *n.* Kürbis, -se *m.*
pun, *n.* Wortspiel, -e *nt.*
punch, 1. *n.* Schlag, -e *m.,* Stoß, -e *m.; (drink)* Punsch *m.* **2.** *vb.* schlagen*, stoßen*; *(make holes)* lochen.
punctual, *adj.* pünktlich.
punctuate, *vb.* interpunktie´ren.
punctuation, *n.* Interpunktion´ *f.*
puncture, 1. *n.* Loch, -er *nt.; (tire)* Reifenpanne, -n *f.; (med.)* Punktion´, -en *f.* **2.** *vb.* durchste´chen*.
pungent, *adj.* stechend, beißend.
punish, *vb.* strafen, bestra´fen.
punishment, *n.* Strafe, -n *f.*
puny, *adj.* mickrig.

pupil, *n.* Schüler, - *m.;* Schülerin, -nen *f.*
puppet, *n.* Marionet´te, -n *f.*
puppy, *n.* junger Hund, -e *m.*
purchase, 1. *n.* Kauf, -e *m.,* Einkauf, -e *m.* **2.** *vb.* kaufen, erwer´ben*.
pure, *adj.* rein.
purée, *n.* Püree´, -s *nt.*
purgative, *n.* Abführmittel, - *nt.*
purge, 1. *n.* Säuberungsaktion, -en *f.* **2.** *vb.* säubern.
purify, *vb.* reinigen, läutern.
puritanical, *adj.* purita´nisch.
purity, *n.* Reinheit *f.,* Echtheit *f.*
purple, *adj.* purpurn; lila.
purport, 1. *n.* Sinn *m.* **2.** *vb.* den Anschein erwecken als ob.

purpose, *n.* Zweck, -e *m.;* Absicht, -en *f.*
purposely, *adv.* absichtlich.
purse, *n. (handbag)* Handtasche, -n *f.; Geldbeutel, - m.*
pursue, *vb.* verfol´gen.
pursuit, *n.* Verfol´gung, -en *f.*
push, 1. *n.* Stoß, -e *m.; (fig.)* Energie´, -i´en *f.* **2.** *vb.* stoßen*, schieben*.
put, *vb.* setzen; stellen; legen.
putrid, *adj.* faul, verfault´.
puzzle, 1. *n.* Rätsel, - *nt.; (game)* Puzzle, -s *nt.* **2.** *vb.* verwir´ren, zu denken geben*.
pyjamas, *n.pl.* Pyja´ma, -s *m.*
pyramid, *n.* Pyrami´de, -n *f.*

Q

quadrangle, *n.* Viereck, -e *nt.*
quadraphonic, *adj.* quadraphon´.
quadruped, *n.* Vierfüßler, - *m.*
quail, *n.* Wachtel, -n *f.*
quaint, *adj.* seltsam; altmodisch.
quake, 1. *n.* Beben *nt.* **2.** *vb.* beben, zittern.
qualification, *n.* Befä´higung, -en *f.,* Qualifikation´, -en *f.; (reservation)* Einschränkung, -en *f.*
qualified, *adj.* geeig´net; *(limited)* eingeschränkt.
qualify, *vb.* qualifizie´ren; *(limit)* ein•schränken.
quality, *n. (characteristic)* Eigenschaft, -en *f.; (grade)* Qualität, -en *f.*
qualm, *n.* Beden´ken *nt.*
quandary, *n.* Dilem´ma *nt.*
quantity, *n.* Menge, -n *f.,* Quantität´, -en *f.*
quarantine, *n.* Quarantä´ne *f.*

quarrel, 1. *n.* Streit *m.,* Zank *m.* **2.** *vb.* streiten*, sich streiten*, sich zanken.
quarry, *n.* Steinbruch, -e *m.*
quarter, 1. *n.* Viertel, - *nt.* **2.** *vb.* ein•quartieren.
quarterly, 1. *n.* Vierteljah´resschrift, -en *f.* **2.** *adj.* vierteljähr´lich.
quartet, *n.* Quartett´, -e *nt.*
quasar, *n.* Quasar *m.*
queen, *n.* Königin, -nen *f.*
queer, *adj.* merkwürdig, sonderbar.
quell, *vb.* unterdrü´cken.
quench, *vb.* löschen, stillen.
query, 1. *n.* Frage, -n *f.* **2.** *vb.* fragen.
quest, *n.* Suche, -n *f.*
question, 1. *n.* Frage, -n *f.* **2.** *vb.* fragen, befra´gen; an•zweifeln.
questionable, *adj.* fraglich, fragwürdig.
question mark, *n.* Frageze-ichen, - *nt.*
questionnaire, *n.* Fragebogen, -e *m.*

quick, *adj.* schnell, rasch.
quiet, 1. *adj.* leise, ruhig, still. **2.** *vb.* beru´higen.
quilt, *n.* Steppdecke, -n *f.*
quinine, *n.* Chinin´ *nt.*
quintet, *n.* Quintett´, -e *nt.*
quip, 1. *n.* witziger Seitenheib, -e *m.,* spitze Bemer´kung, -en *f.* **2.** *vb.* witzeln.
quit, *vb. (leave)* verlas´sen*; *(stop)* auf•hören; *(resign)* kündigen.
quite, *adj.* ziemlich; *(completely)* ganz, völlig.
quiver, 1. *n.* Köcher, - *m.* **2.** *vb.* beben, zittern.
quiz, 1. *n.* Quiz *m.; (school)* Klassenarbeit, -en *f.* **2.** *vb.* aus•fragen.
quorum, *n.* beschluß´fähige Versamm´lung *f.*
quota, *n.* Quote, -n *f.*
quotation, *n.* Zitat´, -e *nt.; (price)* Notie´rung, -en *f.*
quotation mark, *n.* Anführungsstrich, -e *m.,* Anführungszeichen, - *nt.*
quote, *vb.* an•führen, zitie´ren.

R

rabbi, *n.* Rabbi´ner, - *m.*

rabbit, *n.* Kanin´chen, - *nt.*

rabble, *n.* Volksmenge *f.*, Pöbel *m.*

rabid, *adj.* fana´tisch.

rabies, *n.* Tollwut *f.*

race, 1. *n. (contest)* Rennen, - *nt.*, Wettrennen, - *nt.; (breed)* Rasse, -n *f.* **2.** *vb.* rennen*, um die Wette rennen*.

race-track, *n.* Rennbahn, -en *f.*

rack, 1. *n. (torture)* Folterbank, ∺e *f.; (feed)* Futtergestell, -e *nt.; (luggage)* Ständer, - *m.; (train)* Gepäcknetz, -e *nt.* **2.** *vb.* foltern.

racket, *n. (tennis)* Schläger, - *m.; (uproar)* Krach *m.; (crime)* Schiebung, -en *f.*

radar, *n.* Radar *nt.*

radiance, *n.* Glanz *m.*, Strahlen *nt.*

radiant, *adj.* strahlend.

radiate, *vb.* aus•strahlen.

radiation, *n.* Ausstrahlung, -en *f.*

radiator, *n.* Heizkörper, - *m.; (auto)* Kühler, - *m.*

radical, *adj.* radikal´.

radio, *n.* Rundfunk *m.;* Rundfunkgerät, -e *nt.;* Radio, -s *nt.*

radioactive, *adj.* radioaktiv´; **(r. fall-out)** radioakti´ver Niederschlag, ∺e *m.*

radish, *n.* Radies´chen, - *nt.; (white)* Rettich, -e *m.;* **(horser.)** Meerrettich, -e *m.*

radium, *n.* Radium *nt.*

radius, *n.* Radius, -ien *m.*

raffle, 1. *n.* Lotterie´, -i´en *f.* **2.** *vb.* **(r. off)** aus•losen.

raft, *n.* Floß, ∺e *nt.*

rag, *n.* Lumpen, - *m.*, Lappen, - *m.*

rage, 1. *n.* Wut *f.; (fashion)* Schrei *m.* **2.** *vb.* wüten, rasen.

ragged, *adj.* zerlumpt´; *(jagged)* zackig.

raid, 1. *n.* Überfall, ∺e *m.*, Razzia, -ien *f.* **2.** *vb.* überfal´len*, plündern.

rail, *n.* Schiene, -n *f.*

railing, *n.* Gelän´der, - *nt.*

railroad, *n.* Eisenbahn, -en *f.*

rain, 1. *n.* Regen *m.* **2.** *vb.* regnen.

rainbow, *n.* Regenbogen, ∺ *m.*

raincoat, *n.* Regenmantel, ∺ *m.*

rainy, *adj.* regnerisch.

raise, 1. *n. (pay)* Gehalts´erhöhung, -en *f.* **2.** *vb. (increase)* erhö´hen; *(lift)* heben*; *(erect)* auf•stellen; *(collect)* auf•treiben*; *(bring up)* groß•ziehen*.

raisin, *n.* Rosi´ne, -n *f.*

rake, 1. *n. (tool)* Harke, -n *f.*, Rechen, - *m.; (person)* Roué´, -s *m.* **2.** *vb.* harken.

rally, 1. *n. (recovery)* Erho´lung, -en *f.; (meeting)* Kundgebung, -en *f.*, Massenversammlung, -en *f.* **2.** *vb.* sich erho´len; sich sammeln.

ram, 1. *n.* Widder, - *m.* **2.** *vb.* rammen.

ramble, *vb.* umher´•schweifen.

ramp, *n.* Rampe, -n *f.*

rampart, *n.* Burgwall, ∺e *m.*

ranch, *n.* Ranch, -es *f.*

rancid, *adj.* ranzig.

rancor, *n.* Groll *m.*

random, *n.* **(at r.)** aufs Geratewohl´.

range, 1. *n. (distance)* Entfer´nung, -en *f.; (scope)* Spielraum, ∺e *m.; (mountains)* Bergkette, -n *f.; (stove)* Herd, -e *m.* **2.** *vb. (extend)* sich erstre´cken.

rank, 1. *n.* Rang, ∺e *m.* **2.** *vb.* ein•reihen.

ransack, *vb.* durchwüh´len.

ransom, *n.* Lösegeld, -er *nt.*

rap, *vb.* schlagen*, klopfen.

rape, 1. *n.* Vergewal´tigung, -en *f.* **2.** *vb.* vergewal´tigen.

rapid, *adj.* schnell.

rare, *adj.* selten; *(meat)* roh; blutig.

rascal, *n.* Schlingel, - *m.*

rash, *adj.* übereilt´, waghalsig.

raspberry, *n.* Himbeere, -n *f.*

rat, *n.* Ratte, -n *f.*

rate, 1. *n. (proportion)* Maßstab, ∺e *m.; (price)* Preis, -e *m.; (exchange r.)* Kurs, -e *m.; (speed)* Geschwin´digkeit, -en *f.* **2.** *vb.* ein•schätzen.

rather, *adv. (preferably)* lieber; *(on the other hand)* vielmehr.

ratify, *vb.* ratifizie´ren.

ratio, *n.* Verhält´nis, -se *nt.*

ration, 1. *n.* Ration´, -en *f.* **2.** *vb.* rationie´ren.

rational, *adj.* vernunft´gemäß.

rattle, *vb.* klappern.

ravage, 1. *n.* Verwüs´tung, -en *f.* **2.** *vb.* verwüs´ten.

rave, *vb. (fury)* toben; *(enthusiasm)* schwärmen.

raven, 1. *n.* Rabe, -n, -n *m.* **2.** *adj.* rabenschwarz.

raw, *adj.* rauh; *(uncooked)* roh.

ray, *n.* Strahl, -en *m.*

rayon, *n.* Kunstseide, -n *f.*

razor, *n.* Rasier´messer, - *nt.; (safety)* Rasier´apparat, -e *m.*

reach, 1. *n.* Reichweite *f.* **2.** *vb. (tr.)* errei´chen; *(intr.)* reichen.

react, *vb.* reagie´ren.

reaction, *n.* Wirkung, -en *f.*, Reaktion´, -en *f.*

reactionary, 1. *n.* Reaktionär´, -e *m.* **2.** *adj.* reaktionär´.

reactor, *n.* Reak´tor, -o´ren *m.*

read, *vb.* lesen*.

reader, *n. (person)* Leser, - *m.*, Leserin, -nen *f.; (book)* Lesebuch, ∺er *nt.*

readily, *adv.* gern; *(easily)* leicht.

reading, *n.* Lesen *nt.*

ready, *adj.* *(prepared)* bereit´; *(finished)* fertig.

real, *adj.* wirklich, tatsächlich; *(genuine)* echt.

realist, *n.* Realist´, -en *m.*

reality, *n.* Wirklichkeit *f.*

realization, *n.* *(understanding)* Erkennt´nis, -se *f.*; *(making real)* Verwirk´lichung, -en *f.*, Realisie´rung, -en *f.*

realize, *vb.* *(understand)* erken´nen, begrei´fen; **(I r. it)** ich bin mir darüber im klaren; *(make real, attain)* verwirk´lichen, realisie´ren.

realm, *n.* Reich, -e *nt.*; *(fig.)* Bereich´, -e *m.*

reap, *vb.* ernten.

rear, 1. *n.* *(back)* Rückseite, -n *f.*; **(r.-guard)** Nachhut, -en *f.* **2.** *vb.* *(bring up)* erzie´hen*; *(erect)* errich´ten; *(of horses)* sich bäumen.

rear-view mirror, *n.* Rückspiegel, - *m.*

reason, 1. *n.* Vernunft´ *f.*; *(cause)* Grund, ⸗e *m.* **2.** *vb.* überle´gen, denken*; **(r. with)** vernünf´tig reden mit.

reasonable, *adj.* vernünf´tig.

reassure, *vb.* versi´chern; beru´higen.

rebate, *n.* Rabatt´, -e *m.*

rebel, 1. *n.* Rebell´, -en, -en *m.* **2.** *vb.* rebellie´ren.

rebellion, *n.* Aufstand, ⸗e *m.*, Rebellion´, -en *f.*

rebellious, *adj.* rebel´lisch.

rebound, *vb.* zurück´•prallen.

rebuild, *vb.* wieder auf•bauen.

rebuke, 1. *n.* Tadel, - *m.* **2.** *vb.* tadeln.

rebuttal, *n.* Widerle´gung, -en *f.*

recalcitrant, *adj.* starrköpfig.

recall, *vb.* zurück´•rufen*; *(remember)* sich erin´nern an, *(revoke)* widerru´fen*.

recapitulate, *vb.* zusam´men•fassen.

recede, *vb.* zurück´•weichen*.

receipt, *n.* Quittung, -en *f.*; *(recipe)* Rezept´, -e *nt.*

receiver, *n.* Empfän´ger, -m., Empfängerin, -nen *f.*; *(telephone)* Hörer, - *m.*

recent, *adj.* neu.

recently, *adv.* neulich, kürzlich.

receptacle, *n.* Behäl´ter, - *m.*

reception, *n.* Aufnahme, -n *f.*; *(ceremony)* Empfang´, ⸗e *m.*

receptive, *adj.* empfäng´lich.

recess, *n.* *(in wall)* Nische, -n *f.*; *(intermission)* Pause, -n *f.*

recipe, *n.* Rezept´, -e *nt.*

recipient, *n.* Empfän´ger, -m., Empfäng´erin, -nen *f.*

reciprocate, *vb.* aus•tauschen; erwi´dern.

recitation, *n.* Rezitation´, -en *f.*

recite, *vb.* auf•sagen, vor•tragen*.

reckless, *adj.* rücksichtslos; leichtsinnig.

reclaim, *vb.* ein•fordern; *(land)* urbar machen; *(waste product)* aus•werten.

reclamation, *n.* *(land)* Urbarmachung *f.*

recline, *vb.* sich zurück´•lehnen.

recognition, *n.* *(acknowledgment)* Anerkennung, -en *f.*; *(know again)* Wiedererkennung, -en *f.*

recognize, *vb.* *(acknowledge)* an•erkennen*; *(know again)* wieder•erkennen*.

recoil, *vb.* zurück´•prallen.

recollect, *vb.* sich erin´nern an.

recommend, *vb.* empfeh´len*.

recommendation, *n.* Empfeh´lung, -en *f.*

recompense, 1. *n.* Erstat´tung, -en *f.* **2.** *vb.* wieder•erstatten.

reconcile, *vb.* versöh´nen.

reconsider, *vb.* wieder erwä´gen.

reconstruct, *vb.* rekonstruie´ren.

record, 1. *n.* *(document)* Urkunde, -n *f.*; *(top achievement)* Rekord´, -e *m.*; *(phonograph)* Schallplatte, -n *f.*; **(r. player)** Plattenspieler, -m. **2.** *vb.* ein•tragen*; auf•zeichnen; *(phonograph, tape)* auf•nehmen*.

recording, *n.* *(phonograph, tape)* Aufnahme, -n *f.*

recourse, *n.* Zuflucht *f.*

recover, *vb.* wieder•gewinnen*; *(health)* sich erho´hen, gene´sen.

recovery, *n.* Wiedergewinnung, -en *f.*; *(health)* Erho´lung, -en *f.*, Gene´sung, -en *f.*

recruit, 1. *n.* Rekrut´, -en, -en *m.* **2.** *vb.* an•werben*.

rectangle, *n.* Rechteck, -e *nt.*

rectifier, *n.* Gleichrichter, -m.

rectify, *vb.* berich´tigen.

recuperate, *vb.* sich erho´len.

recur, *vb.* wieder•kommen*, zurück´•kommen*.

recycle, *vb.* wieder auf•bereiten).

red, *adj.* rot (⸗).

Red Cross, *n.* Rotes Kreuz *nt.*

redeem, *vb.* ein•lösen; *(eccles.)* erlö´sen.

redeemer, *n.* *(eccles.)* Erlö´ser *m.*, Heiland *m.*

redemption, *n.* Einlösung, -en *f.*; *(eccles.)* Erlö´sung *f.*

reduce, *vb.* verrin´gern, mindern, reduzie´ren; *(prices)* herab •setzen; *(weight)* ab•nehmen*.

reduction, *n.* Vermin´derung, -en *f.*; Herab•setzung, -en *f.*; Ermäßigung, -en *f.*; Reduktion´, -en *f.*

reed, *n.* Schilf *nt.*; *(music)* Rohrflöte, -n *f.*

reef, 1. *n.* Riff, -e *nt.*; *(sail)* Reff, -e *nt.* **2.** *vb.* reffen.

reel, 1. *n.* Winde, -n *f.*, Spule, -n *f.*, Rolle, -n *f.* **2.** *vb.* wickeln, spulen, drehen.

refer, *vb.* (**r. to**) sich bezie´hen* auf; sich beru´fen* auf; verwei´sen* auf.

referee, *n.* Schiedsrichter, - *m.*

reference, *n.* Bezug´nahme, -n *f.*, Hinweis, -e *m.; (recommendation)* Zeugnis, -se *nt.;* (**cross-r.**) Querverweis, -e *m.;* (**r. library**) Handbibliothek, -en *f.*

refill, *vb.* wiederfüllen, nach•füllen.

refine, *vb.* verfei´nern; *(tech.)* raffinie´ren.

refinement, *n.* Verfei´nerung, -en *f.; (culture)* Bildung *f.*

reflect, *vb.* zurück´strahlen; wider•spiegeln; *(think)* nach•denken*.

reflection, *n.* Widerspiegelung, -en *f.*, Reflexion´, -en *f.*

reflex, *n.* Reflex´, -e *m.*

reform, **1.** *n.* Reform´, -en *f.* **2.** *vb.* verbes´sern, reformie´ren.

reformation, *n.* Reformation´ *f.*

refrain, **1.** *n.* Refrain´, -s *m.* **2.** *vb.* sich enthal´ten*.

refresh, *vb.* auf•frischen; erfri´schen.

refreshment, *n.* Erfri´schung, -en *f.*

refrigerator, *n.* Kühlschrank, ⁼e *m.*

refuge, *n.* Zuflucht *f.*

refugee, *n.* Flüchtling, -e *m.*

refund, **1.** *n.* Rückzahlung, -en *f.* **2.** *vb.* zurück´zahlen.

refusal, *n.* Verwei´gerung, -en *f.*

refuse, **1.** *n. (waste matter)* Abfall, ⁼e *m.* **2.** *vb.* verwei´gern; ab•schlagen*.

refute, *vb.* widerle´gen.

regain, *vb.* wieder•gewinnen*.

regal, *adj.* königlich.

regard, **1.** *n.* Achtung, *f.; (greetings)* Grüße *pl.;* (**in r. to**) hinsichtlich. **2.** *vb.* betrach´ten.

regarding, *prep.* hinsichtlich.

regardless, *adv.* (**r. of**) ohne Rücksicht auf.

regime, *n.* Regi´me, -s *nt.*

regiment, *n.* Regiment´, ⁼er *nt.*

region, *n.* Gebiet´, -e *nt.*, Gegend, -en *f.*

register, **1.** *n.* Verzeich´nis, -se *nt.; (music)* Regis´ter, -nt. **2.** *vb.* verzeich´nen; ein•tragen*, an•melden; *(letter)* ein•schreiben*.

registration, *n.* Registrie´rung, -en *f.*

regret, **1.** *n.* Bedau´ern *nt.* **2.** *vb.* bedau´ern, bereu´en.

regular, *adj.* regelmäßig; ordentlich; gewöhn´lich.

regularity, *n.* Regelmäßigkeit *f.*

regulate, *vb.* regeln, ordnen, regulie´ren.

regulation, *n.* Regelung, -en *f.*, Vorschrift, -en *f.*

rehabilitate, *vb.* rehabilitie´ren.

rehearsal, *n.* Probe, -n *f.*

rehearse, *vb.* proben.

reign, **1.** *n.* Herrschaft *f.* **2.** *vb.* herrschen.

reimburse, *vb.* zurück´•erstatten.

rein, *n.* Zügel, - *m.*

reindeer, *n.* Renntier, -e *nt.*

reinforce, *vb.* verstär´ken.

reinforcement, *n.* Verstär´kung, -en *f.*

reinstate, *vb.* wiederein´•setzen.

reiterate, *vb.* wiederho´len.

reject, *vb.* ab•lehnen, verwer´fen*.

rejoice, *vb.* frohlo´cken.

rejuvenate, *vb.* verjün´gen.

relapse, **1.** *n.* Rückfall, ⁼e *m.* **2.** *vb.* zurück´•fallen*.

relate, *vb. (tell)* berich´ten erzäh´len; *(connect)* verknüp´fen; *(be connected with)* sich bezie´hen*; (**r. to**) gemein haben (mit); zurechtkommen* (mit).

related, *adj.* verwandt´.

relation, *n. (story)* Erzäh´lung, -en *f.; (con-*

nection) Bezie´hung, -en *f.; (person)* Verwandt´- *m.& f.*

relationship, *n.* Bezie´hung, -en *f.; (kinship)* Verwandt´schaft, -en *f.*

relative, **1.** *n.* Verwandt´- *m.& f.* **2.** *adj.* relativ´.

relativity, *n.* Relativität´ *f.*

relax, *vb.* sich entspan´nen; lockern.

relay, **1.** *n.* Relais´, - *nt.* **2.** *vb.* übermit´teln.

release, **1.** *n.* Entlas´sung, -en *f.*, Befrei´ung, -en *f.* **1.** *vb.* entlas´sen*; frei´lassen*.

relent, *vb.* sich erwei´chen lassen*.

relevant, *adj.* einschlägig.

reliable, *adj.* zuverlässig.

relic, *n.* Reli´quie, -n *f.;* Überrest, -e *m.*

relief, *n.* Erleich´terung, -en *f.; (social work)* Unterstüt´zung, -en *f.; (replacement)* Ablösung, -en *f.; (art)* Relief´, -s *nt.*

relieve, *vb.* erleich´tern; ab•lösen.

religion, *n.* Religion´, -en *f.*

religious, *adj.* religiös´, fromm.

relinquish, *vb.* auf•geben*.

relish, **1.** *n.* Genuß´, ⁼sse *m.* **2.** *vb.* genie´ßen*.

reluctance, *n.* Widerstre´ben *nt.*

reluctant, *adj.* widerstre´bend.

rely, *vb.* (**r. on**) sich verlas´sen* auf.

remain, *vb.* bleiben*; übrig bleiben*.

remainder, *n.* Rest, -e *m.*

remark, **1.** *n.* Bemer´kung, -en *f.* **2.** *vb.* bemer´ken.

remarkable, *adj.* bemer´kenswert, beacht´lich.

remedy, **1.** *n.* Heilmittel, - *nt.* **2.** *vb.* heilen; ab•helfen*.

remember, *vb.* sich erin´nern an.

remind, *vb.* erin´nern; ermah´nen.

reminiscence, *n.* Erin´nerung, -en *f.*

remiss, *adj.* nachlässig.

remit, *vb.* (*send*) übersen´den*; (*send money*) überwei´sen*; (*forgive*) verzei´hen*.

remittance, *n.* Überwei´sung, -en *f.*

remnant, *n.* Rest, -e *m.*

remorse, *n.* Gewis´senbiß, -sse *m.*

remote, *adj.* entle´gen.

removable, *adj.* abnehmbar, entfern´bar.

removal, *n.* Entfer´nung *f.*, Besei´tigung *f.*

remove, *vb.* entfer´nen, weg•räumen, besei´tigen.

renaissance, *n.* Renaissance´ *f.*

rend, *vb.* zerrei´ßen*.

render, *vb.* geben*; erwei´sen*.

rendezvous, *n.* Stelldichein, - *nt.*, Rendezvous´, - *nt.*

rendition, *n.* Wiedergabe, - n *f.*

renew, *vb.* erneu´ern; (*subscription*) verlän´gern.

renewal, *n.* Erneu´erung, -en *f.*; (*subscription*) Verlän´gerung, -en *f.*

renounce, *vb.* entsa´gen, verzich´ten auf.

renovate, *vb.* renovie´ren.

renowned, *adj.* berühmt´, namhaft.

rent, 1. *n.* Miete, -n *f.* **2.** *vb.* (*from someone*) mieten; (*to someone*) vermie´ten.

rental, *n.* Miete, -n *f.*

repair, 1. *n.* Ausbesserung, -en *f.*, Reparatur´, -en *f.* **2.** *vb.* aus•bessern, reparie´ren.

reparation, *n.* Reparation´, -en *f.*

repatriate, 1. *n.* Repatriiert´- *m.&f.* **2.** *vb.* repatriie´ren.

repay, *vb.* zurück´zahlen.

repeat, *vb.* wiederho´len.

repel, *vb.* zurück´•treiben*; ab•schlagen*.

repent, *vb.* bereu´en.

repentance, *n.* Reue *f.*

repercussion, *n.* Auswirkung, -en *f.*

repertoire, *n.* Repertoire´, - s *nt.*

repetition, *n.* Wiederho´lung, -en *f.*

replace, *vb.* erset´zen.

replenish, *vb.* wieder auf•füllen.

reply, 1. *n.* Antwort, -en *f.* **2.** *vb.* antworten, erwi´dern.

report, 1. *n.* Bericht´, -e *m.*; (*bang*) Knall, -e *m.*; (*rumor*) Gerücht´, -e *nt.* **2.** *vb.* berich´ten; (*complain of*) an•zeigen.

reporter, *n.* Bericht´erstatter, - *m.*, Berichterstatterin, -nen *f.*, Repor´ter, - *m.*, Repor´terin, -nen *f.*

repose, 1. *n.* Ruhe *f.* **2.** *vb.* ruhen.

represent, *vb.* dar•stellen; vertre´ten*.

representation, *n.* Darstellung, -en *f.*; Vertre´tung, -en *f.*

representative, 1. *n.* Vertre´ter, - *m.*, Vertreterin, -nen *f.*; (*pol.*) Abgeordnet- *m.&f.* **2.** *adj.* bezeich´nend, typisch.

repress, *vb.* unterdrü´cken.

repression, *n.* Unterdrü´ckung, -en *f.*, Repression´, -en *f.*

reprimand, 1. *n.* Tadel, - *m.*, Verweis´, -e *m.* **2.** *vb.* einen Verweis´ ertei´len.

reprisal, *n.* Vergel´tungsmaßnahme, -n *f.*

reproach, 1. *n.* Vorwurf, ⸚e *m.* **2.** *vb.* vor•werfen*.

reproduce, *vb.* reproduzie´ren.

reproduction, *n.* Wiedergabe, -n *f.*, Reproduktion´, -en *f.*

reptile, *n.* Reptil´, -e *nt.*

republic, *n.* Republik´, -en *f.*

republican, 1. *n.* Republika´ner, - *m.* **2.** *adj.* republika´nisch.

repudiate, *vb.* ab•leugnen.

repudiation, *n.* Zurück´weisung, -en *f.*, Nichtanerkennung, -en *f.*

repulse, *vb.* zurück´•schlagen*.

repulsive, *adj.* widerwärtig.

reputation, *n.* Ruf *m.*, Ansehen *nt.*

repute, *n.* Ansehen *nt.*

request, 1. *n.* Bitte, -n *f.*, Gesuch´, -e *nt.* **2.** *vb.* bitten*, ersu´chen.

require, *vb.* verlan´gen, erfor´dern.

requirement, *n.* Erfor´dernis, -se *nt.*; Bedin´gung, -en *f.*

requisite, 1. *n.* Erfor´dernis, -se *nt.* **2.** *adj.* erfor´derlich.

requisition, 1. *n.* Forderung, -en *f.*, Requisition´, -en *f.* **2.** *vb.* an•fordern; beschlag´nahmen.

rescind, *vb.* rückgängig machen, auf•heben*.

rescue, 1. *n.* Rettung, -en *f.* **2.** *vb.* retten.

research, *n.* Forschung, -en *f.*

resemble, *vb.* gleichen*, ähneln.

resent, *vb.* übel•nehmen*.

reservation, *n.* vorbehalt *m.*; (*tickets*) Vorbestellung, -en *f.*; (**Indian r.**) Reservation´, -en *f.*

reserve, 1. *n.* Reser´ve, -n *f.* **2.** *vb.* vor•behalten*; (*seats*) reservie´ren.

reservoir, *n.* Reservoir´, -s *nt.*

reside, *vb.* wohnen.

residence, *n.* Wohnsitz, -e *m.*

resident, 1. *n.* Einwohner, - *m.*, Einwohnerin, -nen *f.* **2.** *adj.* wohnhaft.

residue, *n.* Rest, -e *m.*, Restbestand, ⸚e *m.*

resign, *vb.* zurück´•treten*; (**r. oneself**) sich ab•finden* mit, resigne´ren.

resignation, *n.* Rücktritt, -e *m.*; Resignation´, -en *f.*

resist, *vb.* widerste´hen*.

resistance, *n.* Widerstand, ⸚e *m.*

resolute, *adj.* entschlos´sen.

resolution, *n.* Beschluß´, ⸚sse *m.*; Entschlos´senheit *f.*

resolve, *vb.* entschei´den*; beschlie´ßen*.

resonance, *n.* Resonanz´, -en *f.*

resonant, *adj.* resonant´.

resort, *n.* Ferienort, -e *m.;* Kurort, -e *m.*

resound, *vb.* wider•hallen, schallen*.

resources, *n.pl.* Hilfsquellen *pl.;* **(natural r.)** Bodenschätze *pl.*

respect, 1. *n. (esteem)* Achtung *f.; (reference)* Hinsicht, -en *f.* **2.** *vb.* achten.

respectable, *adj.* angesehen, ansehnlich.

respectful, *adj.* ehrerbietig, höflich.

respective, *adj.* entsprechend.

respiration, *n.* Atmung *f.*

respite, *n.* Frist, -en *f.;* Atempause, -n *f.*

respond, *vb. (answer)* antworten; *(react)* reagie´ren.

response, *n.* Antwort, -en *f.;* Reaktion´, -en *f.*

responsibility, *n.* Verant´wortung, -en *f.*

responsible, *adj.* verant´wortlich.

responsive, *adj.* zugänglich.

rest, 1. *n. (remainder)* Rest, -e *m.; (repose)* Ruhe *f.* **2.** *vb.* ruhen; *(be based on)* beru´hen auf.

restaurant, *n.* Restaurant´, -s *nt.*

restful, *adj.* ausruhsam.

restitution, *n.* Wiedergut´machung, -en *f.*

restless, *adj.* unruhig.

restoration, *n.* Wiederher´stellung, -en *f.*

restore, *vb.* wiederher•stellen.

restrain, *vb.* zurück´•halten*.

restraint, *n.* Zurück´haltung *f.*

restrict, *vb.* beschrän´ken, ein•schränken.

restriction, *n.* Einschränkung, -en *f.,* Beschrän´kung, -en *f.*

result, 1. *n.* Ergeb´nis, -se *nt.,* Resultat´, -e *nt.* **2.** *vb.* erge´ben*; zur Folge haben*.

resume, *vb.* wieder auf•nehmen*.

résumé, *n.* Resümee´, -s *nt.*

resurrect, *vb.* wieder•erwecken; wieder hervor´•holen.

resurrection, *n. (eccles.)* Auferstehung *f.*

retail, 1. *n.* Einzelhandel *m.* **2.** *vb.* im Einzelhandel vertrei´ben*.

retain, *vb.* bei•behalten*; zurück´•halten*; auf•halten*.

retaliate, *vb.* vergel´ten*.

retaliation, *n.* Vergel´tung, -en *f.*

retard, *vb.* verzö´gern, zurück´•halten*.

retention, *n.* Beibehaltung, -en *f.*

reticence, *n.* Zurück´haltung *f.;* Verschwie´genheit *f.*

reticent, *adj.* zurück´haltend, schweigsam.

retina, *n.* Netzhaut, ⸚e *f.*

retinue, *n.* Gefol´ge *nt.*

retire, *vb.* sich zurück´•ziehen*; *(from office)* sich pensionie´ren lassen*, in den Ruhestand treten*.

retort, 1. *n.* Retor´te, -n *f.; (answer)* Erwi´derung, -en *f.* **2.** *vb.* erwi´dern.

retract, *vb. (pull back)* zurück´•ziehen*, *(recant)* widerru´fen*.

retreat, 1. *n. (withdrawal)* Rückzug, ⸚e *m.; (refuge)* Zuflucht *f.; (privacy)* Zurück´gezogenheit *f.* **2.** *vb.* zurück´•weichen*.

retribution, *n.* Strafe, -n *f.,* Vergel´tung *f.*

retrieve, *vb.* wieder•erlangen.

retroactive, *adj.* rückwirkend.

retrospect, *n.* Rückblick *m.*

return, 1. *n.* Rückkehr *f.,* Heimkehr *f.;* Rückgabe *f.* **2.** *vb.* zurück´•kehren, zurück´•kommen*; zurück´•geben*.

reunion, *n.* Wiederzusam´menkommen *nt.*

reunite, *vb.* wieder verei´nigen.

reveal, *vb.* offenba´ren; zeigen.

revel, *vb.* schwelgen.

revelation, *n.* Offenba´rung, -en *f.*

revelry, *n.* Schwiegerei´, -en *f.*

revenge, 1. *n.* Rache *f.* **2.** *vb.* rächen.

revenue, *n.* Einkommen, - *nt.*

reverberate, *vb.* wider•hallen.

revere, *vb.* vereh´ren.

reverence, *n.* Vereh´rung, -en *f.;* Ehrfurcht *f.*

reverend, *adj.* ehrwürdig.

reverent, *adj.* ehrerbietig.

reverie, *n.* Träumerei´, -en *f.*

reverse, 1. *n. (opposite)* Gegenteil *nt.; (back)* Rückseite, -n *f.; (misfortune)* Rückschlag, ⸚e *m.; (auto)* Rückwärtsgang, -e *m.* **2.** *vb.* um•drehen; *(auto)* rückwärts•fahren*; *(tech.)* um•steuern.

revert, *vb.* zurück´•kehren.

review, 1. *n.* nochmalige Durchsicht, -en *f.,* Überblick, -e *m.;* **(book r.)** Kritik´, -en *f.,* Bespre´chung, -en *f.* **2.** *vb.* überbli´cken, revidie´ren; bespre´chen*.

revise, *vb.* ab•ändern, revidie´ren.

revision, *n.* Revision´, -en *f.*

revival, *n.* Wiederbelebung, -en *f.,* Neubelebung, -en *f.*

revive, *vb. (person)* wieder zu Bewußt´sein bringen*; *(fashion)* wieder auf•leben lassen*.

revocation, *n.* Aufhebung, -en *f.*

revoke, *vb.* widerru´fen*, auf•heben*.

revolt, 1. *n.* Aufstand, ⸚e *m.* **2.** *vb.* revoltie´ren.

revolution, *n.* Revolution´, -en *f.; (turn)* Umdre´hung, -en *f.*

revolutionary, *adj.* revolutionär´.

revolve, *vb.* sich drehen.

revolver, *n.* Revol´ver, - *m.*

reward, 1. *n.* Beloh´nung, -en *f.* **2.** *vb.* beloh´nen.

rhetorical, *adj.* rheto´risch.

rheumatic, *adj.* rheuma´tisch.

rheumatism, *n.* Rheumatis´mus *m.*

rhinoceros, *n.* Nashorn, ¨er *nt.*

rhubarb, *n.* Rhabar´ber *m.*

rhyme, *n.* Reim, -e *m.*

rhythm, *n.* Rhythmus, -men *m.*

rhythmical, *adj.* rhythmisch.

rib, *n.* Rippe, -n *f.*

ribbon, *n.* Band, ¨er *nt.*

rice, *n.* Reis *m.*

rich, *adj.* reich.

rid, *vb.* los•werden*; sich los•machen.

riddle, *n.* Rätsel, - *nt.*

ride, 1. *n.* (*horse*) Ritt, -e *m.*; (*vehicle*) Fahrt, -en *f.* 2. *vb.* reiten*; fahren*.

rider, *n.* Reiter, - *m.*, Reiterin, -nen *f.*

ridge, *n.* (*mountain*) Grat, -e *m.*; (*mountain range*) Bergrücken, - *m.*

ridicule, 1. *n.* Spott *m.* 2. *vb.* lächerlich machen, bespöt´teln.

ridiculous, *adj.* lächerlich.

rifle, *n.* Gewehr´, -e *nt.*

rig, 1. *n.* (*gear*) Ausrüstung, -en *f.*; (*ship*) Takela´ge, - *n f.*; (*oil*) Ölbohrer, - *m.* 2. *vb.* auf•takeln.

right, 1. *n.* Recht, -e *nt.* 2. *adj.* (*side*) recht-; (*just*) gerecht´; (**be r.**) recht haben*. 3. *adv.* rechts. 4. *vb.* (*set upright*) auf•richten; (*correct*) wiedergut´•machen.

righteous, *adj.* rechtschaffen; (*smug*) selbstgerecht.

righteousness, *n.* Rechtschaffenheit *f.*; Selbstgerechtheit *f.*

right of way, *n.* Vorfahrt´srecht, -e *nt.*

rigid, *adj.* steif; starr.

rigidity, *n.* Starrheit *f.*

rigor, *n.* Härte, -n *f.*

rigorous, *adj.* hart (¨), streng.

rim, *n.* Rand, ¨er *m.*

ring, 1. *n.* Ring, -e *m*; (*circle*) Kreis, -e *m.*; (*of*

bell) Klingeln *nt.* 2. *vb.* klingeln.

rinse, *vb.* spülen.

riot, 1. *n.* Aufruhr, -e *m.* 2. *vb.* in Aufruhr gera´ten*.

rip, *vb.* reißen*; auf•trennen.

ripe, *adj.* reif.

ripen, *vb.* reifen.

ripoff, *n.* Übervor´teilung *f.*

rip off, *vb.* jemand reinlegen.

ripple, 1. *n.* leichte Welle, - *n f.* 2. *vb.* leichte Wellen schlagen*.

rise, 1. *n.* (*increase*) Zuwachs *m.*; (*emergence*) Aufgang, ¨e *m.*; (*advance*) Aufstieg, -e *m.* 2. *vb.* an•steigen*; auf•gehen*; (*get up*) auf•stehen*.

risk, 1. *n.* Risiko, -s *nt.* 2. *vb.* wagen.

rite, *n.* Ritus, -ten *m.*

ritual, 1. *n.* Rituell´, -e *nt.* 2. *adj.* rituell´.

rival, 1. *n.* Riva´le, -n, -n *m.*, Riva´lin, -nen *f.*, Konkurrenz´, -en *f.* 2. *adj.* Konkurrenz- (*cpds.*). 3. *vb.* wetteifern, rivalisie´ren.

rivalry, *n.* Konkurrenz´, -en *f.*, Wettstreit *m.*

river, *n.* Fluß, ¨sse *m.*

rivet, 1. *n.* Niete, -n *f.* 2. *vb.* nieten.

road, *n.* Straße, -n *f.*, Landstraße, -n *f.*

roam, *vb.* umher•schweifen.

roar, 1. *n.* Gebrüll´ *nt.* 2. *vb.* brüllen; brausen.

roast, 1. *n.* Braten, - *m.* 2. *vb.* braten*; rösten.

rob, *vb.* rauben; berau´ben.

robber, *n.* Räuber, - *m.*; Dieb, -e *m.*, Diebin, -nen *f.*

robbery, *n.* Raub *m.*

robe, *n.* Gewand´, ¨er *nt.*

robin, *n.* Rotkehlchen, - *nt.*

robot, *n.* Roboter, - *m.*

robust, *adj.* robust´.

rock, 1. *n.* Stein, -e *m.*; Felsen, - *m.*; (*music*) Rock *m.*, Rockmusik *f.* 2. *vb.* schaukeln.

rocker, *n.* Schaukelstuhl, ¨e *m.*

rocket, *n.* Rake´te, -n *f.*

rocky, *adj.* felsig; (*shaky*) wackelig.

rod, *n.* Stab, ¨e *m.*, Stange, -n *f.*

rodent, *n.* Nagetier, -e *nt.*

roe, *n.* Rogen, - *m.*; (*deer*) Reh, -e *nt.*

role, *n.* Rolle, -n *f.*

roll, 1. *n.* Rolle, -n *f.*; Walze, -n *f.*; (*bread*) Brötchen, - *nt.* 2. *vb.* rollen; (*ship*) schlingern.

roller, *n.* Rolle, -n *f.*; Walze, -n *f.*, Römerin, - nen *f.*

Roman, 1. *n.* Römer, - *m.* 2. *adj.* römisch.

romance, *n.* Roman´ze, -n *f.*; Liebesaffäre, -n *f.*

Romance, *adj.* roma´nisch.

romantic, *adj.* roman´tisch.

romanticism, *n.* Roman´tik *f.*

Rome, *n.* Rom *nt.*

roof, *n.* Dach, ¨er *nt.*

room, *n.* Zimmer, - *nt.*, Raum, ¨e *m.*; (*space*) Raum *m.*

roommate, *n.* Zimmergenosse, -n, -n *m.*, Zimmergenossin, -nen *f.*

rooster, *n.* Hahn, ¨e *m.*

root, 1. *n.* Wurzel, -n *f.* 2. *vb.* (*be rooted*) wurzeln.

rope, *n.* Tau, -e *nt.*, Seil, -e *nt.*, Strick, -e *m.*

rosary, *n.* Rosenkranz, ¨e *m.*

rose, *n.* Rose, -n *f.*

rosy, *adj.* rosig.

rot, *vb.* verfau´len, verwe•sen.

rotate, *vb.* rotie´ren; sich ab•wechseln.

rotation, *n.* Umdre´hung, - en *f.*, Rotation´, -en *f.*; Wechsel, - *m.*

rotten, *adj.* faul; (*base*) niederträchtig.

rouge, *n.* Rouge *nt.*

rough, *adj.* rauh; (*coarse*) grob (¨); (*sea*) stürmisch.

round, 1. *n.* Runde, -n *f.* 2. *adj.* rund. 3. *prep.* um, um . . . herum´.

rout, 1. *n.* wilde Flucht *f.* **2.** *vb.* in die Flucht schlagen*.

route, *n.* Weg, -e *m.* Route, -n *f.*

routine, 1. *n.* Routi´ne, -n *f.* **2.** *adj.* alltäg´lich.

rove, *vb.* umher´•streifen.

row, 1. *n. (line, series)* Reihe, -n *f.; (fight)* Krach *m.* **2.** *vb.* rudern.

rowboat, *n.* Ruderboot, -e *nt.*

royal, *adj.* königlich.

royalty, *n.* Königstum *nt.;* Mitglied eines Königshauses; *(share of profit)* Gewinn´anteil, -e *m.*

rub, *vb.* reiben*.

rubber, *n.* Gummi *nt.*

rubbish, *n.* Abfall, ⸗e *m.; (nonsense)* Quatsch *m.*

ruby, *n.* Rubin´, -e *m.*

rudder, *n.* Steuerruder, - *nt.*

rude, *adj.* rauh, unhöflich.

rudiment, *n.* erster Anfang, ⸗e *m.;* Anfangsgrund, ⸗e *m.*

ruffle, 1. *n.* Rüsche, -n *f.* **2.** *vb.* kräuseln.

rug, *n.* Teppich, -e *m.*

rugged, *adj.* rauh, hart (⸗).

ruin, 1. *n.* Untergang *m.;* Rui´ne, -n *f.; (r.s)* Trümmer *pl.* **2.** *vb.* ruinie´ren.

ruinous, *adj.* verderb´lich, katastrophal´.

rule, 1. *n. (reign)* Herrschaft *f.; (regulation)* Regel, -n *f.* **2.** *vb.* herrschen; entschei´den*.

ruler, *n.* Herrscher, - *m.* Herrscherin, -nen *f.; (measuring stick)* Lineal´, -e *nt.*

rum, *n.* Rum *m.*

rumor, 1. *n.* Gerücht´, -e *nt.* **2.** *vb.* munkeln.

run, 1. *n.* Lauf *m.; (stocking)* Laufmasche, -n *f.* **2.** *vb.* laufen*; *(flow)* fließen*.

rung, *n.* Sprosse, -n *f.*

runner, *n.* Läufer, - *m.,* Läuferin, -nen *f.*

runway, *n.* Startbahn, -en *f.*

rupture, 1. *n.* Bruch, ⸗e *m.* **2.** *vb.* brechen*; reißen*.

rural, *adj.* ländlich.

rush, 1. *n.* Andrang *m..; (hurry)* Eile *f.* **2.** *vb.* drängen; eilen, sich stürzen.

Russia, *n.* Rußland *nt.*

Russian, 1. *n.* Russe, -n, -n *m.,* Russin, -nen *f.* **2.** *adj.* russisch.

rust, 1. *n.* Rost *m.* **2.** *vb.* rosten.

rustic, *adj.* bäurisch.

rustle, *vb.* rascheln.

rusty, *adj.* rostig.

rut, *n.* Rinne, -n *f.;* Radspur, -en *f.*

ruthless, *adj.* erbar´mungslos, rücksichtslos.

rye, *n.* Roggen *m.*

S

Sabbath, *n.* Sabbat, -e *m.*

saber, *n.* Säbel, - *m.*

sable, *n.* Zobel *m.*

sabotage, 1. *n.* Sabota´ge *f.* **2.** *vb.* sabotie´ren.

saboteur, *n.* Saboteur´, -e *m.*

saccharine, *n.* Sacharin´ *nt.*

sack, 1. *n.* Sack, ⸗e *m.* **2.** *vb. (plunder)* plündern; *(discharge)* auf der Stelle entlas´sen*.

sacrament, *n.* Sakrament´, -e *nt.*

sacred, *adj.* heilig.

sacrifice, 1. *n.* Opfer, - *nt.* **2.** *vb.* opfern.

sacrilege, *n.* Sakrileg´, -e *nt.*

sacrilegious, *adj.* gotteslästerlich.

sad, *adj.* traurig.

sadden, *vb.* betrü´ben.

saddle, 1. *n.* Sattel, - *m.* **2.** *vb.* satteln.

sadism, *n.* Sadis´mus *m.*

safe, 1. *n.* Geldschrank, ⸗e *m.* **2.** *adj.* sicher.

safeguard, 1. *n.* Schutz *m.* **2.** *vb.* schützen; sichern.

safety, *n.* Sicherheit *f.*

safety-pin, *n.* Sicherheitsnadel, -n *f.*

sage, *adj.* weise.

sail, 1. *n.* Segel, - *nt.* **2.** *vb.* segeln.

sailboat, *n.* Segelboot, -e *nt.*

sailor, *n.* Matro´se, -n, -n *m.*

saint, 1. *n.* Heilig- *m.& f.* **2.** *adj.* heilig.

sake, *n.* **(for the s. of)** um . . . willen.

salad, *n.* Salat´, -e *m.*

salary, *n.* Gehalt´, ⸗er *nt.*

sale, 1. *n.* Verkauf´ *m.; (bargain s.)* Ausverkauf *m.*

salesperson, *n.* Verkäu´fer, - *m.,* Verkäu´ferin, -nen *f.,* **(traveling s.)** Handelsreisend- *m.& f.*

sales tax, *n.* Umsatzsteuer, - *n f.*

saliva, *n.* Speichel *m.*

salmon, *n.* Lachs *m.*

salon, *n.* Salon´, -s *m.*

salt, 1. *n.* Salz, -e *nt.* **2.** *vb.* salzen.

salty, *adj.* salzig.

salutation, *n.* Gruß, ⸗e *m.;* Begrü´ßung, -en *f.*

salute, 1. *n.* Gruß, ⸗e *m.* **2.** *vb.* salutie´ren.

salvage, 1. *n. (act)* Bergung *f.; (material)* Bergegut *nt.* **2.** *vb.* bergen*, retten.

salvation, *n.* Rettung *f.,* Heil *m.*

salve, *n.* Salbe, -n *f.*

same, *adj.* selb-; **(the s.)** derselbe, dasselbe, dieselbe.

sample, 1. *n.* Probe, -n *f.,* Muster, - *nt.* **2.** *vb.* probie´ren.

sanatorium, *n.* Sanato´rium, -rien *nt.*

sanctify, *vb.* heiligen.

sanction, 1. *n.* Sanktion´, -en *f.* **2.** *vb.* sanktionie´ren.

sanctity, *n.* Heiligkeit *f.*

sanctuary, *n.* Heiligtum, ⸗er *nt.; (refuge)* Zufluchtsort, -e *m.*

sand, *n.* Sand, -e *m.*

sandal, *n.* Sanda´le, -n *f.*

sandwich, *n.* belegtes Brot, -e *nt.*

sandy, *adj.* sandig.

sane, *adj.* vernünf´tig; geistig gesund´.

sanitary, *adj.* Gesund´heits-(*cpds.*).; hygie´nisch.; (**s. napkin**) Damenbinde, -n *f.*

sanitation, *n.* Gesund´heitswesen *nt.*

sanity, *n.* geistige Gesund´heit *f.*

Santa Claus, *n.* Weihnachtsmann, ̈-er *m.*

sap, 1. *n.* Saft, ̈-e *m.* **2.** *vb.* schwächen.

sapphire, *n.* Saphir´, -e *m.*

sarcasm, *n.* Sarkas´mus *m.*

sarcastic, *adj.* sarkas´tisch.

sardine, *n.* Sardi´ne, -n *f.*

sash, *n.* Schärpe, -n *f.*; (*window*) Fensterrahmen, - *m.*

satellite, *n.* Satellit´, -en, - en *m.*

satin, *n.* Satin´, -s *m.*

satire, *n.* Sati´re, -n *f.*

satirize, *vb.* verspot´ten.

satisfaction, *n.* Genug´tuung, -en *f.*; Befrie´digung, -en *f.*

satisfactory, *adj.* befrie´digend, genü´gend.

satisfy, *vb.* befrie´digen, genü´gen.

saturate, *vb.* sättigen.

saturation, *n.* Sättigung *f.*

Saturday, *n.* Sonnabend, -e *m.*, Samstag, -e *m.*

sauce, *n.* Soße, -n *f.*

saucer, *n.* Untertasse, -n *f.*

sausage, *n.* Wurst, ̈-e *f.*

savage, 1. *n.* Wild- *m.&f.* **2.** *adj.* wild.

save, 1. *vb.* (*preserve*) bewah´ren; (*rescue*) retten; (*economize*) sparen. **2.** *prep.* außer.

savings, *n.pl.* Erspar´nisse *pl.*

savior, *n.* Retter, - *m.*; (*eccles.*) Heiland *m.*

savor, 1. *n.* Geschmack´, ̈-e *m.* **2.** *vb.* aus•kosten.

saw, 1. *n.* Säge, -n *f.*; (*proverb*) Sprichwort, -er *nt.* **2.** *vb.* sägen.

say, *vb.* sagen.

saying, *n.* Redensart, -en *f.*

scab, *n.* Schorf *m.*; (*strike breaker*) Streikbrecher, - *m.*

scaffold, *n.* Gerüst´, -e *nt.*; (*execution*) Schafott´, -e *nt.*

scald, *vb.* brühen; verbrü´hen.

scale, 1. *n.* Maßstab, ̈-e *m.*, Skala, -len *f.*; (*music*) Tonleiter, -n *f.*; (*weight measuring*) Waage, -n *f.*; (*fish*) Schuppe, -n *f.* **2.** *vb.* (*climb*) erklet´tern.

scalp, *n.* Kopfhaut, ̈-e *f.*; (*Indian*) Skalp, -e *m.*

scan, *vb.* überflie´gen*; (*verse*) skandie´ren.

scandal, *n.* Skandal´, -e *m.*

scandalous, *adj.* schimpflich, unerhört´.

scant, *adj.* knapp.

scape goat, *n.* Sündenbock *m.*

scar, *n.* Narbe, -n *f.*

scarce, *adj.* selten; knapp.

scarcely, *adv.* kaum.

scarcity, *n.* Knappheit *f.*, Mangel *m.*

scare, 1. *n.* Schreck *m.* **2.** *vb.* erschre´cken; (**be s.d**) erschre´cken*.

scarf, *n.* Schal, -s *m.*, Halstuch, ̈-er *nt.*

scarlet, *adj.* scharlachrot.

scarlet fever, *n.* Scharlach *m.*

scatter, *vb.* zerstreu´en.

scenario, *n.* Inszenie´rung, -en *f.*; (*film*) Drehbuch, ̈-er *nt.*

scene, *n.* Szene, -n *f.*

scenery, *n.* Landschaft, -en *f.*; (*stage*) Bühnenausstattung, -en *f.*

scent, *n.* Geruch´, ̈-e *m.*; (*track*) Spur, -en *f.*

schedule, 1. *n.* Liste, -n *f.*; Programm´, -e *nt.*; (*timetable*) Fahrplan, ̈-e *m.*; (*school*) Stundenplan, ̈-e *m.* **2.** *vb.* an•setzen.

scheme, 1. *n.* Plan, ̈-e *m.*; Schema, -s *nt.* **2.** *vb.* intrigie´ren.

scholar, *n.* Gelehrt´- *m.&f.*

scholarship, *n.* (*knowledge*) Gelehr´samkeit *f.*;

(*stipend*) Stipen´dium, -dien *nt.*

school, *n.* Schule, -n *f.*

science, *n.* Wissenschaft, -en *f.*

science fiction, *n.* Science fiction *f.*

scientific, *adj.* wissenschaftlich.

scientist, *n.* Natur´wissenschaftler, - *m.*, Natur´wissenschaftlerin, -nen *f.*

scissors, *n.pl.* Schere, -n *f.*

scold, *vb.* schelten*.

scolding, *n.* Schelte *f.*

scoop, *n.* (*ladle*) Schöpfkelle, -n *f.*; (*newspaper*) Erstmeldung, -en *f.*

scope, *n.* Reichweite *f.*, Bereich´, -e *m.*

scorch, *vb.* sengen, brennen*.

score, 1. *n.* (*points*) Punktzahl, -en *f.*; (**what's the s.?**) wie steht das Spiel?; (*music*) Partitur´, -en *f.* **2.** *vb.* an•schreiben*; (*mark*) markie´ren.

scorn, 1. *n.* Verach´tung *f.* **2.** *vb.* verach´ten.

scornful, *adj.* veräct´lich.

Scotland, *n.* Schottland *nt.*

Scotsman, *n.* Schotte, -n, -n *m.*

Scotswoman, *n.* Schottin, -nen *f.*

Scottish, *adj.* schottisch.

scour, *vb.* scheuern.

scout, 1. *n.* Kundschafter, - *m.*; (**boy s.**) Pfadfinder, - *m.* **2.** *vb.* erkun´den.

scowl, *vb.* finster blicken.

scramble, *vb.* (*tr.*) durcheinan´der•werfen*; (*intr.*) klettern.

scrambled eggs, *n.* Rührei, -er *nt.*

scrap, 1. *n.* Fetzen, - *m.*; (*fight*) Streit *m.* **2.** *vb.* aus•rangieren; (*fight*) streiten*.

scrape, *vb.* kratzen.

scratch, 1. *n.* Schramme, -n *f.* **2.** *vb.* kratzen; streichen*; (**start from s.**) von Anfang an begin´nen*.

scream, 1. *n.* Schrei, -e *m.*
2. *vb.* schreien*, brüllen.
screen, 1. *n. (furniture)*
Wandschirm, -e *m.;*
(window) Fliegengitter, -
nt.; (movie) Leinwand,
≈e *f.; (TV, radar)* Schirm,
-e *m.; (camouflage)* Tarnung, -en *f.* **2.** *vb. (sift)*
sieben; *(hide)* tarnen.
screw, 1. *n.* Schraube, -n *f.*
2. *vb.* schrauben.
scribble, *vb.* kritzeln,
schmieren.
scripture, *n. (eccles.)*
Heilige Schrift, -en *f.*
scroll, *n.* Schriftrolle, -n *f.*
scrub, *vb.* schrubbern.
scruple, *n.* Skrupel, - *m.,*
Beden´ken, - *nt.*
scrupulous, *adj.* gewis´sen-
haft.
scrutinize, *vb.* genau´ be-
trach´ten.
sculptor, *n.* Bildhauer, - *m.,*
Bildhauerin, -nen *f.*
sculpture, 1. *n.* Skulptur´, -
en *f.* **2.** *vb.* bildhauern.
scythe, *n.* Sense, -n *f.*
sea, *n.* See, Se´en *f.,* Meer, -
e *nt.*
seabed, *n.* Meeresboden *m.*
seal, 1. *n.* Siegel, - *nt.; (animal)* Seehund, -e *m.,*
Robbe, -n *f.* **2.** *vb.*
siegeln, versie´geln.
seam, 1. *n.* Saum, ≈e *m.* **2.**
vb. säumen.
seaport, *n.* Hafen, ≈ *m.*
search, 1. *n.* Suche *f.;*
Durchsu´chung, -en *f.* **2.**
vb. suchen; durch•-
su´chen.
seasick, *adj.* seekrank (≈).
seasickness, *n.* Seekrankheit
f.
season, 1. *n.* Jahreszeit, -en
f.; Saison´, -s *f.* **2.** *vb.*
würzen.
seasoning, *n.* Gewürz´, -e *nt.*
seat, 1. *n.* Platz, ≈e *m.,* Sitzplatz, ≈e *m.; (headquar-
ters)* Sitz, -e *m.* **2.** *vb.*
Sitzplätze haben* für.
seat belt, *n.* Sicherheitsgurt,
-e *m.*
second, 1. *n.* Sekun´de, -n *f.*
2. *adj.* zweit-. **3.** *vb.* **(s. a**

motion) einen Antrag
unterstüt´zen.
secondary, *adj.* sekundär´.
secret, 1. *n.* Geheim´nis, -se
nt. **2.** *adj.* geheim´,
heimlich.
secretary, *n.* Sekretär´, -e
m.; Sekretä´rin, -nen *f.;*
(organization) Schrift-
führer, - *m.*
sect, *n.* Sekte, -n *f.*
section, *n.* Schnitt, -e *m.;*
Teil, -e *m.;* Abschnitt, -e
m.; Abtei´lung, -en *f.*
secular, *adj.* weltlich.
secure, 1. *adj.* sicher. **2.** *vb.*
sichern.
security, *n.* Sicherheit, -en *f.*
sedative, *n.* Beru´hi-
gungsmittel, - *nt.*
seduce, *vb.* verfüh´ren.
seductive, *adj.*
verfüh´rerisch.
see, *vb.* sehen*, schauen.
seed, *n. (individual)* Samen,
- *m.; (collective & fig.)*
Saat, -en *f.*
seek, *vb.* suchen.
seem, *vb.* scheinen*.
seep, *vb.* sickern.
seesaw, *n.* Wippe, -n *f.*
segment, *n.* Segment´, -e *nt.*
segregate, *vb.* ab•sondern.
seize, *vb.* fassen,
ergrei´fen*; *(confiscate)*
beschlag´nahmen.
seldom, *adv.* selten.
select, 1. *adj.* ausgesucht. **2.**
vb. aus•wählen, aus•-
suchen.
selection, *n.* Auswahl, *f.*
selective, *adj.* auswählend.
self, *adv.* selbst, selber.
selfish, *adj.* selbstsüchtig.
selfishness, *n.* Selbstsucht *f.*
sell, *vb.* verkau´fen.
semantic, *adj.* seman´tisch.
semantics, *n.* Seman´tik *f.*
semester, *n.* Semes´ter, - *nt.*
semicircle, *n.* Halbkreis, -e
m.
semicolon, *n.* Strichpunkt, -
e *m.,* Semiko´lon *nt.*
seminary, *n.* Seminar´, -e *nt.*
senate, *n.* Senat´, -e *m.*
senator, *n.* Sena´tor, -o´ren
m., Senato´rin, -nen *f.*
send, *vb.* senden*, schicken.

senile, *adj.* senil´.
senior, *adj.* älter-.
senior citizen, *n.* Senior, -
o´ren *m.;* Senio´rin, -nen
f.
sensation, *n.* Sensation´, -en
f.; (feeling) Gefühl´, -e *nt.*
sensational, *adj.* sensa-
tionell´.
sense, 1. *n.* Sinn, -e *m.;*
(feeling) Gefühl´, -e *nt.;*
(meaning) Bedeu´tung, -
en *f.* **2.** *vb.* fühlen,
empfin´den*.
sensible, *adj.* vernünf´tig.
sensitive, *adj.* empfind´lich;
sensi´bel.
sensual, *adj.* sinnlich.
sentence, 1. *n.* Satz, ≈e *m.;*
(judgment) Urteil, -e *nt.*
2. *vb.* verur´teilen.
sentiment, *n.* Gefühl´, -e
nt., Empfin´dung, -en *f.*
sentimental, *adj.* gefühl´-
voll, sentimental´.
separate, 1. *adj.* getrennt´.
2. *vb.* trennen.
separation, *n.* Trennung, -
en *f.*
September, *n.* Septem´ber, -
m.
sequence, *n.* Reihenfolge, -
n *f.*
serenade, *n.* Ständchen, - *nt.*
serene, *adj.* klar, ruhig.
sergeant, *n.* Unteroffizier, -
e *m.; (police)* Wacht-
meister, - *m.*
serial, 1. *n.* fortlaufende
Erzäh´lung, -en *f.* **2.** *adj.*
Reihen- *(cpds.).*
series, *n.* Reihe, -n *f.*
serious, *adj.* ernst.
seriousness, *n.* Ernst *m.*
sermon, *n.* Predigt, -en *f.*
serpent, *n.* Schlange, -n *f.*
serum, *n.* Serum, -ra *nt.*
servant, *n.* Diener, - *m.,* Dienerin, -nen *f.; (domestic)*
Hausangestellt- *m.& f.*
serve, *vb.* dienen; *(offer
food)* servie´ren.
service, *n.* Dienst, -e *m.;*
(hotel, etc.) Bedie´nung
f.; (china, etc.) Servi´ce
nt.; (church) Gottesdi-
enst, -e *m.*
session, *n.* Sitzung, -en *f.*

set, 1. *n.* *(dishes, tennis)* Satz, ⸚e *m.*; *(articles belonging together)* Garnitur´, -en *f.* **2.** *adj.* bestimmt´. **3.** *vb.* setzen; stellen; legen; *(sun)* unter•gehen*.

settle, *vb.* *(dwell)* sich nieder•lassen*; *(conclude)* erle´digen; *(decide)* entschei´den*.

settlement, *n.* Niederlassung, -en *f.*; Siedlung, -en *f.*; *(decision)* Überein´kommen, - *nt.*

settler, *n.* Siedler, - *m.*, Siedlerin, -nen *f.*

seven, *num.* sieben.

seventeen, *num.* siebzehn.

seventeenth, 1. *adj.* siebzehnt-. **2.** *n.* Siebzehntel, - *nt.*

seventh, 1. *adj.* sieb(en)t-. **2.** *n.* Sieb(en)tel, - *nt.*

seventieth, 1. *adj.* siebzigst-. **2.** *n.* Siebzigstel, - *nt.*

seventy, *num.* siebzig.

sever, *vb.* ab•trennen, ab•brechen*.

several, *adj.* mehrer-.

severe, *adj.* streng; hart (⸚); ernst.

severity, *n.* Strenge *f.*; Härte *f.*; Ernst *m.*

sew, *vb.* nähen.

sewer, *n.* Kanalisation´ *f.*

sex, *n.* Geschlecht´, -er *nt.*; Sexus *m.*

sexism, *n.* Sexis´mus *m.*

sexist, *n.* Sexist´, -en *m.*

sexton, *n.* Küster, - *m.*

sexual, *adj.* geschlecht´lich, sexuell´.

shabby, *adj.* schäbig.

shack, *n.* Bretterbude, -n *f.*

shade, 1. *n.* Schatten, - *m.*; *(color)* Farbton, ⸚e *m.* **2.** *vb.* beschat´ten; schattie´ren.

shadow, *n.* Schatten, - *m.*

shady, *adj.* schattig; *(dubious)* zwielichtig.

shaft, *n.* Schaft, ⸚e *m.*; *(mine)* Schacht, ⸚e *m.*; *(transmission)* Welle, -n *f.*; *(wagon)* Deichsel, -n *f.*

shaggy, *adj.* zottig.

shake, *vb.* schütteln.

shall, *vb.* *(we s. do it)* wir werden* es tun; *(what s. we do?)* was sollen* wir tun?

shallow, *adj.* flach.

shame, 1. *n.* Schande *f.*; *(what a s.)* wie schade. **2.** *vb.* beschä´men.

shameful, *adj.* schandbar.

shameless, *adj.* schamlos.

shampoo, 1. *n.* Schampun´, -s *nt.* **2.** *vb.* die Haare waschen*.

shape, 1. *n.* Form, -en *f.*, Gestalt´, -en *f.* **2.** *vb.* formen, gestal´ten.

share, 1. *n.* Anteil, -e *m.*; *(stock)* Aktie, -n *f.* **2.** *vb.* teilen; teil•haben*.

shark, *n.* Haifisch, -e *m.*

sharp, 1. *n.* *(music)* Kreuz, -e *nt.* **2.** *adj.* scharf (⸚); *(clever)* schlau.

sharpen, *vb.* schärfen.

sharpness, *n.* Schärfe *f.*

shatter, *vb.* zerbre´chen*.

shave, 1. *vb.* rasie´ren. **2.** *n.* Rasie´ren *nt.*; *(get a s.)* sich rasie´ren lassen.

shawl, *n.* Schal, -s *m.*

she, *pron.* sie.

shear, *vb.* scheren*.

shears, *n.pl.* Schere, -n *f.*

sheath, *n.* Scheide, -n *f.*; *(dress)* körperenges Kleid, -er *nt.*

shed, 1. *n.* Schuppen, - *m.* **2.** *vb.* ab•werfen*; *(tears, blood)* vergie´ßen*.

sheep, *n.* Schaf, -e *nt.*

sheet, *n.* *(bed)* Laken, - *nt.*; *(paper)* Bogen, ⸚ *m.*; *(metal)* Platte, -n *f.*

shelf, *n.* Bord, -e *nt.*

shell, 1. *n.* Schale, -n *f.*; *(conch)* Muschel, -n *f.*; *(explosive)* Grana´te, -n *f.* **2.** *vb.* beschie´ßen*.

shellac, *n.* Schellack, -e *m.*

shelter, 1. *n.* Schutz *m.*, Obdach *nt.* **2.** *vb.* beschir´men; beher´bergen.

shepherd, *n.* Schäfer, - *m.*, Hirt, -en, -en *m.*

sherbet, *n.* Sorbett, -e *nt.*

sherry, *n.* Sherry, -s *m.*

shield, 1. *n.* Schild, -e *m.* **2.** *vb.* schützen.

shift, 1. *n.* Wechsel, - *m.*; *(workers)* Schicht, -en *f.*; *(auto)* Schalthebel, - *m.* **2.** *vb.* wechseln; schalten; verschie´ben*.

shin, *n.* Schienbein, -e *nt.*

shine, *vb.* scheinen*, glänzen; *(shoes)* putzen.

shingle, *n.* Schindel, -n *f.*, Dachschindel, -n *f.*

shiny, *adj.* glänzend.

ship, 1. *n.* Schiff, -e *nt.* **2.** *vb.* senden*.

shipment, *n.* Ladung, -en *f.*, Sendung, -en *f.*

shipper, *n.* Verfrach´ter, - *m.*, Verla´der, - *m.*

shipping agent, *n.* Spediteur´, -e *m.*

shipwreck, *n.* Schiffbruch, ⸚e *m.*

shirk, *vb.* sich drücken vor.

shirt, *n.* Hemd, -en *nt.*

shiver, *vb.* zittern.

shock, 1. *n.* Schock, -s *m.* **2.** *vb.* schockie´ren.

shoe, *n.* Schuh, - *m.*

shoelace, *n.* Schnürsenkel, - *m.*

shoemaker, *n.* Schuhmacher, - *m.*, Schuster, -*m.*

shoot, 1. *n.* *(sprout)* Schößling, -e *m.* **2.** *vb.* *(gun)* schießen*; *(person)* erschie´ßen*.

shop, 1. *n.* Laden, ⸚ *m.*, Geschäft´, -e *nt.*; *(factory)* Werkstatt, ⸚en *f.* **2.** *vb.* Einkäufe machen.

shopping, *n.* Einkaufen *nt.*

shore, *n.* Küste, -n *f.*; *(beach)* Strand, -e *m.*

short, *adj.* kurz (⸚); *(scarce)* knapp.

shortage, *n.* Knappheit, -en *f.*

short circuit, *n.* Kurzschluß, ⸚sse *m.*

short cut, *n.* Abkürzung, - en *f.*

shorten, *vb.* kürzen.

shorthand, *n.* Stenographie´ *f.*

shortly, *adv.* bald (⸚).

shorts, *n.pl.* Shorts, *pl.*

shot, *n.* Schuß, ⸚sse *m.*; *(photo)* Aufnahme, -n *f.*

should, vb. sollte; **(s. have)** hätte . . . sollen.

shoulder, 1. n. Schulter, -n f. **2.** vb. schultern.

shout, vb. schreien*.

shovel, n. Schaufel, -n f.

show, 1. n. (theater, film) Vorstellung, -en f.; (spectacle) Thea´ter, - nt.; (exhibit) Ausstellung, -en f. **2.** vb. zeigen; vor•führen; aus•stellen.

shower, n. (rain) Schauer, - m.; (bath) Dusche, -n f.

shrapnel, n. Schrapnell´, -s nt.

shrewd, adj. scharfsinnig; (derogatory) geris´sen.

shriek, vb. kreischen.

shrill, adj. schrill, gellend.

shrimp, n. Garne´le, -n f., Krabbe, -n f.; (small person) Dreikä´sehoch, -s m.

shrine, n. Schrein, -e m.

shrink, vb. schrumpfen; (cloth) ein•laufen*.

shroud, n. Leichentuch, ⸗er nt.

shrub, n. Strauch ⸗er m., Busch, ⸗e m.

shudder, vb. schaudern.

shun, vb. vermei´den*.

shut, 1. vb. schließen*, zu•machen. **2.** adj. geschlos´sen. **3.** adv. zu.

shutter, n. Fensterladen, ⸗ m.; (camera) Verschluß´, ⸗sse m.

shy, 1. adj. scheu, schüchtern. **2.** vb. scheuen.

Sicily, n. Sizi´lien nt.

sick, adj. krank (⸗); **(be s. of)** satt•haben*.

sickness, n. Krankheit, -en f.

side, n. Seite, -n f.; (edge) Rand, ⸗er m.

sidewalk, n. Bürgersteig, -e m.

siege, n. Bela´gerung, -en f.

sieve, n. Sieb, -e nt.

sift, vb. sieben; sichten.

sigh, 1. n. Seufzer, - m. **2.** vb. seufzen.

sight, 1. n. Sicht f.; (vision) Sehkraft f.; (view) Anblick, -e m.; (sights) Sehenswürdigkeit, -en f. **2.** vb. sichten.

sightseeing, n. Besich´tigung (f.) von Sehenswürdigkeiten.

sign, 1. n. Zeichen, - nt.; Schild, -er nt. **2.** vb. unterzeich´nen, unterschrei´ben*.

signal, 1. n. Signal´, -e nt. **2.** vb. signalisie´ren.

signature, n. Unterschrift, -en f.

significance, n. Bedeu´tung, -en f., Wichtigkeit f.

significant, adj. bezeich´nend, bedeu´tend.

signify, vb. bezeich´nen, bedeu´ten.

silence, 1. n. Schweigen nt., Ruhe f. **2.** vb. zum Schweigen bringen*.

silent, adj. still, schweigsam.

silk, 1. n. Seide f. **2.** adj. seiden.

silken, silky, adj. seidig.

sill, n. (door) Schwelle, -n f.; (window) Fensterbrett, -er nt.

silly, adj. albern.

silo, n. Silo, -s m.

silver, 1. n. Silber nt. **2.** adj. silbern.

silverware, n. (silbernes) Besteck´, -e nt.

similar, adj. ähnlich.

similarity, n. Ähnlichkeit, -en f.

simple, adj. einfach, schlicht; (ignorant) einfältig.

simplicity, n. Einfachheit f., Schlichtheit f.

simplify, vb. verein´fachen.

simulate, vb. vor•geben*; nach•ahmen.

simultaneous, adj. gleichzeitig.

sin, 1. n. Sünde, -n f. **2.** vb. sündigen.

since, 1. prep. seit. **2.** conj. seit, seitdem´; (because) da. **3.** adv. seitdem´.

sincere, adj. aufrichtig, ehrlich.

sincerely, adv. **(s. yours)** Ihr erge´bener, Ihre erge´bene.

sincerity, n. Aufrichtigkeit f.

sinful, adj. sündhaft.

sing, vb. singen*.

singe, vb. sengen.

singer, n. Sänger, - m., Sängerin, -nen f.

single, adj. einzeln; (unmarried) ledig.

singular, 1. n. (gram.) Einzahl f., Singular m. **2.** adj. einzig; (unusual) eigentümlich.

sinister, adj. düster, unheimlich.

sink, 1. n. Ausguß, ⸗sse m., Spülstein, -e m. **2.** vb. (tr.) versen´ken; (intr.) sinken*.

sinner, n. Sünder, - m., Sünderin, -nen f.

sinus, n. Stirnhöhle, -n f.

sinusitis, n. Stirnhöhlenentzündung, -en f.

sip, 1. n. Schluck, -e m. **2.** vb. schlürfen.

siphon, n. Siphon, -s m.

sir, n. (yes, s.) jawohl´.

siren, n. Sire´ne, -n f.

sirloin, n. Lendenstück, -e nt.

sister, n. Schwester, -n f.

sister-in-law, n. Schwägerin, -nen f.

sit, vb. sitzen*; **(s. down)** sich (hin•)setzen.

site, n. Lage, -n f.

sitting, n. Sitzung, -en f.

situated, adj. gele´gen.

situation, n. Lage, -n f., Situation´, -en f.

six, num. sechs.

sixteen, num. sechzehn.

sixteenth, 1. adj. sechzehnt-. **2.** n. Sechzehntel, - nt.

sixth, 1. adj. sechst-. **2.** n. Sechstel, - nt.

sixtieth, 1. adj. sechzigst-. **2.** n. Sechzigstel, - nt.

sixty, num. sechzig.

size, n. Größe, -n f., Ausmaß, -e nt.

skate, 1. n. Schlittschuh, -e m. **2.** vb. Schlittschuh laufen*.

skateboard, n. Skatebord nt.; Rollbrett nt.

skeleton, n. Skelett´, -e nt.

skeptic, n. Skeptiker, - m.

skeptical, *adj.* skeptisch.
sketch, 1. *n.* Skizze, -n *f.;* Sketch, -e *m.* **2.** *vb.* skizzie´ren.
ski, 1. *n.* Ski, -er *m.* **2.** *vb.* Ski´laufen*.
skid, 1. *n.* Hemmschuh, -e *m.* **2.** *vb.* rutschen.
skill, *n.* Geschick´, *nt.,* Fertigkeit, -en *f.*
skillful, *adj.* geschickt´.
skim, *vb. (remove cream)* entrah´men; *(go lightly)* flüchtig lesen*.
skim milk, *n.* Magermilch *f.*
skin, 1. *n.* Haut, ⁼e *f.; (fur)* Fell, -e *nt.; (of fruit)* Schale, -n *f.* **2.** *vb.* häuten.
skip, *vb.* springen*; *(omit)* überschla´gen*.
skirt, 1. *n.* Rock, ⁼e *m.* **2.** *vb.* umge´hen*.
skull, *n.* Schädel, - *m.*
skunk, *n.* Stinktier, -e *nt.; (person)* Schuft, -e *m.*
sky, *n.* Himmel, - *m.*
skyscraper, *n.* Wolkenkratzer, - *m.*
slab, *n.* Platte, -n *f.*
slack, *adj.* schlaff, flau.
slacken, *vb.* nach•lassen*.
slacks, *n.pl.* Slacks *pl.*
slam, *vb.* knallen, zu•knallen.
slander, 1. *n.* Verleum´dung, -en *f.* **2.** *vb.* verleum´den.
slang, *n.* Slang *m.,* Jargon´, -s *m.*
slant, 1. *n.* Neigung, -en *f.;* schiefe Ebene, -n *f.;* Aspekt´, -e *m.* **2.** *vb.* neigen.
slap, 1. *n.* Klaps, -e *m.,* Ohrfeige, -n *f.* **2.** *vb.* schlagen*.
slash, 1. *n.* Schlitz, -e *m.;* Schnittwunde, -n *f.* **2.** *vb.* schlitzen.
slat, *n.* Latte, -n *f.*
slate, *n.* Schiefer *m.; (list)* Liste, -n *f.*
slaughter, 1. *n.* Schlachten *nt.;* Gemet´zel, - *nt.* **2.** *vb.* schlachten; nieder•metzeln.
Slav, *n.* Slawe, -n, -n *m.,* Slawin, -nen *f.*
slave, *n.* Sklave, -n, -n *m.,* Sklavin, -nen *f.*

slavery, *n.* Sklaverei´ *f.*
Slavic, *adj.* slawisch.
slay, *vb.* erschla´gen*.
sled, 1. *n.* Schlitten, - *m.; (go sledding)* Schlitten fahren*, rodeln.
sleek, *adj.* glatt (⁼, -); geschniegelt.
sleep, 1. *n.* Schlaf *m.* **2.** *vb.* schlafen*; *(go to s.)* ein•schlafen*.
sleeper, sleeping car, *n.* Schlafwagen, - *m.*
sleeping pill, *n.* Schlaftablette, -n *f.*
sleepy, *adj.* schläfrig, müde.
sleet, *n.* Eisregen *m.*
sleeve, *n.* Ärmel, - *m.*
sleigh, *n.* Schlitten, - *m.*
slender, *adj.* schlank; *(slight)* schwach (⁼).
slice, 1. *n.* Scheibe, -n *f.* **2.** *vb.* in Scheiben schneiden*.
slide, *vb.* gleiten*, rutschen.
slight, *adj.* leicht, gering´; *(thin)* schmächtig.
slim, *adj.* schlank; gering´.
slime, *n.* Schlamm *m.;* Schleim.
slip, 1. *n. (plant)* Steckling, -e *m.; (error)* Verse´hen, - *nt.; (underwear)* Unterrock, ⁼e *m.; (paper)* Zettel, - *m.; (bedding)* Bezug´, ⁼e *m.* **2.** *vb.* gleiten*, aus•gleiten*.
slipper, *n.* Hausschuh, -e *m.,* Pantof´fel, -n *m.*
slippery, *adj.* glatt (⁼, -), schlüpfrig.
slit, 1. *n.* Schlitz, -e *m.* **2.** *vb.* schlitzen.
slogan, *n.* Schlagwort, -e *or* ⁼er *nt.; (election s.)* Wahlspruch, ⁼e *m.*
slope, *n.* Abhang, ⁼e *m.;* Neigung, -en *f.*
sloppy, *adj.* schlampig.
slot, *n.* Schlitz, -e *m.*
slovenly, *adj.* liederlich.
slow, *adj.* langsam; *(be s., of a clock)* nach•gehen*.
slowness, *n.* Langsamkeit *f.*
sluggish, *adj.* träge.
slum, *n.* Elendsviertel, - *nt.*
slur, 1. *n.* Anwurf, ⁼e *m.* **2.** *vb. (speech)* nuscheln.

slush, *n.* Matsch *m.*
sly, *adj.* schlau, verschla´gen.
small, *adj.* klein.
smallpox, *n.* Blattern, *pl.*
smart, *adj.* intelligent´; elegant´.
smash, *vb.* zerschla´gen*, zerschmei´ßen*.
smear, *vb.* schmieren, beschmie´ren.
smell, 1. *n.* Geruch´, ⁼e *m.* **2.** *vb.* riechen*.
smelt, 1. *n.* Stint, -e *m.* **2.** *vb.* schmelzen, ein•schmelzen.
smile, 1. *n.* Lächeln *nt.* **2.** *vb.* lächeln.
smock, *n.* Kittel, - *m.*
smoke, 1. *n.* Rauch *f.* **2.** *vb.* rauchen; *(meat, fish)* räuchern.
smooth, 1. *adj.* glatt (⁼, -). **2.** *vb.* glätten.
smother, *vb.* ersti´cken.
smug, *adj.* selbstgefällig.
smuggle, *vb.* schmuggeln.
snack, *n.* Imbiß, -sse *m.*
snag, *n. (stocking)* Zugmasche, -n *f.; (obstacle)* Hindernis, -se *nt.*
snail, *n.* Schnecke, -n *f.*
snake, *n.* Schlange, -n *f.*
snap, 1. *n.* Druckknopf, ⁼e *m.* **2.** *vb.* schnappen; *(break)* zerrei´ßen*.
snapshot, *n.* Schnappschuß, ⁼sse *m.*
snare, *n.* Falle, -n *f.*
snarl, *vb. (growl)* drohend knurren.
snatch, *vb.* erha´schen, weg•schnappen.
sneak, *vb.* schleichen*.
sneakers, *n.pl.* Freizeitschuhe *m.pl.,* Turnschuhe *m.pl.*
sneer, *vb.* höhnisch grinsen.
sneeze, *vb.* niesen.
snob, *n.* Snob, -s *m.*
snore, *vb.* schnarchen.
snow, 1. *n.* Schnee *m.* **2.** *vb.* schneien.
snub, 1. *n.* Affront´, -s *m.* **2.** *vb.* schneiden*.
snug, *adj.* eng; *(fig.)* mollig.
so, *adv.* so.

soak, *vb.* durchnäs'sen; ein•weichen.

soap, *n.* Seife, -n *f.*

soar, *vb.* sich empor•'schwingen*.

sob, *vb.* schluchzen.

sober, *adj.* nüchtern.

sociable, *adj.* gesel'lig.

social, *adj.* gesell'schaftlich, sozial'.

socialism, *n.* Sozialis'mus *f.*

socialist, *n.* Sozialist', -en, -en *m.*, Sozialis'tin, -nen *f.*

society, *n.* Gesell'schaft, -en *f.*

sociology, *n.* Soziologie' *f.*

sock, 1. *n.* Socke, -n *f.* 2. *vb.* schlagen*.

socket, *n.* (*eye*) Augen-höhle, -n *f.*; (*elec.*) Steckdose, -n *f.*

sod, *n.* Sode, -n *f.*

soda, *n.* Soda *nt.*

sofa, *n.* Sofa, -s *nt.*

soft, *adj.* weich; (*not loud*) leise; (*not rough*) sanft, sacht.

soft drink, *n.* alkoholfreies Getränk', -e *nt.*

soften, *vb.* weich machen*; (*fig.*) mildern.

soil, 1. *n.* Boden, = *m.* 2. *vb.* beschmut'zen.

soiled, *adj.* schmutzig.

sojourn, 1. *n.* Aufenthalt, -e *m.* 2. *vb.* sich auf•halten*.

solace, *n.* Trost *m.*

solar, *adj.* Sonnen- (*cpds.*).

soldier, *n.* Soldat', -en, -en *m.*

sole, 1. *n.* Sohle, -n *f.*; (*fish*) Seezunge, -n *f.* 2. *adj.* allei'nig, einzig.

solemn, *adj.* feierlich.

solicit, *vb.* an•halten* um.

solicitous, *adj.* besorgt'; eifrig.

solid, *adj.* fest; solid', kompakt'.

solidify, *vb.* festigen; verdich'ten.

solitary, *adj.* einzeln.

solitude, *n.* Einsamkeit, -en *f.*

solo, *n.* Solo, -s *nt.*

soloist, *n.* Solist', -en, -en *m.*, Solis'tin, -nen *f.*

so long, *interj.* Wiedersehen.

solution, *n.* Lösung, -en *f.*

solve, *vb.* lösen.

solvent, 1. *n.* Lösungsmittel, - *nt.* 2. *adj.* (*financially capable*) zahlungsfähig.

somber, *adj.* düster.

some, *pron.* & *adj.* (*with singulars*) etwas; (*with plurals*) einig-, ein paar.

somebody, *pron.* jemand.

somehow, *adv.* irgendwie.

someone, *pron.* jemand.

somersault, *n.* Purzelbaum, =e *m.*

something, *pron.* etwas.

sometime, *adv.* irgendwann.

sometimes, *adv.* manchmal.

somewhat, *adv.* etwas.

somewhere, *adv.* irgendwo.

son, *n.* Sohn, =e *m.*

song, *n.* Lied, -er *nt.*

son-in-law, *n.* Schwiegersohn, =e *m.*

soon, *adv.* bald.

soot, *n.* Ruß *m.*

soothe, *vb.* beschwich'tigen.

soothing, *adj.* wohltuend.

sophisticated, *adj.* anspruchsvoll, verfei'nert, weltgewandt; (*tech.*) hochentwickelt.

soprano, *n.* Sopran', -e *m.*

sorcery, *n.* Zauberei' *f.*

sordid, *adj.* dreckig; gemein'.

sore, 1. *n.* wunde Stelle, -n *f.*, offene Wunde, -n *f.* 2. *adj.* wund; schmerzhaft; (*angry*) eingeschnappt; (*be s.*) weh•tun*.

sorrow, *n.* Kummer, - *m.*

sorrowful, *adj.* kummer-voll.

sorry, *adj.* traurig, betrübt'; (*I am s.*) es tut*' mir leid.

sort, 1. *n.* Sorte, -n *f.*, Art, -en *f.* 2. *vb.* sortie'ren.

soul, *n.* Seele, -n *f.*

sound, 1. *n.* Ton, =e *m.*, Laut, -e *m.*, Klang, =e *m.* 2. *adj.* gesund(=, -); (*valid*) einwandfrei. 3. *vb.* klingen*; (*take soundings*) loten.

soup, *n.* Suppe, -n *f.*

sour, *adj.* sauer.

source, *n.* Quelle, -n *f.*

south, 1. *n.* Süden *m.* 2. *adj.* südlich; Süd- (*cpds.*).

southeast, 1. *n.* Südos'ten *m.* 2. *adj.* südöst'lich; Südost'- (*cpds.*).

southeastern, *adj.* südöst'lich.

southern, *adj.* südlich.

South Pole, *n.* Südpol *m.*

southwest, 1. *n.* Südwes'ten *m.* 2. *adj.* südwest'lich; Südwest'- (*cpds.*).

southwestern, *adj.* südwest'lich.

souvenir, *n.* Andenken, -*nt.*; Reiseandenken, - *nt.*

Soviet, 1. *n.* Sowjet, -s *m.* 2. *adj.* sowje'tisch.

sow, 1. *n.* Sau, =e *f.* 2. *vb.* säen.

space, *n.* Raum, =e *m.*

space shuttle, *n.* Raumtransporter, - *m.*

spacious, *adj.* geräu'mig.

spade, *n.* Spaten, - *m.*; (*cards*) Pik *nt.*

spaghetti, *n.* Spaghet'ti *pl.*

Spain, *n.* Spanien *n.*

span, 1. *n.* Spanne, -n *f.* 2. *vb.* überspan'nen.

Spaniard, *n.* Spanier, - *m.*, Spanierin, -nen *f.*

Spanish, *adj.* spanisch.

spank, *vb.* hauen*.

spanking, *n.* Haue *f.*

spar, 1. *n.* Sparren, - *m.* 2. *vb.* boxen.

spare, 1. *adj.* Ersatz'-, Reser've- (*cpds.*). 2. *vb.* sparen, scheuen.

spark, *n.* Funke(n), - *m.*

sparkle, *vb.* funkeln.

spark-plug, *n.* Zündkerze, -n *f.*

sparrow, *n.* Sperling, -e *m.*

sparse, *adj.* spärlich.

spasm, *n.* Krampf, =e *m.*

spasmodic, *adj.* krampfhaft; sprunghaft.

spatter, *vb.* spritzen, besprit'zen.

speak, *vb.* sprechen*, reden.

speaker, *n.* Redner, - *m.*; (*presiding officer*) Präsident', -en, -en *m.*

spear, 1. *n.* Speer, -e *m.*; Spieß, -e *m.* 2. *vb.* auf•spießen.

special, *adj.* beson'der-.

specialist, *n.* Spezialist´, -en, -en *m.*, Spezialis´tin, -nen *f.*

specially, *adv.* beson´ders.

specialty, *n.* Spezialität´, -en *f.*

species, *n.* Art, -en *f.*; Gattung, -en *f.*

specific, *adj.* spezi´fisch.

specify, *vb.* spezifizie´ren; *(stipulate)* bestim´men.

specimen, *n.* Muster, - *nt.*, Exemplar´, -e *nt.*, Probe, -n *f.*

spectacle, *n.* Schauspiel, -e *nt.*; Anblick, -e *m.*; **(s.s)** Brille, -n *f.*

spectacular, *adj.* aufsehenerregend.

spectator, *n.* Zuschauer, - *m.*, Zuschauerin, -nen *f.*

spectrum, *n.* Spektrum, -tren *nt.*

speculate, *vb.* spekulie´ren.

speculation, *n.* Spekulation´, -en *f.*

speech, *n.* Sprache, -n *f.*; *(address)* Rede, -n *f.*

speechless, *adj.* sprachlos.

speed, 1. *n.* Geschwin´digkeit, -en *f.*, Tempo *nt.* **2.** *vb.* hasten; **(s. up)** beschleu´nigt erle´digen; *(auto)* die Geschwin´digkeitsgrenze überschrei´ten*.

speedometer, *n.* Geschwin´digkeitsmesser, - *m.*

speedy, *adj.* schnell; unverzüglich.

spell, 1. *n.* Zauber, - *m.* **2.** *vb.* buchstabie´ren.

spelling, *n.* Rechtschreibung *f.*

spend, *vb. (money)* aus•geben*; *(time)* verwen´den*, verbrin´gen*.

sphere, *n.* Kugel, -n *f.*, Sphäre, -n *f.*

spice, *n.* Gewürz´, -e *nt.*

spider, *n.* Spinne, -n *f.*

spike, *n.* langer Nagel, -= *m.*; *(thorn)* Dorn, -en *m.*, Stachel, -n *m.*

spill, *vb.* verschüt´ten; *(make a spot)* kleckern.

spin, *vb.* spinnen*.

spinach, *n.* Spinat´ *m.*

spine, *n.* Rückgrat, -e *nt.*

spiral, 1. *n.* Spira´le, -n *f.* **2.** *adj.* spiral´förmig.

spire, *n.* spitzer Turm, -=e *m.*

spirit, *n.* Geist, *m.*; *(ghost)* Gespenst´, -er *nt.*; *(vivacity)* Schwung *m.*; **(s.s)** Spirituo´sen *pl.*

spiritual, 1. *n.* Spiritual, -e *m.* **2.** *adj.* geistig, seelisch.

spiritualism, *n.* Spiritualis´mus *m.*; Spiritis´mus *m.*

spit, 1. *n. (saliva)* Speichel *m.*; *(roasting)* Spieß, -e *m.* **2.** *vb.* spucken.

spite, 1. *n.* Trotz *m.*; **(in s. of)** trotz. **2.** *vb.* ärgern.

splash, *vb.* spritzen; planschen.

splendid, *adj.* prächtig.

splendor, *n.* Pracht *f.*

splice, *vb.* spleißen*.

splint, *n.* Schiene, -n *f.*

splinter, *n.* Splitter, - *m.*

split, 1. *n.* Spalt, -e *m.* **2.** *vb.* spalten.

spoil, *vb.* verder´ben*; schlecht werden*; *(child)* verwöh´nen, verzie´hen*.

spoke, *n.* Speiche, -n *f.*

spokesperson, *n.* Sprecher, - *m.*, Sprecherin, -nen *f.*

sponge, 1. *n.* Schwamm, -=e *m.* **2.** *vb. (live off)* nassauern.

sponsor, 1. *n.* Bürge, -n, -n *m.*; Förderer, -en *m.*; *(radio, TV, etc.)* Rekla´meauftraggeber, - *m.* **2.** *vb.* fördern; *(advertising)* in Auftrag geben*.

spontaneity, *n.* Impulsivität´ *f.*

spontaneous, *adj.* spontan´.

spool, *n.* Spule, -n *f.*

spoon, *n.* Löffel, - *m.*

sport, *n.* Sport *m.*; Vergnü´gen, - *nt.*

spot, *n. (place)* Stelle, -n *f.*; *(blot)* Fleck, -en *m.*

spouse, *n.* Gatte, -n, -n *m.*; Gattin, -nen *f.*

spout, 1. *n.* Tülle, -n *f.*; *(water)* Strahl, -en *m.* **2.** *vb.* hervor´•sprudeln; speien*.

sprain, 1. *n.* Verren´kung, -en *f.*, Verstau´chung, -en *f.* **2.** *vb.* verren´ken, verstau´chen.

sprawl, *vb.* sich aus•breiten; alle Viere aus•strecken.

spray, *vb.* spritzen; zerstäu´ben.

spread, 1. *n.* Spanne, -n *f.*; Umfang, -=e *m.* **2.** *vb.* aus•breiten.

spree, *n.* Bummel, - *m.*; Ausflug, -=e *m.*

sprightly, *adj.* munter.

spring, 1. *n. (season)* Frühling, -e *m.*, Frühjahr, -e *nt.*; *(source)* Quelle, -n *f.*; *(leap)* Sprung, -=e *m.*; *(metal)* Feder, -n *f.* **2.** *vb.* springen*.

sprinkle, *vb.* sprengen; streuen.

sprint, 1. *n.* Kurzstreckenlauf, -=e *m.* **2.** *vb.* sprinten.

sprout, 1. *n.* Sproß, -sse *m.* **2.** *vb.* sprießen*.

spry, *adj.* flink.

spur, 1. *n.* Sporn, Sporen *m.* **2.** *vb.* an•spornen.

spurn, *vb.* verschmä´hen.

spurt, *vb.* hervor´•schießen*.

spy, 1. *n.* Spion´, -e *m.*, Spio´nin, -nen *f.* **2.** *vb.* spionie´ren.

squabble, 1. *n.* Zank *m.* **2.** *vb.* zanken.

squad, *n.* Trupp, -s *m.*; *(sport)* Mannschaft, -en *f.*

squadron, *n. (air)* Staffel, -n *f.*; *(navy)* Geschwa´der, - *nt.*

squall, *n.* Bö, -en *f.*

squalor, *n.* Schmutz *m.*

squander, *vb.* vergeu´den.

square, 1. *n.* Viereck, -e *nt.*, Quadrat´, -e *nt.*; *(open place)* Platz, -=e *m.* **2.** *adj.* viereckig, quadra´tisch. **3.** *vb.* quadrie´ren.

squash, 1. *n.* Kürbis, -se *m.* **2.** *vb.* quetschen, zerquet´schen.

squat, 1. *adj.* kurz und dick. **2.** *vb.* hocken, kauern.

squeak, *vb.* quietschen.

squeamish, *adj.* zimperlich.

squeeze, *vb.* drücken; *(juice)* aus•pressen.

squirrel, *n.* Eichhörnchen, -*nt.*

squirt, *vb.* spritzen.

stab, 1. *n.* Stich, -e *m.* 2. *vb.* stechen*; erste´chen*.

stability, *n.* Bestän´digkeit *f.*, Stabilität´ *f.*

stabilize, *vb.* stabilisie´ren.

stable, 1. *n.* Stall, ≃e *m.* 2. *adj.* bestän´dig; stabil´.

stack, 1. *n.* Haufen, - *m.* 2. *vb.* auf•stapeln.

stadium, *n.* Stadion, -dien *nt.*

staff, *n.* Stab, ≃e *m.; (personnel)* Personal´ *nt.; (music)* Notenlinien *pl.*

stag, *n.* Hirsch, -e *m.*

stage, 1. *n. (theater)* Bühne, -n *f.; (phase)* Stadium, -dien *nt.* 2. *vb.* inszenie´ren.

stagflation, *n.* Stagflation´ *f.*

stagger, *vb.* taumeln; *(amaze)* verblüf´fen; *(alternate)* staffeln.

stagnant, *adj.* stagnie´rend.

stagnate, *vb.* stagnie´ren.

stain, 1. *n.* Fleck, -e *m.; (color)* Färbstoff, -e *m.; (paint)* Beize *f.* 2. *vb.* beflé´cken, färben; beizen.

staircase, stairs, *n.* Treppe, -n *f.*

stake, 1. *n. (post)* Pfahl, ≃e *m.; (sum, bet)* Einsatz, ≃e *m.* 2. *vb.* aufs Spiel setzen.

stale, *adj.* alt (≃), schal.

stalk, *n.* Stiel, -e *m.*, Halm, -e *m.*

stall, 1. *n.* Stall, ≃e *m.; (vendor's)* Bude, -n *f.* 2. *vb. (hesitate)* Zeit schinden*; *(engine)* ab•würgen.

stamina, *n.* Energie´ *f.*, Ausdauer *f.*

stammer, *vb.* stammeln.

stamp, 1. *n.* Stempel, - *m.; (mark)* Geprä´ge *nt.; (postal)* Freimarke, -n *f.*, Briefmarke, -n *f.* 2. *vb.* stempeln; prägen.

stand, 1. *n.* Stellung, -en *f.; (vendor's)* Bude, -n *f.; (grandstand)* Tribü´ne, -n *f.* 2. *vb.* stehen*; *(endure)* ertra´gen*.

standard, 1. *n.* Norm, -en *f.*, Standard, -s *m.* 2. *adj.* Standard- *(cpds.).*

standardize, *vb.* standardisie´ren.

standing, *n.* Bestand´ *m.; (reputation)* Ruf *m.*

standpoint, *n.* Standpunkt, -e *m.*

star, *n.* Stern, -e *m.; (movie)* Star, -s *m.*

starch, 1. *n.* Stärke *f.* 2. *vb.* stärken.

stare, *vb.* starren, glotzen.

stark, *adj.* kraß; *(bare)* kahl.

start, 1. *n.* Anfang, ≃e *m.*, Start, -s *m.* 2. *vb.* an•fangen*, starten.

startle, *vb.* erschre´cken, auf•schrecken.

starvation, *n.* Verhun´gern *nt.;* Hungertod *m.*

starve, *vb.* hungern; **(s. to death)** verhun´gern.

state, 1. *n.* Staat, -en *m.; (condition)* Zustand, ≃e *m.* 2. *vb.* dar•legen, erklä´ren.

statement, *n.* Erklä´rung, -en *f.;* Behaup´tung, -en *f.*

stateroom, *n.* Kabi´ne, -n *f.*

statesman, *n.* Staatsmann, ≃er *m.*

static, 1. *n.* atmosphä´rische Störung, -en *f.* 2. *adj.* statisch.

station, *n.* Station´, -en *f.; (position)* Stellung, -en *f.; (R.R.)* Bahnhof, ≃e *m.*

stationary, *adj.* feststehend, stationär´.

stationer, *n.* Schreibwarenhändler, - *m.*

stationery, *n.* Schreibwaren *pl.;* Briefpapier *nt.*

station wagon, *n.* Kombiwagen, - *m.*

statistics, *n.pl.* Statis´tik *pl.*

statue, *n.* Statue, -n *f.*

stature, *n.* Wuchs *m.*, Statur´ *f.; (fig.)* Format´, -e *nt.*

status, *n.* Stand, ≃e *m.*

statute, *n.* Statut´, -e *nt.*, Satzung, -en *f.*

staunch, *adj.* treu, wacker.

stay, 1. *n. (sojourn)* Aufenthalt *m.; (delay)* Einstellung, -en *f.* 2. *vb.* bleiben*; *(hold back)* zurück´•halten*.

steady, *adj.* fest; sicher; bestän´dig.

steak, *n.* Beefsteak, -s *nt.*

steal, *vb.* stehlen*.

stealth, *n.* Verstoh´lenheit *f.*

stealthy, *adj.* verstoh´len.

steam, 1. *n.* Dampf, ≃e *m.* 2. *vb.* dampfen.

steamboat, *n.* Dampfboot, -e *nt.*

steamship, *n.* Dampfer, - *m.*

steel, 1. *n.* Stahl, -e *m.* 2. *adj.* stählern; Stahl- *(cpds.).*

steep, *adj.* steil; *(price)* hoch (hoh-, höher, höchst-).

steeple, *n.* Kirchturm, ≃e *m.*

steer, 1. *n.* Stier, -e *m.* 2. *vb.* steuern.

stellar, *adj.* Sternen- *(cpds.).*

stem, 1. *n.* Stiel, -e *m.* 2. *vb.* stammen.

stenographer, *n.* Stenotypis´tin, -nen *f.*

stenography, *n.* Kurzschrift, -en *f.;* Stenographie´, -i´en *f.*

step, 1. *n.* Schritt, -e *m.; (stair)* Stufe, -n *f.* 2. *vb.* treten*.

stepfather, *n.* Stiefvater, ≃ *m.*

stepladder, *n.* Trittleiter, -n *f.*

stepmother, *n.* Stiefmutter, ≃ *f.*

stereophonic, *adj.* stereophon´.

sterile, *adj.* unfruchtbar; steril´.

sterility, *n.* Sterilität´ *f.*

sterilize, *vb.* sterilisie´ren.

sterling, *adj.* münzecht; *(silver)* echt; **(pound s.)** Pfund Sterling *nt.*

stern, *adj.* streng.

stethoscope, *n.* Stethoskop´, -e *nt.*

stew, 1. *n.* Eintopf, *m.* 2. *vb.* dämpfen.

steward, *n.* Steward, -s *m.*

stewardess, *n.* Stewardess´, -en *f.*

stick, 1. *n.* Stock, ≃e *m.* 2. *vb. (adhere)* kleben; *(pin)* stecken.

sticker, *n.* Etikett´, -e *n.;* Ankleber, - *m.*

sticky, *adj.* klebrig.

stiff, *adj.* steif.

stiffen, *vb.* steif werden*; *(fig.)* verhär´ten.

stiffness, *n.* Steifheit, -en *f.*

stifle, *vb.* ersti´cken.

stigma, *n.* Stigma, -men *nt.,* Schandfleck, -e *m.*

still, 1. *n.* Destillier´apparat, -e *m.* **2.** *adj.* still, **3.** *vb.* stillen. **4.** *adv.* noch; doch; dennoch.

stillness, *n.* Stille *f.*

stimulant, *n.* Reizmittel, - *nt.*

stimulate, *vb.* an•regen.

stimulus, *n.* Anreiz, -e *m.*

sting, 1. *n.* Stache., - *m.; (bite)* Stich, -e *m.* **2.** *vb.* stechen*; *(burn)* brennen.

stingy, *adj.* geizig.

stink, *vb.* stinken*.

stipulate, *vb.* bestim´men.

stir, 1. *n.* Aufregung, - *f.* **2.** *vb.* rühren; erre´gen.

stitch, 1. *n.* Stich, -e *m.; (knitting)* Masche, -n *f.* **2.** *vb.* steppen.

stock, 1. *n. (supply)* Vorrat, ⸗e *m.,* Lager, - *nt.; (lineage)* Fami´lie, -n *f.; (livestock)* Viehbestand, ⸗e *m.; (gun)* Schaft, ⸗e *m.* **2.** *vb.* versor´gen; auf Lager haben*.

stockbroker, *n.* Börsenmakler, - *m.*

stock exchange, *n.* Börse, -n *f.*

stocking, *n.* Strumpf, ⸗e *m.*

stodgy, *adj.* schwerfällig; untersetzt´.

stole, *n.* Stola, -len *f.*

stomach, 1. *n.* Magen, ⸗ *m.* **2.** *vb. (fig.)* schlucken.

stone, 1. *n.* Stein, -e *m.; (fruit)* Kern, -e *m.* **2.** *vb.* steinigen.

stool, *n.* Schemel, - *m.*

stoop, *vb.* sich bücken; *(demean oneself)* sich ernied´rigen.

stop, 1. *n.* Haltestelle, -n *f.* **2.** *vb.* halten*; stoppen; *(cease)* auf•hören.

stopover, *n.* Fahrtunterbrechung, -en *f.*

storage, *n.* Lagern *nt.;* Lagerhaus, ⸗er *nt.*

store, 1. *n.* Laden, ⸗ *m.,* Geschäft´, -e *nt.; (supplies)* Vorräte *pl.* **2.** *vb.* lagern.

storehouse, *n.* Lagerhaus, ⸗er *nt.*

storm, 1. *n.* Sturm, ⸗e *m.* **2.** *vb.* stürmen.

stormy, *adj.* stürmisch.

story, *n.* Erzäh´lung, -en *f.,* Geschich´te, -n *f.*

stout, *adj.* dick; *(strong)* wacker.

stove, *n. (cooking)* Herd, -e *m.; (heating)* Ofen, ⸗ *m.*

straight, *adj.* gera´de; *(honest)* ehrlich.

straighten, *vb.* gera´de machen; in Ordnung bringen*.

straightforward, *adj.* offen.

strain, 1. *n.* Anstrengung, - en *f.;* Belas´tung, -en *f.* **2.** *vb.* an•strengen; belas´ten; *(filter)* seihen.

strait, *n.* Meeresenge, -n *f.*

strand, 1. *n.* Strähne, -n *f.* **2.** *vb.* stranden.

strange, *adj.* merkwürdig; *(foreign)* fremd.

stranger, *n.* Fremd- *m.& f.*

strangle, *vb.* erwür´gen.

strap, *n.* Riemen, -n *m.*

stratagem, *n.* Kriegslist, -en *f.*

strategic, *adj.* strate´gisch.

strategy, *n.* Strategie´ *f.*

stratosphere, *n.* Stratosphä´re *f.*

stratum, *n.* Schicht, -en *f.*

straw, *n.* Stroh *nt.; (for drinking)* Strohalm, -e *m.*

strawberry, *n.* Erdbeere, -n *f.*

stray, 1. *adj.* verein´zelt. **2.** *vb.* ab•weichen; ab•schweifen.

streak, *n.* Strähne, -n *f.*

stream, *n.* Strom, ⸗e *m.; (small)* Bach, ⸗e *m.*

streamlined, *adj.* stromlinienförmig.

street, *n.* Straße, -n *f.*

streetcar, *n.* Straßenbahn, - en *f.*

strength, *n.* Kraft, ⸗e *f.,* Stärke, -n *f.*

strengthen, *vb.* stärken.

strenuous, *adj.* anstrengend.

stress, 1. *n.* Belas´tung, -en *f.; (accent)* Beto´nung, - en *f.* **2.** *vb.* belas´ten; beto´nen.

stretch, 1. *n.* Strecke, -n *f.;* Spanne, -n *f.* **2.** *vb.* strecken; spannen.

stretcher, *n.* Tragbahre, -n *f.*

strew, *vb.* streuen.

stricken, *adj.* getrof´fen.

strict, *adj.* streng.

stride, 1. *n.* Schritt, -e *m.* **2.** *vb.* schreiten*.

strife, *n.* Streit *m.*

strike, 1. *n. (workers')* Streik, -s *m.* **2.** *vb.* streiken; *(hit)* schlagen*.

string, 1. *n.* Bindfaden, ⸗ *m.,* Schnur, ⸗e *f.; (music)* Saite, -n *f.* **2.** *vb.* auf•reihen.

string bean, *n.* grüne Bohne, -n *f.*

strip, 1. *n.* Streifen, - *m.* **2.** *vb.* ab•streifen; entklei´den.

stripe, *n.* Streifen, - *m.*

strive, *vb.* streben.

stroke, 1. *n.* Schlag, ⸗e *m.; (pen, brush, etc.)* Strich, -e *m.; (med.)* Schlaganfall, ⸗e *m.* **2.** *vb.* streicheln.

stroll, 1. *n.* kleiner Spazier´gang, ⸗e *m.* **2.** *vb.* spazie´ren•gehen*.

stroller, *n.* Spazier´gänger, *m.; (baby-carriage)* Kindersportwagen, - *m.*

strong, *adj.* stark (⸗), kräftig.

stronghold, *n.* Feste, -n *f.*

structure, *n.* Struktur´, -en *f.*

struggle, 1. *n.* Ringen *nt.* **2.** *vb.* ringen*.

strut, *vb.* stolzie´ren.

stub, 1. *n.* Kontroll´abschnitt, -e *m.* **2.** *vb.* an•stoßen*.

stubborn, *adj.* hartnäckig; *(person)* dickköpfig.

student, *n.* Student´, -en, - en *m.,* Studen´tin, -nen *f.*

studio, *n.* Atelier´, -s *nt.*

studious, *adj.* eifrig.

study, 1. *n.* Studium, -dien *nt.; (room)* Arbeitszimer, - *nt.* **2.** *vb.* studie´ren; *(do homework)* arbeiten.

stuff, 1. *n.* Zeug *nt.* **2.** *vb.* stopfen.

stuffing, *n.* Füllung, -en *f.*

stumble, *vb.* stolpern.

stump, *n.* Stumpf, ⸗e *m.*

stun, *vb.* betäu´ben; verblüffen.

stunt, *n.* Kunststück, -e *nt.*

stupid, *adj.* dumm (⸗), blöde.

stupidity, *n.* Dummheit, -en *f.*

stupor, *n.* Betäu´bungszustand *m.*

sturdy, *adj.* stark (⸗), stämmig.

stutter, *vb.* stottern.

sty, *n.* Schweinestall, ⸗e *m.; (eye)* Gerstenkorn, ⸗er *nt.*

style, *n.* Stil, -e *m.*

stylish, *adj.* elegant´.

suave, *adj.* verbind´lich.

subconscious, *adj.* unterbewußt.

subdue, *vb.* unterdrü´cken.

subject, 1. *n. (gram.)* Subjekt, -e *nt.; (topic)* Thema, -men *nt.; (of king)* Untertan, -en, -en *m.* **2.** *adj.* unterwor´fen. **3.** *vb.* unterwer´fen*; aus•setzen.

subjugate, *vb.* unterjo´chen.

subjunctive, *n.* Konjunktiv, -e *m.*

sublime, *adj.* erha´ben.

submarine, *n.* Unterseeboot, -e *nt.,* U-Boot, -e *nt.*

submerge, *vb.* unter•tauchen.

submission, *n.* Unterwer´fung, -en *f.*

submit, *vb. (lay before)* unterbrei´ten; *(offer opinion)* anheim•stellen; *(yield)* sich fügen; *(surrender)* sich unterwer´fen*.

subnormal, *adj.* unternormal.

subordinate, 1. *n.* Unterge´ben- *m. & f.* **2.** *adj.* untergeordnet; *(s. clause)* Nebensatz, ⸗e *m.*

subscribe, *vb. (underwrite)* zeichnen; *(take regularly)* abonnie´ren; *(approve)* billigen.

subscription, *n.* Abonnement´, -s *nt.;* Zeichnung, -en *f.*

subsequent, *adj.* folgend.

subside, *vb.* nach•lassen*.

subsidy, *n.* Zuschuß, ⸗sse *m.*

substance, *n.* Substanz´, -en *f.*

substantial, *adj.* wesentlich; beträcht´lich.

substitute, 1. *n.* Ersatz´ *m.;* Vertre´tung, -en *f.* **2.** *vb.* erset´zen; als Ersatz´ geben*; die Vertre´tung überneh´men*.

substitution, *n.* Erset´zung, -en *f.*

subtle, *adj.* subtil´, fein.

subtract, *vb.* ab•ziehen*.

suburb, *n.* Vorort, -e *m.*

subversive, *adj.* zerset´zend, staatsfeindlich.

subway, *n.* Untergrundbahn, -en *f.,* U-Bahn, -en *f.*

succeed, *vb.* erfolg´reich sein*, gelin´gen*; *(come after)* folgen.

success, *n.* Erfolg´, -e *m.*

successful, *adj.* erfolg´reich.

succession, *n. (to throne)* Erbfolge, -n *f.; (sequence)* Reihenfolge, -n *f.*

successive, *adj.* aufeinan´derfolgend.

successor, *n.* Nachfolger, - *m.,* Nachfolgerin, -nen *f.*

succumb, *vb.* erlie´gen*.

such, *adj.* solch.

suck, *vb.* saugen, lutschen.

suction, *n.* Saugen *nt.;* Saug- *(cpds.).*

sudden, *adj.* plötzlich, jäh.

sue, *vb.* verkla´gen; gericht´lich belan´gen.

suffer, *vb.* leiden*.

suffice, *vb.* genü´gen, aus•reichen.

sufficient, *adj.* genü´gend.

suffocate, *vb.* ersti´cken.

sugar, *n.* Zucker *m.*

suggest, *vb.* vor•schlagen*.

suggestion, *n.* Vorschlag, ⸗e *m.*

suicide, *n.* Selbstmord, -e *m.*

suit, 1. *n. (man's clothing)* Anzug, ⸗e *m.; (woman's clothing)* Kostüm´, -e *nt.; (cards)* Farbe, -n *f.; (law)* Prozeß´, -sse *m.* **2.** *vb.* passen; *(be becoming)* stehen*.

suitable, *adj.* passend; angemessen.

suitcase, *n.* Koffer, - *m.*

suitor, *n.* Freier, - *m.*

sullen, *adj.* griesgrämig.

sum, *n.* Summe, -n *f.*

summarize, *vb.* zusam´men•fassen.

summary, 1. *n.* Übersicht, -en *f.* **2.** *adj.* summa´risch.

summer, *n.* Sommer, - *m.*

summit, *n.* Gipfel, - *m.;* Gipfelkonferenz *f.*

summon, *vb.* zusam´men•rufen*, ein•berufen*; *(law)* vor•laden*.

sun, *n.* Sonne, -n *f.*

sunburn, *n.* Sonnenbrand, ⸗e *m.*

sunburned, *adjz.* sonnenverbrannt.

Sunday, *n.* Sonntag, -e *m.*

sunken, *adj.* versun´ken.

sunny, *adj.* sonnig.

sunshine, *n.* Sonnenschein *m.*

superb, *adj.* hervor´ragend.

superficial, *adj.* oberfläch´lich.

superfluous, *adj.* überflüssig.

super-highway, *n.* Autobahn, -en *f.*

superior, 1. *n.* Vorgesetzt- *m. & f.* **2.** *adj.* höher; überle´gen.

superiority, *n.* Überle´genheit *f.*

superlative, 1. *n.* Superlativ, -e *m.* **2.** *adj.* überra´gend.

supernatural, *adj.* übernatürlich.

supersede, *vb.* verdrän´gen; erset´zen.

supersonic, *adj.* Überschall- *(cpds.).*

superstar, *n.* Superstar, -s *m.*

superstition, *n.* Aberglaube(n), - *m.*

superstitious, *adj.* abergläubisch.

supervise, *vb.* beauf´sichtigen.

supervisor, *n.* Aufseher, - *m.*, Aufseherin, -nen *f.*

supper, *n.* Abendbrot, -e *nt.*, Abendessen, - *nt.*; (**Lord's S.**) Abendmahl, -e *nt.*

supplement, *n.* Ergän´zung, -en *f.*, Nachtrag, ⸗e *m.*

supply, 1. *n.* Versor´gung *f.*; Vorrat, ⸗e *m.*; (**s. and demand**) Angebot (*nt.*) und Nachfrage (*f.*). **2.** *vb.* versor´gen, liefern.

support, 1. *n.* Stütze, -n *f.*; Unterstüt´zung, -en *f.* **2.** *vb.* stützen; unterstüt´zen.

suppose, *vb.* an•nehmen, vermu´ten.

suppress, *vb.* unterdrü´cken.

suppression, *n.* Unterdrü´ckung, -en *f.*

supreme, *adj.* oberst-, höchst-; Ober- (*cpds.*).

sure, *adj.* sicher.

surely, *adv.* sicherlich, gewiß.

surf, *n.* Brandung, -en *f.*

surface, *n.* Oberfläche, -n *f.*

surge, *vb.* wogen, branden.

surgeon, *n.* Chirurg´, -en, -en *m.*, Chirur´gin, -nen *f.*

surgery, *n.* Chirurgie´ *f.*; Operation´, -en *f.*

surmise, 1. *n.* Vermu´tung, -en *f.* **2.** *vb.* vermu´ten.

surmount, *vb.* überwin´den*.

surname, *n.* Zuname(n), - *m.*, Fami´lienname(n), - *m.*

surpass, *vb.* übersteigen*, übertref´fen*.

surplus, 1. *n.* Überschuß, ⸗sse *m.* **2.** *adj.* überschüssig; Über- (*cpds.*).

surprise, 1. *n.* Überra´schung, -en *f.* **2.** *vb.* überra´schen.

surrender, 1. *n.* Übergabe *f.*, Erge´bung, -en *f.*

surround, *vb.* umge´ben*; umzin´geln.

surroundings, *n.pl.* Umge´bung, -en *f.*

survey, 1. *n.* Überblick, -e *m.*; (*measuring*) Vermes´sung, -en *f.* **2.** *vb.* überbli´cken; vermes´sen*.

survival, *n.* Überle´ben *nt.*

survive, *vb.* überle´ben.

susceptible, *adj.* empfänglich, zugänglich.

suspend, *vb.* (*debar*) suspendie´ren; (*stop temporarily*) zeitweilig auf•heben*; (*payment*) ein•stellen; (*sentence*) aus•setzen; (*hang*) auf•hängen.

suspense, *n.* Schwebe *f.*; Spannung, -en *f.*

suspension, *n.* Schwebe *f.*; Suspension´, -en *f.*

suspicion, *n.* Verdacht´ *m.*, Argwohn *m.*

suspicious, *adj.* (*doubting*) misstrauisch; (*doubtful looking*) verdäch´tig.

sustain, *vb.* aufrecht•erhalten*; (*suffer*) erlei´den*.

swallow, 1. *n.* (*bird*) Schwalbe, -n *f.*; (*gulp*) Schluck, -e *m.* **2.** *vb.* schlucken.

swamp, 1. *n.* Sumpf, ⸗e *m.* **2.** *vb.* überschwem´men.

swan, *n.* Schwan, ⸗e *m.*

swarm, 1. *n.* Schwarm, ⸗e *m.* **2.** *vb.* schwärmen; (*fig.*) wimmeln.

sway, *vb.* schwingen*; schwanken.

swear, *vb.* schwören; (*curse*) fluchen.

sweat, 1. *n.* Schweiß *m.* **2.** *vb.* schwitzen.

sweater, *n.* Pullo´ver, - *m.*, Strickjacke, -n *f.*

Swede, *n.* Schwede, -n, -n *m.*, Schwedin, -nen *f.*

Sweden, *n.* Schweden *nt.*

Swedish, *adj.* schwedisch.

sweet, *adj.* süß.

sweetheart, *n.* Liebst- *m.& f.*

sweetness, *n.* Süße *f.*; (*fig.*) Anmut *f.*

swell, 1. *adj.* prima. **2.** *vb.* schwellen*.

swift, *adj.* rasch, geschwind´.

swim, *vb.* schwimmen*.

swindle, *vb.* schwindeln.

swindler, *n.* Schwindler, - *m.*

swine, *n.* Schwein, -e *nt.*

swing, 1. *n.* Schaukel, -n *f.* **2.** *vb.* schwingen*, schaukeln.

Swiss, 1. *n.* Schweizer, - *m.*, Schweizerin, -nen *f.* **2.** *adj.* schweizerisch; Schweizer- (*cpds.*).

switch, 1. *n.* (*whip*) Gerte, -n *f.*; (*railway*) Weiche, -n *f.*; (*elec.*) Schalter, - *m.* **2.** *vb.* (*railway*) rangie´ren; um•schalten; (*exchange*) vertau´schen.

Switzerland, *n.* die Schweiz *f.*

sword, *n.* Schwert, -er *nt.*

syllabic, *adj.* silbisch.

syllable, *n.* Silbe, -n *f.*

symbol, *n.* Symbol´, -e *nt.*

symbolic, *adj.* symbo´lisch.

sympathetic, *adj.* mitfühlend; (*med.*) sympa´thisch.

sympathize, *vb.* mit•fühlen.

sympathy, *n.* Sympathie´, -i´en *f.*

symphonic, *adj.* sympho´nisch.

symphony, *n.* Symphonie´, -i´en *f.*

symptom, *n.* Anzeichen, - *nt.*, Symptom´, -e *nt.*

symptomatic, *adj.* symptoma´tisch; charakteris´tisch.

syndicate, *n.* Syndikat´, -e *nt.*

syndrome, *n.* Syndrom´, -e *nt.*

synonym, *n.* Synonym´, -e *nt.*

synonymous, *adj.* sinnverwandt, synonym´.

synthetic, *adj.* synthe´tisch, künstlich; Kunst- (*cpds.*).

syphilis, *n.* Syphilis *f.*

syringe, *n.* Spritze, -n *f.*

syrup, *n.* Sirup *m.*

system, *n.* System´, -e *nt.*

systematic, *adj.* systema´tisch.

table 258 ENGLISH-GERMAN

T

table, n. Tisch, -e m.; *(list)* Verzeich´nis, -se nt.

tablecloth, n. Tischdecke, -n f., Tischtuch, ≈er nt.

tablespoon, n. Eßlöffel, - m.

tablet, n. Tafel, -n f.; *(pill)* Tablet´te, -n f.

tack, 1. n. Stift, -e m.; **(thumb t.)** Heftzwecke, -n f. **2.** vb. *(sew)* heften; *(sail)* kreuzen.

tact, n. Takt m.

tag, n. Etikett, -e nt.; **(play t.)** Fangen spielen.

tail, n. Schwanz, ≈e m.

tailor, n. Schneider, - m.

take, vb. nehmen*; *(carry)* bringen*; *(need)* erfor´-dern.

tale, n. Geschich´te, -n f., Erzäh´lung, -en f.

talent, n. Bega´bung, -en f., Talent´, -e nt.

talk, 1. n. Gespräch´, -e nt.; *(lecture)* Vortrag, ≈e m. **2.** vb. reden, sprechen*.

talkative, adj. gesprä´chig.

tall, adj. groß (≈); hoch (hoh-, höher, höchst-); lang (≈).

tame, 1. adj. zahm. **2.** vb. zähmen.

tamper, vb. herum´-pfuschen.

tan, 1. n. *(sun)* Sonnen-bräune f. **2.** adj. gelb-braun. **3.** vb. bräunen; *(leather)* gerben.

tangle, 1. n. Gewirr´ nt. **2.** vb. sich zu schaffen machen mit.

tank, n. Tank, -s m.; *(mil.)* Panzer, - m.

tap, 1. n. *(blow)* Taps, -e m.; *(faucet)* Hahn, ≈e m. **2.** vb. leicht schlagen*; *(wire)* an•zapfen.

tape, n. Band, ≈er nt.

tape recorder, n. Ton-bandgerät, -e nt., Magne-tophon´, -e nt.

tapestry, n. Wandteppich, -e m.; Tapisserie´, -i´en f.

tar, 1. n. Teer m. **2.** vb. teeren.

target, n. Ziel, -e nt.; Zielscheibe, -n f.

tariff, n. Zolltarif, -e m.

tarnish, vb. *(fig.)* befle´cken; *(silver)* sich beschla´gen*.

tart, 1. n. Törtchen, - nt. **2.** adj. sauer, herb.

task, n. Aufgabe, -n f.

taste, 1. n. Geschmack´, ≈e m. **2.** vb. schmecken, kosten.

tasty, adj. schmackhaft.

taut, adj. straff.

tavern, n. Bierlokal, -e nt.

tax, 1. n. Steuer, -n f. **2.** vb. besteu´ern, belas´ten.

taxi, n. Taxe, -n f., Taxi, -s nt.

taxpayer, n. Steuerzahler, - m.

tea, n. Tee, -s m.

teach, vb. lehren, unterrich´ten.

teacher, n. Lehrer, - m., Lehrerin, -nen f.

tea-pot, n. Teekanne, -n f.

tear, 1. n. Träne, -n f.; *(rip)* Riß, -sse m. **2.** vb. reißen*.

tease, vb. necken.

teaspoon, n. Teelöffel, - m.

technical, adj. technisch.

technique, n. Technik, -en f., Kunstfertigkeit f.

tedious, adj. langweilig, mühsam.

telegram, n. Telegramm´, -e nt.

telegraph, 1. n. Telegraph´, -en, -en m. **2.** vb. telegra-phie´ren.

telephone, 1. n. Telephon´, -e nt., Fernsprecher, - m. **2.** vb. telephonie´ren.

telescope, n. Fernrohr, -e nt.

televise, vb. im Fernsehen übertra´gen*.

television, n. Fernsehen nt.

television set, n. Fernsehap-parat, -e m.

tell, vb. erzäh´len, berich´-ten, sagen.

teller, n. Kassie´rer, - m.

temper, 1. n. Laune, -n f.; Temperament´ nt.;

(anger) Zorn m. **2.** vb. mäßigen; *(steel)* härten.

temperament, n. Gemüts´art, -en f.

temperamental, adj. Gemüts´- *(cpds.)*; tem-perament´voll.

temperate, adj. mäßig.

temperature, n. Temperatur´, -en f.

tempest, n. Sturm, ≈e m.

temple, n. Tempel, - m.

temporary, adj. zeitweilig, vorü´bergehend, proviso´risch.

tempt, vb. versu´chen; reizen.

temptation, n. Versu´chung, -en f.

ten, num. zehn.

tenant, n. Mieter, - m., Mi-eterin, -nen f.; Pächter, -, -nen f.

tend, vb. pflegen, hüten; *(incline)* neigen zu.

tendency, n. Neigung, -en f., Tendenz´, -en f.

tender, 1. n. *(money)* Zahlungsmittel, - nt.; *(train, boat)* Tender, - m. **2.** adj. zart; zärtlich. **3.** vb. an•bieten*.

tenderness, n. Zartheit, -en f., Zärtlichkeit, -en f.

tendon, n. Sehne, -n f.

tennis, n. Tennis nt.

tenor, n. Tenor´, -e m.

tense, adj. gespannt´; kribbelig.

tension, n. Spannung, -en f.

tent, n. Zelt, -e nt.

tentative´, adj. probeweise.

tenth, 1. adj. zehnt-. **2.** n. Zehntel, - nt.

term, n. Perio´de, -n f.; *(of office)* Amtszeit, -en f.; *(college)* Semes´ter, - nt.; *(expression)* Ausdruck, ≈e m.; *(condition)* Bedin´gung, -en f.

terminal, 1. n. *(rail)* Endbahn-hof, ≈e m.; *(air)* Termi-nal, -s m.

terminate, vb. been´den; begren´zen.

terrace, n. Terras´se, -n f.

terrible, *adj.* schrecklich, furchtbar.

terrify, *vb.* erschre´cken.

territory, *n.* Gebiet´, -e *nt.*

terror, *n.* Schrecken, - *m.,* Terror *m.*

terrorism, *n.* Terroris´mus *m.*

terrorist, *n.* Terrorist´ *m.;* Terroris´tin *f.*

test, 1. *n.* Prüfung, -en *f.;* Probe, -n *f.;* Test, -s *m.;* Versuch´, -e *m.* **2.** *vb.* prüfen.

testify, *vb.* bezeu´gen; *(court)* aus•sagen.

testimony, *n.* Zeugnis, -se *nt.;* Zeugenaussage, -n *f.*

text, *n.* Text, -e *m.*

textile, 1. *n.* Textil´ware, -n *f.* **2.** *adj.* Textil´- *(cpds.).*

texture, *n.* Gewe´be, - *nt.;* Aufbau *m.;* Beschaf´fenheit, -en *f.*

than, *conj.* als.

thank, *vb.* danken.

thankful, *adj.* dankbar.

that, 1. *pron.& adj.* der, das, die; jener, -es, -e. **2.** *conj.* daß.

thaw, *vb.* tauen.

the, *art.* der, das, die.

theater, *n.* Thea´ter, - *nt.;* *(fig.)* Schauplatz, ⸗e *m.*

thee, *pron.* dich; dir.

theft, *n.* Diebstahl, ⸗e *m.*

their, *adj.* ihr, -, -e.

theirs, *pron.* ihrer, -es, -e.

them, *pron.* sie; ihnen.

theme, *n.* Thema, -men *nt.*

then, *adv. (after that)* dann; *(at that time)* damals; *(therefore)* dann, also.

thence, *adv.* von da, von dort.

theology, *n.* Theologie´ *f.*

theoretical, *adj.* theore´tisch.

theory, *n.* Theorie´, -i´en *f.*

therapy, *n.* Therapie´ *f.*

there, *adv. (in that place)* da, dort; *(to that place)* dahin´, dorthin´; *(from t.)* daher´, dorther´.

therefore, *adv.* daher, darum, deshalb, deswegen, also.

thermometer, *n.* Thermome´ter, - *nt.*

thermonuclear, *adj.* kernphysikalisch.

these, *adj.* diese.

they, *pron.* sie.

thick, *adj.* dick; *(dense)* dicht.

thicken, *vb.* dicken, verdi´cken.

thickness, *n.* Dicke *f.;* Dichtheit *f.; (layer)* Schicht, -en *f.*

thief, *n.* Dieb, -e *m.*

thigh, *n.* Schenkel, - *m.*

thimble, *n.* Fingerhut, ⸗e *m.*

thin, *adj.* dünn; mager.

thing, *n.* Ding, -e *nt.;* Sache, -n *f.*

think, *vb.* meinen, glauben; denken*, nach•denken*.

thinker, *n.* Denker, - *m.*

third, 1. *adj.* dritt-. **2.** *n.* Drittel, - *nt.*

Third World, *n.* Dritte Welt *f.*

thirst, 1. *n.* Durst *m.* **2.** *vb.* dürsten.

thirsty, *adj.* durstig.

thirteen, *num.* dreizehn.

thirteenth, 1. *adj.* dreizehnt-. **2.** *n.* Dreizehntel, - *nt.*

thirtieth, 1. *adj.* dreißigst-. **2.** *n.* Dreißigstel, - *nt.*

thirty, *num.* dreißig.

this, *pron.& adj.* dieser, -es, -e.

thorough, *adj.* gründlich.

thou, *pron.* du.

though, 1. *adv.* doch. **2.** *conj.* obwohl´, obgleich´.

thought, *n.* Gedan´ke(n), - *m.*

thoughtful, *adj.* gedan´kenvoll; *(considerate)* rücksichtsvoll.

thousand, *num.* tausend.

thousandth, 1. *adj.* tausendst-. **2.** Tausendstel, - *nt.*

thread, *n.* Faden, ⸗ *m.;* Garn, -e *nt.*

threat, *n.* Drohung, -en *f.*

threaten, *vb.* drohen.

three, *num.* drei.

thrift, *n.* Sparsamkeit *f.*

thrill, 1. *n.* Aufregung, -en *f.;* Sensation´, -en *f.;* Nervenkitzel, - *m.* **2.** *vb.* erre´gen, packen.

throat, *n.* Hals, ⸗e *m.,* Kehle, -n *f.*

throb, *vb.* pochen, pulsie´ren.

throne, *n.* Thron, -e *m.*

through, 1. *prep.* durch. **2.** *adj.* fertig.

throughout, 1. *adv.* überall; völlig. **2.** *prep.* durch.

throw, 1. *n.* Wurf, ⸗e *m.* **2.** *vb.* werfen*, schleudern.

thrust, 1. *n.* Stoß, ⸗e *m.;* *(tech.)* Schub *m.* **2.** *vb.* stoßen*.

thumb, *n.* Daumen, - *m.*

thunder, 1. *n.* Donner, - *m.* **2.** *vb.* donnern.

thunderstorm, *n.* Gewit´ter, - *nt.*

Thursday, *n.* Donnerstag, - e *m.*

thus, *adv.* so.

ticket, *n.* Karte, -n *f.,* Billett´, -s *or* -e *nt.; (admission)* Eintrittskarte, -n *f.; (travel)* Fahrkarte, -n *f.,* Fahrschein, -e *m.; (traffic)* Strafmandat, -e *nt.*

tickle, *vb.* kitzeln.

ticklish, *adj.* kitzlig; *(delicate, risky)* heikel.

tide, 1. *n.* Gezei´ten *pl.; (low t.)* Ebbe *f.; (high t.)* Flut *f.*

tidy, *adj.* sauber, ordentlich.

tie, 1. *n. (bond)* Band, -e *nt.; (necktie)* Krawat´te, -n *f.,* Schlips, -e *m.; (equal score)* Punktgleichheit *f.,* Stimmengleichheit *f.* **2.** *vb.* binden*, knüpfen.

tiger, *n.* Tiger, - *m.*

tight, *adj.* eng; *(taut)* straff; *(firm)* fest; *(drunk)* beschwipst´.

tighten, *vb.* straffen, enger machen.

tile, *n. (wall, stove)* Kachel, - *f.; (floor)* Fliese, -n *f.; (roof)* Ziegel, - *m.*

till, 1. *n.* Ladenkasse, -n *f.* **2.** *vb.* bebau´en, bestel´len. **3.** *adv., conj.* bis.

tilt, 1. *n.* Neigung, -en *f.* **2.** *vb.* neigen, kippen.

timber, *n.* Holz *nt.*

time, 1. *n.* Zeit, -en *f.; (o´clock)* Uhr *f.* **2.** *vb.* die Zeit nehmen*.

timetable, *n.* Fahrplan, ≃e *m.*, Kursbuch, ≃er *nt.*

timid, *adj.* ängstlich, schüchtern.

timidity, *n.* Ängstlichkeit *f.*, Schüchternheit *f.*

tin, *n.* (*metal*) Zinn *nt.*; (**t. plate**) Blech *nt.*; (**t. can**) Konser´vendose, -n *f.*

tint, *n.* Farbtönung, -en *f.*

tiny, *adj.* winzig.

tip, 1. *n.* (*end*) Spitze, -n *f.*; (*gratuity*) Trinkgeld, -er *nt.* **2.** *vb.* (*tilt*) kippen; (*give gratuity*) ein Trinkgeld geben*.

tire, 1. *n.* Reifen, - *m.* **2.** *vb.* ermü´den.

tired, *adj.* müde.

tissue, *n.* Gewe´be, - *nt.*; (**facial t.**) Papier´taschentuch, ≃er *nt.*

title, *n.* Titel, - *m.*; (*heading*) Überschrift, -en *f.*

to, *prep.* zu.

toast, 1. *n.* Toast *m.*; (*drink to health*) Trinkspruch, ≃e *m.* **2.** *vb.* rösten; auf Wohl trinken*.

tobacco, *n.* Tabak *m.*

today, *adv.* heute.

toe, *n.* Zehe, -n *f.*

together, *adv.* zusam´men.

toil, 1. *n.* Arbeit, -en *f.*, Mühe, -n *f.* **2.** *vb.* arbeiten, sich ab•mühen.

toilet, *n.* Toilet´te, -n *f.*; (**t. paper**) Toilettenpapier *nt.*

token, *n.* Zeichen, - *nt.*; Symbol´, -e *nt.*

tolerance, *n.* Duldsamkeit *f.*, Toleranz´ *f.*

tolerant, *adj.* duldsam, tolerant´.

tolerate, *vb.* dulden.

toll, 1. *n.* Zoll *m.*; (*highway*) Wegegeld, -er *nt.*, (*bridge*) Brückengeld, -er *nt.* **2.** *vb.* läuten.

tomato, *n.* Toma´te, -n *f.*

tomb, *n.* Grab, ≃er *nt.*, Grabmal, ≃er *nt.*

tomorrow, *adv.* morgen.

ton, *n.* Tonne, -n *f.*

tone, *n.* Ton, ≃e *m.*

tongue, *n.* Zunge, -n *f.*

tonic, 1. *n.* Stärkungsmittel *nt.* **2.** *adj.* tonisch.

tonight, *adv.* heute abend.

tonsil, *n.* Mandel, -n *f.*

too, *adv.* zu; (*also*) auch.

tool, *n.* Werkzeug, -e *nt.*

tooth, *n.* Zahn, ≃e *m.*

toothache, *n.* Zahnschmerzen *pl.*

toothbrush, *n.* Zahnbürste, -n *f.*

toothpaste, *n.* Zahnpaste, -n *f.*

top, 1. *n.* Spitze, -n *f.*, oberstes Ende, -n *nt.*; (*surface*) Oberfläche, -n *f.*; (**on t. of all**) auf. **2.** *vb.* (*fig.*) krönen.

topcoat, *n.* Mantel, ≃ *m.*

topic, *n.* Thema, -men *nt.*

torch, *n.* Fackel, -n *f.*

torment, 1. *n.* Qual, -en *f.* **2.** *vb.* quälen.

torrent, *n.* reißender Strom, ≃e *m.*

torture, 1. *n.* Folter, -n *f.*, Qual, -en *f.* **2.** *vb.* foltern, quälen.

toss, *vb.* werfen*, schleudern.

total, 1. *n.* Summe, -n *f.* **2.** *adj.* gesamt´; total´.

totalitarian, *adj.* totalitär´.

touch, 1. *n.* Berüh´rung, -en *f.*; (*sense of t.*) Tastsinn *m.*; (**final t.**) letzter Schliff, -e *f.* **2.** *vb.* berüh´ren.

touching, *adj.* rührend.

tough, 1. *n.* Rabau´ke, -n, -n *m.* **2.** *adj.* zäh; (*hard*) hart (≃).

tour, 1. *n.* Reise, -n *f.*, Tour, -en *f.* **2.** *vb.* berei´sen.

tourist, *n.* Tourist´, -en, -en *m.*, Touris´tin, -nen *f.*

tourist office, *n.* Fremdenverkehrsbüro, -s *nt.*

tow, *vb.* schleppen.

toward, *prep.* nach; gegen; zu.

towel, *n.* Handtuch, ≃er *nt.*

tower, *n.* Turm, -e *m.*

town, *n.* Stadt, ≃e *f.*, Ort, -e *m.*

toy, 1. *n.* Spielzeug, -e *nt.* **2.** *vb.* spielen.

trace, 1. *n.* Spur, -en *f.* **2.** *vb.* (*delineate*) nach•zeichnen; (*track*) zurück´•verfolgen.

track, 1. *n.* Spur, -en *f.*, Fährte, -n *f.*; (*sports*) Leichtathletik *f.*; (*R.R.*) Gelei´se, - *nt.*, Gleis, -e *nt.* **2.** *vb.* (**t. down**) nach•spüren.

tract, *n.* (*land*) Gebiet´, -e *nt.*; (*pamphlet*) Traktat´, -e *nt.*

tractor, *n.* Trecker, - *m.*

trade, 1. *n.* Handel *m.*; (*exchange*) Tausch *m.* **2.** *vb.* Handel treiben*; aus•tauschen.

trader, *n.* Händler, - *m.*

tradition, *n.* Tradition´, -en *f.*

traditional, *adj.* traditionell´.

traffic, *n.* Verkehr´ *m.*; (*trade*) Handel *m.*

traffic light, *n.* Verkehrs´licht, -er *nt.*, Verkehrs´ampel, -n *f.*

tragedy, *n.* Tragö´die, -n *f.*

tragic, *adj.* tragisch.

trail, *n.* Fährte, -n *f.*

trailer, *n.* Anhänger, - *m.*; (*for living*) Wohnwagen, - *m.*

train, 1. *n.* Zug, ≃e *m.*; (*of dress*) Schleppe, -n *f.* **2.** *vb.* aus•bilden.

traitor, *n.* Verrä´ter, - *m.*, Verrä´terin, -nen *f.*

tramp, *n.* Landstreicher, - *m.*

tranquil, *adj.* ruhig.

tranquillity, *n.* Ruhe *f.*

tranquillizer, *n.* Beruhigungsmittel, -, *nt.*

transaction, *n.* Transaktion´, -en *f.*

transfer, 1. *n.* (*ticket*) Umsteigefahrschein, -e *m.* **2.** *vb.* (*change cars*) um•steigen*; (*money*) überwei´sen*; (*ownership*) übertra´gen*; (*move*) verset´zen.

transfix, *vb.* durchboh´ren.

transform, *vb.* um•wandeln, um•formen.

transfusion, *n.* Transfusion´, -en *f.*

transition, *n.* Übergang, ∸e *m.*

translate, *vb.* überset′zen.

translation, *n.* Überset′zung, -en *f.*

transmit, *vb.* übertra′gen*; übersen′den.

transparent, *adj.* durchsichtig.

transport, 1. *n.* Beför′derung, -en *f.,* Transport′, -e *m.* **2.** *vb.* beför′dern, transportie′ren.

transportation, *n.* Beför′derung, -en *f.*

transsexual, *adj.* transsexuell′.

transvestite, *n.* Transvestit′, -en, -en *m.*

trap, *n.* Falle, -n *f.*

trash, *n.* Abfall, ∸e *m.; (fig.)* Kitsch *m.*

travel, 1. *n.* Reise, -n *f.* **2.** *vb.* reisen.

travel agency, *n.* Reisebüro, -s *nt.*

traveler, *n.* Reisend - *m.&f.*

traveler's check, *n.* Reisescheck, -s *m.*

tray, *n.* Tablett′, -e *nt.*

treacherous, *adj.* verrä′terisch; tückisch.

tread, 1. *n.* Schritt, -e *m.* **2.** *vb.* treten*.

treason, *n.* Verrat′ *m.*

treasure, 1. *n.* Schatz, ∸e *m.* **2.** *vb.* hoch•schätzen.

treasurer, *n.* Schatzmeister, - *m.*

treasury, *n.* Finanz′ministerium, -rien *nt.*

treat, 1. *n.* Extragenuß, ∸sse *m.* **2.** *vb.* gehandeln; *(pay for)* frei•halten*.

treatment, *n.* Behand′lung, -en *f.*

treaty, *n.* Vertrag′, ∸e *m.*

tree, *n.* Baum, ∸e *m.*

tremble, *vb.* zittern.

tremendous, *adj.* ungeheuer.

trench, *n.* Graben, ∸ *m.*

trend, *n.* Trend, -s *m.*

trespass, *vb.* widerrechtlich betre′ten*; übertre′ten*.

triage, *n.* Einteilung je nach Priorität *f.*

trial, *n.* Versuch′, -e *m.; (jur.)* Prozeß′, ∸sse *m.*

triangle, *n.* Dreieck, -e *nt.*

tribute, *n.* Tribut′, -e *m.; (fig.)* Ehrung, -en *f.*

trick, 1. *n.* Kniff, -e *m.,* Trick, -s *m.* **2.** *vb.* rein•legen.

tricky, *adj.* knifflig; heikel.

trifle, *n.* Kleinigkeit, -en *f.,* Lappa′lie, -n *f.*

trigger, *n. (gun)* Abzug, ∸e *m.*

trim, 1. *adj.* adrett′. **2.** *vb. (clip)* stutzen; *(adorn)* beset′zen.

trip, 1. *n.* Reise, -n *f.* **2.** *vb.* stolpern; *(tr.)* einem ein Bein stellen.

triple, 1. *adj.* dreifach. **2.** *vb.* verdrei′fachen.

trite, *adj.* abgedroschen.

triumph, 1. *n.* Triumph′, -e *m.* **2.** *vb.* triumphie′ren.

triumphant, *adj.* triumphie′rend.

trivial, *adj.* trivial′.

trolley-bus, *n.* Obus, -se *m.*

trolley-car, *n.* Straßenbahn, -en *f.*

troop, *n.* Trupp, -s *m.*

troops, *n.pl.* Truppen *pl.*

trophy, *n.* Trophä′e, -n *f.*

tropic, *n.* Wendekreis, -e *m.*

tropical, *adj.* tropisch.

tropics, *n.pl.* Tropen *pl.*

trot, 1. *n.* Trab *m.* **2.** *vb.* traben.

trouble, 1. *n.* Mühe, -n *f.; (difficulty)* Schwierigkeit, -en *f.; (unpleasantness)* Unannehmlichkeit, -en *f.; (jam)* Klemme, -n *f.* **2.** *vb.* bemü′hen; beun′ruhigen.

troublesome, *adj.* lästig.

trough, *n.* Trog, ∸e *m.*

trousers, *n.pl.* Hose, -n *f.*

trousseau, *n.* Aussteuer, -n *f.*

trout, *n.* Forel′le, -n *f.*

truce, *n.* Waffenstillstand, ∸e *m.*

truck, *n.* Lastauto, -s *nt.,* Lastwagen, - *m.,* Lastkraftwagen, - *m.*

true, *adj.* wahr; wahrhaf′tig; *(faithful)* treu.

truly, *adv.* wahrhaf′tig; *(yours t.)* Ihr erge′bener, Ihre erge′bene.

trumpet, *n.* Trompe′te, -n *f.*

trunk, *n. (tree)* Stamm, ∸e *m.; (luggage)* Koffer, - *m.*

trust, 1. *n.* Zuversicht *f.,* Vertrau′en *nt.; (comm.)* Trust, -s *m.; (in t.)* zu treuen Händen. **2.** *vb.* vertrau′en.

trustworthy, *adj.* zuverlässig.

truth, *n.* Wahrheit, -en *f.*

truthful, *adj.* wahr; ehrlich.

try, 1. *n.* Versuch′, -e *m.* **2.** *vb.* versu′chen, probie′ren.

T-shirt, *n.* T-Shirt, -s *nt.*

tub, *n.* Wanne, -n *f.*

tube, *n.* Röhre, -n *f.; (container)* Tube, -n *f.*

tuberculosis, *n.* Tuberkulo′se *f.*

tuck, 1. *n.* Falte, -n *f.* **2.** *vb.* falten.

Tuesday, *n.* Dienstag, -e *m.*

tuft, *n.* Büschel, - *nt.,* Quaste, -n *f.*

tug, *vb.* ziehen*.

tuition, *n.* Schulgeld, -er *nt.; (university)* Studiengeld, -er *nt.*

tulip, *n.* Tulpe, -n *f.*

tumor, *n.* Tumor, -o′ren *m.*

tumult, *n.* Tumult′, -e *m.*

tuna, *n.* Thunfisch, -e *m.*

tune, 1. *n.* Melodie′, -i′en *f.* **2.** *vb.* stimmen.

tuneful, *adj.* melo′disch.

tunnel, *n.* Tunnel, - *m.*

turbine, *n.* Turbi′ne, -n *f.*

turbojet, *n. (plane)* Turbi′nenjäger, - *m.*

turboprop, *n.* Propel′lerturbine *f.*

Turk, *n.* Türke, -n, -n *m.,* Türkin, -nen *f.*

turkey, *n.* Truthahn, ∸e *m.,* Puter, - *m.*

Turkey, *n.* die Türkei *f.*

Turkish, *adj.* türkisch.

turmoil, *n.* Durcheinan′der *nt.*

turn, 1. *n.* Umdre′hung, -en *f.; Wendung, -en *f.,* Kurve, -n *f.; (to take t.s)* sich ab•wechseln; *(it's my t.)* ich bin dran. **2.** *vb.* drehen, wenden*; *(t. around)* um•drehen.

turning point, *n.* Wendepunkt *m.*

turnip, *n.* Steckrübe, -n *f.*

turret, *n.* Turm, ⸗e *m.*

turtle, *n.* Schildkröte, -n *f.*

tutor, 1. *n.* Lehrer, - *m.*, Lehrerin, -nen *f.;* Nachhilfelehrer, - *m.*, Nachhilfelehrerin, -nen *f.* **2.** *vb.* Nachhilfeunterricht geben*.

twelfth, 1. *adj.* zwölft-. **2.** *n.* Zwölftel, - *nt.*

twelve, *num.* zwölf.

twentieth, 1. *adj.* zwanzigst- . **2.** *n.* Zwanzigstel, - *nt.*

twenty, *num.* zwanzig.

twice, *adv.* zweimal.

twig, *n.* Zweig, -e *m.*

twilight, *n.* Dämmerung, - en *f.*, Zwielicht *nt.*

twin, *n.* Zwilling, -e *m.*

twine, 1. *n.* *(thread)* Zwirn, -e *m.; (rope)* Tau, -e *nt.* **2.** *vb.* winden*.

twist, 1. *n.* Drehung, -en *f.; (distortion)* Verdre´hung, -en *f.* **2.** *vb.* drehen; verdre´hen.

two, *num.* zwei.

type, 1. *n.* Typ, -en *m.*, Typus, -pen *m.; (printing)* Schriftsatz, ⸗e *m.; (letter)* Type, -n *f.* **2.** *vb.* kennzeichnen; *(write on typewriter)* tippen.

typewriter, *n.* Schreibmaschine, -n *f.*

typhoid fever, *n.* Typhus *m.*

typical, *adj.* typisch.

typist, *n.* Schreibkraft, -ë *f.*

tyranny, *n.* Tyrannei´ *f.*

tyrant, *n.* Tyrann´, -en, -en *m.*

U

ugliness, *n.* Häßlichkeit *f.*

ugly, *adj.* häßlich.

ulcer, *n.* Geschwür´, -e *nt.*

ulterior, *adj.* höher; weiter; **(u. motives)** Hintergedanken *pl.*

ultimate, *adj.* äußerst-.

umbrella, *n.* Regenschirm, -e *m.*

umpire, *n.* Schiedsrichter, - *m.*

un-, *prefix* un-.

unable, *adj.* unfähig.

unanimous, *adj.* einstimmig.

unbecoming, *adj.* unschicklich; *(of clothes)* unkleidsam.

uncertain, *adj.* ungewiß.

uncertainty, *n.* Ungewißheit, -en *f.*

uncle, *n.* Onkel, - *m.*

unconscious, *adj.* bewußt´los; *(unaware)* unbewußt.

uncover, *vb.* auf•decken; entblö´ßen.

under, *prep.* unter.

underground, 1. *n.* Untergrundbahn, -en *f.* **2.** *adj.* unter der Erde gelegen; Untergrund- *(cpds.).*

underline, *vb.* unterstrei´chen*.

underneath, 1. *adv.* unter, drunter. **2.** *prep.* unter.

undershirt, *n.* Unterhemd, - en *nt.*

undersign, *vb.* unterzeich´nen.

understand, *vb.* verste´hen*, begrei´fen*.

understanding, *n.* Verständ´nis *nt.; (agreement)* Einvernehmen, - *nt.*

undertake, *vb.* unterneh´men*.

undertaker, *n.* Leichenbestatter, - *m.*

underwear, *n.* Unterwäsche *f.*

underworld, *n.* Unterwelt *f.*

undo, *vb.* auf•machen, lösen; ungeschehen machen.

undress, *vb.* entklei´den, (sich) aus•ziehen*.

uneasy, *adj.* unruhig, unbehaglich.

unemployed, *adj.* arbeitslos.

unemployment, *n.* Arbeitslosigkeit *f.*

unemployment insurance, *n.* Arbeitslosenunterstützung *f.*

unequal, *adj.* ungleich.

uneven, *adj.* uneben; ungleich; *(numbers)* ungerade.

unexpected, *adj.* unerwartet.

unfair, *adj.* ungerecht.

unfamiliar, *adj.* unbekannt; ungeläufig.

unfavorable, *adj.* ungünstig.

unfit, *adj.* untauglich.

unfold, *vb.* entfal´ten.

unforgettable, *adj.* unvergeßlich.

unfortunate, *adj.* unglücklich; bedau´erlich.

unhappy, *adj.* unglücklich.

uniform, 1. *n.* Uniform´, -en *f.* **2.** *adj.* einheitlich.

unify, *vb.* verei´nen; verein´heitlichen.

union, *n.* Verei´nigung, -en *f.;* **(labor u.)** Gewerk´schaft, -en *f.*

unique, *adj.* einzigartig.

unisex, *adj.* unisex.

unit, *n.* Einheit, -en *f.*

unite, *vb.* verei´nigen.

United Nations, *n.* Verein´te Natio´nen *pl.*

United States, *n.* Verein´igte Staaten *pl.*

unity, *n.* Einigkeit *f.*

universal, *adj.* universal´.

universe, *n.* Weltall *nt.*

university, *n.* Universität´, - en *f.*

unjust, *adj.* ungerecht.

unknown, *adj.* unbekannt.

unleaded, *adj.* bleifrei.

unless, *conj.* wenn nicht; es sei denn, daß.

unlike, *adj.* ungleich.

unlikely, *adj.* unwahrscheinlich.

unload, *vb.* ab•laden*, aus•laden*.

unlock, *vb.* auf•schließen*.

unlucky, *adj.* **(be u.)** kein Glück haben*, Pech haben*.

unmarried, *adj.* unverheiratet, ledig.

unpack, *vb.* aus•packen.

unpleasant, *adj.* unangenehm.

unqualified, *adj.* *(unfit)* ungeeignet; *(unreserved)* uneingeschränkt.

unsettled, *adj.* unsicher, in der Schwebe.

unsteady, *adj.* unstet.

unsuccessful, *adj.* erfolg´los.

untie, *vb.* auf´knüpfen.

until, 1. *prep.* bis; **(not u.)** erst. **2.** *conj.* bis; **(not u.)** erst wenn; erst als.

untruth, *n.* Unwahrheit, -en *f.*

untruthful, *adj.* unwahr.

unusual, *adj.* ungewöhnlich.

unwell, *adj.* unpäßlich, nicht wohl.

up, 1. *prep.* auf. **2.** *adv.* auf, hinauf´, herauf´.

upbraid, *vb.* schelten*.

uphill, 1. *adj.* (*fig.*) mühsam. **2.** *adv.* bergan´, bergauf´.

uphold, *vb.* aufrecht•erhal´ten*.

upholster, *vb.* bezie´hen*.

upholsterer, *n.* Tapezie´rer, - *m.*

upon, *prep.* auf.

upper, *adj.* ober-.

upright, *adj.* aufrecht.

uprising, *n.* Aufstand, =e *m.*

uproar, *n.* Getö´se *nt.*

uproot, *vb.* entwur´zeln.

upset, 1. *n.* Rückschlag, =e *m.;* **(stomach u.)** Magenverstimmung, -en *f.* **2.** *vb.* **(overturn)** um•werfen*; **(disturb)** über den Haufen werfen, verstim´men; **(discompose)** aus der Fassung bringen*.

upside down, *adv.* umgekehrt, verkehrt´ herum´.

upstairs, *adv.* oben; nach oben.

uptight, *adj.* unsicher, verklemmt.

urban, *adj.* städtisch.

urge, 1. *n.* Drang, =e *m.;* **(sex)** Trieb, -e *m.* **2.** *vb.* drängen, nötigen.

urgency, *n.* Dringlichkeit *f.*

urgent, *adj.* dringend.

urinal, *n.* Harnglas, =er *nt.;* **(public)** Bedürf´nisanstalt, -en *f.*

urinate, *vb.* urinie´ren.

urine, *n.* Urin´, -e *nt.*

us, *pron.* uns.

usage, *n.* Gebrauch´, =e *m.*

use, 1. *n.* Gebrauch´, =e *m.,* Benut´zung, -en *f.* **2.** *vb.* gebrau´chen, verwen´den, benut´zen.

useful, *adj.* nützlich.

useless, *adj.* nutzlos.

user, *n.* Benut´zer, - *m.*

usher, *n.* (*theater, etc.*) Platzanweiser, - *m.;* (*wedding*) Brautführer, - *m.*

usual, *adj.* gewöhn´lich.

usury, *n.* Wucher *m.*

utensil, *n.* Gerät´, -e *nt.*

uterus, *n.* Gebär´mutter, = *f.*

utility, *n.* Nutzbarkeit *f.*

utilize, *vb.* aus•nutzen.

utmost, *adj.* äußerst.

utter, 1. *adj.* völlig. **2.** *vb.* äußern.

utterance, *n.* Äußerung, -en *f.*

V

vacancy, *n.* (*position*) freie Stellung, -en *f.;* (*hotel, etc.*) unvermietetes Zimmer, - *nt.*

vacant, *adj.* frei; (*empty*) leer.

vacate, *vb.* räumen.

vacation, *n.* Ferien *pl.*

vacationer, *n.* Urlauber, - *m.,* Urlauberin, -nen *f.*

vaccinate, *vb.* impfen.

vaccination, *n.* Impfung, - en *f.*

vaccine, *n.* Impfstoff, -e *m.*

vacuum, *n.* Vakuum, -kua *nt.*

vacuum cleaner, *n.* Staubsauger, - *m.*

vagina, *n.* Vagi´na, -nen *f.*

vagrant, 1. *n.* Landstreicher, *m.;* (*worker*) Saison´arbeiter, - *m.* **2.** *adj.* vagabundie´rend.

vague, *adj.* unbestimmt, vage.

vain, 1. *adj.* (*conceited*) eitel; (*useless*) vergeb´lich. **2.** *n.* (*in v.*) umsonst´, verge´bens.

valet, *n.* Diener, - *m.*

valiant, *adj.* tapfer.

valid, *adj.* gültig.

valise, *n.* Reisetasche, -n *f.*

valley, *n.* Tal, =er *nt.*

valor, *n.* Tapferkeit *f.*

valuable, *adj.* wertvoll.

value, *n.* Wert, -e *m.*

valve, *n.* Ventil´, -e *nt.;* (*med.*) Klappe, -n *f.*

van, *n.* (*delivery truck*) Lieferwagen, - *m.;* (*moving v.*) Möbelwagen, - *m.*

vandal, *n.* Vanda´le, -n, -n *m.*

vanguard, *n.* Vorhut *f.;* (*person*) Vorkämpfer, - *m.*

vanilla, *n.* Vanil´le *f.*

vanish, *vb.* verschwin´den*.

vanity, *n.* Eitelkeit *f.*

vanquish, *vb.* besie´gen.

vapor, *n.* Dampf, =e *m.*

variance, *n.* Widerstreit *m.*

variation, *n.* Abwechslung, -en *f.;* Abänderung, -en *f.,* Variation´, -en *f.*

varied, *adj.* verschie´den; mannigfaltig.

variety, *n.* Mannigfaltigkeit *f.;* (*choice*) Auswahl *f.;* (*theater*) Varieté´ *nt.*

various, *adj.* verschie´den.

varnish, 1. *n.* Firnis, -se *m.* **2.** *vb.* firnissen.

vary, *vb.* variie´ren, verän´dern.

vase, *n.* Vase, -n *f.*

vasectomy, *n.* Vasektomie´ *f.*

vast, *adj.* riesig.

vat, *n.* Faß, =sser *nt.*

vaudeville, *n.* Varieté´ *nt.*

vault, *n.* Gewöl´be, - *nt.;* (*burial chamber*) Gruft, =e *f.;* (*bank*) Tresor´, -e *m.;* (*jump*) Sprung, =e *m.* **2.** *vb.* springen*.

veal, *n.* Kalbfleisch *nt.*

vegetable, *n.* Gemü´se, - *nt.*

vehement, *adj.* heftig.

vehicle, *n.* Fahrzeug, -e *nt.*

veil, 1. *n.* Schleier, - *m.* **2.** *vb.* verschlei´ern.

vein, *n.* Vene, -n *f.,* Ader, -n *f.*

velocity, *n.* Geschwin´digkeit, -en *f.*

velvet, *n.* Samt *m.*

veneer, *n.* Furnier´, -e *nt.*

vengeance, *n.* Rache *f.*

venom, *n.* Gift, -e *nt.*

vent, 1. *n.* Öffnung, -en *f.;* *(escape passage)* Abzugsröhre, -n *f.* 2. *vb.* freien Lauf lassen*.

ventilate, *vb.* lüften, ventilie´ren.

ventilation, *n.* Lüftung *f.,* Ventilation´ *f.*

venture, 1. *n.* Wagnis, -se *nt.* 2. *vb.* wagen.

verb, *n.* Verb, -en *nt.,* Zeitwort, ‑er *nt.*

verbal, *adj.* verbal´; *(oral)* mündlich.

verdict, *n.* Urteil, -e *nt.*

verge, 1. *n.* *(fig.)* Rand, ‑er *m.* 2. *vb.* **(v. on)** grenzen an.

verification, *n.* Bestä´tigung, -en *f.*

verify, *vb.* bestä´tigen.

vernacular, 1. *n.* Umgangssprache, -n *f.* 2. *adj.* umgangssprachlich.

versatile, *adj.* vielseitig.

verse, *n.* Vers, -e *m.*

versify, *vb.* in Verse bringen*.

version, *n.* Fassung, -en *f.,* Version´, -en *f.*

versus, *prep.* gegen.

vertebrate, 1. *n.* Wirbeltier, -e *nt.* 2. *adj.* Wirbel- *(cpds.)*.

vertical, *adj.* senkrecht.

very, *adv.* sehr.

vespers, *n.* Vesper, -n *f.*

vessel, *n.* Schiff, -e *nt.;* *(container)* Gefäß´, -e *nt.*

vest, *n.* Weste, -n *f.*

vestige, *n.* Spur, -en *f.*

veteran, *n.* Veteran´, -en, -en *m.*

veterinarian, *n.* Tierarzt, ‑e *m.,* Tierärztin, -nen *f.*

veterinary, *adj.* tierärztlich.

veto, 1. *n.* Veto, -s *nt.* 2. *vb.* das Veto ein•legen.

vex, *vb.* ärgern; verblüf´fen.

via, *prep.* über.

viaduct, *n.* Viadukt´, -e *m.*

vibrate, *vb.* vibrie´ren, schwingen*.

vibration, *n.* Vibration´, -en *f.,* Schwingung, -en *f.;* *(tremor)* Erschüt´terung, -en *f.*

vice, *n.* Laster, - *nt.*

vicinity, *n.* Nähe *f.,* Umge´bung, -en *f.*

vicious, *adj.* gemein´, heimtückisch.

victim, *n.* Opfer, - *nt.*

victor, *n.* Sieger, - *m.*

victorious, *adj.* siegreich.

victory, *n.* Sieg, -e *m.*

videodisc, *n.* Videoscheibe, -n *f.*

Vienna, *n.* Wien *nt.*

view, 1. *n.* Aussicht, -en *f.* 2. *vb.* bese´hen*, betrach´ten.

vigil, *n.* Nachtwache, -n *f.*

vigilant, *adj.* wachsam.

vigor, *n.* Kraft, ‑e *f.,* Energie´, -i´en *f.*

vigorous, *adj.* kräftig, kraftstrotzend.

vile, *adj.* gemein´, niederträchtig.

village, *n.* Dorf, ‑er *nt.*

villain, *n.* Bösewicht, -e *m.,* Schurke, -n, -n *m.*

vindicate, *vb.* rechtfertigen.

vine, *n.* Rebstock, ‑e *m.;* *(creeper)* Ranke, -n *f.*

vinegar, *n.* Essig *m.*

vineyard, *n.* Weingarten, ‑ *m.,* Weinberg, -e *m.*

vintage, *n.* *(gathering)* Weinlese *f.;* *(year)* Jahrgang, ‑e *m.*

viol, viola, *n.* Bratsche, -n *f.*

violate, *vb.* verlet´zen; *(oath)* brechen*; *(law, territory)* übertre´ten*.

violation, *n.* Verlet´zung, -en *f.;* Bruch, ‑e *m.;* Übertre´tung, -en *f.*

violator, *n.* Verlet´zer, - *m.;* Übertre´ter, - *m.*

violence, *n.* Gewalt´tätigkeit, -en *f.;* *(vehemence)* Gewalt´samkeit *f.,* Heftigkeit *f.*

violent, *adj.* gewalt´tätig; gewalt´sam, heftig.

violet, 1. *n.* Veilchen, - *nt.* 2. *adj.* violett´, veilchenblau.

violin, *n.* Geige, -n *f.*

virgin, *n.* Jungfrau, -en *f.*

virile, *adj.* männlich.

virtue, *n.* Tugend, -en *f.*

virtuous, *adj.* tugendhaft, tugendsam.

virus, *n.* Virus, -ren *m.*

visa, *n.* Visum, -sa *nt.*

vise, *n.* Schraubstock, ‑e *m.*

visible, *adj.* sichtbar.

vision, *n.* Sehkraft, ‑e *f.;* *(visual image)* Vision´, -en *f.*

visit, 1. *n.* Besuch´, -e *m.* 2. *vb.* besu´chen.

visitor, *n.* Besu´cher, - *m.,* Besu´cherin, -nen *f.*

visual, *adj.* visuell´.

vital, *adj.* *(essential)* wesentlich; *(strong)* vital´.

vitality, *n.* Lebenskraft *f.,* Vitalität´ *f.*

vitamin, *n.* Vitamin´, -e *nt.*

vivacious, *adj.* lebhaft, temperament´voll.

vivid, *adj.* leben´dig, lebhaft.

vocabulary, *n.* Wortschatz, ‑e *m.;* *(list of words)* Wörterverzeichnis, -se *nt.*

vocal, *adj.* Stimm-, Gesang´- *(cpds.);* lautstark.

vogue, *n.* Mode, -n *f.*

voice, *n.* Stimme, -n *f.*

void, *adj.* ungültig.

volcano, *n.* Vulkan´, -e *m.*

volt, *n.* Volt, - *nt.*

voltage, *n.* Stromspannung, -en *f.*

volume, *n.* Volu´men, - *nt.;* *(book)* Band, ‑e *m.;* *(quantity)* Umfang, ‑e *m.*

voluntary, *adj.* freiwillig.

volunteer, 1. *n.* Freiwillige, -m. & *f.* 2. *vb.* sich freiwillig melden.

vomit, *vb.* erbre´chen*.

vote, 1. *n.* *(individual ballot)* Wahlstimme, -n *f.;* *(casting)* Stimmabgabe, -n *f.;* **(v. of confidence)** Vertrau´ensvotum *nt.* 2. *vb.* wählen, stimmen, ab•stimmen.

voter, *n.* Wähler, - *m.,* Wählerin, -nen *f.*

vouch for, *vb.* verbür´gen für.

vow, 1. *n.* Gelüb´de, - *nt.* 2. *vb.* gelo´ben.

vowel, *n.* Vokal´, -e *m.*

voyage, *n.* Reise, -n *f.*

vulgar, *adj.* vulgär´, ordinär´.

vulgarity, *n.* Ordinär´heit, -en *f.*

vulnerable, *adj.* verletz´bar; angreifbar.

W

wad, *n.* Bündel, - *nt.; (of cotton)* Wattebausch, ⸗e *m.; (roll)* Rolle, -n *f.*

wade, *vb.* waten.

wag, 1. *n.* Spaßvogel, ⸗ *m.* **2.** *vb.* wedeln.

wage, 1. *n.* Lohn, ⸗e *m.* **2.** *vb.* **(w. war)** Krieg führen.

wager, 1. *n.* Wette, -n *f.* **2.** *vb.* wetten.

wagon, *n.* Wagen, - *m.*

wail, *vb.* wehklagen.

waist, *n.* Taille, -n *f.*

waistcoat, *n.* Weste, -n *f.*

wait, 1. *n.* Wartezeit, -en *f.* **2.** *vb.* warten; **(w. for)** warten auf.

waiter, *n.* Kellner, - *m.*

waitress, *n.* Kellnerin, -nen *f.*

waiver, *n.* Verzicht´leistung, -en *f.*

wake, 1. *n. (vigil)* Totenwache, -n *f.; (of boat)* Kielwasser *nt.* **2.** *vb. (tr.)* wecken; *(intr.)* erwa´chen.

walk, 1. *n. (vigil)* Spazier´gang, ⸗e *m.* **2.** *vb.* gehen*, laufen*.

wall, *n.* Wand, ⸗e *f.; (of stone or brick)* Mauer, -n *f.*

wallcovering, *n.* Wandverkleidung *f.*

wallet, *n.* Brieftasche, -n *f.*

wallpaper, *n.* Tape´te, -n *f.*

walnut, *n.* Walnuß, ⸗sse *f.*

walrus, *n.* Walroß, -sse *nt.*

waltz, 1. *n.* Walzer, - *m.* **2.** *vb.* Walzer tanzen.

wander, *vb.* wandern; **(w. around)** umher´⸗wandern.

want, 1. *n.* Mangel, ⸗ *m.; (needs)* Bedarf´ *m.; (poverty)* Armut *f.* **2.** *vb.* wollen, wünschen.

war, *n.* Krieg, -e *m.*

ward, *n.* Mündel, -nt.; *(city)* Bezirk´, -e *m.; (hospital, prison)* Abtei´lung, -en *f.*

ware, *n.* Ware, -n *f.*

warlike, *adj.* kriegerisch.

warm, 1. *adj.* warm (⸗). **2.** *vb.* wärmen.

warmth, *n.* Wärme *f.*

warn, *vb.* warnen.

warning, *n.* Warnung, -en *f.*

warp, *vb.* krümmen; *(fig.)* verdre´hen, entstel´len.

warrant, 1. *n. (authorization)* Vollmacht, -en *f.; (writ of arrest)* Haftbefehl, -e *m.* **2.** *vb.* gewähr´leisten, garantie´ren.

warrior, *n.* Krieger, - *m.*

warship, *n.* Kriegsschiff, -e *nt.*

wash, 1. *n.* Wäsche, -n *f.* **2.** *vb.* waschen*.

wash-basin, *n.* Waschbecken, - *nt.*

washroom, *n.* Waschraum, ⸗e *m.*

wasp, *n.* Wespe, -n *f.*

waste, 1. *n.* Abfall, ⸗e *m.* **2.** *adj. (superfluous)* überflüssig; *(bare)* öde. **3.** *vb.* verschwen´den, vergeu´den.

watch, 1. *n. (guard)* Wache, -n *f.; (timepiece)* Uhr, -en *f.; (wrist w.)* Armbanduhr, -en *f.; (pocket w.)* Taschenuhr, -en *f.* **2.** *vb. (guard)* bewa´chen, passen auf; *(observe)* beob´achten, acht⸗geben; **(w. out)** auf⸗passen; **(w. out!)** Vorsicht!

watchful, *adj.* wachsam.

watchmaker, *n.* Uhrmacher, - *m.*

water, 1. *n.* Wasser, - *nt.* **2.** *vb.* wässern, begie´ßen*.

waterbed, *n.* Matratze mit Wasser gefüllt *f.*

waterfall, *n.* Wasserfall, ⸗e *m.*

waterproof, *adj.* wasserdicht.

wave, 1. *n.* Welle, -n *f.* **2.** *vb.* wellen, wogen; *(flag)* wehen; *(hand)* winken.

waver, *vb.* schwanken.

wax, 1. *n.* Wachs, -e *nt.* **2.** *vb.* wachsen; *(moon)* zu⸗nehmen*.

way, *n.* Weg, -e *m.*

we, *pron.* wir.

weak, *adj.* schwach (⸗).

weaken, *vb. (tr.)* schwächen; *(intr.)* schwach werden*.

weakness, *n.* Schwäche, -n *f.*

wealth, *n.* Reichtum, ⸗er *m.; (possessions)* Vermö´gen, - *nt.; (abundance)* Fülle *f.*

wealthy, *adj.* reich, vermö´gend.

weapon, *n.* Waffe, -n *f.*

wear, *vb.* tragen*, an⸗haben*, *(hat)* auf⸗haben*; **(w. out)** ab⸗tragen*, *(fig.)* erschöp´fen; **(w. away)** aus⸗höhlen.

weary, *adj.* müde, erschöpft´.

weasel, *n.* Wiesel, - *nt.*

weather, 1. *n.* Wetter *nt.* **2.** *vb. (fig.)* durch⸗stehen*.

weather forecast, *n.* Wettervorher´sage *f.*

weave, *vb.* weben(*).

weaver, *n.* Weber, - *m.*

web, *n.* Netz, -e *nt.*, Gewe´be *nt.; (spider w.)* Spinngewebe *nt.*

wedding, *n.* Hochzeit, -en *f.*

wedge, *n.* Keil, -e *m.*

Wednesday, *n.* Mittwoch, -e *m.*

weed, 1. *n.* Unkraut *nt.* **2.** *vb.* jäten.

week, *n.* Woche, -n *f.*

weekday, *n.* Wochentag, -e *m.*

weekend, *n.* Wochenende, -n *nt.*

weekly, 1. *n.* Wochenschrift, -en *f.* **2.** *adj.* wöchentlich.

weep, *vb.* weinen.

weigh, *vb.* wiegen*; *(ponder)* wägen.

weight, *n.* Gewicht´, -e *nt.; (burden)* Last, -en *f.*

weird, *adj.* unheimlich.

welcome, 1. *n.* Willkom´men *nt.* **2.** *vb.* bewill´kommnen, begrü´ßen. **3.** *adj.* willkom´men; **(you're w.)** bitte.

welfare, *n.* Wohlergehen *nt.; (social)* Wohlfahrt *f.*

well, 1. *n.* Brunnen, - *m.* **2.** *vb.* quellen*. **3.** *adv.* gut;

(health) gesund˝(≐, -), wohl.

well-done, *adj.* gut gemacht; *(meat)* durchgebraten.

well-known, *adj.* bekannt´.

west, 1. *n.* Westen *m.* **2.** *adj.* westlich; West- *(cpds.).*

western, *adj.* westlich.

westward, *adv.* nach Westen.

wet, 1. *adj.* naß (≐, -). **2.** *vb.* nässen, näß machen.

whale, *n.* Walfisch, -e *m.*

what, 1. *pron.* was. **2.** *adj.* welcher, -es, -e.

whatever, 1. *pron.* was . . . auch. **2.** *adj.* welcher, -es, -e . . . auch.

wheat, *n.* Weizen *m.*

wheel, 1. *n.* Rad, ≐er *nt.;* **(w. chair)** Rollstuhl, ≐e *m.* **2.** *vb.* rollen.

when, 1. *adv. (question)* wann. **2.** *conj. (once in the past)* als; *(future; whenever)* wenn; *(indirect question)* wann.

whence, *adv.* woher´, von wo.

whenever, 1. *conj.* wenn. **2.** *adv.* wann . . . auch.

where, *adv. (in what place)* wo; *(to what place)* wohin´; **(w. . . . from)** woher´.

wherever, *adv.* wo(hin) . . . auch.

whether, *conj.* ob.

which, *pron.& adj.* welcher, -es, -e.

whichever, *pron.& adj.* welcher, -es, -e . . . auch.

while, 1. *n.* Weile *f.* **2.** *conj.* während.

whim, *n.* Laune, -n *f.*

whip, 1. *n.* Peitsche, -n *f.* **2.** *vb.* peitschen, schlagen*.

whirl, *vb.* wirbeln.

whirlpool, *n.* Strudel, - *m.*

whirlwind, *n.* Wirbelwind, - e *m.*

whisker, *n.* Barthaar, -e *nt.*

whiskey, *n.* Whisky, -s *m.*

whisper, *vb.* flüstern.

whistle, 1. *n.* Flöte, -n *f.,* Pfeife, -n *f.* **2.** *vb.* flöten, pfeifen*.

white, *adj.* weiß.

who, *pron. (interrogative)* wer; *(relative)* der, das, die.

whoever, *pron.* wer . . . auch.

whole, 1. *n.* Ganz- *nt.* **2.** *adj.* ganz; *(unbroken)* heil.

wholesale, 1. *n.* Großhandel *m.* **2.** *adv.* en gros.

wholesome, *adj.* gesund´ (≐, -).

why, *adv.* warum´, wieso´, weshalb.

wicked, *adj.* böse, verrucht´.

wickedness, *n.* Verrucht´heit *f.*

wide, *adj.* weit; breit.

widen, *vb.* erwei´tern.

widespread, *adj.* weit verbrei´tet.

widow, *n.* Witwe, -n *f.*

widower, *n.* Witwer, - *m.*

width, *n.* Weite, -n *f.;* Breite, -n *f.*

wield, *vb.* handhaben*; *(fig.)* aus•üben.

wife, *n.* Frau, -en *f.*

wig, *n.* Perü´cke, -n *f.*

wild, *adj.* wild.

wilderness, *n.* Wildnis, -se *f.*

wildlife, *n.* Tierwelt *f.*

will, 1. *n.* Wille(n) *m.;* *(testament)* Testament´, -e *nt.* **2.** *vb. (future)* werden*; *(want to)* wollen*; *(bequeath)* verma´chen.

willful, *adj.* eigensinnig; *(intentional)* vorsätzlich.

willing, *adj.* willig; gewillt´; **(be w.)** wollen*.

willow, *n.* Weide, -n *f.*

wilt, *vb.* welken, verwel´ken.

wilted, *adj.* welk.

win, *vb.* gewin´nen*.

wind, 1. *n.* Wind, -e *m.* **2.** *vb.* winden*, wickeln; *(watch)* auf•ziehen*.

window, *n.* Fenster, - *nt.*

windshield, *n.* Windschutzscheibe, -n *f.*

windy, *adj.* windig.

wine, *n.* Wein, -e *m.*

wing, *n.* Flügel, - *m.*

wink, *vb.* blinzeln.

winner, *n.* Gewin´ner, - *m.,* Gewin´nerin, -nen *f.,* Sieger, - *m.,* Siegerin, - nen *f.*

winter, *n.* Winter, - *m.*

wintry, *adj.* winterlich.

wipe, *vb.* wischen.

wire, 1. *n.* Draht, ≐e *m.;* *(telegram)* Telegramm´, - e *nt.* **2.** *vb.* telegrafie´ren.

wire recorder, *n.* Drahtaufnahmegerät, -e *nt.*

wisdom, *n.* Weisheit, -en *f.*

wise, *adj.* weise, klug (≐).

wish, 1. *n.* Wunsch, ≐e *m.;* **2.** *vb.* wünschen.

wit, *n.* Verstand´ *m.;* *(humor)* Humor´ *m.*

witch, *n.* Hexe, -n *f.*

with, *prep.* mit.

withdraw, *vb.* zurück´•ziehen*.

wither, *vb.* verdor´ren.

withhold, *vb.* zurück´•halten*; ein•behalten*.

within, 1. *adv.* drinnen. **2.** *prep.* innerhalb.

without, 1. *adv.* draußen. **2.** *prep.* ohne.

witness, 1. *n.* Zeuge, -n, - *m.,* Zeugin, -nen *f.* **2.** *vb.* Zeuge sein* von.

witty, *adj.* witzig; geistreich.

woe, *n.* Leid *nt.*

wolf, *n.* Wolf, ≐e *m.*

woman, *n.* Frau, -en *f.*

womb, *n.* Mutterleib *m.*

wonder, 1. *n.* Wunder, - *nt.* **2.** *vb.* **(I w.)** ich möchte gern wissen.

wonderful, *adj.* wunderbar, herrlich.

woo, *vb.* umwer´ben*.

wood, *n.* Holz, ≐er *nt.;* *(forest)* Wald, ≐er *m.*

wooden, *adj.* hölzern.

wool, *n.* Wolle *f.*

woolen, *adj.* wollen.

word, *n. (single)* Wort, ≐er *nt.;* *(zconnected)* Wort, -e *nt.*

wordy, *adj. (fig.)* langatmig.

work, 1. *n. (labor)* Arbeit, - en *f.;* *(thing produced)* Werk, -e *nt.* **2.** *vb.* arbeiten; *(function)* gehen*, funktionie´ren.

worker, *n.* Arbeiter, - *m.,* Arbeiterin, -nen *f.*

workman, *n.* Arbeiter, - *m.*

work permit, *n.* Arbeitserlaubnis *f.,* Arbeitsgenehmigung *f.*

world, *n.* Welt, -en *f.*
worldly, *adj.* weltlich.
worm, *n.* Wurm, ‑er *m.*
worn-out, *adj.* abgenutzt.
worry, 1. *n.* Sorge, -n *f.* **2.**
vb. sich sorgen.
worse, *adj.* schlimmer,
schlechter.
worship, 1. *n.* Vereh´rung, -
en *f.; (church)* Gottesdienst, ‑e *m.* **2.** *vb.*
vereh´ren, an•beten.
worst, *adj.* schlimmst-,
schlechtest-.
worth, 1. *n.* Wert, ‑e *m.* **2.**
adj. wert.
worthless, *adj.* wertlos.
worthy, *adj.* würdig, ehrenwert.

wound, 1. *n.* Wunde, -n *f.* **2.**
vb. verwun´den.
wrap, 1. *n.* Umhang, ‑e *m.*
2. *vb.* wickeln.
wrapping, *n.* Verpa´ckung,
-en *f.*
wrath, *n.* Zorn *m.*
wreath, *n.* Kranz, ‑e *m.*
wreck, 1. *n.* Wrack, -s *nt.* **2.**
vb. demolie´ren,
kaputt´machen.
wrench, 1. *n.* Ruck *m.; (tool)*
Schraubenschlüssel, - *m.*
2. *vb.* verren´ken.
wrestle, *vb.* ringen*.
wretched, *adj.* erbärm´lich.
wring, *vb. (hands)* ringen*;
(laundry) wringen*;
(neck) ab• drehen.

wrinkle, 1. *n.* Falte, -n *f.,*
Runzel, -n *f.* **2.** *vb.* runzeln; *(cloth)* knittern.
wrist, *n.* Handgelenk, ‑e *nt.*
wrist-watch, *n.* Armbanduhr, -en *f.*
write, *vb.* schreiben*.
writer, *n.* Schreiber, - *m.,*
Schreiberin, -nen *f.; (by
profession)* Schriftsteller,
- *m.* Schriftstellerin, -nen
f.; (author) Verfas´ser, -
m., Verfas´serin, -nen *f.*
writing, *n.* Schrift, -en *f.;*
(in w.) schriftlich.
wrong, 1. *n.* Unrecht *nt.* **2.**
adj. falsch; unrecht; **(be
w.)** unrecht haben*, sich
irren. **3.** *vb.* Unrecht tun*.

X

x-ray, 1. *n.* Röntgenaufnahme, -n *f.* **2.** *vb.* röntgen.

x-rays, *n.pl.* Röntgenstrahlen *pl.*

xylophone, *n.* Xylophon´, -
e *nt.*

Y

yacht, *n.* Jacht, -en *f.*
yard, *n. (garden)* Garten, ‑
m.; (railroad)
Verschie´bebahnhof, ‑e
m.; (measure) Yard, -s *nt.*
yarn, *n.* Garn, -e *nt.; (story)*
Geschich´te, -n *f.*
yawn, *vb.* gähnen.
year, *n.* Jahr, -e *nt.*
yearly, *adj.* jährlich.
yearn, *vb.* sich sehnen.
yell, 1. *n.* Schrei, -e *m.* **2.**
vb. schreien*, brüllen.

yellow, *adj.* gelb.
yes, *interj.* ja.
yesterday, *adv.* gestern.
yet, 1. *adv. (still)* noch; *(already)* schon; **(not y.)**
noch nicht. **2.** *conj.* doch.
yield, 1. *n.* Ertrag´, ‑e *m.* **2.**
vb. ein•bringen*; *(cede)*
nach•geben*.
yoke, *n.* Joch, -e *nt.*
yolk, *n.* Eigelb, - *nt.*
you, *pron.* du, Sie.
young, *adj.* jung (‑).

youth, *n.* junger Mann, ‑er
m., Jüngling, -e *m.;
(young people; time of
life)* Jugend, -en *f.*
youthful, *adj.* jugendlich.
Yugoslav, *n.* Jugosla´we, -n,
-n *m.,* Jugoslawin, -nen *f.*
Yugoslavia, *n.* Jugosla´wien
nt.
Yugoslavian, 1. *n.*
Jugosla´we, -n, -n *m.* **2.**
adj. jugosla´wisch.

Z

zap, *vb. (lit.)* töten; *(slang)*
fertig machen, zer-
schmettern.
zeal, *n.* Eifer *m.*
zebra, *n.* Zebra, -s *nt.*
zero, *n.* Null, -en *f.*

zest, *n. (zeal)* Eifer *m.; (relish)* Genuß´ *m.*
zinc, *n.* Zink *nt.*
zip code, *n.* Postleitzahl, -
en *f.*

zipper, *n.* Reißverschluß,
‑sse *m.*
zone, *n.* Zone, -n *f.*
zoo, *n.* Zoo, -s *m.*
zoological, *adj.* zoolo´gisch.
zoology, *n.* Zoologie´ *f.*

Food Terms

apple	Apfel	lobster	Hummer
artichoke	Artischo´cken	meat	Fleisch
asparagus	Spargel	melon	Melo´ne
bacon	Speck	milk	Milch
banana	Bana´ne	mushroom	Pilz
beans	Bohnen	noodle	Nudel
beer	Bier	nuts	Nüsse
beet	Bete	omelet	Omelett´
bread	Brot	onion	Zwiebel
butter	Butter	orange	Apfelsi´ne
cake	Kuchen	pastry	Gebäck´
carrot	Mohrrübe	peach	Pfirsich
cauliflower	Blumenkohl	pear	Birne
celery	Sellerie	pepper	Pfeffer
cheese	Käse	pie	Obstkuchen
chicken	Huhn	pineapple	Ananas
chocolate	Schokola´de	pork	Schweinefleisch
coffee	Kaffee	potato	Kartof´fel
cookie	Keks	rice	Reis
crab	Taschenkrebs	roast beef	Roastbeef
cream	Sahne	salad	Salat´
cucumber	Gurke	salmon	Lachs
dessert	Nachtisch	salt	Salz
duck	Ente	sandwich	beleg´tes Brot
egg	Ei	shrimp	Garne´le
fish	Fisch	soup	Suppe
fowl	Geflü´gel	spinach	Spinat´
fruit	Frucht, Obst	steak	Beefsteak
goose	Gans	strawberry	Erdbeere
grape	Weintraube	sugar	Zucker
grapefruit	Pampelmu´se	tea	Tee
ham	Schinken	tomato	Toma´te
ice cream	Sahneneis	trout	Forel´le
juice	Saft	turkey	Truthahn
lamb	Lammfleisch	veal	Kalbfleisch
lemonade	Limona´de	vegetable	Gemü´se
lettuce	Kopfsalat	water	Wasser
liver	Leber	wine	Wein

Days of the Week

Sunday	der Sonntag
Monday	der Montag
Tuesday	der Dienstag
Wednesday	der Mittwoch
Thursday	der Donnerstag
Friday	der Freitag
Saturday	der Sonnabend *or* der Samstag

Months

January	der Januar	July	der Juli
February	der Februar	August	der August´
March	der März	September	der Septem´ber
April	der April´	October	der Okto´ber
May	der Mai	November	der Novem´ber
June	der Juni	December	der Dezem´ber

Signs

Vorsicht	Caution	Einbahnstraße	One way street
Achtung	Watch out	Raucher	For smokers
Ausgang	Exit	Nichtraucher	For non-smokers
Eingang	Entrance	Rauchen verboten	No smoking
Halt	Stop	Kein Zutritt	No admittance
Geschlossen	Closed	Damen (*or*)	
Geöffnet	Open	Frauen	Women
Langsam	Slow	Herren (*or*)	
Verboten	Prohibited	Männer	Men
Gesperrt	Road closed	Abort	Toilet

Numerals

Cardinal		Ordinal	
1	eins	1st	erst-
2	zwei	2nd	zweit-
3	drei	3rd	dritt-
4	vier	4th	viert-
5	fünf	5th	fünft-
6	sechs	6th	sechst-
7	sieben	7th	sieb(en)t-
8	acht	8th	acht-
9	neun	9th	neunt-
10	zehn	10th	zehnt-
11	elf	11th	elft-
12	zwölf	12th	zwölft-
13	dreizehn	13th	dreizehnt-
14	vierzehn	14th	vierzehnt-
15	fünfzehn	15th	fünfzehnt-
16	sechzehn	16th	sechzehnt-
17	siebzehn	17th	siebzehnt-
18	achtzehn	18th	achtzehnt-
19	neunzehn	19th	neunzehnt-
20	zwanzig	20th	zwanzigst-
21	einundzwanzig	21st	einundzwanzigst-
30	dreißig	30th	dreißigst-
32	zweiunddreißig	32nd	zweiunddreißigst-
40	vierzig	40th	vierzigst-
43	dreiundvierzig	43rd	dreiundvierzigst-
50	fünfzig	50th	fünfzigst-
54	vierundfünfzig	54th	vierundfünfzigst-
60	sechzig	60th	sechzigst-
65	fünfundsechzig	65th	fünfundsechzigst-
70	siebzig	70th	siebzigst-
76	sechsundsiebzig	76th	sechsundsiebzigst-
80	achtzig	80th	achtzigst-
87	siebenundachtzig	87th	siebenundachtzigst-
90	neunzig	90th	neunzigst-
98	achtundneunzig	98th	achtundneunzigst-
100	hundert	100th	hundertst-
101	hunderteins	101st	hunderterst-
202	zweihundertzwei	202nd	zweihundertzweit-
1,000	tausend	1,000th	tausendst-
1,000,000	eine Million´	1,000,000	millionst´-

271

Weights and Measures

The Germans use the *Metric System* of weights and measures, which is a decimal system in which multiples are shown by the prefixes: Dezi- (one tenth); Zenti- (one hundredth); Milli- (one thousandth); Deka- (ten); Hekto- (hundred); Kilo- (thousand).

1 Zentimeter	=	.3937 inches
1 Meter	=	39.37 inches
1 Kilometer	=	.621 mile
1 Zentigramm	=	.1543 grain
1 Gramm	=	15.432 grains
1 Pfund (1/2 Kilogramm)	=	1.1023 pounds
1 Kilogramm	=	2.2046 pounds
1 Tonne	=	2,204 pounds
1 Zentiliter	=	.338 ounces
1 Liter	=	1.0567 quart (liquid);
		.908 quart (dry)
1 Kiloliter	=	264.18 gallons

Decimals

Instead of a decimal point, a comma is used:
English: 3.82 "three point eight two"
German: 3,82 "drei Komma acht zwei"

Fractions

the half; half a pound	die Hälfte; ein halbes Pfund
one and a half	anderthalb, eineinhalb
the third; two-thirds	das Drittel; zweidrittel
the fourth; three-fourths	das Viertel; dreiviertel
the fifth; four-fifths	das Fünftel; vierfünftel

Useful Words and Phrases

Hello (*or*) **How do you do?**	Guten Tag. Grüß Gott.
Good morning.	Guten Morgen. Grüß Gott.
Good afternoon.	Guten Tag. Grüß Gott.
Good evening.	Guten Abend.
How are you?	Wie geht es Ihnen?
Fine, thanks, and you?	Gut, danke, und Ihnen?
I'm fine, too, thanks.	Auch gut, danke.
Please.	Bitte.
Thank you.	Danke schön.
You're welcome.	Bitte schön.
Pardon me.	Entschul´digen Sie, bitte. Verzei´hung.
I am sorry, I made a mistake.	Es tut mir leid, ich habe mich geirrt.
Do you mind?	Macht es Ihnen etwas aus?
Good luck.	Alles Gute.
Good night.	Gute Nacht.
Good-bye.	Auf Wiedersehen.
Can you please help me?	Können Sie mir bitte helfen?
Do you understand me?	Verste´hen Sie mich?
I don't understand you.	Ich verste´he Sie nicht.
Please speak slowly.	Sprechen Sie bitte langsam.
Please say it again.	Sagen Sie es bitte noch einmal.
I don't speak German very well.	Ich spreche nicht sehr gut Deutsch.
Do you speak English?	Sprechen Sie Englisch?
What do you call that in German?	Wie heißt das auf deutsch?
How do you say . . . in German?	Wie sagt man . . . auf deutsch?
What's your name, please?	Wie heißen Sie bitte?
My name is . . .	Ich heiße . . .
May I introduce . . .	Darf ich Ihnen . . . vorstellen?
What time is it?	Wieviel Uhr ist es?
How much does that cost?	Wie viel kostet das?
I would like . . .	Ich möchte gern . . . ; Ich hätte gern . . .
May I see something better?	Könnten Sie mir etwas Besseres zeigen?
May I see something cheaper?	Könnten Sie mir etwas Billigeres zeigen?
It is not exactly what I want.	Es ist nicht ganz das, was ich suche.
I'd like to buy . . .	Ich möchte gern . . . kaufen.
I'd like to eat.	Ich möchte gern essen.
Where is there a good restaurant?	Wo ist hier ein gutes Restaurant?
I'm hungry (thirsty).	Ich habe Hunger (Durst).
Please give me . . .	Bitte geben Sie mir . . .
Please bring me . . .	Bitte bringen Sie mir . . .
May I see the menu?	Ich hätte gern die Speisekarte.
The check, please.	Bitte zahlen.
Is service included in the bill?	Ist das mit Bedie´nung?
Where is there a good hotel?	Wo ist hier ein gutes Hotel´?
Please help me with my luggage.	Helfen Sie mir bitte mit meinem Gepäck´.
Where can I get a taxi?	Wo bekom´me (finde) ich eine Taxe?
What is the fare to . . . ?	Was kostet die Fahrt nach (bis) . . . ?

Please take me to this address.	Bitte bringen (fahren) Sie mich zu dieser Adres´se.
Please let me off at . . .	Bitte halten Sie . . .
I am lost.	Ich habe mich verlau´fen (verfah´ren).
I have a reservation.	Ich habe . . . reserviert´.
Where is the men's (ladies') room?	Wo ist die Toilet´te, bitte?
How do I get to the station?	Wie komme ich zum Bahnhof?
Where can I check my baggage?	Wo ist die Gepäckauf´bewahrung?
Is this a non-stop flight?	Ist dies ein direkt´er Flug?
I'm sick.	Ich bin krank.
I need a doctor.	Ich brauche einen Arzt.
Where is the nearest drugstore?	Wo ist die nächste Drogerie´?
Where is the next pharmacy?	Wo ist die nächste Apotheke?
Is there any mail for me?	Ist Post für mich da?
Where can I mail this letter?	Wo kann ich diesen Brief einstecken?
I want to send a fax.	Ich möchte gern ein Fax schicken.
Where is the nearest bank?	Wo ist die nächste Bank?
Where can I change money?	Wo kann ich hier Geld wechseln?
Do you accept travelers checks?	Nehmen Sie Reiseschecks?
May I have the bill, please?	Könnte ich bitte die Rechnung haben?
Right away.	Sofort´.
Help!	Hilfe!
Please call the police.	Rufen Sie bitte die Polizei´.
Who is it?	Wer ist dort?
Come in.	Herein´.
Just a minute!	Einen Augenblick, bitte!
Hello (*on telephone*).	Hier . . . (*say your name*).
Look out!	Vorsicht! Achtung!
Stop.	Halt.
Hurry.	Schnell.
As soon as possible.	So bald wie möglich.
To the right.	Rechts.
To the left.	Links.
Straight ahead.	Gera´de aus.